Organizing China

ORGANIZING CHINA

The Problem of Bureaucracy
1949-1976

HARRY HARDING

Stanford University Press
Stanford, California
1981

Stanford University Press
Stanford, California
© 1981 by the Board of Trustees of the
Leland Stanford Junior University

Printed in the United States of America
ISBN 0-8047-1080-5
LC 79-67772

To my parents

Preface

One of the most important trends in the study of contemporary Chinese politics over the past ten years has been a growth in interest in the history of public policy in the People's Republic. In part, this interest has been stimulated by the information about policy debates that became available first during the Cultural Revolution, and then during the official criticism of Teng Hsiao-p'ing and the "Gang of Four" in the 1970's. In addition, specialists on China have come to realize that debates over public policy have played a major role in the political history of modern China, and that the study of individual issues can provide valuable insights into the ways in which Chinese leaders and institutions make policy decisions. In part, too, the concern with Chinese public policy has reflected a broader phenomenon: the interest of political scientists and economists in comparing the approaches taken by a variety of countries toward important issues of public policy. China, as the most populous nation in the world and one of the most self-consciously experimental, has been a natural subject for this kind of inquiry.

The interest in Chinese public policy has been reflected in a series of studies of controversial policy issues, including agriculture, public health, education, cultural and intellectual affairs, military policy, and industrial management. This book is an analysis of still another important issue: organizational policy. Its aim is to examine the problems Chinese leaders have encountered in building and maintaining effective administrative organizations, and the divergent approaches to organizational questions they have taken in the twenty-seven years between the establishment of the People's Republic in 1949 and the death of Mao Tse-tung in 1976.

Readers may not be accustomed to thinking of organizational policy as an important political issue. Although candidates for public office in the United States often campaign on platforms that are highly critical of the national bureaucracy, and although presidents have occasionally proposed the restructuring of the federal government or the reform of the civil-service system, organizational policy has never been a particularly central issue in modern American politics. In China, in contrast, organizational policy has occupied a prominent place on the political agenda ever since 1949, fully comparable to the place assigned to the issues of national security, economic development, and social welfare with which we are more familiar. To Chinese leaders, organizational policy has been important because organizations are important. Effective organizations, they believe, are a crucial prerequisite for success in any public endeavor, whether it is making a revolution or developing the economy.

Organizational policy has been a controversial question as well. To a degree, this is because of the complexity of the administrative problems that the Party and state bureaucracies have presented to Chinese leaders. In part, too, organizational issues have aroused debate because of their implications for socioeconomic policy, and because of their effects on the distribution of power and status among important sectors of Chinese society. Most basic of all, organizational policy has posed an important philosophical dilemma for Chinese leaders: do the efficiency and rationality of modern bureaucracy outweigh the social and political costs that bureaucratization may impose? This book attempts to trace the controversies over all three of these dimensions.

It is important to stress that this book is not intended to be a comprehensive history of organization in China, but rather a history of the organizational issues that have absorbed Chinese leaders. Defining the topic in this way has helped keep to more manageable proportions what might otherwise have been an impossibly broad study. For one thing, the book does not pretend to cover all organizations in China. It does not, for instance, devote much space to the army, the "democratic parties," the trade unions, the neighborhood associations, the scientific and cultural organizations, the industrial and commercial establishments, or the communes and state farms of the country. Instead, it focuses on the Party and the state, for it is they to which Chinese leaders devote particular attention when addressing organizational problems. To be sure, the Chinese have from time to time been concerned with organizational problems in the work place, the mass organizations, and the army. But these have usually been peripheral concerns, of secondary importance when compared with the attention the Chinese have paid to the effectiveness and reliability of the Party and state bureaucracies.

Nor is it the purpose of the book to provide an objective description of the structure and operation of the Party and state. Instead, the book examines Chinese organizations through the eyes of China's leaders, seeking to understand their diagnoses of their country's organizational problems, the debates they have conducted on organizational questions, and the programs they have adopted in their attempts to manage the Party and state bureaucracies. Such an approach has probably overstated some of China's organizational problems and understated others, exaggerating those with which Chinese leaders have been most concerned, and neglecting those to which they have devoted little attention.

The thesis of the book is that Chinese organizational policy between 1949 and 1976 was like a *pu-tao-weng*, the Chinese doll with a weighted base that wobbles when hit but never falls over. Chinese leaders have experimented with a wide range of organizational programs and structures, seeking at some times to rationalize their bureaucracy, at other times to subject it to external supervision, and at still other times to replace it with more participatory forms of organization. But after each experiment, organizational policy, like a *pu-tao-weng*, has found its own center of balance once again. In keeping with much of Chinese tradition, the core organizational program of the Chinese Communist Party has been the recruitment of officials on the basis of their political reliability rather than their substantive skills, the maintenance of bureaucratic loyalty and responsiveness through constant indoctrination and rectification, and the promotion of organizational efficiency through a series of political and economic campaigns. As the concluding chapter argues, this policy has served China reasonably well over the last thirty years. But it has also had its costs, including a stifling conformity among officials, a reluctance to take independent initiatives, a low level of technical and managerial skills, and disillusionment and cynicism at the frequent shifts in official line.

As this book goes to press, Chinese leaders are engaged in their most sweeping reassessment of organizational policy since the early 1950's. In so doing, they have compiled a long list of organizational shortcomings. An unacceptably small number of officials, they now reveal, have received middle-school or university educations. Few understand even the rudiments of administrative science or of substantive policy issues. Cadres are selected on the basis of class background rather than managerial ability, are promoted on the basis of seniority rather than achievement, and enjoy lifetime tenure regardless of performance. Many officials are now too old and feeble to put in a full day's work. And many use the powers of office to gain privileges for themselves and their families, and favors and appointments for their friends and supporters.

These criticisms constitute the acknowledgment that China's administrative organizations are growing old, that they are staffed with aging cadres who do not understand the complex issues now confronting them, and that they are organized around principles that may no longer be appropriate to a modernizing society. The Chinese are now considering a number of significant organizational reforms, including electing top officials at all levels of government to fixed terms of office, retiring cadres who are too old to work efficiently, removing or reassigning officials who do not perform effectively, promoting younger cadres to positions of greater responsibility, and retraining promising men and women in administrative practice, science, and technology.

It is still far too early to know the effect of the reforms that Chinese leaders are now considering. It may be that, with the death of Mao Tse-tung, China's organizational policy has passed a crucial turning point, and that ideological indoctrination and mass campaigns will be set aside in favor of rationalization, formalization, and specialization. Or it may be that we are simply witnessing one more short-lived organizational experiment, after which the *pu-tao-weng* will once again return to its own center of balance, regardless of the suitability of that balance for a more modern and complex society.

In either event, these recent developments illustrate one of the principal conclusions of this study. In describing organizational reform as a prerequisite for economic and scientific modernization, Chinese leaders are once again revealing the importance they have consistently assigned to organizational policy. Like the great movements of the past—the High Tide, the Great Leap Forward, the Cultural Revolution—the current campaign to achieve the "four modernizations" by the year 2000 is believed to require a reassessment of organizational policy and to demand some kind of organizational change.

*

The preparation of this book has passed through three stages, and I am pleased to acknowledge the advice and assistance I received at each step of the way.

In its first incarnation, the book was a Ph.D. dissertation written in the Department of Political Science at Stanford University. I owe a particular debt to my reading committee—Alexander L. George, Chalmers Johnson, John W. Lewis, and Lyman P. Van Slyke—for their encouragement and counsel.

Next, I am grateful to the organizations that provided me with financial support to help turn a doctoral thesis into a publishable manuscript. A leave of absence in 1975–76, under a program of research leaves for junior faculty administered by the Vice-President for Faculty Affairs at Stanford and supported by the Andrew W. Mellon Foundation, enabled me to conduct supplementary research on the 1950's and to write the first draft of this book. A second leave in 1977–78, as a National Fellow at the Hoover Institution on War, Revolution, and Peace, provided a comfortable environment to revise the manuscript thoroughly and prepare a second draft. Additional support during that year was offered by the Center for Research in International Studies and the Arms Control and Disarmament Program, both of Stanford University.

During the second stage, my students played a particularly helpful role. Some of my graduate students at Stanford, especially David Bachman,

Donald Koblitz, and David Yoffie, offered useful suggestions on individual chapters of the manuscript. The participants in a seminar on policy-making and organization in China that I taught at Berkeley in 1977 helped me refine the basic themes of the book. And Rosemary Lodge, then an undergraduate at Stanford, provided admirable research assistance on the organizational heritage of the Chinese Communist Party while I was a National Fellow at the Hoover Institution. I am also grateful for the comments by Lowell Dittmer, Hsiao Liu, Robert Scalapino, James Townsend, and Martin Whyte.

Finally, the manuscript was transformed into a readable book. Here, I am deeply appreciative of the assistance and guidance provided by J. G. Bell and Joy Dickinson of the Stanford University Press, and particularly by my editor, Robert J. Krompart. No author could ask for a finer publisher.

Throughout all three stages, two people have been especially helpful, and deserve a special note of thanks. John W. Lewis has assisted me in more ways than I can possibly recount, first by introducing me to the organizational issues in Chinese politics, then as the chairman of my dissertation committee, and then as my senior colleague in Chinese politics at Stanford. And my wife Roca was, as always, reassuring when I got discouraged, stern when I got lazy, and mischievous when I got too deeply immersed in what must have seemed to be an interminable project. She served neither as typist nor as editor, but her contribution to the book can be found on every page.

Washington, D.C., and Palo Alto   H.H.
August 1980

Contents

1
The Politics of Bureaucracy in Contemporary China

Ever since the founding of their movement, Chinese Communist leaders have seen effective political organization as a prerequisite for success, not only in making one of the most important revolutions in modern times, but also in promoting the social and economic development of the most populous nation in the world. The Chinese Communists have realized that political organization is an essential mechanism for mobilizing popular involvement and support for their Party and its programs, for managing their financial and material resources, for generating the ideas and information needed to address social and economic problems, and for carrying out their national policies. As John Wilson Lewis wrote in his landmark study of Chinese Communist doctrine, "The leadership technique of the Chinese Communists has been to bring all Chinese into formal organizations of various kinds."[1] Or, as Mao Tse-tung succinctly put it in one of his Yenan essays, "Get Organized!"[2]

Under Communist Party rule, therefore, China has been transformed from what Sun Yat-sen described as a "sheet of loose sand" into one of the most highly organized societies in the world. Among the Party's first actions in the early 1950's was to enroll all major sectors of the Chinese population—workers, peasants, youth, women, students, and intellectuals—in a close-meshed system of mass organizations. Chinese leaders also constructed an administrative apparatus, centering on the state and Party bureaucracies, that has exercised broader and tighter control over Chinese society than any previous government in the country's history. In 1955 Mao Tse-tung would describe the result as "a good thing," an achievement that China had not seen in "thousands of years."[3]

Because of the importance assigned to organizations, discussions of this administrative apparatus have occupied a place on the Chinese political agenda comparable in prominence and volatility to problems of economic development and political succession.[4] Almost every year since 1949, Chinese leaders have been engaged in some effort to improve the performance, efficiency, or reliability of the Party and the state. Organizational structure and procedures, administrative expenses, the ideological commitment and technical competence of officials, the relationship between the officials and the public—all have been topics of continuing concern, frequent discussion, and periodic debate among China's leaders. On two occasions, the Hundred Flowers period of 1956–57 and the Cultural Revolution of 1966–69, organizational issues created such political and social tension that they threatened the stability of the regime.

This book suggests three reasons why this has been so. First, in China, as in any complex society, organizations frequently malfunction, giving leaders the task of restoring their efficiency, effectiveness, and reliability. In other words, large political organizations can readily become serious administrative problems for political leaders. Second, organizational staffing, structure, and operations affect the distribution of political power and strongly influence the formation of public policy on a wide range of issues. Organizational policy can thus become a controversial political issue. Third, the expansion of political organization in China has raised a troublesome philosophical problem. As Max Weber pointed out, bureaucracy, because of its theoretically superior efficiency, rationality, and precision, is a form of organization increasingly pervasive in modern society. But the process of bureaucratization may also impose important social and political costs, such as public alienation from government and bureaucratic autonomy from external control. In a revolutionary society like China, where even official ideology has had an antibureaucratic cast, the question of whether the organizational advantages of bureaucracy outweigh the potential social and political disadvantages is particularly likely to become a serious social dilemma.

In this introductory chapter, we will discuss in turn these three dimensions of organizational policy in China, and then summarize the organizational heritage the Chinese Communist Party carried with it to power in 1949.

BUREAUCRACY AS AN ADMINISTRATIVE PROBLEM

As organizational theorists have frequently pointed out, public bureaucracies are susceptible to a variety of organizational maladies, and political leaders must be watchful and inventive managers if they hope to ensure effective organizational performance. We can identify eight organizational pathologies as being of particular importance in the study of Party and state in China; these, in turn, can be grouped in three broader categories, depending on whether they affect the attitudes and values of bureaucratic personnel, the structure and operation of the bureaucracy, or the relationship between bureaucratic officials and the rest of society. The pathologies are closely interrelated but are sufficiently distinct to allow separate discussion.*

*My discussion of bureaucratic pathologies has benefited greatly from Anthony Downs's analysis in *Inside Bureaucracy* (Boston, 1967).

Personnel Problems

Lack of commitment. A basic characteristic of bureaucrats is that they frequently lack the commitment to goals, values, and policies that the regime expects them to hold. The discrepancy between what bureaucratic officials actually value and what they are supposed to value may be manifested in a variety of ways. Officials may be more concerned with preserving or increasing their individual security, power, income, or prestige than with efficient performance. They may be more concerned with maintaining or enlarging their agency's programs, status, authority, or budgets than with disinterestedly serving society as a whole. They may have their own view of what public policy should be. They may advocate policies that would be of benefit to a particular social or economic sector of society that they represent. Or, worst of all from the official point of view, they may subscribe to a political or social philosophy different from that of their leaders.

The problem of commitment, which most organization theorists believe to be inevitable in any complex organization, lies at the root of many other bureaucratic pathologies. Some theories of bureaucratic behavior, such as that of Anthony Downs, have been constructed almost entirely around the assumption that officials are more likely to be motivated by self-interest and personal programmatic and philosophical preferences than by a desire to serve society or by loyalty to their superiors. As we will see, a lack of commitment to official values and goals often explains inefficiency, loss of control, poor communication, and corruption within a bureaucracy.

Lack of zeal. Most managers and political leaders do not want subordinates simply to report and obey. They want subordinates who act with vigor, who pass on information and insights that are useful to the common purpose, and who are innovative and flexible in their work. Chinese Communist organization theory, in particular, places a good deal of emphasis on encouraging active and enthusiastic participation by officials in making and administering policy. In China such desirable behavior is known as "revolutionary zeal" or "revolutionary enthusiasm."

There are several reasons why low zeal and poor morale may emerge in a bureaucratic organization. One of the most basic is lack of commitment: officials who are committed to the organization's goals and policies are more likely to work with enthusiasm than those who are not. Or the reward structure of the organization may trigger morale problems. Officials cannot be expected to have high morale if they are seriously underpaid, if they do not receive recognition for good work, or if they feel the standards for performance change in an erratic or irrational manner. They are unlikely to be eager workers if they fear this will be resented by their coworkers or will antagonize their superiors. Nor are they likely to take the initiative if they fear that mistakes will be punished. Under such conditions, it is more probable that they will carefully follow established procedures and pass responsibility on to their superiors for any deviation from routine. Finally, zeal and morale are related to the style of communication within an organization. Organizations in which superiors talk out workaday problems and policy with subordinates, explain decisions, and actively solicit opinions are likely to have higher morale than organizations with more restrictive styles.

Lack of skill. A third type of bureaucratic pathology emerges when needed administrative and technical skills are either unavailable or underused. For example, a developing country embarking on a program of planned social and economic modernization would require the services of officials schooled in fields ranging from medicine and economics to agronomy and metallurgy. It would also need officials with the training and experience to administer large organizations, to manage the flow of reports and documents, to establish budgeting and auditing procedures, to develop systems of personnel recruitment and training, and to supervise and coordinate organizational activities.

Bureaucracies may fail to meet these needs for a variety of reasons. One obvious problem, of course, may be that skilled people are simply in short supply. Obtaining such officials may require the development of educational and training programs or the solicitation of assistance from abroad. Another problem may be that those who possess the required skills are not considered politically reliable. If specialists are believed not to be fully committed to the goals, values, and programs of the regime, then they may find that their talents are underutilized or ignored altogether. Solving this problem requires reeducating the existing specialists in the political values of the regime, training new specialists who will be both technically proficient and politically reliable, or lowering the standards of political reliability to permit full use of the existing pool of specialists.

Finally, even if skilled and reliable personnel are available, it may still be difficult to integrate them effectively into an organization.[5] Tensions may well develop between the specialists and the generalists with whom they work. The specialists may complain that their advice is unheeded, or that they are supervised and evaluated by people unqualified to judge their performance. The generalists may complain that the specialists are unable to apply their theoretical knowledge effectively to practical problems, or that they are insensitive to the political and budgetary constraints on policymaking. The solution to this problem requires that generalists and specialists be educated to respect each other's contributions and to become aware of the limitations of their own perspectives.

Structural Problems

Loss of control. Because officials often have different commitments from those their political leaders would like them to have, bureaucracies experience problems of discipline and control. No large organization can be completely centralized. Some of the authority to make decisions independently and some of the power to decide how to apply regulations and directives will inevitably be delegated. And the temptation is great to use such discretionary authority to pursue personal goals, promote departmental interests, or uphold individual conceptions of organizational and social interests—all contrary to the intent of the policymakers. The result, according to Anthony Downs, is that "each official will vary the degree to which he complies with directives from his superiors, depending on whether or not those directives favor or oppose his own interest. Subordinates will zealously expedite some orders, carry out others with mild enthusiasm, drag their feet seriously on still others, and completely ignore a few."[6] It is unlikely, therefore, that instructions or regulations will be carried out as issued or acted on as quickly, enthusiastically, or completely as might be wished.

Inadequate information. A fifth type of organizational malady occurs when administrators cannot obtain complete, accurate, or timely information.[7] Just as superiors expect their subordinates to make independent decisions and to carry out organizational regulations and directives, so they rely on them to report on the accomplishments of their departments, the organization's environment, and even their own performance. And just as subordinates may be tempted to misuse their discretionary powers to further their own goals and interests, so will many officials tend to distort the information that they provide their superiors. They may report only information that reflects well on their own performance, that favors the policy options they prefer, or that indicates that departmental resources should be increased. They may also be tempted to supply the sort of information they believe their superiors want to receive. Other information may be withheld altogether, or if that is impossible, its importance may be downplayed. The cumulation of distortions in such information may seriously restrict the ability of administrators to make effective decisions.

Inefficiency. Organizations can be described as inefficient when their performance costs more in time, money, or effort than could reasonably be expected.[8] Three types of inefficiency are particularly important.

The first type is that described in Parkinson's Law: budgets and staff expand "irrespective of any variation in the amount of work (if any) to be done."[9] Such expansion may be prompted by a genuine belief that it will improve performance, but it may also be urged for more selfish motives, for example, the realization that growth will increase an administrator's power and prestige and improve the morale of his subordinates by increasing opportunities for promotion and reward. Political leaders may also see increasing the size of the public bureaucracy as a convenient way of providing political patronage and relieving unemployment.

Poor coordination is a second type of organizational inefficiency. Any large organization divides its tasks among its various departments, but must at the same time coordinate departmental activities so as to ensure efficiency in the work of the organization as a whole. Duplication of effort, failure of departments to share information, and actions by one department that have unintended effects on other departments all are examples of inefficiency produced by poor coordination.

The routinization of organizational operations may produce a third kind of bureaucratic inefficiency. Routine is necessary in any organization to deal quickly and consistently with recurrent problems, but organizations may become excessively committed to established routines and to standard operating procedures. Departures from routine may be seen as inconvenient by individual officials and as costly and disruptive by the organization as a whole. As a result, officials may try to make yesterday's routines serve today's problems, preferring to force the environment to fit the routine instead of changing the routine to fit the environment.

Unfortunately for organizational managers, the three types of inefficiency often reinforce one another. The expansion of organizational staff, for example, usually requires a corresponding increase in the number of departments and levels of authority. The larger the organization becomes, the more difficult it is to coordinate, and the provision of routines may be seen as the best or only way to cope with the problem of coordination. For this reason, many organizational theorists have written of an ossification syndrome, the tendency over time for organizations to become increasingly inefficient as the processes of expansion and the proliferation of routines jointly reduce organizational vitality.

Problems with the Public

Alienation. A seventh type of pathology is public dissatisfaction with the service provided by bureaucratic officials. Although the level of popular support that a government enjoys depends on the programs it has adopted, it also depends on the manner in which bureaucracies deal with the public when they administer those programs. The bureaucracy may not be held responsible if the tax rate is too high, but it will be blamed if it collects taxes in an arbitrary and arrogant fashion.

One of the principal surveys of the relationship between bureaucracy and the public suggests that the public may become alienated from the bureaucracy for any of three reasons.[10] The first is termed "inhumanity," the tendency of officials to be insensitive and abrupt in their dealings with the public. Inhumanity may be due to the press of work or to the monotony of the job, but it may also stem from the officials' belief that they are superior to the public, and that the provision of public services is a favor to be bestowed rather than an obligation to be fulfilled.

The second possible cause of alienation is inflexibility. Officials may hesitate to depart from established procedures because of personal inconvenience or because of fear of punishment. Officials with the power to act may refuse to meet with the people involved, or may neglect to inform them of other agencies that might be of help. This kind of alienation between bureaucracy and the public tends to develop when officials are more committed to personal and organizational considerations than to public service, and when an agency is plagued by poor morale.

The organizational inefficiency that we have just discussed produces a third kind of alienation. People who must fill out many forms and documents, apply at a series of offices to solve a single problem, or wait weeks or months for a reply to their requests may become alienated from the bureaucracy even if the officials they encounter seem concerned with helping them.

In addition to these three problems, which are common to all bureaucracies, there is a fourth that occurs in countries like China that attempt to mobilize active public support for their policies. Such support ideally should be nurtured through education and persuasion, but overworked officials may resort to command and coercion as instruments of mass mobilization. When this happens, the way a policy is applied may breed alienation, even if the policy itself is popular.

Corruption. A final bureaucratic pathology is the misuse of public office for personal gain. Officials may misallocate official funds or property for their own use or for the use of their relatives or friends. They may use their positions to extort money, favors, or services from the public. Or they may accept bribes offered by people seeking special consideration in the making or administration of public policy.

The growing literature on bureaucratic corruption suggests that it is most likely to occur under two sets of circumstances.[11] It occurs, first of all, when the opportunity is present—that is, when prohibitions and penalties are weak, when monitoring mechanisms are ineffective, or when officials have substantial leeway in the interpretation of public policies or the allocation of official funds. It also occurs when the motivation for it is high. Officials who are not paid what they believe to be an adequate salary may be strongly tempted to engage in graft or extortion. Similarly, a group or individual commanding substantial economic resources but unable to ensure favorable action from officials through legal means may be inspired to attempt bribery.

Corruption is commonly seen as a moral and legal problem, but it can also have serious consequences that are purely organizational. Graft by officials wastes public resources and thus increases administrative costs. Officials who accept bribes cannot be expected to administer public policy fairly. And, perhaps most important, corruption can induce substantial alienation in its victims and in those who see others enjoying illegal benefits or dispensations. Although studies have demonstrated that certain types of corruption may actually increase the efficiency and stability of the political system, corruption must generally be considered a measure of poor bureaucratic performance.[12]

BUREAUCRACY AS A POLITICAL ISSUE

The eight problems discussed above can occur in any bureaucracy and can seriously reduce the effectiveness of its performance. Though they demonstrate that managing a bureaucracy can be a challenging problem for political leaders, however, they do not explain why bureaucracies can become controversial political issues. What makes these problems cause for policy debate?

Bureaucracies may become political issues because political leaders differ in their *diagnoses* of the nature and severity of organizational problems. Some may interpret high administrative expenditures as evidence of waste and inefficiency; others may suspect graft and corruption. Some may perceive bureaucratic officials who fail to perform their jobs effectively as well intentioned but inept; others may see them as deliberately insubordinate. Some may believe that the state bureaucracy is reasonably effective overall; others may argue that it is critically diseased with corruption and waste. The differences usually stem from different assumptions about organizational behavior or different views about what constitutes good organizational performance. Whatever the source, different diagnoses are an important reason why organizations become controversial political issues.

Even if leaders agree on the diagnosis of a problem, they may differ over the *remedy*. Faced with corruption and insubordination, for example, one leader may propose a new auditing agency, whereas another may demand a more vigorous indoctrination program. Differences in remedy often reflect different assumptions about the causes of the problems or different views of the workability of alternative remedies.

A related difficulty is that attempts to remedy one problem may simply exacerbate another.[13] Professionalization may increase the level of skills in an organization but may also require the recruitment of people whose political orientation and organizational style are quite different from those of their colleagues. Decentralization may permit greater speed, flexibility, and efficiency in responding to local problems but may also reduce an agency's ability to attain uniformity and coherence in its organizational performance. A relatively democratic organizational structure may help officials obtain information from their subordinates but may be less effective than a strictly hierarchical structure in ensuring coordination and control.

As a result, political leaders may have to make difficult decisions about the price they are willing to pay to solve organizational problems. They may have to strike uneasy compromises among competing organizational goals, making improvements in some problem areas while accepting the creation of new problems in others. In China, for example, a common cleavage has been between the proponents of structural reform and the proponents of motivational reform. Structural reforms are attempts to improve organizational performance by changing the design or procedures of the bureaucracy—its size, the division of labor among its officials, its rules and regulations, its level of centralization, its system of inspection and monitoring, or its incentive structure. Motivational reforms, in contrast, aim at changing the basic values and commitments of bureaucratic officials in the belief that an organization performs best if its staff is committed to its programs, shares the philosophy of its leaders, and is zealous in its work. Debate has typically emerged when one group of leaders argues that motivational reforms are the only way of removing the underlying causes of bureaucractic pathology, and another group responds that it is naive and impractical to attempt to create a selfless corps of officials.

Organizational matters may also become political issues simply because they are so closely connected with substantive *policy concerns*. The structure, procedures, and staffing of a nation's bureaucracies strongly influence its economic, social, and foreign policies. One of these linkages between organization and policy is through the budget: within the financial constraints at work, if more resources are used to pay administrative costs, less will be available to finance substantive programs. Another linkage is through personnel: the kind of people a bureau recruits can strongly influence both the kind of policy proposals it will formulate and the zeal with which it will execute the programs assigned it.

Procedures for gathering information and channels of access to decision makers also may determine which policies are formulated. As Roger Hilsman has argued, "By making it easier for some people to have access than others, by providing for the accumulation of one kind of information and not another, or by following procedures that let some problems rise up to the top of the government's agenda before others—in all these ways some organizational arrangements facilitate certain kinds of policy and other organizational arrangements facilitate other kinds of policy."[14]

Perhaps most important of all, however, are the procedures by which an organization makes and carries out policy. In Graham Allison's words, organizational routines and procedures define a "menu of alternatives" for decision makers that "is severely limited in both number and character." Policymakers quickly discover that organizations can administer quickly and effectively only those policies that they were designed to administer. Radically different policies can be undertaken effectively only by making equally radical changes in organizational procedures or by establishing completely new organizations designed specifically to administer the new programs. Consequently, the very structure of an organization tends to make incremental change seem easier and less costly than radical change.[15]

Since bureaucratic structure, procedures, and staffing have policy consequences, organizational issues and policy questions tend to be intimately intertwined. Discussions of proper remedies for organizational problems will tend to include consideration of what impact alternative organizational reforms will have on policy. Conversely, debates on policy can evolve into debates on organization, since proponents of competing policies will argue for the structures and procedures that they believe will facilitate the adoption of the policies they favor.

Organizational questions are also closely related to the *distribution of resources* such as power, income, and status among officials and political leaders. Decentralization involves shifting power and status from higher-ranking to lower-ranking officials. Professionalization involves shifting power, status, and income from generalists to specialists. Changes in the criteria for promotion will determine which people rise rapidly to positions of power and which do not. Any kind of organizational reform is therefore likely to become controversial within the bureaucracy: it will be supported by those who will benefit and opposed by those who will suffer.

Even more important is the effect of organizational staffing and structure on the competition for power among the political elite. The bureaucracy in China, particularly the Party apparatus, is an essential base of support for contending political leaders. To be sure, leaders can attempt to build power bases elsewhere, such as in the army or the mass organizations, can try to generate widespread popular support, and can try to gain the backing of other influential politicians, but support within the bureaucracy is crucial. Organizational policy, in turn, can help individual political leaders both to win support and to weaken the support available to their opponents. Recruitment and promotion policies can be manipulated to bring supporters into influential bureaucratic positions. Power can be reallocated within the bureaucracy so as to isolate or subjugate elements of the power base of one's opponents. It has often been this factor that has turned an organizational question into a controversial issue on the Chinese political agenda.

BUREAUCRACY AS A SOCIAL DILEMMA

Among Max Weber's great contributions to social science were his identification of bureaucracy as a type of administrative organization and his proposition that bureaucracy would become ever more prevalent in modern society. To Weber, the characteristics of a purely bureaucratic organization were its hierarchical structure, its clear division of labor, its utilization of formal rules and norms, and its appointment of career officials on the basis of technical competence. Weber argued that these characteristics made bureaucracy the most efficient and rational administrative organization yet devised, and thus the only adequate form of organization for modern societies:

Experience tends universally to show that the purely bureaucratic type of administrative organization . . . is, from a purely technical point of view, capable of attaining the highest degree of efficiency and is in this sense formally the most rational known means of carrying out imperative control over other human beings. It is superior to any other form in precision, in stability, in the stringency of its discipline, and in its reliability. It thus makes possible the particularly high degree of calculability of results for the heads of the organization and for those acting in relation to it. It is finally superior both in intensive efficiency and in the scope of its operations. . . . The development of the modern form of the organization of corporate groups in all fields is nothing less than the development and continual spread of bureaucratic administration.[16]

Although Weber was convinced that bureaucratization is an inevitable consequence of modernization, he was ambivalent about the normative implications of such a development. On the one hand, he suggested, bureaucracies recruit solely on the basis of technical competence and not on the basis of class background, and thus contribute to greater equality of opportunity in society. Bureaucrats, he presumed, also perform their duties objectively and dispassionately, treating all members of society equally, without regard to social standing. Weber therefore concluded that "the development of bureaucracy greatly favours the levelling of social classes."[17]

On the other hand, Weber was also aware of the disadvantages of bureaucratization. In almost the same breath that he praised bureaucracy for providing greater equality of opportunity, he cautioned that reliance on technical standards for recruitment might favor the wealthy, who could afford to provide their children with lengthy technical training.[18] He also warned that the division of labor and specialization might create petty people with narrow minds, and urged that society find some way to "keep a portion of mankind free from this parcelling-out of the soul."[19] Most important of all, he identified the problem of maintaining external control over bureaucracy, pointing out that bureaucrats' specialized knowledge and authority to place security classifications on official information make it extremely difficult for anyone outside the bureaucracy to supervise it effectively. He once pessimistically asked, "In view of the growing indispensability of the state bureaucracy and its corresponding increase in power, how can there be any guarantee that any powers will remain which can check and effectively control the tremendous influence of this stratum? How will democracy even in this limited sense be *at all possible*?"[20]

Political scientists, sociologists, and political theorists since Weber have continued to debate the effects of bureaucratization on modern society.* Above all, there has been a recurring concern with whether the disadvantages of bureaucracy outweigh its advantages, and whether, despite its problems, bureaucracy remains a practical necessity for modern society. We will call this enduring issue—the issue of the necessity and desirability of bureaucracy—the bureaucratic dilemma.

The terms of the debate have changed remarkably little since Weber's time. Those who support or accept the inevitability of bureaucracy emphasize the organizational requisites of modern society. As a society becomes more complex, it requires that government undertake a broader range of activities, and that governmental administrative agencies become larger, more differentiated, and more specialized. As society becomes more rational and secular, it demands that scientific and technical expertise be brought to bear on the solution of public problems, and that public policy be administered in the most effective and efficient way possible. Only bureaucracy, it is argued, can meet the organizational demands of modern society.

Those who attack bureaucracy strongly criticize its effects on society. One group of critics points to the bureaucratic pathologies and maladies that we discussed earlier in this chapter. They argue that bureaucracies are not as efficient as Weber claimed, but rather have inherent tendencies toward inefficiency, overstaffing, inadequate flows of information, and loss of discipline. Indeed, some of the most vehement of these criticisms even antedate Weber. As early as 1861 John Stuart Mill warned that routinized bureaucratic governments "perish by the immutability of their maxims."[21] More recently other organization theorists have argued that the

---

*For the influential contributions to the debate that have the greatest relevance to the present discussion, see the works in the Bibliography by Bennis, Berkley, Dunsire, LaPalombara, Montgomery and Siffin, Mouzelis, Toffler, and Waldo.

growing complexity and increasing rate of change in modern society have created an environment in which bureaucratic organizations, because of their commitment to established procedures, simply cannot cope.

These critics have also accused bureaucracy of giving rise to undesirable relationships between officials and the public. "The trained official," wrote Walter Bagehot in 1867, "hates the rude, untrained public. He thinks that they are stupid, ignorant, reckless—that they cannot tell their own interest—that they should have the leave of the office before they do anything."[22] Robert Merton, in his pioneering article on bureaucratic structure and personality, pointed out that bureaucrats are trained to treat all problems in a detached and impersonal manner, even though the problems may be of intense personal concern to the public. Furthermore, the bureaucrat, no matter how lowly his rank, regards himself as a "representative of the power and prestige of the entire structure." This combination of impersonality and self-importance explains why bureaucrats are so frequently charged with arrogance and haughtiness.[23]

And bureaucracies have been characterized as having orientations toward policy problems that may give a distinctive cast to the policies they propose and administer. One of these is goal displacement, the process by which officials realign their aims from the solution of public problems to the defense or aggrandizement of the agency in which they work.[24] This tendency to equate problem solving with organization building has been described by Ivan Illich in the following terms: "Health, learning, dignity, independence and creative endeavor are defined as little more than the performance of the institutions which claim to serve these ends, and their performance is made to depend on allocating more resources to the management of hospitals, schools, and other agencies in question."[25] Bureaucrats have also been accused of preferring stability and predictability to fluidity and change, of favoring incremental change over radical reform, of being more concerned with short-term considerations than with long-term planning, and of stressing the material and quantifiable in social and economic problems rather than the psychological, political, and qualitative.*

All these criticisms derive directly from the organizational pathologies we discussed earlier in this chapter. But there is a second school of criticism that, in some respects, is more telling. Even if bureaucratic performance could be perfected, the second group holds, bureaucracy would still pose the most serious philosophical questions for a free society. For one thing, the very concept of bureaucracy—the assumption that public ad-

---

*Alvin Toffler coined the term "econo-think" to describe some of these orientations. See *Future Shock* (New York, 1970), p. 400; and the discussion of "Consciousness II" in Charles A. Reich, *The Greening of America* (New York, 1970).

ministration is performed best by a corps of specialized, highly trained, career officials—may be fundamentally incompatible with the ideals of community, democratic participation, and self-realization. J. Toulmin Smith, an early proponent of village self-government and a critic of centralized bureaucracy, wrote in 1851:

The wholesome adjustment of practical arrangements suited to the exigencies of the times, and the satisfactory management of administrative functions, must depend on the vital activity of Institutions which give every freeman the full opportunity of discussing, and hearing discussed, all the questions which directly, or indirectly, concern him. . . . Men cannot discuss without having first paid some attention to the subject matter of discussion. As long as everything is done *for* them they have no occasion to think at all, and will soon become incapable of thinking.[26]

Such comments were echoed in the late 1960's by those who demanded that people be given the right of full participation in making the decisions that affected their lives, and that those decisions should not be delegated to impersonal bureaucracies.

Critics of the second group also have been concerned about the bureaucracy's tendency to develop autonomy from external control—the concern that lay at the heart of Max Weber's writings about bureaucracy. Bureaucracy's size, its multiplicity of activities, its tendencies toward secrecy, and its claims to monopolize expertise in its area of operations all make it extremely difficult for any political leader or organization to oversee. This is said to be particularly true in developing countries, where the bureaucracy may be strong and well organized, and any countervailing political institutions weak and ineffectual. The danger is that society becomes dominated by its own administrative organs, which in turn become increasingly unresponsive to the needs of their constituency.

Political leaders and political philosophers have suggested four different approaches to the bureaucratic dilemma, depending on the weight they have assigned to the advantages and disadvantages of bureaucracy. The *rationalizing* response stresses the merits of bureaucratization and denies that the structural principles of bureaucracy contain any inherent organizational, social, or political flaws. Problems emerge only when an organization departs significantly from the bureaucratic ideal-type—when, in Robert Merton's words, it has failed to "live up to the requirements of bureaucratic structure."[27] The solution, therefore, is more bureaucratization, not less; it is to perfect the organization's structure, staffing, and procedures so as to enable it to perform its tasks in a more efficient and effective manner. Typical rationalizing approaches to the bureaucratic dilemma include structural reforms aimed at creating a more efficient division of labor, a more effective allocation of power and responsibility within the bureaucracy, the recruitment of more technically qualified personnel, the adoption of more efficient organizational routines, and the establishment of stringent monitoring and disciplinary mechanisms.

The *radical* response to the bureaucratic dilemma, in contrast, has been to demand that bureaucracies be destroyed and replaced by some nonbureaucratic form of organization. This view is held by those who are most critical of bureaucracy and who most firmly believe it to be fundamentally incompatible with important social, political, and cultural values. According to Dunsire, the radical reaction to bureaucracy "tends to the belief that the unwanted aspects of bureaucracy are inseparable from the positively-valued aspects, and that above a certain size, at least, the unwanted aspects inevitably predominate, so that the costs of bureaucratic structure *as such* outweigh the benefits, and the only cure is the radical one of 'root out and start over.'"[28] Interestingly, those who take this position usually accept the argument that a complex society requires bureaucratization. They often add that society itself must be substantially restructured—made less urban, less industrialized, less materialistic, less complex—so that it can function adequately with nonbureaucratic organizations.

The alternative to bureaucracy most frequently suggested in radical analyses is some kind of communal organization with much less hierarchy, much less specialization, and much more popular participation than bureaucracy. As we will see, both Marx and Lenin singled out the Paris Commune of 1871 as an alternative to bureaucracy. Although Max Weber did not speak specifically of the Paris Commune, he outlined a similar form of political organization, "immediate democracy," which he described as an "anti-authoritarian form of government" in which "imperative powers" would be minimized. In immediate democracy, officials would have short terms of office, would be liable to recall at any time, would be selected by lot or elected, would be rotated frequently so that every citizen would serve in an official capacity at some time, would obtain strictly defined mandates from a popular assembly, and would be under strict obligation to report to the assembly and to request instructions on "every unusual question which has not been foreseen," either from the assembly or from a specialized assembly committee. In addition, governmental powers would be distributed among a large number of offices, and political office would be an avocation, not a vocation.[29]

Weber pointed out, however, that immediate democracy could exist only in communities that are small in size and population, that face only problems the entire populace can understand and discuss, and that have no organized political parties competing for office. In large communities, immediate democracy would be too cumbersome to work effectively. And in communities that had political parties or required the services of specialists, Weber predicted, power would pass inevitably to party leaders and technicians, and the political system would transform itself into a bureaucratic structure. Despite its limitations, however, Weber concluded that immediate democracy could be a rational form of government for those few places where the appropriate conditions were present.[30]

The rationalizing and radical approaches to the bureaucratic dilemma are based on one-sided assessments of the consequences of bureaucratization. There are, in addition, two remedial approaches that see the advantages and disadvantages of bureaucracy as being more evenly balanced, and that suggest reforms designed to retain the advantages while controlling or eliminating the disadvantages.

The *external remedial* approach seeks to subject bureaucracy to effective outside supervision and control. In all political systems, the chief executive—president, monarch, or dictator—can play this role to a degree, but no executive can single-handedly keep an eye on the performance of all the officials in a large bureaucracy. If he relies on the bureaucratic chain of command, or if he establishes a monitoring agency inside the bureaucracy, he has opted, in our analysis, for a rationalizing approach. It is only when a society develops outside mechanisms for supervising a bureaucracy that it can be said to have applied external remedies to the bureaucratic dilemma.

External remedies appear in a variety of forms. In different societies, interest groups, citizen-review boards, community organizations, the secret police, the press, and the judiciary can all play useful roles in exercising supervision over the bureaucracy. But of all the external mechanisms, two are the most important. In democracies control over the bureaucracy has been exercised through techniques of legislative oversight, notably control over administrative budgets, approval of major bureaucratic appointments, the right to make inquiries into bureaucratic activities, and the power to pass laws and make regulations governing bureaucratic performance. In authoritarian systems without active legislatures, the principal form of control over the bureaucracy has been the mass party, particularly its Leninist variant. The Leninist party exercises control over the bureaucracy by managing appointments and promotions, monopolizing leading posts, supervising the indoctrination of state officials, disciplining Party members who hold government positions, and setting the bureaucracy's principal policy guidelines.

Important as these mechanisms are, both may encounter difficulties. As Weber pointed out, the bureaucrat's possession of secret information and technical skills gives him an enormous advantage over the legislator who tries to oversee his work. And as we will see in the Chinese case, the Leninist party may begin to assume policymaking and administrative functions once assigned to the government and may itself become bureaucratized in the process. If legislators find it impossible to penetrate far enough into the bureaucracy, Party *apparatchiks* may find themselves drawn in too far to maintain their distance from day-to-day decision making.

Finally, the *internal remedial* approach to the bureaucratic dilemma introduces nonbureaucratic elements into the staffing and operations of the bureaucracy with the intent of alleviating some of the problems that emerge in purely bureaucratic organization. Unlike the rationalizing approach, internal remedialism does not assume that the solution to an organization's problems is to make it more nearly bureaucratic. Like the radical approach, it seeks to move administrative organizations away from the bureaucratic ideal-type, but its intent is not to destroy bureaucracy: the organizations that remain are still closer to the bureaucratic type than to other organizational forms. The result is quasibureaucracy, not nonbureaucracy.

What are some examples of internal remedial reforms? One is to replace monocratic leadership with a collegial form of leadership. Bureaucratic agencies would be headed not by a single director, but by a collective body representative of a variety of interests. Another might be to reduce the level of specialization by transferring officials from one assignment to another. Or the bureaucracy might be made to rely less on established routines than on informal ad hoc work teams that would deal in a flexible manner with specific problems. In the Chinese case, the most important device has been the establishment of political criteria for public office in addition to, or even in place of, technical and professional standards, and the development of programs of ideological indoctrination for public officials.

In short, there are four distinct approaches to the bureaucratic dilemma in modern society. To restate them concisely, the rationalizing approach believes in perfecting bureaucracy, the external remedial approach advocates controlling bureaucracy, the internal remedial approach proposes modifying bureaucracy, and the radical approach insists on destroying bureaucracy.*

THE ORGANIZATIONAL HERITAGE OF THE
CHINESE COMMUNIST PARTY

When the Chinese Communist Party came to power in 1949, it brought with it a richly variegated assortment of theories and established practices in government and political organization, all of which conditioned the

*For the convenience of the reader, definitions of these and other political and technical terms, together with short descriptions of major organizational programs, appear in the Glossary, which begins on p. 391.

ways it would govern China in the following years. The most firmly em-
placed was China's long history of bureaucratic government.[31] The most
thoroughly tested in a socialist context was the combination of Marxist-
Leninist theory and Leninist-Stalinist practice that constituted the Soviet
tradition of political organization.[32] The most readily available for immediate application was the experience the Chinese Party itself had acquired in administering the rural base areas it had established across China
between 1927 and 1949.[33]

These three sets of organizational theory did not, however, provide
Chinese leaders with clear, positive prescriptions for designing and managing the Party and state bureaucracies after 1949. There was a conflict
among the three, and each contained within itself important ambiguities
and contradictions. The Chinese political tradition had been shaped by the
two-thousand-year tension between Confucianism, with its emphasis on
government by indoctrination and moral example, and Legalism, with its
stress on formal regulations and strict punishment. The Soviet tradition
contained a serious contradiction between some of the antibureaucratic
elements in Marxist-Leninist theory and the bureaucratic cast of Leninist-Stalinist practice. Even the Party's own experience in governing its
rural bases had been marked by friction between its use of mass mobilization at the grass roots and its reliance on bureaucratic patterns of administration at higher levels.

Moreover, Chinese leaders have had an ambivalent attitude toward each
of these three influences. Although Party officials have expressed admira-
tion for certain great Confucian administrators, they have regarded others
as arbitrary, despotic, corrupt, and divorced from the day-to-day life of
the people. Similarly, although Marxist-Leninist theories of organization
have been adopted as Party doctrine and although much of Soviet practice
served as a model for the Chinese Party both before and after 1949,
Chinese leaders have questioned important features of the Soviet heritage,
particularly the violence and terror practiced under Stalin and the Soviet
system's tendencies toward excessive centralism, rigid routine, and strict
specialization. And although the Party has generally sought to preserve the
best of its own pre-1949 organizational policies, some Chinese leaders have
questioned whether organizational techniques that promoted revolution in
relatively backward rural areas could be applied with equal success to the
task of nationwide economic development.

In short, the Party's organizational heritage is unusually complex.
Taken together, Chinese traditional theories of political organization, Soviet theory and practice, and the Party's own revolutionary experience
include all four of the approaches to the bureaucratic dilemma just dis-

cussed. The fact that Chinese leaders have had a wide range of theories from which to choose has greatly heightened contention over organizational issues since 1949.

Internal Remedialism

Parts of all three traditions assume that effective organizational performance depends on indoctrinating officials in a coherent set of philosophical principles so that they will pursue the goals set by the policymakers in a unified and reliable manner.

In traditional China it was Confucianism that most nearly represented an internal remedial approach to the management of bureaucracy. Confucianism, especially during its last five centuries, became the main administrative doctrine of a political order that was largely bureaucratic in character. The imperial government had a clear hierarchy of offices under the emperor, a formal system of ranks, and substantial structural differentiation, particularly at the central and provincial levels. Confucianists also recognized the need for a large body of formal laws and organizational regulations. But Confucianism diverged in important ways from pure Weberian theory. Officials were to be recruited on the basis of moral qualifications, not technical competence. Moral norms were superior to formal rules and regulations and were to override them in case of conflict. Above all, Confucianism held that a purely bureaucratic administration—what the Chinese called government by "rules" or "law"—could never produce a just and stable social order. Government by regulation and routine could only be an adjunct to the informed judgment of officials whose education was firmly grounded in the ethical teachings of the past.

The Confucian principles of government were institutionalized in the civil service examinations that most would-be officials had to pass in order to enter government service. Success in the examinations required not knowledge of techniques of administration, but lengthy study of the Confucian classics, which emphasized moral rectitude, personal abnegation, and service to society. The examinations themselves, successful completion of which might take much of a man's adult life, were rigorous and competitive, and in time came to reward style of writing and beauty of calligraphy more highly than clarity of thought, and to prize normative judgment more highly than simple adherence to regulations. The examination system, in Thomas Metzger's analysis, thus instilled a "probationary ethic" in officials—a belief that they had been entrusted with a high responsibility they did not fully deserve, and that they could merit their status only through diligent and selfless service. If officials performed poorly, the probationary ethic required not only that they accept punishment from their superiors, but also that they confess their misconduct and seek to redeem themselves through exemplary behavior.[34]

The Confucian emphasis on indoctrination, self-cultivation, and redemption has intriguing parallels in the Soviet practice of study, criticism, and self-criticism. In building a professional revolutionary party in the early twentieth century, Lenin used ideological education as a means of ensuring discipline, loyalty, and commitment among his followers. Party members were expected to participate in regular, organized study of doctrine so that they would fully understand the Party's goals and programs. In meetings of their Party cells, members were also supposed to criticize their own shortcomings and denounce the failures of others as a way of maintaining the highest possible level of organizational effectiveness. At times, such as in the early 1920's, Lenin expanded routine criticism and self-criticism into a full-fledged purge of the Party; the unreliable were dismissed, the irresolute reindoctrinated, and the faithful promoted.

Under Stalin this style of Party life was transformed into what Zbigniew Brzezinski has called the "permanent purge." Stalin developed the concept that, even after the seizure of power, there would have to be continuous, violent, and uncompromising struggle to protect the dictatorship of the proletariat against its enemies. With this thesis as justification, between 1927 and 1938 Stalin directed a series of purges against "rightists," "capitalist elements," "Trotskyites," "local nationalists," and "political deviationists." In these purges, carried out in both the Party and the state bureaucracy, the relatively mild techniques of criticism and self-criticism were replaced by imprisonment, terror, and execution.

Alfred Meyer has described the purges as "the bureaucratization of class warfare, the transformation of political struggles into regulated routines and computer-like operations," but Stalinism actually entailed a nearly complete departure from normal bureaucratic routine.[35] Established procedures, administrative regulations, due process, and standard career patterns were all cast aside in the drive to ensure total loyalty to the Vozd. As Leonard Schapiro has pointed out, the administration of both Party and state retained only a few of the characteristics of a pure bureaucracy during the Stalinist period. It was rather "a body of retainers. The source of the authority of every party official was not his office, it was the fact that his continuing to occupy the office when everyone knew he could disappear at any moment was a public mark of the leader's favour."[36] Compared to Party life under Lenin, then, Stalin's "great terror" represented an extreme form of internal remedialism.

The Chinese Communist Party fell under the influence of Stalinist practice in the early 1930's. During the Kiangsi period, violent purges reflected the successive attempts of various factions of the Party to establish dominance over the others. In late 1930, for example, Mao Tse-tung sought to consolidate his control over Party organizations in the Kiangsi Soviet by charging his rivals with membership in an "anti-Bolshevik league." On this pretext he arrested more than four thousand opponents. In other base areas similar purges were conducted against "Trotskyists," "anti-Bolsheviks," and "social democrats." As Jane Price has suggested, one explanation for such tendencies was that young Chinese Communists had returned from training in the Soviet Union with the idea that violent purges were a legitimate way of conducting factional conflict and eliminating political opposition within the Party.[37]

In the early 1940's, during the Yenan period, Stalinist forms of inner-Party struggle were modified to correspond more closely with Leninist concepts and, perhaps not coincidentally, with traditional Chinese views of self-cultivation. The Party's first rectification campaign, the Cheng-feng movement of 1942–44, differed from earlier practice in emphasizing criticism and self-criticism rather than imprisonment and execution. As before, the campaign reflected the effort of one leadership faction, headed by Mao in this case, to consolidate its control over the Party, but it was now recognized that unity and discipline could be more effectively achieved by milder forms of indoctrination and purge.[38]

The Yenan technique of rectification involved, first of all, the compilation of a common body of documents for Party cadres to read and study.[39] Some were drawn from the works of Lenin and Stalin. Others were codifications of the Chinese Communist Party's own emerging theory of political organization, which stressed the need to subordinate one's personal interests to those of the movement, develop commitment to Party programs, investigate concrete local conditions, modify Soviet doctrine to suit Chinese needs, improve communications within the Party, and develop closer links between the Party and the people. Still others were discussions of techniques to be applied in this new form of inner-Party struggle.

The documents were discussed in small groups in which each Party member was expected to demonstrate his understanding of the texts, admit and repudiate the instances in which he had violated them, and criticize the shortcomings of his colleagues. Although these struggle sessions were not supposed to be "rough and rash," Mao warned that they would have to be intense: they were supposed to "administer a shock" and make each cadre "break out in a sweat" before the errant Party members were given "sincere advice on getting treatment." The goal was to "cure the sickness to save the patient," and although the treatment was not as harsh as in Stalin's great purges, it was not to be easy or painless.[40]

A second important technique of organizational management developed by the Party during the Yenan period was the use of mass campaigns to implement Party policies. Such campaigns were, in part, an admission that the Party did not have the manpower, money, or resources to govern its base areas without popular assistance. Mass involvement in such tasks as rent reduction, land reclamation, and the anti-Japanese war was essential if Communist policies were to be successful. But the campaigns were also devices to break the Party and government away from established routine. During the campaigns, administrative agencies were supposed to pay less attention to routine work and concentrate on the goals and problems that were the target of the campaign. Task forces were formed to guide their participation, dispatch officials to temporary leadership posts at lower levels, set higher production targets, and consider ways of improving efficiency. In organizational terms, the campaigns reflected a belief that bureaucratic performance could be improved by temporarily reducing an organization's level of hierarchy, routine, formalism, and specialization.

The "rural work style" the Party developed in Yenan represents yet another form of internal remedialism. The technique involved close, informal contacts between cadres and the peasantry, frequent cadre participation in physical labor, the limitation of income differentials between different grades of officials, and the payment of cadres in kind instead of cash. Organizational structure was relatively informal, specialization was rudimentary, and administrative procedures remained ad hoc and flexible. The rural work style was felt to be well adapted to maintaining the Party's popular support, preserving its financial resources, and coping with changes in the tactical situation.

External Remedialism

External remedialism—the use of external agencies to supervise and control the bureaucracy—was not a significant part of Chinese tradition. It is true that emperors relied on the Censorate to monitor the conduct of officials, but the Censorate, staffed by junior officials, was essentially a branch of the larger bureaucracy that it was supposed to police. No truly independent check on state officials was ever encouraged. Indeed, traditional officials made every effort to suppress or restrict any organization, be it clan, guild, or temple, that threatened to establish a base of political power beyond their control. Only the emperor himself—and, in some dynasties, the eunuchs at court—exercised external control over the bureaucracy. Although Legalists and Confucianists might have differed over the techniques to be employed, they would have agreed that bureaucracy was to be controlled mainly from within, not from without.

For Lenin, however, external controls were necessary to ensure the effectiveness of the bureaucracy. In theory, at least, popular participation was to be one such form of external check on the government. Delegates to local soviets were encouraged to monitor and criticize the work of state officials; so were members of the Workers' and Peasants' Inspection, a network of supervisory agencies that was staffed largely by ordinary citizens and was responsible for reporting any criminal activities, violations of administrative discipline, or departures from the state economic plan that could be traced to government bureaucrats.[41]

But Lenin considered the Party to be the most important instrument of control. In the immediate postrevolutionary period, he authorized the Party to lead the operations of the government, just as it had led the trade unions and other mass organizations during the revolution. Those years witnessed vigorous efforts to increase the proportion of government posts held by Party members and to strengthen Party cells and branches inside the state bureaucracy. In March 1919 the Eighth Party Congress authorized the Party to guide and control the state by issuing directives on policy matters to the Party cells inside the government bureaucracy. The cells were then to see that state officials carried out the directives.

Lenin seemingly did not expect that his emphasis on Party control of the state would lead to the bureaucratization of the Party itself. But by 1924, the year of his death, the Party had expanded its central staff, created a series of central departments to draft policy statements, improved its files on its members, and increased its ability to assign Party personnel to key administrative positions in the government. During the same period Party secretaries came increasingly to be appointed by their superiors, rather than elected by the membership. As Leonard Schapiro has put it, "The national network of Party committees came to be unified and transmuted into an administrative machine, whose backbone was the hierarchy of Party secretaries."[42]

In China before 1949, control over the government in Communist base areas was modeled closely on Leninist theory. During the Kiangsi period (1928–34), the Party emphasized popular supervision of the bureaucracy. In January 1934, for instance, Mao Tse-tung called for more effective mass criticism of the soviet's administrative organs, declaring that "every revolutionary citizen has the right to expose the errors or shortcomings of any Soviet functionary in his work." Since many officials were delegates to local soviets, Mao suggested that popular elections would provide an additional method of removing incompetent or corrupt cadres from office. Echoing Lenin, Mao also suggested that the Worker and Peasant Inspection Commission, a counterpart of the Russian organ, "draw in the broad masses for the critical examination of the work of the Soviet functionaries."[43]

Greater emphasis was placed on Party control of the government bureaucracy in the Yenan period. As part of the Cheng-feng movement,

Party committees at all levels were given the authority to monitor the work of government agencies in the areas under their supervision so that leadership in each base area would be unified.[44]

But the Party continued to experiment with ways of subjecting both the Party and the state to some form of popular supervision. In 1947–48 the Central Committee launched a second rectification campaign, this one aimed principally at corruption and abuse of power by basic-level cadres in North China. The campaign differed from its predecessor, the Chengfeng movement, in that participation by non-Party members was actively encouraged. A February 1948 directive described the campaign as an "open-door" process, in which Party work teams dispatched from higher levels would invite "activists from the non-Party masses" to participate in meetings of local Party branches. These non-Party activists were given the right to demand the dismissal of Party cadres from their posts, "propose their expulsion from the Party, and even hand the worst elements over to the people's courts for trial and punishment." Open-door rectification, it was said, not only helped "remove the impurities in the class composition and style of work in Party organizations," but also "enabled the Party to forge closer ties with the masses."[45]

The Party's experience with open-door rectification in 1947–48 was not altogether happy. The desire of poorer peasants for a more radical program of land redistribution was reflected in harsh criticism of basic-level cadres, resulting in a severe demoralization of Party members. Mao, although he defended the principle that the masses of the people had the right to criticize the Party, warned shortly after the campaign that it would be wrong to forget that "the Party should also educate and lead the masses."[46] The lesson of the 1947–48 rectification campaign was that if external supervision of the Party was to be encouraged, it would also have to be kept under careful control.

Radicalism

Radicalism, in our usage, is a concept with which Chinese Communist leaders were familiar, but as an undercurrent rather than a principal theme. The history of both imperial China and the Soviet Union appeared to suggest that, although radical ideology might offer an impassioned criticism of the irrationalities and inefficiencies of bureaucracy, the radical vision of a society governed by immediate democracy was extremely difficult to realize.

In traditional China radical views of bureaucracy were most clearly embodied in the Taoist ideal of an egalitarian, communitarian society unrestrained by government. Rules, regulations, laws, and administrative organizations were unnatural, the Taoists believed. As the *Lao-tzu* says,

"The more restrictions and prohibitions there are in the world, the poorer the people will be. . . . The more laws are promulgated, the more thieves there will be." Taoism envisioned a society in which people would spontaneously follow their "inherent virtue," and in which there would be no need for government.[47]

But though Taoism provided a rich vocabulary for criticizing the injustices of the prevailing social and political order, and inspired millenarian peasant rebellions against imperial institutions, its radical vision of society proved impossible to put into practice. If national unity were to be maintained, there was simply no practical alternative to bureaucracy in traditional China. Etienne Balazś has pointed out that a "large-scale agrarian society composed of individual cells—peasant families, living by subsistence agriculture, and scattered over an immense territory that was physically undifferentiated— . . . would have disintegrated into hopeless anarchy without the presence of a solid hierarchy of administrators given discretionary powers by a central government."[48] In traditional China, the principal organizational issue was not the choice between bureaucracy and Taoism, but rather the balance to be struck in bureaucratic practice between Confucianist and Legalist principles. For most Chinese Communist leaders, therefore, Taoism was a less important source of radical organization theory than were the theoretical writings of Marx, Engels, and Lenin that suggested bureaucracy would prove to be an obsolete form with no place in socialist society.

In Marxist analysis the origins of bureaucracy lay in the need of the bourgeoisie for an effective form of political organization that could be used first to gain control over the declining elites of feudal society and then to suppress and exploit the emerging proletariat. Marx wrote of this in "The Civil War in France":

The centralized state power, with its ubiquitous organs of standing army, police, bureaucracy, clergy, and judicature—organs wrought after the plan of a systematic and hierarchic division of labor—originates from the days of absolute monarchy, serving nascent middle-class society as a mighty weapon in its struggles against feudalism. . . . At the same pace at which the progress of modern industry developed, widened [and] intensified the class antagonism between capital and labor, the state power assumed more and more the character of the national power of capital over labor, of a public force organized for social enslavement, of an engine of class despotism.[49]

Although Marxists recognized that bureaucracy had first emerged in traditional agrarian societies, especially in Asia, they still linked the development of modern bureaucracy with the emergence of the bourgeoisie. In Lenin's words, bureaucracy was an institution "peculiar to bourgeois society."[50]

Bureaucracy might play either of two roles in capitalist society, neither of them progressive. Most commonly, bureaucracy served as the instrument by which the dominant capitalist class exercised control over the proletariat. Less often, usually in times of stalemate and deadlock between factions of the bourgeoisie, the bureaucracy might win autonomy and rule in its own interests. In both cases, in the Marxist view, it was a repressive institution through which a small minority of capitalists or officials was able to exercise power over the rest of society.

The logical conclusion of this line of argument was that bureaucracy should have no role after the proletarian revolution. Marx, Engels, and Lenin each called for the elimination of bureaucracy under socialism. Marx argued that the working class could not simply take over the ready-made bourgeois state machinery, but would have to change it fundamentally.[51] Engels warned that the working class would have to do away with the old repressive institutions formerly used against it. If it failed to do so, the bureaucrats would transform themselves from servants into masters, and the working class would lose its newly won supremacy.[52] And Lenin declared that the organizational role of the socialist revolution was not one of "perfecting the state machine, but one of *smashing and destroying it*."[53]

For Marx, Engels, and Lenin, one of the most attractive alternatives to a bureaucratic state was the Paris Commune of 1871. After the working class seized power and overturned the bourgeois bureaucracy, it would create a new form of political organization, a proletarian dictatorship. "Do you want to know what this dictatorship looks like?" Engels once asked. "Look at the Paris Commune. That was the dictatorship of the proletariat."[54] Under the Commune all distinctions between executive and legislative organs were eliminated, and all officials, even those occupying purely administrative positions, were chosen by general election. Once placed in office, officials were paid the same wages as ordinary workers, were required to report to their constituents regularly, and were subject to recall at any time. Through these mechanisms, Marx and Engels said, officials were prevented from pursuing their personal interests, and were forced to carry out the mandate given them by their constituents.

In Lenin's view, the workers' soviets that arose spontaneously in Russia during the Revolution of 1905 and the October Revolution of 1917 were latter-day counterparts of the Paris Commune. Both the Commune and the soviets, he wrote in 1917, embodied a form of "revolutionary dictatorship, i.e., a power directly based on revolutionary seizure, on the direct initiative of the people from below." And in both there was a "direct arming of the whole people," the overthrow of the bureaucracy, and the institution of "direct rule of the people themselves."[55] Neither organization was the only guise that the dictatorship of the proletariat might assume, for "the transition from capitalism to communism will certainly create a great variety and abundance of political forms." But Lenin implied that all socialist governments, in their emphasis on direct popular rule, would resemble both the Paris Commune and the soviets, which had continued its work.[56]

Once the Bolsheviks had seized power, however, radicalism played virtually no role in shaping the higher administrative institutions of the Soviet Union. Soviets were formed at the basic levels. But Lenin acknowledged that direct popular rule would be impossible, given the backwardness of the Russian people, and that only prolonged education could bring the people to a standard of literacy and administrative skill that would enable them to participate actively in the work of government: "We are not utopians. We know that an unskilled laborer or a cook cannot immediately get on with the job of state administration."[57]

To justify his departure from the radical vision of direct democracy, Lenin turned to an argument he had made well before the October Revolution, when he had drawn a distinction between the parts of the bureaucracy responsible for the maintenance of law and order and those that administered the economy.[58] The creation of socialism, Lenin now declared, might permit the abolition of the first type of bureaucracy, for the Soviet Union would have less and less need for a "purely administrative apparatus . . . the nature of which is only to give orders." But the economic bureaucracy not only would be preserved, but would grow in size and responsibility: "Apparatus of the type of the Supreme Council of the National Economy is marked out for growth; it will develop and strengthen itself, taking upon itself all the most important activity of organized society."[59]

The resultant growth of the state bureaucracy in the early years of the Soviet Union, and the bureaucratization of the Soviet Party that accompanied it, produced outcries both inside the country and abroad that Lenin had violated the antibureaucratic spirit of Marxism. Critics strongly objected to the restrictions imposed on worker participation in factory management and to the decline of democracy in the Party.* Lenin replied that his opponents were "disarming the proletariat in the interests of the bourgeoisie," and that their criticisms were "ridiculously absurd and stupid." Radical themes in the writings of Marx, Engels, and Lenin himself he now described as an "infantile disorder."[60] Lenin seemed to demonstrate by this shift that although Marxist radicalism, like Taoist

---

*These critics included the Workers' Opposition, the Democratic Centralists, and Leon Trotsky. See Leonard B. Schapiro, *The Communist Party of the Soviet Union*, 2d ed. (New York, 1971), especially chaps. 11 and 15.

radicalism in traditional China, might provide a convenient vocabulary for revolutionaries to criticize an existing regime, it was unlikely to become a program for governing.

Perhaps in consequence, radical views on organization played an extremely small role in the ideology of the Chinese Communist Party before 1949. To be sure, Mao declared that "the ugly evil of bureaucracy must be thrown into the cesspit."[61] And village governments in both Kiangsi and Yenan were deliberately patterned after the Russian soviets. But the Party never promised, as Lenin had, to smash the bureaucracy once the revolution had succeeded. Chinese Communist leaders seemed to accept the notion that a substantial bureaucratic establishment would be necessary under socialism. Liu Shao-ch'i explained in 1938 that bureaucracy could not be "liquidated overnight," and that hierarchy, specialization, and salary differentials could not be eliminated until the gap between mental and manual labor had been closed, and the cultural level of the Chinese people raised. Until then it would only be possible to try to avoid the excesses of bureaucracy by imbuing officials with a democratic spirit.[62]

Rationalization

Once Lenin had concluded that bureaucracy could not be destroyed in the early years of socialism, he went to the other extreme and proposed that it should be regularized, formalized, and perfected. His interest in bureaucratic rationalization had been foreshadowed even in such seemingly radical works as "The State and Revolution." Despite rhetorical flights on smashing bureaucracy and creating new democratic organizational forms, Lenin seems to have envisioned an administrative apparatus modeled on the industrial assembly line and the post office rather than on grass-roots democracy. He argued in "The State and Revolution" that economic development, urbanization, improved communications, and higher levels of literacy had created a situation in which "the great majority of the functions of the old 'state power' have become so simplified and can be reduced to such simple operations of registration, filing, and checking that they can be easily performed by every literate person."[63] Such an administrative organization might indeed be more democratic than its predecessors, in that ordinary workers and peasants would replace representatives of the bourgeoisie in governmental positions, but Lenin apparently did not fully realize that it would be no less bureaucratic.

Lenin's fascination with modeling all governmental organizations on the industrial assembly line increased in the last years of his life, as he became more concerned about the inefficiency, insensitivity, and corruption of the state bureaucracy of the Soviet Union. In 1923, for example, he admitted that "our state apparatus is to a considerable extent a survival of the past and has undergone hardly any serious change. [It has an] utterly impossible, indecently pre-revolutionary form."[64] But having said this, Lenin turned not to radicalism for a solution, but to rationalization. He proposed that a new supervisory agency be created to monitor and reform the bureaucracy, and that it be staffed by a small number of professional organizers selected for their mastery of scientific management techniques. The new agency would be responsible for the study of Western management practices, the development of advanced organization theory, and the compilation of textbooks on public administration.[65] Lenin's growing belief that rationalization offered the proper solution to the problems of socialist bureaucracy is shown by his interest in the works of Frederick W. Taylor, in time-and-motion studies, and in American forms of corporate management. As Paul Cocks has pointed out:

The prescribed medicine for curing creeping and crippling bureaucratic decay, then, was not so much a lesson in party ethics as in administrative skills and organization theory. Indeed, it was this technical conception of and solution to the Communist bureaucratic phenomenon that dominated Lenin's thinking during his last days and his struggle against Stalin and the party bureaucracy. More and more he saw the ultimate remedy for Russia's bureaucratic ills as rationalization, as an administrative revolution from above by experts.[66]

Lenin's interest in rationalization was maintained, at least in theory, by Stalin. Although the great purges of the 1920's and 1930's were the antithesis of organizational rationalization, Stalin continued to endorse many of the characteristics of the bureaucratic ideal-type. At various times Stalin called for a clearer division of labor, greater specialization, a higher level of professionalism, and more stringent systems of monitoring and control.[67] Stalin may have found these concepts attractive as a justification for his replacement of older revolutionaries by a younger, more compliant generation of technicians. Moreover, Stalin appears to have been even less ambivalent about the social and political consequences of bureaucracy than Lenin had been, and to have seen the rationalization of government as an important component in the construction of a powerful industrialized state.

For the Chinese Communists, whatever their inclination, rationalization was not a real possibility in the administration of the Communist base areas before 1949. There were powerful constraints against it in both the Kiangsi and the Yenan periods. In Kiangsi the shortage of skilled and literate officials made it difficult to build a formal government bureaucracy. In Yenan the Party's need to operate from widely dispersed base areas, its limited economic resources, and its involvement in a far-flung mobile guerrilla war made the "rural work style" more appropriate.

Nonetheless, the Party did attempt to regularize its organizational structure whenever possible. In Yenan a degree of bureaucratization was apparent, in part because of the availability of intellectuals from the cities and in part because of the Party's desire to establish a more systematic administration. In the late 1940's, when previously separate base areas in North China were linked together, the Party made further efforts to rationalize its administrative procedures. In 1947–48 the Central Committee required each of its bureaus and sub-bureaus to submit a short bimonthly report on local conditions and special requests for instructions when those conditions changed. Party leaders began to concentrate more authority in the Central Committee and to specify the degree of flexibility local officials would be allowed in interpreting central Party directives.[68] These early efforts at regularization were but a prelude to a more extensive drive for organizational rationalization that was undertaken shortly after the Party assumed nationwide power.

Although the Party's interest in rationalization was shaped primarily by the experience of the Soviet Union and by its own administrative experience, that interest can also be traced to native sources, the policies of the Legalists of the fourth and third centuries B.C. In contrast to Confucianism, Legalism assumed that, in Charles Hucker's words, men were "amorally self-seeking" and would have to be "coerced into obedience by rewards and harsh punishments."[69] It was a theory of government that emphasized the codification of law, rules, and regulations and the strict supervision of official behavior, rather than self-cultivation, moral example, and autonomy of judgment. Its goal was to establish a clear chain of command, not only in the state bureaucracy but also in society as a whole, a chain in which all Chinese would find their places as faithful instruments of the ruler. Legalism contained explicit elements of pure Weberian bureaucracy, particularly hierarchy, formalization, rigor, and impartiality.

The organizational heritage of the Chinese Communist Party was, in short, complex and ambiguous. The morally cultivated generalists of Confucian China found their counterparts in the ideologically committed cadres of Lenin's Bolshevik Party, but the type clashed with Lenin's ideal bureaucrat-as-assembly-line-worker. It also clashed with the Legalist principle that the most effective officials were amoral but disciplined instruments of the emperor. The Taoist desire to abolish all government paralleled the elements of Marxism-Leninism that promised the withering away of the state, but neither provided weaponry to attack the real growth of bureaucracy in the Chinese and the Soviet traditions.

The Party's organizational policy before 1949 combined elements of all four approaches to the bureaucratic dilemma. Radicalism was reflected, although to a limited degree, in the structure of local governments in the base areas. The belief that organizational rationalization should be pursued as far as conditions permitted was reflected in the Central Committee's attempt to regularize and formalize Party structure in the late 1940's. External remedialism was to be found in the open-door rectification campaign of 1947–48, as well as in the use of the Party to penetrate and control the base-area governments in both Kiangsi and Yenan.

But it was internal remedialism that lay at the heart of Chinese Communist organization theory before 1949. The emphasis on indoctrination, rectification, mass campaigns, and the rural work style was intended neither to rationalize bureaucracy nor to destroy it. It was a deliberate effort—by placing limits on hierarchy, specialization, formalization, and routine—to prevent administrative organizations from becoming purely bureaucratic. The issue for the future was whether this strategy would continue to be appropriate after 1949, when the Chinese Communist Party turned from the task of seizing power to the job of economic development and social transformation.

2

Organization Building and Consolidation 1949-1953

The defeat of the Kuomintang and the establishment of the People's Republic of China in 1949 confronted the Chinese Communist Party with an imposing array of new political and economic problems. The first was the task of economic recovery. The Chinese economy had been devastated by years of revolution, foreign invasion, and civil war. Agricultural and industrial production had fallen well below their prewar peaks.[1] The country was suffering from serious urban unemployment and chronic hyperinflation, and was facing the prospect of continued government budget deficits in 1950. It was imperative that the Party balance the national budget, reduce inflation and unemployment, and stimulate the recovery of industrial and agricultural production. Only if China could "achieve a fundamental turn for the better in the financial and economic situation," as Mao put it in June 1950, could the Party expect to maintain its popular support and lay the foundation for planned economic development.[2]

Second was the task of beginning the reorganization and transformation of the Chinese socioeconomic order along the lines indicated by the Party's major programmatic pronouncements in the late 1940's.* The most important program was land reform, which was instituted in the Communist base areas immediately after the Second World War and extended to the newly liberated areas in the early 1950's. But the Party instituted many other major social and economic reforms in the first years of the People's Republic, including a new marriage law, the gradual restriction and regulation of private industry and commerce, the reorganization of the educational system, the extension of Party control over publishing and the arts, and the thought reform of intellectuals, merchants, and industrialists. These measures were believed to be prerequisites for the collectivization of agriculture and the nationalization of industry, even though the socialist transformation of China was still seen as being "quite far off."[3]

*The major pronouncements are Mao, "Report to the Second Plenary Session of the Seventh Central Committee of the Communist Party of China" (5.iii.49), in *Selected Works of Mao Tse-tung*, 5 vols. (Peking, 1967–77), vol. 4, pp. 361–75; Mao, "On the People's Democratic Dictatorship" (30.vi.49), *ibid.*, pp. 411–24; and the Common Program of the Chinese People's Political Consultative Conference, adopted in September 1949.

As a third task, the new Communist government, like all successful revolutionary movements, faced the challenge of stabilizing and consolidating its rule, of consolidating, as Mao put it, "the glorious victory of the Chinese people's revolution."[4] In the Party's eyes, the consolidation of power required the dispossession, imprisonment, or execution of the "enemies" of the new regime—political elements such as landlords, "local tyrants," former high Kuomintang officials, active Kuomintang sympathizers, rural bandits, members of rural secret societies, and common criminals. It required mobilizing the support of the Party's principal constituents, particularly the industrial workers and poorer peasants, through the development of a network of mass organizations and the creation of a nationwide propaganda apparatus.[5] And it required a carefully balanced policy toward the crucial "middle sectors" of Chinese society—intellectuals, technicians, rich peasants, industrialists, and merchants—whose cooperation was essential to economic recovery. Such a policy sought to encourage these sectors to contribute their skills and productivity to the task of economic recovery, and at the same time to reform their political views through an intense program of ideological struggle, criticism, and reeducation.[6] In short, the goal of consolidation was, in Mao Tse-tung's words, that "all the workers, peasants, and small handicraftsmen will support us, and the overwhelming majority of the national bourgeoisie and intellectuals will not oppose us. In this way, the remnant Kuomintang forces, the secret agents, and the bandits will be isolated, as well as the landlord class."[7]

Finally, by late 1950 the new Chinese government also faced an unanticipated strategic problem, ensuring its security against the escalation of American participation in the war in Korea. In October 1950, when United Nations forces approached the Yalu River boundary between North Korea and Manchuria, the Chinese felt obliged to intervene, first in a number of premonitory probes and then in force. By the end of 1951 China and the United States were locked in a stalemate on the Korean peninsula, and the war effort was imposing a significant drain on China's scarce financial and material resources.

Each of these four tasks had important implications for organizational policy in China. Economic reconstruction required the development of a strong administrative apparatus to establish firm and efficient control over the national economy. It also demanded that administrative costs be kept as low as possible so that scarce budgetary resources could be used for productive ends. Socioeconomic transformation required the creation of a strong organizational network that could carry out Party policy effectively and reliably, mobilizing support from the beneficiaries of reform and overcoming opposition from the targets of redistribution. Political consolidation required that both the Party and the government be relatively free of corruption, responsive to popular demands, and restrained in the execution of Party programs. China's entrance into the Korean War simply intensified the existing determination that organizations remain politically reliable, that potentially disloyal officials be dismissed, and that administrative costs be minimized.

Organizational policy reflected these requirements in two ways in the years between 1949 and 1953. First, this was a period of organization building, during which a flexible, relatively informal administrative apparatus was constructed at the central, regional, and provincial levels, and a major recruitment drive was undertaken to staff it. Second, this was also a period of organizational rectification. No fewer than three rectification campaigns were launched in the Party and state administrative bureaucracies in the first four years of the People's Republic. One, conducted in 1950, was directed against "arrogance, bureaucratism, and commandism" in the implementation of land redistribution in the countryside and economic reform in the cities. Another, the San-fan campaign (the campaign against the "three evils") of 1951–52, was aimed at eliminating corruption and waste, particularly in urban economic administration. A third, the so-called New San-fan campaign (the campaign against the "new three evils") of 1953, was intended to reduce commandism, abuse of power, and violations of Party and administrative discipline. The campaigns complemented an ongoing effort to consolidate the rank and file of the Party by weeding out members who did not fully meet Party standards. They were generally effective in creating the organizational basis for economic recovery and socioeconomic transformation in the early 1950's. But as we will see in the conclusion to this chapter, they also produced unintended consequences in the years that followed, consequences that would lead some Party leaders to question the value to postrevolutionary China of further rectification campaigns.

ORGANIZATION BUILDING

Restoring order to a seriously dislocated economy, promoting economic production, implementing land reform, suppressing counterrevolutionaries, mobilizing popular support, fighting a war in Korea—to accomplish these tasks successfully, the Party needed to create an effective and efficient administrative apparatus, and to do so in very short order. On paper this could be done quickly. The central government promptly established the Government Administration Council, a cabinet composed of the heads of a full panoply of ministries and commissions. It also created the People's Supervisory Committee, which was charged with ensuring that the bureaucracy faithfully carried out national policy and with ferreting out and punishing corrupt state officials. Six sets of regional governments

and Party bureaus were established to translate central policy into local
terms and to oversee the operation of the state and Party down to the
township level.* Local governments were also put in place in both urban
and rural China.

Although it was thus a fairly simple matter to establish the outlines of a
national administrative apparatus, the task of organization building was
greatly complicated by a serious shortage of skilled cadres and officials.†
During the revolution the Party's recruitment policies had emphasized
political commitment rather than technical skills or intellectual ability.
Most of its members lacked administrative experience. Fewer than half
had the equivalent of a junior-middle-school education, and a large proportion was illiterate. Thus, though there were some 4.5 million Party
members at the end of 1949, only some 720,000 were even minimally qualified to serve as Party cadres or as government officials—only about one-
third of what was actually needed to staff the Party, government, and mass
organizations, according to one estimate.[8] And the shortage was more
acute at the regional level than even these national figures might suggest.
In the Southwest, for example, the Party was able to fill only 17 percent of
the vacant administrative positions by September 1950. Similarly, in the
Northwest it could recruit only enough cadres to fill 10 percent of the
positions in some branches of the Party and government.[9]

The Party responded to this shortage in two principal ways. In the
months immediately after liberation, it relied heavily on the army for administration, particularly at the regional and provincial levels. Indeed, in
four of the six regions the task of governance was assigned to Military and
Administrative Committees, which were quite explicitly instruments of
military rule. For several years the Party also attempted to compensate for
its shortage of cadres by using mass organizations to carry out social and
economic reforms. Peasant associations, for example, played an important
role in land reform; the Women's Federation educated its members in
their rights under the new marriage law; and the trade unions, together
with the youth and women's organizations, were active in the 1952 campaign against corruption, tax evasion, and other illegal business practices.
As Ezra Vogel has described the early years of Communist rule in Canton,
"Students were organized to carry propaganda messages, consumers to

---

*The six regions, each of which had a Party bureau and a regional government apparatus,
were the Northeast (Manchuria), North, East, Central-South, Southwest, and Northwest.

†Mao referred to the cadre shortage in March 1949, when he pointed out that the Party
did not have enough cadres to administer the "vast new areas" that it would soon control in
South China. Mao said that the army would have to be a major source of new cadres, and that
the "field armies with their 2,100,000 men" should therefore be turned into a "gigantic
school for cadres." He also said that non-Communists would have to be given responsible
positions in the new political system. *Selected Works of Mao Tse-tung*, vol. 4, pp. 363, 373.

check inflation, workers to inspect their employers, [and] housewives to tidy up their neighborhoods."[10]

But reliance on the army and the mass organizations could only be a short-term device. The lasting solution to the problem, as the Party saw it, was to train and recruit career civilian cadres for service in the Party and government. In 1950 Lin Piao, the head of the government in the Central-South region, described the new regime's cadre policy:

Shortages of cadres and the mediocrity of their performance are common in all provinces. This constitutes one of the most difficult problems in our work. Its effective solution is imperative. Training a large group of new cadres should become our first priority. Cadre training classes, people's congresses, and various mass organizations should recommend and train a sufficient number of *worker-peasant cadres* in the provinces and the cities for administrative and management tasks. The previous policies of recruitment and training of *intellectual youth*, technicians, and specialists should be continued. We must cultivate *persons of special talents* [i.e., older intellectuals] in short-term revolutionary colleges and other universities to meet the urgent needs of future production. Based on the directives of the Central Government and Chairman Mao, we should absorb *former military and administrative personnel of the Nationalist government* and, following sufficient training and reform, transform them into new cadres.[11]

As the italicized phrases in Lin's report indicate, the Party recruited its new cadres from four groups: young graduates of middle schools and universities, older non-Party intellectuals and technical specialists, selected officials from the former Nationalist government, and mass activists, particularly those of worker or peasant background, who emerged in the campaigns of the early 1950's. In addition, it also sought to retrain veteran Party members in necessary technical, administrative, and cultural skills so that they could be promoted to administrative positions. What were the strengths and weaknesses of each of these groups of cadres?

The universities and middle schools were an important source of younger administrative cadres for the new regime, but the schools could not come close to filling China's need for administrators during this period. For one thing, all the schools combined turned out a relatively small number of graduates. Between 1950 and 1952, for example, the universities graduated some 66,000 students, the higher technical schools 3,000, and the middle schools and technical schools 200,000.[12] Even if all 269,000 graduates had become administrative cadres, they would have been able to fill only a fraction of the estimated two million vacancies in this period. But these youths were just as badly needed for work in other sectors, including the educational system itself.[13] In fact, most of the 269,000 graduates were assigned to positions outside the government and Party bureaucracies, leaving only a small number to become state or Party cadres.[14]

As a second source of skilled officials, therefore, the Party had to rely on older intellectuals and technicians. Though many were sympathetic to the Party, their class background was usually bourgeois rather than proletarian, and their political ideology tended to be more liberal than communist. Many of these older intellectuals were given administrative posts in the government as part of the united front with the "national bourgeoisie." At the same time, however, it was also considered necessary to carry out appropriate criticism or struggle against their shortcomings, particularly their lack of commitment to Marxism-Leninism and to Party policy and programs. As a result, about 100,000 of these older intellectuals were sent to special "people's revolutionary universities" for thought reform between 1950 and 1952, and others were given ideological training in short courses.[15] These experiences were often unpleasant, but the price the Party exacted of non-Party intellectuals in search of government posts.*

Rather surprisingly, the new regime put its heaviest reliance on officials who had held lower- and middle-level positions in the former Nationalist government. As early as September 1949 the Party had encouraged all officials of the previous regime, except those it defined as reactionaries or Kuomintang agents, to stay on and serve under the Communist government, once they had received short-term ideological training and undergone thought reform.[16] These retained officials played an extremely important administrative role during the early years of the People's Republic, particularly in middle-level positions where political qualifications were relatively unimportant. Retained officials accounted for 70–80 percent of the officials in Shanghai after liberation, for more than 40 percent of the municipal employees in Amoy in 1950, and for fully half of the 180,000 cadres in the whole of the Southwest in mid-1950.[17]

The policy of drawing new cadres from the pool of mass activists, particularly those who emerged during land reform (1950–52) and the Wu-fan campaign against illegal practices by private business (1952), came somewhat later when, at the Third Plenum of the Central Committee in June 1950, some leaders apparently expressed concern at the degree to which the Party was selecting "young intellectuals" fresh out of the middle schools and universities to serve as cadres.[18] The Plenum decided to place greater emphasis on the recruitment of mass activists, particularly those of worker or peasant backgrounds, presumably because of their greater political reliability.[19] Although An Tzu-wen, then minister of personnel and

---

*Most who were sent to "people's revolutionary universities" (*jen-min ko-ming ta-hsüeh*) stayed there for six months, but some were kept on for eight or even twelve months. For a description of these schools and of the thought-reform process, see Robert Jay Lifton, *Thought Reform and the Psychology of Totalism: A Study of "Brainwashing" in China* (New York, 1961), chap. 14.

deputy director of the Party's Organization Department, acknowledged that worker-peasant activists often lacked the culture and skills of college or middle-school graduates, he insisted that once on the job they could learn administrative practice quickly because of their "rich practical experience" and "firm class standpoint."[20] Most of these worker and peasant cadres were probably assigned to basic-level positions in factories, mines, and rural areas, but at least their recruitment freed other officials for reassignment to higher administrative posts.[21]

The Party meanwhile also set out to retrain its own members and cadres for administrative service through programs designed to improve their ideological commitment, understanding of Party and government policy, literacy, arithmetic, and technical and administrative skills. Cadres who had already received a relatively high level of formal education were sent to a university for academic training, to one of the special schools established specifically for cadre retraining by the central, regional, provincial, and municipal governments, or to a short-term training class run by the government ministry or department in which they worked. Cadres who were not qualified for university training were assigned to a regular middle school or, more frequently, to a special "short-course" middle school for instruction to improve their ability to read, write, and calculate. All told, these in-service programs graduated some 1.1 million cadres between 1949 and 1952.[22]

By the end of 1952 these channels for recruiting new officials and retraining veteran Party members had gone a long way toward alleviating the cadre shortage of late 1949. In September 1952, An Tzu-wen claimed that the Party had been able to recruit 2.6 million new cadres since 1949. Adding in the 720,000 cadres already available to the Party in 1949, the new regime now had some 3.3 million officials on the job. An did not indicate the background of this new corps of cadres, but he did suggest that a very small proportion came from the universities. The majority were either retained officials, worker-peasant activists, or veteran Party members who had received administrative or technical training.[23]

Despite these accomplishments, the cadre recruiting and retraining programs produced some serious problems. As might have been expected, cadres recruited from such a wide variety of backgrounds had some difficulty in working together smoothly and cooperatively, and experienced considerable competition over the allocation of power, status, and income. Essentially, the patterns of recruitment and promotion produced two fundamental splits within the Party and state bureaucracies. The first was generational, between older Party members, most of whom had relatively low technical and cultural skills, and younger cadres straight out of middle schools and universities. In some cases, younger, better educated officials were promoted over the heads of older veterans, who responded to the slight with anger and resentment. One older cadre wrote to the journal *Hsüeh-hsi* (Study) to complain that, despite his many years of service, he was now expected to work under young men and women "fresh from school. . . . The fruits of victory, which we paid for with our flesh and blood, are now being enjoyed by those who have contributed nothing and deserve less."[24] Other older Communists coined a slogan containing the bitter phrase, "Old revolutionaries aren't treated as well as new ones."[25] Equally ambitious younger cadres no doubt felt resentful when they found themselves blocked from promotion by older officials who lacked administrative skills but whose years of service to the Party gave them a nearly unassailable claim to the best bureaucratic positions.

The second split was based on political orientation and class background. It set non-Party officials, particularly retained Nationalist cadres and older intellectuals and technicians, against veteran Party cadres and worker-peasant activists. Many of the non-Party officials were contemptuous of the low cultural level and lower-class background of the Party cadres and mass activists, and resented the Party veterans' receiving superior positions in the government. The result often was resistance to attempts to reeducate them in Communist ideology, malingering, and reluctance to offer ideas and suggestions for fear of rejection or even punishment by Party veterans. On the other hand, Communist cadres often complained of the political unreliability of non-Party officials, doubted their willingness to undergo ideological reform, and denigrated their technical skills and administrative abilities. Expanding on the slogan mentioned above, some veteran Party cadres complained not only that "old revolutionaries were not treated as well as new ones," but also that "new revolutionaries [educated youth] were not treated as well as nonrevolutionaries [older intellectuals], and nonrevolutionaries were not treated as well as counterrevolutionaries [retained officials]."

These generational and political rifts were reinforced by a difference in the way the veteran Communist cadres and the retained and new officials were paid. During the revolution cadres in Communist base areas had been paid according to the "supply system," under which their housing and some of their food were provided directly by the government and formed the major portion of their remuneration.* After 1949 the supply system was maintained for nearly all the old Communist cadres, but both

*Cadres also received a living allowance, in cash, to pay for clothing and other daily necessities. They were expected to grow much of their own food and, if possible, to work in supplementary occupations to help support themselves. It is important to keep in mind that the supply system was not totally egalitarian. High-ranking cadres received more food, better housing, and higher living stipends than lower-level cadres.

the officials who had worked under the Nationalist government and many new cadres were paid according to a formal, graduated salary system. Despite a September 1950 reduction in the salaries of the retained cadres and a March 1952 increase in the subsidies paid under the supply system, the gap in the living standards of the two groups remained substantial.[26] Many of the attempts to improve cadre living standards were across-the-board measures that applied equally to supply-system cadres and to wage-system cadres. In July 1952, for example, all cadres received pay increases ranging from 10 to 30 percent and were granted free medical care. But because the level of income of the supply-system cadres was substantially lower than that of the other cadres to begin with, there was little narrowing of the gap.[27]

Officials responsible for organizational policy handled these three problems in different ways. The inequality of wages and salaries was adjusted through the gradual elimination of the supply system and the substitution for all cadres of a common graduated salary scale. That process, justified on the grounds that the salary system was more suitable than the supply system for a society undergoing planned economic development, will be discussed in more detail in the following chapter.

The Party's response to the second problem, the rift between older and younger cadres, was necessarily ambiguous, for the Party needed the support and skills of both groups. To resolve the dilemma, the Party developed a set of policies that acknowledged the roles of both older and younger cadres, but that tended to favor the former. It denied that seniority per se was an acceptable claim to office and denounced the cadres who attempted to invoke seniority as grounds for promotion as "useless and even decadent."[28] Older cadres who seemed particularly incompetent, including those who were unable or unwilling to learn standard Mandarin speech, were gradually removed from office.[29] On the other hand, there was much sympathy for veterans of the revolution and much anxiety about the Party's recruiting "young intellectuals who had neither undergone the steeling of productive labor nor stood the test of pragmatic struggle."[30] Thus, though seniority was rejected in principle as a standard for personnel action, it was considered to be one reliable index of political virtue, which in turn was an important criterion for recruitment and promotion.[31] Moreover, many veteran cadres benefited from the assumption that, because of their revolutionary experience, they could quickly repair any technical, administrative, and cultural deficiencies through on-the-job experience and rotational-training classes. In short, though both groups were said to have important contributions to make to the nation, in practice most of the university and middle-school graduates who entered Party and government service between 1949 and 1952 were assigned lower positions to avoid placing them above the veterans.[32]

The final problem, the tension between Party and non-Party cadres, was managed by adopting a policy of relative lenience toward non-Party intellectuals but increasing strictness toward retained officials. In the spring of 1951 the First National Conference of Secretaries-General was convened to discuss personnel and administrative problems within the government.* Li Wei-han, secretary-general of the Government Administration Council, outlined a policy designed to strengthen the united front within governmental agencies.[33] He began by admitting that government cadres came from widely divergent backgrounds, and that relations between Party and non-Party cadres were not as good as they should be. He called on Party cadres to give their non-Party counterparts greater authority and responsibility, to respect their views and opinions, and to seek their criticism of the Party's work. The principles guiding relations between Party and non-Party officials were to be "honesty, mutual respect, mutual study, and mutual assistance."†

But Li also warned that all cadres should support the policies contained in the Common Program, adopted by the Chinese People's Political Consultative Conference when the People's Republic was established in 1949. To this end Party cadres were duty-bound to educate non-Party officials in the provisions of the Common Program, and non-Party cadres were asked to improve their political understanding through ideological study and by participating in the ongoing mass movements of the period, particularly land reform. The avoidance of sectarianism by Party cadres and the ideological reform of non-Party cadres would produce a unity of views, Li said, as long as there were frequent meetings between the two groups for mutual criticism and self-criticism.[34]

Standards were stricter for retained officials. In February 1951, shortly before the Conference of Secretaries-General, the Politburo held an enlarged meeting to discuss the war in Korea, economic policy, land reform, and organizational matters. Largely as a response to the war, it was decided to conduct a campaign against counterrevolutionaries in the government, in order to uncover enemies of the regime "hiding among the old personnel and among the intellectuals recently drawn into our work."

*The conference was attended by the secretaries-general and directors of the general affairs offices of governmental bodies from the central, regional, provincial, and municipal levels. It was these officials who were principally responsible for administrative and organizational matters within the government bureaucracy. See New China News Agency, 16.v.51, in *Survey of the China Mainland Press*, no. 105 (16–20.v.51), pp. 24–25.

†A month after the close of the conference, the Government Administration Council ordered all levels of government to pay greater attention to improving relations between Party and non-Party cadres. At the provincial and municipal levels the problem was not simply to be assigned to the personnel office, but was to be the personal responsibility of the government secretary-general and the director of the general affairs office. At lower levels, a high-ranking government official was also to be assigned specific responsibility for improving relations between Party and non-Party cadres.

This screening of the middle layer of counterrevolutionaries (the outer layer being counterrevolutionaries in the general population, the inner layer, counterrevolutionaries inside the Party itself) was conducted during the summer and autumn of 1951, first through the self-criticism of intellectuals and retained officials, and then through investigations undertaken by "public security committees" established in each government office.[35] Many retained officials were removed during this campaign, often as a result of exaggerated charges. After the dismissal of two more groups of retained officials, one during the San-fan movement of 1951–52 and another during the later Su-fan campaign of 1955 against "hidden counterrevolutionaries," the process was complete.* From interviews with emigres who served as retained officials in the 1950's, Ezra Vogel has concluded that most had been dismissed by the beginning of 1956.[36]

ORGANIZATIONAL RECTIFICATION

Even as the Party began the long process of recruiting new cadres, it had to cope with the administrative problems caused by the cadre shortage. The three tasks mentioned above—economic recovery, socioeconomic reform, and political consolidation—simply could not wait until a complete new administrative apparatus was in place. Unless the Party could achieve rapid rehabilitation of the economy, Mao had warned in March 1949, "we shall be unable to maintain our political power, we shall be unable to stand on our feet, we shall fail."[37] Land reform was also considered an urgent task in the newly liberated areas of the South, Southwest, and Northwest. Lin Piao declared in July 1949 that in southeastern China the Communists effectively controlled only the cities. The "feudalistic villages" were still dominated by "counterrevolutionary landlords," "bandits," and "Nationalist special agents." Unless land reform could be quickly accomplished and the old order in the villages overturned, China's cities would be deprived of supply, its factories would be in need of raw materials, and its industrial products would lack markets.[38]

But the shortage of skilled and experienced cadres affected the implementation of these urgent economic and social programs. Understaffing led cadres to use compulsion and force rather than persuasion. In the cities, for example, where the government sought to overcome its budget deficit by increasing bond sales, many cadres began to rely on the threat of imprisonment or, in some cases, on physical force to fulfill the high quotas assigned them.[39] Similar problems were evident in agriculture. The peas-

*The "campaign to weed out counterrevolutionaries," abbreviated as the Su-fan campaign, began in June 1955 and ran through October 1957. Some 100,000 "bad elements" and counterrevolutionaries were said to have been discovered hiding inside Party and government organizations.

ants almost certainly would have been willing to adopt new farming techniques if the advantages were clear, but cadres tended to force technical reforms without sufficient explanation or small-group discussion.

These problems at the grass roots were exacerbated by pressures originating at higher levels of the Party and the state. In many cases, the coercive methods of the local cadres were a response to the unrealistic expectations of senior administrators, unfamiliar with local conditions, for rapid or dramatic results. In other cases, local cadres were required to attend so many meetings and file so many reports that they did not have enough time to devote to routine administration.

This situation seems to have caused widespread concern among senior Party leaders that the new government was falling into the ways of the old Nationalist regime. In their view, the Party had to preserve its close relations with the masses. But the commandism of local cadres imperiled that rapport, and the lack of popular support, in turn, seemed certain to endanger their plans for land reform and economic recovery.[40]

The 1950 Rectification Campaign

Accordingly, in the spring of 1950 the Central Committee issued three directives—one on improving relations between the Party and the people, a second on developing criticism and self-criticism in newspapers and journals, and a third calling for a Party rectification campaign to be held during the last six months of 1950 and the first three months of 1951.[41] These directives, together with a fourth on consolidating basic-level Party organizations, were discussed and adopted by the Third Plenum of the Central Committee in June. Mao formally endorsed the rectification campaign in his report to the plenum, expressing the hope that it would help Party cadres overcome "arrogance, bureaucratism, and commandism," and thus "improve the relations between the Party and the people."[42]

The 1950 Party Day editorial of *Jen-min jih-pao* (People's Daily) appearing shortly after the plenum, presented the first detailed public outline of the campaign.* The editorial pointed out that the Party's relations with the people had deteriorated since victory in 1949. The new campaign was being undertaken to remedy commandist work styles, strengthen the relationship between the Party and the people in both city and countryside, and consolidate the united front. Its goal was to facilitate the completion of

---

*The 1950 rectification campaign has received little attention in Western analyses. For a very brief discussion, see Boyd Compton, *Mao's China: Party Reform Documents, 1942–1944*, pp. xlvi–xlix, where the campaign is referred to as the "Three Seasons Reform." For a more detailed discussion in an official Chinese history of rectification campaigns, see Chao Han, *T'an-t'an Chung-kuo Kung-ch'an-tang-ti cheng-feng yün-tung* (A discussion of the rectification campaigns of the Chinese Communist Party), pp. 26–29.

land reform in the villages of the newly liberated areas and the recovery of industry and commerce in the cities.[43]

But the Party Day editorial, the directives issued by regional Party bureaus, and subsequent press reports all stressed that the campaign was to be moderate. The editorial noted that the Party's two previous rectification campaigns, the Cheng-feng campaign of 1942–43 and the Party rectification of 1947–48, had both committed "leftist errors." The 1950 rectification was not to be allowed to commit similar mistakes. In the same vein, one regional directive warned that a harsh campaign would harm the morale of basic-level cadres, and might therefore prevent the smooth accomplishment of land reform, tax collection, and other Party programs.[44]

So from the very beginning Party leaders placed important constraints on the conduct of the campaign. It was, first of all, to be carefully supervised. Party committees at the regional, provincial, municipal, and district levels were to draw up plans and to telegraph them directly to the Central Committee for review; Party committees below the district were also to relay their plans to higher levels for approval. Beyond this, the campaign was also to be limited in intensity. Since one objective was to prevent the press of cadre work from producing commandism and bureaucratism, it was clearly desirable that the campaign itself disrupt normal operations as little as possible. The campaign was therefore designed to complement day-to-day administrative work rather than to compete with it. Third, the campaign was expected to last no more than two months in each unit, and warnings were issued against prolonging it.[45]

Finally, the campaign was to be extremely lenient. To ensure that basic-level cadres alone were not singled out for criticism, and that the responsibility of higher officials for commandism was acknowledged, the campaign was to focus on leading Party cadres at each level and was to be conducted "from top to bottom" (*tzu-shang-erh-hsia*). That is, meetings were first to be called at the regional, provincial, and municipal levels, where high-ranking cadres were expected to admit and correct their own mistakes and shortcomings before criticizing those of their subordinates. Only later would the campaign be extended to the district, county, and local levels.[46] Non-Party cadres were welcome to participate in the campaign and voice criticisms of Party cadres, but it was made clear that they were not expected to meet the strict standards of behavior specified in the Party constitution for Party cadres.[47] At no point in the campaign were quotas set specifying the proportion of cadres to be disciplined, demoted, or dismissed; on the contrary, regional directives and press reports consistently stressed the desirability of leniency and the need to distinguish serious errors from smaller ones. To ensure that the campaign would not get out of hand, punishment was to be determined not by the unit in which the cadres worked, but by control organs at higher levels.

Although the general purposes of the campaign seem to have been widely accepted within the Party, there appears to have been some discussion, perhaps even debate, over certain points, including a precise identification of the problem that the campaign was supposed to resolve. Liu Shao-ch'i's speech to a cadre meeting on May Day, the first public indication that a campaign was in the offing, deplored the basic-level cadres' reliance on a commandist style of administration and warned of the damage that coercion would do to relations between the government and the people. Two months later the Party Day editorial in *Jen-min jih-pao* also identified commandism as the principal problem to be overcome.[48]

In contrast, at the Third Plenum, Mao spoke of the arrogance and complacency among cadres at all levels and of the bureaucratism at the middle levels of the Party and state. And when Hsi Chung-hsün, then the first vice-chairman of the Northwest regional government, spoke to a cadre meeting on May 20 on the theme "Oppose Bureaucratism and Commandism," he deplored the bureaucratic behavior of higher-level cadres and singled out for attack their ignorance of local conditions, unwillingness to listen to advice or criticism, laziness, and inability to delegate responsibility. Hsi also implied that bureaucratism contributed to commandism at lower levels by putting pressure on local cadres to achieve (or at least to report) successes in their work.[49] Jao Shu-shih, secretary of the East China regional Party bureau, gave examples of the way in which such outgrowths of bureaucratism as too many meetings, too many documents, and too much red tape were affecting organizational performance. Moreover, he noted, the arrogance of Communist cadres was damaging the morale of non-Party officials.[50]

As if in response to Hsi and Jao, in late September *Jen-min jih-pao* reiterated the Party Day editorial's earlier emphasis on commandism alone. In an editorial entitled "Resolutely Oppose Commandism," the paper sought to identify and dismiss all possible justifications for commandism, including the bureaucratism of higher-level cadres. True enough, bureaucratism was a problem, but higher-level cadres should not be blamed for the commandism of their subordinates. Indeed, the lower-level cadres shared the blame for bureaucratism at higher levels; after all, was it not up to them to bring their superiors back to "reality"?[51]

A separate issue concerned the allocation of responsibility for organizational problems among different categories of government officials. Party leaders differed markedly over the degree to which veteran Party members should be blamed for shortcomings in bureaucratic performance. Both Hsi Chung-hsün and P'eng Chen, the mayor of Peking, felt that veteran Party cadres were partly responsible, even though retained officials and younger cadres might be charged with most of the problems.[52] Veteran officials, for example, were often ignorant of local conditions in the areas to which they

were assigned, and so might easily issue inappropriate orders and directives. Moreover, these cadres were proving most arrogant, complacent,
and hedonistic in the aftermath of victory. Liu Shao-ch'i disagreed. In his
May Day speech he put the blame squarely on the retained cadres for their
"Kuomintang work style" and on the younger officials, who were inexperienced and ideologically naive. Just as Liu was reluctant to blame
higher-level officials for the emergence of commandism at the grass roots,
so was he apparently unwilling to censure veteran Communist cadres for
the appearance of organizational problems.

Another source of controversy in mid-1950 was the proper format for
the rectification campaign. As we have noted, the Rectification of 1950 was
to be a "top-to-bottom" inner-Party campaign with only limited participation by non-Party officials. In July, however, P'eng Chen proposed the
substitution of a form that had been employed in Peking. The representative conferences (*ko-chieh tai-piao hui-i*) in the city, composed principally
of representatives of the "middle sectors"—intellectuals, professionals,
and technicians—had been asked to identify cadres who were guilty of
particularly serious cases of bureaucratism or commandism. Although the
representative conferences conducted this review under Party leadership,
the solicitation of opinions from non-Party people did introduce an open-
door, "bottom-to-top" element into the campaign in Peking.[53]

P'eng's idea was not enthusiastically received by other leaders. *Jen-min
jih-pao* waited for more than a month before publishing an editorial on the
role of representative conferences in the campaign. After grudgingly acknowledging that this technique added "a democratic component" to what
had been designed as a closed-door campaign, the editorial emphasized its
flaws. If the Party asked for criticism from non-Party representatives, then
it would have to follow through by punishing or criticizing the cadres who
were charged with commandism or bureaucratism. And if it did that, it
would then have to ensure that the cadres who were punished did not seek
revenge against their critics. All in all, the editorial implied, P'eng Chen's
use of representative conferences threatened the Party's ability to keep
the campaign mild, lenient, and controlled.[54] In the end, the representative conferences played little role in the campaign elsewhere in China, and
the description of the 1950 campaign in the official history of rectification
movements does not mention them at all.[55]

This lack of consensus did not prevent the campaign from remaining
limited in format, scope, and duration. In the old liberated areas it lasted
until the spring of 1951, but in other areas it was completed by the end of
the fall of 1950 so that land reform could be conducted during the winter
months. By March 1951 the Party's regional bureaus were claiming that
the campaign had greatly reduced commandism and bureaucratism and
had improved the Party's relations with the people.[56]

But the restrictions placed on the campaign may have limited its effectiveness. The official history of the campaign notes that, though it was "healthy and productive" as a whole, in a few localities it was not conducted in a sufficiently thoroughgoing manner.[57] Indeed, as we will see below, Chinese leaders were pointing to the reemergence of bureaucratism by the end of 1951 and of commandism by the end of 1952. Still, the immediate goal of the campaign had been to facilitate land reform, and land reform was conducted with remarkable ease in China between 1950 and 1952. To that degree, the Rectification of 1950 appears to have accomplished its purpose and can be adjudged a success.

The San-fan Campaign, 1951-1952

A few months after the conclusion of the 1950 rectification campaign, Chinese leaders began to face up to other organizational problems, some political and some economic. By the end of the year their attempts to solve these problems had been combined into the most intensive rectification campaign since 1949, the San-fan movement.[58] At issue was the broad question of consolidating the new Communist regime in China. In the leaders' eyes consolidation required more than the suppression of potential enemies, the mobilization of support, and the conciliation of crucial middle sectors. It also required the purification of the ranks of the Communist movement itself.

The Party had grown from 1.2 million members in April 1945 to some 5.8 million members at the end of 1950. Two million of these joined the Party in 1949 and 1950 alone. Eager to recruit new members in the newly liberated parts of China, the Party had applied lax admissions criteria, and because of the rapid progress of the civil war, had devoted little time to political education. With victory increasingly certain in the late 1940's, many people entered the Party less out of ideological conviction than out of the desire to join the winning side as early as possible. The majority of new members were peasants rather than urban industrial workers.

Even before the establishment of the People's Republic, therefore, Chinese Communist leaders had begun to consider the necessity of purifying the Party. Many of them were aware that the victorious Russian Communist Party, concerned about the loyalty and commitment of its members, not only stopped all recruiting in the years 1917–21, but also purged some 20 percent of its rank and file.[59] Moved by the same concerns, the Chinese Party, at its Second Plenum, held in March 1949, decided to improve its social composition by accelerating recruitment in the cities and restricting it in the countryside.[60]

That decision was confirmed at the Third Plenum in June 1950. By its directive, the recruitment of peasants in the old liberated areas was stopped altogether, and the recruitment of peasants in the newly liberated areas was postponed until after land reform. In contrast, a full one-third of the urban working class was to be absorbed into the Party in the next three to five years, so that the Party might truly become the vanguard of the proletariat. The directive also called for a reexamination of the qualifications of current Party members, more intensive education in Party doctrine and programs, and reorganization of basic-level Party branches throughout the country.[61] These decisions were reaffirmed by an enlarged meeting of the Politburo in February 1951.[62]

To determine the best procedures for fulfilling this program of Party consolidation, a national conference on organizational work was held in Peking in March 1951. The conference drew up plans for a three-year campaign, to be conducted in rural areas mainly during the slack farming seasons, and set as a goal the removal of some 10 percent of the Party's more backward members. The conference also adopted a set of eight criteria for Party membership to tighten the standards set in the 1945 Party constitution.[63]

As originally conceived, Party consolidation was aimed primarily at the rank and file rather than at cadres, but it had implications for Party and government officials as well. After all, the need to ensure their reliability, honesty, and commitment was even more important than purging undesirables from the general membership. And Party leaders were well aware of the temptations of power. As early as the Second Plenum in 1949, Mao had warned that "with victory, certain moods may grow within the Party—arrogance, the airs of the self-styled hero, inertia and unwillingness to make progress, love of pleasure and distaste for continued hard living." Accordingly, "the comrades must be taught to remain modest, prudent, and free from arrogance and rashness in their style of work. The comrades must be taught to preserve the style of plain living and hard struggle."[64]

By early 1951 there were signs that Mao's prophecy was coming true. In the cities, government regulation of industry, commerce, and finance meant that industrialists and merchants were dependent on Party and government cadres for their economic survival. A government contract could mean prosperity for a firm; its withdrawal, serious economic hardship or even bankruptcy. In labor unions, cadres could insist on labor peace or allow worker protests over wages and working conditions. In banking, cadres controlled loans for new investment. These considerations tempted industrialists and merchants to resort to bribery to protect their enterprises. And the inadequacy of the government's control system, headed by the central People's Supervisory Commission, encouraged some cadres to believe that the chances of being caught and punished were acceptably low.[65]

The first steps to cope with these problems were taken in the Northeast. On March 1, 1951, addressing an expanded session of the Northeast People's Government Council, Kao Kang criticized regional government officials for their passivity, arrogance, reluctance to accept criticism, graft, and corruption. Six months later, on August 31, he gave a similar speech to a conference of two thousand regional Party cadres, this time criticizing his listeners' favoritism, nepotism, bureaucratism, hedonism, graft, and corruption. This time he also called for a mass rectification campaign in which rank-and-file Party members, low-ranking officials, and ordinary citizens could all criticize Party cadres for corruption, hedonism, and bureaucratism, implying that the problems were so serious that the campaign would be intense, even harsh.[66]

Kao's proposal apparently encountered substantial resistance both in Peking and in the Northeast. *Jen-min jih-pao* did not report his speech for more than two weeks, and the full text of his address was not released, even in the Northeast, for three months. Even the cadres he addressed evidently did not take the proposal seriously. On September 18, Kao convened a second Party conference to underscore the importance he assigned to the campaign. That conference decided to hold all office heads in the region personally responsible for the successful completion of the campaign. Later accounts indicate that only then was Kao's regional rectification campaign conducted with any vigor.[67]

In addition to these political problems, Chinese leaders faced a set of serious economic difficulties. On the surface, achievements were impressive. By mid-1951 it was evident that China had experienced a very respectable degree of economic recovery. Grain production reached 135 million MT by the end of the year, as compared with 108 million MT in 1949. Cotton production was at 1.03 million MT, two and one-half times the 1949 figure, and steel production had increased more than fivefold, to .9 million MT. In two years' time agricultural production had increased 31 percent, and industrial production, 68 percent. The gross national product had risen 39 percent.[68]

But China's participation in the Korean War was placing an increasing strain on the economy. In 1951, for instance, the central budget allocated as much money to the war effort as to economic development.[69] Moreover, there was an increasing awareness that, despite these gains, the economy was not operating at maximum efficiency. In many enterprises, production costs were high, inventory management was poor, and equipment was not being used to capacity. Many construction projects were being undertaken without adequate planning or supervision, with the result that human, material, and financial resources were being squandered. An improvement in performance was needed, as *Jen-min jih-pao* explained:

The whole nation must fully support the front, support the Chinese People's Volunteers, and ensure supplies to the front on condition that price stability is maintained and no excessive burden is imposed on the people. This [alone] would call for an increase in production and for practicing rigid economy. But, what is more important, to prepare ourselves for the state's large-scale production hereafter and to accumulate funds necessary for various construction [projects], the whole nation must redouble its efforts to increase production and practice rigid economy.[70]

The situation had direct implications for the administrative bureaucracy. Administrative costs still constituted a major share of the national budget (19.3 percent in 1950), and thus represented an important potential source of savings. At the Third Plenum, in June 1950, Mao had urged the reduction of administrative expenses as a means of promoting economic recovery, but this had not proved possible. Since the trend in 1950 and 1951 was to increase the state's administrative force for the land reform and economic recovery programs, it is not surprising that administrative costs rose from 1.3 billion yüan in 1950 to 1.75 billion yüan in 1951.[71]

By the middle of 1951 there was evidence that much of this increase had not been necessary, or at least that it had not been used efficiently. Although the Party and state might, as a whole, be understaffed, it was clear that some agencies had too many personnel, too many offices, and too many levels of administration. In October, Kao Kang reported that certain units in the Northeast had increased their staffs 84 percent between January and July, with the result that some 25 percent of their personnel were now superfluous. Their other operating expenses—from office furnishings and cadre housing to banquet expenses and stationery costs—were higher than necessary too.[72] In some offices efficiency was further reduced because of too many meetings and a proliferation of forms and paperwork.

Given these problems, some regional Party bureaus and regional governments began to reduce administrative expenses on their own in the spring and summer of 1951. In August and September the Central-South regional government reduced the number of cadre meetings, simplified the procedures for issuing official documents, and tried to eliminate unnecessary paperwork.[73]

But it was not until the Third Session of the National Committee of the Chinese People's Political Consultative Conference, held in October, that Chinese leaders decided to expand these regional campaigns into a national effort. In a speech to the National Committee, Mao claimed that the three major mass movements of the previous two years—land reform, the suppression of counterrevolutionaries, and the campaign to aid Korea and resist America—had been successful, and that it was now time to set a new central task for the government's work. That task should be a national campaign to practice greater economy and increase production, both of which were essential if the Korean War was to be successfully prosecuted without damage to the economy.[74] At the same meeting Chou En-lai warned that waste and bureaucratism were threatening to "divorce" the Party and government from the masses. There was still a shortage of personnel in offices responsible for economic affairs and for education, Chou said, but other agencies were too large. Accordingly, the Government Administration Council was planning a conference on governmental reorganization with a view to reducing the size of those overstaffed agencies.[75]

Even at the Third Session of the National Committee, therefore, political and economic problems were still being considered in isolation from one another. Kao Kang had been emphasizing the dangers of corruption, graft, and impropriety in administrative organs in the Northeast, and had sought to launch a rectification campaign to combat them. Central leaders had been concerned with economic inefficiency and waste, and had decided to launch an austerity campaign to help increase production. It was Kao who brought these two threads together and, in so doing, laid down the general outline of what would soon become the San-fan campaign. On October 26, within three days of Mao's speech and while the National Committee was still in session, Kao called yet another meeting of Party cadres in the Northeast. There he gave a speech attempting to link his earlier idea of a rectification campaign to Mao's call for an austerity campaign. Kao made this connection by first redefining the three organizational problems he had discussed in August. Whereas he had then spoken of "corruption, hedonism, and bureaucratism," he now spoke of corruption, "waste," and bureaucratism. Describing these three problems as "the greatest enemy of the production-increase and austerity campaign," he reminded his audience of the rectification campaign he had launched in the Northeast in August and September, and argued that continuing that campaign would be fully in line with Mao's speech. But he continued to insist that the rectification campaign and the austerity drive would have to be open-door campaigns—"mass movements," in his words—and that they should be "drastic and complicated."[76]

By mid-November Kao's idea of linking the austerity campaign with a Party and governmental rectification campaign had won approval in Peking. *Jen-min jih-pao*, declaring that combating extravagance, waste, and corruption in administrative agencies was an important method of saving money, praised Kao Kang for his efforts: "The Northeast has launched an anticorruption and antihedonism campaign and has achieved very great results."[77] The paper implied that Chou En-lai's proposal for a conference on governmental reorganization would not be sufficient, and that Kao was correct in insisting that the problems of administrative inefficiency, waste, and corruption could be handled adequately only through some form of rectification campaign. *Jen-min jih-pao*'s position was reinforced by Mao's statements of late November and early December, which emphasized the importance of eradicating corruption, waste, and bureaucratism, and reiterated Kao's argument for a mass campaign against them.[78]

With this, the San-fan movement developed rapidly. By the first week of December all six administrative regions had held cadre meetings to plan their participation in the campaign.[79] On December 7, at a meeting of the Government Administration Council, Chou En-lai ordered that the movement be launched all across the country, and the Council responded by establishing an ad hoc Austerity Inspection Committee, headed by Finance Minister Po I-po, to lead the campaign in the central governmental and Party organs. On December 29 the National Committee of the Political Consultative Conference issued a directive endorsing the campaign. And on January 1, Mao Tse-tung's New Year's message to the Chinese people called for a nationwide struggle against "corruption, waste, and bureaucratism."[80] The San-fan campaign had begun, and its targets had been clearly identified.

The campaign was conducted along three parallel lines. First, officials at all levels called meetings at which they confessed their own acts of corruption, waste, or bureaucratism and then subjected themselves to the criticism of their subordinates and colleagues. Second, ad hoc austerity inspection committees were formed at all levels and, in turn, dispatched teams to selected units to conduct investigations. And third, the public and office workers were asked to bring forward cases of corruption, waste, or bureaucratism. Those who did so were guaranteed protection against reprisals and offered rewards for providing information. The central Austerity Inspection Committee proposed, and the Government Administration Council adopted, provisions for the criminal or administrative punishment of those found guilty.*

The leaders of the San-fan movement shortly discovered that the "three evils"—corruption, waste, and bureaucratism—were much more serious than they had anticipated. On January 9, 1952, Po I-po made his first public report on the campaign's progress: 1,670 cadres in twenty-seven central government organs had already been identified as guilty of one of the evils. The situation was clearly such, Po warned, that the most serious

---

*The regulations on corruption, waste, and bureaucratism were adopted in provisional form by the Government Administration Council on March 8, 1952, and can be found in *Current Background*, no. 168 (26.iii.52), pp. 4–9. A permanent set of anticorruption laws, which closely followed the relevant portions of the provisional regulations, was adopted by the council on April 18, 1952; see Jerome Alan Cohen, *The Criminal Process in the People's Republic of China, 1949–1963: An Introduction* (Cambridge, Mass., 1968), pp. 308–11.

political and economic consequences would ensue if it was not remedied. Economically, waste and corruption were limiting the pace of national construction. Politically, bureaucratism was reducing the regime's ability to understand and respond to the needs and demands of the people. This raised the threat of counterrevolution. The campaign would have to be intense. It would have to involve mass investigation, and the promise of government protection and rewards if people were to be expected to volunteer information.[81]

An equally somber view was taken by Yeh Chien-ying, the mayor of Canton, in a report to Party cadres in his city somewhat later in January. The three evils were so serious as to be reminiscent of the Nationalist regime, and some people were even saying that they saw very little difference between the Communist Party and the Kuomintang after all. These views were a distortion, Yeh said, but nevertheless the San-fan campaign must be conducted with an intensity unprecedented since the Cheng-feng campaign of 1942–44.[82]

One matter of prime concern to the leaders was the realization that veteran Communist cadres were responsible for much of the corruption and waste. Early accounts of the campaign had optimistically predicted that the overwhelming majority of offenders would be retained officials or new cadres.[83] But early statistics from East China, released in mid-December, indicated that of 615 cases in the region, 226 (37 percent) involved veterans. This was very nearly equal to the number of cases involving retained cadres (256, or 42 percent) and nearly double the number of cases involving new recruits (133, or 22 percent).[84] Indeed, some very high-ranking Communist cadres, including Minister of Justice Shih Liang and Vice-Chairman of the All-China Federation of Trade Unions Liu Ning-i, came forward to make self-criticisms of their wasteful and luxurious lifestyles.[85] And some middle-level Party cadres at the regional, provincial, and municipal levels were dismissed from office.[86]

As more and more cases of corruption were discovered, greater attention was also paid to the bribes offered by merchants and industrialists. By early January Party leaders had begun to blame the bourgeoisie for the high level of corruption in the bureaucracy. Po I-po spoke of the "corroding influence" of the bourgeoisie; and Yeh Chien-ying, charging that the San-fan campaign was a response to a "systematic attack of the bourgeois class [carried out] against Party and government cadres for the past three years," called for a further extension of the targets of the campaign to include "lawless industrialists and merchants." As a result of this redefinition of the problem, the Wu-fan campaign was launched in January against bribery, theft of state property, theft of state secrets, cheating on contracts, and tax evasion. Although the Wu-fan movement came to overshadow the San-fan campaign from which it had sprung, the San-fan itself continued into the summer of 1952.[87]

As Kao Kang had predicted, the campaign was intense. According to An Tzu-wen, of the 3,836,000 cadres who participated at the county level and above, 2.7 percent were prosecuted as criminals, and another 1.8 percent were subjected to administrative discipline. If the figures are accurate, approximately 173,000 cadres received some kind of punishment. The total number charged was even higher, since the regulations on punishment recommended that many minor offenses receive neither criminal prosecution nor administrative sanction.

Moreover, the campaign was apparently a fiscal success. Kao Kang reported a reduction of 33 percent in state expenditures in the Northeast, and Po I-po later credited savings attributable to the San-fan campaign and fines levied during the Wu-fan campaign with having produced a budget surplus in 1952.[88] Mao even claimed that "the moneys that came from the settling of accounts in the movements against the 'three evils' and the 'five evils' can see us through another eighteen months of war."[89]

For all its successes, the San-fan created some serious problems, most of them related to the intensity of the campaign. Later, in 1954, An Tzu-wen revealed that the "spontaneous" rise of the movement in some rural areas in the spring and summer of 1952 so disrupted cultivation that the campaign had had to be postponed until after fall harvest or stopped altogether.[90] In some urban offices so many cadres were dismissed from their jobs that the work had to be performed by replacements dispatched from higher levels. Also, the insistence that the movement be treated as a "shock task" meant that routine duties were neglected. Even before the campaign was over, some Chinese were apparently expressing doubts as to whether it was worth the disruption, and in 1953 Party leaders openly admitted that the campaign had caused serious dislocations.[91]

In fact, the San-fan campaign, far from eliminating bureaucratism and commandism, actually exacerbated the problems. Because of the emphasis on waste and corruption, bureaucratism was effectively ignored.* Higher-level cadres were so preoccupied with the campaign that they had little time to devote to the study and analysis of local problems. And in their effort to comply with the goals of reducing inefficiency and promoting economic growth, they assigned more tasks and higher quotas to local units. Faced with unrealistic orders, basic-level cadres tended to rely on coercive methods to meet their superiors' expectations.[92] Indeed, six

---

*That the San-fan campaign had not really dealt effectively with bureaucratism was admitted, in varying degrees of explicitness, by An Tzu-wen in *People's China*, no. 14 (1953), in *Survey of the China Mainland Press*, no. 622 (31.vii.53), pp. 27–32; and by *Jen-min jih-pao*, 20.ii.53, *ibid.*, no. 511 (11.ii.53), pp. 1–4.

months after the San-fan movement ended, bureaucratism and command-ism had become so serious that they became the target of yet another rec-tification campaign.

The New San-fan Campaign, 1953

In early 1953, after summarizing and evaluating the results of the San-fan campaign of the previous year, Chinese leaders decided to launch the third rectification movement inside the Party and government apparatus since 1949. According to a Central Committee directive issued on January 5 and reportedly drafted by Mao himself, the San-fan movement had sig-nificantly reduced corruption and waste, particularly at the middle and upper levels of the administrative apparatus, but bureaucratism—defined in the directive as the alienation of the cadres from the people—remained a serious problem:

Some leading cadres are ignorant of the people's hardships, of the conditions in subordinate units only a short distance from their offices, and of the fact that among the cadres at the county, district, and township levels there are many bad people guilty of commandism and violations of the law and of discipline. Or they may have some knowledge of such bad people and bad deeds but turn a blind eye to them, feel no indignation, are not aware of the seriousness of the matter, and so take no positive measures to back up good people and punish the bad or to encour-age good deeds and stop the bad.[93]

The bureaucratic style of work (a "reactionary," "antipopular," "Kuo-mintang" style of work) was thus reflected at all levels of the bureaucracy. At the grass roots it was revealed in commandism, abuses of power, and violations of the law by basic-level cadres. Higher up it was manifested in the failure to supervise subordinates adequately, and in "ignorance of and callousness to both the hardships of the masses and the conditions in the grass-roots organizations."[94]

The directive announcing the new movement called for a year-long rec-tification campaign against "bureaucratism, commandism, and violations of law and discipline." Since the new campaign came so soon after the original San-fan movement, and since, like its predecessor, it focused on three organizational problems, it was referred to as the "New San-fan" campaign, the campaign against the "new three evils." But its targets were more reminiscent of the Rectification of 1950 than of the San-fan move-ment.*

*Like the Rectification of 1950, the New San-fan campaign has not received much atten-tion in any published Western analyses. Two available accounts of the campaign are Richard L. Walker, *China Under Communism: The First Five Years* (London, 1956), pp. 80–88; and Thomas Bernstein, "Keeping the Revolution Going: Problems of Village Leadership After Land Reform" in John W. Lewis, ed., *Party Leadership and Revolutionary Power in China* (Cambridge, 1970).

Detailed descriptions of the purposes of the campaign were provided in two speeches by An Tzu-wen, one delivered in his capacity as deputy director of the Party Organization Department to a meeting of central Party officials on January 7, the other delivered in his capacity as minister of personnel to the Fourth Session of the National Committee of the Political Consultative Conference on February 7.[95] Together these speeches provide a clear account of the way in which the three targets of the New San-fan movement had been chosen.

Commandism was described in An's reports and in press accounts in terms strikingly similar to those used three years earlier during the Rectification of 1950. As before, basic-level rural cadres were accused of using harsh methods to collect the grain tax and enforce public health measures. But this time considerable attention was also paid to the use of compulsion in carrying out the Party's agricultural policies. In some areas, cadres were forcing peasants to work on rural construction projects, especially water conservancy projects. An, in his report to the Political Consultative Conference, charged that some cadres had ordered the militia to make the rounds of local market towns to muster peasants attending the markets into labor teams to drill wells. In other cases cadres were compelling the peasants to adopt new seed strains, planting procedures, farm implements, and the like without first demonstrating that the new methods would increase production. The result was grudging adoption of the new techniques by the peasants or, worse, total failure, because the cadres had not attempted to adapt their approach to local conditions. And during the fall of 1952 cadres had used excessively coercive measures in promoting agricultural producers' cooperatives, even denouncing peasants who were reluctant to join as having "capitalist tendencies."[96]

The Party leaders had learned from the Rectification of 1950 that commandism at the basic level was often caused by bureaucratism at higher levels, and so this time bureaucratism was clearly identified as one of the three principal targets of the campaign from the very beginning. Higher-level Party and state officials, particularly at the county level and above, were accused of having committed a by then familiar list of bureaucratic errors: issuing instructions without understanding local conditions, setting goals and targets without specifying the methods for attaining them, requiring basic-level cadres to attend too many meetings and complete too many forms, and failing to supervise their subordinates' performance.[97] Perhaps most important, higher-level officials were said to be tolerant when their subordinates used improper methods but unsympathetic when they were unable to meet their assigned targets. As a result, basic-level cadres were encouraged both to use commandism in dealing with the people and to file false reports about accomplishments. As things stood,

An said, basic-level cadres felt they could report their achievements but not their shortcomings, the good news but not the bad news, and the accomplishments but not the failures.[98]

The third set of problems in the countryside concerned violations of law, departures from Party policy, and misuse of power by certain Party cadres. Some were downright corrupt. Others, according to An's enumeration, cursed and beat people, sanctioned indiscriminate arrests and detentions, interfered with freedom of marriage, persecuted those who criticized them, wrongly accused good people, and even sheltered counterrevolutionaries, drove people to suicide, and resorted to murder.[99] Still other cadres engaged in certain economic activities that, though not illegal, were not proper pursuits for members of the Party. These included hiring others to work their land, renting out or purchasing land, and lending out money at interest.[100]

As important as these problems were, they did not exhaust the list. "Suppression of criticism" by Party functionaries, a problem common to both city and countryside, was the main object of attack. An Tzu-wen pointed out on January 7 that "many of our Party members are rather unaccustomed to criticism. . . . They can tolerate criticism from the upper level but not from the lower level; they can tolerate criticism from the Party but not from the lower level or the masses. They do not consider their work to be subject to the supervision of the masses, so they ignore mass opinion."[101]

As the new campaign got under way, press accounts began to draw a clear distinction between two different types of "suppression of criticism." The first was retaliation by ranking officials against anyone, whether lower-level cadre or ordinary citizen, who dared to criticize them. This problem received nationwide attention at the beginning of 1953, when it was revealed that a regional administrator who was also a university president had attempted to identify and punish a student who had sent an anonymous letter criticizing his work to *Jen-min jih-pao*.[102] An Tzu-wen indicated that similar cases were prevalent in the countryside, particularly among district and township cadres, and that cadres who suppressed criticism from the people actually received protection from their superiors.[103]

A second kind of suppression of criticism involved a less blatant but more widespread problem: the tendency of Party and government offices simply to ignore complaints and suggestions. Campaign spokesmen made much of the large flow of letters to the Party and government that were never read or were shunted from office to office without any action being taken. In January, An attacked both the Shantung provincial government, which had pigeonholed 70,000 letters from people complaining about various problems, and the Shanghai municipal government, which had accumulated more than 22,000 letters in the space of two months and had not acted on a single one of them. In Shanghai "many letter boxes packed full of letters from the masses have been left in the sun and rain for months and months without being touched. The letter boxes are weatherbeaten, and so many of the letters became illegible."[104] One *Jen-min jih-pao* editorial warned that the failure to heed popular opinion could even impede the country's socialist transformation.[105]

The timing of the New San-fan campaign raised some embarrassing questions. An Tzu-wen's report to the Political Consultative Conference also contained a summary and review of the accomplishments of the first San-fan movement and the campaign to reorganize and consolidate basic-level Party branches begun in 1951. The juxtaposition of these two parts of An's report raised the question of why another campaign was needed so soon. Had not the three problems identified by the Central Committee on January 5 all been the targets of earlier rectification campaigns? Had not commandism been one of the principal targets of the Rectification of 1950? Was not the original San-fan campaign directed, at least in part, against bureaucratism? And were not cadres who were guilty of violations of law and discipline identified, criticized, and punished during the campaign to consolidate basic-level Party branches? Why, then, was there a need for another rectification campaign?

Chinese leaders readily admitted that the new campaign was indeed concerned with some familiar organizational problems. And they also admitted that the new campaign was needed because the earlier campaigns had failed to eliminate those problems. One reason for this, according to An Tzu-wen, was that rectification campaigns were becoming ritualized; cadres were learning how to pass through them without having to undergo serious self-examination or reform. He cited the example of the Party's earlier attempts to persuade cadres to pay serious attention to criticism from their subordinates and the people, a feature of virtually every rectification campaign since the Cheng-feng movement. Despite all these efforts, cadres still "act the way they always do, completely ignoring all criticism." Another reason why a further campaign was necessary was that the conditions producing bureaucratism had not yet been eliminated. The Party and state were still attempting to assume a wide range of new political and economic tasks with a corps of cadres who lacked administrative experience and technical skills. Under these circumstances, some degree of bureaucratism was virtually inevitable, and, in An's opinion, the struggle against bureaucratism would have to be a long-term one.[106]

Even more important, the earlier rectification campaigns had actually intensified some of the very problems they set out to solve. For example, by the winter of 1952 some 100,000 cadres had been trained in rectification techniques, formed into work teams, and sent to help consolidate the basic-level Party branches. According to Hsiang Ming, then second secretary of the Shantung Party sub-bureau, this caused a shortage of cadres for routine work in the countryside, particularly at the district level, and thus contributed to the emergence of bureaucratism in the Party and government.[107]

The unintended consequences of the San-fan campaign have already been touched on—the disruption of agriculture, the shortage of cadres caused by the high rate of dismissals, the neglect of routine work at basic levels, the exacerbation of bureaucratism and commandism stemming from the diversion of the upper-level cadres' attention from local conditions and the increased pressure on local cadres. In addition, although the campaign was supposed to deal with bureaucratism, it actually concentrated on eliminating waste and corruption; the problem of bureaucratism received relatively little attention.

These considerations strongly influenced the format, tone, and intensity of the new campaign. Since the First Five-Year Plan was to begin in 1953, Chinese leaders were particularly concerned that the campaign not interfere with economic planning or production management. *Jen-min jih-pao* was unusually candid on March 13 in its comparison of the two San-fan campaigns. The struggle against bureaucratism was important, but was not to be a "shock task. . . . Still less should we use the methods of last year's San-fan campaign." Instead, cadres should understand that economic construction was still the nation's principal task and should conduct the new campaign in ways that would complement, rather than hinder, economic development.[108] In a later editorial summarizing the differences between the results of the new campaign and earlier rectification movements, the paper declared that the New San-fan had been able to avoid some of the deviations of the previous movements because it was conducted in a planned, systematic, and discriminating way. The overall style of the new campaign was to combine "active leadership" (*chi-chi ling-tao*) with "paced advance" (*wen-pu ch'ien-chin*).[109]

Although the tone of the New San-fan campaign was moderate, Chinese leaders apparently hoped to ensure its effectiveness by using a variety of mutually reinforcing techniques. The campaign, complex and multidimensional, combined more remedial devices than any of the new regime's preceding rectification movements. Work teams, study and self-criticism, cadre conferences, mass participation—all these devices were mixed into the new campaign in an attempt to achieve effective results without extensive disruption.[110]

At the higher levels of the Party and state bureaucracies, the campaign emphasized the customary criticism and self-criticism. At the central, regional, provincial, district, and county levels, cadre conferences were called to discuss ways of eliminating bureaucratism. The conferences and study sessions were short affairs, for they were not supposed to interfere with routine work. The Ministry of Commerce, for example, anticipated that this phase of the campaign could be completed within two weeks. Overall the campaign appears to have been concluded at the central level by late March or early April of 1953.[111]

Higher-level officials were organized into work teams and dispatched to the basic levels to check on cadre performance, investigate local conditions, uncover cases of commandism and violations of the law, and educate cadres in mass-line leadership techniques. The central government dispatched more than one hundred such teams (with an average of ten members) to make two- to eight-week tours of subordinate government agencies. To emphasize the importance of the campaign, many of the teams included ministers, vice-ministers, or ministry bureau directors.[112]

Shantung authorities adopted another technique to improve the performance of basic-level cadres. They directed each county to find one "good" cadre and one "bad" cadre whose cases could be discussed in internal bulletins and local newspapers. In addition, basic-level cadre conferences, conferences of Party representatives, local people's congresses, meetings to discuss procedures for handling complaints from the public, and meetings to discuss examples of proper and improper work styles—all were brought into play in the effort to eliminate commandism and create a style of work in which cadres would be "linked to reality and linked to the people."

Like the San-fan, the New San-fan offered opportunities for popular participation, albeit in a more structured way. *Jen-min jih-pao* explained early in the campaign that though the "arousal" of the masses—workers, peasants, and ordinary office cadres—would be beneficial, participation would have to be less extensive, less intensive, and more institutionalized than it had been during the San-fan and Wu-fan movements. Above all, the paper warned, the masses should be made to understand that another mammoth campaign along the lines of those conducted during 1952 would simply not be suitable in a period emphasizing planned economic construction.[113]

The Party leaders identified three formal channels as offering appropriate opportunities for mass participation in the campaign. Since elections were then being conducted to form new local people's congresses and many of the cadres would be candidates, the people could take this opportunity to express their criticisms of the cadres to the local election committees. Those who were guilty of commandism or who had violated state law or Party and government regulations could then be denied renomination.

The government control network, headed by the Committee of State Supervision, provided a second channel for popular participation. Since the San-fan campaign, the supervisory network had recruited more than 20,000 part-time correspondents throughout the country, particularly in factories and administrative offices. These correspondents, at least in theory, could both investigate improper cadre behavior themselves and receive and investigate complaints from other workers and cadres.[114] Finally, ordinary people were encouraged to write letters to the Party and government about cadres with whom they had had contact, and efforts were made to improve the procedures for receiving, processing, and responding to these "letters from the people."

Originally, the New San-fan campaign had been expected to deal equally with commandism at the basic levels of the Party and state, and with bureaucratism at the middle and upper levels. Shortly after the campaign was inaugurated, however, its focus began to change. As in the case of the Rectification of 1950, Chinese leaders gradually became aware of the responsibility that higher-level officials bore for commandism at the grass roots and shifted the emphasis of the campaign to deal more explicitly and forcefully with bureaucratism. During the campaign's final stages, its purposes were almost completely redefined.

This change was first signaled by the circulation of a Central Committee directive to Party members on March 19. The directive's basic premise was that commandism at the basic level could ultimately be traced to "decentralism" and "bureaucracy" at the county level and above, that is, the tendency of middle- and upper-level officials to assign more tasks to basic-level cadres than they could reasonably be expected to perform. This produced what became known as the "five excesses" (*wu-to*)—too many assignments for basic-level cadres; too many meetings and training courses; too many documents, reports, and statistical forms; too many administrative units at the basic levels; and too many concurrent positions for cadres and activists. Although the Central Committee had periodically warned against such practices, the problems had become more frequent and more serious, since the issue had never been "systematically raised in its totality."[115]

As a result, the Central Committee declared that henceforth the emphasis of the New San-fan movement would be on overcoming bureaucratism in the middle and upper levels of the bureaucracy. All undesirable rules and practices that contributed to the five excesses were to be "resolutely abolished." The conduct of the campaign was now to be the responsibility of the Organization Department of the Central Committee and its counterparts at lower levels, and of the Government Administration Council in Peking and its units in the localities. Regional, provincial, and municipal governments were ordered to send out work teams to inspect one or two rural districts and townships and one or two urban districts and neighborhoods to gather reference materials for solutions to the problem of the five excesses.

A month later, in late April, the Kwangsi provincial newspaper published an account of how the five excesses affected one township. In November 1952 the township government had been ordered to conduct no fewer than five "great movements," perform ten "big tasks," and carry out twenty-two "small tasks." Each movement and task was accompanied by cadre meetings and training classes, and each required the filling out of a series of long forms on progress. The township government had been forced to create numerous committees, each responsible for a different phase of the work. Some townships had established as many as forty or fifty. Because of the shortage of cadres, people often held positions on several committees. They were simply overworked. They had too little time to perform their administrative duties, let alone do any production work, and they used commandist methods just to accomplish the tasks they had been assigned. To reduce the burden on local cadres, the article recommended that "all matters to be transmitted to the countryside should be clarified according to their importance."[116]

The article argued, in effect, that organizational problems at the local level should be blamed on the unrealistic expectations and unclear instructions of officials higher up. By the end of June the purpose of the New San-fan campaign had been aligned with this diagnosis of the situation. Commandism and violations of law and discipline, the two problems that had originally been said to characterize the performance of many basic-level cadres, were dropped from the list of "three evils." In their place were substituted two other problems. One was "subjectivism," defined as policymaking without thorough investigation of local conditions and the consequent establishment of unrealistic production targets. The other was "decentralism," the inadequate coordination of various Party and government activities, and the failure to assign clear priorities to competing tasks and programs.[117] The three new targets of the campaign—bureaucratism, subjectivism, and decentralism—were all located in the middle and upper bureaucracy rather than at the base.[118]

The principal organizational problems that confronted the Chinese leaders in the early years of the People's Republic were understandable, even predictable. First, the Chinese Communist Party faced a contradiction between its goals and programs and its limited organizational capabilities. The Party's determination to carry out ambitious social and political reforms and to effect economic reconstruction even before its administrative apparatus was fully in place led inevitably to bureaucratism, waste, and commandism. Second, the Party needed to find ways of maintaining the revolutionary commitment and organizational discipline of its cadres after victory had finally been won. The desire of veteran Party cadres to enjoy the fruits of victory, coupled with the fact that most of those available for recruitment during the Party's rapid expansion had but small commitment to its programs, led predictably to corruption and abuse of power.

Coping with these problems aroused only minor controversy within the bureaucracy and among Chinese leaders. There was, to be sure, a considerable degree of competition for power, income, and prestige among various groups of cadres—the competition between veteran Communists and retained officials and between young intellectuals and worker-peasant activists, for example. But these tensions were not so severe at the time as to trouble the Party (as they would in later years), largely because of the rapid growth of the Party and state administrative apparatus. With the exception of retained officials, most of whom were removed from office by the mid-1950's, there was room for everyone with the slightest administrative, cultural, or technical skill.

Nor was there serious disagreement among Chinese leaders over organizational matters during this period, although there was some discussion over the definition of organizational problems and the selection of proper remedies. In 1950 Party officials differed over whether the principal problem was commandism or bureaucratism and over whether it was local or higher cadres who were to blame. In 1951 they disagreed over whether the main flaw in administrative organs was inefficiency or corruption. And throughout the period they differed over whether the country's organizational problems required a rectification campaign or whether they could be remedied through less disruptive means. But these were not matters of great debate. There appears to have been a consensus that the Party needed to maintain popular support, that certain organizational tendencies within the Party and government threatened that support, and that effective measures should be taken to preserve the prestige of the Party.

The principal remedy chosen was a familiar one, the rectification campaign. The three campaigns launched in the bureaucracy between 1949 and 1953—the Rectification of 1950, the San-fan movement, and the New San-fan movement—differed greatly in scope and intensity. But they all employed techniques that the Party had developed during the 1930's and 1940's: study, criticism and self-criticism, the dispatch of work teams to lower levels, and some degree of mass participation to help identify cadres whose performance was not up to the Party's standards.

Generally speaking, the three campaigns were reasonably effective in maintaining high standards of organizational performance. But there remained some problems, not all of which the Chinese leaders appear to have fully understood. One was an initial bias in the campaigns, a tendency to identify basic-level cadres, retained officials, and new recruits as those most likely to have committed the deviations in question. Inadequate weight was given to the possible culpability of higher officials or veteran Party cadres. In the course of each campaign, the leaders became aware of this initial bias and adjusted for it. In the Rectification of 1950 there was increasing emphasis on the role of bureaucratism at higher levels in producing commandism at all lower levels. In the San-fan movement there was a gradual realization that veteran Communist cadres might be guilty of corruption. And in the New San-fan campaign, there was a gradual understanding that it was incorrect to use local cadres as scapegoats for organizational problems caused by higher bureaucrats.

A second problem involved the unintended consequences of rectification campaigns, particularly the more intensive ones. Campaigns against commandism, such as the Rectification of 1950, could sometimes produce a flight to the opposite extreme, to "tailism" and passivity. Campaigns against rightism and bourgeois ideology, such as the rectification of basic-level Party branches between 1951 and 1953, could similarly lead to excessive zeal among Party cadres. And disruptive campaigns, such as the San-fan movement, could increase the degree of commandism and bureaucratism by distracting large numbers of cadres from their routine administrative duties.

Even in those early years, there was already concern among some Chinese officials that rectification campaigns were less effective than anticipated in maintaining organizational performance. This concern was reflected in the launching of the New San-fan movement, which Chinese leaders acknowledged to be directed against the same problems of bureaucratism, commandism, and misuse of power that had supposedly been controlled by the Rectification of 1950 and the basic-level Party consolidation program of 1951–52. Cadres were learning how to pass through rectification without altering their style of work.

The shortcomings of rectification posed an important, long-term problem for the Party. Did the experience of the early 1950's mean that the organizational techniques of the past, including rectification campaigns, were not appropriate methods of managing the Party and state bureaucracies in the postrevolutionary period? Would it be necessary to develop more formal routines of administration and organizational control? Was it merely that rectification campaigns had to be made still more intense and disruptive to produce the desired result?

3
Organizational Rationalization
1952-1955

Economic recovery occurred more rapidly than Mao had predicted in his June 1950 report to the Third Plenum of the Central Committee.[1] In early August 1952, Finance Minister Po I-po declared that China had revived enough to undertake its first development plan.[2] Three months later the government announced that it had established a State Planning Commission, and that China's First Five-Year Plan would go into effect in January 1953.

Chinese leaders did not claim to have accomplished all of the tasks of consolidation. Although land reform had been completed in most parts of the country, it had not yet been undertaken in some of the more remote provinces inhabited by minority nationalities. Other important social reforms, such as putting the marriage law into execution and reorganizing the educational system, were still underway, and although the government had enjoyed considerable success in increasing industrial production and controlling inflation, urban unemployment remained a serious problem.

But consolidation had gone far enough to warrant a change in national priorities. Accordingly, a series of *Jen-min jih-pao* editorials throughout the summer and fall of 1952 emphasized that the nation's principal task was now to be planned economic development.[3] The January 1, 1953, issue of *Jen-min jih-pao* carried a drawing of Mao Tse-tung, pencil in hand, examining a pile of maps. Behind him was a wall covered with pictures of the new steel mills and hydroelectric plants to be constructed during the First Five-Year Plan.

Chinese leaders recognized that this change in national priorities would require a substantial transformation of China's organizational structure. Between 1949 and 1952, as we saw in the last chapter, the Party had continued to employ the techniques of mass mobilization that it had developed in Kiangsi and Yenan in organizing workers and peasants to participate in land reform, in the suppression of counterrevolutionaries, and in economic production drives, the San-fan and Wu-fan campaigns, and other movements. China was still ruled by the "provisional" central and local governments that had been established in 1949. It lacked a state constitution, and the governmental apparatus remained small, understaffed, and informal. The first three years of Communist rule, in short, had been a period of organizational "ad hoc-racy."

Now, however, Chinese leaders concluded that economic modernization and central planning required the rationalization and regularization of the government and Party apparatus. Just as cottage workshops and traditional farming techniques would soon be replaced by modern factories and collective farms, so the mobilization techniques and irregular organizations of the past would be replaced by systematically structured bureaucracies and formal managerial procedures. As Liu Shao-ch'i explained, "With more people and larger organs, organizations will naturally become more complex. . . . The development from single cells to higher animals is evolution. The higher the animal, the more minute will be the division of labor of its cells. There is division of labor in everything today. Division of labor must be scientific and clearly defined."[4] A variety of government statements and newspaper editorials expressed the same theme in slightly different terms. It would no longer be possible to employ the "organizational forms and work methods of rural state power," or to rely solely on the "direct action of military forces and the masses" in implementing policy. Instead, the new task of economic development required that government become more "systematic and methodical."[5]

Beginning in 1952, therefore, the Party undertook to rationalize its political institutions to a degree unknown in either the revolutionary base areas or the immediate post-Liberation period. Soviet advisers brought blueprints for China's new administrative apparatus along with their plans for new steel mills and machine tool plants. The detailed activities of Russian organizational specialists in China in the mid-1950's have not been thoroughly studied, but they surely played an important, if still inadequately understood, role in the design of China's new state structure. Whole organizational elements, among them the State Planning Commission, the network of science academies, and the Procuracy, were modeled after their counterparts in the Soviet Union. One Russian study of Sino-Soviet relations during this period has claimed that Soviet advisers helped draft the state constitution of 1954 and the First Five-Year Plan, and that their direct participation resulted in 1952 in the reorganization of higher education and the judicial system, in the creation of new ministries (mainly to oversee industrial production), and in the establishment of a system of state planning.[6]

This chapter will examine four of the most important components of the program of organizational rationalization undertaken between 1952 and 1955: the centralization of administration, the regularization of the bureaucracy, the systematization of personnel management in state and Party organizations, and the development of a formal, professional monitoring system for controlling the new bureaucracy. The conclusion to the chapter will discuss the degree to which such rationalization represented a departure from the organizational heritage of the Party.

CENTRALIZATION

When the Party gained nationwide power in 1949, social, economic, and political conditions differed widely from one part of China to another. The areas of Japanese and European penetration in northeastern and eastern China were relatively urban and industrial. The rest was almost exclusively agricultural. In areas where the Party had been in power for several years, land reform had been completed. In other areas the army still pursued remnant Nationalist forces, the Communists as yet had established little rural political organization, and the redistribution of land had not yet begun. Because of these differences, in 1949 the Party established the six regional governments and Party bureaus described earlier. Basic social, economic, and organizational policies were set by the central government in Peking, but the regional authorities were given substantial leeway in adjusting policies to meet local conditions, determining the pace at which they would be carried out, and supplementing them with programs designed to solve specific local problems. The creation of regional governments and Party bureaus was an attempt on the part of the new regime to adapt to diverse local conditions while simultaneously maintaining effective central control.[7]

By late 1952, however, the costs and risks of regional government had become of concern to Chinese leaders. For one thing, the regional governments were increasingly seen as a drain on scarce human and material resources. They and their Party bureaus were staffed by cadres whose services often could have been better employed in the central economic ministries, in local governments, or in industrial enterprises. In addition, the regional governments represented an extra layer of bureaucracy that was expensive to operate; the cost conflicted with the desire to reduce administrative expenditures in order to channel state funds into productive investment.

Regional government was also believed to be incompatible with the kind of economic development that the Party wished to undertake. Apparently with Russian advice, Chinese planners concluded that efficient development required the construction of large-scale industrial projects in order to realize the greatest possible economies of scale, and that balanced modernization required the redistribution of resources from the more developed provinces along the coast to the more backward regions in the interior. Both these considerations made central planning and a strong central government imperative. As Chou Fang, one of China's leading specialists in public administration, put it at the time, economic development under socialism necessitated greater "unity and centralization" in the state and Party structure.[8]

Moreover, there was growing apprehension that, unless restrained, the regional governments established in 1949 might increase their independence from central control. Autonomous regions with political, economic, and military powers of their own had been a feature of Chinese politics since at least the middle of the nineteenth century, and had formed the basis of warlordism in the first half of the twentieth. That this old regionalism still posed a threat to national unity was evident to some Chinese leaders by the middle of 1953. In August, Mao Tse-tung warned of tendencies toward excessive decentralization in China and criticized the "handful" of Party cadres who, he said, "flatly reject collective leadership . . . and always prefer to be left alone."[9]

Although Mao did not mention them by name, he almost certainly was referring to Kao Kang of Manchuria and Jao Shu-shih of East China, both of whom were showing signs of increasing independence in the early 1950's. After their dismissal in February 1954, Kao and Jao were accused of establishing tight personal control over their regional governments and Party bureaus and of then using their local power to demand changes in the central Party and state leadership. The two men also may have had policy differences with other leaders in Peking. It is likely, for example, that they were more willing than others to adopt Russian methods of enterprise management and less eager to transfer financial and material resources from their own regions into the interior of the country. But whatever its cause, the Kao-Jao affair illustrated the danger that ambitious regional leaders might decide to challenge the authority of the Party center.[10]

Happily, even as the costs became more and more apparent, the need for regional government was becoming significantly reduced. By late 1952 the administrators of the newly liberated areas—the Central-South, the Southwest, and the Northwest regions—were successfully completing their campaigns to redistribute land, establish local governments, suppress local bandits, and expose counterrevolutionaries. They had begun to catch up with the eastern, northern, and northeastern areas that had been liberated well before 1949. This made it possible to impose central policies in all of them at approximately the same time. As the differences among the six regions narrowed, the possibility of effecting administrative centralization correspondingly increased.

These developments encouraged Chinese leaders to impose greater central control over the regional governments between 1952 and 1954. Administrative centralization was accomplished in four steps. In November

1952 the regional governments were reorganized as administrative committees, and some of their bureaus were placed under the direct control of their corresponding ministries in Peking. The new administrative committees continued to have a large degree of independence in cultural and educational matters, but they had much less autonomy than their predecessors in interpreting economic and financial policy. This reorganization of regional government was undertaken, the central government explained, because large-scale economic construction made it necessary to "further unify and centralize leadership over various phases of work."[11]

In August 1953, at the National Conference on Financial and Economic Work, Mao Tse-tung referred approvingly to the measures that the Central Committee had taken in the late 1940's to strengthen control over its regional and local Party bureaus and strongly implied that similar measures were required once again.[12] In response to Mao's instructions, in the following month the Central Committee convened a national Party conference on organizational work that adopted a set of principles to govern relations between the Party and the government and between the Party center and the local Party bureaus and committees. These principles stipulated that the Central Committee alone had the authority to make basic policy decisions, and that although local Party and government leaders might adapt central policy to local conditions, they should never deviate from the guidelines established by the Party center. These principles were later described as having been formulated for the purpose of combating excessive decentralization.[13]

A third step in the process of administrative centralization involved the establishment sometime in 1953 of procedures for national economic planning. The First Five-Year Plan was notable for imposing tight central control on the industrial sector of the economy. State-owned industries, almost without exception, were placed under the jurisdiction of the central ministries. Each ministry, in turn, specified a wide range of targets and quotas for the enterprises it controlled, including gross value of output, volume of output, product mix, product quality, costs, profits, employment, wages, and labor productivity. Monitoring of economic performance was the responsibility of the State Statistical Bureau, established in October 1952, which specified the forms, data, and computation methods to be used by each production unit in filing its regular reports.

In June 1954 the Party finally abolished the regional administrative committees and Party bureaus altogether, explaining that planned economic development once again required the "strengthening of the concentrated and unified leadership of the central government."[14] The new state constitution, adopted in September of the same year, differed from Soviet precedent in establishing a unitary rather than a federal state system: all legislative powers were explicitly reserved for the central government, which was granted the authority to change or revoke any decisions by provincial or local government that it deemed to be inappropriate.[15]

The elimination of the regional governments and Party bureaus was accompanied by a low-keyed rectification campaign to explain why greater administrative centralization was necessary. The most important texts studied during the campaign were the "Resolution on Party Unity," adopted by the Fourth Plenum in February 1954, and the "Resolution on the Kao Kang–Jao Shu-shih Anti-Party Alliance," adopted by the National Party Conference held in March 1955. These two documents, written to criticize Kao Kang and Jao Shu-shih, were used to impress local and provincial cadres with the need to obey central Party direction and to refrain from creating "independent kingdoms."[16]

REGULARIZATION

A second type of organizational rationalization undertaken between 1952 and 1955 was the regularizing of administrative procedures. Chinese leaders recognized that planning the national economy would be much more complex than administering the subsistence economies of the revolutionary base areas—or even than engineering the economic recovery of the early 1950's. Vast amounts of information and data would have to be gathered and ordered. New industries would have to be planned, constructed, and managed. Plans for the various sectors of the economy would have to be coordinated. All of this required that the state bureaucracy would have to become more regular and formal in its operation than it had been during the consolidation period.

As early as 1951 the central government had convened a conference of officials responsible for administrative affairs at the central, regional, provincial, and municipal levels. The primary purpose of the conference, discussed in the previous chapter, was to improve relations between Party and non-Party cadres in government agencies. But the conference also drafted a decision, adopted by the Government Administration Council on July 26, that called for regularizing administrative procedures and clarifying the division of labor among government offices. The decision foresaw a gradual transition from the flexible, ad hoc governmental institutions of the 1949–51 period, which it described as the "former large and all-inclusive organizational set-up," to a more formal, systematic, and regular bureaucracy.[17]

The 1952 decision to emphasize economic development simply accelerated these trends toward administrative regularization. Within a week of the 1952 Party Day editorial, which announced that economic construction was now to be the Party's principal task, the North China bureau of the Party held a conference on organizational work to discuss the editorial's implications for administrative affairs. The conference called on the regional government's economic departments to develop more precise systems of accounting and auditing, to codify organizational rules and procedures, to establish routines for inspection and reporting, and to specify the responsibilities of their various sub-agencies and personnel.[18] Soon thereafter the central government began to issue a series of decisions on such topics as the establishment of a national statistical system, the management of state archives, the classification and protection of confidential materials, and the transmission of government documents. It also clarified the organizational structure of the provincial governments and the size and design of various central ministries and bureaus.[19] To supervise the process, committees on administrative organization (*pien-chih wei-yüan-hui*) were established at the central and provincial levels and charged with determining the size and structure of the state bureaucracy.

Regularization also promised to affect the style of policy implementation in China. The Party had continued to employ mass campaigns as a technique for carrying out policy in the early 1950's. In part this was a response to the serious shortage of reliable cadres, but it also reflected the belief that many of the policies of the period—land reform, the marriage law, the suppression of counterrevolutionaries, and economic recovery— could effectively be enforced only through mass mobilization.

In the mid-1950's, however, a number of Party leaders began to suggest that the campaign techniques of the past were no longer appropriate in an era of planned economic development. At both the National People's Congress in 1954 and the Eighth Party Congress in 1956, for example, Tung Pi-wu argued that mass campaigns tended to produce excesses and contrasted them with the more formal and regular procedures for policy implementation that would soon be established. At the National People's Congress, Tung described mass movements as an "overly simple" way of linking the government to the people.[20] At the Eighth Party Congress, though acknowledging that the land reform, San-fan, and Wu-fan campaigns of the early 1950's had achieved greater results than expected, he warned that because they did not rely on the law, they had "possibly promoted the growth of a hostile and distrustful attitude among the people toward state administration and resulted in greater difficulties for the Party."[21]

Unofficial sources suggest that similar views were expressed even more bluntly in speeches and reports not intended for public distribution. At a national conference on public security work in May 1954, for example, P'eng Chen is said to have declared that large-scale economic development would require that mass campaigns against counterrevolutionaries be brought to an end, and that judicial work would thereafter have to be conducted according to formal, legal procedures. Tung Pi-wu is reported to have said, in a meeting that year of the Political and Legal Affairs Committee of the Government Administration Council, "We used to live on movements. After the constitution is passed, we shall live by law."[22]

PERSONNEL MANAGEMENT

By the end of 1952 the cadre shortages of the early years of the People's Republic had largely been overcome. As discussed in the previous chapter, the Party was able to recruit approximately 2.6 million new cadres into the Party and government in the three years between 1950 and 1952, producing a total corps of some 3.3 million officials. To be sure, the need for more cadres continued through 1954 and 1955, as the government assumed greater responsibility for economic management, and as the Party extended its supervision over the state bureaucracy. But by the time the First Five-Year Plan began in 1953, Chinese leaders believed that their principal personnel problem was no longer to recruit large numbers of new officials; instead they sought to upgrade the skills of the existing corps of Party and state cadres and to manage them more effectively. In an article listing accomplishments in personnel work over the preceding three years, Minister of Personnel An Tzu-wen complained in September 1952 that China's personnel management program was still not sufficiently "rational and systematic."[23] The cadre policies of the next three to four years can best be understood as an attempt to introduce greater system into China's personnel practices.

Perhaps the most important change was the institution in 1955 of a graduated wage scale for all state and Party cadres.[24] As described in the last chapter, veteran Communist cadres were paid according to a modified version of the Yenan supply system and were given room and board by the agencies for which they worked. Retained officials and newly appointed cadres were given a monetary wage. Over the years the problems associated with the concurrent use of two different systems of remuneration became increasingly apparent. Cadres on the supply system generally received less than officials who were paid cash wages. However, supply-system cadres with many dependents received cash supplements that occasionally brought them more income than comparable officials on the wage system. All this was both confusing and unfair, and the cases of inequity produced tension and discontent.

In theory the Party might have solved these problems by putting everyone on the supply system, but that was impossible for several reasons. The supply system, with its complicated schedule of supplementary payments for dependents, travel, education, and the like, was more difficult to administer than the wage system. And the conditions for which the supply system had been originally designed—feeding and housing highly dedicated cadres during a period of economic scarcity—no longer held. The bulk of China's officials could not be assumed to be intensely committed to the cause. Many were holdovers from the previous government, others were only recent recruits, and most were not even Party members. Normative appeals would therefore have to be supplemented by a system of material incentives beyond those the supply system could offer.

Perhaps most important, Chinese leaders believed that the supply system could not efficiently reward cadres for improving performance, acquiring technical skills, or assuming greater responsibilities. It violated the principle "to each according to his work" because it gave roughly the same income to skilled and unskilled alike.[25] A wage system, it was argued, would better encourage workers to raise their level of technical competence, strengthen their enthusiasm for work, increase their efficiency, and "fulfill and surpass the great responsibilities of the First Five-Year Plan sooner." Economic constraints had prevented the universal application of the wage system in the early 1950's, but with economic recovery now well under way, and with inflation under control, it would now be possible to give monetary incentives to cadres who worked more skillfully and efficiently.[26]

For all these reasons, the supply system was gradually phased out between 1953 and 1955.* In 1952, 90 percent of China's cadres were still on the supply system, but in August 1955 only 33 percent remained, most of them rural cadres at the county and district levels.[27] Later that year the supply system was finally eliminated, along with free housing, free utilities, and supplementary payments for dependents and travel.[28] All government and Party employees were assigned to one of thirty ranks (the upper twenty-six were administrative grades, the lower four, nonclerical service grades), and a range of grades was established for each government and Party post. The salary for grade-thirty nonclerical service personnel was 20 yüan per month; the salaries for administrative cadres ranged from 30 yüan per month for grade twenty-six to 560 yüan per month for grade one.[29]

The establishment of a comprehensive salary system required that Party cadres be given a personal rank based on seniority, experience, and administrative position. The process created a good deal of tension and resent-

---

*The supply system was retained in a few areas in which supplies were short and where it would therefore be desirable to ensure that cadres received enough foodstuffs. An explanatory article appeared in *Jen-min jih-pao*, 14.x.55, and is translated in *Survey of the China Mainland Press*, no. 1134 (21.ix.55), pp. 13–17.

ment. In his interviews with former cadres from Kwangtung, Ezra Vogel discovered that this "rational approach to civil service administration" created a "wave of discontent among cadres disappointed with their new ranks."[30] The announcement of the wage system was phrased to defuse this resentment through inclusion of a prediction that wages would increase 65.7 percent during the course of the First Five-Year Plan.[31] Although this promise was never kept, the majority of cadres, particularly those at the bottom of the salary system, did receive a wage increase in April 1956, and in an attempt to reduce salary differentials between high-ranking and low-ranking officials, cadres above grade eleven (cadres at and above the level of department head in the central government and bureau chief in the provinces) received salary reductions in December 1956.[32]

Other personnel policies adopted between 1952 and 1955 concerned the training of Party and state cadres. Officials responsible for personnel matters readily admitted that in the early 1950's they had been almost exclusively concerned with adding to the number of cadres and had not devoted enough attention to verifying political reliability or professional qualifications.* This had been understandable, even unavoidable, during consolidation, but the emphasis on quantity rather than quality had produced a corps low in average education. Of 5.3 million cadres in service in 1955, some three million had only the equivalent of a junior or senior middle-school education, and another two million had received only a primary-school education or less.[33]

The shift of national priorities toward economic development placed greater demands on administrators and managers. It was necessary, therefore, to upgrade the cultural, technical, administrative, and ideological skills of China's cadres so that they could master the technological aspects of industrialization and agricultural modernization, administer large and complex organizations, and make policy decisions that conformed to the basic tenets of Marxism-Leninism. The 1952 Party Day editorial in *Jen-min jih-pao* offered assurances that the Party would be fully capable of giving leadership in the work of state economic construction but cautioned that this would be true only if Party cadres were able to master the relevant skills. Leadership by unskilled and ignorant officials could waste scarce material and financial resources, or even cripple China's development effort.[34]

---

*One of the most outspoken was Lin Feng, who as director of the Second Staff Office of the State Council was responsible for cultural and educational affairs, but who had also served in various regional organization departments. See his speech to the second session of the National People's Congress in *Jen-min jih-pao*, 25.vii.55, in *Current Background*, no. 351 (29.viii.55), pp. 1–7; and his report to the Eighth Party Congress in September 1956 in *Jen-min shou-ts'e* (1957), pp. 130–32.

A number of institutions provided in-service technical, administrative, and cultural education in the mid-1950's. As a result of a series of decisions on cadre training adopted by the Central Committee and the central government between 1952 and 1955, universities accepted applications from cadres aged thirty or less and provided special tutorials to help them prepare for the college admissions examinations.[35] Specialized schools and classes were established for older cadres and for younger officials who were not able to go on to university training. The cadre schools, often specializing in a particular aspect of government or Party affairs, usually enrolled students for a relatively lengthy, full-time course, and the training classes, which were run by various agencies in the bureaucracy, offered cadres four to six hours of instruction each week in reading, writing, arithmetic, and technical subjects.

The increased attention to technical skills was paralleled by greater concern with the political qualifications of China's cadres. In January 1953 An Tzu-wen warned that though administrative talent and technical skills were both crucial to success in economic development, there was a danger in ignoring "revolutionary virtue." It was not enough for some cadres to have talent and others to possess revolutionary commitment, or for the government to concern itself with technical skills and administrative expertise while the Party was responsible for political supervision. All officials should possess at least a modicum of both "talent" (*ts'ai*) and "virtue" (*te*), that is, administrative ability and political reliability.[36] Two years later Mao Tse-tung expressed the same point somewhat differently, pointing out that expertise in political and economic work could only be successful if achieved on the basis of "a higher level of Marxism-Leninism." If cadres could not be turned into a powerful corps of theoretical workers, Mao said, "we will not have a common language or any common method, and we may keep arguing back and forth without making things any clearer."[37]

With this in mind, both Party and state personnel departments began to develop new programs for political study to accompany established programs of technical education. Not surprisingly, political training at that time tended to emphasize materials of direct relevance to economic development. Senior and intermediate-grade cadres, for instance, began studying Stalin's *Economic Problems of Socialism in the USSR*, the *History of the CPSU (Bolshevik)*, and other Soviet writings on economic development, as well as documents on the Chinese economy and Party policy.[38]

A final set of personnel reforms completed between 1952 and 1955 was intended to ensure that cadres be given jobs in which their talents could be used to the fullest advantage, and that key positions in industry and the bureaucracy be filled by well-qualified officials. Those in charge of personnel work admitted that in the early 1950's skilled people had often been given inappropriate job assignments and that other cadres had been placed in jobs they were not qualified to handle. Now that planned economic development was underway, it was time to tidy up the system of assignments and promotions.

One aspect of this program was the creation of a more formal network of personnel agencies. Party organization departments at the central, provincial, and county levels were given the responsibility of making appointments to administrative posts in the Party. Together with the Party committees and Party branches inside the state bureaucracy, they also maintained the files of all government officials who were Party members, assigned Party members to positions in the government, and supervised the work of the state personnel apparatus. A parallel system of state personnel agencies—consisting of the Ministry of Personnel (renamed the Bureau of Personnel in 1954), the provincial and county personnel departments, and the personnel sections within government ministries and departments—was formally responsible for the appointment, promotion, transfer, dismissal, and punishment of all government officials. In practice, however, state personnel agencies deferred to the Party in the management of Party members and in the selection of important government officials.

Like the workings of the rest of the administrative apparatus during the time of the First Five-Year Plan, personnel management was highly centralized. In August 1952 the central authorities were given control over the allocation of college and university graduates. In 1956 similar control over the assignment of technical specialists was given to a central Bureau of Experts. Throughout the period the central personnel organs made or approved all appointments of county magistrates and Party first secretaries, all provincial appointments above the level of bureau director, and all central government and Party appointments above the level of deputy bureau director. This meant, in fact, that all cadres in the top thirteen grades of the twenty-six-grade salary system for administrative cadres were directly controlled by personnel agencies in Peking.[39]

With this structure in place, the Party next attempted to specify more clearly the criteria for assignment and promotion of state and Party officials. Articles on personnel matters complained that administrators used improper standards in deciding which cadres to hire and which to promote. Some were accused of discriminating against women, non-Party cadres, officials from bourgeois backgrounds, or members of minority nationalities. Still others were criticized for showing favoritism to those with whom they had some kind of personal or familial relationship. It was incorrect, personnel managers were told, to believe that cadres could be

promoted only one grade at a time, and it was also incorrect to give preference to cadres who had joined the Party early in the revolution or had
served in administrative posts for a long period of time. Although seniority
was important in determining retirement benefits, it was not to be the
standard for promotion. Instead, personnel departments were told to consider only a cadre's administrative ability and political reliability.[40]

Those responsible for personnel work were particularly concerned with
the misallocation of China's limited supply of skilled technicians. Because
of the shortage of educated officials in the early 1950's, many cadres with
technical backgrounds had been assigned to administrative positions in the
middle levels of the bureaucracy or had been asked to work in a specialty
other than that in which they had been trained. The personnel departments were therefore ordered to identify cadres' technical skills and make
sure that they were reassigned to more appropriate positions. Technicians
who believed that their jobs did not make use of their specialized training
were urged to appeal for reassignment to personnel departments at a
higher level.[41]

Many cadres were transferred from middle-level administrative work to
basic-level management in the mid-1950's. This program began in 1951 as
part of the preparation for the First Five-Year Plan, but it was greatly
intensified in 1953. Administrative offices above the county level were reduced in size, and cadres were transferred to managerial positions in factories and mines on the "industrial front." Officials who had worked in
regional Party bureaus and administrative committees were particularly
likely to receive this type of reassignment when those agencies were
abolished in 1954.[42]

The substantial number of reassignments between 1952 and 1955 appears to have aroused considerable resistance, both from the cadres about
to be reassigned and from their immediate superiors. Despite assurances
that they would be performing important service in the cause of economic
development and that the experience would win them promotion later,
many cadres objected to being shifted down to basic-level positions in factories, mines, and commercial enterprises. Middle-level officials in Party
and government agencies opposed the reassignment of subordinates because they feared that their departments would suffer if they lost experienced staff members.

As a result, the program had mixed results. To be sure, large numbers
of cadres were reassigned, some 70,000 being transferred in 1952–53 and
over 90,000 more by July 1954.[43] But in early 1955 there were complaints that the job had been done poorly, and a census of state workers
and employees made the same year indicated that 11.7 percent of the en-
gineers who had graduated from college and 17.7 percent of those who had

graduated from technical middle school still had not been given appropriate job assignments.[44]

CONTROL

Organizational regularization was also involved in the methods by which Chinese leaders attempted to maintain control over the Party and state bureaucracy. As we have seen, in the early 1950's control had been exercised primarily through a series of rectification campaigns, each addressing a different set of bureaucratic problems: bureaucratism and commandism in 1950, waste and corruption in 1951–52, and bureaucratism and commandism once again in 1953. Now, however, Chinese leaders began to wonder whether such rectification campaigns could continue to provide a reliable mechanism for ensuring the dependability, efficiency, and effectiveness of the bureaucracy. For one thing, the experience of the early 1950's had turned up disturbing evidence that rectification campaigns tended to lose their impact over the years as cadres quickly learned to pass through them relatively unscathed. In addition, the San-fan campaign had demonstrated that intense rectification movements might distract the attention of lower-level cadres from routine work, and thus intensify the very problems they were designed to solve. And it was also apparent that economic planning would require a new kind of organizational control: routine auditing of the allocation of material and financial resources, reduction of administrative costs, and some mechanism for ensuring that all departments and agencies should operate in accordance with the national plan.

Consequently, the Party began to develop a new organizational control system between 1952 and 1955. The system was based on the assumption that such motivational control mechanisms as indoctrination and rectification would have to be supplemented by stringent, overlapping devices of structural control. At the heart of the new control system were four monitors: the Procuracy, the Ministry of Supervision, the Party, and a network of Party control commissions. The performance of the government was to be overseen by the Procuracy, the Ministry of Supervision, and the Party, while the behavior of the Party itself was to be supervised by the Party control commissions. All four monitors, in turn, were to incorporate a number of mechanisms by which the bureaucracy would be made responsive, at least to a degree, to popular demands and pressures.

Of the four organizational monitors, the weakest was the Procuracy.[45] Modeled after the procuratorial organs in the Soviet Union, its principal responsibility was to review recommendations from public security offices concerning the arrest of suspected criminals, and to act as the equivalent of a state attorney in criminal cases. But the Chinese Procuracy was also given the job of ensuring that the activities of the government complied with the law and of investigating and prosecuting serious crimes committed by state officials. Although the control function of the Procuracy was focused particularly on the public security system, the whole state bureaucracy technically fell within its purview.

In the early years of the People's Republic, the growth of the Procuracy was stunted by a shortage of cadres, as well as by the new regime's emphasis on mass campaigns and military control to suppress counter-revolutionary and criminal activity. As a result, the Procuracy did not play an important role in criminal justice in the early 1950's, let alone act as an effective instrument of organizational control. But between 1954 and 1955 the size of the Procuracy nearly doubled as a result of the Party's new policy of promoting "socialist legality," and a special branch was established with the sole function of supervising the work of other government agencies. Furthermore, the Procuracy gradually gained greater freedom from interference by local Party and state leaders and greater autonomy in its investigations of the criminal acts of government officials. Even so, the Procuracy was still hobbled because organizational supervision was not its primary function, because of widespread confusion about the extent of its jurisdiction, and because its mandate extended only to the investigation of serious breaches of the criminal code and not to violations of administrative procedure.[46] As a result, though the mid-1950's may be called the Procuracy's heyday, it was still the least powerful and least active of the four organizational monitors.

The Ministry of Supervision and the network of state supervisory offices under its jurisdiction, like the Russian Control Commissariat, was responsible for investigating cases of administrative malfeasance involving officials who made improper use of state funds, who failed to carry out the decisions and regulations of higher levels, or who departed from state budgets and economic plans.[47] It also looked into minor crimes that the Procuracy decided not to prosecute and investigated officials who were making light of their duties, causing delay in their work, stirring up dissension, or acting in a "rotten and decadent" manner. In each such case, the Ministry of Supervision would make an investigation of the officials responsible for the problem and recommend appropriate punishment to the personnel office that controlled the cadre in question.

In a word, the division of labor between the Procuracy and the Ministry of Supervision roughly followed the distinction between criminal offenses and administrative infractions, except that the ministry was not given jurisdiction over the Party apparatus. A *Jen-min jih-pao* editorial of June 20 explained the scope of the supervisory system:

Supervisory organs are administrative control organs whose task is to supervise the execution of government decisions by state organs and public functionaries, and to indict organs and functionaries who violate the law and administrative discipline or are derelict in the performance of their duties. Supervisory organs are not responsible for supervising nonpublic functionaries [including cadres in the Party bureaucracy], and the action they take is administrative action; cases that call for legal action are referred to prosecuting organs [i.e., the Procuracy].[48]

Like the Procuracy, the Ministry of Supervision (then known as the People's Supervisory Committee) had relatively few cadres in the early 1950's and was only able to send inspection teams into government offices on a random, ad hoc basis. With the onset of administrative rationalization, however, the supervisory system was enlarged and strengthened. Its control was pushed deeper into the bureaucracy, with supervisory offices established in thirteen central ministries and in the financial and economic departments of the provinces and major municipalities. The responsibilities of the supervisory organs were simultaneously expanded, so that they had the authority not only to evaluate bureaucratic performance after the fact, but also to approve departmental plans and budgets before they were promulgated. And the supervisory system gradually won greater independence from the agencies it was supposed to monitor. At first supervisory offices were responsible both to the Ministry of Supervision and to the departments in which they were located, with the latter retaining the right to decide which cadres and offices would be audited. During the middle 1950's, however, a number of supervisory offices in the central government ministries were placed under the sole jurisdiction of the Ministry of Supervision and empowered to investigate possible infractions and derelictions without prior approval of the agencies involved.[49]

A network of control commissions was established within the Party in the aftermath of the Kao-Jao affair, first at the central, provincial, and county levels, then in factories and enterprises, and finally in central Party departments and state ministries.[50] Although the commissions' jurisdiction was limited to monitoring the conduct of officials who were members of the Party, they had jurisdiction over violations not only of Party discipline and the Party constitution but also of state laws and decrees. In practice they tended to supplant both the Procuracy and the Ministry of Supervision in overseeing the investigation and punishment of Party members.

Beyond this, remarkably little is known about the procedures and powers of the Party control commissions.[51] It appears, however, that they never gained much autonomy from the rest of the Party apparatus, perhaps because of fears that independent control commissions might become the instrument of an aspiring Chinese Stalin. Although the Ministry of Supervision might recommend punishment of an errant cadre to the appropriate personnel department, and although the Procuracy's cases were presented to a court, the control commissions worked in a more dependent manner. Investigations and preliminary judgments on Party members were made by the Party branches to which they belonged or by a superior Party committee, and only then were they submitted to the Party control commissions for approval. The control commissions thus acted to verify disciplinary actions undertaken elsewhere rather than to initiate investigations on their own.

The most important component of the control system was the Chinese Communist Party itself, which was responsible for overseeing all operations of the government. Until 1952 Party control over the government had been remarkably limited, being exercised primarily through high-ranking Party cadres who held concurrent positions as government officials, and through the Party's rectification campaigns against the state administrative apparatus. After the San-fan campaign, however, Chinese leaders greatly increased the power of Party committees to coordinate and inspect government work on a regular basis. In part, this reflected the belief that the Party could coordinate government activities at the local level more effectively than could the local people's councils. In part, too, increasing Party control over the government was seen as a necessary device for ensuring the execution of Party programs.

With these considerations in mind, Chinese leaders took two steps after the San-fan campaign to strengthen the Party's role in government affairs. In May 1952 the Central Committee issued a "Directive on the Reorganization and Expansion of the Party on the Foundation of the San-fan Movement," a document that, among other things, proposed recruiting more government cadres into the Party, increasing the Party's educational activities among government officials, convening more regular conferences of Party members inside government agencies, and reorganizing the Party branches inside the state apparatus.[52]

Then, on March 10, 1953, the Central Committee adopted a resolution on strengthening Party leadership over government work. Although the text of the directive was not published, Mao Tse-tung later noted that it required that all policy or important issues should first be discussed and decided by the appropriate Party committee before being referred to the government for action.[53] It is likely that this resolution provided the basis for the provisions, adopted by the Second National Conference on Organizational Work held later the same year, that "decisions are to be taken by the Party committees and to be carried out by all concerned," and that "Party committees have the responsibility to inspect [government] work."[54]

The impact of these two resolutions on Party involvement in government affairs was analyzed in an article published in March 1954 by the

Party Committee for Government Organs in Hopei, which was responsible for overseeing Party work within the provincial government apparatus.[55] The article cautioned that the Party should not attempt to exercise administrative authority directly, but it also claimed that the Party did have responsibility for the work of the government and that its own activities should therefore be coordinated with state affairs. Within government agencies, Party committees and branches should define the central task, find and correct any ideological obstacles to its successful completion, supervise the performance of Party members, help establish efficient administrative procedures, identify and report organizational problems, conduct campaigns against improper work styles, and organize political study programs for government officials. In this way, although the details of administrative work were still outside the Party's purview, the Party assumed substantial responsibility for organizational, personnel, ideological, and policy matters within the government. A study of the Southwest region during this period indicates that the Party convened conferences on economic work and issued directives on economic problems, in addition to continuing its traditional interest in problems of propaganda, rectification, culture, and education.[56]

These increasing powers and responsibilities required the Party to develop functional departments to formulate Party programs in substantive areas. Until 1952 central and regional Party committees had offices responsible for propaganda, organizational matters, united front work, and women's work, but not for economic problems. At some point between July 1952 and July 1953, the period of the campaign promoting agricultural cooperatives, the Party established its first such bureau, the Rural Work Department. In 1956 a comparable bureau was established to supervise work in the industrial and communications sectors. Together with the increase in the power of the Party's organization departments over personnel matters and the responsibility of the propaganda departments for cadre training programs, the creation of these two economic departments advanced the Party's effort to improve its ability to monitor and control the operation of the state administrative apparatus.

In addition to instituting these four channels of organizational control, Chinese leaders also sought new ways of making the bureaucracy more answerable to popular pressures and demands. During the revolution, accountability had been incorporated in the mass line, with its emphasis on informal, face-to-face contacts between cadres and the people. In the late 1940's and early 1950's accountability had also been built into such open-door campaigns as the Rectification of 1947–48 and the San-fan movement of 1951–52. But in the mid-1950's such methods, like mass mobilization itself, were increasingly seen as relics of an earlier and simpler era. To meet the changed circumstances, Chinese leaders attempted to design and substitute more orderly procedures for channeling mass opinion to the bureaucracy and for preventing alienation between the leaders and the led.

One procedure was to encourage citizens with complaints to write letters of protest to the appropriate Party or government office, or even to visit that office directly. In fact, an important element of the New San-fan campaign of 1953 was to ensure that such letters and visitors were processed correctly: each visitor was to receive an enthusiastic and helpful reception, each letter was to be answered promptly, and summaries of the most common complaints and suggestions were to be relayed to officials at higher levels. The significance that the Party assigned to this link between the bureaucracy and the people was underlined by an editorial in *Jen-min jih-pao* in January 1953 that described letters from the people as "the most practical, the most economical, and the most direct method" of mass participation in post-liberation China.[57]

Another procedure, popular participation in the organizational control system, has been described above. A network of "mass correspondents" was established under the Ministry of Supervision in factories, offices, mass organizations, and rural areas. It was the correspondents' job to observe the performance of government officials, investigate possible cases of criminal activity or infractions of administrative regulations, and solicit suggestions and criticisms from fellow workers and peasants. They could then report such cases to the supervisory office in the agency concerned, which would then investigate and recommend appropriate action. This system was described as a way of ensuring both that public complaints would be properly attended to and that cadres would be unable to retaliate. Similar networks of correspondents were created under the Procuracy, and the public was permitted to address complaints directly to the Party control commissions.[58]

Besides these two channels of direct public participation, there were also a number of indirect methods by which Chinese leaders proposed to allow popular review of the bureaucracy.[59] The public was encouraged to write letters to the provincial and national press, which in turn was expected to investigate particularly important national or local problems and make suggestions either in mass circulation journals or in periodicals whose distribution was restricted to ranking Party and government cadres. Mass organizations—trade unions, student and youth organizations, peasant associations, and the women's federation—were also identified as mechanisms by which public opinion on important policy issues could be conveyed to the Party and the government. And the deputies elected to the local, provincial, and national people's congresses were given authority to oversee the work of the government in their own constituency and elsewhere. In a decision announced in August 1955, national and provincial deputies were also authorized to make two inspections of government work each year (one after the spring planting and one after the autumn harvest), to demand briefings from local government officials, to attend local government meetings, and to receive petitions and complaints from their constituents. They were not, however, to overrule the decisions of local government directly; they were only to make suggestions as to how government leaders might improve their work.[60]

Most of these mechanisms for popular supervision were relatively ineffectual. In retrospect, it is clear that they were never intended to be devices for ensuring extensive popular control over the government and Party or for allowing the public to challenge basic Party principles and programs. But they are nonetheless significant for at least two reasons. They further illustrate the ways in which organizational control was gradually becoming more institutional and formal in the mid-1950's. Though Chinese leaders continued to insist that officials must be continually aware of the needs and demands of the people, their actions suggested that the methods for soliciting popular opinion would become both more routine and more controlled than they had been in the past. Even more important, the very existence of these mechanisms, weak as they were, took on political significance in the Hundred Flowers period of 1956–57 when, as we will see in Chapter 5, a number of leaders both inside and outside the Party proposed that these mechanisms for popular involvement in politics be strengthened as a way of preventing the alienation of the Party from the people.

Chinese political organizations underwent a transformation between 1952 and 1955. Administrative authority was centralized, rules and regulations were drafted, chains of command were formalized, and the division of labor among specialized agencies was more clearly specified. Chinese leaders redefined procedures and standards for recruiting and training cadres, established a single, nearly uniform system of ranks and salaries, and paid increasing attention to improving the technical and administrative skills of the nation's officials. They constructed a complex organizational control network and gave it responsibility for monitoring bureaucratic performance. Moreover, by announcing their intention to reduce reliance on mass campaigns as a method for implementing policy, Chinese leaders indicated that they were going to assign higher priority to regularized bureaucratic practice than to mass mobilization.

The extent of rationalization during these years should not be exaggerated; the formalization and regularization of organizational structures and procedures remained limited. Political criteria were still important in personnel decisions. The state administrative apparatus was subjected to increasing control and supervision by the Party, which was only partially bureaucratized. Mass mobilization, while deemphasized in the cities, was still used to carry out specific programs in rural areas. And despite the greater attention to structural methods of organizational control, Party and state cadres still experienced such rectification campaigns as the New San-fan movement of 1953 and the campaign against hidden counterrevolutionaries, the Su-fan, in 1955. Ezra Vogel was certainly correct in insisting that the Party and state in the mid-1950's can better be described as "semi-bureaucracies" than as fully bureaucratized organizations.[61] Nonetheless, when compared with the Party and state organizations of the revolutionary period and with China's organizational structure just after liberation, the degree of bureaucratization that had occurred by 1955 was pronounced. Moreover, for the first and only time during Mao's lifetime, Chinese leaders appeared to be committed to rationalization as the principal strategy for building and managing their nation's political structure.

When it began, this process of rationalization generated remarkably little controversy. It did, to be sure, produce resentment and tension among Party and state cadres. Regional leaders resisted the gradual centralization of administrative and financial controls between 1952 and 1954.[62] Officials responsible for economic affairs feared the growing power and independence of the Ministry of Supervision and its increasing ability to monitor their work.[63] Cadres disliked being transferred from administrative positions in the state bureaucracy to managerial positions in factories or from assignments in coastal cities to new projects being built in the interior. The assignment of personal ranks and salaries in 1955 aroused further discontent, and the preferential treatment given to wives of ranking officials, to Party members, and to demobilized servicemen in making appointments and promotions continued to generate bitterness and acrimony.

Despite these problems within the ranks, the rationalization process in the beginning produced little disagreement among top Chinese leaders, who seem to have agreed that it was a necessary concomitant of China's program of economic development. Even Mao Tse-tung, a lifelong foe of officialdom, openly endorsed the formalization and centralization of China's administrative structure and supported the development of greater technical skills within the bureaucracy.[64]

Nevertheless, there is evidence that some leaders were more enthusiastic about the process than others. Although P'eng Chen and Tung Pi-wu both called for greater attention to "socialist legality," Public Security Minister Lo Jui-ch'ing warned against giving the public security organs total responsibility for the Su-fan campaign and proposed continued mass mobilization to root out "hidden counterrevolutionaries."[65] Similarly, Mao never expressed wholehearted enthusiasm for regularization and systematization, but suggested the need for continuing to mount rectification campaigns against the conceit, complacency, and rightist opportunism that he saw developing among Party and state officials.[66] Mao's attitude was probably one of passive acquiesence: he was willing to preside over rationalization, and he was ready to endorse parts of it, but he was not uncritically committed to the process.

By the end of 1955 these latent differences had begun to surface and widen. As bureaucratic problems emerged, Chinese leaders began to consider whether further rationalization was the best solution, and as the shortcomings of the First Five-Year Plan became evident, they also began to ask if China might need a different strategy of development and thus a different set of organizational principles. The resulting debates over organization in the mid-1950's are the subject of the next two chapters.

4

The Origins of the First Crisis
1955-1956

By late 1955, at the end of only the sixth year of the People's Republic, Chinese leaders were losing confidence in their political organizations. Even before completing the organizational rationalization outlined in the last chapter, some had begun to reconsider the effectiveness of a regularized, bureaucratic structure in promoting rapid economic development and in guiding China toward communism.

The crisis of confidence did not emerge in isolation from other issues. The unease that Chinese leaders felt about political organizations in the mid-1950's was closely linked to their growing uncertainty about Soviet strategies of economic development, their awareness of the shortcomings of the First Five-Year Plan, and their concern about the effects of de-Stalinization on the international communist movement. Because these domestic and international developments did not occur simultaneously, China's first organizational crisis developed gradually between early 1955 and the middle of 1957. During the first stage of the crisis, January 1955 to June 1956, concern about China's bureaucracy was not yet severe, disputes over organizational issues remained minor, and the reforms undertaken in response were incremental. As the problems produced by bureaucratic inefficiency, economic imbalance, and de-Stalinization continued to accumulate, however, the sense of crisis deepened, and between June 1956 and June 1957 Chinese leaders began to disagree more sharply and openly over organizational issues. Some began to propose sweeping changes in China's political structure. The crisis culminated in the dramatic Hundred Flowers episode of the spring of 1957, when Party leadership came under unprecedented criticism from non-Party intellectuals, government officials, and students.

The present chapter discusses the origins of the crisis of confidence and the incremental reforms undertaken during the first phase. Chapter 5 will deal with the intense debates of the Hundred Flowers period.

ORIGINS OF THE CRISIS

The organizational crisis of the mid-1950's began with two domestic developments that came to the attention of Chinese leaders in early 1955.

One was the growing inefficiency in China's state and Party bureaucracies. The other was the poor performance of agriculture during the First Five-Year Plan.

By the spring of 1955 the Chinese press had begun to express concern that the new cadres recruited since 1949 were not being used efficiently. For one thing, the middle levels of the bureaucracy were growing faster than the basic levels. To be sure, expanding the provincial and municipal governments and Party committees was a convenient way of absorbing some of the urban unemployed, who constituted a major economic problem during the period. It also helped satisfy the demands of rural cadres and factory officials for promotion to office jobs in the cities. Although the central government sought to restrict the expansion of the middle levels of the bureaucracy, resourceful provincial and municipal officials could find ways of circumventing the center's controls. A report from Heilungkiang, for example, revealed that the provincial government had contrived to employ 57 percent more cadres than the center had authorized simply by tapping the profits of provincial enterprises and factories, a maneuver over which central authorities seem to have had no veto.[1]

As a result, the bureaucracy began to suffer from "a heavy head and weak feet"—too many officials in the middle levels and too few skilled and dedicated cadres at the basic levels. What is more, cadres in the cities apparently had little to do:

New offices are more crowded than ever. But over half the sixty-one cadres in the [retraining] division have not received any work assignment for at least half a year. Work that should and can be done by one cadre is now divided among four or five or even ten persons. Worse still, no one is in charge and no one is responsible. The cadres ordinarily spend hours reading newspapers or just gossiping every day. When they get bored at the office, they go out wandering the streets in the name of "business coordination" or "field inspection." The morale of the division has dropped so low that two cadres were specially assigned to show movies eight times a month in order to cheer up the bored cadres.[2]

No less than one-third of the officials in some agencies had no work at all.[3] The cadre shortage of the early 1950's, it seems, had been overcome with a vengeance.

The expansion of the bureaucracy also permitted a large number of cadres to be assigned to unnecessary staff positions. In Heilungkiang the Party had begun to duplicate the state structure, and there were Party offices charged with supervising the excavation of mineshafts and the installation of structural metals in construction projects. Provincial economic bureaus, in turn, were establishing policy-research sections, financial sections, and personnel offices that duplicated similar agencies directly attached to the governor's office.[4] Reports from other provinces complained that too many officials were being assigned to work in state guest houses, nurseries for officials' children, rest homes for cadres, and other nonproductive positions. A nationwide survey in 1956 revealed that one-third of all Chinese government cadres were working in staff rather than line positions, that is, they were not "directly involved in handling business in the administrative organs of the state."[5]

There was another problem. By 1955, the gradual strengthening of central planning and control had begun to produce troublesome problems at several levels of administration. At the center neither the Politburo nor the State Council could effectively coordinate the large number of ministries established to manage the economy under the First Five-Year Plan. The ministries therefore issued instructions to the provinces without securing the approval of the Central Committee or the State Council. At the ministerial level the various departments and planning agencies were deluged with a flood of reports and forms from the localities. And at the provincial level, where government agencies were responsible primarily to their corresponding ministries in Peking, rather than to the provincial authorities, it was difficult for provincial leaders to coordinate government programs, and there came to be substantial duplication of effort and overlapping of activities. In addition, ministerial instructions often did not adequately consider the variation of economic conditions from province to province. In early 1956, Mao complained that excessive centralization was placing provincial and local governments in a strait jacket. "Scores of hands" were reaching down from the center to interfere in local affairs.[6] One of China's principal economic planners charged that central planning was suffering from a double malady: it was not comprehensive or thorough, but it was still overly restrictive and rigid.[7]

A second cause for the organizational crisis was the mixed performance of the Chinese economy under the First Five-Year Plan. Following Soviet experience, the Chinese had attempted to achieve rapid industrialization by channeling the bulk of investment into heavy industry. The results of this policy, in retrospect, seem predictable. Industrial production rose impressively, growing at an average rate of 16 percent per year during the 1952–55 period, but agricultural output grew at an average annual rate of only some 4 percent during the same period. Grain output fell behind the targets set by the five-year plan, and the production of cotton actually suffered an absolute decline. The result was that peasant living standards increased only slowly, and the gap between city and countryside grew; that light industry experienced shortages of agricultural raw materials and was forced to operate at less than full capacity; that urban demand for foodstuffs and consumer goods began to exceed supply; and that China, which was then importing large amounts of machinery from the Soviet

Union, was unable to expand its exports of agricultural products rapidly enough to meet the payments on its debt.

Chinese planners faced serious constraints in attempting to solve these problems. They did not want to reduce their overall rate of growth, since that would limit China's ability to improve living standards and strengthen national defense. Nor were they eager to revise the basic premises of the five-year plan, for fear that doing so on a piecemeal basis might have unpredictable consequences. They therefore concluded that, at least in the short term, the pace of industrialization, the allocation of investment between industry and agriculture, and the distribution of investment between light and heavy industry should be maintained essentially as defined in the plan. Debate focused, therefore, on ways of increasing agricultural output without altering those investment ratios. In the spring of 1955 a set of policies was adopted that permitted wealthier peasants to withdraw from the cooperative farms and granted them direct material incentives for increasing output. But this program failed to produce quick results and also tended to increase inequality in the countryside. So Mao insisted in late July on a speedup instead of a slowdown of the pace of agricultural cooperativization. Mao argued that cooperatives—in addition to increasing output immediately by generating economies of scale, and raising productivity in the long run by facilitating agricultural mechanization— would stimulate investment by pooling local financial resources and would increase state accumulation by facilitating government purchase of agricultural products at artificially reduced prices. At the same time, the cooperatives would provide peasants with important material incentives by financing local public health and educational facilities. Best of all, these incentives would be of a collective rather than an individual nature, and therefore would not increase the degree of class differentiation in the countryside.[8]

These economic problems, together with the July decision to accelerate agricultural collectivization, had implications for China's political organizations. In the short run, they heightened the Party's concern with the administrative efficiency of the bureaucracy. The swollen administrative budget seemed to be an important source of potential savings that could be channeled into agricultural investment. One article published in the autumn of 1955, for instance, insisted that although no funds could be diverted from industry into agriculture, any savings generated by reducing administrative expenses could be reallocated directly to land reclamation work.[9] Furthermore, the creation of agricultural collectives and the state purchase of agricultural products both required an increasing number of skilled cadres at the basic rural levels. This made the phenomenon of "heavy head and weak feet" even more intolerable, and increased the pressure to reassign middle-level officials to the countryside.

In the longer term, China's economic problems raised some important questions about the capability of the bureaucracy to plan—questions, that is, about the bureaucracy's ability to allocate the nation's scarce human and material resources effectively, economically, and creatively. Chinese leaders saw two different ways for increasing this type of organizational efficiency. One, advocated forcefully by Mao, was to reintroduce campaign techniques into the planning and policy-implementation procedures of the increasingly rationalized bureaucracy. The other, favored by the planners themselves, was to increase the bureaucracy's ability to draw on the professional skills and expertise of China's non-Party intellectuals.

ADMINISTRATIVE RETRENCHMENT

The growth of bureaucratic overstaffing and inefficiency, the desire to channel funds from administration into agriculture, and the shortage of skilled cadres at the basic levels all argued for a major effort to reduce administrative staffs and budgets in the middle and upper levels of the bureaucracy.

Such an effort had two precedents in the history of the Party. The first was the campaign for "better troops and simpler administration" (*ching-ping chien-cheng*) that had been mounted in 1942–44 in response to economic and financial problems brought on by Japanese military pressure. The aim of that campaign had been to promote "simplification, unification, efficiency, economy, and opposition to bureaucracy" by reducing the size of administrative organs and transferring middle-level officials to leadership positions at the basic levels.[10] The second precedent was the program in late 1953 and early 1954 to transfer cadres from administrative posts to schools, factories, mines, and other productive enterprises. We have already discussed the latter program as part of the broader policy of reallocating skilled cadres to meet the needs of a planned economy. But the program had as another aim the streamlining of the middle levels of the country's administrative structure.

Both precedents suggest that administrative retrenchment was difficult to accomplish. Mark Selden points out that the number of full-time administrative officials in Yenan was actually greater in early 1943 than when the campaign to simplify administration began in December 1941. Although the campaign was intensified in 1943–44, the failure to publish final statistics on the number of cadres reassigned suggests that the goal of reducing the number of administrative officials by 20 percent was never attained.[11] Similarly, after the 1953–54 retrenchment effort, it was admitted that although 150,000 cadres had been reassigned in the first half of 1954, the work had not been done carefully, the middle levels of the bureaucracy were still overstaffed, and many cadres had not been given appropriate assignments after they had been transferred.[12] In neither case were rank-and-file cadres or middle-level administrators enthusiastic about administrative retrenchment. Cadres resisted reassignment to lower positions, particularly in rural areas. Administrators were afraid that reducing the size of their staffs would hamper the agencies' ability to complete their work on schedule.

Despite these rather discouraging examples, a major retrenchment drive was launched with considerable publicity in early 1955. In January the State Council established a national Committee on Organization and Wages and assigned it the tasks of investigating the efficiency of central Party and state agencies and recommending measures for administrative retrenchment. The campaign was organized under three headings: organizational retrenchment, staff reduction, and adjustment of cadre assignments. Originally scheduled for completion in mid-1955, it was slowed by the simultaneous campaign against hidden counterrevolutionaries, and its conclusion was postponed until January 1956.

The purposes and accomplishments of the campaign were described in detail in two lengthy reports by the officials most directly responsible. One was by Hsi Chung-hsün, the secretary-general of the State Council, and was delivered to the National People's Congress in July 1955; the other was by Ho Lung, director of the Committee on Organization and Wages, and was presented to the State Council in late December of the same year.[13] The two reports not only summarize the organizational reforms undertaken in the name of administrative retrenchment, but also provide insight into the way in which Hsi and Ho understood China's organizational problems.

According to the reports, the inefficiency of the Party and state bureaucracies could be traced to three problems: structure, personnel, and work style. As for structure, Hsi and Ho complained that the division of labor among the various central agencies, and between the central ministries and the provinces, had never been clearly defined, a circumstance that produced much confusion and duplication of effort. In addition, the internal structure of many ministries had become too complicated. This created problems in coordination and long delays in reaching decisions, for all bureaus and sub-bureaus concerned with each problem had to be consulted before action could be taken. As for personnel, there were too many officials at the central and provincial levels, and careful plans would have to be devised for reassigning them. As for work style, both Hsi and Ho said that the bureaucracy emphasized processing documents rather than personal investigation and direct experience, a style that rewarded stolid performance of routine rather than creativity and initiative.

In Hsi's and Ho's analysis, the three problems were closely interrelated. The more complex and ill-defined the division of labor within the bureaucracy, the more officers would be needed to run it. The larger the number of officials, the more complex the internal structure of each ministry would have to be. The more complex the internal structure of its units, the more likely the bureaucracy would be to foster "documentism" (*kung-wen-chu-i*), and the less able its cadres would be to investigate problems personally. They concluded that increasing organizational efficiency through administrative retrenchment required that each problem be attacked in turn.

The first step in the retrenchment campaign was to define each agency's tasks, to decide which were primary and which were secondary, and to determine which responsibilities should be transferred to other departments or to local authorities. Government and Party agencies were encouraged to readjust their tables of organization, strengthening those units which were responsible for the agency's primary tasks, eliminating other units altogether, and changing the assignments of still others. Ho Lung emphasized the desirability of reducing the number of levels within each ministry from four or five to two or three and of severely reducing or eliminating all ministries' provincial branch offices. By so doing, the government could reduce the number of layers of bureaucracy separating the central government from the basic levels.

By the end of December this aspect of the campaign had achieved impressive results on paper. Ho Lung reported that the forty-eight government agencies that had participated had abolished no fewer than 2,200 of their offices and sections. The Second Ministry of Machine Building, for example, had eliminated 468 of its original 647 divisions, sections, and groups. The Ministry of Public Security had managed to do away with more than 50 percent of its 345 subdivisions. Of the twelve ministries with offices in the provinces, six had abolished their provincial offices altogether, and the other six had reduced their size—the overall staff reduction was 1,100.*

---

*The retrenchment campaign of 1955–56 concerned the internal structure of existing ministries rather than the structure of the central government as a whole. To deal with the latter question, the State Council convened a conference on governmental organization in the spring of 1956 to reconsider the government's ministerial structure. The result was the creation of seven new ministries and commissions, the division of one old ministry into three new ones, and the renaming of two others. According to the official account of the reorganization, new ministries were created when an existing ministry had too wide a sphere of responsibility (explaining the division of the Ministry of Heavy Industry into Ministries of Metallurgical Industry, Chemical Industry, and Building Materials), when economic activities formerly controlled by the provinces needed to be more closely controlled by the center (explaining the creation of the Ministries of Urban Construction and Urban Services), when the nationaliza-

The second step in administrative retrenchment was to be a reduction of government and Party officials at the central level commensurate with each agency's simplified table of organization. The emphasis was placed on reducing the number of administrators, clerks, and secretaries. At the same time, however, it was considered necessary to reassign about 25 percent of the technicians and college graduates to factories and to transfer some 15 percent of department heads, section chiefs, and the like to strengthen local government.[14]

Acting on the recommendation of the Committee on Organization and Wages, the State Council then established a set of criteria for determining where these officials might be sent. Technical personnel and college graduates were to be sent to factories. Administrative cadres with middle-school training who were in good health and of good political character were to be sent to administrative positions at lower levels in the bureaucracy, often in such border provinces as Tibet and Sinkiang. A number of younger cadres were to be transferred to universities or government schools for further training. And some elderly and less competent officials were to be persuaded to retire or to return to their native villages to find work in agriculture. To encourage cadres to accept their new assignments, the State Council provided that transferred officials would receive their old salary, at least temporarily, even if their new posts were at a lower salary grade. On the other hand, if a new position carried a higher salary, then the cadre transferred to it would be eligible to receive the higher rate immediately.[15]

According to Ho Lung's report, the second component of the retrenchment campaign also achieved considerable success. The Ministry of Agriculture reduced its service staff by 74.5 percent, and the Ministry of Forestry, by 63.8 percent. Overall, during 1955 the central Party apparatus reduced its personnel by more than 43 percent, and central government agencies, by 40 percent, from 90,490 to 54,228. On the other hand, many had not yet received new assignments. By the end of November 34,000 government officials had been released from their original positions, but only 10,000 had received new jobs.* And some central

---

tion of industry put new areas of the economy under government control (explaining the creation of the Ministry of Food Industry), or when the central government wanted to promote the development of a neglected area of work (explaining the formation of the Ministry of State Farms and Land Reclamation and the Ministry of Aquatic Products). See New China News Agency, 11–12.iv.56, translated in *Survey of the China Mainland Press*, no. 1291 (17.v.56), pp. 4–6; and *Shih-shih shou-ts'e*, no. 11 (1956), translated in *Extracts from China Mainland Magazines*, no. 46 (7.viii.56), pp. 7–9.

*Of these, 6,000 were being sent to factories; 2,500 were being transferred to local government and Party offices, especially in Tibet, Tsinghai, and Sinkiang; and 1,000 were being assigned to schools for further training.

ministries managed to evade the campaign entirely. When it was established in July 1955, the Ministry of Coal Industry had been allotted 821 cadres, but it already had more than 900 when the retrenchment campaign reached it later in the year. Under its own reorganization plan, the ministry promised to reduce its staff by some 100 officials, but it was reported in June 1956 that the ministry was actually employing more than 1,200 cadres. For that ministry, at least, "retrenchment" meant nearly a 50 percent increase in staff over twelve months.[16]

The third phase of the retrenchment campaign was a series of measures to improve work style. According to Ho Lung, its goals were to reduce meetings and reports, improve the circulation of documents, and simplify statistical reporting. In addition, all cadres were supposed to conduct personal investigations of the problems for which they were responsible, exercise more initiative and creativity, and act with greater zeal and dispatch. This latter aspect, however, was almost immediately taken into the campaign against "waste and conservatism," which will be discussed in the next section.

Once these three sets of reforms had been completed, the final step was to ensure that the bureaucracy did not simply grow back again. To this end, the State Council issued a regulation providing that any change in the number of bureaus within a ministry, or any increase in a ministry's staff, would have to be approved directly by the State Council.[17] Ho Lung's report added that, to enforce this provision, the Committee on Organization and Wages and the Ministry of Finance would both strengthen their monitoring of the organizational structure and the administrative expenses of the central ministries.

At the same time that the Committee on Organization and Wages was supervising administrative retrenchment in central agencies, comparable efforts were being made to reduce the size of the Party and state bureaucracy at the provincial and local levels. Provincial committees on organization and wages were established early in 1955 to draw up retrenchment plans by May. By the end of the year, however, there had apparently been little progress in most provinces. Although the State Council was able to report "conspicuous results" for the campaign in central Party and government agencies and in Peking municipality, it could only say that provincial retrenchment programs were "in progress" or "under preparation." Accordingly, the deadline for provinces and municipalities was postponed until February 1956.[18]

To stimulate and guide retrenchment outside Peking, the State Council issued a directive on December 29, 1955, that in substance echoed the reports of Hsi Chung-hsün and Ho Lung but indicated more specifically how to carry out retrenchment in government organizations in the provinces and localities.[19] As at the center, the main procedure was to study the existing organizational structure, clarify the responsibilities of various agencies, and draw up plans for reducing the number of government organs and decreasing their staff. These plans were then to be submitted to higher levels for approval: provincial plans were to be reviewed by the State Council; county and special district plans, by provincial governments. The State Council directive established different goals for each level of government. Provinces and special districts, like the central organs, were to emphasize both organizational retrenchment and reduction of staff. Counties were to pay most attention to simplifying their organizational structure; few reductions in personnel were anticipated. Below the county, smaller districts and townships were gradually to be amalgamated into larger units. Once the reorganization was completed, any further changes in organizational structure or additions of staff would have to receive advance approval from the next higher level of government.

The State Council directive notwithstanding, the 1955–56 retrenchment campaign had only limited success outside the capital. For one thing, some of the components of the retrenchment program conflicted with each other. One major element of the campaign, for example, was to reduce the size of administrative staffs in the special districts and provinces. However, another aspect of retrenchment was to amalgamate the rural districts into larger units, a program that produced a pool of cadres without jobs, many of whom were promptly reassigned to new positions in the special districts or provinces. One reform negated the other.[20]

More important, just as in earlier retrenchment campaigns, there was substantial opposition to staff reduction within the bureaucracy. It is doubtful that many cadres really wanted to be transferred to factories or to retire early. It is virtually certain that very few were anxious to be reassigned to Sinkiang or Tsinghai. To avoid being transferred, some cadres feigned illness or grumbled so bitterly that they were exempted from the program. Some accepted transfer but stayed at their new assignments for only a few days before returning to their original posts.[21] Even cadres who did not receive transfers often opposed the retrenchment campaign because they were afraid that their own work loads would be increased if their colleagues were reassigned. As one postmortem of the campaign explained, there were comrades who simply felt that it was easier to get things done with more people.[22]

Opposition from below greatly limited the effect of the 1955–56 retrenchment, as provincial officials found ways to escape its provisions. Some officials simply turned to trickery to maintain the size of their staffs. But there were also legitimate devices that could be used. As we have seen, the first step in the campaign was to define the administrative and programmatic responsibilities of the agency in question. If a department could demonstrate that its work was crucial, it might avoid a reduction in its staff, or even win an increase. According to later charges, provincial departments were able to circumvent the campaign by "onesidedly stressing the importance of their own establishment."[23] Appeals for exemption from the campaign were often accompanied by the argument that retrenchment was incompatible with rationalization; rationalized organizations were apparently seen as those with large staffs and complex structures. As one cadre cynically put it in 1956, there seemed to be an "unwritten law of regularization," according to which a reduction in the number of administrative levels or in personnel was equated with failure to regularize.[24]

THE CAMPAIGN AGAINST "CONSERVATISM"

As we have already seen, one of the principal economic problems confronting Chinese leaders in 1955 was the poor performance of the agricultural sector. By late July, after several months of discussion and debate, Mao concluded that the best method of stimulating agricultural production was to accelerate the formation of agricultural cooperatives. He reached this conclusion over the objections of many colleagues, including Teng Tzu-hui, Li Hsien-nien, Ch'en Yün, and very likely Liu Shao-ch'i. Mao's opponents warned that creating cooperatives in the absence of agricultural mechanization would actually decrease production by disrupting traditional farming patterns and alienating wealthier (and more productive) peasants.

Faced with this opposition, Mao appealed to provincial leaders for support. At a work conference on July 31, Mao caricatured his opponents as "tottering along like women with bound feet, always complaining that others are going too fast." He urged provincial Party secretaries to look into the matter of accelerating cooperativization, and to "work out appropriate plans in accordance with the concrete conditions and report to the Central Committee within two months." After reviewing these reports, the Central Committee would discuss the matter again and make a final decision. The Party had originally planned to increase the number of agricultural cooperatives by 55 percent between October 1955 and October 1956. Mao now suggested that it might be possible to obtain a 100 percent increase in the same period of time. His speech to the July work conference was, in effect, a plea to provincial leaders to provide evidence that his optimism was justified.[25]

The Central Committee's review of cooperativization occurred at the Sixth Plenum in October. The meeting heard a series of presentations by local leaders about the prospects for cooperativization in their provinces, and Mao then announced his conclusions in a summary speech. The re-

ports had shown that cooperativization provided a way of increasing agricultural output even without capital investment—without, in Mao's
words, "funds, carts, oxen, . . . and farm machinery." Furthermore, as
he had argued in July, cooperativization could be accelerated so that it
could be accomplished, in the main, by 1960. Finally, he suggested for the
first time that China's economic shortcomings stemmed from an underlying organizational problem. In Mao's analysis, the Party and state bureaucracies had become "conservative," that is, they had begun to fall
behind the times and had "failed to keep pace with current developments." He charged specifically that the doubts about rapid
cooperativization expressed by the Party's Rural Work Department under
Teng Tzu-hui constituted a "conservative work style" and "right-deviationist mistakes."[26]

Mao's position after July 1955 became increasingly explicit: China's
major problem was an unnecessarily slow pace of economic growth and
social change, the result of a "right deviation" caused by conservatism
within the bureaucracy. His speeches in the late summer and fall contained numerous contrasts between leaders who were willing to "get on the
socialist horse" and support socialist transformation and agriculture and
those who insisted on "getting off."[27] Mao also drew a clear distinction
between Party committees that were "committees for promoting retrogression" and those that were "committees for promoting progress."[28]

After the Sixth Plenum, in order to prove that the bureaucracy was
being unnecessarily conservative, Mao intervened personally on two issues
crucial to China's future, agricultural development and the nationalization
of industry. In his speech to the plenum, Mao had set relatively cautious
targets for cooperativization. But once the plenum was over, he began
supervising the compilation of a twelve-year program of agricultural development that presented more ambitious goals: basic cooperativization
was to be achieved by the end of 1956 rather than by 1960, and collectivization was to be accomplished by 1960 (or even 1959) rather than by 1967.
The twelve-year program also contained longer-range targets for water
conservancy, control of plant diseases and pests, land reclamation and af-
forestation, fertilizer use, education, public health, transportation and
communication, and grain yields. Mao apparently was convinced that the
most likely source of support for his agricultural program was the provincial Party leadership, and the draft plan was first presented and discussed
in meetings with provincial Party secretaries in Hangchow and Tientsin in
November.[29]

At the same time that he was compiling the twelve-year program for agriculture, Mao was also proposing an acceleration of the nationalization of
industry. In late October he called a symposium on socialist transformation

of industry that was attended by central Party and government leaders, by representatives of the democratic parties and mass associations, and by members of the Federation of Industry and Commerce. This was followed by additional meetings the following month. The industrialists and merchants accepted the idea of rapid nationalization more readily than might have been expected, in part because of the attractive terms offered by the Party (including a guaranteed 5 percent interest on their investment for at least seven years), but doubtless in part because of the futility of resistance. As a result of their cooperation, Mao was able to advance the deadline for completing the nationalization of industry from 1967 to 1957. What his more cautious colleagues had said would take twelve years, Mao was prepared to accomplish in two.[30]

By December, Mao had concluded that much of the Party and state bureaucracy was indeed guilty of "right-deviationist empiricism." The speed with which the socialist transformation of both agriculture and industry was occurring proved that "we have underestimated our own strength," and that "the thought of leading cadres has fallen behind reality." Leadership organs were supposed to "promote the development of undertakings," but certain departments "did not pay attention to the development of the objective situation, and thus underestimated the possibility of change."[31]

All this was very likely true in other sectors of the economy as well as in industry and agriculture. It would therefore be necessary to conduct the same kind of critical examination of the rest of the economy:

The problem facing the whole Party and people is no longer that of criticizing right-conservative ideas about the speed of the socialist transformation of agriculture. That problem has been solved. Nor is it the problem of the speed of transforming the whole of capitalist industry and commerce trade by trade into joint state-private enterprises. That problem too has been solved. . . . The problem today . . . lies in agricultural production; industrial production; . . . handicraft production; the scale and speed of capital construction in industry, communications, and transport; the coordination of commerce with other branches of the economy; the coordination of the work in science, culture, education, and health with our various economic activities; and so on. *In all these fields there is an underestimation of the situation, a shortcoming which must be criticized and corrected if our work is to keep pace with the development of the situation as a whole. People must adapt their thinking to the changed conditions.*[32]

Mao's argument was that the sluggish pace of Chinese economic development was due not to objective constraints, but to the conservatism of planners and bureaucrats. All previous plans would have to be set aside, and new ones drafted. The rapid pace of cooperativization "makes it clear to us that in scale and tempo China's industrialization and the development of its science, culture, education, health work, etc., can no longer proceed exactly in the way previously envisaged, but must be appropriately expanded and accelerated."[33] The immediate task was "to oppose conservatism, right deviation, passivity, and arrogance, . . . to speed up the tempo, . . . and to achieve faster, greater, and better results in all work projects."[34]

Conveniently for Mao, the administrative retrenchment campaign provided the ideal opportunity for conducting the struggle against "right conservatism" in the bureaucracy. The third stage of the retrenchment drive—the improvement of work style—could easily be redefined to meet Mao's needs. The goal could be not simply to promote a correct work style, but more specifically to develop a style of work that would be antirightist and anticonservative.

The "progressive work style" Mao had in mind had already been roughly outlined in his speech to the Sixth Plenum. In early December it was described more fully in the talk "Oppose Right-Deviationism and Conservatism," which served as a summary of the aims of this new campaign. First of all, a progressive work style would involve more investigation of local conditions, particularly by Party secretaries and deputy secretaries at all levels. The careful study of specific units and localities selected as representative of certain problems would help uncover "new and advanced experiences" to be applied as exemplars elsewhere. If, on the other hand, cadres adhered to the style of "sitting in the office," they could never achieve more than conservative, conventional results.

Second, a progressive work style would include steps to circulate information rapidly throughout the bureaucracy. Mao proposed several techniques for improving the flow of information within the Party and state. One was to "hold large or small meetings yearly to solve current problems." Another was to increase the number of inner-Party publications: "Each province and autonomous region might compile a book every year or every six months, with one article from each county, so that the experience of all counties can be exchanged." Still another was for each level to submit regular bulletins on the progress achieved in cooperativization: "The leadership at various levels will acquaint itself with the situation through these bulletins and be able to find solutions to problems when they arise."* A fourth technique was "to use the telephone"—that is, to

---

*Mao's interest in inner-Party communications is reflected in detailed instructions he issued on the typeface to be used in Party publications: "The type used . . . should not be too small, and the lines should not be run too close together. Don't use the New No. 5 type, but use the Old No. 5 type to make them easy to read." See *Miscellany of Mao Tse-tung Thought*, Joint Publications Research Service, Nos. 61269–1, –2 (Arlington, Va., 1974), p. 21. He also commented on style in writing: "To be logical, to be grammatical, and to have a better command of rhetoric—these are the three points I would like you to bear in mind when you write." See *Selected Works of Mao Tse-tung*, vol. 5, p. 233.

take advantage of the extension of telephonic communication deeper into the countryside.[35] Later press reports commented on the time saved by substituting telephone conference calls for meetings and by phoning instructions down the chain of command.*

A third characteristic of the progressive work style was comprehensive planning. Mao recommended that each level of administration, from agricultural cooperative through province, should draw up a series of long-range plans that would guide their work for a minimum of three years, an optimum of seven years, or, as an ideal, twelve years. Each level should formulate sectoral plans for agricultural production, cooperativization, culture and education, public health, and Party and Youth League work; and then each should combine its sectoral plans into a single comprehensive plan.[36] In the process, leaders should try to "balance upward"—that is, they should have advanced units and sectors set the pace and not allow the weakest units and sectors to act as bottlenecks: "We grasp the progressive and bring up the others in the midst of imbalance so as to make progress. . . . To break through and then seek balance is dialectics. Only in this way can we inspire the initiative of the masses, and advance socialist construction to an early date."[37]

The campaign against rightist conservatism resulted in a period of crash planning throughout the Party and state bureaucracies.† After his consultations with the provincial Party secretaries in November, Mao circulated a revised draft of his twelve-year agricultural program on December 21, requesting that it be discussed by "the secretaries of all the prefectural [special district] Party committees and . . . of some of the county Party committees," and that opinions be ready by January 3, 1956.[38] A twelve-year plan, in other words, was to be formulated in about twelve days, surely insufficient time for prudent deliberation. Other sectors of the

---

*In Shensi, for example, it had once taken thirty days to convene all the necessary meetings to relay instructions from the province to the basic levels. Now, with telephone conferences, the process could be completed in five days. See *Jen-min jih-pao*, 6.i.56, in *Survey of the China Mainland Press*, no. 1261 (19.i.56), pp. 33–35. For the effects of telephones on the bureaucracy, see Michel Oksenberg, "Methods of Communication Within the Chinese Bureaucracy," *China Quarterly*, no. 57 (January–March 1974), pp. 1–39.

†The campaign was launched even without the publication of Mao's speech on opposing rightist deviation. Indeed, that speech still has not been officially released. But the 1956 New Year's Day editorial embodied all of what Mao had been saying. Entitled "Strive for the Overall Fulfillment and Overfulfillment of the Five-Year Plan Ahead of Schedule," it underscored the accelerated goals for cooperativization and nationalization and declared that these developments were making possible "greater, faster, better, and more economical" progress in all other sectors of work. It also summarized Mao's views on the importance of work style, calling for more investigation and research, discovery and popularization of "advanced experience," struggle against conservative thinking, and attention to positive factors, not just negative ones, when drawing up plans. *Jen-min jih-pao*, 1.i.56, in *Survey of the China Mainland Press*, no. 1201 (1.v.56), pp. 8–13.

economy were forced to draw up their long-range plans under similar time pressures, for their deadlines likewise fell in January.

The crash planning process faced a tight schedule, and also was undertaken with the clear expectation that extremely ambitious goals would be announced. The previous plans had, after all, been denounced as representing underestimations of the situation, and the new ones were to be free of right-conservative thinking. Mao's discussions of planning had clearly stated that there should be "balance upward," and that the most advanced units should set the pace for the rest of the country. In fact, the twelve-year agricultural program also set advanced goals for sectors of the economy other than agriculture. Public health agencies, for example, were urged to eliminate schistosomiasis within seven years; education departments were ordered to "wipe out illiteracy" in seven years; and communications agencies were told to connect every township and cooperative in the country by a landline broadcasting network within the same period of time. The political context made it clear that despite Mao's request for "opinions," the stated goals were to be taken as givens: any plans that did not pledge to attain them would be considered unnecessarily conservative.

It is not surprising, therefore, that the planning of late 1955 and early 1956 produced some extremely optimistic assessments of what China could achieve in twelve years. The Ministry of Education put forward a two-year plan for eliminating illiteracy among employees of government, Party organs, and mass organizations; a three-year plan for eliminating illiteracy among industrial workers; and, just as Mao had requested, a seven-year plan for eliminating illiteracy among peasants.[39] The Youth League pledged to see that all young people could read and write within seven years.[40] The Ministry of Education promised to achieve universal junior-middle-school education in large and medium-sized cities and universal primary-school education throughout the rest of the country, both within twelve years.[41] The Ministry of Public Health produced a twelve-year plan for rural health, the State Planning Commission and the Academy of Sciences drew up a twelve-year plan for scientific development, and the State Planning Commission began work on a fifteen-year plan for the national economy.

These documents, moreover, were seen not simply as plans for the distant future, but as measures with immediate implications for the Chinese economy in the coming year. Once the seven- and twelve-year plans were formulated, various ministries and departments began to increase their annual targets for 1956. Teacher-training programs were accelerated.[42] Production targets for agriculture were raised.[43] The Ministries of Building Construction, Coal Industry, Heavy Industry, and Railways all revised their plans for 1956 upward.[44] Finally, it was announced that the First

Five-Year Plan, originally scheduled to end in 1957, could be fulfilled in 1956 by completing two years' work in the space of one.[45]

Many of these long- and short-term national targets, particularly those for agriculture, were doubtless unrealistic to begin with. Moreover, the campaign against conservatism placed additional pressures on the lower levels of Party and government to raise the already inflated targets handed down from higher up. In January the central authorities announced that there should be a 10 percent increase in grain output in 1956. When that target reached Fukien, the provincial leadership raised it to 16 percent, and by the time the plans reached the township level, the target had become 40 percent.[46] Similarly, although the plan of the Ministry of Education was to eliminate illiteracy within seven years, some provinces promised to do so in four or five, and some counties announced plans to make everyone literate in three.[47] As soon as a central plan was announced, in other words, "all organizations vied with each other to set . . . high targets lest they should be accused of rightist conservatism."[48]

The results of the campaign were uneven. It was successful in the area of socialist transformation. Collectivization of agriculture was achieved far ahead of schedule, and in relatively smooth fashion. The conversion of private industry into joint state-private operation (nationalization, in effect if not in name) was completed in the largest cities by the end of January, and in most of the rest of China by June. But the campaign had serious consequences for output planning. Unrealistic targets were set for agriculture and capital construction. Factories increased production as quickly as possible but ignored efficiency and quality. Local cadres were presented with ambitious plans for every sector of their work but were not told which should have priority.[49]

The campaign against conservatism was therefore brought to an end by April 1956. The transformation of industry, particularly the combination of smaller enterprises into larger ones, was slowed down.[50] It was announced that spring planting should take precedence over collectivization.[51] Mao himself called on local leaders to resist "inoperable, impractical, and subjective orders" from the ministries.[52] And in June, *Jen-min jih-pao* published a series of editorials criticizing hastiness and "reckless advance," and proposing a more deliberate pace of economic development.* But the damage had been done, for the economy had already become overheated. The consequences of the economic imbalance produced

*Some of these editorials, especially the one published on June 20, went beyond what Mao had envisioned. In fact, when a draft of the editorial was presented to Mao for his approval, he wrote, "I don't want to read it" (*pu-k'an-le*) at the top. See Parris H. Chang, *Power and Policy in China* (University Park, Pa., 1975), p. 27; and *Miscellany of Mao Tse-tung Thought*, p. 83.

by the High Tide of 1955–56, particularly its consequences for organizational policy, will be discussed at length in the next chapter.

PROFESSIONALIZATION

It was becoming increasingly apparent in early 1956 that China would depart from the Soviet model of development and begin to devise its own style of social and economic modernization. For one thing, as Chinese leaders became more aware of the shortcomings of their First Five-Year Plan, it was inevitable that the Soviet model, on which the plan had been based, would become less attractive. At the same time, the contrast between collectivization in China, which had been relatively smooth and effective, and collectivization in the Soviet Union, which had been prolonged and violent, gave Chinese leaders greater confidence that they could draw on their own experience and insights to chart their future independently. The Party was also becoming concerned about the risks of continued dependence on the Soviet Union. Moscow had already revealed that it would not supply China with as much technical and economic assistance during the Second Five-Year Plan as it had during the first, and the Soviet Union's international economic policy now stressed a division of labor within the socialist bloc that threatened to relegate China to the position of supplying agricultural products and raw materials to other socialist countries and to restrict the development of China's own industrial base.[53]

These considerations were reflected in a growing willingness to criticize the shortcomings of the Soviet Union and to reassert China's pre-liberation refusal to copy the Soviet example slavishly. For example, in an address to the Politburo in April 1956, Mao warned that although "there is still much that merits our study," China should not follow the Soviet Union "blindly, but should subject everything to analysis." He listed a series of policies—the system of one-man leadership in factories, the suppression of counterrevolutionaries, and the departure from the mass line in policy implementation—in which the Russians had made many mistakes, and charged that China had "committed many errors because of their direct leadership." As a symbol of China's growing independence, Mao announced that the Soviet Party's May Day slogans need not be posted in China in 1956.[54]

Mao sounded a similar theme in his speech "On the Ten Major Relationships," delivered the same month to a central work conference in Peking. Certain "defects and errors" had been committed by the Russians in the course of building socialism. These included the Soviet Union's "prolonged failure to reach the highest pre–October Revolution level in grain output, . . . the glaring disequilibrium between the development of heavy industry and light industry in some Eastern European countries," and the

Soviet Party's tendency to extract "too much from the peasants at too low a price." The Chinese "must learn with an analytical and critical eye, not blindly, and we mustn't copy everything indiscriminately and transplant mechanically." In fact, China would have to learn from the valuable experience of all nations, including capitalist nations, and not simply from the Soviet Union.[55]

Mao's speech confronted Chinese planners with a dilemma. If China chose to rely more on its own resources, there were two ways in which it could undertake economic planning. One was to draw up new plans quickly, to base them on the most optimistic assumptions, to rely primarily on generalists at all levels of the administrative hierarchy, and to encourage them to criticize conservative thinking. As we have seen, the plans formulated in late 1955 and early 1956, notably the twelve-year agricultural program, resulted from such a crash-planning process.

But the unrealistically high targets and the economic imbalances produced by the High Tide had graphically illustrated the shortcomings of crash planning. By the time of Mao's speech, the Chinese had already begun to shift to a second style of planning: plans were to be drawn up more slowly and thoughtfully, specialists consulted more fully, and efforts made to set realistic and attainable goals. This more deliberately paced planning process culminated in a long series of Politburo meetings in March and April at which no fewer than thirty-four government agencies reported on their work and made proposals for the Second Five-Year Plan. And at about the same time active discussion of the twelve-year agricultural program virtually ceased. These two events demonstrated that power over planning had shifted markedly away from the generalists in the provincial Party committees, those who had participated so actively in crash planning during the High Tide, to the specialists in the central state ministries.

This growing interest in a more professional planning process required a reassessment of China's policy towards intellectuals, whose active participation in the process would be crucial to its success. A major conference on intellectuals was consequently convened by the Central Committee in January. Interestingly, few if any non-Party intellectuals were present at the meeting; those attending were national and provincial Party leaders and Party representatives from various scientific, industrial, and cultural establishments. But the conference did hear Chou En-lai present an important report that promised both an improvement in the treatment of intellectuals and a change in the role of intellectuals in the political process.[56]

Chou provided a frank account of China's shortcomings in scientific and technical work. For one thing, he acknowledged that it had too few specialists, and that those it did have were lagging behind world standards. For another, while many specialists were already employed by government or Party agencies, their skills were often wasted through improper assignments. Some were "assigned one task today, and another task the next, but never sent to the job for which they are qualified"; others were given administrative positions that did not permit them to make use of their technical or scientific skills; others were "idle to the point of having no work to do"; and still others were denied promotion and were underpaid. In short, despite the attempt made in 1953–54 to allocate skilled manpower as effectively as possible, the talents of Chinese intellectuals were still not being employed efficiently.

Even where intellectuals had been given appropriate assignments, Chou said, they sometimes were not given the respect and authority that they deserved. Some Party and Youth League members refused to take orders from non-Party intellectuals, even if they were their legal superiors, because of their bourgeois backgrounds. In addition, the presence of Russian experts provided a ready excuse for Party and government generalists to ignore Chinese specialists.

Chou admitted that the political consciousness of Chinese intellectuals was not as high as the Party would like. He estimated that 40 percent were "middle-of-the-road elements" who supported the Party but were "politically not sufficiently progressive"; somewhat more than 10 percent were "backward elements who lack political consciousness or ideologically oppose socialism"; and a minor percentage were "counterrevolutionaries or other bad elements." There remained 45 percent, however, who could be considered progressives who actively supported the Party and were committed to socialism. Chou estimated that, by the end of the Second Five-Year Plan, gentle political suasion would increase the proportion of progressive intellectuals from 45 percent to 75 percent and reduce the proportion of "backward elements" from 10 percent to about 5 percent.

Chou announced three sets of reforms based on his assessment of the political attitudes and organizational status of intellectuals. One promised alleviation of the shortage of specialists: university enrollments would be expanded, more students would be sent to the Soviet Union for training, postgraduate education in China would be strengthened, and new research agencies would be set up to train scientists and technicians. Another altered the working conditions of scientists, technicians, and educators: intellectuals were promised higher salaries, more research materials, better facilities, more time to conduct research, and greater freedom to examine scientific questions independently of previous work done in the Soviet Union; furthermore, efforts were to be made to locate unemployed intellectuals and to match the job assignments of specialists with their training.

For our purposes, however, the most important reforms were those of the third set, which affected the role of intellectuals in the Party and in government. The recruitment of intellectuals into the Party was to be accelerated, partly by modifying the criteria for admission to Party membership. In the future, *Jen-min jih-pao* explained, Party organization departments should be less concerned with the political and class background of intellectuals—a major obstacle for many who had come from bourgeois backgrounds and worked for the Nationalist government—and should emphasize the intellectuals' present political orientation.[57] Chou En-lai's report proposed that one-third of the country's higher intellectuals (college graduates) become Party members by 1962, and, indeed, the percentage of Party members classified as intellectuals rose appreciably in 1956 and 1957.

Even those intellectuals who were not Party members were to be given a larger role in decision making. Chou's report emphasized that certain government agencies, particularly those in the fields of geology, industry, agriculture, water conservancy, transportation, national defense, and health, should employ more specialists in policy research. The goal was to ensure that "as rapidly as possible, the world's most modern technology will be installed in different departments of our country." In keeping with this reform, the Shanghai municipal Party committee adopted a work program for intellectuals in March 1956 that provided that the Party should invite intellectuals who are "advanced politically" to attend Party work conferences as observers, and that Party leaders should keep in contact with higher intellectuals and consult them on policy matters.[58] Throughout 1956 and early 1957 press reports indicated that the policymaking process was in fact becoming more professionalized, and that economic problems were being discussed more actively and openly in meetings with non-Party specialists.

DECENTRALIZATION

At the beginning of this chapter, we summarized the organizational problems that were created by the introduction of highly centralized planning during the First Five-Year Plan. Central planning encountered three major difficulties: the central planning agencies could not control the ministries, the ministries could not handle the flood of information sent in from the provinces, and the provinces lacked authority to modify central directives or even to coordinate economic activities that were directed from the center. All of these problems were apparent by the middle of

1955, and the High Tide of 1955–56 only served to make them worse. The nationalization of industry substantially increased the number of enterprises and the number of goods that were to be included in central planning, a development that made it more difficult for central planning agencies to coordinate the economy, and that increased the amount of information reaching central government ministries. Furthermore, centralized planning could not cope effectively with the bottlenecks produced by the High Tide. Material shortages could be filled and surpluses reallocated within ministries, but only the overburdened central planning agencies could transfer materials from one ministerial system to another. Finally, local cadres were deluged with ambitious targets for the economy, each drawn up by a different ministry, and at no time was any clear indication forthcoming from the center or the provinces as to which sectoral plans should be given precedence.

As a result, at the same time that the crash-planning phase of the High Tide began to give way to a more professional style of planning, Chinese leaders also were beginning to consider ways of decentralizing the planning and management of the economy. The topic was first discussed at the series of Politburo conferences on the economy in March and April, and Mao's summary of those deliberations, "On the Ten Major Relationships," contains an entire section discussing central-provincial relations.[59] Mao revealed that the Politburo conferences had concluded that it would be necessary to enlarge the powers of the local authorities to some extent, give them greater independence, and "let them do more." Decentralization would not be permitted to disrupt the "strong and unified central leadership and unified planning and discipline throughout the country," but, given China's size and the complexity of its economy, it would be "far better to have the initiative come from both the central and the local authorities than from one source alone."

Mao's speech did not present a detailed program of decentralization, but it did suggest that the amount of power to be transferred to the provinces would vary from one sector of the bureaucracy to another. At one point Mao made a distinction between matters in which centralization was necessary and matters in which it was not. In industrial work, for example, centralized leadership was actually to be strengthened, but in social services it was not to be imposed at all. After decentralization, industrial ministries would share power with provincial and municipal authorities, but would still "exercise leadership right down to the enterprises." The educational and cultural ministries, by contrast, would simply "lay down guiding principles and map out work plans while the local authorities assume the responsibility for putting them into operation."

Mao concluded this section of his report by admitting that Chinese experience in matters of decentralization was "still insufficient and immature." He proposed that there be a review of the organization and responsibilities of the State Council and the central ministries, and that a new policy be formulated to define the organization and responsibilities of local governments. To this end the State Council convened a series of meetings on governmental reorganization between May and August 1956.[60] The meetings produced a draft plan for decentralization, the text of which has never been published but was circulated to the provinces and major municipalities for comment.[61]

The formulation of the draft stimulated a lengthy debate that continued until November 1957, when a series of decentralization reforms was finally adopted by the Central Committee at its Third Plenum.[62] Although much of the discussion of decentralization appeared in professional journals on economics, finance, and planning, the debate was also reflected in speeches and reports presented at the Third Session of the National People's Congress in June and at the Eighth Party Congress in September. A few officials seemed to want no decentralization at all, but they were in a small minority.* The principal question was not whether decentralization was desirable, but rather how it should be undertaken.

The most detailed statements of the competing views presented during the debate were contained in two documents: Chou En-lai's report on the Second Five-Year Plan, which was presented to the Eighth Party Congress,[63] and an article by Hsüeh Mu-ch'iao, director of the State Statistical Bureau, that appeared in the September 1957 issue of *Chi-hua ching-chi* (*Planned Economy*).[64] For the sake of clarity, I will summarize the two documents before analyzing the differences between them.

The basic principle in Chou En-lai's discussion of decentralization was that local government, particularly the provinces and provincial-level municipalities (Peking and Shanghai, at the time), would be given greater control over planning, finance, enterprise management, personnel, and the allocation of materials in their areas. This authority would be exercised

---

*At a meeting of the National People's Congress in June 1956, for example, Sha Ch'ien-li, the minister of local industry, referred to the State Council's conferences on the administrative system, but expressed the hope that "the various industrial ministries of the center will . . . strengthen their leadership over local industry [so as] to promote activism and avoid blind development [and] to facilitate the continued emergence and growth of new technical forces within local industry." See *Chung-hua jen-min kung-ho-kuo ti-i-chieh ch'üan-kuo jen-min tai-piao ta-hui. ti-san-tz'u hui-i wen-chien* (Documents of the Third Session of the First National People's Congress of the People's Republic of China) (Peking, 1956), pp. 339–46. That there was opposition to any form of decentralization is acknowledged by Ch'en Ta-lun. See *Ching-chi yen-chiu* (Economic Studies), no. 3 (1958), pp. 35, 37.

through four mechanisms. First, "ownership" of a large number of enterprises would be transferred from the ministries to the provinces. Only the highly capital-intensive factories (the ones, in Chou's terms, that were "concentrated"), or factories that produced commodities essential to the national economy, would remain under central control. Second, enterprises that remained under central "ownership" would come under the principle of "dual rule," that is, would be subject to control both by the relevant ministry and by the provincial government. Third, local governments would be presented with a single draft plan drawn up by the State Council to include all sectors of the economy, rather than with a series of separate plans from each ministry. This would make it easier for the provincial authorities to analyze the plan, comment on it, and coordinate economic activities within the province. Finally, provincial governments would be given greater leeway in adjusting plan targets and in shifting personnel and materials from one sector to another in the course of the year.

In contrast, Hsüeh Mu-ch'iao's article in *Chi-hua ching-chi* was based on the notion of "echelon-by-echelon management" (*fen-chi kuan-li*) and "level-by-level responsibility" (*ts'eng-ts'eng fu-tse*). Under these principles, the center would grant provinces, ministries, and regions a "fixed degree of autonomy" (*i-ting ch'eng-tu-ti tzu-chu ch'üan-li*) in planning and management. More specifically, Hsüeh suggested that only a small number of major economic activities (such as investment allocation, wage standards, and the production, procurement, sale, and pricing of major products) should be directly controlled by the central planning agencies. Less important activities might be guided according to targets determined by the center, but the ministries, provinces, or enterprises should be allowed flexibility in meeting those targets. Alternatively, some decisions might be made directly by the enterprises in accordance with market conditions, with the market, in turn, to be regulated by the state's commercial departments. Hsüeh concluded by proposing that targets be divided into categories, some to be set by the State Council, some by the ministries, and some by the provinces. Certain categories would be mandatory, alterable only with the concurrence of the agency that set them. Others would be adjustable according to changing conditions. Still others would be merely advisory.

Basically, the detailed proposals presented by Chou and Hsüeh differed in two dimensions. The first concerned the mechanisms for decentralization. Chou's report envisioned a reform of the state administrative system by which responsibility for entire sectors of the economy would be transferred from the center to the provinces. This administrative decentralization would have created a two-tiered economy, divided between primary sectors (including heavy industry, defense industry, and higher education), which would remain under the control of the central government, and secondary sectors (including light industry, primary and secondary education, public health, and agriculture), which would become the responsibility of the provinces. Although this reform would not necessarily have produced a cellular economy composed of relatively autarchic provinces, it certainly would have laid the groundwork for such a development.

Hsüeh Mu-ch'iao's article, in contrast, proposed a reform of the planning system by which the power to set and adjust plan targets would be transferred from the central planning agencies to the ministries, the provinces, and the individual enterprises. This form of decentralization would have preserved a single, national economic system, but it also would have moved responsibility for detailed planning and administration away from the center. Compared to Chou's proposals, Hsüeh's plan would have transferred power not just to the provincial authorities and their planning departments, but to the central ministries and to enterprise managers, as well. Hsüeh's proposals also envisioned a greater role for the market in regulating the Chinese economy, although the market, in turn, would itself have been regulated by the state.

A second difference between Chou's and Hsüeh's proposals concerned the degree of authority to be given to provincial Party and government leaders. To facilitate a comparison of the two proposals—and a comparison of the decentralization decisions of 1957 with later reforms conducted during the Great Leap Forward—we isolate six possible measures for transferring power from the center to the provinces, listed here in increasing order of magnitude:

1. Grant the provinces authority to adjust the targets set by central planning agencies.

2. Reduce the number of targets set by the center.

3. Transfer the "ownership" of industrial enterprises from the center to the provinces.

4. Grant the provinces more authority to determine their own levels of expenditure and make independent investment decisions.

5. Base the national economic plan on comprehensive provincial plans rather than on separate sectoral plans—that is, organize the economy by geographic area rather than economic or industrial sector.

6. Undertake planning from the bottom up (*tzu-hsia-erh-shang*) rather than from the top down (*tzu-shang-erh-hsia*). Under top-down planning, production and financial targets are set mainly by the center on the basis of its appraisal of local capabilities. Under bottom-up planning, production and financial targets are set principally by the provinces; the role of the center is restricted to approving local plans and striking a national balance.

A comparison of Chou's report with Hsüeh's article reveals that Chou was willing to grant substantially more power to the provinces. Hsüeh proposed that the provinces have the right to adjust certain less crucial targets (measure 1), and that the number of targets set by the center be reduced (measure 2). Chou agreed, but proposed that a significant number of central enterprises be transferred to provincial "ownership" (measure 3), and that the center be required to publish comprehensive provincial plans as well as sectoral plans (measure 5). In addition, Chou hinted that the provinces should be assigned greater control over their own finances and budgets (measure 4).

In short, Hsüeh proposed that central control remain all-encompassing, but that it become less stringent. Chou recommended a substantial reduction in the scope of central control and a start to shifting economic planning to the provinces.

The available evidence suggests that both proposals found adherents among the central Party elite, particularly those with responsibility for economic affairs. A brief reference to decentralization in Li Hsien-nien's budget report to the National People's Congress in June 1956 appears to indicate that Li supported Chou En-lai's proposals.[65] Hsüeh's proposals, in contrast, were described as being based on principles set forth by Vice-Premier Ch'en Yün and were virtually identical to views expressed to the Eighth Party Congress by Li Fu-ch'un.[66] Of the other members of the Politburo, the only one to present specific views on decentralization during this period was Liu Shao-ch'i, who seemed to take a position midway between Chou and Hsüeh in his political report to the Eighth Party Congress in September 1956.[67] Liu said that enterprises should be given appropriate powers to make their own decisions in such matters as the management of plans, finances, and personnel; the allotment of workers and employees; and the provision of welfare facilities. The terms were totally in keeping with the proposals presented to the Congress by Li Fu-ch'un and later expressed by Hsüeh Mu-ch'iao in his article. However, Liu also stated that it would be "absolutely necessary for the central authority to delegate some of its administrative powers and functions to the local authorities," along the lines suggested by Chou En-lai:

As regards a good deal of the work of the state, such as agriculture, small and medium industries, local transport, local commerce, primary and secondary education, local health services, local finance, and so forth, the central authority should only put forward general principles and policies and map out general plans, while the actual work should be referred to the local authorities for them to make arrangements for carrying it out in a manner suitable to the particular place and time. . . . The provinces, municipalities, counties, and townships should be given a definite range of administrative powers and functions.[68]

Liu's report suggested that the two sets of proposals should be viewed not as mutually contradictory but as providing the raw materials for compromise.

The decentralization reforms approved by the Third Plenum in September 1957 reflected the kind of compromise that Liu had in mind.[69] On the first question—whether to decentralize the administrative system or the planning system—the plenum took an eclectic approach. Much of light industry, and some less important factories within the heavy industrial system, would be transferred to provincial control (measure 3), and provincial authorities would be given more authority over the allocation of materials to industrial plants operating in their provinces (measure 1), even those remaining under central "ownership." All this agreed with Chou En-lai's proposals. But the plenum's reforms also introduced important changes into the planning system by reducing the number of obligatory targets to be set by the State Council and by granting both ministries and local authorities the right to lay down additional "nonflexible" targets (measure 2). In this respect, the Third Plenum agreed with Hsüeh Mu-ch'iao's recommendations for decentralizing the planning system.

The decentralization reforms increased the economic and financial powers of the provinces, but they still set important limits on provincial authority. As Nicholas Lardy has shown, the center kept close control over provincial finances. Although the provincial governments were given access to part of the profits of both centralized and decentralized industry, they could tap those profits only to balance the provincial budget. Since the central government retained the power to determine the level of normal expenditure of the local governments, it retained the right to decide what would constitute a balanced budget and what part of the profits of the enterprises should flow into provincial treasuries. In short, decentralization gave provincial leaders greater autonomy in deciding how to allocate labor, materials, and financial resources among various industries and projects in the province, but it did not give them much leeway in deciding how much to spend. Wealthier provinces were still forced to turn over a large part of their income to the center for redistribution to poorer provinces.[70]

Furthermore, the planning system was still organized into sectors whose annual and long-range economic programs were based on plans drawn up by the ministries. Chou En-lai's proposal that comprehensive provincial plans also constitute a part of the planning process (measure 5) was not adopted in 1957. In fact, the central authorities went out of their way to explain that decentralization would not mean the creation of autonomous, quasi-autarchic provinces. *Jen-min jih-pao*'s description of the decentralization measures stressed that coordination of provincial activities by the center was to remain an important feature of planning.[71] There was, as yet, no indication that China would become a cellular economy.

As China began to encounter serious economic difficulties in 1955, Chinese leaders became concerned with improving the efficiency and reducing the cost of the administrative bureaucracy, and with developing its ability to deal creatively and independently with economic problems. Since China had undergone considerable organizational rationalization between 1952 and 1955, it is not surprising that most of the reforms undertaken in 1955 and 1956 reflected the same philosophy. The goal was to perfect the Party and governmental structures, not to replace them with something less bureaucratic. Thus, if organizations were overstaffed at the upper and middle levels, the solution was to transfer officials to other positions. If administrative costs were too high, the solution was to reduce them through economy measures. If the bureaucracy was too centralized, and if planning was, as Hsüeh Mu-ch'iao said, "overly restrictive and rigid," then the answer lay in some form of decentralization. If economic problems required new solutions, then the proper approach was to give experts and specialists more influence in policymaking. All this still accorded with the basic assumption of rationalization: China's organizational problems showed that the Party and government were "failing to live up to the requirements of bureaucratic structure."[72]

The major exception to this trend was the campaign against conservatism launched in late 1955 at the personal initiative of Mao Tse-tung. It would be incorrect to imply that Mao perceived the problem very differently from other Chinese leaders. Like the other organizational reforms of the period, Mao's campaign against conservatism reflected a concern with China's economic problems and a desire to make the Party and state organizations more efficient and effective engines of economic development. Nor is it true that he opposed the attempts at retrenchment, decentralization, and professionalization undertaken in 1955 and 1956. Quite the contrary. It was he who told the Politburo in April 1956 that the Party and government bureaucracies should be "cut by two-thirds," and that they must "not follow the example of the Soviet Union in concentrating everything in the hands of the central authorities, [thus] shackling the local authorities and denying them the right to independent action."[73] And it was he who admitted in January 1957 that the Party needed expert advice on major policy questions—that it could not "rely on us loutish fellows alone."[74]

But Mao wanted to go further. He seemed to believe that the country's economic problems demonstrated that rationalization had gone too far, not that it remained incomplete, and that bureaucratization was producing conservatism. Officials who "bury themselves in office work and do not study problems" are unable to "sense the political climate," and so fail to "see what is already widespread and abundant."[75] And officials who "know no better than to keep to the old routine even in times of revolution" do not understand the potential for more rapid development.[76] He therefore sought to reintroduce mobilizational techniques—the campaign style of policymaking and policy implementation—into an administrative structure that was becoming too bureaucratic. His plea was to halt rationalization and return to some form of remedialism.

Thus, in 1955 and 1956 two currents of organizational theory, rationalization and remedialism, began to flow in the Chinese Communist Party. The remedial heritage of the Party had been suppressed at the height of rationalization in 1953 and 1954, but now it was resurrected with Mao's endorsement. There was surprisingly little controversy over this development at the time. Mao's colleagues seemed willing to accept his call for a campaign against bureaucratic conservatism, although the vigor with which they criticized "reckless advance" and crash planning in the spring of 1956 may suggest that their support was tentative. In the next chapter, however, we will see how further domestic and international developments intensified this nascent controversy, and how open debate over organizational issues grew among Chinese leaders.

5
The First Crisis: The Hundred Flowers 1956-1957

For about a year and a half, the organizational problems described in the previous chapter remained relatively mild. Dissatisfaction with bureaucratic performance was limited, debate over organizational policy was muted, and the measures chosen to reform the bureaucracy were moderate. Rationalization had been shown to have its drawbacks, but Chinese leaders were still optimistic about the effectiveness of their Party and state organizations.

In 1956, however, the problems that had once seemed quite manageable were exacerbated by dramatic developments at home and abroad. Economic imbalances created by the High Tide revived concern about the inefficiency of the Chinese bureaucracy. In his denunciation of Stalin in February, Khrushchev acknowledged the possibility that a ruling Communist party might become alienated from its own people—a danger that was even more clearly illustrated by the protests that broke out in Poland and Hungary later in the year. By December, China itself was experiencing a considerable amount of popular dissent, stimulated both by the country's own economic problems and by the example of political protest in Eastern Europe.

The result of these three developments was intense debate within the Party over its relations with the Chinese people. Characteristically, Mao Tse-tung believed that the Party's relationship with the rest of society could be improved most effectively through an open-door rectification campaign in which non-Party intellectuals would be encouraged to criticize the Party's performance since 1949. At Mao's urging, and over substantial opposition from his own colleagues on the Politburo, the Party called in April 1957 for a period of "blooming and contending," in which the views of these non-Party intellectuals could be freely expressed and openly discussed. But students, professors, and government officials used this opportunity, known as the Hundred Flowers, to question not only the organizational structure of the Party but also its leadership role in Chinese society. Their criticism of the Party proved so intense that, after little more than a month, the Party brought "blooming and contending" abruptly to an end.

THE IMPACT OF DE-STALINIZATION

In a report to a closed session of the Twentieth Congress of the Communist Party of the Soviet Union, held on the night of February 24–25, 1956, Nikita Khrushchev delivered a long and impassioned account of Stalin's "intolerance, brutality, and abuse of power."[1] He admitted that Stalin had executed large numbers of innocent people, including high-ranking leaders of the Soviet Party, and called for the elimination of the "cult of the individual" in Soviet politics. Khrushchev's secret speech stunned the entire Communist world, not only because of its revelations about Stalin, but also because of its failure to explain fully how such repression and brutality could have occurred in a socialist state. Were Stalin's crimes simply the result of one man's megalomania, as Khrushchev implied? Or could the terror and savagery of Stalinist Russia be traced, as some European Communists began to suggest, to flaws inherent in the very concepts of "dictatorship of the proletariat" and "vanguard party"?

Like their counterparts in other socialist countries and in nonruling Communist parties in the West, Chinese leaders were forced to provide their own Party and people with an answer to these troubling questions, and to offer some explanation of the dramatic developments in the Soviet Union. They also had to consider the implications of Khrushchev's revelations for the political situation in China. The Chinese response was arrived at in a series of Politburo meetings in March and was made public in an important editorial in *Jen-min jih-pao* on April 5.[2] Although Mao probably did not write the editorial himself, it is likely that he closely supervised its drafting.

The editorial, entitled "On the Historical Experience of the Dictatorship of the Proletariat," reflected the Politburo's concern that Khrushchev's secret speech would demoralize the socialist bloc and the international Communist movement. Compared with Khrushchev's report, therefore, the Chinese response placed much greater emphasis on Stalin's contribution to Soviet development and to international Communism, and provided only a brief account of his "erroneous decisions." As Mao later explained privately in a speech to the Second Plenum of the Party Central Committee, the one-sided nature of Khrushchev's speech was tantamount to "discarding the sword of Stalin" and giving the West (and certain revisionists in Europe) ammunition with which to criticize socialism. Stalin had indeed made errors, Mao admitted, but they represented only 30 percent of his total work. Stalin remained a "great Marxist," and it would be wrong (or, at least, inexpedient) to "defame and destroy" him.[3]

The editorial also differed from Khrushchev's report in its explanation of Stalin's crimes. It agreed with Khrushchev that Stalin's personality, particularly his tendency to "exaggerate his own role and counterpose his individual authority to the collective leadership," was an important reason for his behavior. Unlike Khrushchev, however, the Chinese editorial went on to suggest that the equivalent of Stalinism might emerge in any socialist system, including China itself, if its leaders managed "contradictions" within the society incorrectly. In the Chinese analysis, there were two types of error to be avoided. On the one hand, Stalin had exaggerated the degree of class struggle in socialist society, and had constructed an unnecessarily repressive and dictatorial regime in the name of suppressing counterrevolutionary forces. On the other hand, the editorial warned in a veiled reference to Khrushchev, some people with "naive ideas" were suggesting that no serious social contradictions of any kind could exist under socialism. This was equally incorrect. The task for leaders in socialist countries was to identify contradictions correctly and resolve them appropriately. In particular, they would have to make a clear distinction between the "antagonistic contradictions" dividing those who supported the socialist system from those who opposed it and the "nonantagonistic contradictions" among those who basically supported the regime.*4

In its final section, the editorial attempted to spell out the implications of Stalinism for China. It warned that the Party, now that it had seized and consolidated power, might misuse its authority just as Stalin had misused his. In the ideological sphere, the Party might become dogmatic—it might try to copy the Soviet example in rigid and inappropriate ways, or use coercion rather than persuasion to gain public acceptance of Marxist-Leninist principles. In day-to-day affairs, Party leaders faced the "great danger of using the machinery of the state for arbitrary acts, of alienating themselves from the masses and collective leadership, resorting to commandism, and violating Party and state democracy."5

How might these problems be avoided? Here the editorial spoke in only the vaguest terms. It might be possible to "establish certain systems" to preserve inner-Party democracy, collective leadership, and closer ties with the people. Although these systems could not completely prevent errors of judgment by individual leaders, they could prevent local and isolated mistakes from becoming "mistakes of a nationwide or prolonged nature, doing harm to the people." Nowhere, however, did the editorial explain clearly just what those systems might be.

When the Eighth Party Congress opened in Peking in mid-September,

---

*The editorial thus contained in embryo the conceptual framework that Mao was to develop more fully in two speeches over the next ten months. "On the Ten Major Relationships," delivered in April 1956, would identify what he considered to be the most important political, social, and economic contradictions in China; and "On the Correct Handling of Contradictions Among the People," given in February 1957, would elaborate the distinctions between antagonistic and non-antagonistic contradictions and identify the proper methods for resolving them.

the first national Party congress since the Communist victory in 1949, little had happened to alter the first Chinese response to Khrushchev's speech. But an important element had been added. The socialist transformation of industry and agriculture during the High Tide had been accomplished much more swiftly and smoothly than had been anticipated. This, in turn, meant that "the question of who will win in the struggle between socialism and capitalism in our country has now been decided."[6] And, since intense class struggle had come to an end, the main task facing the country was now economic modernization—"to build a great socialist country" and "catch up with the United States."[7]

These two implications were linked through a new emphasis on political unity. The resolution of the struggle between the proletariat and the bourgeoisie made unity possible, and the task of economic development made unity necessary. In Mao's formulation, China's ambitious economic goals could be achieved only if all members of the Party would "strive hard to unite with the masses, unite and work with all those that can be united."[8]

This interest in political unity made it even more imperative that the Party learn how to handle "contradictions among the people" correctly. In his opening address to the congress, Mao emphasized that it would be necessary to take determined action to get rid of "unhealthy manifestations . . . detrimental to the unity between the Party and the people." He specified three such problems: unrealistic and inappropriate policies (subjectivism), arrogant and inefficient officials (bureaucratism), and discriminatory treatment of government officials and intellectuals who were not Party members (sectarianism). "Among many of our comrades there are still standpoints and styles of work which are contrary to Marxism-Leninism, namely, subjectivism in their way of thinking, bureaucratism in their way of work, and sectarianism in organizational questions. Such standpoints and such styles of work alienate us from the masses, cut us off from reality, and harm unity both within and without the Party."[9]

Mao's criticism of the Party may not have been warmly received by the delegates to the congress, most of whom had doubtless come to Peking expecting to congratulate themselves on their accomplishments during the revolution and since liberation.[10] But, given the disturbances in Poland over the summer, few could deny the possibility that a ruling Communist party might become divorced from the people, or that contradictions between the party and the people could have explosive consequences. Given the gravity of the problem, the identification of these "systems" became the subject of extensive discussion both during and after the Eighth Party Congress.

The proposals presented in this debate can be divided into four groups: (1) proposals to improve the systems of planning, communication, and control within the bureaucracy (rationalization), (2) proposals to strengthen the commitment of Party members and government officials to such traditional organizational principles as the mass line and democratic centralism (rectification), (3) proposals that mass organizations and representative institutions be given a greater role in policymaking (democratization), and (4) proposals that intellectuals, technicians, and managers outside the Party (the so-called non-Party democrats) be given greater opportunities to criticize Party and government policies (external criticism). In their fullest form these four sets of proposals were introduced by second-echelon leaders: ministers of the State Council, chairmen of mass organizations, and directors or deputy directors of departments of the Central Committee. They were then combined into quite different policy packages by such first-echelon leaders as Chou En-lai, Liu Shao-ch'i, Teng Hsiao-p'ing, and Mao Tse-tung.

Proposals for Rationalization

The first position presented at the Eighth Party Congress envisioned relatively minor structural improvements in the bureaucracy's mechanisms for planning, communication, and control. Vice-Premier Li Fu-ch'un, the chairman of the State Planning Commission, expressed the view that organizational problems were partly to blame for shortcomings in implementing the First Five-Year Plan.[11] Li endorsed two groups of reforms to prevent these problems from recurring. As mentioned in the preceding chapter, he called for a program of decentralization that would give the provinces, ministries, and enterprises more authority to set their own targets and to adjust some of the goals and quotas set by their superiors. In addition, Li reviewed some changes in the central planning apparatus that had been made earlier in the year: the establishment of a State Economic Commission to formulate annual plans and the redefinition of the functions of the State Planning Commission to emphasize long-term planning. Li added that these agencies would have to improve their understanding of the Chinese economy. Planners, Li said, should

intensify their efforts to understand conditions at the primary level, make more systematic investigations into and study the trends of economic development, ascertain the immediate and long-term needs of the various departments and areas, acquire a clear idea of the potentialities and weak links in the national economy, analyze the situation in fulfilling the various technical-economic quotas, and summarize and popularize advanced experience in production and construction.[12]

A somewhat different set of proposals, but a set that still qualified as proposals for organizational rationalization, was presented by Ch'ien Ying, the minister of supervision.[13] Ch'ien argued that the organizational control system—including both the Party control commissions and the state supervisory network—could conduct a "resolute struggle against bureaucratism." She also suggested that because oversized and overlapping state agencies were an important cause of bureaucratism, there should be a continuation of the retrenchment and administrative simplification begun in 1955. Sending cadres in rotation to lower levels would enable them to investigate problems personally, improve their understanding of local conditions, and suggest changes in state and Party policy.

In short, Li's and Ch'ien's speeches called for further organizational rationalization through decentralization, reorganization of planning, retrenchment, or tightening of administrative and Party controls. No one of their proposals was particularly controversial, despite the differences in detail between Li's proposals and the decentralization reforms adopted in 1957. What was significant was that they did not go further. With the exception of a passing reference in Ch'ien Ying's speech to the need for "rectification," neither advocated any further measure to improve the ability of the Chinese political system to handle "contradictions among the people."[14]

Proposals for Rectification

Other leaders, in contrast, took the position that the earlier emphasis on bureaucratization had produced serious political problems that further rationalization could hardly be expected to solve. They argued that in recent years the Party had seemed to abandon much of its own organizational heritage—particularly the mass line, democratic centralism, and collective leadership—in favor of rationalization. Since this had harmed the relationship between the Party and the people, the remedy was to revive the Party's traditional work style, particularly its techniques of acquiring information about public attitudes and demands through direct contact with the people.

Some leaders seemed to believe that a strengthening of routine political education within the Party would suffice to improve the Party's work methods. Lin Po-ch'ü, a senior member of the Politburo, suggested that senior cadres should study Marxism-Leninism systematically.[15] Sung Jen-ch'iung, then deputy secretary-general of the Party under Teng Hsiao-p'ing, made a particularly eloquent appeal for emphasizing the mass line in Party education programs. After Khrushchev's secret speech, virtually all socialist countries had reasserted the principle of collective leadership.[16] But this, he said, was not enough:

It is clear that the crux of the matter is not the form, but the essence of collective leadership; that is to say, the crux lies in whether or not collective leadership rests

on the solid foundation of the mass line. . . . To be effective, collective leadership
. . . requires the committee to rely on the masses, to keep closely to the mass line,
to make vigorous efforts to further the growth of democracy, and to be very keen
about gathering and summing up opinions from the masses. It is not enough that
the masses should be consulted before decisions are taken. They should also be
consulted while the decision is being actually carried out.[17]

Others called not simply for more attention to political education, but
for a vigorous rectification campaign against unhealthy tendencies in the
bureaucracy. Liu Lan-t'ao, the deputy secretary of the central Party Control Commission, agreed with Ch'ien Ying's call for a strengthening of
Party discipline, but immediately added that routine disciplinary action
could not substitute for a rectification campaign directed against the
"temporary and partial errors" in organizational work committed by the
Party since 1949, including factionalism, bureaucratism, commandism,
suppression of criticism, and false reporting. He expressed support for the
Central Committee's request that middle and upper cadres reread Mao's
major speeches from the 1942–44 Cheng-feng movement.[18] Chu Te,
another of the Party's elder statesmen, joined in the call for a rectification
campaign, as long as it did not damage the solidarity and unity of the
Party.[19]

Proposals for Democratization

A third group of leaders argued that China's organizational problems
could not be solved by either rationalization or rectification, but required
that mass organizations and representative bodies be given a degree of
control over the Party and state. Many of these proposals to "improve the
democratic life of the people" had first been introduced during the discussions of popular participation in the period of organizational rationalization a year or so before.

Several institutions were identified at the Eighth Party Congress as possible mechanisms of external control over the bureaucracy. Tung Pi-wu
argued that the system of people's congresses could provide an effective
check against subjectivism and bureaucratism, particularly if the congresses at the local levels met more regularly, if provincial and local governments listened to the opinions of the deputies, and if they encouraged
the deputies to express the sentiments of the masses.[20] He developed his
proposals in more detail some six months later. Addressing the National
Committee of the Political Consultative Conference, he suggested that the
congresses examine government budgets and programs more critically,
and make more proposals about government policy. Deputies to the congresses could become a major avenue of communication between the government and the people if they would visit their constituents more often,

hold public forums, open offices at the grass roots, and relay popular opinion to the government.[21] In the same vein, P'eng Chen reportedly suggested that the people's congresses at all levels establish standing committees to supervise the work of the government in various policy areas.[22]

Although Teng Hsiao-p'ing's report on the revision of the Party constitution will be discussed in more detail later, it is pertinent to point out here that Teng made proposals for strengthening Party congresses that closely paralleled Tung Pi-wu's recommendations for increasing the role of people's congresses.[23] He noted that, even at the central level, formal Party congresses had been infrequent, and that even the central work conferences that had been held frequently since 1949 could not really substitute for them. Teng pointed out that the new Party constitution set terms of office for delegates to Party congresses and specified how frequently the congresses should meet. The intent of these provisions was to ensure that the Party's most important decisions could all be brought before the congresses for discussion.

The Central Committee and the provincial and county committees must submit annual reports to their respective congresses, listen to their criticisms, and answer their questions. And since the delegates are elected for a fixed term and are responsible to the bodies that elected them, they will be in a better position to bring together regularly the views and experiences of the lower organizations, of rank-and-file Party members, and of the masses of the people.[24]

The congresses, as he conceived them, would not become active policy-making bodies but would be able to provide some oversight over Party activities, and would greatly help to develop inner-Party democracy.

The third, and certainly the most controversial, proposal for democratization was that of Lai Jo-yü, the chairman of the All-China Federation of Trade Unions.[25] Lai warned that bureaucratism was hindering the successful resolution of the contradictions between the interests of the workers and the interests of the state, and suggested that bureaucratism might be prevented through mass supervision. To this end, two institutions should be developed to represent the workers' interests. One was the conference of workers and employees in factories and enterprises; the other, and the one to which Lai devoted most attention, was the trade union system. Lai listed three specific tasks for the trade unions: seeing that the policies of the Party and laws of the state were not violated by officials or managers; finding out the masses' problems in their work and life and solving them; and seeing that the sound proposals and criticism of the masses were treated with respect and handled without reprisals.

Lai acknowledged that his proposals constituted a substantial redefinition of the functions of the trade unions. Trade unions had previously helped carry out the directives of the Party and the government, but had done very little to understand the opinions and demands of the people and relay them to the Party. This would have to be changed. The work of carrying out Party and government directives was necessary, but it was even more important for the trade unions to "work from below." This would require that the trade unions be allowed to present the workers' interests to Party leaders at the highest levels, and that they be given greater independence from Party controls so that they could reflect their members' views more objectively.*

Proposals for External Criticism

A fourth set of proposals, which would soon become the most controversial of all, envisioned giving a greater political voice to intellectuals, technicians, managers, and professionals. Despite their willingness to accept the nationalization of industry and commerce in the High Tide of 1955–56, these groups were considered part of the bourgeoisie, and thus of doubtful political reliability. Most were not members of the Party, many belonging instead to the small "democratic parties" that had been allowed to exist since 1949 and were represented in the Political Consultative Conference. To call on these "non-Party democrats" to help remedy the organizational problems of the Party was controversial because the criticism would be coming not only from outside the Party, but, even worse, from outside the worker-peasant alliance.

At the Eighth Party Congress, the principal spokesman for the fourth proposal was Li Wei-han, the director of the Party's United Front Work Department.[26] Reminding his audience that Mao had been calling for unity throughout the country, Li argued that unity could only be obtained by broadening the Party's consultation with non-Party people, even to the point of seeking their criticisms of Party programs.

---

*In a later article Lai made the same point in slightly different terms. In the past, he said, the trade unions had always adopted the viewpoint of the Party and of management. This was an "overly simple viewpoint." Instead, the trade unions should recognize that they were essentially an "organization of the masses" that should side with their members if their views were correct, and that should "mediate between the leaders and the masses." *Kung-jen jih-pao*, 9.v.57, in *Survey of the China Mainland Press*, no. 1535 (22.v.57), pp. 8–12. Lai's proposals were rebutted at the Eighth Congress by Li Hsüeh-feng, director of the Central Committee's Department of Industrial and Communications Work. Apparently alarmed at the specter of more independent trade unions, Li proposed that trade union conferences in factories be abolished and replaced by conferences of workers and employees. Li was willing to grant greater authority to these conferences—they could criticize management, make recommendations on policy, and even request that higher authorities discipline or remove managerial personnel—but he did not want worker complaints sponsored and articulated by a trade union organization that extended beyond the factory. See *Eighth National Congress of the Communist Party of China, Vol. 2: Speeches* (Peking, 1956), pp. 304–317.

We need supervision by the various democratic parties and by democrats without party affiliations. This is because they represent the views and demands of a section of our society and possess certain political experience and professional skills. They often give us well-directed criticisms and valued suggestions. . . . We must create all the necessary conditions to help them supervise us.[27]

This supervision, which Li acknowledged would have to be coupled with continued programs to educate and remold the bourgeoisie, could take several forms. It could occur in the people's congresses, as Tung Pi-wu had suggested, and also in the Political Consultative Conference and in informal meetings between non-Party democrats and Party and government leaders. All such devices had proved effective and should be extended in scope and intensity so that they would become an established institution.

An even more outspoken proposal was made somewhat later by Chang Po-chün, then minister of communications. Since Chang was not a member of the Party, his proposals were not presented to the Eighth Party Congress, but rather to a meeting of the Political Consultative Conference in March 1957.[28] He suggested that the Conference gradually be turned into a "democratic link" in a strengthened "parliamentary system"—in other words, that it be transformed into the upper chamber of a national parliament in which the National People's Congress would serve as the lower house. Capitalist countries and other socialist states both had bicameral legislatures, Chang said, and though Chinese should not force themselves to be the same as others, he clearly favored adopting bicameralism in China as well.

The conversion of the Political Consultative Conference from a consultative body into a legislative one would have greatly increased the formal role of the democratic parties in China, and Chang, as vice-chairman of the Democratic League, was not reluctant to make that conclusion explicit. The democratic parties should be allowed to expand, he said, and compete directly with the Communist Party in recruiting younger members; they should not be restricted to seeking members only from among older intellectuals and industrialists. Chang paid proper deference to the principle that the democratic parties should be under the supervision of the Communist Party, but he urged that the Party should be prevented from exercising total control over them. Instead, that control should be shared with the masses of the people and with the members of the democratic parties themselves. Chang Po-chün's proposals thus went far beyond those of Li Wei-han. He sought to weaken the control of the Communist Party over the democratic parties, to strengthen the smaller parties' power base, and to give them legislative as well as consultative power.

Alternative Policy Packages: Chou, Liu, Teng, and Mao

As different as they were, these four sets of proposals were not mutually exclusive, but were combined into different packages by the Party's top leaders. This was particularly evident in the principal reports presented to the Eighth Party Congress: the summary of the Second Five-Year Plan by Chou En-lai, the political report by Liu Shao-ch'i, the report on the revision of the Party constitution by Teng Hsiao-p'ing, and the opening remarks by Mao Tse-tung.

Chou En-lai took the most conservative position on organizational questions.[29] He recognized that many economic problems could be attributed to organizational causes, particularly to subjectivism and bureaucracy among the leadership and commandism at lower levels, but he endorsed only a few of the proposals for dealing with those problems.[30] He suggested that a further retrenchment of the bureaucracy should be undertaken to eliminate overstaffing and red tape in the State Council.[31] He further advocated closer contact between the government and the people, and better investigation and study of local conditions. And as mentioned in the preceding chapter, he gave detailed recommendations about decentralization, proposing that a large number of industrial enterprises be transferred to provincial control.[32]

Chou's report was the least obviously "political" of the four, and thus was least obligated to consider proposals for organizational reform. But he could have chosen to use his section on the "further improvement of the people's life" to comment on managing contradictions in Chinese society, and perhaps to talk about reforming political life in China. Instead, he only made some perfunctory remarks about the need to "rectify our bureaucratic style of work" and "concern ourselves more about the life of the masses."[33] And he could have criticized sectarianism in discussing relations with "the former industrial and merchant capitalists," but again he chose not to do so.[34] Thus, although Chou would later come to accept the need for a rectification campaign, and even Mao's proposal that it involve criticism of the Party by people outside it, he initially echoed Li Fu-ch'un's view that organizational problems could be controlled through restructuring and further rationalization of the bureaucracy.

In contrast to Chou, Liu Shao-ch'i presented a much more comprehensive and eclectic report, as befitted its status as the keynote address.[35] He dealt separately with the organizational problems of the state and the Party—the former in a section on "the political life of the state," and the latter in one on "the leadership of the Party."

The principal problem in the state apparatus was its tendency toward bureaucratism, towards a style of "armchair leadership that does not understand but suppresses the opinions of subordinates and the masses, and that pays little attention to the life of the masses." To eliminate bureau-cratism within state agencies, Liu advocated, first of all, "earnest, sys-tematic efforts" to simplify organization, clearly define each cadre's re-sponsibility, and promote investigation of local conditions. He next en-dorsed the idea that central authority be passed down both to individual enterprises and to local governments. Up to this point, his recommen-dations were virtually identical to those of Chou En-lai. But he went on to suggest that "in order to combat bureaucracy effectively, we must strengthen supervision of the work of the state through several channels at the same time." And he listed the channels—presumably in decreasing order of importance—as Party leadership, supervision by people's con-gresses and their deputies, bureaucratic discipline, monitoring by the Ministry of Supervision, and supervision by the masses and by low-ranking government workers.[36] Earlier, Liu had made passing reference to the desirability of accepting supervision by non-Party democrats but, significantly, he did not incorporate this idea into his summary list.[37] In short, when speaking of the state, he seconded Li Fu-ch'un and Ch'ien Ying on rationalization, and Tung Pi-wu and Lai Jo-yü on democratiza-tion, but not Li Wei-han on external criticism of state policy.

In discussing the shortcomings of the Party, Liu focused on subjec-tivism.[38] His solutions were in some ways more limited than his proposals for combating bureaucratism in the state apparatus. They emphasized the need to strengthen education in Marxism-Leninism and in the organiza-tional principles of the Party. The Party should intensify the systematic study of Marxism-Leninism by high-ranking cadres; further the education of new Party members "so as to enable them to understand step by step the Marxist-Leninist standpoint, viewpoint, and method"; assign the Party's theoreticians to study "major problems and basic experience in the socialist transformation and socialist construction of our country"; strengthen investigation and research into actual conditions; adhere to the Party's principles of collective leadership; and broaden democratic life in the Party.[39] And it should continue to reeducate cadres who had made mistakes in their work, rather than simply taking disciplinary action against them. On organizational problems in the Party, then, Liu sounded much like other leaders who recommended vigorous inner-Party educa-tion, but he did not go as far as Liu Lan-t'ao or Chu Te in actually calling for a rectification campaign against bureaucratism and subjectivism.[40]

Teng Hsiao-p'ing's proposals for reforming the Party offered some in-teresting contrasts to Liu's. Although he also took an eclectic approach—endorsing intensified inner-Party education, investigation and research in advance of policy decisions, organizational retrenchment, development of the "democratic life" of the Party and state through the representative congresses, improvements in the Party control commissions and the state supervisory system, and strengthened Party leadership over the state bureaucracy—his report differed from Liu's in two important respects. First, Teng emphasized a reform measure that Liu had ignored: extra-Party criticism. Strengthening the ideological education of Party members, the measure that Liu had stressed, was important, but Teng added that "the Party has an even more important task, namely . . . to make appropriate provisions in both the state and the Party system for a strict supervision over our Party organizations and Party members . . . by the masses and by non-Party personalities."[41] His report contained two lengthy paragraphs on the desirability of accepting criticism from non-Party members:

In the struggle to carry out the mass line and combat bureaucracy, it is of vital importance to strengthen still further our cooperation with non-Party people, and to draw as many of them as possible into the struggle. . . . Of course, there are struggles in this kind of cooperation. But the point is that these democratic personalities can provide a kind of supervision over our Party which cannot easily be provided by Party members alone; they can discover mistakes and shortcomings in our work which may escape our own notice, and render us valuable help in our work.[42]

A second difference between Teng and Liu was Teng's strong advocacy of a revival of the mobilizational style of policy implementation in China, a stand that paralleled the defense of the mass line by Teng's deputy, Sung Jen-ch'iung. Teng listed a series of accomplishments—the defeat of the Nationalists, land reform, suppression of counterrevolutionaries, the elimination of corruption, the eradication of opium smoking, and the promotion of public health. He then asked which could have been won if the movement or the task in question had not "actually reflected the demands of the broad masses and been translated into conscious and voluntary action by them."[43] Where Tung Pi-wu and P'eng Chen had called in earlier speeches for an effective end to mass movements, Teng was advocating their continuation: the mass line could not mean simply the bureaucratic formulation and administration of policies in the people's interest, but must continue to embody the leadership style "from the masses, to the masses" elucidated by Mao in 1944. Although he did not reject rationalization—indeed, he endorsed the specialization of personnel and the formalization of disciplinary procedures in his report—he was proposing a restoration of the mobilizational aspects of organizational life in China.[44] On this issue, Liu Shao-ch'i was silent.

Most intriguing of all was the position that Mao Tse-tung took at the Eighth Party Congress. It was he, after all, who had introduced the concept of managing contradictions between the Party and the people, had defined the purpose of the congress as promoting national unity, and had called for a struggle against subjectivism, sectarianism, and bureaucratism. But at this point Mao did not forcefully endorse any particular solution to the problems he had identified. In his opening address to the congress, he said only that "the serious shortcomings in our ranks must be vigorously corrected by strengthening ideological education in the Party," and then vaguely that "in the various organs of state and in public affairs a lot of work has to be done by non-Party people."[45] These passages might be interpreted as an endorsement of political education, an oblique nod toward extra-Party criticism, and a lack of interest in democratization and rationalization. But it would be more prudent to conclude that Mao either had not made up his mind, or had not yet decided to speak out. Only after the developments in Eastern Europe and in China in late 1956 did Mao bring forward his own proposals.

THE IMPACT OF ECONOMIC IMBALANCE

Despite intensive discussion of organizational matters, the Eighth Party Congress ended without taking any concrete steps toward organizational reform. The most striking characteristic of the congress's final resolution was its lack of urgency. It simply repeated the major points that Liu had made in his analysis of the Party and state, adding only that the Party should consult more frequently with the democratic parties, non-Party intellectuals, and the Political Consultative Conference. It called for no rectification campaign against subjectivism or bureaucratism, or for any other extraordinary measures to alleviate organizational problems. It implied that the reforms Liu had endorsed could be effected in a gradual, cautious, and unhurried manner.[46]

But when the Central Committee met in its second plenary session in mid-November, serious economic problems created by the High Tide had altered this rather complacent assessment. Although collectivization had proceeded relatively smoothly, it was clear that agricultural production would not show the same rate of increase in 1956 as in 1955. And although industry was experiencing spectacular growth—including a 57 percent increase in steel output from 1955 to 1956—production increases were uneven, and serious bottlenecks and supply shortages were already apparent. Moreover, given the lag in agriculture, the rapid acceleration of industrial output would be impossible to sustain.

Even worse, the Chinese economy was beginning to face a threat of inflation. One source of inflationary pressure was a shortage of capital equipment and construction goods demanded by the hyperactive industrial sector. Two other sources were the 15.4 percent wage increase given Chinese workers in 1956 and overemployment in urban factories and enterprises, which during the High Tide had taken on more workers than originally authorized. These two factors produced an urban demand for foodstuffs and consumer goods that the agricultural and light industrial sectors simply could not satisfy.

The Second Plenum decided to try to slow the economy down in an attempt to redress the imbalances between industry and agriculture and between supply and demand. According to the communiqué issued at the end of the session, Chou En-lai told the plenum that "because there are certain items that are not satisfactory and there is overspending on certain items in the current year's plan, there must be suitable retrenchment in certain fields in the coming year's plan." This meant, the plenum decided, that "production should be increased only where supplies of raw materials were definite and the increase was needed by the community." It also required, as Chou further stated, "an energetic economy campaign in government organizations."[47]

Why was another campaign for administrative retrenchment necessary so soon? One reason was that the retrenchment drive of 1955–56 had achieved only limited success. More important, however, were the ways in which the High Tide had nullified many of the accomplishments of the earlier effort. For one thing, the higher targets of the High Tide and the new responsibilities assumed by the government after the nationalization of industry and collectivization of agriculture once again gave officials a legitimate reason for increasing their staffs. For another, it is likely that the mobilizational style of the High Tide nullified attempts to assert stringent controls over administrative finances as envisioned in the 1955 reforms. For whatever reason, the High Tide's effect on China's administrative budget was alarming. Although the 1956 budget already allowed for a 16 percent increase in administrative costs, the actual expenditures would be more than 10 percent over budget by the end of the year.[48]

Given these unexpected expenditures and the inflationary pressures the Chinese economy was already experiencing, it is not surprising that the Second Plenum called for a renewed effort at administrative retrenchment. On November 16, the day after the plenum concluded, the State Council issued a directive prohibiting any increase in the size of government staffs or the number of government agencies. The directive explained that a new retrenchment drive would help alleviate the country's economic problems not only directly, by reducing administrative expenses, but also indirectly, by increasing the government's ability to manage the economy efficiently.[49]

In broad outline, the retrenchment campaign of 1956–57 was similar to that of 1955–56. The press was filled with articles offering evidence of inefficiency and overstaffing. Bureaucracy in Shanghai had grown so fast that there was a shortage of office space.[50] Szechwan had so many officials that some worked only two hours a day.[51] Conferences for county-level cadres were so poorly organized that some officials read documents or signed letters while listening to reports.[52] And the state trading offices in Hopei had managed to double their staff despite the retrenchment effort of 1955–56.[53] As before, the goal was to clarify the responsibilities of Party and government agencies, eliminate duplication of assignments and unnecessary offices, reduce "administrative" (as opposed to "business") staff, and send a large number of cadres to new positions at lower levels. But despite these general similarities, there were some important differences between the first and second rounds of retrenchment.

The 1956–57 retrenchment drive was given much more publicity at the provincial levels. Aware that the 1955–56 campaign had been much less successful in the provinces than in central government and Party agencies, Chinese leaders apparently decided to concentrate the second round outside Peking. Specific targets for provincial retrenchment were published in the press, and sometimes targets for large municipalities and special districts were specified, as well. The most common goal was a 20–30 percent reduction in administrative staffs, but some provinces set even higher goals. (A selection of provincial retrenchment targets is presented in the accompanying table.)

The 1956–57 campaign also established quantitative measures for strengthening leadership at the basic levels. Shansi, for example, decided

Retrenchment Targets for Selected Administrative Units, 1956–1957

Province or municipality	Proposed reduction in administrative staff
Heilungkiang[a]	38%
Honan	33
Hupei[b]	20–30
Kwangtung	30
Shantung	33
Canton	20
Shanghai	20–25

SOURCES: Heilungkiang, *JMJP*, 15.xii.56, in *SCMP* 1442 (3.i.57), pp. 14–15. Honan, NCNA, 26.xii.56, in *SCMP* 1448 (11.i.57), pp. 21–22. Hupei, NCNA, 16.xii.56, in *SCMP* 1442 (3.i.57), pp. 22–23. Kwangtung, NCNA, 20.xii.56, in *SCMP* 1442 (3.i.57), p. 22. Shantung, *JMJP*, 7.xii.56, in *SCMP* 1442 (3.i.57), pp. 18–19. Canton, NCNA, 2.xii.56, in *SCMP* 1442 (3.i.57), pp. 23–24. Shanghai, *Hsin-wan jih-pao*, 28.xii.56, in *SCMP* 1456 (23.i.57), pp. 16–18.
[a] Refers only to the provincial department of water conservancy.
[b] Includes retrenchment at the special-district level.

to transfer two "good cadres" to each township.[54] Kiangsi decided one goal of its campaign would be to ensure that 30 percent of the townships in the province received cadres from the county level; and another, that 90 percent of the counties would, in turn, have a cadre from the special district level serving as Party secretary.[55]

A third difference was that the 1956–57 round gave more attention to reducing the level of administrative expenditures than to reducing the number of administrative cadres. Particular emphasis was placed on cutting government expenditures on telephone calls, telegrams, buildings, furniture, banquets, and automobiles. To investigate ways in which this could be done, the Ministry of Finance held a special forum on administrative expenses in January 1957 that issued a series of recommendations on minimizing travel costs, reducing meeting expenses, and economizing on building maintenance.[56] Although fewer specific goals were announced for this aspect of the campaign, Honan province did propose to reduce its administrative expenses by 20 percent, and Shanghai announced plans to reduce its costs by 16 percent.[57] The central government, in turn, set as its goal the saving of 40 million yüan in administrative expenses in 1957, primarily by reducing office supplies and the number of meetings held, and by using up inventories and using letters instead of telegrams.[58] In Kwangtung T'ao Chu announced that the provincial government would no longer host official banquets, except for visiting foreign delegations.[59]

Fourth, the 1956–57 campaign introduced a system of transferring cadres to lower levels on a rotational, rather than a permanent, basis. As we have seen, part of the resistance to the 1955–56 retrenchment drive was the reluctance of many cadres to accept permanent transfer from the urban bureaucracy to the countryside. To help meet these objections, the 1956–57 Hsia-fang campaign established the policy of sending officials to the basic levels for a fixed tour of duty, after which they would return to their original posts. The details varied among the provinces, but in many areas this system of rotational transfer was conducted level by level throughout the bureaucracy. Cadres at the provincial and special-district levels might be sent to county offices for a year's assignment, and county cadres might be ordered to spend two-thirds of their time working at the grass roots.[60] In other provinces, high-ranking cadres were sent directly to basic-level units for a period of "investigation and study," often for as long as one year.[61]

This aspect of the retrenchment campaign was of more use in increasing bureaucratic effectiveness than in reducing administrative expenditures. Since transferred officials retained their original rank and salary, the Hsia-fang program could not generate a decrease in the total administrative wage bill. Nevertheless, reducing the upper levels of the bureaucracy was seen as a way of increasing administrative efficiency, and Chinese leaders believed that what officials learned during their period of rustication would improve their performance in their permanent posts.[62] To fully realize the benefits of the program, the Kansu provincial government specified that rotational transfers should be to a variety of villages—some officials would be sent to mountain areas, others to drought areas, others to villages inhabited by national minorities. After this experience, cadres would return with a collective enhancement of their understanding of conditions in the provinces.[63]

Like its predecessor, the retrenchment campaign of 1956–57 had some serious obstacles to overcome. Cadres still resisted being sent to the basic levels, even on a rotational basis. Department heads continued to dislike reducing the size of their staffs.[64] Some cadres argued that these organizational problems could not effectively be solved in a campaign-like atmosphere: they opposed the arbitrary targets set by provincial governments, warned against "hasty and blind measures," and called for a more gradual and lasting reform rather than momentary enthusiasm.[65]

As a result, many provinces were slow in meeting their retrenchment targets. When the twenty-odd provincial departments in Kwangtung were asked to submit their plans for staff reduction, one proposed a cut of 10 percent, three asked that their staffs be kept as they were, and all the rest requested a staff increase averaging 25.4 percent.[66] In Chekiang a county magistrate and his two deputies wrote an article for *Jen-min jih-pao* claiming that it would be impossible to reduce the size of their administrative staff unless the province first simplified its administrative structure, reduced the number of meetings, clarified the division of labor between Party and government, and stopped telling county cadres to take personal charge of every campaign that came along.[67] Thus, in mid-January of 1957, when the New China News Agency prepared a summary of the campaign's progress, it could identify only nine provinces that had successfully completed their retrenchment programs.[68]

Yet another problem was the use of political criteria in determining which cadres would be rotated to the countryside. During the antirightist campaign of 1957–58, it was charged that some provincial-level officials who took "rightist" positions on major political and economic issues— who opposed accelerated collectivization and who favored a reduction in the intensity of class struggle—used the retrenchment drive to consolidate their support within the Party and government. Officials who shared their views were kept in provincial and special district positions, and cadres who took more "leftist" positions received transfers to lower levels.[69]

Nonetheless, over a period of ten months the campaign was able to record some successes. By April the central government could announce that its administrative expenses had been reduced by 10 million yüan in the first quarter of 1957, an accomplishment that gave promise of meeting the goal of saving 40 million yüan over the course of the year.[70] By June, Li Hsien-nien could claim that government administrative expenses had been reduced 31 percent below 1956.[71] And by September it could be announced that 300,000 Party and government cadres had been transferred, 200,000 to "production posts" and the rest to lower administrative positions.[72] Compared to the 1955–56 retrenchment drive, this second round had been a considerable success.

THE IMPACT OF POPULAR DISSENT

In June the Poznan riots in Poland sparked a wave of political protest that forced changes in the composition of the Polish government and the leadership of the Polish Communist party. In October an uprising in Hungary secured the temporary installation of a more moderate government, although it was crushed by Soviet intervention in early November. On November 11, Tito issued a strong condemnation of Stalinism and called for greater freedom for all socialist countries to follow their own paths toward communism.

These events in Eastern Europe might, by themselves, have encouraged expression of similar grievances in China in any case, but they were particularly threatening because of the psychological impact of economic retrenchment on the Chinese people. The retrenchment announced at the end of the Second Plenum affected capital construction and administrative expenses, of course, but it also had a strong impact on consumer welfare and social services. The expansion of educational enrollments was halted; wage increases in the cities were forbidden; and the cloth ration was reduced. In a series of articles and editorials in late 1956 and early 1957, the Chinese press began to warn that expectations raised during the High Tide of 1955–56 would now have to be reduced. Parents and students were told that, although the nation's goal was universal college education, most middle-school graduates would not be able to go on to college in 1957 or even to find jobs in the cities, but would instead be sent to the countryside.[73] Peasants were cautioned not to let the rapid completion of collectivization create economic expectations that could not be satisfied.[74] And the 1957 New Year's Day editorial acknowledged that "the improvement of the people's living conditions can only be gradual."[75]

The expectations produced by the High Tide of 1955–56, the shattering of those expectations after the Second Plenum, and the example of popular protest in Eastern Europe combined to produce a wave of strikes and demonstrations in China in late 1956 and early 1957. In rural areas the disappointing harvest of 1956, coupled with the tendency of the new collectives to allocate a relatively high proportion of their output to investment rather than consumption, led to complaints that peasant incomes were falling rather than rising. These were views naturally held by the peasants, but they also, according to Mao, "found an echo among certain Party cadres."[76] The government attempted to marshal evidence to prove that 75 percent of the peasants were continuing to enjoy an increasing level of income after collectivization, but the same statistics revealed another aspect of the problem: the urban wage increases of 1956 meant that worker incomes were rising much faster than peasant incomes. Worker consumption increased by 9.1 percent between 1955 and 1956 while peasant consumption rose only 2.7 percent.[77] The growing gap between workers and peasants led to charges that the Chinese Party, like Stalin, was ignoring the peasants in favor of welfare and investment in the urban areas.

This did not mean, however, that urban residents were satisfied with their economic conditions. In Canton alone there were thirteen strikes at the end of 1956, and Mao admitted that some workers were going on strike because of the government's failure to satisfy their demands for material benefits.[78] Students, as well, were creating disturbances in the fall and winter of 1956–57. In the Shihchiachuang middle school, students who had been scheduled to graduate in June 1956 were forced to stay on for an additional year because there were not enough jobs for them. At some point in the fall, probably as it became clear that their prospects would not be much better the following June, they organized a demonstration and threatened to seize the provincial radio station, demanded the "overthrow of fascism," and charged that socialism was "in no way superior" to other political systems.[79] In Chengtu over a hundred students attempted to travel to Peking to present a petition to the central government but were turned back en route.[80] At Tsinghua University in Peking another student declared that he would like to see "thousands and tens of thousands of people" (presumably Communist officials) shot after the Party was overthrown.[81] These protests and demonstrations graphically illustrated the need to find better ways of managing such "contradictions among the people" and forced a reconsideration of the proposals for political and organizational reform presented at the Eighth Party Congress.

It was at this point that Mao Tse-tung began to express more fully his own views on China's organizational problems. From the Second Plenum on Mao made it increasingly clear that, although he was not opposed to administrative retrenchment or to rotating officials to country posts, his main interest was in an open-door rectification campaign in which intellectuals, the democratic parties, and "non-Party democrats" would play a particularly important role. Mao's views on Party rectification were expressed in a series of major speeches between November 1956 and April

1957.[82] The details of his presentation differed somewhat from one occasion to another, but the essentials of his argument can be summarized as follows.

Mao began with the premise, first expressed in April 1956, that China's principal goal was to "build a great socialist country" in the shortest possible time, and that the attainment of this goal required the mobilization of the broadest possible united front within China. There were, in Mao's view, three possible obstacles to achieving popular unity and promoting socialist construction. One was the counterrevolutionaries, who might try deliberately to obstruct China's modernization. But, Mao argued, this was less a problem for China than for Eastern Europe. Because the Chinese Party, unlike its European counterparts, had relied on mass mobilization to identify and suppress counterrevolutionaries earlier in the 1950's, the bulk of them had already been "cleared out."[83] A more important obstacle to national unity, therefore, was the tendency within the Party and state organizations to develop bureaucratism, subjectivism, and sectarianism, all of which had reduced the Party's ability to formulate, explain, and implement policy effectively, and had given the principal impetus to the disturbances and protests of late 1956.[84] A third problem hindering national unity was the undeveloped political consciousness of the intellectuals, most of whom were not entirely committed to Marxism and were thus "prone to vacillate politically." The emphasis on professionalization in 1956 had brought more intellectuals into the Party and had given them more influence in policymaking, but inadequate attention had been paid to their political reeducation.[85]

Mao also believed that the organizational problems of the Party and state could best be remedied through a form of open-door rectification that would allow people who were not Party members to criticize Party and government policies and officials. It was wrong that so many localities and units in China should have "no democracy of any kind."[86] The resultant gap between leaders and led should be bridged through criticism: "In matters within the purview of the people, the people should have the right to criticize."[87] Moreover, in places where bureaucratic problems were particularly serious, it would be all right to use "supplementary" methods to regulate the social order, and Mao specified strikes, demonstrations, and petitions as acceptable methods.[88] Such protests would "help get the festering sore cured."[89] Even if they forced the removal of some officials from office, that, too, would be a positive achievement.[90]

Mao placed particular emphasis on the role of intellectuals and non-Party democrats in this open-door rectification movement. Though acknowledging that the majority of intellectuals still had doubts about Marxism, Mao nonetheless insisted that they would support the socialist system "in varying degrees" and could be relied upon to "criticize us Communists and give us their suggestions."[91] Encouraging the non-Party intellectuals to participate actively in the open-door rectification campaign would have several advantages. For one, their criticism might help identify and eliminate instances of subjectivism, bureaucratism, and sectarianism in the Party and government. For another, such a gesture of confidence would convince them of the superiority of the socialist system, and the process of debate, discussion, and criticism during rectification would convince them of the validity of Marxism-Leninism. "The classes of their birth have now been destroyed, so they hang in mid air," Mao explained. "If we reach out warmly, it can go a bit faster."[92] Thus, relying on the non-Party democrats in the rectification campaign would ameliorate two of the most important problems blocking the way to Mao's goal of national unity: it would help solve the Party's organizational problems, and it would hasten the political reeducation of some "wavering" elements.

Mao's proposals for open-door rectification offered some intriguing comparisons with the four sets of proposals presented to the Eighth Party Congress. Mao verbally endorsed some elements of rationalization, particularly administrative retrenchment, but in fact he went far beyond them. He also endorsed the concept of a Party rectification campaign, but he insisted that opportunities to participate be offered to those who were not members of the Party. Like the proponents of democratization, Mao was interested in finding ways for the people to exercise some degree of supervision over the Party and the government, but unlike them, he was not convinced that the best method would be to increase the power of representative assemblies and mass organizations. Like the proponents of external criticism, Mao sought the views of non-Party democrats, but unlike Chang Po-chün, at least, he did not seem to believe that this would require any formal change in the structure of the Chinese political system. Indeed, at the Second Plenum Mao explicitly rejected Chang's proposals for turning the Political Consultative Conference into a second parliamentary chamber, saying that, for Chang and his followers, "great democracy" meant the adoption of "the bourgeois parliamentary things of the West and the imitation of such Western stuff as 'parliamentary democracy,' 'freedom of the press,' and 'freedom of speech.'"[93] Instead, Mao's notion of "great democracy" resembled the San-fan and Wu-fan campaigns, except that now mass mobilization would be directed not against capitalists but against "bureaucrats." Of all the views on organizational problems expressed at the Eighth Party Congress, Mao's most closely paralleled those of Li Wei-han and Teng Hsiao-p'ing.

DEBATE OVER RECTIFICATION

Mao's proposals for open-door rectification generated the Party's most serious controversy over organizational questions since 1949. At the height of the debate, Mao himself estimated that 90 percent of the Party membership opposed him.[94] A number of central leaders, most notably P'eng Chen and Liu Shao-ch'i, sought to dissociate themselves from Mao's ideas.* And in mid-April a tough editorial in *Jen-min jih-pao* admitted that there was resistance to the rectification campaign throughout the Party, resistance that it traced to some "mistaken conceptions" about the role of the Party in Chinese society. If leaders did not learn how to deal with contradictions among the people, the editorial warned, they would be "in danger politically."[95]

Opposition forced Mao to circumvent the Central Committee and seek political support elsewhere, just as he had during the debate over agricultural collectivization in 1955. Mao held no less than three special meetings in early 1957 to explain his proposal for open-door rectification. In January he called a meeting of provincial-level officials. In late February he convened a session of the Supreme State Conference at which he delivered his speech "On the Correct Handling of Contradictions Among the People," the purpose of the session being to seek support from non-Party leaders. And in March, at a national conference on propaganda work, Mao met separately with delegates from different geographic regions and with journalists and publishers attending the conference.

Despite Mao's attempts to mobilize political support, there was still an unusual delay in getting the rectification campaign underway. The national press carried no reports on Mao's address to the Supreme State Conference, or on his speech to the national propaganda conference. Only in mid-April, after Mao sarcastically suggested that *Jen-min jih-pao* be renamed the *Nationalist Daily*, and demanded that it be "rectified," did the first editorials on the rectification campaign appear.[96] The Central Committee was equally slow in approving a formal directive on rectification; Mao had initially hoped that the campaign could formally be launched early in 1957, but the Central Committee's directive was not issued until April 27.[97]

*As Roderick MacFarquhar has pointed out, the *Jen-min jih-pao* photograph of the rostrum of the Supreme State Conference in February, taken on the day Mao delivered "On the Correct Handling of Contradictions Among the People," failed to show several important leaders, including Liu Shao-ch'i, Chu Te, Lin Piao, Lin Po-ch'ü, Lo Jung-huan, and P'eng Te-huai. MacFarquhar believes that many of these men actually attended the conference but refused to be photographed on the rostrum (*The Origins of the Cultural Revolution, Vol. 1: Contradictions Among the People, 1956–1957* [New York, 1974], pp. 191–92). He also argues that P'eng Chen opposed Mao's ideas on rectification (pp. 181–82, 195, and chapter 15). MacFarquhar's attempt to identify "the balance of forces within the Politburo" is on pp. 241–49.

Why was Mao's proposal so controversial? One possible issue was whether a rectification campaign was necessary. There is substantial evidence that many Party officials resisted Mao's basic premise that the relations between the Party and the people had become so strained that a major Party reform movement was required to improve them. One article in the Party's youth journal, for example, insisted that bureaucratism was not a major problem in China, that those who exaggerated the dangers of bureaucratism were doing so out of the "narrowmindedness and prejudices" of the petty bourgeoisie and were effectively practicing "rejection of revolution."[98] Similar doubts were expressed at a propaganda conference in Kwangtung in April, where some officials apparently argued that if problems arose between the Party and the people, the object of rectification should be the people, not the Party, and that if mass education failed to resolve these contradictions, then pressure against dissenters would be perfectly legitimate.[99]

Another issue concerned the targets of the rectification campaign. As Roderick MacFarquhar has demonstrated, central and provincial leaders did not always list the three objects of rectification—bureaucratism, sectarianism, and subjectivism—in the same order as did the Central Committee directive. Some even deleted one or two of these "three evils," or added other organizational problems, such as dogmatism, to the list of targets.[100] Although MacFarquhar's finding may be significant, it is also important to add that Mao himself was not consistent in his listing of the evils. So it may not be wise to read too much into the tendency of other officials to list them in "improper" order.[101]

Alternatively, as Richard Solomon has argued, Chinese leaders may have differed over the type of subjectivism to be combated by rectification. In Chinese Communist ideology, subjectivism can be of two kinds: divorce from reality (dogmatism) or divorce from theory (empiricism, which becomes revisionism if it develops to the point of departing from Marxist-Leninist principles). Although Mao repeatedly criticized dogmatism in late 1956 and early 1957, particularly the uncritical adoption of Soviet policies, he also became increasingly concerned with revisionism after the Hungarian uprising. At the national conference on propaganda work in March he said that revisionism was "more pernicious than dogmatism," and that those who were severely critical of dogmatism often neglected to criticize revisionism as well.[102] By contrast, an article published on March 3 by Lu Ting-i, the Party's propaganda chief, differed substantially from Mao's views in that it stressed the continuing danger of dogmatism and made only passing reference to a need to combat revisionism.[103] Solomon has taken this to indicate basic differences in the way Chinese leaders identified the country's ideological problem—differences between those who believed that extreme dogmatism was the basic cause both of the Eastern European uprisings and of popular protest in China, and those who believed that de-Stalinization should not be permitted to erode China's strict adherence to basic Marxist-Leninist principles.[104]

Though both MacFarquhar's and Solomon's analyses are plausible, the most important issue at stake was neither the necessity for a rectification campaign nor the targets at which it was to be directed; it was rather the nature of the rectification methods Mao proposed. Many central Party leaders questioned Mao's emphasis on soliciting criticism from non-Party intellectuals and his willingness to tolerate strikes and demonstrations by students and workers. They sought, instead, a more limited rectification campaign in which criticism and self-criticism would occur primarily within the Party with only restricted participation by outsiders. In short, where Mao wanted open-door rectification—to let, in his famous phrase, a "hundred flowers bloom"—many of his colleagues sought only a closed-door campaign.

The resistance to open-door rectification was apparent in statements, published and unpublished, by a number of Politburo members in early 1957. Lu Ting-i's article on rectification mentioned above said nothing about the desirability of external criticism. Indeed, by choosing to write an article commemorating the 1942–44 Cheng-feng movement—rather than, say, the 1947–48 rectification or the San-fan campaign—Lu was expressing his support for closed-door techniques.[105] Similarly, Liu Shao-ch'i gave a number of speeches in the first half of 1957 that reflected his doubts about the wisdom of "big democracy." Mao had expressed willingness to tolerate strikes and demonstrations, but the most Liu was willing to accept, to judge by a talk he gave in January, was large-scale struggle sessions.[106] In an address delivered in June to the graduating class of the Peking Institute of Geology, Liu acknowledged that there was bureaucracy in the country, but claimed that "the Communist Party has found a way to deal with it—rectification." The role of outsiders in rectification should be limited: extensive democracy was unsuitable, limited democracy, better.[107]

Of particular concern to Mao's opponents was the role of non-Party intellectuals in the rectification campaign. If these groups were politically unreliable, as Mao himself admitted, then why should they be given a prominent role in criticizing the Party? One of the first public expressions of this viewpoint was an article by four army officers published on January 7. It charged that the more liberal policy toward intellectuals had already reduced the number of novels, stories, and plays that "reflect the glory of socialist construction" and had encouraged writers to produce pieces that "restore the old."[108] Although the article dealt specifically with literature and art, it implicitly raised a political question: If the intellectuals could not even be trusted in the artistic sphere, how could they be relied upon in a Party rectification campaign?

Several *Jen-min jih-pao* editorials published in April took a similar position. One on policy toward intellectuals took its title, "Educators Must Receive Education," from the speech Mao had made to the national conference on propaganda work one month before. But by stressing that China's intellectuals needed political remolding and ignoring Mao's proposal that they be encouraged to criticize the Party, it subtly distorted the point of Mao's speech.[109] It was two and one-half weeks later that the first major editorial on the rectification campaign finally accepted the notion of some role for non-Party people in rectification, and even then the paper did not identify intellectuals as the most important participants. Instead, it resurrected the proposals for democratization made at the Eighth Party Congress. Calling for an expansion of the "democratic life of the people," it suggested that ordinary people be given more opportunity to participate in decision making in such basic-level organizations as factories, schools, and collectives. The door had been opened a crack, but the manner of its opening and the people invited in differed greatly from Mao's proposals.[110]

At the end of April this long period of debate finally came to an end with a series of decisions on the reform of the Chinese political system. The decisions indicated that the Politburo had assembled a program that drew on all four sets of proposals presented to the Eighth Party Congress the preceding September. They also showed that Mao had been forced to compromise with his opponents on the issue of open-door rectification.

The April decisions had little new to say about rationalization. The planning for decentralization was still under way, and the retrenchment campaign launched at the Second Plenum was already achieving some success. But they did define a series of steps to democratize various institutions in Chinese society. A Central Committee directive on the democratization of the agricultural producers' cooperatives provided that accounts be made public, that cadres be elected, that peasants be consulted in planning and decision making, and that special forums be called periodically for peasants to discuss current problems.[111] Editorials discussed ways of increasing the power and representativity of the congresses of cooperative members.[112] At about the same time, the Party adopted Li Hsüeh-feng's proposals for broadening the role of workers' congresses in factories and enterprises by giving them the right to advise and criticize factory managers on production plans and policies, to recommend policies concerning worker welfare and safety, to suggest the dismissal of cadres whom they believed to be incompetent or inattentive to worker concerns, and to appeal to higher levels if managers ignored their proposals.[113] A more active role was also assigned to the Standing Committee of the National People's Congress, and newspaper accounts began to describe its members' questioning of reports from the government ministries.[114]

The key issue at stake, however, was not rationalization or democratization, but the fate of the proposals for rectification and external criticism. Here the Central Committee's April 27 directive on rectification reflected a compromise.[115] It presented the rationale for rectification that Mao had been offering for more than six months—that the Party's goal should be to mobilize all "positive forces" and transform China into a modern socialist state; that a major obstacle to this unity was the tendency of many Party members to use "administrative measures" (compulsion) to solve political and social problems; and that it was therefore necessary to launch a rectification campaign against bureaucracy, sectarianism, and subjectivism. But the directive went on to impose several important limits on rectification, limits that may have been necessary to secure the consent of Mao's opponents within the Politburo. The campaign was to be conducted "as gently as a breeze or as mild rain": there was no sanction given for large-scale struggle sessions, let alone strikes and demonstrations. Instead, the directive stipulated that no cadres were to be punished unless they had actually committed illegal acts or had violated Party discipline. Inefficiency, arrogance, sectarianism, or errors in judgment were not to be punished—just remedied. And the directive stressed that the campaign should not be so intense as to interfere with the day-to-day work of the Party and government.

A second set of limits involved the role of external criticism in rectification. Although officials were to study the two speeches that most fully presented Mao's proposals for open-door rectification—"On the Correct Handling of Contradictions Among the People" and his speech at the Party's National Conference on Propaganda Work in March—the directive envisioned a campaign that would open the door only part way to external criticism of the Party. The main forum for conducting rectification would be the Party committees at various levels, which might invite non-Party representatives to attend. There was no hint that the democratic parties might call their own meetings independently of the Party to express criticism of Party policies. Moreover, the importance of extra-Party criticism was further reduced by the fact that the directive placed nearly equal emphasis on physical labor by cadres as a way of bridging the gap between the Party and the people. All in all, the Central Committee directive allowed for external criticism, but it did not encourage or emphasize it.

Despite these limitations, the rectification campaign did not develop along the lines laid out in the Central Committe directive. With the apparent support of the Party's United Front Work Department, Mao was able to keep the idea of external criticism alive through another meeting of the Supreme State Conference held on April 30. The Chinese press reported that even before the publication of the April 27 directive, the democratic parties had begun to hold meetings to discuss Mao's two speeches, and that they had started to criticize some local Party committees and officials for sectarianism. A *Jen-min jih-pao* editorial of April 26 had endorsed this arena of criticism, saying that it should be welcomed as a manifestation of Mao's policy of "long-term coexistence and mutual supervision" between the democratic parties and the Communist party.[116] In a very close paraphrase of a key passage from Li Wei-han's report to the Eighth Party Congress, the editorial explained:

Of course, we need first and foremost the supervision of the rank-and-file members of the Party and the broad masses of the working people. But at the same time we need supervision by other democratic parties and non-Party democrats. This is because they each represent the views and demands of one sector of society, and moreover they have certain political experience and professional skill. Hence, they are often able to put forward views and criticisms that go right to the point.[117]

Yet the editorial also admitted that this additional arena of rectification would be unpopular among Party members, who could still not understand why the democratic parties had the right to criticize the Party.

In essence, then, the rectification campaign was to develop along two parallel tracks. One was that envisioned by the Central Committee's directive. At the center, rectification meetings were called, under Party leadership, for high-ranking officials of the Party and government.[118] In the provinces, Party committees began to work out detailed procedures for the campaign.[119] Although there were substantial variations from province to province, the plans generally provided for a two-stage rectification—first of Party committees at the county level and above and in larger factories, mines, and universities; then, in late 1957 or early 1958, of the basic level. The reporting of these meetings indicated that this first track was concerned primarily with explaining the general purposes of the campaign and drawing up plans for rectification, not with criticizing particular Party policies or individual leaders. Nor were non-Party intellectuals described as playing a particularly active role in the movement.

The second track of the campaign was quite diffcrent. To provide a format for hearing criticism from intellectuals, the United Front Work Department called two series of forums of non-Party personages in Peking, and the State Council convened a meeting of its non-Party employees in late May and early June.[120] The locus was not the Party, but more neutral ground; the participants were not Party cadres, but mostly non-Party officials and intellectuals; the topic was not the procedures for rectification, but substantive issues; and the criticisms of the Party were not vague and general, but sharp and specific. Indeed, the complaints voiced at these forums were much more severe and sweeping than anyone, including Mao, had ever expected.

A third arena of criticism, which had not been anticipated by any prominent Chinese leader in late 1956 or early 1957, was the major universities, where students revealed themselves to be intensely critical of the Party. When Mao, Teng Hsiao-p'ing, and Li Wei-han proposed soliciting criticism, they had in mind judicious statements by prestigious senior non-Party intellectuals—scholars, managers, and officials. And yet the spirit of criticism soon spread beyond these limits. The first wall posters appeared in Peking universities on May 19, and daily student meetings to discuss the rectification campaign began on May 23. Students organized their own clubs and study groups to criticize the work styles of Party officials and the policies of the government. These clubs and study groups, in turn, began to forge links with other universities. Peking was the center of the student movement, but protests and demonstrations also took place in Nanking, Chengtu, Tsingtao, Tsinan, Kweilin, Soochow, and Nanchang.[121]

The student movement posed a more serious challenge to the Party than did the criticisms of senior intellectuals and non-Party officials. Not only did the students express sweeping opposition to some of the most basic premises of Party rule, but many did so in a blunt and earthy manner that was both alarming and offensive to Party leaders. Student demonstrations and protests often involved assaults on cadres and the police, and one evolved into a full-scale riot at the Hanyang Middle School in Wuhan.[122] Nor did the Party dare underestimate the significance of the student movement. Some officials drew parallels between events at Peking University in 1957 and at the beginning of the May Fourth Movement in 1919, implying that the former posed as dangerous a threat to the Party in the 1950's as the latter had to the warlord regimes earlier. Not surprisingly, then, the first indications that open-door rectification would be brought to an end appeared on May 25, when Mao said to the delegates to the Third Congress of the National Democratic Youth League, "The Chinese Communist Party is the core of leadership of the whole Chinese people, . . . and any word or deed at variance with socialism is completely wrong." As Roderick MacFarquhar has pointed out, Mao's choosing to make his remark to youth leaders shows that it was youth that was causing most concern.[123]

BLOOMING AND CONTENDING: ORGANIZATIONAL ISSUES

Many of the criticisms expressed in the meetings of the democratic parties, by non-Party members working in the State Council, in the United Front Work Department forums, and by university students dealt with economic policy, foreign policy, and the Party's policies toward science, education, and culture. A full discussion of these criticisms is beyond the scope of this study. What is relevant here are criticisms of the structure and staffing of the Party and state bureaucracies, and of the distribution of power among the Party, the government, and the democratic parties.

Some of the most cautious and conservative criticisms dealt with the unwieldiness and inefficiency of the government. One non-Party official pointed out that the regulations issued by various ministries were not always consistent, and that they often conflicted with the more general directives issued by the State Council.[124] Another complained that the planning process was too centralized, and that even the ministries had little influence in setting the goals and quotas they received.[125] A counselor of the State Council expressed his concern that the structure of state organs embodied too many levels, that a directive from the State Council only reached the primary level after going through channels "even longer than descending an eighteen-story pagoda."[126] Since these problems had been acknowledged by the Party itself more than a year before, comments such as these could not have been particularly ill-received.

More pointed and irritating criticisms concerned the cadre policy of the Party.[127] The Hundred Flowers period revealed five serious cleavages within the ranks of government and Party cadres, many of which had arisen during the period of organization building in the early 1950's. The first of these was the tension between local cadres and "outsiders." Cadres working in their native county or province complained that they were given less authority than cadres sent in from outside. Presumably, this was because in the People's Republic, as in traditional China, outsiders were considered to be less susceptible to local pressure, less wedded to local interests, and thus more loyal to central direction. Local cadres charged that the outsiders did not attempt to learn local conditions or the local dialect, but remained aloof from the local people and from local cadres.[128]

A second tension was that between the educated and the noneducated. Cadres with university training, many of whom came from bourgeois backgrounds, complained that they were discriminated against in appointments and promotions. They charged that, despite the Party's policy of giving equal weight to "skills" and "virtue," personnel decisions were made primarily on the basis of political reliability without reference to administrative or technical ability. Moreover, the assessment of an official's "virtue" was always subjective. Some alleged that virtue was measured not by considering a cadre's political attitudes, but by reference to class background and personal connections. One pointed out that people with no education and little visible ideological merit were still being promoted. He concluded that in the Party's eyes the definition of virtue must be "absence of talent." Another charged that the maxim "employ only the good and the talented" had been superceded by "employ only relatives and Party members."[129]

The third tension was between junior and senior cadres, particularly now that the expansion of the bureaucracy had been halted and the opportunities for promotion were decreasing. This was closely related to that between educated and noneducated cadres, for officials who entered the bureaucracy after 1949 tended to have higher academic qualifications than those who had become cadres before. But even junior cadres with little education—those appointed from the ranks of workers and peasants in the early 1950's—apparently also believed that their chances for promotion were being restricted. Junior officials complained that upward mobility was being blocked by a corps of veterans who received and maintained their positions solely by dint of their length of service to the Party. They charged that the political longevity of incompetent older officials showed that the Party's cadre policy was based on neither skills nor virtue, but purely on seniority.

Fourth was the deep division within the government between Party and non-Party officials. This problem, despite all the criticism of sectarianism, had not been ameliorated since the early 1950's. Non-Party cadres complained that even when they held positions of formal authority they could exercise very little power because they were denied access to documents and information necessary in their work. And non-Party officials also had difficulty in getting promotions. A Party member might get promoted three or more steps a year, one non-Party official complained, but non-Party men, however assiduous, were not promoted for three to five years.[130]

Finally, there were tensions between high- and low-ranking cadres over the hierarchy of rewards and privileges established during the period of rationalization between 1952 and 1955. People both inside and outside government expressed resentment at the privileges enjoyed by high officials: vacation villas and lighted tennis courts, better quality food and clothing, chauffered limousines, preferential treatment at theatrical performances, access to special hospitals, and success in gaining admittance for their children to higher quality schools.[131] As a leader of one of the democratic parties put it:

Privilege . . . is not simply an infection that spread [to veteran Communists when they entered the cities] following liberation, it is also a by-product of the absurd hierarchical system which besets the whole country. For instance, the discrepancy in material rewards between a minister, a director of a bureau, a director of a department, a head of an office, a chief of a section, and the ordinary rank-and-file cadres is far too excessive, and the distinction between them far too marked. . . . Talk of sharing hardships with the masses in a hierarchical system such as ours![132]

Still another group of criticisms concerned the structure of the Chinese political system, and particularly the distribution of power among the Party, the government, and the democratic parties. One recurring theme was the steady transfer of power from the government to the Party. The Political Consultative Conference and the National People's Congress were described as impotent organs, ignored by the Party, that could do nothing but unanimously approve proposals submitted by the Central Committee.[133] Party members considered documents from these organizations to be so unimportant that they did not even read them, but simply circulated them to non-Party cadres. A leader of one of the democratic parties complained:

In the meetings of the National People's Congress standing committee and bills committee, quorums were generally only barely achieved. Absentees included more members of the Communist party than any other party, and this led people to feel that these Communist party members did not respect the supreme organ of state power. [Was this] because some members of the Communist party thought that decisions were generally reached inside the Party, and that the National People's Congress standing committee merely passed them as a formality[?][134]

Relations between Party and government were also strained at the provincial and local levels. It was said that Party committees and functional departments could annul decisions made by government agencies and could even override or supersede orders received from higher levels of the government.[135]

Because of complaints such as these, the Party's critics made a number of proposals that, if adopted, would have produced major changes in China's political system. It was suggested that Party control over government personnel be eliminated, and that the Party's files on government employees be destroyed. And it was proposed that Party committees be abolished below the provincial level, that Party factions in government offices be eliminated, and that the Party's functional departments be redesignated functional committees of the National People's Congress.[136] Chang Po-chün repeated his proposal that the Political Consultative Conference become the second house of a Chinese parliament and suggested that, as an interim measure, representatives of the congress, the conference, the

Party, the democratic parties, and the mass organizations form a "political design department" to discuss all major policies and programs.[137]

Startling as they were, these proposals still represented a call only for the adjustment of China's existing political system, for granting more authority and power to the Political Consultative Conference and the National People's Congress and less to the Party. Other proposals went further, demanding more fundamental changes in the political system. Some critics charged that bureaucratism and abuses of power were the inevitable consequences of the dictatorship of the proletariat the Party had imposed on Chinese society. As one intellectual put it, the dictatorship of the proletariat was the root of it all. "Unless we go to the source of the troubles we will only aggravate bureaucratism and sectarianism by trying to combat them."[138] For those who took this position the solution was drastic: to eliminate the "absolute leadership of the Party," to allow for a free press "even if it means opposition to the Communist party," and to permit democratic parties to attempt to control the government through free elections.[139] Theirs was, in short, a proposal to institute liberal democracy.

Needless to say, criticisms such as these were totally unacceptable to either Mao or the central leadership of the Party. Beginning on June 8, therefore, little more than a month after it had begun, the "blooming and contending" of the Hundred Flowers period was brought to an abrupt end. Editorials appeared questioning the motives of the Party's critics and refuting their analysis of Party programs and policies. Mao's speech "On the Correct Handling of Contradictions Among the People," which had been paraphrased but not published, finally appeared in *Jen-min jih-pao* on June 19.[140] But it had additions clearly limiting criticism of the Party and of the Chinese political system.* From then until mid-October a brief but intense antirightist campaign was conducted throughout China against Party members and non-Party intellectuals whose criticisms had violated Mao's retroactive guidelines. Some prominent "rightists" made self-criticisms before the National People's Congress in June; some were subjected to struggle sessions and then sent off to penal camps to receive "reeducation through labor." For others, the antirightist campaign created such humiliation and anguish that they committed suicide. Nor were Party members spared harsh punishment. In at least twelve provinces of-

---

*The limitations on acceptable criticism were contained in the six criteria for "distinguishing fragrant flowers from poisonous weeds" that appeared in the June version of Mao's speech; words and deeds should help to unite, not divide, the people of all China's nationalities: should be beneficial, not harmful, to socialist transformation and socialist construction; should help to consolidate, not undermine or weaken, democratic centralism; should help to strengthen, not "shake off" or weaken, the leadership of the Communist Party; and should be beneficial, not harmful, to international socialist unity and the unity of the peace-loving people of the world. *Selected Works of Mao Tse-tung*, vol. 5, p. 412.

ficials who had taken "rightist" positions on collectivization in the preceding years, or who had joined non-Communists in criticizing the Party during the Hundred Flowers period, were either dismissed from their posts or
expelled from the Party altogether. This aspect of the antirightist campaign, which occurred in late 1957 and early 1958, led to the dismissal of
one provincial first secretary, four governors, ten vice-governors, and
eighteen members of the standing committees of provincial Party committees, and some forty other high-ranking provincial officials. It also led to
the dismissal of lower-level cadres linked to them either by personal connections or by common policy preferences.[141] All told, according to Frederick Teiwes, between 15 percent and 40 percent of the leadership of the
democratic parties, and between 2 percent and 3 percent of the members
of the Communist Party itself, were labeled as "rightists" during the antirightist campaign.[142] The label, in many cases, was not removed until
after Mao's death.

The Hundred Flowers period of May and early June 1957 marked the
climax of the most serious debate over organizational questions since the
establishment of the People's Republic in 1949. To conclude our discussion of China's first organizational crisis, let us consider the ways in which
the Party and state became administrative problems, raised political issues, and posed social dilemmas during this dramatic period.

In the formative stage of the crisis, discussed in the preceding chapter,
Chinese leaders believed their principal organizational problems to be the
high cost and limited planning capability of the Party and state bureaucracies. Consequently, the organizational policies discussed or adopted in
1955–56—retrenchment, decentralization, mobilization, and professionalization—were all efforts to improve the skills and efficiency of the nation's
political organizations.

These same problems continued to plague Chinese leaders in 1956–57.
The debate over decentralization continued, and the final decisions on the
matter were not taken until the Third Plenum in September 1957. By
increasing the economic responsibilities of the Party and government, the
High Tide of 1955–56 effectively nullified the accomplishments of the retrenchment drive of 1955–56 and forced the Party to launch a second such
campaign in 1956–57.

But the second stage of the crisis was less concerned with skills and efficiency than with the alienation of the Chinese people from the Party and
the government. In the first ten months of 1956 a series of domestic and
foreign developments began to undermine the authority of the Party
and the political system it had created—the High Tide produced popular
expectations that the economy could not meet, de-Stalinization brought

the superiority of socialist political structures into serious question, and the uprisings in Hungary and Poland gave tacit sanction to the expression of popular dissent in China. Together, these events forced the Chinese leadership to confront a problem they had not had to face since 1952: the need to maintain close relations between the Party and the people, to preserve the Party's prestige, and to sustain popular support for the Party's programs.

Virtually all Chinese leaders could agree on the nature of the problem they faced; thus, unlike later arguments, the hot debate of 1956–57 was less over the diagnosis of the country's political malady than over the most suitable remedy. The proposals for reform presented during and after the Eighth Party Congress varied in two familiar dimensions. First, should the Party rely on structural or motivational reforms? Those who favored further rationalization of the bureaucracy and those who advocated democratization both agreed that the need was for structural change that would make governing organizations more responsive to popular demands. The proponents of political education and rectification, in contrast, argued that the solution could be found in changing the attitudes and work styles of Party cadres so that they would work better with non-Party officials, understand local conditions more fully, and resolve social and economic problems through discussion and debate, rather than through coercion.

A second issue was whether the Party and government could reform themselves or whether they would have to be subjected to criticism from the outside. Should organizational reforms, in other words, be implemented through an open-door or closed-door process? The proponents of democratization and of external criticism agreed that closed-door approaches would not suffice, and that the bureaucracy needed outside supervision. They disagreed, of course, over the source. Some favored greater roles for legislative bodies and popular representatives, others for trade unions and mass organizations, and still others for non-Party intellectuals and the democratic parties. The proponents of rationalization and rectification, in contrast, seemed to believe that internal reform would suffice, and some argued strongly that external criticism, especially from intellectuals, would tend to exacerbate the problem rather than solve it.

The proposals presented by various Party and government officials in late 1956 and early 1957 corresponded very closely to their official responsibilities. As Graham Allison might have predicted, "where they stood" was strongly influenced by "where they sat."[143] Thus, the minister of supervision argued for more stringent bureaucratic controls over errant cadres; important Party administrators like Liu Shao-ch'i and Liu Lan-t'ao advocated rectification; Li Wei-han, the director of the United Front Work Department, supported criticism by non-Party intellectuals and the

democratic parties; the head of the trade unions, Lai Jo-yü, argued that
mass organizations could be a powerful weapon against bureaucratism;
and Chou En-lai and Li Fu-ch'un, the principal government managers,
sought to rationalize the bureaucracy through decentralization of power
and reorganization of the economic planning system. This correlation between official position and political stand was not perfect. Tung Pi-wu,
although in charge of the Party's control system, emphasized the role of
people's congresses, not discipline or rectification, in preventing popular
alienation from the Party. Teng Hsiao-p'ing, although a Party administrator like Liu Shao-ch'i, favored external criticism, while Liu did not. Despite these exceptions, however, the distribution of opinion on the organizational issue did suggest that bureaucratic specialization was producing
divergent views on organizational problems.

Mao's own reservations about the place of bureaucracy in a revolutionary state developed a step further during the Hundred Flowers
period. In the preceding chapter we saw that he had concluded by late
1955 that rationalization had produced an undesirable degree of economic
and political conservatism. This he still believed, but he also offered three
additional criticisms of bureaucracy during the winter of 1956–57. First,
rationalization, despite its emphasis on regular reports and inspections,
had actually reduced the amount and adequacy of information circulating
in the Party and government. Mao complained that "leading comrades" at
the central and provincial levels were no longer aware of problems at the
grass roots and did not understand "ideological trends among the masses."[144] One reason for this was that the institution of ranks and hierarchy
was preventing subordinates from offering criticism, or even expressing
opinions, to their superiors.[145]

Second, rationalization was contributing to the alienation of the people
from their governing institutions. At the Second Plenum, Mao expressed
his concern that the privileged life style and routine work style of the
bureaucracy were creating officials who "have not a single kind word for
[the masses] but only take them to task, and . . . don't bother to solve any
of the problems the masses may have." He warned that if Party and government officials continued to employ a bureaucratic style of work, they
might "grow into an aristocratic stratum divorced from the people."[146]

Finally, and most basically, Mao was convinced that rationalization had
promoted selfishness among officials, rather than a selfless commitment to
principle or to service to the people. He had been appalled by the behavior
of some Party cadres when they were assigned civil service ranks in 1955
and 1956. Some had complained about their low ratings, and others even
had gone on hunger strikes in protest. In January 1957 Mao pointed out
that "some cadres now scramble for fame and fortune and are interested

only in personal gain."[147] A month later he noted "a dangerous tendency
. . . among many of our personnel—an unwillingness to share weal and
woe with the masses, a concern with personal fame and gain."[148] He had
warned in 1949 that such developments might occur after the revolution
had triumphed, but his statements in 1957 indicated that he traced the
problem not just to the fact that the Party was now in power, but more
specifically to the establishment of bureaucratic ranks and the elimination
of the supply system.[149]

The Hundred Flowers period marked the end of the Party's brief flirtation with organizational rationalization. It is significant that those who
believed that the problems of popular alienation could be solved by further
rationalization were in the minority—and it is even more telling that their
views did not prevail. Instead, there was widespread agreement that it was
time to restore some abandoned elements of the Party's own organizational
heritage. In the first stage of the crisis Mao revived the campaign style,
despite the opposition of those who believed it was not an appropriate way
to promote economic development. In the second stage it was open-door
rectification that he attempted to resurrect. And even though his proposal
that criticism should be especially sought from non-Party intellectuals
caused controversy, his call for a Party rectification campaign received
widespread support.

But the emerging consensus that the Party should return to its organizational heritage did not constitute a radical critique of bureaucracy. No one,
except for a few disgruntled students and university professors, was yet
ready to suggest that bureaucracy in China should be destroyed and replaced by some other form of organization. That demand would not
emerge until China's second organizational crisis, the Great Proletarian
Cultural Revolution.

6

The Great Leap Forward and Its Aftermath 1957-1962

The intense criticism by students, non-Party intellectuals, and even younger Party cadres during May 1957 required not only that Party leaders bring the Hundred Flowers period to an end, but that they also reassess the broader rectification campaign of which it had been part. What had been the results of the movement to date? Had the choice of open-door rectification techniques been appropriate? Should the campaign be continued or terminated? If the decision was made to continue, what form should the movement take?

Not surprisingly, Mao Tse-tung, as the principal sponsor of open-door rectification, tried to present the Hundred Flowers period in the best possible light.* It only appeared, he argued, that the Party had been placed on the defensive by the criticism expressed in May and early June. In fact, the Party had maintained the initiative throughout. He claimed, somewhat unconvincingly, to have fully anticipated that "poisonous weeds" would emerge during the course of the campaign and to have deliberately invited criticism as a way of exposing and uprooting them. In this way dissent had been isolated in "many small Hungarian incidents," rather than being allowed to coalesce into a single major outbreak that might have posed a real danger to the regime.[1]

Thus, in Mao's analysis the Hundred Flowers period had actually produced significant accomplishments. Party and government officials were "discarding the Kuomintang style of work and their uppity airs."[2] The antirightist campaign had isolated and weakened those who opposed the regime and had actually won over perhaps 80 percent of those who had doubted the superiority of socialism. And through the exposure and criticism of the rightists, the political consciousness of the people had risen to a considerable degree.[3]

---

*The development of Mao's assessment of the Hundred Flowers period can be traced in the following 1957 speeches printed in the *Selected Works of Mao Tse-tung*, vol. 5, pp. 448–513: "Things Are Beginning to Change" (May 15), "Muster Our Forces to Repulse the Rightists' Wild Attacks" (June 8), "Beat Back the Attacks of the Bourgeois Rightists" (July 9), "The Situation in the Summer of 1957" (July), "Be Activists in Promoting the Revolution" (October 9), and "Have Firm Faith in the Majority of the People" (October 13).

Mao refused to admit that to encourage criticism had been a mistake, and he even asserted that similar open-door rectification campaigns should be repeated in the future. Since the results of the campaign would probably be relatively transient ("That's how people are; they have a short memory"), rectification campaigns would have to be repeated from time to time, perhaps as often as every two or three years.[4] Subsequent campaigns might be briefer and, accordingly, less intense.[5] However, they would still use the same format, that of speaking out freely, airing views fully, holding great debates, and writing big-character posters. "It is a new form created by the masses which is different from other forms employed by our Party in the past."[6] Mao concluded that the revolution had "found a form well suited to its content."[7]

Based on this optimistic analysis of the campaign's progress, Mao proposed not only that rectification be continued, but that it be extended to the basic levels of the Party and state where it had not yet begun. At a conference of provincial Party secretaries in Tsingtao in July, Mao argued that the two purposes of rectification had been to reform the work style of the Party and government through "a free airing of views," and to persuade the bourgeoisie to accept "socialist transformation" through an antirightist campaign. The rectification campaign could therefore be divided into a number of stages. The first stage, directed against the bureaucracy, had occurred in May and early June; the country was then, in July, in the middle of the second stage, directed against the rightists. But once the antirightist campaign was over, the Party and government would once again become the principal targets of rectification. In a third stage, the bureaucracy would be expected to adopt the "correct" suggestions presented by its critics. And in a final stage, officials should study the campaign's major documents, engage in criticism and self-criticism, and raise their individual consciousness.[8] Thus, the antirightist campaign should not mean the end of rectification. Indeed, rectification could proceed more smoothly now that "the rightists' wild attacks had been repulsed by the people."[9]

Mao recognized that not everyone was likely to agree with his analysis of the outcome of the Hundred Flowers period, or with his proposal that rectification be continued. He acknowledged that there were those who wished to halt the rectification campaign for the sake of political stability: "Some comrades have been afraid that chaos would spread across the land." He admitted, too, that others wanted to stop the campaign to avoid criticism of their own performance: "Everybody says he wants [tempering]. To talk about it is very easy, but when it comes to the real thing, when it means being 'forged' with a pneumatic hammer, he backs away, scared stiff."[10]

Such opposition did indeed exist. There were Party leaders who refused to accept Mao's conclusion that the political consciousness of the people had risen. In their view, the people's confidence in the Party's leadership and in the superiority of the socialist system had been shaken and had to be restored. As Roderick MacFarquhar has shown, P'eng Chen, Lu Ting-i, and their subordinates in the Peking municipal apparatus and in the Party's propaganda department insisted that the main task now should be continued criticism of the rightists, not rectification of the Party and the government, and both publicly and privately they gave vent to loosely veiled criticisms of Mao's management of the rectification campaign.[11]

Still, Mao was able to win some important supporters for his proposal that rectification be continued. At the National People's Congress in June, in a political report devoted primarily to criticism of the rightists, Chou En-lai loyally agreed that bureaucratism still existed in China to a serious degree.[12] The following month, Chou's State Council adopted a resolution that the government would therefore resume rectification even before the antirightist campaign had been brought to an end.[13] Similarly, K'o Ch'ing-shih, the first secretary of Shanghai, said in August that rectification definitely would not be abandoned halfway because of the antirightist struggle. K'o sought to disillusion anyone in Shanghai who might have hoped that P'eng Chen, Lu Ting-i, and their supporters might bring the rectification campaign to an end. Indeed, by warning that there was no basis for doubting that rectification ("contending and blooming") would continue, K'o not only supported Mao's proposal for proceeding with rectification, but also defended Mao's original choice of method.[14]

RECTIFICATION REDEFINED

A compromise was reached by early fall between these conflicting positions, and was described in Teng Hsiao-p'ing's report on rectification to the Third Plenum on September 23.[15] On the one hand, as Mao had proposed at the Tsingtao Conference, the antirightist campaign would be brought to a close, and rectification would move on to the third and fourth stages (reform and study) in Party and government offices at the county level and above. Rectification would also be started at the basic levels, although by methods different from those used in the middle and upper levels of the bureaucracy. Speaking to those who wanted to bring rectification to a halt, Teng argued that "the movement should be carried on to a still further stage and on a still broader scale. It should not be wound up hastily, and should not be started strong and ended weak." Indeed, in Teng's analysis, the stages of reform and study should be considered even more important than the antirightist campaign.[16]

On the other hand, in response to the concern many Party leaders felt about the effects of the Hundred Flowers period on popular opinion, the rectification campaign was modified in three important respects: its targets were broadened, its purposes were redefined, and its methods were almost completely transformed.

The principal targets of the rectification campaign had originally been Party cadres, despite Mao's argument that permitting non-Party intellectuals to participate in the campaign would help remold their political outlook. Now, however, the campaign was expanded to encompass the entire society. It was transformed from a Party rectification campaign into a nationwide socialist education movement.

The intellectuals, predictably, were the prime focus of this retargeting. But workers and peasants were targets as well. In the more liberal atmosphere of late 1956 and early 1957, wealthier peasants had engaged in speculation, had refused to sell their surplus grain to the state, had sought to withdraw from membership in the agricultural producers' cooperatives, and had tried to return to private farming. Even poorer peasants were said to be wavering in their commitment to collectivization because of the growing gap between rural and urban incomes and the poor performance of the agricultural sector in both 1956 and 1957. And as we have seen, workers had also expressed dissatisfaction with both their material standard of living and the authoritarian manner in which some Party officials managed the factories. Workers were not expected to hold such views in a socialist country, so Teng Hsiao-p'ing had to explain that their discontent reflected the peasant, student, and city-poor origins of a large number of workers, particularly the younger ones, and the influence of petty bourgeois ideology. To deal with these problems, a "socialist education campaign" was to be launched in both factories and villages in late 1957 to strengthen the workers' and peasants' "determination to walk the socialist road."[17]

In a related development, much greater emphasis was now placed on the reeducation of younger cadres, particularly those with intellectual backgrounds, in discussions of cadre rectification. The complaints many younger officials had expressed about the Party's personnel policies—their criticism of the seniority principle and their denigration of older cadres as being uneducated and fossilized, for instance—were taken as evidence of "liberalism," "selfishness," "anarchism," "egalitarianism," and "lack of consciousness."[18] In fact, senior Party leaders now warned that the large numbers of young cadres with intellectual backgrounds posed a real danger to the Party. Hupei provincial authorities, for example, complained that fully 40 percent of their 220,000 cadres were young intellectuals who had assumed office since 1949.[19] Similarly, in Shanghai, 80 percent of the city's 267,000 officials had entered the bureaucracy since liberation, and most of these were recorded as being from bourgeois rather than worker-peasant backgrounds.[20] These younger cadres were described as being ignorant of the basic processes of production, particularly in agriculture; unfamiliar with the life, thinking, and feelings of the working people; and unaware of the strength and intelligence of the masses.[21] To rely on such young people before their political consciousness had been raised would be to act "like the peasant in the fable who tried to help the rice grow quicker by pulling at the young plants."[22]

These changes in the targets of the rectification campaign were closely linked to changes in the purposes of the movement. Originally, rectification had been designed to combat subjectivism, sectarianism, and bureaucratism among cadres. At the Third Plenum, however, two of these three problems underwent a significant redefinition.

When the problem had first been identified in April 1956, following Khrushchev's denunciation of Stalin, subjectivism had essentially meant dogmatism: the mechanical application of Russian, particularly Stalinist, principles and policies to China, and the suppression of dissent and criticism by administrative measures. In China after the Hungarian uprising, and especially after the Hundred Flowers period, subjectivism came to mean not dogmatism, but rather revisionism and bourgeois ideology. And these rightist deviations were said to be characteristic not only of workers, peasants, and intellectuals, but also of many cadres—cadres who had allegedly sponsored the attempts of wealthier peasants to withdraw from the collectives, shared the doubts of poorer peasants about the superiority of collectivized agriculture, and supported the demands of workers for higher wages. The problem was no longer seen as political rigidity, but rather as political vacillation and as a lack of genuine socialist consciousness within the ranks of cadres.

Sectarianism, too, was redefined. Sectarianism had originally referred to strained relations between Party officials and non-Party intellectuals and between Party members and non-Party members within the government and mass organizations. Now, however, because non-Party intellectuals were considered less essential to China's development than they had been in 1956, this aspect of sectarianism received much less attention. Instead, sectarianism had come to mean the alienation of Party officials from the ordinary people as reflected in their failure to engage in physical labor, their higher living standards, and their tendency toward special privileges. Within the bureaucracy it was also used to describe the tensions between local cadres and outside cadres that had been revealed in a large number of provinces during the Hundred Flowers period.

Only the definition of bureaucratism survived this process relatively unchanged. In his report to the Third Plenum, Teng Hsiao-p'ing spoke of irrational regulations in the bureaucracy, the excessive number of functionaries in the Party and government organs, and the tendency of many officials to ignore the reasonable, different, and opposing views of the people—all of which had been important targets for criticism during earlier phases of the rectification campaign.[23]

These changes in the targets and purposes of rectification led quite logically to changes in the methods by which the campaign would be conducted. At Mao's insistence, open-door rectification, free discussion, and wall posters (*ta-tzu-pao*) were all retained. But there was still ample room for change within this fixed framework. First of all, the special role of non-Party intellectuals in open-door rectification was abolished. Henceforth, rectification in middle- and upper-level Party and government offices was to involve not criticism of Party leaders by non-Party members, but criticism of superiors by their subordinates, who might or might not be Party members. Second, the balance of power between leaders and led—between the targets of criticism and their critics—was substantially shifted in favor of the leaders. In the past the emphasis had been on the rectification of leaders; now equal stress was to be placed on the rectification (or "socialist education") of the populace and of younger officials. Leaders were still supposed to accept criticism, but they were also authorized to reject and refute incorrect views.[24] Third, the importance of criticism and open-door techniques as instruments of rectification was reduced. As we will see below, physical labor, which had been mentioned in the original directive on rectification in late April but had been overshadowed by the "blooming and contending" that followed, was reintroduced into the rectification campaign on a mammoth scale.

RECTIFICATION CONTINUED

The rectification campaign now had three components: at the basic levels, rectification of cadres was coupled with socialist education of workers and peasants; at the provincial and central levels, blooming and contending was resumed, but with lower-level officials, rather than non-Party intellectuals, as the principal participants; and throughout the bureaucracy, an intense hsia-fang campaign was begun combining the goals of organizational retrenchment and political reeducation. In this section we will discuss each of these three components in turn.

Rectification at the Basic Levels

The Central Committee in its April 27 directive had envisioned a rectification of all Party and government cadres from the center to the basic levels. But it supplied clear guidelines only for the conduct of the campaign at the county level and above and indicated that basic-level rectification would come later, as the second stage in a rather lengthy campaign. Accordingly, the provincial directives on rectification that appeared in May all provided that rectification would not begin at the basic levels until the fall, or even January 1958, only after it had been completed at the middle and upper levels of the bureaucracy.

By the time fall came, much had changed, and the agenda for political and organizational work at the basic levels had become a lengthy one: to conduct a socialist education movement among the workers and peasants, to carry out a purge of any rank-and-file members of the Party who had exhibited rightist tendencies during the Hundred Flowers period, to correct the cadres' inclinations toward rightism and localism, and to halt their commandist treatment of the masses. Of these, rightist tendencies among the cadres were described as the most serious problem. As one article explained, many rural cadres had become uncertain about the superiority of collectivization, or suspected that the majority of peasants now opposed collective farming. As a result, they were hesitant to conduct a vigorous struggle against the "landlords and bad elements" who were allegedly responsible for leading the poor and middle peasants astray. "The fundamental fact here," the article said, "is that since the Party organizations and Party cadres in the rural areas are constantly exposed to the bad influence of the peasants, particularly the well-to-do middle peasants, they can easily be affected by the rightist mentality." Thus, the success of socialist education depended on the rectification of rightist tendencies among the cadres: "The more thoroughly the rightist mentality is criticized within the Party, the better able we are to criticize capitalist thought [among the peasants]."[25]

The Party leadership decided that a single mechanism, "guided mass debate," could solve all these political and organizational problems at the basic level. In such a debate, workers and peasants would be encouraged to express their doubts about Party policies and their criticisms of the performance and attitude of individual cadres. If the criticisms were "correct," the cadres were supposed to accept them. But if they were "incorrect," the cadres were to subject them to criticism at an opportune moment and then guide the discussion until the masses recognized that "truth is on the side of the Party."*

Guided mass debates combined Mao's continuing interest in open-door

---

Cheng-chih hsüeh-hsi, no. 9 (1957), in *Extracts from China Mainland Magazines*, no. 106 (4.xi.57), pp. 3–5. More specifically, the goals of the guided mass debates were as follows. In the rural areas, peasants were to "recollect the past and make comparisons" with the present, and thus to understand the relative superiority of the socialist system; to study the living standards of peasants in the Soviet Union, and thus to realize that an even better future lay ahead; and to discuss the need to consolidate the collectives, restrict private farming, and support state purchases of grain. In the factories, the workers were to be led to understand the need for discipline and for responsibility to the collective, and to realize that improved standards of living could not be achieved in the absence of increases in industrial productivity. The purposes of the mass debates are well summarized by Teng Hsiao-p'ing, in Robert R. Bowie and John King Fairbank, eds., *Communist China, 1955–1959: Policy Documents with Analysis* (Cambridge, Mass., 1962), pp. 341–63.

rectification with the Third Plenum's decision to promote socialist education among workers and peasants. Most discussions of this technique,
however, emphasized the second purpose, political indoctrination. In the
past, one article explained, propaganda had merely been education from
above. Cadres simply propagated Party principles and policies and told the
peasants what they should do and what they should not do. The peasants
played a passive role in this process, and there was no way of exposing and
refuting their negative views. Now the peasants and workers would be
encouraged to speak up, but they were to be firmly guided to correct conclusions. In case anyone missed the point, the article assured those who
feared that the mass debates would be as disorderly as blooming and contending had been that "to encourage debate is just a good method of incul-
cating obedience in the minds of the peasants."[26]

The guided mass debates were supplemented by two additional forms of
rectification. To deal with the most serious instances of rightism among
cadres, meetings were to be held at the county seats and attended by cadres from the county and its districts and townships. As Teng Hsiao-p'ing
described them, the meetings would criticize various rightist ideological
trends, and would struggle against cadres who "seriously violate the law
and Party discipline."[27] Second, the efforts to democratize basic-level organizations, particularly by establishing workers' congresses and congresses of agricultural producers' cooperatives, were continued. But once
again the emphasis was placed as much on mobilizing and maintaining
mass support as on checking abuses by local officials. Teng Hsiao-p'ing
described the democratization of the cooperatives:

It must be borne in mind that even if all the enterprises we promote are fully
correct and greatly successful, if they have not been decided after earnest discussion by the masses, there will be dissatisfaction. And in fact there will be portions
of our work which fail or do not produce the desired effects. If they have not been
discussed by the masses, the masses will blame us. But if everything is done
through the decision of the masses, even losses will be borne by all, all will learn
the lesson, and unity and correction [of mistakes] will be easier.[28]

These new forms of political participation at the basic levels, guided
mass debates and the democratization of basic-level organizations under
continuing Party leadership, were described as a version of the mass line.
But compared to the process of blooming and contending in the spring,
they represented a quite different balance between leaders and led. There
was not to be any mobilization of unrestricted criticism by people who
were known to be wavering in their political commitment; there was rather
to be guided and restricted criticism by those who, as Mao had put it, were
assumed to be "on our side."[29] Liu Shao-ch'i explained that this kind of
participation constituted a guided form of democracy, in contrast to the

unlimited or anarchic democracy of blooming and contending, and thus could promote basic-level rectification and socialist education without creating national turmoil.[30]

Rectification at the Center and in the Provinces

As we have seen, the first phase of rectification in the spring of 1957, proceeded on no fewer than three tracks. One, the official track, consisted of meetings called by central and provincial Party agencies to discuss ways in which the bureaucracy's style of work might be improved. The second, a semiofficial track, was sponsored by Mao and Li Wei-han and consisted of a series of forums, held outside the Party, in which non-Party intellectuals were asked to present their criticisms of Party officials and policies. The third, an unofficial track, consisted of the student movement that emerged spontaneously in Peking and at universities and middle schools in other major cities.

The antirightist campaign marked the end of the second and third types of rectification, but it simultaneously saw the intensification of the first. In part, this was because many Chinese leaders still believed that the performance of the bureaucracy could stand improvement, and that some form of rectification would be necessary to achieve it. Leaders as different as Hsi Chung-hsün and K'o Ch'ing-shih expressed this view in remarkably similar terms. In November 1957 Hsi justified continued rectification of the State Council by warning against "attempting to overcome bureaucratism by bureaucratic means."[31] The following month, in a report to the Shanghai Party Committee, K'o declared, "We cannot fight bureaucratism with bureaucratism."[32] But the continuation of rectification after the antirightist campaign also reflected the Party's desire to demonstrate that it was still willing to undertake necessary reforms despite the criticisms it had received the previous spring.

When rectification at the upper and middle levels resumed after the antirightist campaign, the emphasis was initially placed on sifting through the criticisms made by non-Party intellectuals during the Hundred Flowers period, separating the correct from the incorrect, and adopting constructive criticisms and proposals. This effort was in line with Mao's assessment that, overall, more than 90 percent of the views aired in the spring were valid, and the rightist ones were a tiny fraction.[33] As early as July it was reported that various ministries of the central government had established ad hoc task forces to review the proposals made during the Hundred Flowers period, and that some had already decided to require more physical labor of cadres, revise the procedures for handling letters from the people, improve the reception of visitors, and end various kinds of preferential treatment and perquisites for high officials.[34]

Within a few months, however, it was decided to generate more suggestions and criticisms. The same methods were used as in the spring: wall posters, rallies, forums, and study groups. But the participants were different. Rather than calling on non-Party intellectuals, the Party now asked middle- and low-level cadres and office workers to air their views. In essence, then, late 1957 saw a return of the Hundred Flowers, but without the "poisonous weeds." The Party sought to demonstrate that ordinary bureaucrats could make suggestions for change that were more numerous, more valid, and more workable than those presented by the non-Party intellectuals in the spring.

After the end of the antirightist campaign in October, the effort to solicit suggestions from within the bureaucracy took on an almost frantic tone. By October 22, cadres in Hupei had presented 40,000 suggestions and criticisms. In Honan officials in provincial, municipal, and special district offices had written 90,000 wall posters containing more than 300,000 suggestions.[35] In offices of the central government cadres had displayed 200,000 posters by November 21.[36] The press claimed that the number of criticisms and suggestions had far surpassed the number presented during the Hundred Flowers period. And, of course, the percentage of "correct" or "valid" statements was also much higher.

The flood of bureaucratic self-criticism confronted government and Party leaders with a real problem. The point of this phase of the campaign was to show that the bureaucracy could generate its own recommendations for reform and then put them into practice. But how could such a mass of suggestions be processed effectively? By December 5, faced with more than 855,000 suggestions presented in some 325,000 wall posters and 34,000 meetings, Hsi Chung-hsün finally acknowledged that the central government was in danger of being "overwhelmed by big-character posters."[37] The Party committee responsible for the central government complained that some senior officials were trying to cope with this mass of criticisms by responding to each poster, "The suggestions are correct. We humbly accept them. We hope that you will continue to make suggestions." This, the committee said, was not enough. It was time to launch a "high tide of administrative improvement"—that is, to institute bureaucratic reforms. To this end, the committee demanded on December 5 that the central government agencies adopt 80 percent of the suggestions (some 684,000) within the next ten days.[38]

Although the goal was impractical, the committee's decision turned the rectification campaign from the collection of suggestions to the consideration of reform. Some units began to concentrate on the life style of high-ranking officials and the problem of relations between cadres and the people. This was a logical point of emphasis in Shanghai because, according to K'o Ch'ing-shih, no fewer than 50 percent of the suggestions made by cadres and 35 percent of the wall posters in factories had criticized the arrogance and aloofness of some cadres, their perfunctory attitude when dealing with complaints from the people, their higher standards of living, and their use of personal contacts in determining job assignments and promotions. K'o argued that these problems should be the focus of administrative reform because they were relatively easy to solve and because to do so would demonstrate the Party's sincerity in conducting rectification. To ignore them, on the other hand, would amount to committing new errors and "contracting new debts." Such debts "snowball through compound interest and become heavier and heavier."[39]

Other units, such as the State Economic Commission, dealt with policy questions and work style. Po I-po instructed the commission to consider nine sets of issues: Does the annual plan embody the principle of achieving greater, faster, better, and more economical results? Does it assign the proper priorities to industry and agriculture? Is the planning process based on full understanding of economic conditions or does it reflect subjectivism? Does the plan adequately take Soviet experience into account? Has the commission carried out its administrative retrenchment campaign? Is there still sectarianism in the relations between Party and non-Party officials? Are some officials still behaving in a bureaucratic and authoritarian manner? Are personnel policies and wage policies being implemented properly? And is the work of the commission affected by bourgeois ideology?[40] Similar questions concerning policy, personnel, and work methods were posed to the State Planning Commission by Li Fu-ch'un.[41]

In early 1958, then, the rectification campaign began to turn from addressing the relationship between the bureaucracy and the people, its original purpose, to considering China's policies for social and economic development. Resolving contradictions among the people became less important than combatting waste and conservatism in economic planning. As we will see below, the redefinition of the rectification campaign at the upper and middle levels of the bureaucracy provided the organizational link between the Hundred Flowers and the Great Leap Forward.

Hsia-fang

The Central Committee's April 27 directive on rectification had indicated that criticism and self-criticism were to comprise only one facet of the Party's rectification campaign. Another was to be a program of physical labor for cadres instituted on the assumption that the contradiction between leaders and the led stemmed in large part from the fact that cadres engaged primarily in mental labor while the masses worked principally with their hands, and that cadre participation in manual labor would therefore help bridge the gap between the officials and the people. Given the political drama and tension generated by the blooming and contending of May, it is not surprising that, despite the publication of a supplementary Central Committee directive on physical labor on May 14, the first phase of the rectification campaign saw little attention to this side of the plan.[42] After the Third Plenum, however, what had been a distinctly secondary aspect of rectification suddenly assumed greater importance. In October and November alone, 510,000 cadres were sent to engage in physical labor, followed by another 520,000 in December and January.[43]

In some ways, this program of physical labor for cadres was an extension of the Hsia-fang campaign of 1956–57, but there were two important differences. For one thing, the number of cadres participating in the movement was significantly greater in late 1957 and early 1958 than it had been in 1956–57. As we saw in the previous chapter, it took seven months (mid-November 1956 to mid-June 1957) to transfer 300,000 cadres during the earlier campaign. More than three times that many were transferred during the four months between October 1957 and early February 1958. For another, the purposes of the two campaigns were substantially different. The earlier movement had been aimed at reducing administrative costs and strengthening local leadership by shifting unneeded urban bureaucrats to positions in the countryside and in factories, but the campaign of 1957–58 was seen as a method of political reeducation. Indeed, one editorial in the Liaoning provincial newspaper explicitly told cadres that hsia-fang should no longer be seen simply as a mechanism for organizational retrenchment, but also as a new way of raising the political consciousness of deskbound officials.[44]

These changes in the purposes of the new Hsia-fang campaign were reflected in changes in the type of cadres reassigned and the destinations to which they were sent. In 1955 and in 1956–57, when administrative retrenchment was the principal rationale for reassignment, the cadres who were selected to participate in the campaign were usually officials of worker or peasant background who had recently been promoted to middle-level positions. These cadres were ideal candidates to be sent back to the countryside or to factories to strengthen leadership at the basic levels. In 1957–58, however, when political education was the principal purpose of hsia-fang, the emphasis was placed on the reassignment of younger cadres, especially those from bourgeois backgrounds. These cadres were believed to be particularly susceptible to bourgeois ideology and to rightist influences, and it was expected that a stint of physical labor would be necessary if they were to develop a "revolutionary character."

There was a corresponding change in the destinations to which transferred officials were sent. In the earlier retrenchment campaigns most officials had been sent to factories, rural areas, or lower-level Party and government posts to serve in leadership positions. Only some 33 percent of the 300,000 Party and government cadres participating in the 1955–56 Hsia-fang movement were assigned to production posts. In 1957–58, however, the overwhelming majority of participants were sent to serve as physical laborers rather than as leaders. Press accounts stressed that they received such assignments as construction work, office cleaning, and planting and harvesting.[45] In Kwangtung it was reported that 83 percent of the cadres involved in the Hsia-fang campaign were engaged in physical labor; in Anhwei the proportion was 90 percent.[46] On a nationwide basis, it is likely that between 70 and 80 percent of the cadres receiving reassignments during the 1957–58 Hsia-fang campaign were sent down to do manual work. Even those who were not transferred to new assignments were expected to spend at least one month each year in physical labor.[47]

Despite these important differences, there was at least one major similarity between the Hsia-fang campaigns of 1955–56 and 1957–58, the need to overcome the reluctance of most cadres to participate. There was public acknowledgment, for example, that reassignment to a period of physical labor represented a cataclysmic change in a cadre's life.[48] To make that change more tolerable, cadres were sent to suburban areas or to their native districts whenever possible, rather than to assignments in the border provinces, or else were given some degree of choice in deciding their destination. Once they arrived, their reception and treatment was jointly the responsibility of their original offices and the local Party committees, and they were periodically visited by cadres who were not participants in the program.[49] Most important, cadres were promised that their assignments would be temporary, and that enthusiastic participation in the campaign would be rewarded. Hsi Chung-hsün, who was in charge of the central government's hsia-fang task force, pointed out that "a few years hence, the state will want more cadres."[50] Those who did not have labor experience could expect no further promotions; those who participated grudgingly might have to spend a longer stint than normal; but those who took part enthusiastically could expect to return to the cities after twelve months.[51]

RETURN TO THE CAMPAIGN STYLE

Sometime between the Third Plenum in September and the end of the year, Chinese leaders decided to try, once again, to accelerate the country's rate of economic growth through mass mobilization. Such a decision was considered feasible for a variety of political, economic, organizational, and international reasons. Politically, Mao Tse-tung argued, the Hundred Flowers campaign, the antirightist movement, and the socialist education campaign had all clarified a great many questions and promoted activism.

The result was that the Chinese people were ready for more rapid progress: "The masses' tide of enthusiasm," he said, "is like atomic energy."[52] Economically, the retrenchment of 1957 had brought the state budget back into balance and had generated a surplus of some 1.1 billion yüan, which could now be channeled into productive investment.[53] Organizationally, the decentralization of 1957 had relaxed the degree of central control over the provinces, and thus was judged to have increased the initiative and creativity of local leaders. Internationally, the Soviet sputnik, it was argued, had demonstrated the superiority of the socialist system and had thus allayed some of the doubts that had plagued the socialist countries after de-Stalinization. The Moscow Conference in November had strengthened the unity of the socialist camp, and the capitalist world, in contrast, was seen to be increasingly weakened and divided by the movements for independence in Africa. As Mao put it in November 1957 during his visit to Moscow, it was not the west wind that was prevailing over the east wind, but the east wind prevailing over the west wind.[54]

Moreover, Chinese leaders apparently believed that an acceleration of economic growth was necessary for domestic political reasons. The protests and demonstrations of late 1956 and early 1957 had shown the political consequences of an economic slowdown, and Chinese leaders may have felt that the way to prevent similar crises of legitimacy from recurring was to maintain high rates of economic growth. Liu Shao-ch'i explained in May 1958 that the economic retrenchment policies of late 1956 and early 1957, intended to reduce tension in the economic sphere, had actually produced tension in the country's political life. "Some say that speeding up construction makes people feel tense, and so it's better to slow down the tempo," Liu told the second session of the Eighth Party Congress. "But are things not going to get tense if the speed of construction is slowed down? Surely one should be able to see that a really terribly tense situation would exist if more than 600 million people had to live in poverty and cultural backwardness for a prolonged period."[55] Similarly, in late 1957 Mao began to develop his concept of "uninterrupted revolution," which held that mass enthusiasm could be sustained only if new tasks and higher targets were constantly put forward after previous goals had been attained. Mao explained it in January 1958: "In making revolution one must strike while the iron is hot—one revolution must follow another, the revolution must continually advance."[56] Or, as he rephrased the same point somewhat later, "Our revolutions are like battles. After a victory, we must at once put forward a new task. In this way, cadres and the masses will forever be filled with revolutionary fervor instead of conceit."[57]

It was clear, too, that despite the shortcomings of the High Tide of

1955–56, mass mobilization might be the only feasible way to achieve higher rates of growth in the short run. Most students of Sino-Soviet relations believe that at the Moscow Conference the Soviet Union made it clear that China could not expect to receive any additional credits during the Chinese Second Five-Year Plan, scheduled to begin in 1958. At the same time, despite better weather in 1957 than in 1956, the material incentives introduced in late 1956 and early 1957 to increase agricultural production did not seem to be working. In fact, the growth in agricultural output was lower in 1957 than in 1956; grain production was only 1 percent greater in 1957 than in 1956, and was not even keeping pace with increases in population.[58]

In late 1957 and early 1958 Chinese leaders adopted a series of decisions based on these assessments that laid the foundation for the Great Leap Forward. At the Third Plenum Mao reintroduced the slogan "greater, faster, better, and more economical results"—the 1955–56 High Tide theme that had been set aside during the economic retrenchment of 1956–57.[59] At the same time Teng Hsiao-p'ing announced that Mao's twelve-year agricultural program would be resurrected and that, in line with its provisions, a mass movement to construct water conservancy projects would be conducted during the slack winter farming season.[60] In December Li Fu-ch'un revealed that the draft Second Five-Year Plan, which had been based on the principles of smooth and balanced growth, reasonable targets, and respect for financial limitations, would have to be adjusted.[61] He set a new goal: China was to overtake Great Britain in the output of major industrial products within fifteen years.[62] This new mood of optimism was summarized in the 1958 New Year's Day editorial, appropriately entitled "Full Steam Ahead!": "The world is what man makes it. Pessimism, doubt, and conservatism [should be eliminated]. We ride with the wind and march forward."[63]

Shortly thereafter Mao Tse-tung began an extended tour of China during which he visited a variety of basic-level units throughout the country and attempted to plumb the mood of the country, gather ideas, and generate enthusiasm for the coming campaign. The Party also convened a series of conferences to discuss plans for the campaign—a second session of the Eighth Party Congress in May and central work conferences in Hangchow and Nanning in January, Chengtu in February and March, Hankow in April, and Peitaiho in August. At first glance, these work conferences of provincial leaders seemed reminiscent of the July 1955 conference on agricultural collectivization, the November 1955 conferences on the twelve-year agricultural program in Hangchow and Tientsin, or the January 1957 conference on Party rectification—conferences at which Mao attempted to circumvent opposition at the center by appealing for support to provincial Party secretaries. In early 1958, however, Mao faced relatively little opposition in either Peking or the provinces. The provincial leaders who would have been most likely to resist had been silenced by the antirightist campaign. At the same time, a surprising number of central leaders, including such economic planners as Li Hsien-nien, Li Fu-ch'un, and Po I-po, seemed to support the call of Mao and Liu for an acceleration of economic growth. Only Chou En-lai, Ch'en Yün, and Teng Tzu-hui appear to have been skeptical, but Chou was probably loyal to Mao once the decision had been made, and Teng and Ch'en could rather easily be bypassed as long as other economic planners were willing to cooperate.*

These conferences produced the major concepts behind the Great Leap Forward. By the time of the Chengtu conference in February and March, the first two principles had been formulated. First, rapid economic growth could be sustained only if China developed industry and agriculture simultaneously ("walking on two legs"). Second, agriculture could be developed by using the mobilization of rural labor power and local financial and material resources to construct water conservancy projects and rural industry ("the basic transformation of the rural areas after three years of struggle"). By the Peitaiho conference in August, a third principle had been added. Only through the reorganization of the countryside into communes could there be effected the communitarian and egalitarian social and economic policies needed to generate and sustain mass support and to mobilize and concentrate financial and material resources for the development of rural industry. Together these principles assumed an agricultural sector that would modernize itself self-reliantly. Rural communes would implement their own water-conservancy and land-reclamation projects and produce their own tools, construction materials, and agricultural supplies in local industries. None of this would require the importation of large amounts of machinery or capital from the industrial sector. As a result, the profits generated by industry, combined with the agricultural surpluses extracted from the rapidly modernizing agricultural sector, could be invested almost totally in further industrialization.

These principles provided a broad outline for the Great Leap Forward, but they did not supply much concrete detail. Mao Tse-tung told the Chengtu conference that they already had the basic ideas for the Leap, but that the specifics—the line for building socialism—were still being created. Nor was there any assurance that the new policies were correct. "The

*For discussions of the political controversies surrounding the Great Leap Forward, see Roderick MacFarquhar, "Communist China's Intra-Party Dispute," *Pacific Affairs*, 31 (1958): 323–35; and Jürgen Domes, *The Internal Politics of China, 1949–1972* (London, 1973), chap. 6.

line has already begun to take shape," Mao said, "but it has yet to be perfected and verified in practice. . . . Mistakes will inevitably be committed."[64]

Given the schematic and tentative nature of these guidelines, it was obvious that much of the concrete planning for the Great Leap Forward would have to be done by the ministries and provinces. But how could the bureaucracy, given its tendencies towards conservatism and routinization, adopt its planning procedures to the Great Leap atmosphere? As in the High Tide of 1955–56, the answer seemed to lie in the reintroduction of campaign techniques into bureaucratic operations.

The resurrection of the campaign style began at the Third Plenum, Mao's address to which dealt as much with the bureaucracy's style of work as with the Hundred Flowers period or with the ongoing rectification campaign. At the Hangchow and Nanning conferences, the elements of the campaign style were codified in an important document, "Sixty Points on Working Methods," which was circulated within the Party on February 19.[65] The work style of the Great Leap Forward can be summarized under five headings: (1) a more flexible and rapid policymaking process, (2) a campaign against "waste and conservatism," (3) the assertion of Party control over every aspect of policy, (4) the denigration of the role of specialists and intellectuals, and (5) decentralization of power to the provinces beyond that provided in the November 1957 reforms described in Chapter 4.

More flexible and rapid policymaking. At the heart of the policymaking process advocated during the Great Leap Forward was an emphasis on personal investigation of conditions at the basic levels throughout China. At a Supreme State Conference in January 1958, Mao proposed that, in addition to the ongoing Hsia-fang program, responsible people of the Communist Party, except the old and the sick, should leave Peking for four months every year, "seek the sutras" from the working people, and then return and process what they had learned. Peking—and, by extension, all the rest of the upper and middle levels of the bureaucracy—were like "processing plants," Mao explained. All they could do was to process information and ideas provided from below. And all the raw materials for decision making came entirely from the workers and peasants. "After I've stayed in Peking for a long time, I feel my brain has become empty, but as soon as I leave Peking there is something in there again."[66]

Mao's own extended national tour in early 1958 was seen as the example of personal investigation for other central Party leaders to emulate. Liu Shao-ch'i made his own national tour. Officials attending the Chengtu conference adjourned to make inspections of the surrounding countryside before reconvening. Cadres were encouraged to cultivate their own experimental fields, in which new agricultural techniques could be tested, and to study representative units closely in order to understand the problems and the potential existing at the local levels. Many conferences were held in basic-level units, rather than in government and party offices.[67] All this embodied the notion that better information about local conditions would contribute to more efficient and effective leadership, and thus would promote an upsurge in production.

The information acquired through personal investigations was then to be processed in a series of planning conferences that were to follow new methods. At the central level, planning meetings were to be held more frequently, with participants drawn both from the central departments and from the provinces, and also from selected counties and urban districts. Many of the conferences were to be relatively small so as to encourage free discussion. And the ministries and departments were told to present their ideas in draft form so that revisions could be made on the basis of the personal experiences of the participants. Similarly, outside Peking, regional and provincial conferences were to be held as often as every other month to review accomplishments and to compare "province with province, city with city, county with county, commune with commune, factory with factory"—to see which policies and techniques were achieving the best results.[68]

There was also a return to the system of comprehensive, multilevel planning introduced during the High Tide. At the Third Plenum Mao directed that all six levels of administration outside Peking—province, special district, county, district, township, and cooperative—should draw up comprehensive plans that would "bring industry, agriculture, commerce, culture, and education together and coordinate them."[69] "Sixty Points on Working Methods" added more detail on the items to be incorporated into these comprehensive plans and provided that there should be five-year as well as annual plans. The plans were to be examined level by level. To facilitate comparison, a provincial committee was to select the best and worst from the county, district, township, and collective plans and submit them to Peking for consideration.[70] The important implications of this new planning process for decentralization will be discussed below.

During the High Tide the targets set in these comprehensive plans had frequently been inflated as they passed down the organization hierarchy. This inflation of targets was formally identified in the Sixty Points as a desirable feature of campaign-style planning. The Sixty Points provided that the center would draw up two plans: the public plan would indicate the minimum targets to be attained; another, unpublished, would indicate more ambitious targets that the center expected the provinces to fulfill. Indeed, it was the second plan, not the first, that was binding on the provinces. The provinces were to use the targets set in the second plan as their own minimum and set even higher targets for the special districts and counties to fulfill. So it would go through the levels of the bureaucracy, a deliberate stage-by-stage inflation of plan targets.[71]

This policymaking process was summarized in the Sixty Points as "overall planning, regular inspection, and annual reviews and comparisons"—although the rest of the document made it clear that the reviews and comparisons were to be conducted more frequently than every twelve months. According to the Sixty Points, the advantage of the method was that both the overall situation and the details would receive appropriate attention, experiences be summed up, and outstanding achievements made known in good time. In this way morale could be heightened in order to make "concerted progress." The key was to identify advanced experiences and popularize them as quickly as possible.[72]

The campaign against waste and conservatism. One of the most interesting similarities between the High Tide and the Great Leap Forward was the way in which both campaigns made use of ongoing efforts to improve the performance of the bureaucracy. The High Tide had transformed the final stage of the retrenchment drive of 1955, originally intended simply to improve the bureaucracy's efficiency, into a campaign against conservatism. In the same way, the Great Leap transformed the final stages of the rectification campaign of 1957, originally intended to resolve contradictions between the Party and the people, into a campaign against waste and conservatism. This redefinition of the rectification campaign began in January and February 1958, when such economic agencies as the State Planning Commission and the State Economic Commission started to consider ways in which economic policies might be improved.[73] It was then announced formally on March 3, by a Central Committee directive that predicted that a campaign against waste and conservatism could produce "miraculous surprises" in terms of economic productivity.[74]

The assault on waste involved, quite predictably, attempts to find and use idle material and financial resources, to reduce administrative and production costs, and to maintain high rates of output in the early months of the year, a time of slackened effort in many factories. But the main focus of the campaign was against "irrational rules and regulations." A major proponent of this effort was Liu Shao-ch'i, who contributed a section on the subject to "Sixty Points on Working Methods."[75] Some of the rules, regulations, and procedures drawn up since 1949 were still applicable, Liu said, but a considerable number of them had become obstacles to heightening the "activism of the masses" and to the "development of productive forces." Liu suggested that, as a general principle, the Party and government should encourage workers and officials to break those rules and regulations that restricted the development of the productive forces and then should summarize and popularize the revisions that proved effective.[76]

This aspect of the campaign was conducted primarily in factories and other basic-level enterprises. The campaign against conservatism, on the other hand, was more relevant to higher levels of the administrative bureaucracy. For the first time since late 1956, dogmatism reappeared as a major target for criticism. As before, dogmatism referred to the mechanical and uncritical adoption of Soviet policies and programs in China. But now the emphasis was placed more on economic dogmatism than on political dogmatism, more on the Soviet principles of economic development than the Stalinist tendency to view all tensions in society as instances of class struggle. At the Chengtu conference in March, Mao complained that

dogmatism [has] made its appearance both in economic and in cultural and educational work. . . . In economic work, dogmatism primarily manifested itself in heavy industry, planning, banking, and statistics. . . . Since we didn't understand these things and had absolutely no experience, all we could do in our ignorance was to import foreign methods. . . . Many of our comrades . . . do not consider whether there might be alternative formulae, and that they should choose those which are more suited to Chinese conditions and reject the others.[77]

By November, after a careful reexamination of Stalin's *Economic Problems of Socialism in the Soviet Union,* which had been used as a basic textbook for cadres since 1953, Mao had concluded that Stalin had paid attention only to half of the factors that promote economic development: technique, but not politics; cadres, but not the masses; industry, but not agriculture; the constraints imposed by objective conditions, but not the potential created by man's subjective will.[78]

If uncritical reliance on the Soviet experience represented, in Mao's view, a kind of superstition, the way to eliminate it was to force officials to examine the fundamental political and economic assumptions with which they approached their work. To stimulate this kind of discussion, conferences were held in a number of central ministries to consider "politics" rather than "business," the "abstract" rather than the "concrete," and "theory" rather than "reality." According to accounts in the Chinese press, these ministerial conferences discussed such questions as these: Whom do we serve in our work? How can we follow the mass line in our agency? Is gradual, incremental change necessarily better than radical change? Can the contradictions between quantity and quality and between speed and economy be resolved by creating a "unity of opposites"? In planning, should we permit the weak links to hold back the rest, or can the strongest links propel the rest of the economy forward?[79] In a sense, this aspect of the Great Leap Forward was a harbinger of the Cultural Revolution's attempt to put "politics in command" of policy planning; in fact, Mao introduced that very slogan at the Hankow conference in April.[80]

In addition to these ministerial forums, the campaign against waste and conservatism continued the use of wall posters, which had begun during the Hundred Flowers period and carried over into the rectification of the upper levels of the bureaucracy in late 1957. If the latter phase of the campaign had been somewhat frantic, the campaign against waste and conservatism was even more so. It may be recalled that 325,000 posters had been displayed by December 5, 1957. Now, during the campaign against waste and conservatism, that number increased more than tenfold, to 2.4 million by March 3, and to 5 million by March 23. During a period of twenty days, in other words, government officials wrote an average of 130,000 posters each day. In some ministries, each cadre wrote an average of 30 posters, and the national record was apparently held by one prolific official who wrote some five hundred. Cadres competed with one another to see who could come up with the most criticisms of waste and conservatisms, and officials who failed to make their contributions to the campaign were criticized by name by their colleagues.[81]

Party control. A third aspect of policymaking during the Great Leap Forward was the assertion of almost total Party control over the entire planning process. The assumption was that the Party, because it was less bureaucratized and routinized, was less conservative than the government. Mao himself paid particular attention to establishing this control at the central level; at the Nanning conference he complained that the Central Committee and the Politburo had been able to supervise only revolution and agriculture effectively. In other issue areas, particularly in finance and economics, the ministries made policy directly, consulting the Politburo only as a matter of form. They presented the Politburo members with finished drafts of policy decisions, instead of a list of options. "Ten minutes before the conference opens," Mao charged, "the document is produced for resolution. This is a Stalinist method. This is a blockade." Mao demanded that thereafter the ministries should provide a constant stream of information and advice to the Politburo, a "steady drizzle" instead of a sporadic "heavy downpour." This would enable the Politburo and the Central Committee to make policy on all major issues, the state bureaucracy serving simply to administer the Politburo's decisions.[82]

Mao admitted that this new division of labor between the Party and the government would arouse opposition. During the Hundred Flowers period, he recalled, some government officials, particularly those working in legal affairs, had complained that the Party was constantly encroaching on the independence of the state. But this, Mao insisted, was as it should be. "How," he asked, "will such things as the forty-article program [i.e., the twelve-year agricultural program] be divided? Twenty for the Central Committee and twenty for [the Ministry of] Agriculture? This cannot be done. . . . We cannot have the Central Committee operating under one constitution and other organizations operating under another."[83]

While Mao was emphasizing Party control over central policymaking in his speeches in early 1958, other leaders were trying to strengthen Party control over the government at lower levels of administration. The Central Committee's "Sixty Points on Working Methods" began by instructing Party committees at the county level and above to take charge of fourteen issue areas: industry, agriculture, handicrafts, rural sideline production, forestry, fishery, animal husbandry, transport and communication, commerce, finance, labor and population, science, culture and education, and public health. Number 28 of the Sixty Points specified that "essential powers should be concentrated in the hands of the Party committees of the center and the localities, so as to combat diffusion of power."* And, in his report at the second session of the Eighth Party Congress in May, Liu Shao-ch'i explained that "the Central Committee of the Party and local Party committees at all levels must be the leading core of the government at all levels. In the past few years, the leadership of the Party concentrated its efforts mainly on the socialist revolution. While we shall continue to pay attention to this work, we now can and must concentrate greater efforts on socialist construction."[84]

Denigration of specialists. A few months after the blooming and contending of the spring of 1957, Chinese leaders began to reassess their previous policy of cooperating with the nation's intellectuals and of professionalizing the policymaking process. By mid-1958 what had begun as skepticism of intellectuals had turned into open denigration. A representative article in the newspaper for Chinese youth charged that many of China's intellectuals were both politically and professionally backward, and had proved themselves unwilling to take up problems that were of real relevance to China's economic development. It would be totally wrong, the article concluded, to say that the Great Leap had to rely on intellectuals.[85] Instead, the Leap was based on the premise that if they studied hard, veteran Party cadres were perfectly capable of mastering the necessary technical skills and becoming, in the famous phrase, "both red and expert" (*yu hung yu chuan*). Rather than co-opting intellectuals, as in 1956

---

*See Jerome Ch'en, *Mao Papers: Anthology and Bibliography* (London, 1970), pp. 68–69. To enable the Party to exercise this power effectively, two important economic planners, Li Fu-ch'un and Li Hsien-nien, were added to the Party Secretariat at the Fifth Plenum in May.

and early 1957, the Party's goal was now to cultivate a "working-class intelligentsia" by training workers and peasants to take the place of intellectuals.[86]

Accordingly, one of Mao's most frequent themes in the first months of 1958 was his rejection of the notion that scientific and technical knowledge was beyond the ability of ordinary Party cadres to master, and that Party cadres were somehow inferior to the intellectuals. "Professors? We have been afraid of them ever since we came into the towns. . . . When confronted by people with piles of learning, we felt we were good for nothing. . . . I believe this attitude is another example of the slave mentality. . . . We must not tolerate it any longer." This situation could be changed if new journals and books were published to convey scientific and technical information in relatively simple language to ordinary Party cadres and Party members: "We only need to read a dozen or so books and we can beat them." Younger people would be particularly capable of raising their technical skills: "Ever since ancient times, . . . young people without too much learning . . . [have] had the ability to recognize new things at a glance and, having grasped them, open fire on the old fogeys."[87]

With Mao's optimistic views of the intellectual potential of Party cadres in mind, leaders placed renewed emphasis in early 1958 on part-time training classes for cadres from worker-peasant backgrounds. A representative plan was drawn up by Tangshan municipality. Cadres who had not yet acquired a junior middle-school education would obtain one within five years. Cadres who had achieved a junior middle-school standard would begin to undertake theoretical and technical studies, and some would be sent to universities. Henceforth, according to the Tangshan program, the goal would be to train workers to be experts, not to rely totally on older intellectuals.[88]

Further decentralization. In Chapter 4 we identified six measures for transferring power from the center to the provinces: (1) to permit provinces to adjust central targets, (2) to reduce the number of central targets, (3) to transfer the "ownership" of enterprises from the center to the provinces, (4) to give the provinces greater control over their own budgets, (5) to base the national economic plan on comprehensive provincial plans, and (6) to undertake planning from the bottom up rather than from the top down. The decentralization reforms discussed at the Third Plenum and promulgated in November 1957 enacted the first three of these measures. Within only a few months of their adoption, however, the Central Committee and the State Council jointly announced new reforms that carried the decentralization of planning and management much further.

In mid-April the first of these joint decisions provided that more industrial enterprises would be transferred to provincial "ownership" than originally planned—in fact, all enterprises, except for certain principal, special, and "experimental" enterprises, would be turned over to local control.* Cultural, educational, political, and judicial affairs, which had not been mentioned in the 1957 reforms, were also transferred to the provinces. The decline of the center's role in the economy was symbolized by the simultaneous reduction in the number of central ministries, particularly in the areas of capital construction and heavy and light industry, and in the division of the country into six "economic cooperation regions" to serve as the focus of economic planning.† The directive provided that after this reorganization of the State Council, only 30 to 40 percent of the effort of the surviving ministries should be devoted to the direct management of the remaining centrally controlled enterprises, or to any form of planning. The rest should be channeled toward helping the localities manage their enterprises successfully through the provision of technical data and designs, the training of technical staff, and the exchange of "advanced experiences" and research.[89]

A second directive from the Central Committee and the State Council on September 24, however, carried decentralization even further in the direction of organizing the economy by region rather than by sector. According to this decision, provinces were permitted to retain any budgetary surplus they could generate, as long as they continued to remit an agreed amount of money to the center each year. Through the use of these funds and any surplus raw materials not committed to the central authorities, the provinces could begin to make their own investment decisions and start their own construction projects (measure 4). Moreover, under the principle of "taking regional balance as the key" (*i ti-ch'ü p'ing-heng wei-chu*), provinces were authorized to draw up their own comprehensive plans, including plans for the centrally controlled enterprises remaining under their jurisdiction (measure 5). Even the factories remaining under ministerial control would have to apply to the provinces for the supplies and materials they needed. And finally, perhaps as a result of Mao's proposal at the Third Plenum that all levels of administration engage in economic planning, the directive specified that plans were henceforth to be compiled from the bottom up, each level to set its own targets and input-output balances (measure 6). These local plans would become the raw material for planning at the next higher level:

*Shortly before this decision was announced, the number of central ministries had been substantially reduced, particularly in the areas of construction, heavy industry, and light industry. See New China News Agency, 11.ii.58, in *Survey of the China Mainland Press*, no. 1713 (14.ii.58), pp. 1–2.

†These economic regions—Northeast, North, East, Central-South, Southwest, and Northwest—corresponded to the administrative regions that existed between 1949 and 1954.

The economic and cultural construction of each district, township, and commune should be entered into the county's unified plan; after the counties' and the special districts' plans have been balanced, they should be entered into the unified plan of the provinces, autonomous regions, and [provincial-level] municipalities; after the provincial, regional, and municipal plans have been balanced by the economic cooperation regions, they should be brought into the national plan; on the basis of the regional balance, the ministries should draft national sectoral plans to form a component of the unified national plan; on the basis of the regional and sectoral balances, the central planning organs should create a comprehensive balance, and draw up a unified state plan.[90]

Although the directive warned against "localism, blind construction, and lack of coordination between provinces," the 1958 decentralization measures still constituted a major step towards creating an economic system composed of relatively autarchic provinces. Under its provisions, provinces would contract to deliver a certain amount of surplus output and money to the center for redistribution to other provinces; other than this, they were quite independent of central interference.

The decentralization of economic planning and management was accompanied by an increasing role for provincial leaders in central decision making. The major decisions of the Great Leap Forward were made in a series of work conferences, most of them held outside Peking, in which provincial Party secretaries played a major part. Two first secretaries, Li Ching-ch'uan of Szechwan and K'o Ch'ing-shih of Shanghai, were added to the Politburo in May, and the Chinese press in 1958 was filled with essays and articles by provincial leaders—men who were acting as the innovators and spokesmen for the Great Leap.

The common thread linking all these five sets of changes in policymaking, planning, and organizational structure was that they were all intended to "break down superstition," increase the creativity of the bureaucracy, and thus contribute to the Great Leap in economic production. Some of the measures were attempts to change the basis on which officials made decisions: to provide them with more rapid feedback, to present them with achievements to emulate, to force them to consider the political premises behind their decisions, to encourage them to break away from established routines and procedures and strive for goals once assumed to be unattainable. Other measures, however, represented a major shift of power within the bureaucracy. Power passed from specialists to generalists, from the government to the Party, and from the center to the provinces. In this way, the reforms of the Great Leap Forward were intended to take authority from those who were likely to be conservative in outlook and transfer it to those who dared to set ambitious goals.

SHORTCOMINGS OF THE CAMPAIGN STYLE

Despite the optimism and enthusiasm with which it was launched, the Great Leap Forward proved unable to attain the extraordinarily high production goals that were set through the campaign style of policymaking. Agricultural production did increase impressively in 1958, but then it fell sharply in 1959, and it continued to decline until it bottomed out in 1961 at approximately the same level of output as in 1952. Industrial production rose steadily between 1958 and 1960 until it, too, suffered serious losses in 1961. Rural social services, such as the hospitals and schools established in the early months of the Leap, were forced to close for lack of financial resources. There were reports of food shortages and unrest, even of armed banditry and starvation in several provinces.[91] In the end, the Leap produced an economic recession from which China did not fully recover until 1965.

The question of why the Great Leap failed to achieve its economic goals still arouses considerable controversy. The Chinese themselves point to the natural disasters which struck the nation's rural areas in 1959 and 1960. These clearly contributed to the steep declines in agricultural output in those years, but they cannot explain why it took agriculture so long to recover. The Chinese also blame the Russians for withdrawing their technicians and advisers in 1960. This, too, must have had some effect on industrial production, but it is doubtful that industrial output could have remained unaffected by the depression in the agricultural sector even if the Russian advisers had remained.

Many Western analyses point to the "irrationalities" in the basic premises of the Great Leap. There is an important insight here, but one that should not be overstated. It is true, for example, that Chinese leaders vastly overestimated the potential of mobilized rural labor to create sustained increases in agricultural production and of ordinary workers to sweep away unrealistic and unnecessary rules and regulations. Similarly, they overestimated the extent to which the rural sector could generate its own investment and the degree to which it could create, through local industry, the capital inputs required to modernize agriculture. But many of the principles behind the Leap were not irrational. The idea that local industry, using relatively simple technologies, could absorb surplus rural labor and produce needed inputs for agriculture was not unreasonable. The recognition that the agricultural bottleneck could not be broken simply by another reorganization of peasant communities, but required investment in fertilizer, water conservancy, and tools was also sound. The notion that the rural economy could support certain social services without depending on state assistance was an important insight. Indeed, many of the more successful rural programs of the Cultural Revolution were based on some of the principles of the Leap.*

A full account of the shortcomings of the Great Leap must also take organizational problems into consideration. The program of the Leap was, after all, both experimental and schematic. It required an organizational structure that could keep a close watch over conditions at the grass roots, gather accurate information, popularize successes, and correct failures. Unfortunately, the organizational structure and procedures created during the Great Leap Forward were unable to meet these requirements. Instead, organizational shortcomings magnified the weaknesses in the underlying concepts of the Leap, carried even sound ideas to unworkable extremes, and prevented Chinese leaders from recognizing and correcting failures as they occurred.

First of all, the technique of popularizing advanced experiences on a nationwide basis meant that programs that might have been workable in some parts of China were adopted too quickly and uncritically in other areas of the country. Liu Shao-ch'i said in January 1962:

Many movements have been unfolded during the past few years. Most were set in motion on the spur of the moment. Some were even without official documents; they were simply set in motion on hearing some not very accurate news from somewhere. Such a way of doing things is not good. . . . The practice of daring to think, speak, and act should not be followed on a nationwide scale but should be tried out on a small scale with typical experiments conducted first.[92]

Communes, for example, grew out of ad hoc decisions by local leaders to amalgamate several cooperatives to enable them to cooperate more efficiently in the construction of water-conservancy projects. Once the first communes had been established, they were copied in other provinces, until in the end the formation of communes was adopted as a national policy at the Peitaiho conference. During his self-criticism at the Lushan conference in July 1959, Mao himself admitted that China had "communized too quickly." He assigned some of the blame to his chief agricultural lieutenant, T'an Chen-lin, but he also accepted some of the responsibility himself. Mao recalled that, after having visited one of the first communes established in Shantung early in 1958, he told a reporter from the New China News Agency that he thought the "people's communes good"—a commonplace pleasantry that became an important slogan in the drive to promote communes. Mao learned a lesson from this, he said: "In the fu-

---

*A well-balanced attempt to understand the economic logic of the Great Leap Forward is to be found in Victor D. Lippit, "The Great Leap Forward Reconsidered," *Modern China*, 1 (1975): 92–115.

ture reporters should keep away."[93] An even more costly example of the shortcomings of popularizing advanced experiences was the campaign to build backyard steel furnaces, one of the symbols of the Great Leap. Here a basically sound idea (local industry) was transformed into an impractical one (producing steel at the commune level without proper equipment or skilled labor), and was promoted throughout the nation before any careful analysis was made of its feasibility.[94]

Second, program goals set in accordance with the principles of balancing upward and combating waste and conservatism were continually adjusted upward to the point where they became virtually useless as realistic targets.[95] It is true that from the beginning there were editorials calling for a matter-of-fact spirit as well as for "revolutionary vigor," and that Mao himself reminded cadres that the Party must deal in reality as well as in "revolutionary romanticism."[96] Despite these cautionary remarks, however, the prevailing spirit was of virtually unchecked optimism and enthusiasm. In the same speech at the Chengtu conference in which he spoke of the need to confront reality, Mao also predicted that the twelve-year agricultural program, whose implementation was just beginning, could be fulfilled "within the next year, two years, or three to five years."[97] Even as they called for a matter-of-fact spirit, editorials spoke of economic miracles and promised that Chinese society would enter communism within one or two decades.

The effective result of planning in a campaign atmosphere was that provincial and local Party committees were put under intense pressure to set their targets as high as possible. Ezra Vogel's study of Canton has revealed that Canton raised its industrial production targets three times in the space of two months. The original goal for 1958 was to increase industrial output 5.8 percent over 1957. In January 1958 that target was raised twice, first to 12.4 percent and then to 15 percent. By February the goal had reached 33.2 percent. A similar escalation of production targets was occurring simultaneously at the provincial level. In early February Kwangtung's plan was to double industrial output over the next five years. One week later the goal was to triple output, and in three more weeks it was to quadruple it.[98]

In agriculture some of the provincial plans were even more utopian. Hopei, to cite a rather extreme example, adopted a directive that proposed to meet the output targets of the twelve-year program (400 catties per mou for grain) in 1958, achieve a level of grain output some five to eight times higher than that (two to three thousand catties per mou) within three to five years, establish a university in each commune within ten to fifteen years so that "all people now under twenty-five may reach the cultural standard of university students," and, probably within the same period of time, to construct an airstrip in each commune and a railway line in each county.[99]

The pressures on lower-level cadres to set unrealistically high targets were equalled by similar pressures on officials to meet or exceed targets set by their colleagues in other agencies or other localities. The principle of balancing upward implied that the high agricultural targets of the Leap would be matched by equally high targets in every other sector of the economy. After all, if bottlenecks occurred, the proper response was to push the lagging sector forward, rather than to hold the leading sector back. So when commune factories and water-conservancy projects demanded more iron and steel than could immediately be provided, the response was to raise the target for iron and steel output for 1958 from a 16 percent increase over the previous year to a 100 percent increase.[100] And when the first indications of higher agricultural and industrial output began to appear after the summer harvest, it was argued that the economic base was outstripping the cultural, educational, and scientific superstructure. New targets for these sectors were drawn up so that they could keep pace with the progress of the rest of the economy. According to the National Day editorial on October 1, illiteracy was to be eliminated in two to three years (as compared with five to seven years in the twelve-year agricultural program), middle-school enrollment was to be doubled in the fall, university enrollment was to increase 60 percent, and the twelve-year plan for science was to be fulfilled five to seven years ahead of schedule.[101]

Third, decentralization was carried even beyond the formal reforms of 1958. In some places, "ownership" of industrial enterprises was not simply passed from the center to the provinces, but further transferred from the provinces to the municipalities in which the industries were located.[102] Although the center was supposed to have retained control over the total amount of investment in the country, and thus over the amounts to be spent on construction projects by each province, many provinces were able to use the principle of rejecting unwarranted restrictions to undertake investment without any central approval at all.[103] In addition, though the center still theoretically regulated transfers of resources from one province to another, in fact the provinces used their authority over resource allocation to direct materials to their own industries and refused to meet their commitments to factories in other provinces. Neither the economic cooperation regions nor the ministries proved able to restrain the provinces, and the center's effective control over the economy was substantially reduced.[104]

The result was that central planning virtually ceased. At the Lushan meeting in July 1959 Mao complained that the State Planning Commission and the central ministries had decided not to concern themselves with planning after the Peitaiho conference the previous August: "They dispensed with overall balances and simply made no estimates of how much coal, iron, and transport would be needed." Although he laid the blame on the central economic agencies, they may have simply been responding rationally to their loss of control over the provinces.[105] The bottom-upward planning process was resulting in provincial autarchy. Given circumstances in which plan targets would have to be repeatedly revised upward, it should not be considered surprising that central planners felt their task a futile one.

Fourth, and perhaps most crippling of all, the bureaucracy lost its ability to correct its own errors. Lower levels were reluctant to report failures to their superiors. Instead, while still increasing pressure on the basic levels to meet inflated targets, they would file false reports stating that the plans had been not only fulfilled but overfulfilled. This would force other sectors and geographic areas to adjust their own targets upward to balance the reported (but nonexistent) advance. The result was to create a bubble of error, failure, and misinformation that swelled as it traveled through the bureaucracy. As early as November 1958 Mao was complaining that false reporting had become one of the country's principal organizational problems. Other reports indicated that the national statistical system was in a state of total disarray.[106]

RETREAT FROM THE CAMPAIGN STYLE

The difficulties in acquiring accurate information from the bureaucracy did not prevent Chinese leaders from learning, quite early on, that the Great Leap Forward was producing serious economic and social dislocations across the country. They attempted to address these problems in two distinct ways. On the one hand, the Central Committee began in late 1958 to issue more specific guidelines on the structure and operation of the communes and to set more realistic targets for agricultural and industrial output. On the other, the central leadership also started to replace the campaign style in the bureaucracy with a more regular set of organizational procedures. Both measures were temporarily interrupted by the brief campaign against rightist opportunism that was launched after P'eng Te-huai's ill-fated critique of the Great Leap Forward at the Lushan meeting in July 1959.[107] But the retreat from the campaign style of leadership resumed in mid-1960 and was the most important feature of organizational policy in China from then until early 1962.

Some of these remedial measures were directed against basic-level officials, to whom the responsibility for many of the Great Leap's shortcomings was assigned. As early as November and December 1958 Mao criticized the tendency of basic-level cadres to exaggerate achievements, report inaccurate output statistics, conceal failures, and administer Party policies through coercion.[108] In a circular letter written on April 29, 1959 and addressed to cadres throughout the country, Mao acknowledged that these problems stemmed, in large part, from "pressure from above." Mao therefore told basic-level officials that they could ignore unrealistic directives from their superiors and concentrate on practical possibilities. Mao acknowledged that his advice was low-keyed but he stated that it was better to set realistic goals and report successes and failures accurately than to listen to the "high-sounding talk currently making the rounds."[109]

These efforts to rein in basic-level officials were transformed into a full-scale rectification campaign in the winter of 1960–61. Begun on an experimental basis at the Peitaiho conference in July and August 1960 and then expanded into a nationwide movement at the Ninth Plenum in January 1961, the campaign was relatively mild, was conducted area-by-area across the country, and was undertaken during the slack winter season so as to avoid any interference with agricultural production.* Called the campaign against the "five styles" (*wu-feng*), it was directed against egalitarianism (ignoring differences in performance in calculating remuneration, or transferring productive resources from wealthier production teams and brigades to poorer ones), commandism (achieving production quotas through compulsion), blind direction of production (ignoring objective conditions in managing production), exaggeration of accomplishments, and the tendency of cadres to claim special prerogatives in a time of economic hardship.[110] All these problems had been produced by the reintroduction of the campaign style of work in 1958 and by the economic overextension created by the Great Leap Forward.

The campaign style at the middle and upper levels of the bureaucracy was also the target of decisions taken between 1959 and 1962. At the Seventh Plenum in April 1959, Mao began work on another document on bureaucratic work methods that could be interpreted as a replacement for,

---

*The campaign is discussed in the communiqué of the Ninth Plenum, in *Current Background*, no. 644 (27.i.61), pp. 1–4. Although primarily conducted at the basic levels, the campaign did not spare higher-level officials altogether: Party first secretaries in five provinces (Honan, Kansu, Tsinghai, Shantung, and Anhwei) were demoted or removed from office. See Parris H. Chang, *Power and Policy in China* (University Park, Pa., 1975), p. 130. Of these five leaders, two were well known in China as strong advocates of the Great Leap. Wu Chih-p'u of Honan had sponsored the communes; Tseng Hsi-sheng of Anhwei had introduced the slogan "Transform the entire country after three years of hard struggle!" and was accused by Mao of having set excessively high targets for water conservancy. See Wu Chih-p'u, "On People's Communes," *Chung-kuo ch'ing-nien pao*, 16.ix.58, in *Current Background*, no. 524 (21.x.58), pp. 1–15; and Mao Tse-tung, "Speech at the Sixth Plenum of the Eighth Central Committee," 19.xii.58, in *Miscellany of Mao Tse-tung Thought*, pp. 141–42.

or at least a substantial revision of, the Sixty Points drawn up in February 1958. A rather dull and lifeless document, the "Sixteen Articles Concerning Work Methods" called on cadres to be resourceful and decisive, strive for the greatest effect, be adept at observing the situation, decide at the crucial moment, be responsible, and look at problems from the historical point of view. In essence, it was a warning against excessively high targets and a justification of a more deliberate rate of economic growth. As Mao put it, "We cannot have a high tide everyday."[111]

A more sweeping transformation of the policy process came in the following year, when a decision was made to reexamine policy in every major issue area and to summarize the results of these reappraisals in a series of systematic policy guidelines. Between March 1961 and September 1962, policy reviews were conducted for agriculture, industry, finance and trade, science, education, and literature and art. The resulting documents circulated privately within the Party.[112] The assumptions underlying the policy review were diametrically opposed to those underlying the Leap. At the height of the Leap the emphasis had been on unleashing the creative potential of the masses throughout the country. Now, however, attention was shifted to respecting the "objective laws" that would limit "man's subjective ability to mold nature."[113] As the 1962 New Year's Day editorial explained, "Lofty aspirations and ambitions [are all to the good], but at the same time we must keep our feet on the ground, . . . proceed from concrete conditions at all times, and be practical."[114] During the Great Leap, one of the fundamental principles of planning was balancing upward; after the Ninth Plenum, held in January 1961, the principle was changed to read "readjustment, consolidation, filling out, and raising standards"—a principle that, in effect, called for holding the advanced sectors and areas back so that the lagging sectors could catch up.[115] At the height of the Leap, the emphasis had been on achieving utopian goals in miraculously short periods of time. Now it was acknowledged that China would remain in the socialist stage for a long period of time, that development would be paced, and that communism was a goal to be achieved only in the distant future. "Play it safe," *Jen-min jih-pao* editorialized in early 1962, and "advance step by step"—a view that four years earlier would have almost certainly been regarded as an instance of rightist conservatism.[116]

The policy reviews of 1961 and 1962 also marked a significant change in the participants in the policymaking process. Given the greater concern with objective constraints on policy and the need for a sophisticated understanding of the environment, it was logical that specialists and experts would play a greater role in policymaking, and generalists somewhat less. These years saw a loosening of restraints on Chinese intellectuals. Chou

En-lai called on the Party to develop democracy still further and unite further with all patriotic intellectuals, and Ch'en I decried the lack of technical experts and political interference with scientific and scholarly work.* The greater freedom given to intellectuals was reflected in the policymaking process as well. The radical policies of 1955 and 1958–59 appear to have been decided upon at small, informal gatherings of generalists, selected Politburo members and provincial secretaries, who shared many of Mao's policy predispositions and whom the Chairman was able to manipulate quite effectively. In the early 1960's, however, these meetings were replaced by larger, more formal central work conferences attended both by regional generalists and by high-ranking specialists from the ministries, the Central Committee departments, and the Secretariat. Moreover, in preparing the new policy guidelines for discussion at these central work conferences, the Secretariat frequently consulted specialists and experts outside the bureaucracy, either by calling national conferences of intellectuals or by consultations with the appropriate professional associations.[117] In short, policy was now made in forums at which Mao's influence was substantially restricted, or so he would later complain.†

Finally, the 1959–61 period was characterized by attempts to bring the provinces back under tighter central control. The first sign that the process of decentralization was to be reversed came in 1959 with the introduction of the slogan "take the whole country as a single chessboard" and with measures to strengthen central control over the level and nature of provincial investment.[118] In late 1960 the regional Party bureaus abolished in 1954 were reestablished to "act for the Central Committee in strengthening leadership over the Party committees in various provinces, municipalities, and autonomous regions."[119] Just as the centralization measures of 1954 had been followed by a mild campaign against "independent kingdoms," so was the recentralization process of 1960–61 followed by a campaign to "strengthen the centralized, unified leadership of the Party and state." Local and provincial leaders, who during the Great Leap had been encouraged to display their local activism, were now warned against such

*For a discussion of this "second Hundred Flowers campaign," see Merle Goldman, "Party Policies Toward the Intellectuals: The Unique Blooming and Contending of 1961–2," in John W. Lewis, ed., *Party Leadership and Revolutionary Power in China* (Cambridge, 1970). Chou En-lai's comments, quoted above, were drawn from his address to the third session of the Second National People's Congress in March and April 1962. See *Current Background*, no. 681 (28.iv.62), pp. 1–3. Ch'en I's comments are contained in his speech to Peking college graduates given in September 1961, in *Chung-kuo ch'ing-nien pao*, 2.ix.61, in *Survey of the China Mainland Press*, no. 2581 (19.ix.61), pp. 1–7.

†Mao was particularly critical of Teng Hsiao-p'ing's alleged failure to consult with him on major issues. Mao's views were expressed in two central work conferences in October 1966. See Mao, in Jerome Ch'en, ed., *Mao* (Englewood Cliffs, N.J., 1969), pp. 96–97; and in Ch'en, *Mao Papers*, p. 40.

deviations as "laissez-faire dispersionism" and "putting the interests of the part above the interests of the whole." Local initiative, in effect, was restricted to adding supplementary provisions to central policy and was no longer a justification for provincial independence.*

These preliminary attempts to recentralize the economy were followed by more wide-ranging measures between 1962 and 1965. A number of economic ministries that had been abolished in the late 1950's were reestablished in the mid-1960's, a sure sign that Peking now sought to exercise greater control over economic planning and management. In 1964 state corporations were established on an experimental basis in four sectors of the industrial economy. These state corporations, responsible solely to the relevant ministries of the central government, regained jurisdiction over the factories and enterprises that had been transferred to provincial ownership in 1957–58. Their goal was to maximize economic efficiency by creating a single, national system of production and distribution for their sector of the economy, thus eliminating or reducing the duplication of effort by factories in different provinces that had characterized Chinese industry during the Great Leap Forward. By 1965 another eight state corporations, or "trusts," were formed in other branches of industry, so production and management were again centralized in such sectors of the economy as motor vehicles, tractors, engines, steel, petroleum, textiles, rubber, aluminum, and petrochemicals. All in all, according to Marianne Bastid, some 70–80 percent of the country's industrial production was back under central direction by 1966.[120]

To summarize, then, the attempt to reintroduce campaign styles of leadership in the bureaucracy was effectively ended during the "three hard years" (1959–61). Political power was largely recentralized, the role of specialists and experts in decision making was restored, what was once denounced as "conservatism" was now seen as an appropriate response to "objective limitations," and the policymaking process was slowed down and tightened up. These changes did not, however, undo all of the organizational reforms of 1957–58. First of all, despite the extension of greater

---

*Representative articles on democratic centralism from this period include *Jen-min jih-pao*, 1.i.62, in *Survey of the China Mainland Press*, no. 2653 (8.i.62), pp. 1–6; "Oppose Dispersionism and Departmentalism," in *Nan-fang jih-pao*, 2.v.52, *ibid.*, no. 2750 (1.vi.62), pp. 1–3; Liu Ch'ung, "Strengthen Centralization and Unity, Develop Democracy Within the Party," in *Jen-min jih-pao*, 3.iv.63, *ibid.*, no. 2727 (30.iv.62), pp. 1–7; and Li Te-sheng et al., "There Must Be Centralized, Unified Leadership Over Socialist Construction," in *Ta-kung pao*, 21.iii.62, *ibid.*, no. 2717 (11.iv.62), pp. 1–6. These articles were commentaries on speeches given by Mao and Liu Shao-ch'i at large conferences in January and early February. For analysis, see Byung-joon Ahn, "Adjustments in the Great Leap Forward and Their Ideological Legacy, 1959–62," in Chalmers Johnson, ed., *Ideology and Politics in Contemporary China* (Seattle, 1973), pp. 138–39, 157–62.

central control over the economy, there was no return to the highly centralized ministerial system that had existed before November 1957. Most of industry remained under provincial control. The new regional bureaus were staffed largely by former provincial officials and thus tended, over time, to become as much an arena for articulating provincial demands as an instrument of central authority. Most important, national policy continued to be hammered out in central work conferences attended by provincial as well as central officials. As a result, although central direction was increased, and although specialists were consulted, central leaders and technical specialists still had to share power with provincial generalists.

Nor did the organizational changes between 1959 and 1962 involve any reduction in the role of the Party, a role which had been greatly increased during the Great Leap Forward. During the codification of new policy guidelines in the early 1960's, it was the Central Committee and the Party Secretariat, not the State Council, that played the most important part. The regional bureaus were Party agencies, not government organs, and they were given extensive powers to coordinate and manage the economy. At lower levels, there was little evidence that the ability of local Party committees to dominate policymaking and administration was declining. Indeed, in an article on the Party written for the tenth anniversary of the People's Republic in 1959, Liu Lan-t'ao, an alternate member of the Party Secretariat, reiterated that the Party should exercise leadership over all other organizations, including the government; that this leadership should be "organizational" as well as "political and ideological"; and that, for government officials outside Peking, the principal source of supervision should be the local Party committee rather than the local government or the central ministries. Though still paying ritual deference to the principle that the Party could not take all the daily routine of such non-Party organizations completely into its own hands—a principle that was increasingly ignored—Liu nonetheless declared that it was perfectly proper to "mix the Party with the government." Under the leadership of the proletariat, he explained, "there can be only one 'political planning department,' not two."[121]

THE GREAT LEAP FORWARD AND THE BUREAUCRATIC DILEMMA

The Great Leap Forward was, by any standard, a radical period in China's social and economic development. Chinese leaders spoke of closing the gap between mental and manual labor, of eliminating differences between city and countryside, of breaking the connection between work performed and wages received, and of catching up with the West in industrial output—and they promised all this in a very short period of time. At the height of the Leap, editorials in *Jen-min jih-pao* seriously forecast China's achievement of communism within perhaps fifteen years.

One might reasonably have expected that such utopianism in socioeconomic policy would have found parallels in organizational policy as well. In fact, discussions of bureaucracy and of organizational policy during the Great Leap Forward contained remarkably few radical components, certainly many fewer than would emerge during the Cultural Revolution a decade later.*

Analyses of organizational policy during the Great Leap Forward, to be sure, contained many criticisms of bureaucracy. As during the Hundred Flowers period, there was concern that bureaucracy tended to alienate leaders from the led: to produce officials who were divorced from the people, who rarely visited basic-level units, or who assumed an "expressionless look" when hearing of the day-to-day problems of ordinary Chinese. In January 1958, for example, a *Jen-min jih-pao* editorial went so far as to argue that the most dangerous enemy then facing the Chinese Communist Party was not the Kuomintang, the United States, the landlords, or the bourgeoisie, but rather bureaucratism.[122] The Great Leap also saw the repetition and amplification of complaints first expressed during the High Tide of 1955–56: bureaucracy tended toward economic and administrative inefficiency, it became attached to outdated and inappropriate ways of doing things, it failed to discover and popularize advanced techniques, and it lost sight of the political goals it was supposed to pursue. There was also growing criticism of bureaucratic specialization and the desire of bureaucratic agencies for autonomy. Mao complained at the Nanning conference in January 1958 that the Politburo was growing less and less able to understand the policy proposals presented by the various state ministries, let alone provide effective policy guidance.[123] Later, in October 1959, Liu Lan-t'ao noted the tendency of the functional departments of government to win de facto independence from Party supervision and control, and their desire to transform the Party from a unified vanguard organization ("an organ of supreme power of the proletariat") into a bargaining arena in which the interests of various specialized agencies could be reconciled ("a free federation of individual organizations").[124]

These criticisms of bureaucracy were reflected in the organizational reforms of the Leap, which represented an important departure from each of the components of rationalization that were discussed in Chapter 3. Dur-

---

*The analysis that follows conflicts with that of Meisner but is similar to that of Starr. See Maurice Meisner, *Mao's China: A History of the People's Republic* (New York, 1977), pp. 238–41; and John Bryan Starr, "Revolution in Retrospect: The Paris Commune Through Chinese Eyes," *China Quarterly*, no. 49 (January–March 1972), pp. 109–10.

ing the period of regularization between 1952 and 1955, the political system had been centralized; during the Leap, it underwent substantial decentralization. During the period of regularization, rules and regulations had been formalized; during the Leap, these same procedures were denounced as being outmoded relics that produced only waste and conservatism. During the period of regularization, cadres had been encouraged to develop administrative and technical skills and to become specialists; during the Leap, skills were still considered important, but specialists were seen as having tendencies toward conservatism, and cadres were urged to become jacks-of-all-trades. During the period of regularization, Chinese leaders had constructed a complex web of control agencies; during the Leap, however, the Ministry of Supervision and the Procuracy were both accused of seeking to win independence from the Party. Accordingly, the Ministry of Supervision was abolished in 1959, its functions being transferred to the Party and to the Party's control commissions, while the supervisory work of the Procuracy, which had never been well developed, virtually ceased altogether.*

Despite the criticism of the bureaucracy, and despite the departure from the principles of organizational regularization, the Great Leap Forward produced very few proposals that the bureaucracy be replaced by a nonbureaucratic form of organization. There were few demands, in other words, that qualified as radical in their approach to China's bureaucratic dilemma. In fact, one of the most striking aspects of the Leap was that the opportunities for organizational radicalism that presented themselves were quite deliberately passed by.

The talk of the imminence of communism in China might, for example, have sparked a detailed discussion of the process by which the state would begin to "wither away." It is true that some of the more utopian editorials did state that, once communism was attained, the only function left for the state to perform would be national defense.[125] But there was virtually no discussion of the organizational aspects of the transition to communism, of what form administration would assume under communism, or of what organizational changes would have to occur during the few years of socialism that remained.

As another example, consider the organizational structure of the rural people's communes. The term "commune," of course, was borrowed from

---

*The fullest critique of the Ministry of Supervision is in *Jen-min jih-pao*, 5.xii.57, in *Survey of the China Mainland Press*, no. 1679 (27.xii.57), pp. 2–7. The article charged that leading officials in the ministry not only paid little attention to complaints from the masses or to popular correspondents, but, more important, sought to expand the functions of the ministry so that it could supervise planning as well as policy implementation, and budgets as well as final accounts. For analysis, see Franz Schurmann, *Ideology and Organization in Communist China*, rev. ed. (Berkeley and Los Angeles, 1968), pp. 355–64.

the Paris Commune of 1871, and the historical experience of the Paris Commune received some attention during the Great Leap Forward. But the Paris Commune served much more as a socioeconomic model for the people's communes than as a political or organizational prototype. Like the Paris Commune, the people's communes were supposed to combine industry and agriculture, civilian and military affairs, and political leadership and economic management.[126] But the organizational principles of the Paris Commune—direct election and recall of all officials, the assumption of official positions by ordinary workers or peasants by rotation, the integration of legislative and executive functions, and the elimination of salary differentials between officials and ordinary citizens—were almost completely neglected. Indeed, the Hopei directive on forming communes, a remarkably radical document when discussing socioeconomic questions, was downright conservative when it came to considering organizational matters. It did provide that communes should have elected administrative and supervisory committees. But commune officials were still to be appointed, not elected: "Cadres of a people's commune shall be suitably provided by the higher Party committee." Cadres sent from outside the commune would still receive their old salaries, based on the graduated wage system. And, in general, the original structure of local government would not be "disturbed all of a sudden." The requirement that cadres must participate in productive labor hardly reduces one's feeling that the organizational program of the Great Leap Forward could claim few links with the Paris Commune.[127]

There was, however, one important instance in which the elements of a radical critique of bureaucracy were presented during the Great Leap Forward. The issue at stake concerned the methods by which bureaucratic officials should be paid, and the participants in the discussion and the views they expressed represented an important link between the Great Leap Forward and the Cultural Revolution.

The debate apparently began at Peitaiho in August 1958 when Mao Tse-tung raised the question whether the wage system, which had been fully implemented in 1955, was truly more desirable than the supply system that it had replaced, or whether the supply system should be reintroduced as the principal method for paying Party and government officials.[128] Mao's interest in the subject appears to have been stimulated by the discussion of the communes at the Peitaiho conference. He may have believed that, if peasants were soon to be paid by a supply system, there was no reason why cadres, presumably more ideologically advanced, could not be paid by the supply system too. It is very likely that an undated commentary written by Mao, "Some Opinions on the Supply System," was composed at the Peitaiho conference or shortly thereafter.[129] The short commentary made three points: the wage system was promoting selfishness within the bureaucracy ("contesting for rank" and "contesting for position"); the supply system had been one of the keys to victory in the revolution; and although the supply system could be seen as reflecting a rural work style and "guerrilla attitudes," it was nevertheless applicable to post-1949 China.*

On the basis of Mao's commentary, Chang Ch'un-ch'iao, a propaganda officer in Shanghai who would later achieve national prominence during the Cultural Revolution, wrote an article in late September or early October for the Shanghai journal *Chieh-fang* (Liberation). His essay, entitled "Break Away from the Idea of Bourgeois Rights," provided an elaboration of the ideas that had been presented in outline form in Mao's unpublished commentary.[130] Chang began by asserting that equality between the army and the people, between officers and men, and between higher and lower levels had always been taken as a fundamental principle for handling the relations within the ranks of the people, and that the supply system had "ensured the victory of the Chinese revolution." Despite this, the supply system was "condemned by some people as a serious offense," and was eliminated in the mid-1950's. This was a mistake, Chang said. It not only was based on the erroneous notion that only material incentives could inspire people to work hard (the notion, in Chang's words, that "money talks"), but it also reflected the fact that many veteran Communists had been infected by bourgeois ideas after 1949 and had become interested in pursuing their own material interests. In Chang's analysis, the regularization of the bureaucracy in the early 1950's had produced only waste, selfishness, laziness, and estrangement from the people. His conclusion, stated implicitly, was that the reintroduction of the supply system in the communes pointed the proper way for the bureaucracy, as well, and that it was time to follow the example of the Paris Commune and begin gradually to destroy hierarchy, inequality, and the principle of material interests on which they were based.

Since Chang's article was almost certainly an elaboration of Mao's own ideas, it is hardly surprising that the Chairman was pleased, although Chang may have stated the issue more simply than Mao would have liked. Mao ordered that the article be reprinted in *Jen-min jih-pao*, and he personally added an editorial note saying that the article, while it was one-sided and reflected some misunderstanding about the course of history, was at the same time basically correct and very readable.

---

*At the first Chengchow conference in November 1958, Mao added, "In 1953 [sic] we changed the supply system to the wage system. Basically it was the right thing to do. It was necessary for us to compromise. But there were defects. . . . The grade-level system is the father-son relationship, the cat-mouse relationship. It must be destroyed." See *Miscellany of Mao Tse-tung Thought*, p. 131.

The publication of Chang's article in *Jen-min jih-pao* on October 13 launched a debate on the supply system that lasted for three months. Some participants agreed with Chang. Eight graduate students in the economics department at the People's University in Peking wrote that they, too, believed the change from the supply system to the wage system to have been retrogression, and that the supply system should have been expanded in the early 1950's, not restricted.[131] Other writers totally disagreed. One pointed out correctly that the supply system had also been hierarchical, in that some cadres received more supplies than others. Another said that the institution of the wage system was actually progressive, because it helped develop China's "technical forces"; to eliminate it now would represent "absolute egalitarianism," for which China was not yet ready.[132] Still others sought to find a middle ground. Party propagandist and historian Hu Sheng, for example, agreed with those who said that it was proper to have switched from the supply system to the wage system, but he also accepted Chang Ch'un-ch'iao's assertion that it was wrong to have done so in so complete a fashion and to have denigrated the supply system as an example of rural work habits. Hu suggested that there should be a mixed system in which cadres would receive part of their income through the supply system and part through the wage system, and that gradually the role of the supply system should be increased.[133]

This debate in *Jen-min jih-pao* also attracted the attention of some senior Party officials. The director of the Party's Organization Department, An Tzu-wen, took a position virtually identical to that of Hu Sheng. In an article published in *Kuang-ming jih-pao* in early December, An acknowledged that the shift from the supply system to the wage system in the early 1950's had probably gone too far, and he proposed that cadres be paid by a system that combined free supplies with a graduated wage. This would maintain the incentive effects produced by the wage system, but it would narrow the difference in income among cadres and between cadres and the people, and would therefore help promote "communist thinking." An hastened to assure Party and government officials that the total income they would receive under this hybrid system would be higher than what they had earned under the supply system during the revolution, and that the effect on their present standards of living would therefore be minimal.[134]

Although this compromise had important backers, the wind soon shifted against it. The Sixth Plenum, held somewhat later in the month, recognized the difficulty of administering the supply system in the communes and decided that "in the income of commune members, the portion constituting the wage paid according to work done must occupy an important place over a long period and will, for a certain period, take first place."[135] This decision, when applied to the question of cadre remuneration, seems to have ended any possibility of a return to the supply system. In late December Mao asked Hu Ch'iao-mu, then an alternate member of the Party Secretariat and a deputy director of the Propaganda Department, to convene a meeting to decide the issue. At that meeting, which ran into January 1959, both Hu Ch'iao-mu and Teng Hsiao-p'ing stated their opposition even to An Tzu-wen's compromise proposal. Teng said that it was "difficult to say" whether the supply system was more progressive than the wage system and warned that if the supply system were carried out, it would cost more money than the wage system and the government would "bear a big burden"—presumably because under An's scheme salaries would have to be leveled upward, not downward. Hu, citing Lenin's *State and Revolution,* added that it would still be necessary for society to "retain bourgeois rights," and that it was those who demanded the reinstatement of the supply system, not those who had abandoned it, who were infected by "bourgeois" (in this case "petty bourgeois") ideas.

This viewpoint carried the day at the meeting. Chang Ch'un-ch'iao was instructed to help write a summary of its conclusions, in effect renouncing his own earlier views, but refused to do so. As for Mao, he apparently did not agree but chose not to challenge the decision. As Wu Leng-hsi, the editor-in-chief of *Jen-min jih-pao,* explained during the Cultural Revolution, "Chairman Mao consented to the summary not being written for the time being, but my subsequent impression was that Chairman Mao was dissatisfied. On many occasions he mentioned the incident in which the summary was not worked out."[136]

With this one exception, then, the Great Leap did not produce many radical proposals for solving China's bureaucratic dilemma. Instead, the Leap, like the Hundred Flowers before it, represented a resurgence of the organizational heritage of the Party—a remedial heritage that the tide of rationalization between 1952 and 1955 had suppressed but not eliminated. The Hundred Flowers had seen the rediscovery of rectification as an instrument of organizational control. The Great Leap Forward—together with its predecessor, the High Tide of 1955–56—marked the return to the principle that the introduction of mobilizational techniques into the bureaucracy could boost China's rates of economic growth and social modernization. As Teng Hsiao-p'ing expressed it:

Our basic method of work is as follows: to integrate the leadership with the masses, to pursue the mass line in all fields of work, to mobilize the masses boldly, to develop energetic mass movements under the guidance of the leadership, to sum up the views and pool the wisdom of the masses and rely on the strength of the masses to carry out the policies of the Party. . . . Hence it is obviously an erroneous view to ignore the initiative of the masses, to maintain that it is no longer necessary to organize mass movements since everything can be done from above by relying on the state apparatus, . . . or to consider mass movements necessary in the revolution but maintain that it is a different matter in [economic] construction.[137]

Like the Hundred Flowers, the Great Leap Forward also illustrated what would happen when the remedial heritage of the Party was carried too far. The Hundred Flowers demonstrated that open-door rectification campaigns, when they actively solicited external criticism of Party structure, staffing, and policies, could generate serious social unrest and political instability. The Leap showed that mass mobilization had to be guided by effective, disciplined, and restrained leadership. When the campaign style was applied to the bureaucracy as well as to the masses, the result was economic dislocation and organizational collapse.

7

The Origins of the Second Crisis
1962-1966

By 1962 a new set of economic and organizational programs had engineered China's recovery from the recession that had followed the Great Leap Forward. In the countryside, authority over agricultural production had been transferred from the communes back to the production brigades, then to the production teams, and even in some places to individual families. Overly ambitious plans for rural industrialization and social services had been scaled down or set aside. Material incentives had been restored to both peasants and workers, and scarce financial and material resources were once again being concentrated in the most productive sectors of the economy. Industry was undergoing reorganization to restore greater central control over planning and management. And, as we saw in the last chapter, the Party and state bureaucracies were being restructured so as to restore more systematic, institutionalized, centralized, and pragmatic methods of policymaking and administration.

Once the "three hard years" had passed and economic recovery was clearly underway, China's leaders turned yet again to the evaluation of their country's administrative organizations. The reassessment produced sharp controversy as they arrived at different diagnoses of the health of the Party and state bureaucracies and prescribed different remedies for organizational ills.

The principal issues at stake were familiar ones. One was whether the bureaucracy was simply inefficient and ineffective, or whether the new economic policies it had adopted since the Great Leap Forward demonstrated that it was leading China along a revisionist course. The other was whether the Party and state could be revitalized through a mixture of rationalization and rectification, or whether reform required that the bureaucracy once again be subjected to some form of popular supervision.

These two issues were joined during the Socialist Education Movement of 1962–66, a nationwide rectification campaign directed both at basic-level organizations in rural China and at the middle and upper levels of the state and Party bureaucracies. As Party leaders experimented with different procedures for organizational reform and drafted and redrafted the guiding principles for the Socialist Education Movement, the disputes among them became more and more intense. The People's Republic of China faced its second organizational crisis not because the Party was facing the sort of economic pressures and popular dissatisfaction it had encountered in 1956–57, but because the consensus among its highest leaders over economic programs and organizational policy had collapsed.

EMERGING ORGANIZATIONAL PROBLEMS

As Chinese leaders began their reassessment of the Party and state bureaucracies in 1962, they came to focus on three problems. One was serious corruption and demoralization among basic-level administrative and Party cadres, particularly in the rural communes. The effect of the Great Leap Forward on the countryside had been so devastating that the organizational network so painstakingly constructed in the early and middle 1950's was now experiencing a high degree of decay and deterioration. Another problem was ossification at the middle and upper levels of the Party and state bureaucracy, a condition reflected in overstaffing, poor coordination, and excessive routinization. Just as they had been confronted with the consequences of the campaign style of administration during the "three hard years," now Chinese leaders began to be faced with the results of what Maurice Meisner has called the "bureaucratic restoration" of the early 1960's.[1] And some leaders, particularly Mao Tse-tung, saw a third problem in what they perceived as the emergence of revisionist tendencies in the bureaucracy. More than at any previous time, organizational policy became intricately entwined in debates over social and economic issues as Mao and his supporters attempted to use rectification campaigns to undermine or reverse the decisions reached during the reviews of economic, cultural, and educational policy in the early 1960's.

Basic-Level Decay

One of the most serious organizational problems to emerge in the early 1960's was decay and corruption among the ranks of administrative and Party cadres at basic levels throughout the country, particularly in the communes. Some cadres had become so demoralized by the Great Leap Forward that they resigned their posts, or else performed their duties in a passive and perfunctory way. Others had taken advantage of their official positions to engage in various kinds of corruption and embezzlement. Still others had exceeded the Party's rural policies by condoning or actively encouraging the abandonment of collective production in favor of individual family enterprise.[2]

Some of these problems can be traced to the disastrous effects of the Great Leap Forward on industrial and agricultural production. The serious economic crisis of the early 1960's made it virtually inevitable that some basic-level cadres would use the leverage of their official positions to appropriate extra food for themselves, to allocate public funds and collective land for their personal use, or to profiteer by lending money to poorer peasants, often at usurious interest rates. In addition, despite the Party's attempt to attribute the decline in agricultural production between 1959 and 1961 to natural disasters, many peasants and cadres blamed Party policy for these reverses and argued that the agricultural sector could recover only if greater leeway were allowed for private farming and sideline household production.

Moreover, some of the Party's efforts to correct the economic and organizational errors of the Great Leap served to exacerbate basic-level organizational problems. The 1960–61 rectification campaign against the "five communist styles," mentioned in the last chapter, increased the disillusionment and demoralization among rural officials, who concluded justifiably that they were being blamed for policies for which they had little responsibility. The decentralization of power within the communes, through which control over accounting and production was transferred from commune to brigade to team, created a demand for skilled and committed basic-level leadership that was greater than the supply. Despite the attempt to fill this shortage by sending cadres from higher levels to settle in the countryside, rural leadership frequently passed to former middle and rich peasants who, despite their questionable political credentials, at least possessed a knowledge of local conditions, rudimentary literacy, and practical managerial skills.[3]

Upper-Level Ossification

At the upper and middle levels of the bureaucracy, there were growing signs of red tape and inefficiency, inadequate information about local conditions, and inability to ensure control over lower-level Party and government agencies. The bureaucratic restoration of the early 1960's had, in essence, produced an "ossification syndrome" highly reminiscent of that which had emerged from the period of rationalization between 1952 and 1955.

For one thing, as in the middle 1950's, there was a proliferation of new governmental agencies, particularly at the ministerial level. By 1965 the State Council encompassed some fifty ministries and major commissions, thereby becoming as large as it had been in May 1956 before the streamlining of government that took place during the Great Leap Forward. In just three years between 1963 and 1965, no fewer than ten new ministries and commissions were created or reestablished, many of them with counterparts at the provincial level. A similar proliferation of offices and sections was also taking place within each ministry and department. The result was that it became increasingly difficult to coordinate governmental programs effectively or to make decisions quickly. By 1965 Peking municipal government cadres were complaining that bureaucratic inefficiency was inevitable because there were too many sections and because the division of labor was drawn too fine.[4]

There was also evidence of serious overstaffing at the middle levels as cadres who had entered the bureaucracy in the 1950's worked their way up the ranks. Between 1957 and 1965, for example, despite the hsia-fang movements, the number of cadres in the Heilungkiang provincial system of supply-and-marketing cooperatives who were assigned to offices at the county level and above increased by some 8,500, while only 1,500 new cadres were being added to the basic-level offices. This meant that the proportion of supply-and-marketing cadres working in the middle-level administrative positions rose from 20 percent in 1957 to 30 percent in 1965. At the same time, however, the basic levels continued to be understaffed; of 6,000 supply-and-marketing offices in the province, more than 1,900 were staffed by only two cadres. Many were staffed by only one. The result was top-heavy organization with inefficiency at the middle levels and poor service at the bottom.[5]

Another problem was the extension of routine. Cadres were becoming preoccupied more with the mechanical application of established procedures than with creative solutions to new problems. With increasing frequency, articles in the Chinese press criticized the cadres' tendency to "seek only the passable" in their work, their refusal to take risks, and their lack of enterprise.[6] At the same time, the bureaucracy was accused of producing too much paperwork and holding too many meetings, so that even if cadres did try to initiate more adaptive policies, they would simply not have had the time to do so effectively. In September 1963, for instance, a Central Committee directive complained that although the Party had repeatedly given orders to simplify meetings and exercise strict control over statistical reports and forms, the problem of too many meetings and too much paperwork had still not been solved.[7]

Finally, serious problems of information gathering and organizational control affected the entire bureaucracy. According to press reports published in the mid-1960's, county Party committees and government agencies lacked adequate information about rural conditions, largely because county officials were too lazy or too preoccupied with routine to make tours of inspection. When they did go down to the basic levels, the reports charged, they preferred to visit advanced communes and brigades rather than more typical ones because these units had "better conditions and fewer problems."[8] County cadres were also accused of blindly carrying out unrealistic directives from their superiors for fear that they would be pun-

ished if they dared to question a provincial order. One county official pro-
fessed himself to be greatly shocked to learn that Mao considered the
mechanical implementation of such orders to be a "subtle way of opposing
or sabotaging directives from higher levels."[9]

A somewhat different set of problems seemed to characterize Peking's
relationship with the regions and the provinces. Even after the efforts in
the early 1960's to recentralize the economic system and to reestablish
central control over the Party, provincial and regional leaders maintained
substantial influence in the policymaking councils in Peking, and a degree
of economic autonomy. At the same time, the growing disputes within the
Politburo over socioeconomic policy meant that fewer clear and un-
equivocal directives were being sent out from Peking. Taken together,
these considerations made it possible for provincial and regional leaders to
ignore or evade central directives with which they disagreed, distort central programs to suit their own ends, and turn their localities into what
would later be described as "independent kingdoms."[10]

Revisionism?

As central policymaking became increasingly pragmatic, and as policymakers showed less concern with doctrinal considerations and more
willingness to let objective conditions determine socioeconomic programs,
the process began to produce a set of social, economic, and cultural
policies that some leaders, particularly Mao, considered to be dangerously
close to revisionism. In agriculture, for example, experiments with various
forms of private farming—dividing collective land among households, as-
signing production quotas to individual families rather than to the production teams, expanding the size of private plots, and the like—not only
developed spontaneously in the countryside, but were also sanctioned by
some provincial and central leaders. Meanwhile, rural investment was
concentrated in the most productive counties, and agricultural machinery
was provided only to those counties and communes that could afford to
pay for it. In industry, worker participation in factory management was
curtailed, material incentives were reinstated, rules and regulations were
reestablished, and investment decisions were made on the basis of profita-
bility rather than of social or political criteria. Peasants were given temporary urban jobs that required few skills, but that provided lower wages
and fewer benefits than those available to full-time industrial workers. In
public health, resources were concentrated in urban hospitals, and rural
clinics established during the Great Leap Forward were closed. In education, a two-track system was developed under which students with the best
academic qualifications attended elite institutions while others, often from
worker-peasant backgrounds, attended part-work, part-study programs of

lower prestige and quality. In culture, traditional forms of literature and art reappeared, and writers and artists employed allegorical techniques to make veiled criticisms of the Great Leap Forward and Mao's leadership. The common thread that linked these policies, in Mao's view, was that they sacrificed socioeconomic equality, popular participation, and ideological orthodoxy for the sake of technical efficiency, economic growth, and political liberalization.*

Mao came to regard the policies of the early 1960's as both undesirable and unnecessary. They were undesirable because they threatened to increase the degree of inequality and privilege in China; they were unnecessary, he was convinced, because mass mobilization and ideological zeal could promote economic growth more effectively. As a result, although the Chairman had agreed that new policy guidelines should be drawn up in the early 1960's, he became increasingly dissatisfied with the results of that review. Between 1962 and 1965 he intervened on four sets of issues, each of which had long been of particular interest to him, in an attempt to alter the policy directions set in 1961–62. In agriculture, he tried to halt the trends toward private farming and to place agricultural mechanization under local, rather than central, control. In education, he suggested reforms in teaching methods and in the examination system, called for a simplification of the curriculum, and proposed that university students spend less time in class and more time in physical labor and political movements at the grass roots. In public health, he criticized the urban orientation of the Ministry of Public Health (suggesting dryly that it be renamed the "Ministry of Health for Urban Gentlemen"), and instructed that the focus of medical work be concentrated on the countryside. In culture, he repeatedly criticized both the resurgence of traditional forms and historical themes and the appearance of allegorical criticisms of the Great Leap Forward, and warned that some people in China's literary circles were sliding "right down to the brink of revisionism."[11]

American specialists on contemporary China disagree as to how successfully Mao intervened in the Chinese policymaking process between 1962 and 1965. Some point to changes in policy toward agriculture, education, public health, and culture and conclude that his attempts to reverse the policy directions of the early 1960's were relatively effective.[12] Others believe that he achieved only minor changes in policy but blame the inertia of the bureaucracy and the ambiguity of his own instructions rather than any conscious opposition by powerful state and Party officials.[13] Still others argue that he encountered stubborn resistance at the highest levels of the

---

*The secondary literature now available on the policy adjustments of the early 1960's is too voluminous to list here. The best single account is in Byung-joon Ahn, *Chinese Politics and the Cultural Revolution: Dynamics of Policy Processes* (Seattle, 1976), chaps. 3–8.

Politburo from men who believed that the policies set in the early 1960's were sound, effective, and totally in keeping with socialist principles.[14]

Whatever the assessment of outside observers, it is clear that Mao himself was dissatisfied with his ability to effect policy change through the periodic interventions he made between 1962 and 1965. Nor was he satisfied that either Party cadres or the Chinese people were sufficiently aware of the danger of revisionism in China. For both these reasons, he became convinced as early as the fall of 1962 that it was necessary to launch a nationwide campaign against revisionism.[15] On the one hand, such a campaign would increase his ability to change the policies with which he disagreed. By reintroducing doctrinal considerations into bureaucratic decision making, he could place his opponents on the defensive and mobilize Party and state officials to join him in demanding the modification of revisionist policies. On the other hand, as Lowell Dittmer has pointed out, casting the policy debates of the time as a monumental conflict between "proletarian" and "revisionist" lines would help cadres and masses alike to understand the significance of the struggle and would help explain and justify the policy changes Mao wanted to promote.[16] His call for a "socialist education movement," then, was partly a tactical device for outflanking his opponents in the Central Committee and in the provinces and partly a strategy for innoculating the entire country against the virus of revisionism.

Mao's desire for a new rectification campaign, which stimulated the sharpest debate over organizational questions since the Hundred Flowers, laid the groundwork for the Cultural Revolution. Although Chinese leaders had become concerned about basic-level decay and upper-level ossification in the Party and state organizations, they did not all agree with Mao that the policy adjustments of the early 1960's constituted revisionism. Some consequently opposed his plans for rectification and sought to divert it to safer targets. Moreover, Mao's proposals for rectification—particularly basic-level rectification—involved substantial reliance on mass mobilization as a means of supervising the performance of Party officials. They therefore reopened a question that had divided the Party ever since the 1950's: Should the reform of the Party and state be undertaken by open-door or closed-door techniques?

THE SOCIALIST EDUCATION MOVEMENT
AT THE BASIC LEVELS

In August 1962, at a central work conference in Peitaiho, Mao Tse-tung vetoed proposals for any further departures from a policy of collectivized agriculture and ordered that the use of private plots and rural markets be held to existing levels. The following month, again on Mao's initiative, the

Tenth Plenum decided to launch a campaign to rectify basic-level rural Party organizations.[17] This rural rectification campaign had three purposes. First, it was to ensure that trends toward individual farming were halted, and that, in the words of the plenum's resolutions on rural work, rural officials would "respect the directives of the Central Committee." Second, as a "socialist education movement," the campaign would explain the theoretical and ideological reasons that made it necessary to defend and consolidate a collective system of agriculture. And finally, the rectification campaign would serve to punish cadres who had engaged in corruption and to strengthen rural Party organizations that had decayed in the years following the Great Leap Forward.

As a preliminary step in the campaign, investigations were undertaken in selected areas across the country to determine the amount of corruption among basic-level Party cadres, the extent to which the Party's agricultural policy had been violated, and the degree to which capitalist and superstitious practices had reemerged among the peasants. These investigations also provided an opportunity for experimentation with different methods of conducting a socialist education movement among peasants and rural cadres and for determining which techniques would best be able to correct the problems in the countryside. Reports from these experiments were relayed to Peking, where they were discussed in two Central Committee work conferences in February and May 1963. Mao took an active part in these two work conferences, and the regulations they produced, known as the Early Ten Points, closely reflected the Chairman's views.[18]

The Early Ten Points

The aim of the Early Ten Points was to provide an explanation of the necessity for a socialist education movement in rural China and to indicate the basic principles that would guide the campaign. The first part of the document, echoing the views that Mao had stated at the work conference in May, warned that though the economic situation in the countryside had greatly improved since 1959, political and organizational problems were still serious. Speculation, profiteering, usury, corruption, land purchase, and hired labor were common in some areas, and, even more important, many cadres had adopted an attitude of indifference toward these phenomena, thereby letting them continue to develop. Nonetheless, the ten points continued, the experiments undertaken since the Tenth Plenum indicated that a properly conducted socialist education movement could basically eliminate the problems of corruption and "antisocialist thinking" within three years' time.

The program envisioned two methods of organizational reform. All cadres at the county level and below, and particularly the Party secretaries, were to participate regularly in collective productive labor. This would eliminate the possibility of alienation between the cadres and the masses and ensure that, in Mao's words, cadres would "no longer be toplofty, no longer be bureaucrats and overlords, no longer be divorced from the masses." In addition, regular physical labor would also offer a means for officials to acquire accurate information about the relations between classes, socioeconomic problems, and the production situation in the localities for which they were responsible.

A more controversial method of organizational reform spelled out in the plan was the creation of "poor and lower-middle peasant associations." The associations were to provide a mechanism for mobilizing a "revolutionary class army" of politically reliable peasants to monitor the performance of basic-level rural cadres. In the short term, the associations were given the authority to investigate commune accounts, identify corrupt cadres, and even initiate disciplinary actions against errant officials. Over the longer term, they were supposed to "assist and oversee the work of the commune and brigade administrative committees" by regularly sending delegates to discuss important policy problems with basic-level cadres.

The recruitment standards for the associations were quite lenient. Poor and lower-middle peasants who had become "corrupt elements, thieves, speculators, and [political] degenerates" or who had collaborated with "landlords, rich peasants, counterrevolutionaries, and undesirable elements" were not to be admitted to membership unless they could show they had truly reformed. But the program also warned that maintaining the purity of the associations could not be used as a pretext for excluding peasants who had made "minor errors in their daily life."

What was potentially controversial about the Early Ten Points was not its diagnosis of the rural situation, but the remedy that it proposed. The plan envisioned a virtually unrestrained open-door rectification in which the power to monitor and discipline basic-level cadres would pass from the Party to the peasants. To those concerned with maintaining production and those who believed in the vanguard role of the Party, the degree of authority given to the associations by the Early Ten Points must have seemed excessive.

The Later Ten Points

It is not surprising, then, that the attempt to establish effective poor and lower-middle peasant associations in the summer of 1963 encountered some serious difficulties.[19] For one thing, peasants often feared that local cadres, or the higher-level Party committees that had appointed them, would retaliate against anyone who dared to speak out against corruption or deviations from Party policy. They thus were reluctant to use the associations as instruments to supervise the cadres. For another, many local cadres redefined the functions of the associations to strip them of their supervisory powers and transform them into auxiliaries of the local Party branch and administrative committee. Even though it directly contradicted the provisions of the Early Ten Points, this policy often had support at higher levels as well. Within five days of the publication of the plan, the *Nan-fang jih-pao* published a statement of the responsibilities of the peasant associations in Kwangtung. They were

to act as the assistant to the management committee of the production team; under the leadership of the Party, to conduct class education and education in Party policy among the poor and lower-middle peasants as well as the broad masses of commune members; to raise the ideological consciousness of the poor and lower-middle peasants; to consolidate the collective economy; and to take the lead in accomplishing various production tasks.[20]

Nothing at all was said about the supervisory functions of the associations.

From the beginning, the Early Ten Points had been regarded as a provisional document that was to be modified on the basis of practice and further experimentation. Increasingly aware of the difficulties in establishing peasant associations independent enough or strong enough to rectify basic-level cadres, the Party Secretariat, under the direction of Teng Hsiao-p'ing and P'eng Chen, drafted a second document on the rural Socialist Education Movement in September 1963. Much longer, much more concrete, and much more detailed than the earlier formulations, this document, known as the Later Ten Points, attempted to resolve a number of problems concerning concrete policies that had emerged in the course of "spot-testing at various places."[21]

The Later Ten Points differed from the earlier program on three major issues. First, they voiced considerable skepticism about the possibility of establishing peasant associations that could serve as reliable agents of organizational reform in the countryside. Compared to the Early Ten Points, the new program was more concerned about the "impurity of class ranks" among the poor and lower-middle peasants, less sanguine that all poorer peasants would support Party policy, and therefore more insistent on the need for strict recruitment criteria when forming peasant associations. As a result, the later points argued that the formation of associations would be a protracted process, and warned, "Any poor and lower-middle peasant association that is established . . . only by administrative order will exist only nominally and will not function well. Some time ago, in some places, poor and lower-middle peasant associations were set up overnight. Most of these organizations exist in name only or are seriously impure." The new program clearly implied that the associations could be established, therefore, only after the Socialist Education Movement had been completed and the peasants had undergone "education and examination." Since this was the case, although the associations might be able to play a supervisory role in the future, they could hardly play a major role in the rectification of basic-level cadres during the Socialist Education Movement.

This pessimistic view of the difficulties of forming effective peasant associations in the countryside led logically to a second difference between the Early and the Later Ten Points over the role of work teams in the Socialist Education Movement. The earlier plan, relying on peasant associations formed quickly and spontaneously at the local levels to conduct rectification of basic-level cadres, provided for the dispatch of work teams from higher-level Party committees only in the most exceptional cases. The later program, which saw the formation of associations as a complicated and lengthy process, called for the dispatch of work teams to selected communes for a three-month tour of duty. These work teams—composed of intellectuals, students, and office workers, and led by higher-level cadres—would ensure both that corrupt and inefficient cadres would be identified and punished, and that the mass movement would proceed in correct directions. Selected peasant representatives might still help the work teams, but their power to supervise their own cadres had been greatly reduced.

Furthermore, the role of the peasant was even more limited in communes that did not receive work teams. Cadres from these units, together with peasant representatives, were summoned to commune or district headquarters. At these meetings, lasting some twenty days, the cadres would be told the purpose of the movement, encouraged to correct their mistakes voluntarily, and instructed to rely on the poor and lower-middle peasants when they returned to their units. Although not saying so explicitly, the Later Ten Points strongly implied that permanent peasant associations would not be established in communes that had not received work teams, presumably because purity of peasant organizations could not be guaranteed.

A third difference between the Early and the Later Ten Points was that the latter document called not only for rectification of the basic-level rural cadres, but also for rectification of their superiors at the county, special district, and provincial levels who were accused of having "impure thoughts and work styles" of their own. The Later Ten Points provided that these middle-level cadres should first correct their own class standpoint and improve their own work style before the Socialist Education Movement could be undertaken at the basic levels. To this end, middle-level cadres were to be subjected to the urban component of the Socialist Education Movement, a so-called five-anti movement, whose targets were corruption and theft, speculation, extravagance and waste, poor coordination, and bureaucratism.* This was to be a mild, closed-door rectification campaign; and the later points did not in any way suggest that these problems at the middle levels of the bureaucracy were nearly as significant as those at the basic levels.

Despite these differences between the two programs, Mao seemed willing to accept the change in emphasis that the second embodied. Work teams were, after all, a commonly accepted device for carrying on rectification campaigns; some degree of peasant participation in the Socialist Education Movement was still provided for; and it appeared that the campaign would not be successful without the use of work teams.[22] But though Mao may have found the Later Ten Points to be an acceptable reformulation of the procedures to be employed in rural rectification, there is reason to believe that he was less satisfied with the way in which they were implemented. Refugee accounts indicate that the work teams dispatched to the countryside under the later program devoted most of their energies to investigating cases of cadre corruption and showed little interest in mobilizing the peasantry to participate in the movement or to form peasant associations.[23]

The first sign that Mao was dissatisfied with the course of the Socialist Education Movement came in June 1964, nine months after the Later Ten Points had been published, when he drew up six criteria for evaluating the progress of the movement.[24] Mao's first criterion was whether "the poor and lower-middle peasants have been truly mobilized." By placing it first on his list, Mao seems both to have been indicating the importance he placed on popular participation in the campaign and to have been implying that he was not satisfied with this aspect of the movement. As Richard Baum has concluded in his careful study of the Socialist Education Movement:

Mao undoubtedly had reason to be concerned; for in the first half of 1964, mass peasant mobilization had not (despite numerous official protestations to the contrary) held a high priority among rural work-team personnel. . . . Consequently, peasant mobilization had not occurred on a large scale; and mass struggles against corrupt cadres had in general been minimized—with major emphasis being placed instead upon quiet and discreet [i.e., closed-door] investigations, criticism, and discipline, under the tight control of the work teams, local Party organs, and higher authorities.[25]

The Revised Later Ten Points

The Early and the Later Ten Points had both emphasized the need for high-ranking cadres to participate personally in the Socialist Education

*There was no relationship between the "five-anti" movement of the early 1960's and the Wu-fan campaign of 1952, beyond the coincidence that both campaigns were directed against "five evils."

Movement in order to gain firsthand knowledge of socioeconomic conditions and organizational problems at the basic levels. And both Liu Shao-ch'i and his wife, Wang Kuang-mei, heeded this advice. Liu spent eighteen days in a commune in Honan in the first half of 1964.[26] Wang spent the full five months between November 1963 and April 1964 in the T'ao-yüan production brigade near Tientsin.[27]

Before Wang Kuang-mei left for T'ao-yüan, Liu allegedly warned her that the brigade would be so tightly controlled by its cadres that it would be impossible to persuade the peasants to criticize them. Liu reportedly told his wife that "the poor and lower-middle peasants do not tell us the truth," and that therefore "the method of holding investigation meetings no longer produces any results." Rather than organizing open mass meetings, therefore, the work teams would have to "do some secret work. It is only by 'putting down roots' and linking up with the villagers that they will have their fears allayed and will dare to speak out." Following her husband's advice, Wang Kuang-mei visited T'ao-yüan under a pseudonym, posing as a secretary of the Hopei provincial public security department, and conducted the rectification as if it were a secret investigation. As a Cultural Revolution account put it, "Protected by security personnel who followed her about in secret, she made secret investigations in a furtive way, 'putting down roots' and linking up with the villagers and carrying out secret activities in a big way." Wang treated T'ao-yüan like a "Kuomintang-ruled area" and established "a dictatorship of the work team, which monopolized all work, manipulated the masses, and did everything itself."

On the basis of her investigation, Wang Kuang-mei wrote a report of some sixty or seventy thousand characters. One conclusion was that the poor and lower-middle peasants could not be relied upon to conduct the movement on their own because they lived in fear of the cadres and because their own political standpoint was not firm. As Wang is said to have described them, "No matter how much you teach the poor and lower-middle peasants, hardly any of them lack defects. Bandits, KMT members, puppet army men, big Buddhists, old priests. . . . There's hardly anyone over 35 who is any good. . . . Try as you will you can hardly find any poor and lower-middle peasants who are without defects."* Wang further concluded that the T'ao-yüan Party branch was "basically not Red at all," and that a full 85 percent of the brigade's cadres were corrupt (the Later Ten Points had estimated that only 5 percent of the cadres would be found guilty of corruption or other mistakes). "All of them, big or small,

---

*This quotation refers, in fact, to Wang's experiences in a different commune, but is probably representative of her opinion of T'ao-yüan. It appeared in *Tung-fang hung* (Peking) on May 7, 1967. It is quoted from Schurmann, *Ideology and Organization in Communist China*, pp. 538–39.

are questionable and can not be trusted," she reportedly said. Her recommendation was that to reform the countryside, the Party should rely even more on work teams dispatched from higher levels.

Influenced by his wife's report, which he circulated widely within the Party, Liu Shao-ch'i began to express a highly pessimistic view of the rural situation in a series of speeches in Peking and Hopei in mid-1964.[28] In these speeches Liu accepted his wife's conclusion that a large percentage of basic-level cadres—higher than that previously admitted—had become corrupt or lax. On July 2, 1964, addressing a forum of district Party committee secretaries in Hopei, Liu declared, "The problems of some grassroots cadres are serious, and political power is not in the hands of the Communist Party. You say that they [corrupt cadres] made up 30 percent, and I am afraid that in the general sense this is the actual percentage." Of the other 70 percent, Liu said, only 30 percent were quite good, while 40 percent were mediocre.

Liu also warned that rooting out these bad cadres would be extremely difficult. For one thing, basic-level cadres were protected by the stipulation in the Later Ten Points that only 5 percent of the cadres were to be criticized. "The grassroots cadres have a way to deal with us, since uniting more than 95 percent of the cadres is called for." Furthermore, they could use their influence and authority to deny information about their activities to all but the most powerful, most persistent work teams: "Don't belittle the grassroots cadres, for you must know that the strength of our work teams is inferior to theirs. Nothing is clear to the work teams, but [the basic-level cadres] have a clear knowledge of everything, because they have their own gangs." Finally, in his rather vague observation that "the county committees cannot lead the movement," Liu seemed to imply that corrupt basic-level cadres were able to rely for protection on their superiors in the county seats who were responsible for their appointments.

Liu's conclusion was that the work teams would have to be strengthened to make the Socialist Education Movement effective. More care would have to be taken in recruiting them, and they would have to be given more power once they arrived in the countryside. Explicitly repudiating the provision in the Later Ten Points that the work teams should serve as the staff of the basic-level cadres, Liu said, "It won't do for a work team merely to serve as staff. . . . It must exercise leadership as a plenipotentiary and should serve as the representative of the Party at a higher level." He also proposed increasing the size of the work teams so that they could be large enough to fight a "battle of annihilation" against corrupt rural officials.

In September 1964 the Later Ten Points were revised to take into account new experience that had come to the attention of the Central Committee. The "new experience" reflected in the document, commonly known as the Revised Later Ten Points,[29] was almost certainly that of Liu and Wang, for the revised draft embodied the same assessment of the rural situation that Wang Kuang-mei had provided in her report on T'ao-yüan and Liu had presented in his speeches earlier in the summer.

The most striking feature of the revision was its pessimism. This was in sharp contrast with both earlier plans, but quite in keeping with the rather gloomy characterization of the rural situation that Liu had provided in his speeches in Peking and Hopei. It was now estimated that the rural Socialist Education Movement would require six months in each commune and, as a whole, "five to six years, or even longer." (The Later Ten Points had estimated three months and two to three years, respectively.) Even more important, the revision expressed doubts about the Party's ability to conduct the campaign successfully. Describing the Socialist Education Movement as "more widespread, more complicated, and more meaningful than the land-reform movement," the text went on to warn:

At present, the enemy's methods of opposing the proletarian dictatorship and socialism are becoming even more cunning. They associate with and corrupt cadres, implement peaceful transition, and establish a counterrevolutionary two-faced regime. They also utilize certain articles of our documents to carry out legal struggle against us. These are the main forms of the enemy's opposition to us. We are still very unfamiliar with class struggle under these new conditions, and with this new revolution. If one does not personally go deeply into practice, one will not be able truly to understand this class struggle and this revolution, and naturally will not correctly lead them.

One of the grounds for concern, according to the Revised Later Ten Points, was that class ranks in the countryside had become hopelessly muddled. Many of those who claimed to be poor or lower-middle peasants in fact were not. It would be impossible, therefore, to let the poorer peasants, or the peasant associations, play any important role in the Socialist Education Movement. In particular, any hasty attempt to form associations would permit false poor and lower-middle peasants to "sneak into the organizations." In view of the impurity of the class ranks, the revision stressed the importance not so much of mobilizing the peasants, but of "controlling the mass movement." And it called for nothing less than a complete review of the class background of every peasant: "Since there is widespread confusion about class backgrounds in the villages, it is necessary to clearly define class ranks as a part of the work of the Socialist Education Movement. The background of each rural household should be examined and classified after full discussion by the masses, and a class file be established." The clear implication was that the peasant masses could be only targets of the Socialist Education Movement, not its instrument.

If the peasants were unreliable, the cadres were even worse. Where the Later Ten Points had cautioned against exaggerating the cadres' problems, the revision warned of ignoring the seriousness of problems among basic-level cadres, and of being not stern enough in the education and criticism of cadres who had committed mistakes. Although the revised points still spoke in terms of uniting 95 percent of the cadres, they said that the successful rectification of cadres who had made errors could "only be a hope."

In short, the Revised Later Ten Points reflected a serious dilemma in the thinking of its drafters. Both the cadres and the peasants were seen as corrupt or antisocialist, and in serious need of reform, but neither could be relied upon to reform the other. Corrupt cadres could not educate the peasants, nor could backward peasants straighten out the cadres. To resolve this dilemma, Party strategists were forced to rely heavily on work teams dispatched from higher levels and to downplay the role of local cadres and local peasants—let alone local peasant associations—in the Socialist Education Movement. "The whole movement should be led by the work team," the revised plan declared, and the document paid special attention to ensuring the quality and capability of work-team members. No cadres who were politically unreliable or seriously questionable in ideology and behavior were to be permitted to join the teams, for if the purity of the teams was not maintained, the entire movement would surely founder.

The differences between the Revised Later Ten Points and the Later Ten Points are clear. What is less certain is whether Mao had serious objections to the revised points at the time they were formulated. In 1964 Mao himself had arrived at an analysis of the rural situation that was as pessimistic as those of Liu and the Revised Later Ten Points. As early as March Mao had acknowledged that the Socialist Education Movement could probably not be completed within the two to three years stipulated in the Later Ten Points and had expressed his willingness to extend the campaign to five to six years.[30] In August Mao also indicated his agreement with Liu Shao-ch'i's assessment that 30 percent of the rural cadres were corrupt. In Mao's words, "In our nation now, about one-third of the power is controlled by the enemy or by those who sympathize with them." He noted that many branch Party secretaries could be bribed with a few packs of cigarettes, and went on to complain that there was no telling "what one could achieve by marrying his daughter off to such a person." His conclusion was that in the rural areas "there are more than a few problems at the present time."[31]

As with the Later Ten Points, Mao may have objected more to the way in which the revised program was implemented than to the words in which it was formulated. Refugee interviews and documents from the Cultural Revolution both indicate that after the publication of the revised points, extremely large work teams were sent to fight what Liu termed a "war of annihilation" against corrupt cadres and "bad elements."[32] In Hopei, for example, work teams in the first stage of the movement comprised 120,000 people, or one team member for every five to six households in the communes to which they were sent. During the second stage the number on work teams was increased to 180,000, or one for every three to four households.[33] In the central-south area there were two or three work-team members in every production team, or one for every ten to twenty "labor-power units." These work teams, according to the Red Guards, went to the villages in a mood to suspect everything, and took over all work in the brigades, including day-to-day accounting: "All powers were exercised by the work teams."[34]

As a result of such techniques, the Socialist Education Movement became, in Richard Baum's words, "the most intensive purge of rural Party members and cadres in the history of the Chinese People's Republic." Overall, between 1.25 and 2.5 million basic-level cadres were dismissed from office. Although this figure may represent only between 5 and 10 percent of China's total rural leadership at the time, the proportion of cadres purged in the villages visited by the work teams may have been as high as 50 or even 80 percent. As Baum has put it, "Never before . . . had such a thoroughgoing attempt been made to fully expose and criticize . . . corruption."[35]

The Twenty-three Articles

The effect of the Revised Later Ten Points on the Socialist Education Movement came under intense criticism at a central work conference on rural work convened by the Politburo in December 1964 and January 1965. Mao's comments at the conference were reflected in a document called the "Twenty-three Articles" that was disseminated by the Central Committee in mid-January.[36] That this new formulation represented a significant change in policy was indicated in the Secretariat's introduction, which acknowledged that it might well "contradict previous Central Committee documents concerning the Socialist Education Movement" and emphasized that it would supersede all earlier directives on the campaign.

In essence, Mao had three sets of objections to Liu's conduct of the Socialist Education Movement and to the way it had been implemented in the three months since the publication of the Revised Later Ten Points. First, Mao had come increasingly to believe that the campaign had lost sight of its true purpose—rectifying revisionist tendencies among cadres and peasants—and had become obsessed with the narrower problem of cadre corruption. Liu had contended in mid-1964 that the focus of the campaign should be the resolution of the "contradiction between the four cleans and the four uncleans"—a circumspect way of saying that it should deal with the question of cadre corruption. By the end of 1964, however, Mao had concluded that the "four cleans and the four uncleans" did not explain the nature of the problem. His reasoning was that corrupt officials and clean officials could be found in any society, including capitalist and feudal societies. What was more important than corruption, therefore, was the political stance that cadres took on major policy issues. In Mao's view, the principal contradiction in rural areas was between socialism and capitalism—the degree to which both cadres and peasants were committed to socialist principles and socialist policies—just as he had stated in the Early Ten Points.

Mao's return to the original definition of the Socialist Education Movement was signaled by two key passages in the Twenty-three Articles. In one, Liu's formulation of the "contradiction between the four cleans and the four uncleans" was explicitly repudiated (although it was not attributed to Liu personally) and the assertion was made that the Marxist-Leninist way of describing the movement would be to recognize that it involved the "struggle between the two roads of socialism and capitalism." In a second and even more significant passage, the target of the Socialist Education Movement was defined as "people in the communes, districts, counties, special districts, and even in the provincial and Central Committee departments, who oppose socialism." The emphasis on provincial and Central Committee departments was significant. The Revised Later Ten Points, with their emphasis on corruption, had referred to higher-level cadres (particularly at the county level) only insofar as they had "instigated, protected, and supported" corruption of cadres at the basic levels. The Twenty-three Articles, on the other hand, emphasized the problem of revisionism and suggested that revisionists (or, at least, people who "oppose socialism") might even be found at the highest levels of the Party.

Mao's second concern was the number of cadres who were being accused of corruption by the work teams, and the severity with which they were being punished. The Revised Later Ten Points had called for a rectification of both Party cadres and state officials, but Mao now advocated restricting the movement, at least at first, to the Party committees. The revised points had demanded that cadres who had engaged in corruption be forced to repay all the money that they had taken, but Mao said that this was a futile attempt to "squeeze out all the toothpaste." In other words, Mao saw the cadre problem not as a "war of annihilation" against some enemy, but as a temporary difficulty within the ranks of the people, a difficulty to which united-front tactics could be applied. Accordingly, the Twenty-three Articles stipulated that most cadres were "good" or "relatively good"; that after criticism and struggle most cadres would be reformed enough to "go to battle" once again; and that cadres who had embezzled funds but who had admitted their crimes could have their indemnities reduced, delayed, or even cancelled. Where Liu had called for strict, even harsh, treatment of corrupt officers, Mao seemed to advocate great leniency.

Mao reserved his greatest vehemence for a third issue: the way in which the work teams had controlled the Socialist Education Movement, employed "human-wave" tactics, and emphasized secret investigations instead of mass mobilization. On January 3, 1965, he called this an "insipid method" that could only obstruct the success of the movement, and expressed amazement at the size of the work teams and disgust at the constant pleas of work-team leaders for more manpower. He declared that, in the future, if anyone asked to increase the size of a work team, he would order it cut in half; if they asked again, he would have the work team abolished altogether. Instead of this "dreary" method of work, he recommended that the movement rely on the masses, not on the work teams.

Mao did not propose abolishing the work teams completely, but he did suggest that they reduce their size and change their style of work. He would begin with one cadre—for instance, his long-time adviser Ch'en Po-ta. If this was not enough, Ch'en might "bring another fellow." The two would then enter a production brigade, and Ch'en would say, "My name is Ch'en Po-ta, and I won't visit your village if you don't have any problems. If you have, a meeting should be held. Most of the people are innocent, and only a few are guilty. Let's rely on the majority." Then the work team would let the peasants themselves decide whether or not they wanted to launch the Socialist Education Movement in their village. If they chose to do so, the work team would encourage them to mobilize 70 to 80 percent of the households and select their own leaders during the course of the struggle. This way a tiny work team could mobilize five thousand people. Under the Revised Later Ten Points a work team of five hundred people was not mobilizing the masses and therefore was achieving nothing. "If we make revolution this way," Mao concluded, "the revolution will take a hundred years."

In line with Mao's recommendations, the Twenty-three Articles retained provisions enabling work teams to guide the Socialist Education Movement at selected communes, but forbade them to engage in the "human-wave" tactics or secret investigations characteristic of the T'ao-yüan experience. Instead of behaving mysteriously or confining their activities to a small minority of people, the work teams were to "boldly unleash the masses" to conduct rectification of basic-level Party cadres.

In short, the Later Ten Points and the Revised Later Ten Points had gradually transformed the Socialist Education Movement from the relatively spontaneous mass movement envisioned by the Early Ten Points into a rectification campaign dominated by work teams. The Twenty-three Articles halted this trend and once again gave initiative and authority to the peasants. "Cadres must be supervised both from above and below," the document said, but the "most important supervision is that which comes from the masses." It reiterated that among the most significant goals of the Socialist Education Movement was the design and construction of "effective supervisory and political work systems," such as the peasant associations, that could monitor the ideological orientation and the performance of basic-level cadres on a long-term basis.

The County Reform Campaign

The publication of the Twenty-three Articles affected the way in which the Socialist Education Movement was conducted both at the basic levels and in the county Party committees. At the local level there was some effort to reduce the numbers of cadres purged in the campaign, even if that meant reversing the verdicts on some of those who had been dismissed in late 1964. The goal was to conform to Mao's instruction that only 5 percent of the cadres should be criticized and only 1 or 2 percent punished. In early 1965, for example, a widespread reversal of verdicts apparently took place in Tung-hsien, Peking municipality. According to P'eng Chen, Peking's Party first secretary, 40 to 60 percent of the rural cadres had been purged earlier in the Socialist Education Movement. To conduct so extensive a purge was impermissible, P'eng said, and the cadres should be reinstated. "If half the members of the municipal Party committee or the county Party committee were replaced, would problems arise? Those who replace others may feel that no problem would arise, but those who are replaced certainly feel that this is not right."*

The Twenty-three Articles also changed the focus of the campaign at the basic levels, though not in the way Mao had intended. If the campaign was no longer described as a purge of corrupt cadres by large work teams, neither did it become the occasion for mass mobilization to monitor the Party. In many provinces the Twenty-three Articles were distorted in the

---

*P'eng is quoted in "Counterrevolutionary Revisionist P'eng Chen's Towering Crimes of Opposing the Party, Socialism, and the Thought of Mao Tse-tung," published by the "Liaison Center for the Thorough Criticism of Liu, Teng, and T'ao" on June 10, 1967; see *Survey of China Mainland Magazines*, no. 639 (6.i.69), pp. 19–20. Ironically, the Red Guards later criticized P'eng's so-called reversal of verdicts as an attempt to protect corrupt cadres, though P'eng actually was trying to conform to the provisions of the Twenty-three Articles.

same way that the Early Ten Points had been: the formation of peasant associations was resumed, but their function was defined as serving as an auxiliary of the Party and as helping to promote agricultural production. Only in a few provinces, such as Honan, were class struggle and mass mobilization strongly emphasized.[37]

In addition to redefining the Socialist Education Movement at the basic levels, the Twenty-three Articles also spoke of the need to combat revisionism at higher levels of the Party organization. After some delay, a rectification campaign was launched in October 1965 at the county level. But the county reform movement never addressed the question of revisionism directly. Instead, it focused almost exclusively on ways of increasing the efficiency of the nation's two thousand county Party committees.

The first stage in the campaign consisted of extensive documentation in the Chinese press of the organizational problems faced by various county Party committees throughout the country. County cadres were variously described as afraid of hardship, fatigue, and illness; as unreceptive to criticism; as lacking an enterprising spirit in their work; as fearing to take risks; as being reluctant to conduct extensive investigations of conditions in the communes under their jurisdiction; and so forth.[38] The general thrust of the criticisms was that the work of county Party committees had become much too bound by routine, and that the committees had failed to maintain close communications with cadres at the basic level. At a time when basic-level organizations were being reformed through the Socialist Education Movement, a vigorous campaign to rectify the county committees was necessary if they were to keep pace with the development of the situation.[39]

Once these problems had been identified, the next step was to encourage the county cadres to rectify them. In general, the county reform campaign was conducted with considerable restraint. Some counties reportedly held meetings, attended by basic-level cadres and representatives of poor and lower-middle peasants, at which county cadres listened to criticisms of their work. But these were hardly struggle sessions. Accounts of the meetings indicate that the county cadres were well in command of the situation, and that the meetings usually concluded with the basic-level cadres criticizing their own errors in an attempt to match the "fine example" set by their superiors.[40] No county cadres were reported to have been purged, or even punished. Instead, the main focus of the campaign was a movement to emulate Chiao Yü-lu, a model county cadre who had served in Lan-t'ao county, Honan province. The exemplary Comrade Chiao was described as a man without a trace of egoism who constantly studied Mao's writings and was a model in the implementation of the mass line and of democratic centralism. Stricken with liver cancer, Chiao refused to heed advice to take sick leave and continued his work until he died at his post.[41] Having been made aware through Chiao's example of their own lackluster performance, county cadres would presumably reform themselves voluntarily, and an intense sequence of struggle sessions and purges would thus be unnecessary.

The county reform campaign does not seem to have achieved particularly striking results. Articles written in March and April 1966 indicate that many county cadres still refused to listen to criticism from their subordinates and steadfastly denied that they were in need of reform.[42] Even if it had been effective, however, the campaign had limited goals. It focused on questions of work style—on the bureaucratism, laxness, and passivity of many county cadres—and it sought to persuade county officials to streamline their procedures, perform regular manual labor, and spend more time investigating local conditions. The question of whether county cadres had antisocialist ideas, or were implementing revisionist policies, was never raised. The main goal of the movement was an upsurge in production, not the rectification of revisionism.

In the spring of 1966 the county reform campaign was subsumed by a broader campaign of ideological study being conducted throughout the middle and upper levels of the bureaucracy. That study movement, in turn, was the culmination of a long series of efforts undertaken between 1962 and 1966 to fight ossification—and, in Mao's eyes at least, to halt revisionism—in the urban bureaucracy in China. It is to this second aspect of the Socialist Education Movement that we now turn.

THE SOCIALIST EDUCATION MOVEMENT
AT HIGHER LEVELS

Although primarily directed against organizational problems in rural China, the Socialist Education Movement also included measures directed against inefficiency and revisionism at higher levels of the state and Party bureaucracies. In the eighteen months between the Tenth Plenum in September 1962 and the spring of 1964, these measures were limited in scope and intensity and received much less emphasis than the campaign against corruption and decay that was simultaneously underway in the countryside. In 1965–66, however, the rectification of the urban bureaucracy and the debate that it engendered began to overshadow the Socialist Education Movement in the rural areas.

In its initial period the rectification of the urban bureaucracy involved a series of piecemeal reforms, each of which dealt rather ineffectually with a particular aspect of organizational ossification. In order to improve communications and coordination within the bureaucracy, the Central Committee decided at the Tenth Plenum to begin a "planned interchange of important leading cadres of Party and government organs at various levels."[43] Ranking officials were thus to gain a broader view of the operations of Party and state agencies.* In order to strengthen factory and enterprise leadership and to improve the operations of the agencies responsible for economic management and planning, the "five-anti" movement mentioned earlier was also launched after the Tenth Plenum to combat corruption, speculation, waste, lack of coordination, and, of course, bureaucratic inefficiency. In order to half the overstaffing of central administrative offices, the center ordered in June 1964 that no more cadres were to be transferred to Peking from the provinces.[44] And in order to improve the flow of information from the basic levels and strengthen control over the grass roots, a hsia-fang campaign for middle-level cadres was begun in 1964–65.[45] Systematic procedures were established to ensure that cadres would spend a certain amount of time each week in manual labor and in investigating conditions at the lower levels of their organizations.† Some cadres, presumably those who filled superfluous positions in the provinces or at the center, were sent to work in communes, factories, and mines for a full year.[46]

These limited reforms were supplemented, however, by three more extensive campaigns launched in 1964, 1965, and 1966, respectively. The first was the establishment of political departments, modeled after those in the army, in the agencies of government responsible for economic affairs. The second was a campaign to promote the study of Maoist doctrine throughout the bureaucracy. And the third was a purge of "revisionist" officials in culture and education—and, to a lesser degree, in the economic sphere as well. We will see that all three of these campaigns encountered serious resistance within the bureaucracy from the cadres at whom they were directed. Even more important was a growing dispute at the highest levels over the purposes to which these campaigns should be put. Should they be directed against inefficiency, ossification, and corruption, like the piecemeal reforms that had preceded them? Or, as Mao Tse-tung clearly intended, should they be used to initiate a critical examination of the putatively revisionist policies that had been adopted in 1961–62?

Political Departments

Of all major Chinese organizations in the early 1960's, the People's Liberation Army could make a strong claim to being the most efficient and

---

*In 1963 this program involved exchanges between financial and trade departments and the People's Liberation Army. See Ralph L. Powell, "Commissars in the Economy: The 'Learn from the PLA' Movement in China," *Asian Survey*, 5 (1965): 125–38.

†The campaign was only partly successful. *Jen-min jih-pao* admitted on January 28, 1965, that only a "rather small number of units" had implemented it well; see *Survey of the China Mainland Press*, no. 3387 (28.i.65), pp. 1–7.

effective. After his appointment as minister of defense in 1959, Lin Piao had undertaken a variety of measures to reinvigorate the military bureaucracy and to place "politics in command" of military strategy and operations. Under Lin's guidance, the basic-level Party committees in the army were strengthened, Party membership in the army was increased, and the control of the Party's Military Affairs Committee over military matters was enhanced. At the same time, political indoctrination of both officers and enlisted men was intensified under an innovative set of regulations issued in March 1963. The techniques for political education used in the military included the compilation and publication of a set of quotations from Mao Tse-tung, a campaign for the "living study and living application" of Marxism-Leninism and the thought of Mao Tse-tung, the formulation of criteria by which to evaluate the performance of military units and individual soldiers, and a series of campaigns to publicize the accomplishments of model soldiers and model units.[47]

These efforts to place politics in command were prominently reflected in two sets of reforms announced in the early 1960's. First, Lin reasserted such traditional organizational principles of the revolutionary Red Army as military democracy and collective leadership, principles that in the mid-1950's had been believed to be incompatible with a modern army's need for rapid, decisive, and technically proficient command. The most visible symbol of the return to a less hierarchical form of military organization was the elimination of personal ranks in 1965. Officers no longer wore the stiff hats, gold braid, and epaulets that had been copied from the Soviet Union; instead, they again donned the simple khaki uniforms of the Kiangsi and Yenan periods. In addition, new military manuals prepared in the early 1960's attempted to codify the military strategy of the revolutionary period and to adapt it to conditions of modern warfare. Chinese military strategy in these years assigned great importance to the development of a modern air force and atomic bombs, weapons that were not available to the Red Army in the 1930's and 1940's. But as far as the ground forces were concerned, Lin stressed the primacy of the infantry over more specialized services, called for a resurrection of the militia, and proposed a return to the infantry tactics, close fighting and night fighting, that had been denigrated in the 1950's.

Thus, to those concerned about the health of the civilian bureaucracy, the People's Liberation Army stood in striking contrast to the Party and state organizations. Although the Party organizations in rural China were seriously decayed, basic-level Party organizations in the army had been reorganized and strengthened by mid-1961. Although the Party and state bureaucracies were increasingly rigid, the army appeared to have restored the vigor and efficiency of the revolutionary years. And although the policy reviews undertaken by the civilian sectors in the early 1960's seemed to some Chinese to have produced revisionist policies, the comparable policy reviews conducted by the army had reasserted many Maoist strategic and tactical principles. At the same time, however, the army remained an effective force. Despite the emphasis on political indoctrination, Lin Piao still insisted that more time be spent on military training than on political work. The successful campaign against India in 1962 and the detonation of China's first nuclear device in 1964 both demonstrated that the army was "expert," as well as "red."

Given these accomplishments, it is not surprising that the army was soon selected as a model for the civilian bureaucracies to copy. The emulation of the army began in 1963, when a model soldier, Lei Feng, and a model unit, the Good Eighth Company of Nanking Road, were selected for national publicity. On February 1, 1964, this campaign was broadened into a nationwide movement to "learn from the People's Liberation Army."

The component of this campaign that was of particular significance for the civilian bureaucracy was the decision to establish political departments modeled after those in the army in each agency of the state bureaucracy concerned with economic affairs, and to make them responsible for the political indoctrination of government officials. By May 1964 political departments had been set up in six ministries in the industrial and communications system: the Ministries of Metallurgical Industry, Agricultural Mechanization, Petroleum Industry, Textile Industry, and Railways; and the First Ministry of Machine Building. Later in the same year more political departments were established in the industrial and communications system, in the agricultural and forestry system, and in the Ministry of Foreign Affairs.[48] And in 1965 the system of political departments was extended from the central level down to provincial and municipal government agencies and to factories and enterprises. By October, 80 percent of the administrative offices in the finance and trade system had set up political departments, and 60 to 70 percent of the country's banks and enterprises were reported to have appointed political instructors.[49]

Not much is known about the politics behind the decision to establish political departments in the civilian bureaucracy. The decision itself can be traced to a directive by Mao Tse-tung, issued in January 1964, in which the Chairman ordered that the "industrial departments at all levels (from the ministries to the factories and communes) throughout the country should learn from the People's Liberation Army by setting up political departments and political bureaus and by appointing political commissars." He described this method as "the only way to arouse the revolutionary spirit of millions of cadres and workers in the industrial (as well as agricultural and commercial) departments," and as a device for ensuring that the economic agencies would intensify their political work.[50] His intention was not only to increase the efficiency and vigor of the bureaucracy, but also to establish an institutional mechanism for guaranteeing that concrete economic policy conformed with ideological principles.

But the decision to establish political departments was not made by Mao alone. In his January directive Mao indicated that certain of his advisers had suggested that the civilian bureaucracy form political departments, and it would seem plausible to conclude that Lin Piao was one of them. There is no reason to doubt that Lin was genuinely convinced of the efficacy of political departments as a means for solving China's organizational problems. But, beyond this, the establishment of political departments illustrated Lin's personal success in building the army into a model of organizational vigor and ideological orthodoxy, a marked contrast to the organizational and ideological shortcomings of civilian Party leaders. In addition, as minister of defense, Lin almost certainly would have favored any new organizational arrangement that offered influential bureaucratic posts to demobilized army cadres. In short, while Mao was turning to the army to provide an organizational model for other bureaucracies, it would also seem that the army, through Lin Piao, was turning to Mao for support for a proposal to increase its own power and prestige.

If Lin Piao was one of the principal advocates of political departments, Liu Shao-ch'i may have been one of their chief opponents. During the Cultural Revolution Liu was accused of having resisted the formation of political departments altogether, probably on the grounds that political education in the bureaucracy had traditionally been the responsibility of the Party's propaganda department. When he was overruled, he then allegedly tried to ensure that the political departments would be controlled by the Party, not by the army. Later accounts indicate that there had been a proposal in early 1964, perhaps by Lin Piao, that the political departments be placed under the control of the General Political Department of the army, but that Liu Shao-ch'i had successfully insisted that they be placed instead under the supervision of the economic departments of the Party Central Committee and of the Party committees in the provinces and municipalities.[51] Though the army provided many of the cadres needed to staff the political departments, Liu had been able to ensure that the civilian bureaucracy remained under Party, rather than army, control.*

---

*Lin Piao's continuing attempts to influence the political departments may be reflected in the "Letter on Living Study and Application of Chairman Mao Tse-tung's Works on the Industrial and Communications Front" that he wrote on March 11, 1966. The letter is innocuous in content—it simply says that the study of Maoism can ensure that officials maintain their fervor and preserve a correct political orientation—but it represents Lin's assertion of his right to speak out on questions affecting the civilian bureaucracy. The letter is in Michael Y. M. Kau, ed., *The Lin Piao Affair: Power Politics and Military Coup* (White Plains, N.Y., 1975), pp. 321–22.

Immediately after their establishment in 1964 and 1965, the new political departments began to encounter problems. The first of these was a serious shortage of cadres to staff the political departments in the middle levels of the bureaucracy and to serve as political instructors in basic-level factories and enterprises. Attempts were made to relieve this shortage in two ways. In some organizations the need to assign cadres to political work stimulated a long overdue simplification and reduction of administrative staff. Elsewhere large numbers of military cadres were transferred in to lead the political work of the civilian bureaucracy, where they provided between 30 and 40 percent of the political commissars and political instructors in the economic sector. But many of these army cadres had little idea how to perform economic work, despite crash training programs offered by the Chinese military academies. As a result, despite the transfer of military cadres and civilian administrators to political work, nearly one-third of the political departments "established" in Honan province had had no cadres assigned to them in June 1965. There is no way to estimate how many of the others were so understaffed as to be ineffective.[52]

Another problem encountered by the political departments was substantial opposition from the bureaus in which they were established. Even though the political departments were intended to be the administrative arm of the Party committees at various levels, Party cadres perceived, quite accurately, that the formation of political departments in their localities was an implicit criticism of their own performance and of the policies they were implementing. Government administrators, on the other hand, saw the political departments as further interference by ideologues and generalists in their work; some sarcastically suggested that, to ensure that politics be brought to the fore, the political departments ought to be given responsibility for management, as well as for supervising policymaking and conducting political education.[53] And both groups of officials—Party cadres and state administrators—appear to have resented the need to adjust their agencies' budgets to provide manpower and financial support for the new political departments. During the Cultural Revolution it was charged that the Peking municipal Party committee, to give but one example, had first refused to make appropriations for wages and administrative funds for the political departments under its jurisdiction, and then had called for a "simplification of administrative structure" in an attempt to abolish the political organs that had already been established.[54]

Third, and perhaps most important, the proposed functions of the political departments appear to have been seriously distorted in practice, most likely at the instigation of the central Party cadres responsible for the supervision of political work in the economy. We can presume that Mao's intention in establishing political departments was to modify some of the revisionist policies he believed were being carried out in the economic sphere. His method was to form an organizational hierarchy specifically charged with maintaining consistency between ideological principles and concrete policies. But the political departments, in fact, were never encouraged to assume such a role. Press reports of 1965 and early 1966 indicate that the political departments instead were concerned primarily with raising organizational efficiency and productivity by conducting ideological study classes, by establishing regular programs of manual labor for cadres, and by simplifying the organizational structure of the bureau, factory, or enterprise to which they were attached. The goal of all this was usually defined as increasing production, rather than as waging class struggle.* In this way, the function actually assigned to the political departments appears to have been the enthusiastic, flexible, and efficient implementation of existing Party policies, rather than the critical evaluation of economic policy in the light of Maoist ideological values. Whether this reflected a deliberate attempt at sabotage on the part of high-level Party cadres can not be known with certainty. It is highly probable, however, that the political departments were never permitted to do the job that Lin and Mao expected them to do.

Finally, the political departments failed to fulfill even the limited tasks we have just described. Part of the problem was their inability to sustain a rectification campaign within the civilian bureaucracy. Many bureaus and enterprises gave lip service to the goals of improving organizational efficiency and flexibility when the political departments were first established, but then let the campaign die out before any concrete results had been achieved. In January 1966, for instance, *Ta-kung pao* complained that "although great achievements have been made in the finance and trade departments' political work, it still does not adequately meet the demands of the favorable situation at home and abroad, and there still is a wide gap between political work in the finance and trade departments and in the People's Liberation Army." The problem, according to *Ta-kung pao*, was that bureaus that had put political work in the right position at the beginning of the campaign were unable to keep it there for long.[55]

The fault would seem to lie not simply with the economic bureaus, however, but also with the political departments themselves. After some experimentation with alternative methods of conducting political work, the Party called at the end of 1965 for the regularization of the work of the

---

*The production orientation of the political departments was particularly evident in the reports of the National Work Conference on Industry and Communications and the National Political Work Conference in the Fields of Industry and Communications, both held in February 1965. See *Jen-min jih-pao*, 25.ii.65, in *Survey of the China Mainland Press*, no. 3414 (11.iii.65), pp. 1–4.

political departments, so that "the position of political work will be further adjusted, a set of experiences for doing political and ideological work will be summed up, and a set of measures for giving prominence to politics and implementing the 'four firsts,' as well as a set of systems for carrying out regular political and ideological work, will be devised."[56] The effect of this decision was the rapid routinizing of the political departments themselves. Political cadres, now that political work had been regularized, came to assume that their very presence in a bureau ensured that political and ideological work was being successfully undertaken and organization problems were on the way to solution. Lulled by this assumption, some political cadres showed a style of "drifting along," as *Jen-min jih-pao* complained.[57] As a result, only two years after their establishment, the political departments became the targets of a campaign directed at their "arrogance" and "isolation from the masses." The instruments intended to reinvigorate a bureaucracy numbed by routine and ossification had apparently themselves fallen victim to the same malaise.

The Campaign to Study the Thought of Mao Tse-tung

By the fall of 1965 it was all too clear that Mao's warnings about revisionism, the establishment of political departments, and the rectification of county cadres had all failed to change the socioeconomic policies to which Mao had objected. At a central work conference in September, he therefore renewed his criticism of revisionism and intensified his demands that the policies adopted in 1961–62 be modified.

Mao focused his attention on a play, entitled *Hai Jui Dismissed from Office*, that constituted a thinly veiled attack on the 1959 dismissal of P'eng Te-huai. It had been written by Wu Han, a vice-mayor of Peking, and in order to conduct a campaign against Wu and other "bourgeois reactionaries" in cultural and propaganda circles, Mao turned to a five-man "Cultural Revolution Group" headed by P'eng Chen, Party first secretary of Peking, and Lu Ting-i, director of the Party's Propaganda Department, that had been established a year earlier to supervise the "revolutionization" of Peking opera. Both Lu and P'eng were now put to the test: Would they attack the writers, plays, and articles that Mao found so objectionable, or would they seek to defend and protect them?[58]

Although Wu Han and *Hai Jui* were the most prominent of Mao's targets, the Chairman's renewed assault on revisionism in China had important implications for the rest of the bureaucracy as well. The central work conference of September 1965 was followed by an ideological study campaign in which all cadres, from the basic levels to provincial and central officials, were supposed to participate. This campaign began in earnest during the first three months of 1966, when many provinces and regions published programs of systematic ideological education for leading cadres at and above the county level.[59] The Central-South Party bureau, for example, ordered that leading cadres at and above the county level spend one full month a year in study, and government cadres, two to four days each month.*

The basic theme of the campaign was the proper relationship between "politics" and "business," the basic goal being to ensure that politics was "placed at the fore." Press accounts of the campaign charged that many cadres gave little attention to political or ideological considerations when they made decisions or carried out policy, holding such views as "production is a hard task but politics is a soft one," "good production is good politics," or "production and politics are of equal importance."[60] As in the earlier rectification campaigns discussed in this chapter, there was initially some question as to what "placing politics to the fore" actually meant. Many of the press accounts, and even some of the regional and provincial decisions on ideological study, emphasized the importance of political work in promoting production. The 1966 New Year's Day editorial in *Hung-ch'i*, for instance, argued that placing politics in command would ensure the successful accomplishment of the Third Five-Year Plan.[61] Other articles stressed the role of political work in remedying such organizational problems as routinization, departmentalism, complacency, and commandism.[62]

But a relatively large number of press reports indicated that the campaign was beginning to call into question some of the economic and social policy decisions that had been made during the policy review of 1961–62. An early report in *Kuang-ming jih-pao* noted that ideological study and careful attention to doctrinal principles in decision making would be necessary if the "vestiges of private economy" were to be kept in their proper place.[63] In April 1966 *Jen-min jih-pao* went so far as to summarize the inconsistencies between doctrinal principles and existing economic policy, noting that if politics were truly placed in command, then material incentives would be deemphasized, workers would be given a greater role in industrial management, the role of profit in economic planning would be reduced, and greater efforts would be made to lessen inequalities be-

---

*The attempt by the Central-South bureau to systematize the study of Mao's works, which seemed quite radical at the time, was nonetheless criticized during the Cultural Revolution in the following terms: "By devoting several days a month to concentrated study of Chairman Mao's writings as a task, was this a call on all people penetratingly to launch activities for the study of Chairman Mao's writings? No! By calling on people to study Chairman Mao's writings for a while and not to read them every day, the design of T'ao Chu and his ilk was extremely venomous." This was "setting confines and calling the tune" for the study of Chairman Mao's writings. See the statement of the "Canton Liaison Center of the Wuhan Revolutionary Rebel Headquarters of the Red Guards for the Thought of Mao Tse-tung" published on January 14, 1967; in *Current Background*, no. 824 (27.iv.67), p. 8.

tween rural and urban areas.[64] And on February 5, in an unmistakable reference to Teng Hsiao-p'ing, a *Yang-ch'eng wan-pao* editorial criticized "those who regard all cats, whether black or white, as good cats as long as they catch mice"—a phrase from Teng's defense in 1962 of household contract production in agriculture.[65]

More was at stake, therefore, than the problem of ensuring a regular program of ideological study. High-ranking cadres could not but be aware that their committees and bureaus, and the very policies they had supported in the early 1960's, were rapidly coming under assault. Accordingly, these officials resisted the campaign before it began—and sought to derail it once it was underway. In August 1965, a month before the campaign was approved by the central work conference, both Liu Shao-ch'i and Teng Hsiao-p'ing had expressed opposition to "rigid" or "formalistic" study programs on the grounds that they would obstruct the work of Party and state agencies.[66] The Honan provincial propaganda department is said to have threatened to ignore the campaign altogether unless some of its own cadres and some county Party secretaries in the province could be identified as models in the study and application of Maoist ideology.[67] The Party committee of the Seventh Ministry of Machine Building, reluctant to launch a campaign that might encourage criticism of its past policies, decided that it would "neither promote nor oppose the study of Chairman Mao's works."[68] And Liu Chien-hsün, the Party first secretary of Honan, insisted that although he did not sit and study every day, he did not necessarily "compare unfavorably" to those who did.[69]

Despite the fact that here and there a few editorials and agencies began to raise some of the questions Mao wanted discussed, the campaign as a whole was no more effective in achieving Mao's goals than the establishment of political departments had been. By the end of March *Jen-min jih-pao* was complaining that some places, despite many meetings on the subject, had still not placed politics to the fore.[70] And in June, in a candid description of the results of the campaign, the southwest bureau of the Party acknowledged that, despite two years of effort, "there has been no basic change. Only a few . . . are really good at studying and applying Chairman Mao's works creatively; the majority . . . are not studying the works earnestly or combining study with application and theory with practice sufficiently closely."[71] In other words, the county and upper-level cadres were talking about Maoist ideology, but they were not allowing its premises to affect their day-to-day actions.

The Fifty Days

By June 1966 events in China had reached a crisis. On the one hand, Mao's latest attempts to deflect the bureaucracy from its "revisionist" course had produced few lasting results. On the other, in Mao's eyes P'eng

Chen, Lu Ting-i, and the Cultural Revolution Group had turned the campaign against "bourgeois reactionaries" in propaganda and art into a purely academic debate and had refused to denounce the allegorical criticisms of Mao and the Great Leap Forward that had been published in the early 1960's. On June 4 Peking announced the dismissal of both P'eng and Lu and the reorganization of the Peking municipal Party committee, the Party Propaganda Department, and the Cultural Revolution Group. This demonstrated Mao's determination to have his way on the policy issues that concerned him most deeply and his ability to secure the dismissal of those Party leaders, whatever their rank, who did not comply.

At the same time, however, Mao also indicated that he now wanted a thoroughgoing purge of the entire Party and state to rid them of the "revisionists" who had thwarted him ever since the Great Leap. This was to be another antirightist campaign, similar to those conducted in 1957 and 1959, but on an even larger scale. Mao did not take personal charge of this campaign, or even clearly indicate what results he expected or what methods he wanted employed. He remained in Hangchow, leaving Liu Shao-ch'i in Peking in charge of the day-to-day affairs of the Party. The responsibility for purging China of revisionism was thus assigned to the very man whom Mao had suspected since January 1965 of promoting it in the first place.

Liu faced a serious dilemma. To survive he would have to show zeal and determination in combating revisionism, but he would also have to prevent the campaign from escalating to a point where he and his associates might come under criticism. In most universities, and in many government and Party bureaus, young leftists were prepared to voice severe criticisms of revisionist policies and of the cadres they considered to be responsible for them. In many places these leftists were in contact with the central Cultural Revolution Group, which was now headed by Ch'en Po-ta and Chiang Ch'ing, a change that doubtless encouraged them to pursue the issues to as high a level in the bureaucracy as possible.

Liu's solution to this dilemma was to launch an intense but controlled rectification campaign throughout the bureaucracy during the fifty days from early June to mid-July. His aim was probably to identify enough "revisionists" to convince Mao of his sincerity, but to limit the scope of the purge to lower-level officials.[72] The principal targets of the campaign were university administrators and central and provincial officials responsible for propaganda, culture, and education. But the campaign was conducted in other areas of the bureaucracy as well, including the agencies responsible for finance, trade, industry, and communications.[73] To keep things under control, Liu ordered the formation of some four hundred work teams, totaling about ten thousand people, to be supervised and coordinated by the Party Secretariat, and by the Party control commissions at the regional levels.[74]

The operating procedures of the work teams during what came to be called the "Fifty Days" were remarkably similar to the procedures used by the work teams under the Revised Later Ten Points. Indeed, many of the members of the work teams had previously participated in the Socialist Education Movement. The work teams worked under the assumption that the majority of cadres, particularly in the universities, had serious political problems, and that these basic-level officials, rather than their superiors, should be the principal targets of the campaign. In the Ministry of Finance, 90 percent of the cadres reportedly came under attack. In the Ministry of Culture, under the slogan "plow the garden three feet deep, gather the dirt, and sweep it out the gate," the work teams were reportedly ordered to dismiss two-thirds of the cadres, retaining mainly those who had recently been transferred to the ministry from the army.

The work teams also were under instructions to maintain control of the rectification campaign in each unit and prevent it from falling into the hands of leftists. On June 24, for example, a *Jen-min jih-pao* editorial entitled "The Sunlight of the Party Illuminates the Road of the Great Cultural Revolution" urged the leftists to submit to Party (i.e., work team) leadership:

Only with leadership by the Chinese Communist Party can the Chinese people possibly be victorious in any undertaking or struggle. . . . It is under the leadership of the Chinese Communist Party alone that the Great Cultural Revolution is able to triumph. . . . The Great Cultural Revolution can take the correct direction, the revolutionary people can see and think clearly, and the movement can develop in a healthy way only with the correct leadership of the Party.[75]

And on July 9 an editor's note in *Jen-min jih-pao* declared, "Since only organized action under proper leadership constitutes the most effective revolutionary action, our revolutionary masses should strive to get organized more correctly under Party leadership."[76] The same goal was stated even more baldly by Li Pao-hua, the Party first secretary of Anhwei, on July 14. "In general, the Party committees at all levels have strengthened leadership over the campaign. . . . For units where the leadership is not in our hands, work teams must be sent immediately to win it back."[77]

Armed with this authority, the work teams sought to channel mass participation into acceptable, controlled, and organized activities. In some units the work teams prohibited any demonstrations or wall posters altogether; in others they permitted people to write wall posters, but told them to obtain the permission of the work team before posting them. Students and faculty in the universities, and working staff in government agencies, were prohibited from discussing the campaign with people in other units.[78]

Having conducted this whirlwind rectification and having purged large numbers of low-level administrators from central and provincial offices, Liu Shao-ch'i claimed that the Great Cultural Revolution had achieved its purpose and should be concluded. The Party Day editorial on July 1, for example, proclaimed that the "counterrevolutionary clique" had been "exposed and smashed," and that this represented an "immense new victory for Mao Tse-tung's thought."[79] There was no hint that there were more revisionists in China yet to be discovered.

The restrictions imposed by the work teams were probably accepted by the majority of ordinary Chinese.[80] But many leftists in universities and government agencies concluded that the work teams had been dispatched solely to repress the masses and to protect the established Party leadership, a charge that was very likely true in most instances. As the leftists began to criticize the work teams, the work teams shifted the focus of the movement from the Party committees, which they had been sent to rectify, to the leftists, whom they described as being "a few people trying to make trouble."[81] A particularly dramatic confrontation between work team and leftists occurred in the Second Bureau of Mechanical and Electrical Industry in Shanghai. There the leader of the work team, Huang Ch'ih-po, who was director of public security in the city, accused the leftists of rejecting Party leadership in their criticism of the work team and of the bureau's leading cadres. When one of the leftists denied the charge, according to a Red Guard account Huang

sprang off the couch so fast that he left his shoes behind. "Do you still want to argue the point, you stupid young punk? You've forgotten all about Party leadership! You don't give a damn about the work team! You say you want the Party to lead, but you really think we're not revolutionary enough. *You're* the only revolutionaries around here, I suppose. . . . You've tried to create chaos. You've made things so difficult for the Party cadres that their work has been paralyzed. What kind of people are you? If you thought about your position, you'd break out in a cold sweat!"

When the leftists still tried to argue with Huang, he lost his patience completely:

"I've tried to talk to you. . . . Now I'm *telling* you: If you don't obey my orders, I have the police, I have the Security Bureau, I have the dictatorship of the proletariat. You youngsters had better smarten up!"[82]

The conduct of the work teams and the resistance of the leftists soon came to Mao's attention. Dissatisfied with Liu Shao-ch'i's management of the rectification campaign, Mao left Hangchow, went for a celebrated swim in the Yangtze River on July 16, and arrived in Peking shortly there-after. On July 22, at a meeting of regional Party secretaries and the mem-bers of the Cultural Revolution Group, Mao criticized the work teams and, as in the Early Ten Points, called on the masses in each unit to conduct the rectification themselves:

The Great Cultural Revolution must be led by the Cultural Revolution teams of schools as organized by the revolutionary teachers and students. . . . The work teams know nothing. Some work teams have even created trouble. . . . Work teams only hinder the movement. . . . [Affairs in the schools] have to be dealt with by the forces in the schools themselves, not by the work teams, you, me, or the provincial committees.[83]

Mao's views were amplified in a speech by K'ang Sheng on July 28. Some work teams, K'ang admitted, might have acted in a restrictive manner because they had no knowledge of the units to which they were sent and were "jittery," but others went to the schools intending not to lead but to obstruct the mass movement. K'ang went on to say, "Revolution cannot be monopolized, and the masses must be allowed to rise and make revolu-tion themselves. Monopoly and substitution by work teams is not 'from the masses, to the masses.' . . . Lots of experiences prove that there is something wrong with this method and that the work teams should be recalled. . . . The decisions of the work teams are worthless. . . . To hell with the work teams!"[84]

The work-team question was the immediate issue—although probably not the most important one—in Liu Shao-ch'i's dismissal from the Stand-ing Committee of the Politburo at the Eleventh Plenum in August. In the course of the plenum, Mao published a wall poster in which he described the Fifty Days as a period in which "some leading cadres enforced a bourgeois dictatorship, . . . encircled and suppressed revolutionaries, . . . imposed a white terror, and felt very pleased with themselves. . . . How poisonous!"[85] And he drew the obvious parallel with the Revised Later Ten Points, which he characterized as "the wrong tendency in 1964, Left in form but Right in essence." Both the Revised Later Ten Points and the Fifty Days, he implied, demonstrated Liu's reluctance to freely mobilize the masses to criticize the Party, his desire to restrict party recti-fication campaigns to lower levels of the bureaucracy, and his unwilling-ness to confront squarely the issue of revisionism in China.

Following the Great Leap Forward, Mao Tse-tung's role in Chinese politics underwent a significant transformation. In the mid-1950's Mao had principally been China's chief executive. Deeply involved in the day-to-day affairs of the country, Mao listened to conflicting analyses and rec-ommendations concerning social, economic, and political problems, and then made the authoritative decisions about the course the Party would take. In the early 1960's, however, Mao moved back to a "second line" of leadership from which, no longer responsible for day-to-day decision making, he was free to devote more time to theoretical questions and to take a broader view of the course of the Chinese revolution. Mao's role thus changed from arbiter to initiator. From his position on the second line he would periodically intervene on the issues of most concern to him, often to the consternation of those officials who believed that his proposals lacked a full awareness of the constraints imposed by China's social and economic conditions.[86]

Mao's interventions in the early 1960's occurred across a wide range of issues: foreign policy, agriculture, education, culture, and public health. Of most relevance to this study, of course, were his attempts to influence organizational policy. Mao's organizational program between 1962 and 1966 can be summarized under two broad headings: his conviction that revisionism, at the highest levels of the Chinese Party and state as well as at local levels, was an immediate threat to the goals and values of the Chinese revolution; and his proposal that revisionism be combated through a combination of devices that gave first priority to mass mobilization. The fundamental feature of organizational politics in the early 1960's was a muted but intense debate over the appropriateness of Mao's organizational program.

Earlier in this chapter, we identified three problems that afflicted the Chinese state and Party organizations in the early 1960's: decay and corruption at the basic levels, ossification and routinization at the middle and upper levels, and the emergence of revisionism throughout the bureaucracy. Mao's speeches and writings between 1962 and 1966 showed his concern with all three of these problems. His interest in basic-level decay and corruption was evident in his initiation of the Socialist Education Movement and in his personal involvement in the formulation of both the Early Ten Points and the Twenty-three Articles. His concern with routinization and ossification was reflected in a lengthy directive written in December 1963 in which he criticized arrogance among cadres, challenged their complacency with existing social and economic conditions, and urged them to cultivate a desire to make "ceaseless progress" in the improvement of their work and the development of the country.[87] Mao's awareness of overstaffing was apparent in his remarks at the Hangchow Conference of May 1963, in which he proposed a 60 to 70 percent reduction in the staff of the Kiangsu provincial Party offices and described administrative retrenchment as "an old problem that for a long period of time has not been resolved."[88]

Mao's central concern, however, was with the emergence of revisionism in China. His speech at the Tenth Plenum, the Early Ten Points, "On Khrushchov's Phoney Communism," the Twenty-three Articles, his interviews with Edgar Snow and André Malraux in the winter of 1964–65, and his comments to the central work conference in September 1965—all these warned of revisionist tendencies throughout the Party.[89] At first Mao's warnings were relatively low-keyed. At the Tenth Plenum, for example, he said that the Party should tackle the problem of revisionism, but he added that this class struggle should not "interfere with our work . . . or be placed in a very prominent position. . . . We have to engage in the class struggle, . . . but there are special people [i.e., public security personnel] to take care of this kind of work."[90] By 1965, however, he had become convinced that revisionism posed an imminent danger to China, and also that it existed at the highest levels of the bureaucracy. "Among those at higher levels," the Twenty-three Articles declared, "there are some people in the communes, districts, counties, special districts, and even in the . . . provincial and Central Committee departments who oppose socialism." His talk at the September 1965 work conference was even more pointed. "If revisionism appears in the Central Committee, what are you going to do? It is probable that it will appear, and this is a great danger."[91]

The first element in Mao's organizational program, then, was to launch a nationwide struggle against revisionism in China. The explicit purpose of such a movement, as indicated by the Twenty-three Articles, was to "straighten out those people in positions of authority within the Party who take the capitalist road." Implicitly, the Socialist Education Movement was also Mao's attempt to reverse the policies in education, culture, public health, and economic affairs adopted during the policy reviews of the early 1960's with which he disagreed.

Mao's cause enjoyed the support of a number of central and provincial leaders, among them Lin Piao, Ch'en Po-ta, K'ang Sheng, and, from the end of 1964, Chou En-lai. Other officials, however, differed with Mao's reading of conditions and supported the socioeconomic policies formulated after the Great Leap Forward, believing them to constitute a sound and viable program for China's modernization. Additionally, some may have genuinely believed that the principal organizational problem in China was not revisionism but the decay of basic-level organizations in the countryside and the ossification of the higher levels of the bureaucracy. Given the ideological nature of the issue as Mao posed it, and the depth of his involvement with it, it was virtually impossible for any Chinese leader to say openly that revisionism was an unimportant problem, or that China was free of revisionist tendencies. But those who supported the policies of the early 1960's and who wanted to defend them against Mao's criticism could still use a more subtle stratagem: to divert Mao's campaigns toward other targets—targets that they thought were more important, or less threatening.

Many officials thus tried to direct the Socialist Education Movement against corruption rather than revisionism, tried to assign the peasant associations the task of promoting production rather than supervising basic-level cadres, tried to ensure that the political departments remained under the control of the Party rather than of the army, and tried to keep the ideological study campaigns of 1965–66 focused on problems of work style rather than on substantive policy questions. This explains one of the most persistent patterns of the 1962–66 period, the tendency for movements that began as campaigns against revisionism to be transmuted into campaigns for higher production or for greater organizational efficiency.

And yet one of the great ironies of the period is that, even after they were redefined, the campaigns to rectify county staffs, establish political departments, and study Mao's writings did not seem to have much impact on the bureaucracy. The one exception to this trend is the dramatic impact of the Socialist Education Movement on basic-level cadres, particularly when it was operating under the guidance of the Revised Later Ten Points. Enjoinders to simplify forms, reduce meetings, engage in labor, take the initiative, simplify organizational structure, pare office staffs, listen to criticism, solicit advice—none of these had much impact. This may have meant that China's bureaucrats were aware of the divisions among Party leaders over the purpose of the campaigns, and that they therefore felt no need to take them seriously. In part, too, it may have demonstrated that the rectification techniques themselves, after fifteen years of use in the People's Republic and nearly thirty years of use in the Party, had become too routine to remain effective.

The second element in Mao Tse-tung's organizational program was the belief that the problems of corruption, ossification, and revisionism could all be combated, at least in part, by some form of mass mobilization. This is not to say that he was opposed to ideological study or physical labor, or that he wished to circumvent such internal control mechanisms as public security forces and Party control commissions. Quite the contrary. But compared to other Party officials he seemed to assign a smaller role to such control devices and to give greater prominence to mobilizing peasants, students, and lower-level cadres to serve as monitors of Party and state officials.

Mao's position on mass supervision was very similar to the stand he had taken during the Hundred Flowers period. In 1956–57 he had recognized that non-Party intellectuals were wavering in their political commitments, but he still believed that they could be relied upon to rectify the Party. In 1962 he had a similar view of the peasantry—the communiqué of the

Tenth Plenum described them as being subject to the small producers' "spontaneous tendency toward capitalism," but he was nonetheless prepared to assign to the peasant associations principal responsibility for eliminating corruption among basic-level cadres.[92] And in 1965 he told Edgar Snow that since the youth of China had not experienced the revolution personally, they might "make peace with imperialism, bring the remnants of the Chiang Kai-shek clique back to the mainland, and take a stand beside the small percentage of counterrevolutionaries still in the country."[93] And yet he was still willing to mobilize students to attack revisionism during both the Fifty Days and the Cultural Revolution. As before, he not only advocated open-door rectification but was willing to rely on seemingly unreliable sectors of the society to carry it out.

This component of Mao's organizational program also engendered substantial opposition within the Party—opposition that came from different sources, with different goals, at different times. During the Socialist Education Movement, lower-level officials, particularly in the counties, feared the consequences of unrestricted mass mobilization through the formation of powerful peasant associations. At best such mobilization would make political leadership and production management difficult; at worst it could lead to the wholesale condemnation of basic-level leaders as corrupt or incompetent. The goal of these officials was therefore to make sure that the peasant associations remained under the leadership of local Party committees, served as the auxiliaries of basic-level leaders, and concerned themselves more with production than with mass supervision.

At the same time, central leaders—Teng Hsiao-p'ing, P'eng Chen, and especially Liu Shao-ch'i—became convinced that the peasants were simply not sophisticated enough or reliable enough to play the role in rectification that Mao had assigned them in the Early Ten Points. Unlike lower-level officials, Liu, Teng, and P'eng were not directly threatened by the mobilization of the poor and lower-middle peasants. Instead, their resistance to Mao's proposals stemmed from their fear that peasant associations would be impure, inept, or impotent, that they could readily be co-opted and controlled by local officials, and that the entire Socialist Education Movement would therefore fail. Thus, Liu wanted to rely heavily on work teams to conduct the rectification in the countryside and to assign the peasants a clearly subordinate role.

During the Fifty Days, provincial and central leaders also became aware of substantial leftist opposition to prevailing policies, particularly among students, and knew that the opposition was being encouraged, if not directly mobilized, by the new Cultural Revolution Group under Ch'en Po-ta and Chiang Ch'ing. At this point provincial and central leaders experienced the same concerns that their rural subordinates had experienced during the Socialist Education Movement, and they, too, attempted to keep the mass movement under tight control, to deflect it toward safe targets, and to minimize the threat to their own political positions.

Because of this opposition, the peasant associations never developed to the point where they played an important role in the Chinese countryside, and Mao concluded that his attempts to halt revisionism, either by intervening personally or by promoting organizational rectification, had accomplished little. As he complained in October 1966, "I could do nothing in Peking; I could do nothing at the center. Last September and October I asked, if revisionism appeared at the center, what could the localities do? I felt my ideas couldn't be carried out in Peking."[94] By mid-1966, therefore, Mao had decided that even more drastic measures were needed to deal with revisionism in the Party and state bureaucracies. But Mao still believed that these measures could be effective only if they allowed for a high level of mass supervision over the bureaucracy.

8
The Second Crisis:
The Cultural Revolution
1966-1968

To Mao Tse-tung, the purpose in launching the Great Proletarian Cultural Revolution in August 1966 was, in the broadest terms, to halt the emergence of revisionism in China. So ambitious a goal had implications for every aspect of Chinese society. It meant the dismissal and often the persecution of officials who had demonstrated their opposition to Mao and his policies; the formulation of new programs for education, public health, industry, agriculture, and science; sweeping changes in literature and the arts; and the education of all Chinese, officials and ordinary citizens alike, in the danger of a "capitalist restoration" and the need to prevent it by "continuing the revolution under the dictatorship of the proletariat through to the end."

The Cultural Revolution also had important organizational components. "On Khrushchov's Phoney Communism" is a tract written in July 1964 under Mao's supervision that remains the most comprehensive and authoritative discussion of the problem of revisionism in socialist countries. It identifies the "degeneration of the leadership of the Party and the state" as creating the greatest threat of capitalist restoration.[1] Given this analysis, Mao's concern was to undertake organizational reforms that could make this degeneration less likely—to create, in other words, a form of political organization that could help prevent the emergence of revisionism.

Mao's writings on the eve of the Cultural Revolution suggest two approaches to solving this problem. "On Khrushchov's Phoney Communism," and some speeches and articles written at about the same time, implied that capitalist restoration could be prevented if China were more diligent in following some of the Party's traditional organizational principles: regular cadre participation in physical labor, the practice of criticism and self-criticism, the minimization of administrative staffs, decentralization, a democratic style of work, promotion of younger officials, simplification of bureaucratic structure, and the reduction of the gap between the salaries of high officials and the incomes of ordinary working people.[2] This aspect of the Cultural Revolution—the restoration and reinvigoration of the Party's organizational heritage—will be discussed further in the next chapter.

A second, more innovative, aspect of Mao's proposals for organizational reform was his emphasis on restructuring the Party and state to increase popular participation in the Chinese political process. The idea of controlling the bureaucracy through mass mobilization was hardly new. It had its precedents in both the Hundred Flowers period and in the Socialist Education Movement. But the form that popular participation took during the Cultural Revolution, and the intensity to which it developed, both were unprecedented in the history of the People's Republic.

Mao favored greater mass participation in Chinese politics for two reasons. The most immediate was the need to identify, criticize, and, if necessary, dismiss revisionist officials. Mao believed, at least in the beginning, that the Chinese people would carry out such a rectification campaign reliably. His 1963 proposal to form poor and lower-middle peasant associations to supervise basic-level rural cadres reflected his assumption that the masses, particularly those from certain class backgrounds, could be depended upon to discipline corrupt or errant officials. Now, during the Cultural Revolution, he extended the principle to other organizations as well—first to middle schools and universities, then to factories and enterprises, and finally to Party and state offices at all levels of administration. In furthering this strategy, he declared in July 1966 that cadres should actually mobilize the masses to criticize their own leadership.* They should smash all restrictions on mass criticism, depend on the masses, trust the masses, and "be prepared for the revolution to strike."[3] In the same vein, editorials in *Jen-min jih-pao* warned that cadres could retain their right to speak and their right to lead only if they responded positively and sincerely to mass criticism.[4]

A second purpose of increasing mass participation in politics was to educate ordinary citizens, particularly youth, in revolution, revisionism, and "affairs of state." For although Mao was optimistic about the masses, his view was not completely sanguine. He believed that, because the youth of China had not experienced revolution, they were now wavering in their commitment to socialist principles. The Cultural Revolution would provide young Chinese with such a revolutionary experience, which would temper them in the same way that Mao's generation had been molded by the revolutionary struggles of the 1920's and 1930's. As the Eleventh Plenum's decision on the Cultural Revolution put it, the masses would

---

*Later, in evaluating the results of the Cultural Revolution, Mao would stress the degree to which it had successfully increased popular participation in political life. In the fall of 1967 he declared, "The situation in the Great Proletarian Cultural Revolution throughout the country is not just good but excellent. The entire situation is better than ever before. The important feature of this excellent situation is the full mobilization of the masses. Never before in any mass movement have the masses been mobilized so broadly and deeply as in this one." Stuart R. Schram, *The Political Thought of Mao Tse-tung*, rev. ed. (New York, 1969), p. 370.

"educate themselves in the movement . . . , heighten their consciousness in the midst of struggle, increase their capacity for work, and distinguish between right and wrong and [between] the enemy and ourselves."

It is important to recognize that the extension of popular participation Mao had in mind was to be a permanent feature of Chinese politics, not simply a temporary one. Although the Cultural Revolution might deal revisionist influences a sharp blow, he apparently believed that revisionism would simply reappear in a few years' time if China's political structure was left unchanged. His intent, therefore, was to institutionalize mass involvement in politics on a simple premise: the greater the level of continued popular participation, the less the likelihood revisionism will emerge. This feature of the Cultural Revolution was stated most clearly in the resolutions of the Eleventh Plenum in August 1966. It would take a "very, very long time" to eliminate the old ideas, culture, customs, and habits that were the source of revisionism in Chinese society. Accordingly, the resolutions provided that the cultural revolutionary groups, committees, and congresses—the organizations that at the time provided the format for mass participation—would not be temporary organizations, but "permanent, standing mass organizations."[5]

Although one major goal of the Cultural Revolution was to increase popular participation in the Chinese political process, there was no clear vision of how extensive that mass participation should be, nor of the institutional arrangements that would be necessary to accommodate it. In fact, the Cultural Revolution witnessed experimentation with no less than four organizational forms—the Cultural Revolution committees, the Red Guard movement, the Paris Commune, and the revolutionary committees—each of which provided a different definition of the scope, extent, and format of mass participation. In this chapter we will describe each of these four forms, discuss the assumptions upon which they were based, describe their implementation, and explain the abandonment of one form for another.

CULTURAL REVOLUTION COMMITTEES: THE MASSES AS MONITORS

From the very beginning of the Cultural Revolution, the Paris Commune offered a compelling model for those concerned about the tendencies toward revisionism in Chinese bureaucracy and those who believed that expanding popular participation would be an effective means of combating them.* A lengthy article in the April issue of *Hung-ch'i*, written in commemoration of the ninety-fifth anniversary of the Paris Commune,

---

*For an excellent summary of the role of the Paris Commune in the Cultural Revolution, see John Bryan Starr, "Revolution in Retrospect: The Paris Commune Through Chinese Eyes," *China Quarterly*, no. 49 (January–March 1972), pp. 106–25.

summarized the Commune's major characteristics: direct election of officials, provisions for referendum and recall, and restriction of official salaries to the level of an average worker's wage. The article also recommended that their organizational policies be adopted in China, noting that this would help prevent the state organs in the dictatorship of the proletariat "from becoming the opposite of what was intended—from degenerating."[6] Even more important, Mao himself enthusiastically referred to the first wall poster written in Peking University during the Fifty Days as the "declaration of the Chinese Paris Commune of the 1960's."[7]

Despite these endorsements, however, there was no suggestion in the first six months of the Cultural Revolution that China would follow the example of the Paris Commune in a literal way—no indication, that is, that Chinese bureaucracy would be totally abolished and replaced by "Chinese Paris Communes." Instead, the first format for popular participation adopted during the Cultural Revolution was the so-called Cultural Revolution committee. These committees, along with Cultural Revolution groups and Cultural Revolution congresses, were supposed to be established in basic-level units throughout China to serve as the forum for popular criticism of revisionism.* It is true that these committees were to be modeled after the Paris Commune. But they were intended to supplement, not to replace, the Party and state bureaucracies. And it was only the committees, not the Party and state, that were to be organized on Paris Commune principles.

The first Cultural Revolution committees were formed in schools and universities during the Fifty Days in keeping with the long-standing practice of establishing ad hoc organizations to manage important political campaigns. Initially, these committees had little in common with the Paris Commune, for the selection of committee members was tightly controlled by the work teams.[8] When the work teams were withdrawn, however, both the structure and the role of the Cultural Revolution committees were transformed. In speeches to university students in Peking in late July, K'ang Sheng and Ch'en Po-ta proposed that the Cultural Revolution committees take over the management of the Cultural Revolution from the disgraced work teams.[9] Ch'en implicitly recommended that the committees thereafter be patterned on the Paris Commune, for he suggested that

---

*The names of these organs depended on the size of the units in which they were formed. Cultural Revolution groups were to be established in the smallest units in Chinese society (workshops, offices, classes, production teams, and the like). Cultural Revolution congresses were to be formed in larger units (factories, enterprises, schools, and communes) and were to elect Cultural Revolution committees as their standing organs. For the sake of simplicity, I have decided to use the term "Cultural Revolution committee" to refer to all of these variants. They should not be confused with the "revolutionary committees" formed later in the Cultural Revolution.

the committee members should be elected by the masses (although from an established list of candidates), should be subject to recall at any time, and should be "service personnel" for the students and staff and not "ride on your backs." Accordingly, when the Peking municipal Party committee formally ordered the disbandment of the work teams on July 28, it simultaneously called for the election of Cultural Revolution committees in every school and university in the city.[10]

The Eleventh Plenum of the Central Committee, meeting in August 1966, decided to extend the Cultural Revolution from the educational and cultural sectors, which until then had been the principal locus of the movement, to "all other parts of the superstructure not in correspondence with the socialist economic base." The scope of the movement was now to include virtually every economic and political organization in urban China. The plenum also ordered that Cultural Revolution committees be established in factories, mines, and urban districts and neighborhoods, as well as in schools, universities, and government and Party organs. The plenum decision explicitly provided that the committees should be modeled after the Paris Commune: their members would be chosen by a system of general elections, could be criticized by their constituents at any time, and could be recalled from office if they proved incompetent. The committees were to serve as the "organs of power of the proletarian cultural revolution."[11]

At the same time, however, the plenum also stipulated that the Cultural Revolution committees should not replace the Party committees or the administrative structure in the units in which they were established. Instead, they were described as a bridge between the Party and people—as an organization that would still be under the leadership of the Communist Party, but that would keep the Party in close contact with the masses. In this sense, the Cultural Revolution committees were intended to be an urban analogue of the peasant associations of the Socialist Education Movement. Both were organizations through which ordinary citizens could monitor and criticize the performance of local officials. Both were assigned the responsibility of discovering and criticizing "those persons in authority who are taking the capitalist road."

This first model of popular participation in the Cultural Revolution did not last long. The Cultural Revolution committees were soon replaced as the "organs of power of the proletarian cultural revolution" by the Red Guards and other "revolutionary rebel" organizations, composed of high school and college students, urban workers, and, to a lesser degree, suburban peasants. This constituted a major change in the conduct of the Cultural Revolution, for the Cultural Revolution committees and the Red Guards were completely different kinds of organizations. Both emerged during the Fifty Days, but the first Red Guards were linked to the central Cultural Revolution Group, while the earliest Cultural Revolution committees were linked through the work teams to the Party center administered by Liu Shao-ch'i. Both were supposed to criticize revisionist officials, but the Cultural Revolution committees focused their attention on basic-level cadres, while the Red Guards took on the task of attacking higher-level officials. The Cultural Revolution committees represented the entire membership of the factory, school, or office in which they were formed; the Red Guards were self-consciously factional organizations. The Cultural Revolution committees were placed under Party leadership; the Red Guards usually rejected such leadership.

Despite these differences, both types of organization received Mao's personal approval. Mao's endorsement of the Cultural Revolution committees was given in a speech to regional Party secretaries on July 22; his approval of the Red Guards, in a letter he sent to the Red Guards of the Tsinghua University Middle School on August 1.[12] In contrast, the Eleventh Plenum approved the formation of Cultural Revolution committees but did not mention, let alone endorse, the Red Guards. This may indicate that the Central Committee did not share Mao's willingness to legitimate factional organizations that appeared to reject the principle of Party leadership.

Within ten days of the adoption of the plenum's Sixteen-Point Decision on the Cultural Revolution, however, Mao Tse-tung personally reviewed the first of a series of enormous Red Guard rallies in T'ien-an-men Square in Peking. This apparently caused great confusion, particularly in the schools and universities attempting to adhere to the Sixteen-Point Decision.[13] Two very different types of organization had now been endorsed—one by the Central Committee collectively, the other by Mao personally. The Central Committee decision made it necessary to establish Cultural Revolution committees, but Mao's appearance at the Red Guard rally simultaneously removed any doubt that mass organizations similar to the guards would also be formed throughout China.

Organizers were thus faced with a dilemma: What was the relationship between these two kinds of organizations supposed to be? Some units tried to cope with the problem by establishing both Cultural Revolution committees and Red Guard (or revolutionary rebel) organizations. Quite rapidly, however, the Red Guards began to eclipse the Cultural Revolution committees, primarily because of three constraints on the committees' ability to serve as effective critics of revisionist cadres. The provision that the committees should accept the leadership of the Party often made it possible for basic-level Party officials or their superiors at the municipal level to control or co-opt them. In his discussion of the Cultural Revolution in Shanghai, Neale Hunter has referred to the Cultural Revolution committees as mere "appendages of the Party committees," and William Hinton has written that the Cultural Revolution committee established at Tsinghua University in Peking was simply "a work team without the Work Team."[14] As the Cultural Revolution escalated, this close connection between the Cultural Revolution committees and the Party establishment made the committees increasingly suspect.

And, in addition, the Cultural Revolution committees, just as intended, were broadly representative of all the members of each basic-level unit. This inevitably meant that there would be sharp divisions within the committees between those who supported local officials and those who opposed them. Originally, Mao himself had endorsed this feature of the committees, saying that they should have the Left, the neutrals, and the Right as members, and should contain "an opposition."[15] But this, too, restricted the ability of the committees to undertake vigorous, unified action in dealing with local cadres.

Finally, Cultural Revolution committees were supposed to deal principally with cadre problems and policy questions in their own units, whereas Red Guard organizations could attack a much broader range of targets. As the Party establishment sought to regain control over the Cultural Revolution, this feature of the Cultural Revolution committees became an important disadvantage. The committees could rather easily be split, controlled, or co-opted. But the Red Guards could be dispatched to investigate conditions in other units or even, as was frequently the case, in other cities and provinces where they would be less susceptible to pressure from local Party officials. The Red Guards could therefore provide the Cultural Revolution with a shock force that was much more flexible, mobile, and powerful than the Cultural Revolution committees.

RED GUARDS AND REVOLUTIONARY REBELS:
THE MASSES AS REBELS

So although the Cultural Revolution committees lingered on for a few months, it was the Red Guards and similar mass organizations that became the principal vehicle for popular participation in the Cultural Revolution.* The Red Guards, composed at this point principally of students from high schools and universities, eagerly assumed the role Mao had assigned them, first engaging in a campaign to destroy all remnants of feudal and

---

*In November and December, for instance, the central Cultural Revolution Group and the Central Committee continued to call for the formation of Cultural Revolution committees in communes, factories, and other industrial enterprises. But there is little evidence that these committees were influential in the Cultural Revolution. See *CCP Documents of the Great Proletarian Cultural Revolution, 1966–1967* (Hong Kong, 1968), pp. 113–20, 131–42.

bourgeois culture and then going on to confront and denounce "revisionist" officials. Editorials urged Party cadres to trust the masses and accept their criticism in a humble and nonvindictive spirit, while encouraging the students to rise up in revolution and "pay attention to state affairs."[16]

Nevertheless, the Red Guard movement encountered a series of serious problems in August and September 1966 that Mao and the central Cultural Revolution Group were unable to solve. Part of the difficulty stemmed from the reluctance of many students to express strong criticism of higher-level Party committees and cadres, whether out of respect for the Party's authority or fear of punishment and reprisals. Part of the difficulty also stemmed from the extraneous interests of many Red Guards, their concern with matters within their own schools, and their delight at the opportunity to engage in "nonrevolutionary tourism."[17] Of greater importance, however, was the active resistance to the movement by municipal and provincial Party leaders.*

Many Party leaders at first attempted to prohibit or restrict Red Guard activities, using as their pretext the failure of the Eleventh Plenum's decision on the Cultural Revolution to sanction Red Guard organizations. In some places officials outlawed the Red Guards altogether; in others they permitted Red Guards to organize but denied them the right to conduct parades or demonstrations, display wall posters, or publish their own newspapers. Somewhat more subtly, many officials sought to evade criticism by arguing that attacking local Party committees was the same as attacking the Party as a whole, the Central Committee, or even Chairman Mao.[18] In these ways local Party leaders attempted to manipulate the widespread uncertainty as to the permissible scope of the movement.

To clarify the situation, the center used a variety of methods to demonstrate its approval of Red Guard activities. Perhaps most important was the series of mammoth Red Guard rallies in Peking reviewed by Mao and organized by the People's Liberation Army. Many Red Guards were given army uniforms, and Mao himself donned a Red Guard armband. The rallies conveyed the message that the movement had the support of Mao—and of the army, as well. In addition, editorials reasserted the right of students to form Red Guards, to criticize Party committees at all levels, to engage in parades and demonstrations, and to publish newspapers. The Central Committee apparently issued a directive granting Red Guards the right to use printing presses.[19] And Mao donated a sample of his own

---

*For an excellent discussion of this resistance, see Parris H. Chang, "Provincial Party Leaders' Strategies for Survival During the Cultural Revolution," in Robert A. Scalapino, ed., *Elites in the People's Republic of China* (Seattle, 1972).

calligraphy for the Red Guard journal *Hsin Pei-ta* to use as its masthead.[20]

Finally, the center attempted to deny to local Party committees the immunity from criticism enjoyed by the Party as a whole. One editorial, in instructing all Party committees to "follow the mass line and accept supervision and criticism by the masses," noted, "The Party Central Committee is the center of the Party. The Party organ of an area or unit is merely the Party organ of that area or unit. Why should the Party organ of an area or unit not be criticized if it has turned against the correct leadership of the Party Central Committee headed by Comrade Mao Tse-tung and against the thought of Mao Tse-tung?"[21]

Once the legitimacy of the Red Guards had been established, however, local Party officials simply switched tactics. Rather than attempt to halt the formation of Red Guards, they now encouraged the formation of additional mass organizations that would support the local establishment. The mobilization of leftists to criticize Party officials was matched by the countermobilization of moderates and conservatives to defend them. In this process of competitive mobilization, the local Party leaders appear to have had a considerable advantage. Their extensive local contacts and their power over local patronage gave them important resources in mobilizing supporters and discouraged local students from committing themselves to an "anti-Party" position. To break the local leaders' control over their own areas and units, the Cultural Revolution Group encouraged Red Guards to "exchange revolutionary experience." By dispatching Red Guards from other areas to a given city, the central leaders hoped to provide a core of students less susceptible to the threats of local Party leaders. This tactic was successful in some areas.[22] But it backfired in others, for these newly arrived Red Guards could easily be portrayed as arrogant outsiders, ignorant of local conditions, who had come to make trouble.[23]

Moreover, the Cultural Revolution Group's own regulations for conducting the Cultural Revolution in factories and communes tended to favor local officials and hamper Red Guards in their attempts to gain support among workers and peasants. In September, for example, urban Red Guards were ordered to stay out of the countryside unless specifically authorized by the provincial or special district Party committee.[24] And until November 1966 students were generally discouraged from entering factories to recruit workers to join assaults on local Party committees. On the other hand, the local Party committees were not prevented from using the commune and factory Party branches, and even the work teams still participating in the Socialist Education Movement, to mobilize workers for assaults on the Red Guards.[25]

As a result, by the end of October, the Cultural Revolution had achieved, at best, a standoff. Despite the clear calls from Peking for criticism of provincial and municipal cadres, and despite the dispatch of leftist Red Guards from the capital in answer to those calls, local Party officials had been able to mobilize substantial support from among students, workers, and peasants. This is not to say that local Party officials were completely unaffected by the movement. Many found it necessary to attend Red Guard rallies and issue self-criticisms and confessions. But, in general, local Party leaders still found it possible to live with the movement by making a concession here or a self-criticism there, or by sacrificing an unpopular subordinate when necessary. Describing the accomplishments of the Cultural Revolution in Shanghai, Neale Hunter has written, "By November, the movement had been going on for six months, yet in a city like Shanghai not a single high Party official had been discredited."[26]

The frustration of Mao and other central radicals with the progress of the Cultural Revolution was apparent at a central work conference held October 8–25. Lin Piao's speech to the conference, along with Mao's two informal talks, indicate the dual strategy employed in a final attempt to secure the compliance of Party leaders with the Cultural Revolution.[27] On the one hand, Mao and Lin sharply criticized Party officials who failed to subject themselves to criticism by Red Guards. Mao, for instance, commented that most cadres "are incoherent, daren't see the Red Guards, don't speak truthfully with the students, and are bureaucrats. . . . Years of revolution have made them more stupid than ever." He added that "only a very few people firmly place the word 'revolt' in front of other words. Most people put the word 'fear' in first place." In the same vein, Lin began his speech by noting that although there was great enthusiasm "at both ends"—enthusiasm, that is, on the part of both Mao and the masses—there was not enough enthusiasm "in between." He attributed the resistance of the Party to "some leadership comrades in the Central Committee—said to be Comrades Liu Shao-ch'i and Teng Hsiao-p'ing—who have been engaged in another line that is contrary to Chairman Mao's line." And he revealed that the work conference had been called in order to cope with "setbacks" in the movement.

But at the same time that they denounced officials who obstructed the Cultural Revolution, Mao and Lin also sought to reassure cadres that they could most likely pass the test if they would only consent to take it. Mao admitted that many cadres were understandably anxious, but said that he was just as anxious as they were, and that he sincerely hoped and expected that they would pass the test. "Who wants to knock you down?" he asked. "I do not. And I do not believe that the Red Guards want to do that either." Mao said that many cadres had lost the initiative when they first opposed the Red Guards and next mobilized other "Red Guards" in their own support, but that the lost initiative could be recovered if cadres would now change their attitudes toward the Cultural Revolution.

As a concrete manifestation of this dual policy, Mao insisted that Liu Shao-ch'i and Teng Hsiao-p'ing present self-criticisms to the work conference, but he commented later, "Not everything Comrade Shao-ch'i has done is bad. If they [presumably Liu, Teng, and other ranking cadres] have made mistakes, they can probably correct them! When they have corrected them, it will be all right, and they should be allowed to come back and go to work with fresh spirit." Mao may still have been hoping that Liu would accept the Cultural Revolution, and that Liu's example would inspire other cadres to do the same.

Although Mao expressed satisfaction with the outcome of the work conference, few cadres appear to have been convinced by the arguments presented there. Within several weeks the Maoists decided upon a major intensification of Red Guard activity to force the compliance that persuasion had been unable to obtain.

This new stage of the Cultural Revolution was inaugurated at yet another massive Red Guard rally in Peking. There Lin Piao repeated the call for the students to criticize and supervise the leadership institutions and leaders of the Party and government at all levels.[28] This time, however, the radical forces were to be enlarged. At the beginning of the Red Guard movement the recruitment of leaders, and in some cases members, of Red Guard organizations had been restricted to students and staff with "five-red" family backgrounds: the sons and daughters of workers, poor and lower-middle peasants, soldiers, revolutionary martyrs, and revolutionary cadres. This provision had limited the size of the Red Guard organizations, for only a fraction of students in most schools came from "five-red" backgrounds. Moreover, it also served to moderate the movement, since leadership in Red Guard organizations often passed to the children of the same officials who were supposedly under attack. In October and November, these restrictions were lifted. In one middle school in Canton, membership in the various Red Guard organizations immediately rose from 30 percent to 80 percent of the student body.[29] Even more important, students were now given the authority to enter factories and communes to mobilize the workers and peasants against municipal and provincial Party leaders, subject only to the restriction that they not disrupt production or attempt to control the workers' and peasants' own Cultural Revolution activities.[30]

With the ranks of the Red Guards thus reinforced, the center began to designate more precisely the targets it had in mind. A second wave of Red Guards was sent out from Peking to other major cities, apparently with quite definite instructions as to which local officials should be criticized and "tested."* The purpose of these central emissaries was to prevent the movement from focusing only on lower-level cadres, many of whom were being deliberately sacrificed by their superiors. At this point, the idea that an entire municipal or provincial Party committee should be the target of the Cultural Revolution was incredible, even to many Red Guards; specific instructions to the contrary were necessary if the movement were not to be confined to minor targets. To reinforce the point that extremely high-ranking cadres should be subjected to careful scrutiny, the center began to leak the information that Liu Shao-ch'i and Teng Hsiao-p'ing had opposed Mao's line on the Cultural Revolution and were attempting to protect local revisionist cadres. Finally, in December Yang Shang-k'un, Lo Jui-ch'ing, Lu Ting-i, P'eng Chen, and Ho Lung—all Party cadres of the highest rank—were paraded before public rallies of condemnation in Peking. It was now clear that the scope of criticism was to be virtually unbounded.

MASS UPRISING AND PARIS COMMUNE: THE MASSES SEIZE POWER

The effects of this new wave of assaults varied from province to province and city to city, but virtually nowhere did the intensification of the Red Guard movement produce the results that Mao and the Cultural Revolution Group had intended: voluntary self-criticism by Party and state officials. Instead, many local leaders intensified their resistance to the Cultural Revolution. Some encouraged workers to leave their jobs and travel to Peking to present their views to the Central Committee. Others, particularly in Shanghai, granted raises, bonuses, and other material incentives to workers to secure their support. The result was that in many cities the economy was seriously disrupted, but no political settlement was in sight.[31]

In mid-January 1967, therefore, the surviving central leaders abandoned the notion of securing the Party establishment's compliance with the Cultural Revolution and the Red Guard movement. As Mao put it, most cadres had simply refused to submit to criticism by the Red Guards and had "failed to come to grips with the Great Cultural Revolution."[32] Accordingly, the "proletarian revolutionaries" were now encouraged to move beyond criticism and actually overthrow the local Party committees. A Central Committee directive, issued on January 23, told them to "form a great alliance to seize power from those in authority who are taking the capitalist road" and instructed the army to give "active support . . . to the

---

*Nieh Yüan-tzu, for example, was sent to Shanghai with instructions to mobilize criticism of the mayor and the director of the municipal education department. Neale Hunter, *Shanghai Journal: An Eyewitness Account of the Cultural Revolution* (New York, 1969), pp. 152ff.

broad masses of revolutionary leftists in their struggle to seize power."[33] A *Jen-min jih-pao* editorial on January 22 attributed what it called the "setbacks" of the past several months to the fact that revisionist Party cadres still possessed the "seals of power."* It declared:

The handful of representatives of the bourgeoisie are vicious and dare to bully people to such an extent precisely because they still have power! Of all the ways for the revolutionary masses to take their destiny into their own hands, in the final analysis the only way is to take power. Those who have power have everything; those who are without power have nothing. Of all the important things, the possession of power is the most important. Such being the case, the revolutionary masses, with a deep hatred for the class enemy, make up their mind to unite, form a great alliance, seize power! Seize power!! Seize power!!! All the Party power, political power, and financial power usurped by the counterrevolutionary revisionists and those diehards who persistently cling to the bourgeois reactionary line must be recaptured![34]

The role of the masses in the Cultural Revolution thus changed. No longer were they simply to serve as critics and monitors of the Party and state organizations—to "criticize and supervise the Party and government leadership institutions and leaders at all levels," as Lin Piao had said in November 1966. Now they were to unite in a great alliance, rise in rebellion, and depose those who had usurped power and departed from the proletarian revolutionary line. In a speech on January 24, Ch'en Po-ta declared that this form of revolution would be very different from the seizure of power in urban China at the time of liberation. Then, Ch'en said, the way to make revolution had been to send the military into an area, establish a new government, and issue orders from the top down. During the Cultural Revolution, in contrast, "it is the masses who take over": the workers, peasants, soldiers, students, and traders would seize power, establish a provisional "political consultative conference," and elect a more permanent representative conference modeled after the Paris Commune.†

There were problems, however, in trying to carry out this policy in China. In speaking of a single "great alliance" of proletarian revolutionaries, the Maoists were assuming that the Chinese people formed a single social force, united by their common interest in ridding China of revisionism. As the events of the previous six months had already demonstrated, however, such an assumption was unwarranted. The masses, far from being a unified social force, were divided into innumerable factional

*Power seizures had already occurred in Shansi and Shanghai before this editorial was written, as local leftists attempted to restore order to a collapsing economy.

†Ch'en's speech was delivered to representatives from Peking University and other educational institutions in the Peking area. See *Huo-ch'e-t'ou*, no. 7 (ii.67), in *Survey of the China Mainland Press*, no. 3898 (14.iii.67), pp. 4–7.

organizations, each with its own particular interests. The Cultural Revolution Group proved unable to forge their leftist supporters into an effective, united movement. The groups that seized provincial power in late January, therefore, were frequently small and unrepresentative coalitions of a handful of mass organizations. In a few cases the groups that seized power appear to have been instruments of the provincial Party committee, which hoped to maintain its control of provincial affairs following a staged seizure of power. In other provinces there were several competing coalitions, each claiming to be more revolutionary than the others and each seeking support for its claims from the local military commands and from Peking. As a result, few of the provincial power seizures in late January 1967 were acceptable to the center. Of the thirteen power seizures reported by the provincial press, only four—Shansi, Kweichow, Shanghai, and Heilungkiang—were mentioned by the central media.

But even where power had been seized by groups acceptable to Peking, there remained the problem of exercising the authority that had been won. It soon became apparent that mass organizations did not have the political experience or administrative knowledge necessary to manage provincial affairs. In some cases representatives of mass organizations would "seize power" by entering provincial Party and state offices, demanding and receiving the official seals, and then simply leaving. The mass organizations were able to seize the symbols of power, but they were unable effectively to exercise its substance.

In short, the model of the mass uprising failed in two respects. It failed to provide for an authoritative method of analyzing the competing mass organizations in a province, forming the broadest possible coalitions, and excluding from it those organizations whose membership or programs were unacceptable to Peking. Moreover, it also failed to provide for the administrative skills necessary to maintain governmental operations once power had been seized. Only some nine days after it had been announced, the model of a mass uprising was abandoned.

The new model for the seizure of power to replace the mass uprising was announced in an important *Hung-ch'i* editorial published on February 1.[35] The editorial stated that thereafter power should not be seized simply by an alliance of mass organizations, as the January 22 *Jen-min jih-pao* editorial had implied, but by a coalition to consist of "members of the leadership of local Liberation Army units and revolutionary leadership cadres of Party and government organs." This "three-in-one combination" was intended to overcome the difficulties posed by the model of a mass uprising. The army was responsible for suppressing any opposition to the seizure of power and making sure that it was undertaken by acceptable groups. The presence of "revolutionary cadres" in the coalition was to provide it with members who were politically more mature and who had greater ability in organizational work than the leaders of mass organizations. If they were not included, one editorial pointed out, "the proletarian revolutionaries will not be able to solve the problem of seizing and wielding power in their struggle . . . , nor can they consolidate power even if they seize it." In short, the editorial concluded, experience had demonstrated that in seizing power "it will not do to rely solely on the representatives of these revolutionary mass organizations."*

But once the proper methods for seizing power had been determined, another problem emerged: Through what organizational forms should power be exercised? On January 24 Ch'en Po-ta had said that the new "political consultative conferences" produced by the Cultural Revolution should be based on the Paris Commune model.[36] Similarly, the *Hung-ch'i* editorial of February 1 pointed out that the old Party and governmental organs could not simply be taken over as they were, but that completely new forms were necessary. Moreover, by repeating Mao's comment that Nieh Yüan-tzu's wall poster in May had inaugurated a Paris Commune in Peking, *Hung-ch'i* strongly implied that the new forms should be modeled after the Paris Commune. Thus, *Hung-ch'i*, which very likely represented the views of Ch'en Po-ta and the Cultural Revolution Group at this time, appeared ready to carry the concept an important step further. The example of the Paris Commune was not simply to guide the formation of Cultural Revolution committees, as suggested by the decisions of the Eleventh Plenum, but was to lead to a fundamental restructuring of the Party and state bureaucracies as well.

Accordingly, most of the provisional provincial governments announced that they would adopt the Commune's organizational principles. The Shansi "revolutionary rebel general headquarters," for instance, claimed that its members had been democratically elected at a congress "jointly sponsored by the revolutionary mass organizations, the local army units, and the revolutionary leading cadres." Shansi also pledged that all the members of the headquarters staff were subject to supervision and criticism by the revolutionary masses and could be recalled at any time if they were found incompetent.[37] Heilungkiang's revolutionary committee, in describing its organizational structure, stated that it had been designed to accord with the experience of the Paris Commune. The revolutionary committee's staff members would not receive any official title or special treatment; they would be elected "in accordance with the election system

*_Jen-min jih-pao_, 10.ii.67, in *Peking Review*, 17.ii.67, pp. 17–19. A few days later Mao endorsed this point by saying that "for the purpose of seizing power, the three-way alliances were essential." Stuart R. Schram, *Chairman Mao Talks to the People: Talks and Letters, 1956–1971* (New York, 1974), p. 277.

of the Paris Commune under extensive democracy," and would be subject to dismissal and recall.[38] Similarly, the Kweichow revolutionary committee announced that the proletarian revolutionaries had the authority to supervise the revolutionary committee and to remove from office any member of the revolutionary committee who was unfit for his position.[39] It is clear, then, that explicit references to the Paris Commune were by no means restricted to Shanghai.

Some cities went even further and proclaimed themselves communes. Shanghai established a "people's commune" on February 5; Tsingtao, a "political and judicial commune" on February 9; and Harbin, a "people's commune" on February 16.[40] But there was no essential difference between their organizational principles and structures and those of the three provincial revolutionary organs. The only distinction was semantic: the cities declared themselves to be communes, the provinces did not. Nevertheless, the distinction, however slight, was to have crucial political importance.

The formation of a "people's commune" in Shanghai apparently gave Peking pause, even though the principles of the Paris Commune had been endorsed only a few weeks before. Although Radio Shanghai claimed that the commune had been established with "the great solicitude and support of Chairman Mao," Peking carefully avoided using the word "commune" in its accounts of events in Shanghai. One New China News Agency dispatch, in an attempt to find a suitable circumlocution, chose the rather awkward phrase, "the provisional highest organ of authority of the Shanghai revolutionary rebels."[41] Chang Ch'un-ch'iao and Yao Wen-yüan, leaders of the Shanghai commune and members of the central Cultural Revolution Group, were called back to Peking to discuss the problem with Mao. In a series of three meetings with these two Shanghai leaders between February 12 and February 18, the Chairman announced that no further communes could be established in China, asked Chang and Yao to change the name of Shanghai's political structure to something else, and strongly implied that the organizational principles of the Paris Commune were not to be applied to the new provisional governments.[42]

Mao probably had several reasons for asking Shanghai to give up the name "people's commune."* First, the principle that new leaders should be chosen by general elections—a cornerstone of the Paris Commune model—was unrealistic under the circumstances. The mass movement in China's cities was deeply fragmented and divided, and no one could be

---

*In addition to the points noted, Mao also gave a less substantial reason. He argued that if Shanghai called itself a commune, every other locality in China would want to follow suit, and the name of the country would have to be changed from the People's Republic of China to the "Chinese People's Commune." This, Mao said, might cause other states to withdraw their diplomatic recognition from China.

sure that leaders acceptable to Peking could be selected in any such elections. In fact, none of the cities and provinces that claimed to have followed the model of the Paris Commune had actually conducted general elections. They had instead selected their new leadership through bargaining and consultation. Shanghai itself promised only that general elections might eventually be held "when conditions become ripe."[43] As Ch'i Pen-yu, a member of the central Cultural Revolution Group, was later to comment: "If it depended on balloting, our Communist Party would not have won the victory [in the Revolution]. From the start, revolutionaries are always in the minority."[44]

Second, the Paris Commune model was potentially incompatible with the three-in-one combination, and particularly with the continued participation in government of high-ranking cadres. After all, one of the principles of the Paris Commune was to turn official positions into "a form of worker's job" that could be performed by anyone. This vision was hardly congruent with Peking's claim that veteran cadres must still participate in the new organs of power because they were politically more mature than ordinary citizens and had greater ability in organizational work. In discussing the Shanghai commune with Chang Ch'un-ch'iao and Yao Wen-yüan, Mao had warned of the anarchical tendencies that were emerging in the Cultural Revolution—particularly the desire to eliminate all formal positions of leadership and authority—calling them "most reactionary." Thus, when Chang Ch'un-ch'iao announced in Shanghai that the city would abandon the name "people's commune," he simultaneously attempted to refute those who argued that "we can do without revolutionary leading cadres":

Why do we need old cadres who have assumed leadership work before? The reason is very simple. For instance, some workers perform very well. They dare to break through and rebel; they are able and have made significant contributions to the Great Cultural Revolution. But if we turn over to them a city such as Shanghai or a province such as Kiangsu, then they would find it very difficult to manage it because of lack of experience.[45]

Third, the Paris Commune model contained no provisions for a vanguard party. To be sure, commentaries on the history of the original commune usually pointed to the absence of a vanguard party as one of the reasons for its collapse, but they did not explain what the relation between such a party and the highly participatory governmental institutions of the commune might have been. In his discussions with Chang and Yao, Mao Tse-tung seemed acutely aware of the implications of this problem for China. "If everything were changed into a commune, then what about the Party? Where would we place the Party? . . . There must be a party somehow! There must be a nucleus, no matter what we call it. Be it called the Communist Party, or Social Democratic Party, or Kuomintang, or I-kuan-tao, there must be a party."

Mao's conclusion, therefore, was that it was better not to change the name and call it a commune. He justified his position by saying that the name given to the new form of government produced by the Cultural Revolution was less important than the way in which it operated. "What we want to see," he said, "is not the changing of titles, because the problem lies not with titles but with practice, not with form but with content." Nonetheless, he was also concerned about the practical consequences of adopting the Paris Commune as a model. His conclusion appears to have been that the commune promised too much democracy and too little centralism for China's circumstances.

THE REVOLUTIONARY COMMITTEES:
THE MASSES SHARE POWER

On February 19, the day after Mao's last meeting with Chang Ch'un-ch'iao and Yao Wen-yüan, the Central Committee issued a notification explicitly forbidding any further use of the term "people's commune" at the provincial and municipal levels.[46] Almost immediately mention of the Paris Commune as a model for the state began to disappear from the official Chinese press.* A little less than a month later, Mao formally confirmed that the new "revolutionary, responsible, and proletarian provisional power structures" that were being formed in the Cultural Revolution should be called, not "communes," but "revolutionary committees."† These new organs of power were to be established at all levels of administration from communes and urban neighborhoods to provinces, replacing, at least temporarily, both the government and the Party apparatus.‡

---

*The use of the Paris Commune as a model for mass organizations continued a bit longer. See, for instance, *Peking Review*, 10.iii.67, pp. 6–7.

†Jerome Ch'en, *Mao Papers: Anthology and Bibliography* (London: 1970), pp. 136–37. The term "revolutionary committee" (*ko-ming wei-yüan-hui*) can be traced to the early Yenan period, when revolutionary committees were provisional governments established in areas that had just been incorporated into Communist base areas or that remained militarily insecure. These revolutionary committees, like their later namesakes, were "three-in-one combinations" of local activists, outside Communist Party cadres, and military personnel. They were replaced by elected village soviets once military security was assured, land reform completed, and peasant associations organized. See Mark Selden, *The Yenan Way in Revolutionary China* (Cambridge, Mass., 1971), pp. 114–15.

‡No "national revolutionary committee" was formed at the center, although there were revolutionary committees established in a few central ministries. Nor were revolutionary committees established in the regions, for regional Party bureaus were abolished in 1968. In the countryside, revolutionary committees were not established in production teams and were formed in brigades only "where needed." See *CCP Documents of the Great Proletarian Cultural Revolution, 1966–1967* (Hong Kong, 1968), pp. 627–33.

As a model for popular participation in politics and as a model of political organization, the revolutionary committees differed from the Paris Commune in two important ways. First, as far as the composition of government bodies was concerned, the revolutionary committees abandoned any implication that ordinary citizens would now accede to all official positions, or that all cadres would be dismissed from their posts. Instead, the revolutionary committees were based on the same principle of the three-in-one combination that had earlier been applied to the seizure of power. The revolutionary committees were to embody a coalition of three groups: "responsible persons from those revolutionary mass organizations that really represent the broad masses," representatives of local Liberation Army forces, and representative revolutionary leading cadres from Party and government organs.[47] The masses, in short, now were told to share power both with representatives of the bureaucracy (who had administrative skills and a detailed knowledge of local social and economic conditions) and with representatives of the military (who could enforce discipline on unruly mass organizations).

Second, the revolutionary committees were not formed on the basis of general elections, as provided in the Paris Commune model. Instead, the composition of the revolutionary committees was determined by a complex, and often lengthy, process of negotiation and bargaining among mass representatives, local officials, and military officers.[48] Throughout this process, it was the army that played the critical role. Immediately after the seizure of power from the former Party authorities, the local garrison forces would establish a military control committee, charged with responsibility not only for maintaining order and continuing production, but also for supervising the formation of the revolutionary committees. This involved the suppression and disbandment of mass organizations that they considered to be counterrevolutionary or ultraleftist, the solicitation of nominations for revolutionary committee membership from mass organizations and cadre groups, the recommendation of military representatives to serve on the revolutionary committees, and the composition of a final slate of representatives that would be acceptable, or at least tolerable, to all major parties. In a way, the army served as a nationwide work team with substantial power not only to determine which cadres had passed the test of the Cultural Revolution and therefore deserved to serve on the revolutionary committees, but also to decide which mass representatives were worthy of sharing political power.

For the most important revolutionary committees—those in the provinces and in the major cities—this complicated process was supervised by the central authorities in Peking. Peking could veto the revolutionary committees nominated by the provinces. It could resolve provincial disputes by sending emissaries to the provinces in question or by calling representatives of provincial factions to the capital to participate in study groups.[49] It could, after investigation, label mass organizations as "revolutionary" and "counterrevolutionary," even if this meant overriding the previous judgment of the military control committees. It could dismiss the military control committees and the local military commanders if they proved unresponsive to central orders.[50] And, if all else failed, Peking could dispatch central military units to troubled provinces to serve as district instruments of central authority.[51]

At the same time, Peking could act more indirectly to influence the formation of revolutionary committees throughout the country. Central leaders soon realized that the main dynamic in the process was the tension between the local military officers responsible for forming the revolutionary committees and the representatives of the various mass organizations. At times when the center felt that local military commanders were too strict or authoritarian in trying to impose unity and order on the mass organizations, it could therefore give the Red Guards and revolutionary rebels the authority to criticize the Liberation Army; at times when Peking felt that the mass organizations had become too unruly and anarchic, it could give the army the right to suppress them and to restore order. This strategy created a cyclical pattern in the formation of revolutionary committees between February 1967 and August 1968, a pattern in which periods of radicalism, when mass organizations were dominant, alternated with more moderate periods, when the army was dominant.

The revolutionary committees, then, were not "created by the masses"; the masses were not permitted, as they had been promised in January, to take their destiny entirely into their own hands. Instead, formation of revolutionary committees involved negotiation and bargaining in which mass organizations and representatives were only one type of participant, in which mass organizations were often in serious conflict with one another, and in which close control by higher authorities and local military headquarters was a sine qua non.

Once they were formed, however, the new revolutionary committees did permit a substantial degree of mass representation. Predictably, the degree of mass participation on the revolutionary committees varied over time, with more mass representatives appointed in radical phases of the Cultural Revolution, fewer in moderate periods.[52] Overall, however, 28 percent of the members of the standing committees of the provincial revolutionary committees were mass representatives, as were more than one-third of the vice-chairmen. It was these mass representatives who were supposed to ensure that the benefits of popular participation in politics were won—that the workings of government would be supervised by its constituents, and that policies would follow the proletarian rather than the revisionist line. As one of the most authoritative descriptions of the revolutionary committee model put it, the system of mass participation on revolutionary committees

> provides the revolutionary committees . . . with a broad mass foundation. Direct participation by the revolutionary masses in the running of the country and the enforcement of revolutionary supervision from below over the organs of political power at various levels plays a very important role in ensuring that our leadership groups at all levels always adhere to the mass line, maintain the closest relations with the masses, represent their interests at all times, and serve the people heart and soul.[53]

Nonetheless, the new revolutionary committees encountered serious opposition in several provinces during late 1967 and early 1968 from leftists who were quite possibly supported by some members of the central Cultural Revolution Group. The leftists disapproved of the revolutionary committees for several reasons. Perhaps their most basic complaint concerned the extent to which the concept of the revolutionary committee departed from the ideal of the Paris Commune. Many leftists felt that the decision of the Eleventh Plenum in August 1966 and, in addition, various editorials appearing in the central media in January 1967 had promised completely new organs of political power modeled after the Paris Commune, organs in which the people would govern themselves free of interference and exploitation by professional bureaucrats. The abandonment of the commune model in February and the introduction of the principle that the masses would have to share power with the military, and with representatives of that very bureaucratic class against which the Cultural Revolution was directed, appeared to many leftists to be a betrayal of one of the most basic goals of the Cultural Revolution.

Further, the leftists objected not only to the composition of the revolutionary committees but also to the process by which they were formed. Even if a three-in-one combination were necessary, the leftists argued, the selection of military and civilian cadres to serve on the revolutionary committees should be made by general election. In November 1967, for example, a delegation of Red Guards from Canton asked Chou En-lai how he could justify the appointment of a Kwangtung provincial preparatory group by the center when the principles of the Paris Commune clearly indicated that all political leaders should be elected by the masses. To this Chou could only respond that, in his opinion, elections were "a bourgeois thing," and that he and the Chairman always relied on "consultations" rather than "balloting" in resolving political issues.*

*Chou's remarks are contained in the pamphlet published on November 5, 1967, by the "liaison headquarters" of the Central-South bureau; see *Survey of China Mainland*

A third cause for concern was the widespread tendency during the second half of 1967 and the first quarter of 1968 to appoint a relatively small number of mass representatives to revolutionary committees, and to assign them comparatively unimportant positions. At the provincial level, military commanders were reluctant to approve the appointment of representatives of those mass organizations that had criticized, or even assaulted, the army after the Wuhan incident in late July, and Peking, for its part, was willing to accede to the army's demand for a tougher line toward mass organizations. As a result, the level of military representation on provincial revolutionary committees rose substantially between August 1967 and April 1968, primarily at the expense of mass representation. The problem of inadequate mass representation was even more serious below the provincial level, where the center's ability to exert its influence was considerably less. In Shanghai, for instance, some middle-level revolutionary committees had allegedly made "all possible excuses" to exclude mass representatives, and others had considered the mass representatives to be unimportant partners and assigned them jobs of secondary importance. Furthermore, these same middle-level revolutionary committees had successfully limited mass participation at lower levels by rejecting all proposed revolutionary committee membership lists on which the number of mass representatives exceeded the number of cadres.[54]

Finally, it was also soon apparent that the mass organizations would be assigned a clearly subordinate role once the revolutionary committees were established. In February 1967, in the early months of the Cultural Revolution when such questions were still undecided, the Kweichow revolutionary committee had promised that the provincial "proletarian revolutionary rebel general headquarters," which had seized power in January, would continue to be "the supervisory organization of the proletarian revolutionaries," presumably with the power to continue to supervise the revolutionary committee itself.[55] By late 1967, however, the policy toward the mass organizations had begun to change. The Red Guard and revolutionary rebel organizations were stripped of their power to supervise the revolutionary committees and were told that they should now submit to

---

Magazines, no. 611 (22.i.68), pp. 12–18. In a talk a few months before to a group of foreign visitors, probably a military delegation from Mali, Mao had once again rejected the radicals' demands for general elections of revolutionary committee members. "Some members say that elections are very good and democratic," he said. "I, myself, do not admit that there is any true election. I was elected a People's Deputy for Peking district, but how many people are there in Peking who really understand me? I think the 'election' of Chou En-lai as Premier [actually] means his appointment as Premier by the center." Mao's comments can be found in an untitled pamphlet reprinted in September 1967 by the "Proletarian Revolutionaries of Factory No. XXXX of the Chinese People's Liberation Army"; see *Survey of the China Mainland Press*, no. 4200 (18.vi.68), p. 5.

the "proletarian dictatorship" of the new governmental organs. The mass organizations were told that they had been correct in rebelling against the "bourgeois" authority of the former Party committees and government agencies, but that if they continued to act independently, they would be guilty of anarchism.*

For all these reasons—the composition of the revolutionary committees, the process through which they were formed, the persistent indications of military predominance in the committees, and the attempts to restrict the longer-term influence of the mass organizations—the revolutionary committees aroused considerable opposition. Leftists complained that the revolutionary committees did not, in the final analysis, represent an essential change in either the structure or composition of the organs of government in China. The most strident objections were raised in Hunan by a group calling itself the "Hunan provincial proletarian revolutionary great alliance committee," or Sheng-wu-lien. In three important documents published between its formation in mid-October 1967 and its suppression in January 1968, the Sheng-wu-lien presented a scathing critique of the organizational and political aspects of the revolutionary committees and called for an armed revolution to overthrow the revolutionary committees and establish communes throughout China.†

The basic premise of the Sheng-wu-lien was that continued participation by experienced cadres in Chinese political organs was not necessary to prevent a total collapse of civil administration. The Sheng-wu-lien argued that the January Revolution in Shanghai and the brief experimentation with the Paris Commune model had demonstrated conclusively that in the absence of bureaucrats, the people could not only go on living, but could live better and develop more quickly and with greater freedom:

It was not at all like the intimidation of the bureaucrats who, before the [cultural] revolution, had said: "Without us, production would collapse, and the society would fall into a state of hopeless confusion." As a matter of fact, without the bureaucrats and bureaucratic organs, productivity was greatly liberated. After the Ministry of Coal Industry fell, production of coal went on as usual. The Ministry of Railways fell, but transportation was carried on as usual. . . . For the first time, workers had the feeling that "it is not the state which manages us, but we who manage the state." For the first time, they felt that they were producing for them-

---

*Attempts to restore discipline over mass organizations and to combat "anarchic" tendencies began as early as January 1967 and continued throughout the Cultural Revolution. For a representative article from the period under discussion here, see New China News Agency, 25.ii.68, in *Survey of the China Mainland Press*, no. 4130 (4.iii.68), pp. 1–3.

†The three documents are the "Program" (issued sometime between October and December 1967), the "Resolutions" (December 21, 1967), and the polemic "Whither China?" (January 6, 1968). All are in Klaus Mehnert, *Peking and the New Left: At Home and Abroad*, Center for Chinese Studies, Monograph No. 4 (Berkeley, Calif., 1969).

selves. Their enthusiasm had never been so high, and their sense of responsibility as masters of the house had never been so strong.[56]

Given this attitude, the Sheng-wu-lien concluded that the abandonment of the Paris Commune model and the establishment of revolutionary committees was completely unnecessary. Even more, the step was counterrevolutionary because it returned the political power seized by the masses to China's "Red" capitalist class* and to the army, which had become a tool used by the capitalist-roaders to suppress the revolution.[57] Under the revolutionary committees, political power remained in the hands of the army and local bureaucrats; the seizure of power for which the masses had struggled had become merely a "change in appearance."[58]

From the Sheng-wu-lien's point of view, therefore, the Cultural Revolution was only just beginning. Their program was to organize and arm the masses, overthrow 90 percent of the cadres, and form the "People's Commune of China," despite Mao's earlier repudiation of such a concept. The new state they envisioned, which would be modeled after the Paris Commune, was one in which cadres would be members of the commune, with no special privileges, who could be dismissed or replaced at any time at the request of the masses.[59] In addition, there would be a new distribution of property and power and the egalitarian and communitarian vision contained in Mao's May Seventh Directive would be fully realized.† The ultimate aim of the Cultural Revolution, according to the Sheng-wu-lien, was to create nothing less than full communism in China.

In discussing their utopian goals and the means they felt necessary to achieve them, the Sheng-wu-lien revealed a curiously ambivalent attitude toward Mao. He was, after all, the author of the May Seventh Directive and the initiator of the Cultural Revolution who "foresaw the commune as the political structure which must be realized by the first Cultural Revolution." But why, then, did he endorse the revolutionary committee? Why did he suddenly oppose the establishment of the Shanghai people's commune? This was something "hard to understand." The Sheng-wu-lien gamely sought to rationalize the retreats ordered by the "Supreme Commander" as wise tactical measures aimed at avoiding a premature attempt to carry out "unrealistic demands of immature revolutionaries." But their hearts were clearly not in it; their efforts to explain Mao's endorsement of

---

*The Sheng-wu-lien charged that Chou En-lai was "at present the chief representative of China's 'Red' capitalist class," and that the revolutionary committees were Chou's idea. If this "bourgeois plan" had been achieved, the Sheng-wu-lien claimed, and if revolutionary committees were successfully established throughout China, then the proletariat would have "retreated to its grave." See "Whither China?" in Mehnert, *Peking and the New Left*, p. 88.

†The directive, in essence, called for a society in which everyone is simultaneously a worker, a peasant, a soldier, and a student. The text can be found in Ch'en, *Mao Papers*, pp. 103–5.

the revolutionary committees were riddled with contradictions and inconsistencies.* The outcome of their attempts to understand Mao is suggested by the last sentence in "Whither China?"—not "Long Live Chairman Mao!" but rather "Long Live Mao Tse-tung-ism!" The clear implication was that Mao was no longer a Maoist. By betraying the Paris Commune model, which the Sheng-wu-lien felt was the essence of the Cultural Revolution, Mao was simultaneously betraying his own thought.

Although the Sheng-wu-lien was perhaps the most extreme in its demand for the restoration of the principles of the Paris Commune, other leftists expressed similar criticisms of the revolutionary committees in somewhat more cautious language. In January 1968 Wang Shao-yung, a vice-chairman of the Shanghai revolutionary committee, acknowledged that the revolutionary committees throughout the city had been assailed by people who felt that "everything remains the same after the establishment of the revolutionary committee—the same old faces, the old leading group, the old style of work, and the old way of doing things." Wang also asserted that he thought such criticism was correct. He indicated that Chang Ch'un-ch'iao, chairman of the Shanghai revolutionary committee, had proposed that "revolutionary people's representative conferences" be established to "adjust, regulate, and purge the leading organs" of the revolutionary committees. In effect, these representative conferences were to serve the revolutionary committees in the same way that the poor and lower-middle peasant associations and the Cultural Revolution committees had been intended to serve the Party.[60] To Wang and Chang, Shanghai had already come full circle: the revolutionary committees were already divorced from the masses and in need of new organizational devices to link them once again with their constituents.

These criticisms of the revolutionary committees had a limited but noticeable effect: the center did initiate or authorize measures to meet some of the criticisms raised by the leftists. The level of mass participation on provincial revolutionary committees formed after March 1968 was substantially increased, and the level of military participation was reduced. In addition, several provincial revolutionary committees were purged of those held to be responsible for the lenient policies toward cadres and the harsh policies toward mass organizations of which the Sheng-wu-lien and others had complained.[61]

At lower levels, too, there was criticism of what was described as an excessively lenient policy toward errant cadres and an unnecessarily critical attitude toward popular representatives. Shanghai, in particular,

---

*For instance, at one point they described the revolutionary committees as an intermediate step on the path to a commune state, at another as unacceptable "bourgeois reformism."

sought to ensure high levels of mass participation on the revolutionary committees yet to be formed in the city. One editorial, though upholding the right of superior revolutionary committees to approve the composition of lower committees, insisted that any mass representatives who were disqualified should be replaced by other mass representatives. "Under no circumstances should the proportion or the number of representatives of revolutionary masses be diminished."[62] Another editorial stipulated that of the representatives of the cadres, the armed forces, and the masses on revolutionary committees, "the representatives of the revolutionary masses must make up a bigger proportion."[63]

However, these changes did not in any way constitute a repudiation of the revolutionary committees. In fact, a major editorial appearing on March 30, 1968, depicted the revolutionary committees as an organizational form, created by the masses and approved by Mao, that deserved the support of "all revolutionary comrades." In tacit rebuttal of the charges made by the Sheng-wu-lien, the editorial denied that the revolutionary committees had anything in common with the "overstaffed bureaucratic apparatus of the old exploiting classes."[64] With this editorial and the simultaneous suppression of the Sheng-wu-lien by the Hunan provincial authorities, the proponents of the Paris Commune suffered their final rebuff.

THE FATE OF MASS PARTICIPATION

If the members of Sheng-wu-lien were dissatisfied with the level of popular participation in China in late 1967 and early 1968, they must have become even more disgruntled about the political trends that emerged between August 1968 and December 1970. A coalition of military officers and civilian officials who had survived the Cultural Revolution, almost certainly with Mao's support, succeeded in greatly reducing the role of mass representatives in the Chinese political process. This was accomplished in three steps: the termination of the Red Guard movement, the reduction of the responsibilities of the mass representatives on revolutionary committees, and the virtual exclusion of mass representatives from the new Party committees organized at the provincial level in 1970–71.

The first of these measures was a direct result of the intensification of factional conflict in the summer of 1968 among Red Guard organizations in Peking, Kwangtung, and Kwangsi over the composition of the municipal and provincial revolutionary committees. In Peking, according to Jean Daubier, the university district had been turned into a virtual battleground, with contending factions employing firearms, bricks, and roofing tiles in their assault on buildings occupied by their opponents.[65] In Kwangtung and Kwangsi the bodies of victims of the fighting were dumped into the Pearl River, many floating downstream to be discovered in Hong Kong.[66] In an emotional meeting with Red Guard leaders from Peking on July 28, Mao complained that the continued fighting was disappointing everyone in China: "The people are not happy. The workers are not happy. The peasants are not happy. Peking residents are not happy. The students in most of the schools are not happy. Most students in your school are also not happy. Even within the faction that supports you there are people who are unhappy. Can you unite the whole country this way?" If the fighting did not cease, Mao warned, resort might be made to military control, and Lin Piao might take command of the universities.[67]

Within a few days Mao reached his decision. "Worker propaganda teams," usually under military control, were sent into the universities to "exercise leadership in everything."[68] Red Guard and revolutionary organizations were disbanded, their publications outlawed, and their members forcibly dispatched to the countryside, in some cases to join production and construction units in border provinces far from any major city. The former Red Guards, once lauded as "proletarian revolutionaries," were now described as "petty bourgeois intellectuals" who needed physical labor in the countryside as a way of receiving "education" from the working class.

Within a year the termination of the Red Guard movement was accompanied by a restriction of the role of mass representatives on middle-level revolutionary committees. In those instances in which mass representatives belonged to revolutionary committees at two or three levels simultaneously (say, a factory, a city, and a province), they were advised to give up their membership on the higher-level committees and to retain only their membership on the revolutionary committee in their own place of work.[69] Even where mass representatives had no other administrative responsibilities, they were increasingly told to return to their own units and stay at their own production posts, rather than spend full time in their revolutionary committee assignments.[70] Otherwise, it was argued, they would become divorced from the masses and could no longer be considered to be mass representatives. Although they were assured that they would be consulted on important matters—that they would be summoned to attend important revolutionary committee meetings and would be contacted by telephone—it was clear to the mass representatives themselves that their influence over committee decisions would be substantially reduced. Some reportedly argued that they would become delegates in name only if they were forced to return to their units;[71] others said that they could continue to hold onto power only if they were permitted to remain at work in the revolutionary committee offices.[72] Although the measure was explained as an attempt to ensure close contacts between the mass representatives and their constituents, it seems more likely to have been an effort by military and civilian cadres to remove unskilled and frequently contentious mass representatives from important roles on the revolutionary committees.

The restriction of popular participation in the post–Cultural Revolution political order reached its logical conclusion with the formation of new Party committees throughout the country in the aftermath of the Ninth Party Congress. While the revolutionary committees were to remain as arenas for the detailed specification of policy and as instruments of policy implementation, it soon became clear, as we will see in the next chapter, that the responsibility for policymaking was to be transferred from the revolutionary committees to the reconstructed Party apparatus.

As a result, the question of mass participation on the new Party committees became one of considerable importance. For a brief period during the formation of some of the first county committees in 1969, the three-in-one combination of military officers, revolutionary cadres, and mass representatives that had been used to form the revolutionary committees was applied to the Party as well. Then a second version of the three-in-one combination was introduced: a two-way triple alliance in which secretaryships on Party committees would be assigned according to age (old, middle-aged, and young) as well as occupation (military, cadre, and mass representative).[73] When the first provincial Party committees were formed at the end of 1970, however, yet a third version of the three-in-one combination was said to apply: a combination only of the old, the middle-aged, and the young. No mention was made of the desirability of guaranteeing positions to mass representatives. Given the political context, this reformulation of the three-in-one combination was clearly a way of allowing the Party to draw new blood into leadership positions without granting any representation to the mass organizations of the Cultural Revolution. The Party's new secretaries could, under this formulation, be selected exclusively from the ranks of younger cadres and younger military officers.

Unfortunately, little is known about the composition of municipal or county Party committees during this period. At the provincial level, however, the reconstruction of the Party saw little attention paid to the principle of mass representation. Of the 158 secretaries appointed to the committees in 1970–71, 94 (59 percent) were military officers, 55 (35 percent) were civilian cadres, and only 9 (6 percent) could conceivably be considered to be mass representatives. Of these 9, 6 were low-ranking cadres, 1 was Mao Tse-tung's nephew, and 2 were workers. Not one was a peasant. Although the full Party committees might have contained a higher proportion of workers and peasants, effective provincial power was denied to mass representatives.* The formation of the Party committees, in effect, ended China's brief experiment with expanded, institutionalized mass participation.

THE CULTURAL REVOLUTION AND THE
BUREAUCRATIC DILEMMA

The Cultural Revolution was the most radical period in the history of the People's Republic, a violent and disruptive time that witnessed extreme levels of mass mobilization and the most sweeping purge of Party and state officials since 1949. What is even more important for our purposes is that the Cultural Revolution was also a "radical" period in an organizational sense, in that it involved proposals for the destruction of bureaucracy and its replacement with loosely structured, highly participatory administrative organizations patterned after the Paris Commune. These proposals, in turn, reflected the belief that bureaucratic organizations were an important locus of revisionism in a socialist society, and that new, nonbureaucratic organizations would be required if China were to avoid taking a revisionist path.

In these two respects the Cultural Revolution was significantly different from any previous period in post-liberation China. Although the Hundred Flowers period had also produced proposals for a thorough restructuring of the Chinese political system, the Hundred Flowers had been much less antibureaucratic than the Cultural Revolution. In addition, the Hundred Flowers campaign had focused on the problem of the alienation of a successful revolutionary elite from the people, whereas the Cultural Revolution was more concerned with the problem of the departure of that elite from its revolutionary vision. Nor was the Cultural Revolution's fascination with the Paris Commune particularly reminiscent of the Great Leap Forward. During the Leap only the socioeconomic aspects of the Paris Commune received much attention; during the Cultural Revolution, in contrast, the organizational and political elements of the commune model received the greatest emphasis.

What is surprising about the Cultural Revolution is the limited degree to which Mao Tse-tung associated himself with this radical critique of bureaucracy. The most systematic expression of the view that bureaucracy was the locus of revisionism was written not by Mao, but by Lin Piao. In

*The Ninth Central Committee, elected in April 1969, did contain a substantially higher percentage of mass representatives than the Eighth Central Committee, since 20 percent of the full members and 26 percent of the alternate members were workers or peasants. But none of them was elected to the Politburo. See Donald W. Klein and Lois B. Hager, "The Ninth Central Committee," *China Quarterly*, no. 45 (January–March 1971), pp. 37–56.

an undated essay entitled "On the Social Foundation of Revisionism," Lin attributed revisionism in China to such bureaucratic characteristics as hierarchy, routinization, and graduated salary systems. Hierarchy, Lin complained, "permits the people at the subordinate level only to follow orders, but does not allow them to use the thought of Mao Tse-tung as the supreme directive to command everything." Routinization, in turn, leads to a decline in the fighting will of the cadres, causing them to seek no further progress but be content with the status quo. Specialization prevents cadres from participating in labor and "mingling with the masses." And a graduated pay scale enlarges the differences between worker and peasant, and creates in the cadres a desire for personal privileges, making them "conceited and egotistical." Lin's conclusion, echoing Engels, was that an organizational policy that simply "inherits the bureaucratic system of the exploiting classes . . . is the historical origin and social foundation of the reactionary line."[74]

In contrast, Mao's writings during the Cultural Revolution contain surprisingly few strong criticisms of bureaucracy as an organizational form, and contain nothing as systematic as Lin Piao's essay on the social foundation of revisionism. For the most part, Mao was content to repeat the piecemeal criticisms that he had issued earlier in the 1960's: there were revisionists in the Party and state, the bureaucracy had become bloated and divorced from the masses, and veteran cadres were resting on their laurels and not striving hard enough for new accomplishments. Mao's one major statement on bureaucracy during the Cultural Revolution was an extraordinarily vitriolic document called "Twenty Manifestations of Bureaucracy." It described bureaucrats as "brainless, dishonest, irresponsible, lazy, conceited, arbitrary yes-men"—but it did not present a detailed analysis of how they came to be that way.[75]

Nor did Mao advocate that bureaucracy be totally destroyed and replaced by participatory organizations like the Paris Commune. The support for the Paris Commune model came first from leaders of the central Cultural Revolution Group like Ch'en Po-ta and later from leftist Red Guard and revolutionary rebel organizations like the Sheng-wu-lien. For his part, Mao actually vetoed the attempt to establish a similar political structure in Shanghai, describing it as having too many anarchistic, and thus reactionary, characteristics. The Sheng-wu-lien's perception that Mao did not want to replace the bureaucracy in China with Paris Communes was totally accurate.

To the extent that Mao had any clear organizational program in mind at the beginning of the Cultural Revolution, that program was much more remedial than radical. What Mao wanted was some kind of mechanism for mass supervision that would have served to check and control, but not to replace, the existing Party and state bureaucracies. Mao was willing to endorse the Red Guards as a shock force for criticizing revisionism, but his ideal was very likely the ill-fated Cultural Revolution committees of late July and early August 1966. Together with the poor and lower-middle peasant associations in the countryside, the urban Cultural Revolution committees would have provided an institutionalized form of mass control over the bureaucracy, but in a way that would not have negated Party leadership. With such structures in place, the Chinese political system would not have been fully Leninist, for the Cultural Revolution committees and the peasant associations would have actively supervised the Party and state, particularly at the basic levels. Nor would it have been completely populist, for these new organizations would have coexisted with the Party and would, in theory at least, have followed Party leadership. As Maurice Meisner has pointed out, the dialectical character of this organizational arrangement—the blend of Leninism and populism—is characteristically Maoist.[76]

These remedial and dialectical features also characterized the organizational arrangement that received Mao's final endorsement, the revolutionary committee. Although the revolutionary committees placed mass representatives in policymaking bodies at all levels from the commune to the province, they still kept the former state bureaucracy in place to execute policy. And although mass representation on the revolutionary committees introduced a populist element into the Chinese political structure, Mao made it clear from early 1967 that the Party would eventually be rebuilt and resume its vanguard role.

All four of the models for popular participation developed during the Cultural Revolution encountered serious difficulties. The Cultural Revolution committees, Mao's ideal, could not develop enough independence from the established Party leadership at the basic levels or from the work teams. The Red Guards were more easily mobilized than controlled: the Cultural Revolution Group at the center was unable to mold the Red Guards into a unified mass movement or to prevent local officials from forming their own Red Guards to defend themselves against attack. The Paris Commune, as we have seen, did not provide a realistic model after which to pattern effective administration, and its system of general elections was too serious a departure from the Leninist principle of the vanguard party to be acceptable. The revolutionary committees, for their part, did offer a viable format for mass participation in the Chinese political process, but the degree of popular participation on the revolutionary committees gradually declined, and the principle of mass representation was not extended to the new Party committees. As far as mass supervision was concerned, therefore, the political system that emerged from the Cultural Revolution looked very similar to the system that had existed before.

In this chapter, however, we have discussed only one aspect of the organizational reforms of the Cultural Revolution, those that aimed at increasing mass supervision over the bureaucracy. Another set of reforms was concerned with change within the bureaucracy. The formation of the revolutionary committees commenced a period of organizational reconstruction that stressed returning to the organizational heritage of the Chinese Communist Party and revitalizing and reinvigorating the Party and state apparatus. Those reforms are the subject of the next chapter.

9
Attempts at Organizational Revitalization
1967-1969

In organizational terms, the purpose of the Cultural Revolution was to reform and restructure the Party and state bureaucracies in order to halt what Mao Tse-tung saw as their degeneration into revisionism. The expansion of popular participation discussed in the last chapter was only one part—albeit the most innovative and dramatic part—of the organizational program of the Cultural Revolution. A second was the revitalizing of the bureaucracy from within: the transformation of the Party and state into more efficient and energetic organizations, and the strengthening of the commitment of Party and government officials to Maoist principles and programs.

This chapter will discuss five elements of the revitalization of the bureaucracy between 1967 and 1969: (1) the reassessment of the qualifications and performance of administrative officials to identify and remove from all levels of the bureaucracy "persons in authority" who were "taking the capitalist road"; (2) the codification of new standards of behavior for cadres to stress ideological study, selfless service, regular physical labor, and close ties with the masses; (3) the establishment of May Seventh cadre schools to provide a new mechanism for the evaluation of cadres and a new format for physical labor and political indoctrination; (4) the retrenchment of the bureaucracy through reduction of administrative staffs, simplification of organizational structure, and redefinition of the relationship between the Party and the state; and (5) the decentralization of planning and management of the economy by shifting authority from the central and regional levels to the provinces. The conclusion will consider the extent to which these reforms represented a departure from, or a restoration of, the organizational traditions of the Party.

REASSESSMENT OF ADMINISTRATORS

Upon the publication of the Twenty-three Articles in January 1965, Mao Tse-tung began repeatedly to describe the rectification of cadres who had "taken the capitalist road," "opposed socialism," or "degenerated into revisionists" as the principal focus of the Cultural Revolution. Mao's major concern, of course, was with the highest officials at the various levels of Party and state, for it was they who had the greatest power over the formulation and implementation of public policy. Accordingly, it was these cadres—members of the Central Committee, ministers of the State Council, provincial and regional Party secretaries, county magistrates—who were the chief targets of the Red Guard movement in late 1966, and who were removed from office during the seizures of power in early 1967. But this still left a large number of lower-echelon administrators—vice-ministers, assistant ministers, department heads, section chiefs—whose political qualifications and reliability would also have to be evaluated. In this section we will examine the procedures employed during the Cultural Revolution to reassess and correct the performance of these administrative officials.*

The methods for evaluating the performance of administrators changed with each stage of the Cultural Revolution. After the publication of the Twenty-three Articles, the rectification of county and provincial cadres was conducted through relatively mild programs of political education and self-criticism. During the Fifty Days, as we have already seen, the rectification campaign was greatly intensified by sending work teams into central and provincial offices responsible for culture, education, industry, and finance. After the Eleventh Plenum the assessment of administrative officials was supposed to be administered by the Cultural Revolution committees, which in theory at least were established by general elections in all government and Party organs. But the Cultural Revolution committees proved to be no more effective in the bureaucracy than in schools and universities. By the fall of 1966, revolutionary rebel organizations patterned after the Red Guards began to be formed within Party and government agencies. Some of these were composed of students in the colleges and universities run by the central ministries, such as the Public Finance College, the College of Construction Engineering, and the Foreign Affairs Institute. Other revolutionary rebel organizations consisted of lower-level cadres and office workers who began to criticize the leading administrators in the agencies in which they worked.

Cultural revolutionary activities inside the bureaucracy escalated in January 1967 from the criticism of ranking administrators to the actual seizure of power. Central and provincial administrative offices were taken

---

*The distinction between "level" and "echelon" is drawn from Donald W. Klein, "Sources for Elite Studies and Biographical Materials on China," in Scalapino, *Elites in the People's Republic of China*, p. 612. "Level" refers to the geographical unit to which an official is attached: commune, city, special district, province, region, and so on. Officials at each level can then be divided into "echelons" according to their rank and responsibility. By "administrative officials" or "administrators," I am referring to second- and third-echelon cadres at each level.

over by groups of Red Guards and revolutionary rebels, some of whom were lower-ranking cadres and some of whom were students and workers from outside the bureaucracy. By January 21 such power seizures had occurred in more than thirty ministries and bureaus in the central government alone.[1] As with the provincial Party committees, the results of these seizures of power were not always satisfactory. In many offices routine work virtually ceased as cadres and office workers engaged in continuous political discussion and debate. In some agencies ranking administrators encouraged loyal subordinates to stage their own seizures of power, hoping thereby to prevent more radical groups from overthrowing them.

In an attempt to prevent these power seizures from producing complete chaos in the bureaucracy, and to maintain some degree of coherent administration, the central authorities developed a set of rules in January and February to guide the conduct of the Cultural Revolution in administrative offices.* First, the bureaucracy was largely insulated against power seizures by external Red Guard groups. Mass organizations of workers and students might overthrow a county magistrate or a provincial Party committee, but they were not supposed to take over the work of the functional Party and government agencies. As one *Hung-ch'i* editorial explained in February, outside mass organizations would be permitted to send representatives to a bureaucratic agency, but they would not be allowed to "monopolize" that agency's affairs. Cultural revolutionary activities within the bureaucracy should depend, *Hung-ch'i* said, on the cadres and office staff within each department, since they had the best knowledge of the department's administrators and of the quality of their work. Therefore, the editorial concluded, "in the struggle to seize power in the Party and government organs, it is utterly wrong and impracticable that revolutionary mass organizations from other departments should take things over instead."[2] Illustrating this same point, the Kweichow revolutionary committee reported approvingly that the seizure of power within municipal and provincial government and Party agencies—as opposed to the seizure of power from the people's councils and Party committees themselves—had been accomplished primarily by the "revolutionary Left" within each department concerned, and that outside mass organizations had not employed any method of doing things "like a savior" on their behalf.[3]

Although policy allowed outside mass organizations to serve as spectators in most parts of the bureaucracy, the most sensitive agencies were

---

*For a different set of "rules"—one that does not distinguish between power seizures at the policymaking level and power seizures within administrative offices—see Thomas W. Robinson, "Chou En-lai and the Cultural Revolution," in Thomas W. Robinson, ed., *The Cultural Revolution in China* (Berkeley and Los Angeles, 1971), pp. 206–9, 234–35.

totally isolated from outside intervention. On February 21 the Central Committee identified as inviolable the ministries responsible for the defense industry (the Second through the Seventh Ministries of Machine Building), the Ministries of Public Security and Finance, the commissions responsible for economic planning (the State Planning, Economic, and Capital Construction Commissions), the Science and Technology Commission, all the departments of the Central Committee, all banks, and all the central news media. In these agencies cadres and office workers might form their own revolutionary rebel organizations, but people who worked in other units were ordered to "clear out at once."[4]

Second, cultural revolutionary activities within the bureaucracy were placed under the supervision of higher authorities. In the provinces such activities were monitored by the local military control committee or, if it had already been formed, the revolutionary committee itself. At the center, government and Party agencies were divided into three broad functional groups, each of which was placed under the guidance of a separate supervisory committee. Agencies responsible for propaganda, culture, and education were assigned to the central Cultural Revolution Group; agencies that handled political and legal matters were placed under the leadership of a committee headed by Hsieh Fu-chih, the minister of public security; and agencies responsible for economic affairs were put under the jurisdiction of a "Cultural Revolution Direction Committee for Central Organs" that was chaired by Chiang Ch'ing and had Chou En-lai as an "adviser."[5]

Once this supervisory network had been established, it was possible to impose strict controls over any attempt to seize power within an administrative agency. Some agencies were explicitly and unequivocally exempted from seizures of power, even by their own staffs. At the center these included the general offices of the Central Committee and the State Council, the Cultural Revolution Group, and the headquarters of the People's Liberation Army. Seizures of power were also prohibited in military leadership organs at the regional and provincial levels.[6] In other agencies power seizures were allowed, but only if permission had been received from the appropriate authority. Seizures of power that did not receive the necessary authorization were suppressed. In the Ministry of Finance, for example, a vice-minister named Tu Hsiang-kung organized a group of revolutionary rebels that seized operational control of the ministry from Li Hsien-nien and retained it until Chou En-lai declared the seizure of power invalid and ordered the army to arrest Tu.[7] The legitimacy of a preemptive seizure of power by Vice-Premier T'an Chen-lin in the departments responsible for agriculture and forestry was discussed by the Politburo itself, which ultimately ruled against T'an.[8] And an unauthorized power seizure in the

Foreign Ministry by a group of leftists under Yao Teng-shan was forcibly ended in August.[9]

Finally, a new collective leadership was to be established in each bureaucratic agency to conduct the evaluation, rectification, and purge of its own cadres. As elsewhere, these new organs of power were to be called "revolutionary committees." But, unlike the revolutionary committees of the policymaking echelons, those inside the bureaucracy were at first to be composed entirely of cadres. An early *Hung-ch'i* editorial provided that in Party and government organs the revolutionary committees were to be composed of "revolutionary leading cadres, revolutionary middle-level cadres, and revolutionary masses"—the last presumably referring to low-ranking cadres and office staff.[10] Chou En-lai would later describe this as an alliance of the old, the middle-aged, and the young.[11] Representatives of workers, students, and the army were all to be kept out of the revolutionary committees.

The formation of revolutionary committees in the bureaus proved more difficult than expected. Factionalism among opposing cadre organizations and competition for influential positions between junior and senior cadres greatly delayed the formation of the revolutionary committees, particularly in some of the central ministries. As a result, in mid-March *Hung-ch'i* changed its mind about the composition of the three-in-one combination in the bureaucracy and called for direct military participation in cultural revolutionary activities in governmental and Party organs.[12] Although the evidence is fragmentary, it would appear that several central ministries, and possibly certain provincial bureaucratic agencies as well, were placed under some form of military control. That Chou En-lai was not entirely pleased by the introduction of military representatives into the bureaucracy is suggested by a talk he gave at a mass rally at the Academy of Sciences on May 26, 1967.[13] There he continued to insist that both forms of the three-in-one combination, the one that contained military representatives and the one that did not, had been approved by Mao for use in administrative agencies.*

Because of Peking's preoccupation with the formation of provincial revolutionary committees, it could not turn its attention to the formation of revolutionary committees within the central bureaucracy until early 1968. At that time Chou En-lai held separate meetings with cadres from the various functional sectors of Party and government—national defense industry, industry and communications, finance and trade, agriculture and

---

*Chou repeated the point in February 1968, when he implied that the normal three-in-one combination of cadres, military officers, and mass representatives might not be suitable for administrative agencies. See *Supplement to the Survey of the China Mainland Press*, no. 224, pp. 1–18.

forestry—to try to accelerate the formation of "great alliances" among competing cadre organizations and thus facilitate the establishment of revolutionary committees.[14] In January, for example, Chou singled out the two cadre organizations in the Seventh Ministry of Machine Building for sharp criticism:

I wonder how long the 916 and 915 factions of the Seventh Ministry of Machine Building are going to fight it out among themselves. Don't you people feel ashamed at all? Factionalism is nothing but reactionary, and since the central Cultural Revolution Group and I have intervened on many occasions, why don't you people form alliances? . . . How much of the production quota did you fulfill last year? You know the answer very well! Do you think you have lived up to the expectations of our great leader Chairman Mao and of our people? I am indeed very upset! Very, very upset![15]

Chou attributed factionalism to overstaffing in the central ministries, saying that if there were too many people in one unit and they had nothing better to do, then they would fight one another. He also complained that the result of this factionalism was that the central ministries had fallen greatly behind the rest of the country in forming revolutionary committees, that leadership in the ministries consisted only of "two-in-one" combinations of ranking administrators and military representatives, and that young and able-bodied people who had emerged from revolutionary struggles during the past eighteen months were being excluded.

Although Chou's intervention did accelerate the formation of leadership groups in the bureaucracy, it is doubtful that more than a few ministries actually created revolutionary committees. In December 1972, for example, a "responsible person" of the general editorial department of the New China News Agency visiting the United States expressed impatience when asked whether the agency had established a revolutionary committee. "We have a leading organ," he replied. "Does it matter what it is called?" Instead, reorganized Party "nuclei," usually incorporating the three-in-one combination of senior administrators, junior cadres, and military representatives, provided leadership for cultural revolutionary activities within the bureaucracy.[16]

Once an administrative agency had established its new collective leadership, it could then begin a review of its staff to determine who should be retained in office, who should be promoted, and who should be purged. The evaluation and reeducation of cadres took two principal forms. One made use of the May Seventh cadre schools (to be discussed later in this chapter), to which cadres were sent for extended periods of physical labor and ideological study. The other involved the establishment of study classes to be attended not only by the administrators under review, but also by representatives of the revolutionary cadre organizations, the army, and in some cases Red Guard and revolutionary rebel groups from outside the bureaucracy. These study classes were occasions for lower-ranking cadres to criticize their superiors, for higher administrators to make self-criticisms, and for military representatives and mass representatives to evaluate the cadres' past conduct and future potential.

One such study class, held in Canton, was attended by 153 provincial cadres and 60 municipal officials who met for a month with 30 representatives of cadre organizations and outside mass organizations. In this case the atmosphere in the study class was described as relatively relaxed, for the cadres were told, even before the class started, that it was not proposed to "overthrow" any of them. Instead, they were to regard the study class as a course that, once completed, would qualify them to become cadres of a three-way alliance.[17] Another study class was conducted in Hotsing county, Shansi province. Here cadres met together with representatives from mass organizations, the army, the militia, and poor and lower-middle peasants. When the class ended in February 1968, it was reported that most of the cadres had "passed the test" and would remain in office.[18]

The tone of these model study groups reflected the lenient cadre policy that the Central Committee had sought to impose on the Cultural Revolution from the very beginning. In the sixteen-point decision on the Cultural Revolution adopted by its Eleventh Plenum in August 1966, the Central Committee had established four categories of cadres: the good, the comparatively good, those who had made serious mistakes but had not become anti-Party or antisocialist elements, and a "small number" of anti-Party rightists. "Under general conditions," the decision had stated, "the first two types of cadres are in the majority."[19] Throughout 1967 and 1968 central editorials stressed that most cadres were expected to pass the test of the Cultural Revolution, that only a few were to be demoted or dismissed, and that to regard all persons in authority as untrustworthy was incorrect.[20] The Cultural Revolution, in other words, was to be a rectification and reeducation movement for the vast majority of officials—a purge for only a few.

Despite these repeated demands from the center for leniency, a combination of opportunism, uncertainty, and factionalism produced a situation in which large numbers of leading officials were suspended or dismissed from office, some suffered serious physical and psychological abuse, and some were killed or committed suicide. Opportunism led many participants in the evaluation process to try to see that few leading administrators passed the test. Lower-ranking cadres, for instance, doubtless saw the Cultural Revolution as an opportunity for dramatic upward mobility and may therefore have tried to create as many vacancies in higher positions as possible. Military officers, both at the center and in the provinces, appear to have believed that demobilized servicemen had been discriminated against in cadre recruitment during the early 1960's and may have tried to find as many civilian positions for army men as possible. Similarly, representatives of outside mass organizations may also have seen the Cultural Revolution as a chance for "lateral entry" into the bureaucracy. All these considerations made it unlikely that the lenient cadre policy formulated by the center would enjoy quick and unquestioning compliance.

But more than opportunism was at work. Some participants in the study classes, particularly lower-level officials, may have believed that it was safer to take a leftist position than a rightist one, and that it was therefore wiser to be critical of leading administrators than lenient. As a result, some were "even reluctant to sit side by side" with ranking cadres at a meeting, for fear that any sign of sympathy or friendliness would cause them to be labeled as "restorationists" or "supporters of the bourgeoisie."[21] In other cases militant rebels may have genuinely believed that the need for a Cultural Revolution proved that the vast majority of administrators had made serious mistakes, and that their attempts at self-criticism represented little more than "sham rebellion."[22]

Finally, factionalism among the mass organizations both inside and outside the bureaucracy prevented the study classes from reaching agreement on the names of cadres to be recommended for administrative positions. Competing mass organizations scrambled to obtain key appointments for people they favored and sought to exclude members of rival groups from obtaining positions of power and influence. As one *Wen-hui pao* editorial described the attitude of the mass organizations:

If one gets control of these "vital departments," then his "position of strength" will be considerably improved. If he is short of manpower, he may just ask for it and get it; if he wants money, he may have the desired amount allocated to himself; if he needs authorization, he may use his own seal. In short, he may do whatever he likes, and suffer no restriction. Moreover, he may hold his opponent by the neck, pin him down, issue orders to him, and force him to obey.[23]

As a result, evaluations of cadres frequently ended in deadlock. In Kwangtung, for example, a special committee that had been formed to decide the fate of administrators in provincial government and Party organs had been consulting the two competing cadre organizations in the province. Both had wanted to dismiss a large number of administrators (some 38 percent, by one account), but they were unable to agree on who should be retained in office. Fully 44 percent of the cadres under review either were supported by one organization and opposed by the other or had become so demoralized by the Cultural Revolution that they were no longer willing to serve as officials.[24]

By 1969, therefore, the fate of the officials who had held important administrative positions before the Cultural Revolution remained largely unresolved. Only a small number of administrative cadres had been fully "liberated" and returned to work. At the same time, relatively few had actually been dismissed outright. The vast majority were in organizational limbo: some had been suspended from office and were performing menial clerical or service work until their cases were decided, others were undergoing "reeducation" at May Seventh cadre schools, and still others remained at their posts but were working under "supervision." None of these fates could have been pleasant.

What is more, the future of these officials was becoming an increasingly controversial issue among central leaders. As the struggle for the succession to Mao Tse-tung began to intensify in 1969 and 1970, some leaders began to advocate a wholesale rehabilitation of veteran cadres, while others supported a much less lenient policy toward those who had held office before the Cultural Revolution. We will return to this question, and its relationship to the struggle for power between 1969 and 1976, in the next chapter.

CODIFICATION OF WORK STYLE

Organizational revitalization during the Cultural Revolution involved more than a reassessment of administrative officials. It also required that the cadres who would staff the new revolutionary committees and Party committees have a clear understanding of the kind of behavior expected of them and a firm commitment to Maoist principles and programs. As Mao reportedly said in August or September 1967 while on a tour of the provinces, it was a combination of incorrect policies and poor work styles that had produced such great mass resentment against the bureaucracy:

Why were some cadres subject to mass criticism and struggle? One reason is that they have carried out a counterrevolutionary and bourgeois line so the people are angry. The other is that, being high officials, they put on airs and were haughty. They would not consult the masses and treat the people with equality. They did not practice democracy and were in the habit of instructing and berating the people. They had seriously alienated themselves from the people. So the people had reactions but could not express them. These reactions exploded during the Cultural Revolution. Once they erupted, the situation became serious, and the officials were embarrassed.[25]

There was, indeed, an attempt to create a corps of officials who would be neither counterrevolutionary nor haughty. Soon after the establishment of the first revolutionary committees in early 1967, several provinces began to set down concise descriptions of the ideal work style for officials. The movement began in Shantung, which adopted a set of ten regulations on cadre work in June 1967. It soon spread to other provinces, typically in the form of endorsements of the Shantung regulations with added provisions. By mid-March 1968 at least seven provinces and one city had published summaries of what constituted ideal performance in office.[26]

These provincial regulations, taken together, contained six principal components.* In first place was the regular study of the writings of Mao Tse-tung and the application of Maoist ideological principles to every decision a cadre might make. "All our words and deeds," the Shantung regulations provided, "must be gauged by the supreme criterion of whether or not they are in conformity with the thought of Mao Tse-tung." Accordingly, the study of Mao's writings was described as a necessary task that should be undertaken on a systematic, daily basis. Each of the provincial directives on cadre work style therefore contained a section calling for daily ideological study, the most common formula being an hour of study each day with two additional half days of study each week.[27]

The format for ideological study was patterned after that popularized in the army by Lin Piao. The most common texts were the book of quotations originally compiled by the army's General Political Department; the "three constantly read articles," which set out in a concise and popular way the Maoist values of service, self-sacrifice, and revolutionary zeal;[28] and the terse and enigmatic directives issued by Mao from time to time over the course of the Cultural Revolution.[29] These works were then discussed in ideological study classes that ranged in membership from 20 to 100 cadres and were described in a *Jen-min jih-pao* editorial in October 1967 as the best form for the "creative study and application" of the thought of Mao Tse-tung. For veteran administrators the classes were said to provide the opportunity to sum up experience, correct their mistakes, and consolidate their achievements "so as to catch up with the proletarian revolutionary ranks." For new cadres the classes were a way to learn Maoism in a systematic way and to develop a better understanding of the work style expected of officials. For the units in which they were held, the study classes provided a format for beginning the process of "criticism and transformation": the examination of the work of the past years to identify bureaucratic work habits and revisionist policies and the formulation of new policies and styles of work that would adhere to the proletarian line.[30]

The second element in the regulations on cadre work styles was regular participation in collective physical labor. Physical labor was described as a

---

*A seventh element was added later in the Cultural Revolution. On March 14, 1969, Mao issued a directive on "summing up experience" that discussed the procedures cadres should use when going to a unit to get to know the situation there. This directive served as the basis for a campaign in 1969–70 to teach cadres the advantages of selecting typical units for detailed examination and then making decisions on the basis of the information thus gathered. *Peking Review*, 21.iii.69, p. 2.

way of ensuring that cadres would integrate themselves with the masses, would remain like rank-and-file workers, and would gain a true understanding of life in the communes and the factories. As one press account put it, physical labor would guarantee that cadres would not "float" on the surface, divorce themselves from the masses and reality, and act like a "headquarters in the air."[31] Accordingly, most of the provincial regulations called on cadres to do some physical labor on a regular basis. Few had provisions that were as specific as the passages on ideological study, but one commonly accepted formula, contained in the Heilungkiang regulations, was that cadres should spend roughly one-third of their time in physical labor at the basic levels.

Third, the provisions placed considerable emphasis on the mass line as a technique for gathering information, making decisions, and implementing policy. The Shantung regulations provided that cadres should set aside a certain amount of time for interviews with ordinary citizens, should deal personally with letters from the masses, should call meetings and forums with their constituents and invite them to express their opinions, and should listen to popular criticisms willingly and sincerely. In the summer of 1967, in the same talk quoted at the beginning of this chapter in which he described the two principal reasons for the Cultural Revolution, Mao identified the improvement of relations between higher and lower levels and between cadres and the masses as one of the major goals of the movement. "From now on," he said, "all cadres must go to the lower level to see [things] for themselves and to consult the masses more."[32]

Fourth, many of the regulations on work style called for frequent small-scale rectification campaigns to ensure that cadres would remain zealous, efficient, and humble. As the Shantung regulations put it, "The revolutionary committee should undertake periodic rectification campaigns (once every two months or so). Some representatives of the mass organizations should be invited to participate in each rectification campaign as necessary." The provisions adopted by the Heilungkiang revolutionary committee were even stricter on this point. They called for "persistent blooming and contending" involving constant use of debates and wall posters as a means for expressing criticism, opinions, and dissent. Every office was urged to hold a "democratic-life meeting" once a month, every department was told to hold one every three months, and the revolutionary committee as a whole was supposed to hold a "democratic mass meeting" every six months. In addition, small-scale rectification campaigns were also to be conducted, presumably on a less regular and somewhat less frequent basis.

Fifth, cadres were told to adhere to the Party's traditional principles of democratic centralism and collective leadership. The Kweichow revolutionary committee, for example, called for "extensive democracy" within all its administrative organs; Heilungkiang insisted that major policy decisions could only be made at a plenary session of the entire revolutionary committee or at a meeting of its standing committee, and that the chairman could not speak on behalf of the committee without its express consent.

A sixth component of these provincial regulations was an attempt to create a totally selfless corps of officials. These provisions were based on the premise that selfishness not only was the cause of many of the organizational problems that had plagued the Party during the early 1960's, such as inefficiency, insubordination, false reporting, and corruption; but also, because it promoted a desire for privilege and inequality, was the foundation of revisionism. One of Mao's most widely quoted instructions during the Cultural Revolution—"fight selfishness, criticize revisionism" (*touszu, p'i-hsiu*)—expressed the relationship in capsule form. He apparently believed that official positions, because of the status and privileges attached to them, tended to promote greed and competitiveness among cadres. Any one of these privileges, one editorial warned, could be "the opening of a small hole" in the wall of resistance to selfishness.[33] As K'ang Sheng put it, when people do not hold power and are oppressed, it is easy for them to remain revolutionary, but there is a tremendous change after seizing power—"You fight for houses, desks, chairs, and secretaries. This is undesirable!"[34]

The danger, therefore, was that official privileges would corrupt the people who held public office, thereby reducing the efficiency and responsiveness of the bureaucracy and increasing the possibility that officials would tolerate, or even promote, revisionist policies. To meet this danger, the regulations on cadre work style were designed to deny cadres any of the psychological or material perquisites that had been awarded to officials in the past. Cadres were not to be praised for their work, addressed by their official titles, photographed without the consent of the entire revolutionary committee, applauded at public gatherings, or sent off or received when they went on trips—and their names were generally not to appear in the press. It was as a result of these provisions that cadres, whatever their rank or position, began to be described merely as "responsible persons" of the agency for which they worked—a job title that caused considerable consternation and amusement among Western observers. For those who sought material satisfaction and physical comfort from public office, the regulations were equally severe. Cadres were not to use automobiles unless on official business, they were not to receive gifts, they were not to have secretaries, they were supposed to help clean their own offices, and they could not give banquets. But there was no mention of the possibility that, in accordance with the model of the Paris Commune, their salaries might be reduced to the level of ordinary workers or peasants.

The work style for cadres described in these provincial regulations was, in many respects, similar to the work style developed during the Kiangsi and Yenan periods. Cadres were to be selfless, live a simple life, and engage in regular physical labor. In making decisions they were to rely on direct investigation of local conditions and on experiments conducted in representative units. They were to take the initiative in their work, act with vigor and imagination, and have the courage to raise questions and criticize defects in the work of their superiors. They were supposed to undergo periodic rectification and to maintain close ties with the masses. Communications between leaders and led and among cadres was to be open, regular, and unconstrained.

At the same time, however, the regulations envisioned a style of policymaking and administration that was much more influenced by doctrine than that of the Yenan years.[35] Cadres were encouraged to study ideology constantly, to apply it to all policy questions, and to consider the ideological implications of every action they took. Differences of opinion that emerged during discussions of policy were presumed to reflect not different understandings of a complex and uncertain situation or different estimates of the costs, risks, and benefits attached to competing policy options, but rather the ongoing clash between "bourgeois" and "proletarian" lines in the Party.

This kind of doctrinal decision making contributed greatly to the political polarization that emerged during the Cultural Revolution, and that continued through the purge of the "Gang of Four" in 1976. The assumption was that differences of opinion reflected class struggle within the Party, and that, if two officials disagreed, one must be a class enemy, or at least following the incorrect line. In such a situation it would be morally wrong to compromise. It would also be wrong to accept any method of decision making, such as majority rule, that ignored the ethical and ideological nature of the choices involved. Instead, all Chinese were urged to decide for themselves which policies and programs conformed to Maoist ideology and which did not. Under these circumstances it was virtually inevitable that most debates would escalate, factionalism would persist, and unity would be elusive.

Interestingly, the work style advocated during the Cultural Revolution had relatively few points in common with the campaign style of 1955–56 and 1957–58. As during the High Tide and the Great Leap Forward, some articles published during the Cultural Revolution argued that a reliance on manpower, self-confidence, and human will could act as a substitute for scarce human and technical resources, and asserted that China's progress toward communism could be accelerated. Compared to the High Tide and the Great Leap, however, these references were relatively muted. The key problem in the late 1960's was believed to be the tendency of officials to accept or advocate policies that Mao and his followers regarded as revisionist. It was not, as in the 1950's, the sluggish pace of China's economic development. Accordingly, although the High Tide and the Great Leap Forward both advocated that cadres return to the campaign style in their work, the work style developed during the Cultural Revolution placed much more emphasis on ideological orientation than on speed.

The attempt to promote this style of work encountered some serious obstacles, largely because of contradictions with other organizational reforms undertaken at the same time. Most striking was the inconsistency between the attempt to improve cadres' work styles and the campaign, to be discussed later in this chapter, to reduce the size and complexity of the bureaucracy. On the one hand, cadres were told to carry out careful investigation and research before coming to decisions, to consult fully with their colleagues and their subordinates, to deal with each problem on an individual basis rather than in terms of routine, to engage in regular physical labor and ideological study, to hold frequent forums to fathom popular opinion and hear public criticism, and so forth. Clearly, to be a good cadre would require large amounts of time. And yet organizational staffs were being substantially reduced, sometimes on the order of 60 to 80 percent. This meant that the work previously done by five cadres would now have to be performed by one or two. As a result, cadres began to complain that the burden of work placed on them in their newly straitened circumstances was preventing them from performing their tasks in the manner that the campaign to improve work style intended.[36]

Similarly, it was difficult for cadres to be zealous and innovative in their work after the intense criticism—even persecution—that they had endured from the Red Guards, the revolutionary rebels, and their own colleagues and subordinates. Many officials were reluctant to assume the responsibility for decisions or to take on positions of authority after the Cultural Revolution for fear of being criticized once again. One editorial complained that many cadres performed their work in a half-hearted manner, "carrying only five hundred catties of a thousand-catty load."[37] In this sense the Cultural Revolution inadvertently did serious damage to cadre initiative and morale.

MAY SEVENTH CADRE SCHOOLS

A third organizational reform instituted during the Cultural Revolution was the establishment of May Seventh cadre schools between 1968 and 1972.[38] Although significant enough to be considered in their own right, the schools must also be understood in conjunction with the three other organizational programs discussed in this chapter. Like the ideological study classes organized in government and Party departments, the schools served as an important format for the criticism, reeducation, reassessment, and reassignment of administrative officials. In addition, the curriculum of the May Seventh cadre schools embodied many of the components of the work style advocated during the Cultural Revolution, in that the schools provided cadres with an opportunity for ideological training, physical labor, and close contact with ordinary citizens. Finally, at a time when administrative offices were undergoing a major organizational simplification and a reduction in staff, the May Seventh cadre schools provided a convenient way of relocating cadres whose jobs had been eliminated.

The first May Seventh cadre school was established by the Heilungkiang provincial revolutionary committee in Liuho, a rural area of the province, on May 7, 1968. May 7 was the second anniversary of one of Mao's most important directives on the Cultural Revolution, one that had called on cadres to learn to do industrial, agricultural, and military work as well as administration.[39] By October some five hundred cadres, mostly from provincial offices, had settled at Liuho and opened a farm. The school's curriculum included daily ideological education and physical labor in farm work, land reclamation, and water conservation. To maintain close contact with the people, the cadres attending the school would hold discussion sessions with workers, peasants, and soldiers living in the neighboring areas; would participate in labor in nearby communes and factories; and would invite mass representatives to give lectures at the school on their experience during and after the revolution.

On October 4, 1968, Mao Tse-tung issued yet another directive, this time on the need for cadres to participate in physical labor:

It is necessary to maintain the system of cadre participation in collective productive labor. The cadres of our Party and state are ordinary workers and not overlords sitting on the backs of the people. By taking part in collective productive labor, the cadres maintain extensive, constant, and close ties with the working people. This is a major measure of fundamental importance for a socialist system; it helps to overcome bureaucracy and to prevent revisionism and dogmatism.[40]

The success of the Liuho school convinced Chinese leaders that the institution was an effective embodiment of Mao's directive on physical labor for cadres. Accordingly, after Mao's October 4 directive was published, the Liuho school received national publicity and was identified as a model for other provinces to imitate. Once this was done, the system of May Seventh cadre schools expanded rapidly. By November 1968 there were one hundred such schools in Heilungkiang alone with a total enrollment of nearly 21,000 cadres.[41] By 1973, according to one report, some three thousand May Seventh schools had been established throughout China.[42]

The May Seventh schools were set up by all upper and middle levels of the Party and government, from central Party departments and government ministries down to the provinces, special districts, counties, cities, and even urban districts. Schools run by the central authorities tended to take in students from only one functional system. Cadres with responsibility for agricultural work, in other words, would attend different schools from those attended by cadres responsible for culture and education. In contrast, May Seventh schools established at lower levels took in a broader cross section of cadres. A school run by an urban district, for example, might include administrative officials from all the district's departments; leading cadres from hospitals, stores, and factories in the district; and teachers and staff members from the district's schools. This feature was seen as a useful mechanism for cadres from different lines of work to exchange information and ideas.

Students attending May Seventh cadre schools divided their time among three kinds of activities. Given the fact that the schools were established in response to Mao's October 4 directive on physical labor, it is not surprising that considerable emphasis was placed on manual work. Although the first students to attend a school might live with peasant families temporarily, it was expected that they would eventually construct their own facilities. Often the schools were located on hitherto unusable land—in a marshy area, for instance—so the students had to participate in land reclamation as well as build the schools' classrooms, mess halls, and dormitories. Once the schools were constructed, students spent a major part of their time working in the fields or in whatever small-scale industry the school had established.

Another aspect of the May Seventh schools' curriculum was regular ideological study. Characteristically, a student might spend at least half an hour a day studying works by Mao Tse-tung and, especially after the fall of Lin Piao, works by Marx, Engels, and Lenin. These self-study sessions would be supplemented by lectures and group discussions.

Students were also expected to establish and maintain close ties with the peasants living in the areas surrounding the schools. One article on the schools described various ways in which students might become familiar with the attitudes and day-to-day life of the peasants—by working for a time in neighboring production teams, by participating in the peasants' ideological study classes, by helping nearby communes deal with floods and pests, or by assisting local propaganda teams in the rectification of rural Party branches.[43]

The curriculum and facilities of the May Seventh cadre schools were explicitly contrasted with the institutions for cadre education that existed before the Cultural Revolution. Before 1966 cadres might be sent to basic-level units or to experimental farms to engage in physical labor, and might even spend a fairly long period of time there. But these hsia-fang programs, it was now charged, had ignored ideological training. Conversely, the pre–Cultural Revolution cadre schools had emphasized only ideological and technical training and had included little opportunity for physical labor or for contact with ordinary citizens. The older schools were now described as practicing "self-cultivation behind closed doors—divorced from reality, from the masses, and from productive labor."[44] In addition, the former cadre schools apparently had much more comfortable and elaborate facilities than the May Seventh cadre schools, and none of the new schools' punitive connotations.[45]

In the beginning the time cadres would spend at a May Seventh cadre school might vary significantly. Those who could demonstrate a "correct" political attitude, whose skills were urgently needed within the bureaucracy, or whose family responsibilities were heavy might expect to return to work relatively soon. Those from offices whose staffs were being trimmed, who had been charged with antisocialist activities before the Cultural Revolution, who had resisted the Red Guard movement, or who did not possess important administrative skills, would have to stay in the schools for a longer period. The first students stayed as little as three months or as long as three years. Throughout this period, cadres were reportedly paid their regular salaries and were allowed to return home to their families for two days every two weeks.*

By 1971 or 1972 virtually all of the original students had moved on, and the operation of the May Seventh schools had become more routine. Cadres now applied for admission to the schools for periods of reeducation ranging from three to twelve months. In contrast to the earlier students, who might well have received totally new work assignments upon "graduation," later students usually returned to the office or unit from which they had come. The May Seventh cadre schools thus became institutions of rotational training under which administrative cadres at various levels would be given a "revolutionary sabbatical" every eight years or so during which they could concentrate on ideological study, physical labor, and the reestablishment of contacts with ordinary laborers.[46] The facilities at the May Seventh schools remained spartan, but there is every reason to believe

---

*Nonetheless, some cadres were understandably reluctant to attend the May Seventh cadre schools. See *Jen-min jih-pao*, 18.viii.69, in *Survey of the China Mainland Press*, no. 4489 (5.ix.69), pp. 6–8; and *Jen-min jih-pao*, 8.ix.69, *ibid.*, no. 4499 (19.ix.69), pp. 10–11. As we will see in the next chapter, Lin Piao may have used this reluctance as a basis for mobilizing political support within the bureaucracy.

that by 1971–72 attendance at the schools was considered an important upward step in a cadre's career and no longer a demotion or punishment.*

ADMINISTRATIVE RETRENCHMENT

A fourth aspect of the organizational revitalization undertaken during the Cultural Revolution was a wide-ranging program of administrative retrenchment aimed at reducing the size and complexity and increasing the efficiency of the Party and state organizations.

Of the structural reforms instituted between 1967 and 1969, perhaps the most far-reaching was a redefinition of the relationship between the Party and the government, a relationship that by the mid-1960's had become almost hopelessly confused. In theory, the Party was not to set policy directly. Rather, it was charged in its own constitution with responsibility to "supervise ideologically and politically" all Party members who held government positions.[47] The Party was to be an ideological vanguard and a monitoring agency, but it was not supposed to assume policymaking and administrative functions.

In practice, of course, the relationship between the Party and government was substantially different. One of the themes of this book has been the growing role of the Party in governmental affairs, beginning with the San-fan movement and continuing through the Great Leap Forward. By the early 1960's the Party had created a network of functional departments that paralleled the functional bureaus of the government and enabled the Party to play an extensive role in policymaking at all levels of Chinese society. In such circumstances it was inevitable that power would flow steadily from the government to the Party, and that the entire state apparatus would become largely redundant—a "duplicate administrative structure," as Lin Piao described it in 1969.[48]

The Cultural Revolution attempted to solve this problem in the most logical way possible: it formally recognized the policymaking functions of the Party, and thus changed theory to correspond with practice. The solu-

---

*We do not know what proportion of all cadres in China attended May Seventh schools. There is, however, some fragmentary evidence. A report from Shanghai in March 1972 said that 60 percent of the city's district-level cadres had attended the schools. And a report from Canton in February 1972 revealed that 160,000 cadres had attended schools in Kwangtung province to that time. This would represent some 32 percent of the 500,000 officials in Kwangtung in 1957. See Radio Shanghai, 29.iii.72, in Foreign Broadcast Information Service, *Daily Report: Communist China*, 4.ix.72, pp. C1–2; and Radio Canton, 29.ii.72, *ibid.*, 2.iii.72, pp. D1–2. The number of cadres in Kwangtung in 1957 is drawn from Ezra F. Vogel, *Canton Under Communism: Programs and Politics in a Provincial Capital, 1949–1968* (Cambridge, Mass., 1969), p. 378. Maurice Meisner has cited an estimate that three million cadres attended May Seventh schools in the first year alone, and that "many millions more" attended later; but he does not provide a source for his figures. See Meisner, *Mao's China: A History of the People's Republic* (New York, 1977), p. 355.

tion was termed "unified leadership" and involved, in schematic form, three concentric circles of authority. At each level the smallest and most powerful of these three circles was the Party committee, which would serve as the locus of policymaking. The middle circle was the revolutionary committee, which would discuss and ratify the policies determined by the Party committee and begin the task of formulating the specific measures for carrying them out. To ensure continuity between policymaking and policy implementation, virtually all members of the Party standing committee would be ex officio members of the revolutionary committee, and the first secretary of the Party committee would serve, virtually without exception, as the revolutionary committee chairman. Finally, the outermost circle was the administrative staff of the revolutionary committee, organized into functional departments, which would present plans and data to the Party committee and the revolutionary committee and would work out the detailed measures for the implementation of policy. This administrative staff was drawn primarily from the Party and government departments that had existed before the Cultural Revolution.

The system of unified leadership had the advantage of permitting a substantial simplification of bureaucratic structure. The size of the Party's own functional staffs was considerably reduced. Although a Party committee might retain a propaganda department, an organization department, and a united front work department, the Party agencies formerly responsible for economic affairs (the political departments for agriculture and forestry, industry and communications, finance and trade, and so forth) were abolished during the Cultural Revolution. Instead, the Party was to rely on the revolutionary committee departments for its economic staff work, thus eliminating some of the most important redundancies that had existed between the Party and the government before the Cultural Revolution.

Logical though it was, this redefinition of the relationship between the Party and the government encountered opposition during the later years of the Cultural Revolution. An important source of opposition was the mass representatives still serving on the revolutionary committees; they realized that they were being put in a position subordinate to the Party and argued that the revolutionary committees, not the Party, should be the principal locus of policymaking. The Party's response was to try to define the role of the revolutionary committee more clearly. As the press reports have it, on the one hand, the revolutionary committees were to recognize that they did not have the authority to set basic policy guidelines; on the other, the Party committees were not to attempt to monopolize policymaking, but were to consult regularly with the revolutionary committees.[49]

The readjustments of Party-government relations helped lay the groundwork for a second structural reform, the retrenchment of administrative staffs and the simplification of bureaucratic structure.In our discussion of organizational problems of the early 1960's in Chapter 7, we described the concern of Chinese leaders with the increasing size of the Party and state bureaucracies and with the proliferation of administrative agencies. It is not surprising, therefore, that a consistent theme in Mao's directives during the Cultural Revolution should have been the need to reduce the size and complexity of the bureaucracy. In July 1966, for example, Mao complained that the Peking municipal Party committee had too large a staff, and that the State Council had too many ministries.[50] In March 1968 he said that the revolutionary committees should "achieve a unified leadership by cutting through duplicative administrative structures" and should follow the principles of "better troops and simpler administration."[51] In August he spoke once more of the need to simplify administration and send office personnel down to lower levels.[52]

In keeping with Mao's statements, a large number of editorials on organizational matters published during the Cultural Revolution criticized the excessive size and complexity of the bureaucracy. Some articles complained that as the size of the bureaucracy increased, the amount of time and energy spent on administrative matters also increased and the attention paid to policy questions declined. One *Hung-ch'i* editorial stated: "Once the number of men in higher-level organs is large, paperwork would increase. The following consequences would arise: the leadership members would rely on the administrative personnel in everything; more time would be spent on administrative affairs and less guidance given with respect to politics, ideology, and policy."[53]

Other articles noted that policy coordination became more difficult as bureaucracies became larger. One radio broadcast compared the operation of a "clumsy, huge, and repetitive" bureaucracy to playing football: documents are passed back and forth and "travel hither and thither" with no one taking the responsibility for making decisions.[54] Still other press reports expressed concern that large, complex bureaucracies inevitably produced alienation between leaders and led. An editorial complained that "the plural form of organization . . . bars the leaders from going among the masses and hinders the organization of a revolutionized leading group that keeps in close contact with the masses."[55] And *Jen-min jih-pao* predicted that if the bureaucracy continued to grow in size, "more and more cadres will be taken away from actual production. . . . Cadres will stay high above as officials and overlords, to be divorced from reality, labor, and the masses, gradually 'evolve peacefully,' and gradually become a special privileged class."[56]

The simplification of organizational structure and the reduction of administrative staffs received the most attention at the upper and middle levels of the bureaucracy, that is, in agencies from the center down to the counties. When the restructuring of the central bureaucracy was completed in January 1975, the number of ministries had been reduced from forty-nine to twenty-nine, most of the cuts having been made in the areas of agriculture and forestry, science and education, light industry, and planning.* Of the seven State Council staff offices, each responsible for coordinating the ministries within a different functional system, six were abolished.[57] At the provincial and county levels the revolutionary committees identified as administrative models had amalgamated the various bureaus and departments of the former Party and government bureaucracies into as few as four agencies, which were responsible for production, political affairs, administration, and defense and security. And throughout the country the remaining bureaucratic monitoring agencies established during the period of rationalization in the mid-1950's were abolished. Just as the Ministry of Supervision had been eliminated in 1959, so now were the Party's control commissions and the Procuracy, with its limited responsibility for supervision over the governmental apparatus. This did not reflect only the assessment that these agencies had not adequately prevented revisionism in the years before the Cultural Revolution. It also reflected the belief that physical labor, ideological indoctrination, and mass supervision would be more effective methods of organizational control than bureaucratic monitoring agencies.

The import of these changes is, of course, open to question. As Doak Barnett has pointed out, the establishment of new ministries and the amalgamation of old agencies had occurred several times since 1949, giving an impression of "a fairly high degree of administrative instability at the national level." At the same time, however, bureaus and other subministerial bodies had often remained relatively intact, continuing to perform many of their basic tasks despite mergers or splits at the ministry level.[58] It is highly likely that the ministries and provincial departments that were nominally abolished in the Cultural Revolution actually survived as bureaus or departments of the agencies into which they were merged. In Heilungkiang, for example, the former department of finance and trade was technically eliminated, but it soon reappeared as the "finance and trade section" of the production office of the revolutionary committee.[59]

Consequently, the readjustment of bureaucratic structure would be less important than the reduction of administrative staffs. Here the evidence is

*But three ministries that were abolished in the early years of the Cultural Revolution had already been reestablished by the time of the National People's Congress in January 1975. These were the Ministries of Railways, Posts and Telecommunications, and Coal Industry.

somewhat contradictory. Reports published during the Cultural Revolution indicate that an extremely high number of cadres were being removed from office at the upper and middle levels of the bureaucracy. In an interview with Edgar Snow in late 1970, for example, Chou En-lai claimed that the number of officials working in central agencies had been reduced from 60,000 to 10,000—a reduction of more than 80 percent.[60] Descriptions of the new revolutionary committees included comparable reductions of staff at the provincial level: 86 percent in Inner Mongolia, 75 percent in Heilungkiang, and 67 percent in Honan.[61] At the county level an intensive campaign to pare administrative staffs began in July 1968 with the publication of the experiences of Lingpao county, Honan province, which had reduced the number of cadres working in county offices from one hundred before the Cultural Revolution to thirty after. Throughout 1968 reports appeared from other counties that had implemented similar reforms indicating that reductions in staff ranged from 92 percent to 75 percent, the average being around 80 percent.*

But at the same time that it was reporting these large staff adjustments, the Chinese press was also insisting that 95 percent of the cadres be permitted to "pass the test" of the Cultural Revolution and resume work. If few cadres were being dismissed from office outright, where were central, provincial, and county officials being sent after the administrative retrenchment in their offices? Doubtless some were being sent to the local levels, but no large-scale hsia-fang of officials was reported at the time. It is more likely that cadres whose jobs were eliminated during the Cultural Revolution were sent to May Seventh cadre schools for retraining, and that, once their reeducation was completed, most of them returned to the offices from which they had come.[62] The administrative retrenchment of the Cultural Revolution, in other words, was almost certainly a temporary reform, the significant effects of which probably lasted only some two or three years. Once the bulk of cadres began returning to their offices from the May Seventh cadre schools, the size of the urban bureaucracy was

---

*The following are some of the model counties: Lingpao, Honan—*Jen-min jih-pao*, 1.vii.68; Yench'ing, Peking—*Pei-ching jih-pao*, 13.vii.68, in *Survey of China Mainland Magazines*, no. 654 (12.v.69), pp. 28–30; Hsinlo, Hopei—New China News Agency, 15.vii.68, in *Survey of the China Mainland Press*, no. 4222 (22.vii.68), pp. 16–17; Chuansha, Shanghai—New China News Agency, 21.vii.68, *ibid.*, no. 4266 (26.vii.68), pp. 14–16; Chingyen, Szechwan—*Jen-min jih-pao*, 22.x.68, *ibid.*, no. 4301 (19.xi.68), pp. 1–5; and Hsiangch'eng, Honan—*Hung-ch'i*, no. 4 (1968), in *Survey of China Mainland Magazines*, no. 634 (22.xi.68), pp. 1–5. A Japanese scholar who visited China after the Cultural Revolution reported that in thirty counties the number of cadres had been reduced from an average of 155 to an average of 33—an average reduction overall of 79 percent. See Atsuyoshi Niijima, "The Establishment of a New Commune State," *Chinese Law and Government*, 4 (1971): 38–60.

doubtless restored to something similar to what it had been before the Cultural Revolution.

DECENTRALIZATION

Even before the onset of the Cultural Revolution, Mao Tse-tung had begun to express his reservations about the recentralization of industrial management and economic planning that had occurred between 1960 and 1965. In 1966 he complained that too many of the decentralization measures undertaken in 1957 and 1958 had been abandoned after the Great Leap Forward and proposed that they should be reinstated. "It will not do to have everything concentrated at the central level," he said. The factories that had been placed under the control of the central ministries and their economic trusts should be turned back to the provinces "lock, stock, and barrel." The provinces should be given greater control over their own financial resources, thus altering the situation in which "everything belongs to the state treasury." The center, in turn, should only be responsible for "major administrative policies."[63]

Mao's criticism of the recentralization of the early 1960's seems to have originated in two considerations. At a time when the conflict in Vietnam was rapidly escalating and the threat of an American attack on China could not be ignored, Mao believed that a dispersed, decentralized economy would be better able to survive a war than a concentrated, centralized one. If the Americans attacked, he warned, the center would not be able to send soldiers, commanders, clothing, food, or weapons quickly enough or in sufficient quantities to help the provinces. Instead, each province would have to fight its own battles. To accomplish this the provinces would have to develop enough industrial capacity to support their own troops in relative independence. Every province would have to have "a small iron and steel plant," or even "several dozen steel plants." And, by implication, these dispersed industrial enterprises could make their contribution to China's military preparedness only if they were not only spread across the country but also controlled by the provincial authorities.[64]

Mao's second concern was with the effects of recentralization on agricultural mechanization, a subject that had long been one of his principal personal interests. One of the economic trusts established in 1964–65 was the China Tractor and Internal Combustion Parts Company, which was responsible for agricultural mechanization. Through the trust, production of agricultural machinery was placed under the control of the Ministry of Agricultural Machinery, later renamed the Eighth Ministry of Machine Building, and was effectively insulated from provincial supervision or interference. Moreover, the tractors were assigned to machine-tractor stations, also under central direction, that provided mechanical services to selected counties and communes on the basis of their ability to pay for them.

Mao believed that the gaps between city and countryside and between industry and agriculture could be better bridged if communes owned and operated their own machines, rather than relying on centrally controlled machine-tractor stations. To make this arrangement financially and technically feasible, greater emphasis would have to be placed on the design and production of smaller and simpler machines that the communes could afford to purchase and could learn to operate and maintain. This form of semimechanization, Mao believed, could be undertaken by the provinces and even by the counties, which could produce simple walking tractors, pumps, and harvesters that were well suited to local conditions. Thus, in March 1966 Mao proposed a careful investigation of experiments undertaken in Hupei on the manufacture of agricultural machinery by the provincial government, declaring that having everything united under the central government and strictly controlled by the central authorities was not a good method.[65]

The Cultural Revolution, then, transferred back to the provinces some of the authority that the center had gained over the economy in the early 1960's. To be sure, in the first years of the Cultural Revolution (1967–68) some of this decentralization occurred without any central decision or authorization. In those years the central planning process was crippled by Red Guard activities in the economic ministries and by the disruption of production and communications in the provinces. As it became virtually impossible to produce meaningful central plans, power to manage the economy inevitably passed to the military control committees and revolutionary committees in the provinces. Nevertheless, as political order was slowly reestablished in late 1968 and early 1969, it became clear that decentralization was not to be simply an accidental result of economic and political disorder, but was to be the outcome of a deliberate attempt to restructure the economy.

Details of the decentralization measures adopted during the closing months of the Cultural Revolution are scarce. No formal directives on the subject were ever announced, and there were few comprehensive discussions of the problem in the Chinese press. But the evidence does suggest that three sets of reforms were undertaken.[66]

To begin with, the regional Party bureaus, established in the early 1960's to reassert central control over the provinces, were abolished. Although mention of cultural revolutionary activities in these bureaus appeared in the press as late as mid-1968, the draft Party constitution discussed at the Twelfth Plenum in October contained no mention of the regions. The elimination of the regions probably stemmed from two conflicting considerations. Under some circumstances the size of the regions threatened to give regional Party secretaries an unacceptable degree of independence from central control; under other circumstances the regional bureaus would impose too many restraints on the economic initiative of the provinces.

Next, the economic trusts established in 1964–65 were also dismantled, and the industrial enterprises they controlled were transferred back to the provinces. At the same time, a large number of small-scale industries were set up under provincial supervision to take responsibility for food processing, fertilizer production, and the manufacture of the machinery, tools, and construction materials required by agriculture. The result of these changes was that the output of industry directly controlled by the center declined from some 70–80 percent of total national production in 1965 to approximately 50 percent in 1972.

Finally, the planning and budgeting process established under the decentralization reforms of 1958—a process that also appears to have been modified or ignored during the period of retrenchment following the Great Leap Forward—was reinstated. The center retained supervisory powers over provincial budgets, but the provinces were given the authority to adjust them as long as the total amount of expenditure for either productive or nonproductive purposes was not increased. Moreover, if a province was able to achieve a budgetary surplus by increasing its income or by reducing its expenditures, it was given the right to make additional investments as long as those investments could be undertaken without increasing the total provincial labor force and without increasing the province's demand for centrally regulated materials and commodities.

Economic planning, too, returned to the procedures established in 1958. Planning was once again to proceed from the bottom up, rather than from the top down. Each locality was to try to strike its own product balances and to consider trade with other localities as a residual element in its planning. The province was to become a particularly important locus of economic planning, for, in conformity with Mao's 1966 proposals, each province was to become a small but complete economic unit that would develop both industry and agriculture and be as self-reliant as possible. Press accounts indicated that under this program provinces in northern China were gradually becoming self-sufficient in grain, and that relatively under-developed provinces were beginning to develop their own industrial infrastructure.

Under these arrangements the responsibilities and powers of the central ministries and planning agencies were less than they had been before the Cultural Revolution. In addition to managing centrally controlled industry, each ministry was responsible, as in 1958, for general policy planning, research and development, and coordination and technological exchange among enterprises in its sector of the economy. The planning commissions were responsible for setting production targets, allocation plans, and prices of key commodities; for supervising provincial budgets; and for determining the total amount of investment and wages throughout the country. They could also establish ratios to guide the provinces in drawing up their local plans—to suggest, for example, ratios between agricultural and industrial investment, or the proportion that administrative expenditures might occupy in a total provincial budget. At the apex of the entire planning process, of course, stood the Politburo, the Central Committee, and the State Council, which retained control over the basic course of social and economic policy.

There is some reason to suppose that, again as in 1958–59, the decentralization measures adopted at the end of the Cultural Revolution were not always administered as intended.[67] There is evidence, for example, that some provinces wanted to undertake a more drastic decentralization than the center was willing to permit. In January 1968 Heilungkiang proposed that all provincial industry be further decentralized to municipal and county control, and it is likely that some provinces wanted all central industry, not just half of it, transferred to the provinces. Furthermore, some provincial leaders were slow to respond to central policies with which they disagreed. Visitors to China in 1970 and 1971 reported that certain provinces had very different priorities than others, and that variations in socioeconomic policy were evident from one province to another. The ability of the center to exercise effective supervision over provincial budgets and investments during this period is also open to doubt.[68] As a result, the question of whether the decentralization measures instituted during the Cultural Revolution should be maintained or modified would become a controversial issue later in the 1970's.

After the first seizures of power in the January revolution, the Chinese press took great pride in identifying differences between the new administrative organs established by the "revolutionary masses" and the ossified "revisionist" bureaucracies that they replaced. An early description of the Shanghai people's commune, for example, described its administrative staff in the following terms:

The new organ is basically different from the economic leading organ of the former Municipal People's Council. It uses politics to run the economy and is not a purely professional department. Nor has it large structures such as bureaus, sections, and offices. The number of its personnel is less than that employed by some offices of the former Municipal People's Council. They do not spend the entire day sitting in the office reading documents, listening to reports, and making telephone calls, but they go out among the masses every day. . . . They make policy decisions following a timely study of the class struggle on the economic front. They publish a bulletin to publicize Mao Tse-tung Thought, linking it with their work and using it as a guide. They make on-the-spot investigations every day at the grass-roots level. . . . Most of the workers in the Front-Line Command have had no experience in leading economic work. But by taking Mao Tse-tung Thought for their guide, relying on the masses, and practicing criticism and self-criticism, they are doing it successfully.[69]

Reports such as these, together with the vehement criticisms of pre–Cultural Revolution bureaucracy and the early experiments with the Paris Commune model, led a few outside observers to conclude that the Cultural Revolution had actually eliminated bureaucracy in China. The Japanese sinologist Atsuyoshi Niijima wrote in 1968, for example, that "the Great Proletarian Cultural Revolution is making the abolition of bureaucracy—which was reiterated by Lenin—come true." On visiting Canton at the height of the Cultural Revolution, Niijima came across a poster bearing Mao's words, "The dictatorship of the proletariat must be the dictatorship of the masses." He says, "Their impact was so strong on me that I could literally hear my heart pounding. Right here, I thought, I was witnessing a commune state—the state withering away."[70] A more dispassionate view, however, would suggest that the effects of the Cultural Revolution on the Party and state organizations were much more limited than Niijima thought.

It is true, as indicated in Chapter 8, that articles such as Lin Piao's "On the Social Foundation of Revisionism" did question the desirability of some of the structural characteristics of Weberian bureaucracy.[71] It is also true that the Cultural Revolution generated some significant organizational reforms. By giving the Party formal responsibility for decision making, the Cultural Revolution eliminated much of the overlap between the Party and state bureaucracies. Substantial control over industrial management and economic planning was passed from the center back to the provinces. Mass representatives were placed on revolutionary committees at all levels from factory and commune to the province. Bureaucratic control agencies, such as the Party control commissions and the Procuracy, were abolished. And cadres were sent to May Seventh cadre schools to receive ideological reeducation and to engage in physical labor. At least three of these reforms—the inclusion of mass representatives in governing bodies, the establishment of May Seventh cadre schools, and the redefinition of the relationship between the Party and the state—were important organizational innovations.

But these reforms did not constitute the elimination of bureaucracy in

China. By any reasonable standard, the Chinese political system remained nearly as bureaucratic after the Cultural Revolution as it had been before. There was still a formal hierarchy of offices. There were still large and complex administrative organizations governed by formal rules and regulations and characterized by a division of labor. Despite the presence of mass representatives on revolutionary committees, China was still ruled by a career officialdom paid salaries differentiated on the basis of personal rank.

What the Cultural Revolution represented, therefore, was not the abolition of bureaucracy but another attempt to create a bureaucracy that was more ideologically committed, efficient, flexible, and responsive than it had been in the past. The last two chapters have discussed the two sets of remedial reforms undertaken during the Cultural Revolution—the extension of mass control over the bureaucracy and the intensification of such techniques as ideological study and physical labor. These devices were accompanied by efforts at greater rationalization through decentralization, retrenchment, and reorganization. Despite all the rhetoric, then, the approach taken by the Cultural Revolution to the bureaucratic dilemma was primarily remedial and rational—not radical.

Indeed, what is most striking about the Cultural Revolution is how many of these reforms were familiar. The mass line, an important component of the cultural revolutionary work style for cadres, had been formulated during the Kiangsi period. The reduction of staffs, open-door rectification, and intense indoctrination of officials were all techniques developed in Yenan. Manual labor and the hsia-fang had been introduced in the mid-1950's. Decentralization in the Cultural Revolution was largely a reassertion of reforms adopted in 1957–58. The May Seventh cadre schools may have been a new phenomenon, but their components—ideological study, manual labor, and close ties with the masses—were hardly novel.

Despite its early flirtation with radical reforms, therefore, the Cultural Revolution ended as an organizational restoration in the traditional Chinese sense. With the exception of the introduction of mass representatives to revolutionary committees, which was perhaps the most innovative reform of the period, the heart of the organizational program of the Cultural Revolution was much less an attempt to create new forms or develop new procedures than an effort to revitalize the familiar remedial traditions of the Chinese Communist Party.

But the effects of the restoration were fleeting. By 1971 institutionalized mass participation in decision-making bodies had been effectively abolished, except at the grass-roots level. By the end of the same decade, each of the other reforms described above—from the merger of the Party and state bureaucracies to the establishment of May Seventh cadre schools, and from the decentralization of economic management to the reduction of administrative staffs—had been abandoned as unworkable. Even worse, the price of the Cultural Revolution had been enormous, not only in terms of its damaging effects on organizational efficiency and bureaucratic morale, but also in terms of social justice and human life. As innovative as some of its organizational programs had been, the Cultural Revolution's achievements could hardly justify its cost.

10

Bureaucracy and the Struggle
for Succession
1969-1976

For more than seven years, from the Ninth Party Congress in April 1969 to the death of Mao Tse-tung in September 1976, the single issue dominating Chinese politics was the question of political succession, both in the narrow sense of the succession to Mao as chairman of the Chinese Communist Party, and in the broader sense of the succession to an entire generation of aging Party leaders. The issue was bound to be complex and tendentious. Like most authoritarian regimes, China had not developed an institutionalized method for transferring authority from one group of leaders to another. And, like victorious revolutionaries in other societies, Mao was preoccupied by the fear that power would pass to leaders less committed to his revolutionary vision than he was.

Mao saw the Cultural Revolution as his final opportunity to ensure that the succession would give power to those who deserved it. One of its purposes, then, was to purge "persons like Khrushchev" who were being "trained as our successors" in the 1950's and early 1960's.[1] They were to be replaced with more worthy "successors to the revolutionary cause of the proletariat."[2] In consequence of Mao's pursuit of this elusive goal, China witnessed first the demotion and then the dismissal of Mao's heir apparent, Liu Shao-ch'i; the selection of Lin Piao as "Comrade Mao Tse-tung's close comrade-in-arms and successor" by the Ninth Party Congress; and the replacement of large numbers of Politburo members, Central Committee members, and provincial Party officials between 1969 and 1971.

But none of these developments provided a final solution to the succession question. The purges of the Cultural Revolution produced not a united Party but a divided one in which a deep schism of hostility and suspicion separated those who had led the movement and those who had been its victims. Despite Mao's endorsement, Lin Piao lacked a secure base of support in either the civilian Party apparatus or the government; and he had aroused substantial opposition from a growing number of civilian leaders who resented the role of the army in nonmilitary affairs. And, as the Cultural Revolution itself so clearly demonstrated, Mao might easily grow disenchanted with arrangements he had made, dispense with his heir apparent, and select a new successor. If there was any lesson to be learned from the Cultural Revolution, it was that no succession arrangement should be considered final or unchallengeable.

For all these reasons, the issue of succession remained unresolved at the end of the Ninth Party Congress. Indeed, three groups of leaders engaged in a continuing struggle for power from 1969 until Mao's death in 1976. One was a group of central military leaders, associated with Lin Piao, who occupied key command positions in the headquarters of the People's Liberation Army and in the Military Affairs Commission of the Party. A second group of contenders consisted of senior civilian officials—symbolized at the central level by Chou En-lai, Teng Hsiao-p'ing, and Li Hsiennien—many of whom had been severely criticized during the Cultural Revolution for their support of "revisionist" policies in the early 1960's. We will follow convention and call this group the "moderates." Third, there was a group of more junior civilian leaders who had either played important roles in the central Cultural Revolution Group between 1967 and 1969 or emerged out of the mass movements of the Cultural Revolution. In Peking the most prominent of these officials were Chiang Ch'ing, Chang Ch'un-ch'iao, Wang Hung-wen, and Yao Wen-yüan. To avoid confusion with the technical definition given the word "radical" in this book, we will call this group the "leftists."

To identify these three groups as the principal contenders for power in China in the early 1970's is, of course, to oversimplify a much more complicated reality.[3] To so group them does not imply that they held divergent views on all issues, that the differences among them were always wide, or that their views were consistent over time. It does not mean that we can clearly identify which leaders were associated with which groups, although the core membership of all three factions is quite well known. Nor are the terms "moderate" and "leftist" totally appropriate, for they invite misleading analogies with comparably named tendencies in Western political thinking. But despite these drawbacks, the approach does provide a useful way of explaining a period of political struggle that would otherwise be difficult to understand.

Most important of all, to identify these groups as the principal contenders in the succession struggle does not exhaust the list of participants in Chinese politics between 1969 and 1976. Mao Tse-tung stood somewhat apart, seeking to strike the appropriate balance among the three sets of contenders while providing a strong sense of support for the leftists. The majority of military region commanders neither sided fully with Lin Piao and his military faction nor sought political power on their own, but rather threw their weight behind whichever group seemed most deserving of their support. Similarly, a large number of civilian leaders, particularly those who had occupied second-echelon positions before the Cultural Revolution but who had risen to prominence as "revolutionary cadres" during the late 1960's, resisted firm attachments to any of the three factions. Paradoxically, although this group—represented by Hua Kuo-feng, Wu Te, and Chi Teng-k'uei—did not appear to be actively seeking central political power in the early 1970's, it was one of the principal beneficiaries of the succession struggle, at least at first. Although in this chapter we will focus on the three groups actively contending for power, we also will frequently refer to the positions taken by Mao, the military regional commanders, and the second-echelon "centrists."

In the struggle for political power that swept China between 1969 and 1976, organizational issues were only one element.[4] The three groups of contenders also used social, economic, and foreign-policy issues to mobilize popular support. They formed personal alliances for self-protection and self-aggrandizement. They fomented violence and, in at least one instance, allegedly plotted to assassinate or kidnap Mao and other central leaders. They sought to influence the Chairman through rumor and intrigue. Nonetheless, organizational issues did play an important role in the succession struggle in the years before Mao's death, for the contenders fully recognized the way in which organizational policy could influence the outcome of that struggle. The main theme of this chapter is that each of the three groups attempted to manipulate organizational policy in ways that would provide it with a firm base of bureaucratic support, that would weaken the power base of its rivals, that would facilitate the adoption and implementation of the policies it favored, and that would obstruct or block the policy programs advocated by its opponents. Organizational policy became paramount between 1969 and 1976, in a word, because it was linked with the struggle for power and with the debate over socioeconomic policy that accompanied that struggle.

In describing this connection between organizational issues and the struggle for the succession, our analysis will proceed chronologically and will center on five organizational programs presented by the three contending factions: the military faction's of 1969–71; the moderates' program of 1971–73; the leftists' counterproposal of 1973–75; the moderates' program of 1975; and the leftists' counterproposal of 1976.

As one might expect, the strategies and programs of these three groups varied over time, the variations corresponding with changes in the political climate. But each group's approach to organizational issues also had characteristic elements that remained relatively constant throughout the period under consideration. The military's strategy was to increase the number of army officers appointed to civilian positions, preserve the army's autonomy from civilian Party control, and institutionalize these arrangements to the greatest degree possible. The moderates' strategy, in contrast, was to assign senior civilian officials dismissed during the Cultural Revolution to positions of authority in the Party and the state, to maintain tight Party control over all mass organizations, to restrict mass criticism of Party policy, and to launch a vigorous rectification campaign inside the bureaucracy against the policies and assumptions associated with the Cultural Revolution. The leftists' strategy was to describe the rehabilitation of veteran cadres as a plot to restore revisionism, to demand the rapid promotion of younger officials to leadership positions, and to continue intense mass criticism of the moderates' policies—even if this meant a degree of social unrest, organizational disorder, and political anarchy.

THE MILITARY PROGRAM, 1969–1971

Lin Piao's strategy for strengthening his position as Mao's successor rested on the premise that the People's Liberation Army would constitute his most powerful and most effective base of political support. Lin could not assume that his control over the army was complete. As we have already indicated, many of the regional commanders did not support his political ambitions. But by the end of the Cultural Revolution Lin had been able to effect some major changes in the military command. He had removed many commanders and commissars at the central, regional, and provincial levels, replacing some of them with close personal associates from the Fourth Field Army, which he had commanded during the revolution; he had created within the Military Commission an "administrative unit" that was staffed almost exclusively with his own supporters; and in 1969–70 he was advancing the proposition that, as vice-chairman of the Party and minister of defense, he should be the legal commander-in-chief of all the armed forces. All of these steps had served to give him greater influence, though not total control over the army.

Lin had also put forward a set of foreign and domestic policies that he believed would be attractive to the military officers on whose support he depended. In international affairs, Lin opposed Chou En-lai's rapprochement with the United States in 1970–71, arguing that military preparations, rather than diplomatic maneuver, would be the most effective way of ensuring Chinese security against a Soviet attack.[5] In economic policy, Lin sought to find the financial and material resources to support a substantial increase in military procurements. This led him to propose the rapid development of the electronics industry, to oppose the mechanization of agriculture on the grounds that it would divert resources from the defense industry, and to advocate the revival of mobilizational techniques in the countryside as an alternative strategy for agricultural development.[6]

That Lin's power base rested in the army had implications for his organizational programs as well as for his economic and foreign policy proposals. Simply put, his political survival required that he expand and institutionalize the army's role in Chinese politics. As Jürgen Domes has pointed out, he sought to create an army-Party relationship that would be essentially similar to the Party-government relationship in other Leninist political systems, including pre–Cultural Revolution China. Before the Cultural Revolution, the Party had provided most of the leaders of the government: the leading Party members in each government agency met in Party branches to discuss policy in the absence of non-Party members, the policy decisions reached by the Party and the Party branches were binding on the government, and the Party committee or branch in each government agency controlled the recruitment, promotion, and education of that agency's officials. Now, in the late 1960's, Lin Piao and his supporters were trying to recast the relationship between the Liberation Army and the Party. As Domes explains, "The party was about to become a mass organization of the PLA, particularly at basic-unit, county, and provincial levels."[7] The syllogism was clear: if Lin controlled the army, and the army controlled the Party, then Lin's power over civilian affairs would be vastly expanded.

Lin sought to achieve this goal through four specific organizational policies. First, he endeavored to extend close military control over the reconstruction of the Party apparatus that began shortly after the conclusion of the Ninth Party Congress in April 1969. This objective was relatively easy to attain. In the aftermath of the Cultural Revolution, the army was the only nationwide organization that could claim to be disciplined and reliable. It was logical, therefore, that it would be given responsibility for supervising the reconstruction of the Party at every level from the grass roots to the provinces.

The army fulfilled this responsibility in different ways at different levels of the political system. For instance, it sent work teams to the lower levels—to factories, schools, and communes—to help reregister Party members, organize new Party branches and committees, and select new Party secretaries. At the middle levels, military representatives on the revolutionary committee would often form a Party "core group" to supervise the rectification and reorganization of the Party committee. In addition, army-sponsored congresses of mass activists and model workers and peasants provided useful instruments for identifying candidates for membership on middle-level Party committees, and thus for influencing the rebuilding of the Party.

As a second goal, Lin sought to increase the number of military representatives appointed to central governmental positions, to the Central Committee, and to provincial Party committees. Here again, he was able to achieve impressive results. Five of the eight ministerial positions filled between 1969 and September 1971 (the Ministries of Agriculture and Forestry, Foreign Trade, Communications, and Physical Culture, and the First Ministry of Machine Building) were given to military officers. Of the 170 members and 109 alternate members of the Central Committee elected at the Ninth Party Congress, approximately 45 percent (74 members and 55 alternatives) were military representatives. Military officers were assigned to 59 percent of the 158 secretaryships on the provincial Party committees formed in late 1970 and 1971. And of the 29 provincial Party first secretaries, 21 were either military commanders or professional military commissars. Not all of these men were necessarily personal followers or political supporters of Lin Piao, but Lin had succeeded in raising military participation in the Party and government to a level unknown since the early 1950's.

A third element in Lin's organizational program was to ensure that this high level of military representation in civilian Party and government positions would be a permanent phenomenon. Military officials were quoted as asserting that involvement in Party rectification and participation on revolutionary committees and Party committees would be a "fundamental task of the army during the entire historical period of socialism"—a period that Mao had said in 1964 might last as long as "one to several centuries."[8] The attempt to institutionalize military involvement in civilian politics was reflected in two provisions of the draft State constitution adopted by the Second Plenum in August 1970. One formalized the military's participation on revolutionary committees by a reference to the three-in-one combination of civilian cadres, mass representatives, and military officers. The other provided the army with a mandate to engage in civilian political and economic work and to "safeguard the socialist revolution and the achievements of socialist construction."[9]

Finally, as a fourth policy, Lin appears to have created conditions under which the military representatives on the Party committees could serve as a separate leadership core that could act independently of their civilian Party secretaries. Discussions of civilian-military relations after Lin's purge revealed that some military representatives had refused to consult with their civilian colleagues or to be bound by Party discipline, but had regarded themselves as subject only to the military chain of command.[10] Mao himself complained that decisions nominally made by the Party committee were later referred to local military commanders for discussion and approval.[11] And there were reports that the Ministry of National Defense had begun to organize a number of new bureaus that, like the former functional departments of the Party, could monitor the government's implementation of socioeconomic policy.[12]

Lin was also accused of advocating a decision-making style that he himself had described as "united effort without unity of minds."[13] This meant that decisions would be made by the military representatives on a Party committee, dissenting opinions would be ignored or suppressed, and a strict, martial discipline would be imposed on the civilian committee members. In apparent reference to this style of work, Mao said that although strict discipline might be appropriate for the army, it could not be applied to the political and ideological matters that a civilian Party committee would discuss.[14]

By the time the Central Committee convened its Second Plenum in August 1970, Lin's organizational program had begun to arouse the opposition of both the moderates and the leftists. These two groups may have differed substantially on issues such as the desirability of agricultural mechanization and the wisdom of the rapprochement with the United States, but as civilians they could both agree that Lin Piao was attempting to perpetuate an unacceptable degree of military involvement in Chinese civilian politics.

As a result, civilian cadres began to express open displeasure with the degree of military participation in Chinese politics. In an interview with Edgar Snow in late 1970, Chou En-lai implied that plans were already afoot to reduce the military's involvement in civilian affairs. As Snow reported, "On one point the Premier wished to be clearly understood. The foreign press had greatly misinterpreted the role of the army by presenting it as dominating both the Party and government. That had not been and would never be the case, he said; in the future it would become even further evident to those who wished to analyze the Party leadership."[15]

What is more, Chou's view was shared by Mao, who had begun to conclude that his heir apparent was showing an unseemly degree of personal ambition. In his tour of the provinces in the summer of 1971, Mao complained that the army had become a "cultural army," that it devoted too much time to civilian affairs and neglected its military responsibilities. "You can't just be a civilian official," Mao told provincial and regional military commanders. "You . . . must also be a military official."[16]

The civilians' opposition to Lin's organizational program was reflected in increasing criticism, both public and private, of the work style of the military representatives on Party and revolutionary committees. Mao called two central work conferences, one in December 1970 and the other in April 1971, in which he demanded self-criticism from some of Lin's ranking generals for their "arrogance and complacency."[17] Early in 1971, *Hung-ch'i* carried several articles that attacked the way in which the army was conducting its civilian responsibilities. One rebuked those who suppressed democracy within Party committees for the sake of "unity"—a veiled criticism of Lin Piao's theory of "united effort without unity of minds."[18] Another explicitly called upon the army to be modest and prudent, and to "continue to make revolution"—presumably against defects in its own style of work.[19] These themes were summarized by a joint editorial, published on May Day, 1971, that called on the "whole Party, the whole Army, and the people of the whole country" to launch a campaign to criticize revisionism and rectify their style of work. In so doing, they would learn to "be modest and prudent, guard against arrogance and rashness, study more assiduously, and work harder."[20]

With the new campaign to rectify work style as a framework, the provincial press began to publish articles in the summer of 1971 that were outspokenly critical of the army. Canton claimed that some military officers failed fully to respect the leadership of the Party committees and the revolutionary committees, and ignored Party directives with which they disagreed.[21] Changsha criticized the army for attributing all the achievements of the Cultural Revolution to itself, and warned military officers against "regarding themselves only as the motive force of the revolution and not as its targets."[22] Nanning, in a formulation later attributed to Mao personally, said that the army must learn from civilian cadres and the civilian masses, just as the civilians were supposed to study the accomplishments of the army.[23]

Faced with these clear signs of increasing opposition among civilian Party officials to de facto military rule, some of Lin's supporters began to draw up a rather amateurish plan for a coup d'etat.[24] The plan was given the code number "571," a near homophone for three Chinese characters meaning "armed uprising." The naiveté of the document suggests that Lin and the senior commanders around him were not directly involved, and that the plot was formulated by a group of younger air force officers, possibly led by Lin's son, Lin Li-kuo.[25] The drafters of the document suggested that, to forestall his own purge, Lin would be well advised to make a quick accomodation with the moderates and then move against the leftists, who were described as the "Trotskyist group wielding the pen."

In keeping with this analysis, the organizational policy outlined in the "571" document was designed to appeal to the veteran cadres who formed so important a part of the moderates' power base. "Cadres who were rejected and attacked in the course of the protracted struggle within the Party [during] the Cultural Revolution are angry but dare not speak," the document claimed. "Administrative cadres were retrenched and sent to May Seventh cadre schools, which amounted to losing their jobs." The implication was that Lin would now support the rehabilitation of large numbers of veteran officials, as advocated by the moderates. But though it identified the areas in which the military faction and the moderates might reach an accord, the "571" document still argued for continued military

participation in politics. The drafters of the document complained that the
army was being oppressed by the campaign against arrogance and complacency that had followed the Second Plenum, and warned that, unless
countermeasures were taken, the "activities and influence of the 'civilians'
are bound to expand."

It is still not known whether Lin Piao actually adopted the "571" plan,
and whether, as some Chinese reports have claimed, he actually ordered
assassination attempts against Mao Tse-tung.* It is clear, however, that
important civilian leaders learned of the plot, and that Mao made a tour
of the provinces to explain his differences with Lin and to lay the
groundwork for a purge of his erstwhile successor. Realizing that his political situation was hopeless, Lin attempted to flee, apparently toward the
Soviet Union, in a commandeered military jet transport. It crashed in
Outer Mongolia early on September 13, 1971, killing all on board.

THE MODERATES' FIRST PROGRAM, 1971–1973

The purge of Lin Piao created an excellent opportunity for the moderates to formulate their own program for China after the Cultural Revolution. Although Lin Piao may have moved closer to the moderates in the
last months of his life in a desperate attempt at political survival, his association with the Cultural Revolution still marked him as a leftist in the
eyes of most Chinese. The death of Lin therefore created a political climate
in which leftism was suspect and in which moderate programs might receive a more sympathetic hearing.

Like the program presented by Lin Piao between 1969 and 1971, the
program developed by the moderates between 1971 and 1973 contained
socioeconomic, international, and organizational components.[26] In agriculture, the moderates favored attention to mechanization, remuneration
according to individual productivity, the retention of the production team
as the basic unit of accounting, and preservation of private plots. In industry, they advocated the reintroduction of rules and regulations, greater
attention to quality control and labor discipline, and a more lenient policy
toward managers and technicians. In education, they proposed that
academic qualifications be given more consideration in selecting students
for university training, and that entrance examinations be restored as a
way of measuring academic potential. In foreign policy, they suggested the

---

*For accounts claiming that Lin did try to assassinate Mao, see the abridged version of the
"Communiqué of the Central Committee of the Chinese Communist Party Concerning Lin
Piao's 'September 12' Anti-Party Incident," in Kau, *Lin Piao Affair*, pp. 69–70; Chou En-
lai's report in *The Tenth National Congress of the Communist Party of China (Documents)*, p. 6;
and Wilfred Burchett, "Lin Piao's Plot—The Full Story," *Far Eastern Economic Review*,
August 20, 1973, pp. 22–24. For the contrary view, see Philip C. Bridgham, "The Fall of
Lin Piao," *China Quarterly*, no. 55 (July–September 1973), pp. 427–29.

development of the broadest possible united front against the Soviet Union and improved relations with both the United States and Japan. All these programs represented substantial departures from the policies and assumptions of the Cultural Revolution.

Of greatest interest to this study, of course, are the parts of the moderates' program that would have affected the Party and state bureaucracies. The first of these was to alter the recruitment and staffing policies of the Party and state bureaucracies to the disadvantage of the military officers then holding civilian positions. The moderates argued that, in his speech to the Eleventh Plenum in 1966, Lin had deliberately distorted the criteria for revolutionary successors that Mao had set down in "On Khrushchov's Phoney Communism." Lin's three criteria for selecting, promoting, and employing cadres had emphasized only their commitment to the revolution and to Maoist ideology.[27] In contrast to Mao's formulation, they made no reference to collective leadership, service to the people, or modesty. It was not surprising, the moderates argued, that the army had become arrogant and authoritarian, for Lin Piao had ignored the question of work style in his discussions of cadre policy.[28] One radio broadcast stated, "Nothing was said about the political orientation of persisting in Marxist-Leninist principles, about the basic goal of serving the majority of Chinese and world people, about the work method of 'from the masses, to the masses,' about the principle of persisting in revolutionary unity, and about the attitude of being modest and prudent and the style of self-criticism."[29]

This rather abstract discussion of recruitment standards was used to justify the gradual removal of military officers, particularly those personally associated with Lin Piao, from civilian positions at both the central and provincial levels. At the Tenth Party Congress in August 1973, the proportion of Central Committee seats held by military representatives was reduced from around 45 percent to approximately 32 percent.[30] By the end of 1973, the ratio of provincial Party secretaryships occupied by military officers had decreased from about 60 percent at the time of Lin's purge to around 50 percent, thanks largely to a rotation of military regional commanders in December.* Most of these officers had been concurrent Party first secretaries in the provinces where their regional command was headquartered, but they were not given comparable civilian positions when they reported to their new assignments. In addition, when vacancies appeared on provincial Party committees, military represen-

---

*For analyses of the shift in the composition of the provincial elites during this period, see Frederick C. Teiwes, *Provincial Leadership in China: The Cultural Revolution and Its Aftermath*, East Asian Paper No. 4 (Ithaca, N.Y., 1974); and Robert A. Scalapino, "The CCP's Provincial Secretaries," *Problems of Communism*, 25.4 (July–August 1976): 18–35.

tatives were given a disproportionately small share of the appointments made to fill them. Through these mechanisms the level of military participation in civilian affairs was reduced, albeit in a deliberate and measured fashion.

It is highly unlikely that this first aspect of the moderates' organizational program aroused much opposition from the leftists. Few regional or provincial military officials had supported leftist socioeconomic policies. And the army had generally used its influence over the reconstruction of the Party to exclude mass representatives from the provincial Party committees and from Party secretaryships.[31] That Shanghai, one of the leftists' most important political bases, had never had much military participation on its revolutionary committee suggests that the leftists may not have regretted the departure of military representatives from Party committees in other provinces.

A second aspect of the moderates' organizational program was much more controversial. In their attempt to reduce the civilian authority of the military the moderates tried also to transfer that power to civilian officials who had been severely criticized, or even dismissed from office, during the Cultural Revolution. The moderates accused Lin Piao of having turned the Cultural Revolution into a movement to dismiss all Party officials rather than simply the small number who were capitalist roaders.*

With ulterior motives, swindlers like Liu Shao-ch'i [i.e., Lin Piao] confused the two different kinds of contradictions and turned the Great Proletarian Cultural Revolution into a campaign to repudiate the cadres, both the powerholders taking the capitalist road and those taking the socialist road. . . . Swindlers like Liu Shao-ch'i regarded all the leadership of the Party as "jackals of the same lair," and cried that it was necessary to fire and do away with all the revolutionary cadres.[32]

What Lin failed to recognize, the moderates claimed, was that Mao had consistently said that the overwhelming majority of cadres, as many as 95 percent, should be retained in office. The Chairman, according to moderates, had always advocated a lenient and patient line toward officials who had "made mistakes" during the early 1960's. By refusing to admit that these officials had been tempered by the Cultural Revolution and reeducated in May Seventh cadre schools, and by preventing veteran cadres from assuming positions of leadership after the Cultural Revolution, Lin Piao was in direct opposition to Mao's views on cadre policy.[33]

*New China News Agency, 24.i.72, in Foreign Broadcast Information Service, *Daily Report: Communist China*, 2.ii.72, pp. G1–3. These charges were not unjustified. On August 10, 1966, Lin had put forward a rather harsh line on the cadre question: "Our cadre policy from now on should be that whoever opposes Chairman Mao will be discharged. Whoever does not give prominence to politics will be discharged. It does not matter how much ability he may have." See "On the Question of the Cadre Line," in Kau, *Lin Piao Affair*, pp. 351–54.

With this criticism of Lin Piao as justification, the moderates were able to reappoint veteran Party officials to important posts in both Peking and the provinces in the years following Lin's purge. Of the new appointments made at the provincial level between 1971 and the end of 1973, over two-thirds were veteran cadres who had been rehabilitated only after Lin's fall from power. By 1975 fully half of the civilian officials serving on provincial Party committees were cadres who had been criticized or dismissed during the Cultural Revolution.[34] The most visible symbol of this wave of rehabilitation was the April 1973 reappearance of Teng Hsiao-p'ing, who had been described during the Cultural Revolution as the "number two Party person in authority taking the capitalist road."

It was this aspect of the moderates' recruitment program that aroused intense leftist opposition. The leftists feared that the rehabilitation of so many veteran cadres would strengthen support within the bureaucracy for the moderates' social and economic policies. They had already been disappointed in their hope that the removal of military officers from civilian positions would permit the appointment of more mass representatives, who had been effectively excluded from political power ever since the formation of the new provincial Party committees, and who would be more likely to be sympathetic to the leftist political cause. By 1972, therefore, there were already signs that the leftists were displeased with the wave of rehabilitations. Leftists at lower levels described the moderates' cadre policy as a "restoration of the old."[35] The Shanghai media began publicizing an alternative to the rehabilitation of senior officials: younger cadres, often from worker backgrounds, should be selected to serve in leading positions on revolutionary and Party committees.[36] In this way were planted the seeds of an issue that would emerge with greater force within a few months' time.

A third element in the organizational policy developed by the moderates between 1971 and 1973 was the reassertion of Party leadership over all other organizations in China, particularly the army and the mass organizations. Lin Piao, predictably, was charged with having attempted to abolish the leadership of the Party over the army in order to place the army above the Party. The subordination of the army to civilian authority was, therefore, an important theme in Chinese politics throughout 1972 and 1973.[37] But the same issue also applied to the large mass organizations—the trade unions, the Communist Youth League, the Women's Association, and the peasant associations—whose operations had been suspended during the Cultural Revolution but whose reconstruction was now underway.

The activities of the Red Guard and revolutionary rebel organizations during the Cultural Revolution had thrown the relationship between mass organizations and the Party into confusion. Were the mass organizations to become transmission belts once again, responsible for carrying Party policy to the people and generating popular support? Or were the mass organizations, like the Red Guards, to have the right to criticize Party policies and officials that they believed to be revisionist and to refuse to carry out policies with which they disagreed? Although the leftists took the second position, the moderates held closely to the first. Moderate leaders in Hupei province argued that mass organizations, in this case the trade unions, "must place themselves under the Party's absolute leadership and actively accept Party leadership. On no account can they be allowed to shake off or weaken Party leadership, nor can they be permitted to lord it over the Party."[38] Similar views were expressed in other provinces about the roles to be assigned to the peasant associations and the Communist Youth League.[39]

In taking this position, the moderates recognized that many mass organizations still had leftist leadership and were likely to defend the social and economic policies of the Cultural Revolution if given the chance. If those policies were to be modified, as the moderates hoped, the mass organizations would have to be kept under tight Party control. As a result, the moderates opposed any extensive open-door rectification campaigns in the early 1970's. Instead, they sought in the name of political unity and organizational discipline to confine mass criticism to routine denunciations of Lin Piao and his "ultraleftist" line.[40]

Finally, a fourth aspect of the moderates' program concerned the rectification campaign that was being conducted in the Party, the state, and the mass organizations to explain and justify Lin Piao's fall from favor. The moderates proposed that this campaign be organized around the criticism of leftism, idealism, and apriorism—all terms denoting the tendency to rush utopian programs without sufficient attention to the constraints imposed by objective conditions and without recognizing the need for a protracted period of socialist development before communism could be attained. By calling Lin a leftist and associating him with the Cultural Revolution, the moderates laid the foundation for a criticism of the egalitarian programs that had emerged from the movement, particularly in industry, agriculture, education, and science. By extension, this tactic also set the stage for the moderates to introduce the socioeconomic policies outlined at the beginning of this section.[41]

But to call Lin a leftist and an idealist was a controversial decision, for it opened the way to criticism of all the programs and leaders produced by the Cultural Revolution. As a result, the leftists began to challenge the moderates' description of Lin's political deviation. They charged that Lin had been a rightist rather than a leftist, and that he was guilty of empiricism and pragmatism, not of idealism or apriorism.[42] In their view, Lin's error was not that he had overemphasized the application of doctrinal principles to policymaking, as the moderates were charging, but that his program for the practical study and practical application of the thought of Mao Tse-tung was "a vain attempt . . . to limit our study to day-to-day trivialities while neglecting the basic line and other specific tasks of the Party."[43] Nor did the leftists associate Lin with the excesses of the Cultural Revolution. Instead, they pointed out that the "571" document had contained some critical comments about such programs as the May Seventh cadre schools, the *hsia-hsiang* ("transfer to the countryside") of urban youth, and the freeze on the salaries of industrial workers.* This indicated, the leftists argued, that the principal danger confronting China was the tendency to deny the accomplishments of the Cultural Revolution, and that the chief target of rectification in the early 1970's should be those who held such a view.

By the beginning of 1973 the leftists had secured a reassessment of Lin Piao: the provincial press gradually began to deny that Lin could properly be considered an ultraleftist and started to describe him as an ultrarightist.[44] Lin's class standpoint, one broadcast claimed, was indicated by his attempt to "unite with the landlords, rich peasants, counter-revolutionaries, bad elements, and rightists to exercise the fascist dictatorship of the landlords and comprador-bourgeoisie."[45] And a broadcast from Szechwan asserted that Lin's policy had been intended to "erase the fruits of struggle, criticism, and transformation on all fronts of the superstructure"—that is, to undo all the reforms instituted in the course of the Cultural Revolution.[46] In this way, the leftists had turned back one of the principal elements of the moderates' political strategy.

THE LEFTISTS' FIRST COUNTEROFFENSIVE, 1973–1975

The leftists believed that the foreign, socioeconomic, and organizational policies developed by the moderates between 1971 and 1973 were unacceptable—that they constituted nothing less than the reemergence of revisionist tendencies in China. Between 1971 and mid-1973 the leftists had been primarily on the defensive, resisting and criticizing the program put forward by the moderates, despite some degree of success, particularly in securing a redefinition of Lin Piao as a "rightist." In the summer of 1973, however, the leftists went on the attack in earnest, presenting their own views on the issues that the moderates had raised. The leftist counteroffensive had two components. On the policy level, the leftists identified specific programs and institutions that had appeared during the Cul-

---

*For a history of the *hsia-hsiang* program, see Thomas P. Bernstein, *Up to the Mountains and Down to the Villages* (New Haven, Conn., 1977).

tural Revolution, gave them the label "socialist newborn things," and defended them against modification or abandonment. On the organizational level, the leftists presented a program designed to build their power base within the Party apparatus, weaken that of the moderates, and ensure support for their own socioeconomic policies.

The leftists' counteroffensive between 1973 and 1975 was conducted in two separate campaigns, each linked to a major national political meeting. The first, the campaign to criticize Lin Piao and Confucius, followed the Tenth Party Congress of August 1973. The second, the campaign to study the dictatorship of the proletariat, followed the Fourth National People's Congress of January 1975. For the sake of clarity, we will deal with each campaign separately.

The Campaign to Criticize Lin Piao and Confucius

In August 1973 delegates from all over China arrived in Peking to attend the Tenth Party Congress. One of the purposes of the congress was to endorse the official explanation of the purge of Lin Piao, to approve the dismissal of Lin's followers from the Politburo and from their military positions, and to select a new central Party leadership. At the same time, the moderates hoped to win the Congress's endorsement for the policy package they had been advocating—and, in large measure, implementing—since 1971.

Even before the congress opened, the leftists began to publish a series of articles criticizing the moderates' programs, praising the "newborn things" of the Cultural Revolution, and charging that the moderates, in trying to modify those things, were trying to turn back the wheel of history. Two articles presented themes that would later be developed in greater detail. One, a criticism of Confucius by the Chungshan University historian Yang Jung-kuo, referred to Confucius' policy of "reviving states that had been extinguished, restoring families whose line of succession had been broken, and calling to office those who had retired into obscurity."[47] Yang's article was a denunciation by analogy of the moderates' policy of rehabilitating veteran officials who had been "retired into obscurity" during the Cultural Revolution. A second article, written by a group of students of Tsinghua University's middle school on the anniversary of the first 1966 Red Guard rally in Peking, declared that the Cultural Revolution had demonstrated the necessity and feasibility of mobilizing the masses to rebel against revisionist tendencies in the bureaucracy.[48]

These themes were presented more formally in Wang Hung-wen's address to the Tenth Party Congress and in an unpublished report Wang gave to a study class for high-ranking central officials the following January.[49] Wang, a security official in a textile factory in 1966, had played an active role in the Shanghai workers' movement during the Cultural Revolution, had become a member of the Shanghai municipal revolutionary and Party committees, and had been elected to the Central Committee at the Ninth Party Congress in 1969. Now, at the Tenth Congress, he was dramatically elevated to the third-ranking position in the Party, following Mao and Chou En-lai, and was chosen to give the report on the revision of the Party constitution.

Wang's two reports presented, first of all, the thesis that class struggle was continuing in China, and that revisionism was already reappearing in the aftermath of the purge of Lin Piao. To combat the reemergence of revisionism it would be necessary in the future to carry out more cultural revolutions in which the masses would be mobilized to criticize revisionist tendencies in the bureaucracy. In his report to the Tenth Congress, Wang placed "special emphasis" on the question of accepting criticism and supervision from the masses. In terms reminiscent of the communiqué of the Eleventh Plenum in August 1966, he called on the Party to "have faith in the masses, rely on them, and constantly use the weapons of arousing the masses to air their views freely, write big-character posters, and hold great debates." He also endorsed an instruction from Mao, incorporated in the new Party constitution, that permitted the masses to reject incorrect Party leadership: "Going against the tide is a Marxist-Leninist principle." Only revisionists, Wang argued, would fear these principles of mass supervision and "going against the tide."

In both his speeches, Wang Hung-wen spoke of "leading cadres"—presumably those rehabilitated since the Cultural Revolution—as needing pointed criticism. In his report to the Tenth Party Congress, he accused these officials of trying to win special privileges, such as admission to universities and choice jobs in the cities for their children (the practice of "going in by the back door"), and of suppressing criticism from the masses (a phenomenon Wang said was quite serious in some individual cases). In his address to the central study class in January, he complained that many of these veteran cadres remained "passive, superficial, and hesitant" because of the criticism they had received during the Cultural Revolution.

Accordingly, Wang called for more rapid recruitment and promotion of younger cadres. At the Tenth Congress he expressed this view in relatively veiled terms, referring only to the need to train "millions of revolutionary successors" from among the workers and peasants and to place them in leading posts at all levels. At the central study class, however, Wang was much more blunt. He charged that some comrades in the revolutionary ranks looked down upon the "children's corps" of younger officials, thereby ignoring the fact that the vast number of young cadres were full of vigor, eager to learn and to progress, and not afraid to go against the tide. It was extremely unfair that younger cadres should be severely criticized for a single mistake in their work, while the Party's policy was lenient toward veteran officials who had committed errors that were both more numerous and more serious.

The distinctive features of the leftists' position on organizational issues became even clearer if we compare Wang's two speeches with the report presented to the Tenth Congress by Chou En-lai.[50] The differences should not be exaggerated, for Chou's presentation had much in common with Wang's. Like Wang, Chou endorsed the principle of "going against the tide," and he referred to the three-in-one combination of the old, the middle-aged, and the young as the model to guide recruitment and promotions in the Party, thus indirectly endorsing the appointment of younger cadres to leading positions. Despite these similarities, however, his position on the danger of revisionism and the desirability of open-door rectification was significantly different from Wang's. Although he acknowledged that for a long time to come there would still be two-line struggles within the Party, he did not describe the Cultural Revolution as a model for waging such struggles. Nor did his report contain any reference to the need for the Party to accept criticism and supervision from the masses, the very point that Wang had made with special emphasis.

The disagreements between leftists and moderates on these issues continued to be reflected in the press during the fall of 1973.[51] Leftist articles cautioned against relaxing vigilance against revisionism, warned that revisionist tendencies had begun to reappear since the fall of Lin Piao, and defended the principle of mass supervision and criticism of Party cadres. Moderate articles pointed out that if the masses were given the right to go against the tide, they might mistakenly end up criticizing a correct policy. The moderates, therefore, placed greater emphasis on unity and discipline under Party leadership than on going against the tide. When they spoke of class struggle, their articles usually failed to mention mass supervision or the need for future cultural revolutions.

Despite the opposition of the moderates, the leftists succeeded, most likely with Mao's support, in winning two important victories in early 1974. First, they secured agreement that their campaign against the continuing influence of Confucianism in contemporary China would be one of the central features of Chinese politics for the coming year.[52] Indeed, by February the leftists' anti-Confucian campaign, with its criticism of retrogression and restoration, was being described as equal in importance to the moderates' campaign to criticize Lin Piao, and the two campaigns were thereafter merged into a single effort, the campaign to criticize Lin Piao and Confucius.[53]

The leftists' second achievement was to conduct the criticism of Lin Piao and Confucius as a "revolutionary great debate" over the course China had been taking since the Cultural Revolution. A revolutionary great debate was, in essence, a new form of open-door rectification campaign, similar to the Red Guard movement during the Cultural Revolution, but less disruptive. Like the Red Guard movement, the debate was guided by the mass media, over which the leftists exercised a great deal of influence, rather than by the Party apparatus, in which the leftist imprint was much weaker. Also like the Red Guard movement, the debate was intended to prevent the emergence of revisionism in China by mobilizing mass criticism of the socioeconomic programs of the moderates. But the debate was to be considerably milder in tone than the Cultural Revolution had been. Restrictions were imposed against factional organizations and "fighting groups" in order to prevent organizations like the Red Guards from disrupting the economy and promoting violence and disorder. And, unlike the Red Guards, the participants in the debate were never encouraged to seize power from the Party apparatus.*

The revolutionary great debate began early in 1974 when dockworkers in Shanghai put up wall posters complaining that the managers of the harbor expected them to be "slaves to tonnage," rather than masters of the wharves. This was followed by other posters in other factories complaining about the restoration of material incentives, the increasing size of administrative staffs, and the neglect of political work.[54] The campaign intensified dramatically in mid-June when wall posters appeared in Peking and in some provincial capitals criticizing such provincial leaders as Wang Chia-tao of Heilungkiang, Li Jui-shan of Shansi, and Hua Kuo-feng of Hunan for allegedly supporting the rightist policies of the moderates.[55]

Some of the posters, particularly those written in Peking, returned to an organizational issue that had been troubling leftists for four years. Mass representatives on the Peking revolutionary committee complained that the committee had not held a plenary session since 1970, and that the concept of mass participation in a three-in-one combination had therefore become meaningless. They also pointed out that a number of mass representatives at the municipal and district levels had been charged with "ultraleftism" and dismissed from the revolutionary committees since 1970. The wall posters also once again invoked the model of the Paris Commune;

---

*The format for the revolutionary great debate was apparently defined in a set of central directives, issued in early April, that permitted mass criticism of policy decisions, but that also prohibited the formation of factional organizations and fighting groups, placed restrictions on the number of meetings that could be held, prohibited any form of armed struggle, and urged that the campaign not be permitted to disrupt the economy or production. See *China News Summary*, nos. 513 (18.iv.74) and 514 (25.iv.74).

they demanded the direct election of leaders at all levels, the abolition of the privileges of rank, and the reduction of official salaries to the same level as those of ordinary workers.[56]

Shortly after these wall posters began to appear, the revolutionary great debate suffered the same abrupt termination that had characterized the blooming and contending of May and early June 1957. As early as June 21, wall posters began to complain that mass criticism was being suppressed. One charged that the police were discouraging people from writing post-ers. Another claimed that the authorities were insidiously sabotaging the display of wall posters by stealing the critics' glue.[57] Then, on July 1, *Jen-min jih-pao*, *Hung-ch'i*, and *Chieh-fang-chün pao* announced the end of the period of mass criticism in their joint Party Day editorial. Although acknowledging that the Party should have faith in the masses and should welcome their criticism and supervision, the editorial went on to say that the debate should be conducted under the centralized leadership of the Party committees, and that the Party should give the masses guidance when they expressed "wrong ideas running counter to Marxism."[58]

The same day the Central Committee issued its "Notice Concerning Grasping Revolution and Promoting Production," which pointed out that the revolutionary great debates had created serious economic problems on some railway lines and in heavy industry.[59] The notice supported the abstract concept of going against the tide, but it denounced most of the concept's concrete manifestations, such as rebelling against the leadership, withdrawing from work, and refusing to produce for the "wrong" line. Most significant of all, the notice insisted that most cadres were good and demanded that all questions of wage policy and economic policy should immediately be shelved. On this note, and amid strong calls for unity and order throughout the rest of the year, China's first revolutionary great debate gradually came to an end.

The impact of the campaign was less than the leftists would have liked. Many of the popular demands raised during the campaign were not those that the leftists wanted expressed. Some workers used the opportunity to press not for egalitarianism, but for higher wages; some people in Peking made unrealistic demands for the Paris Commune–style organizations that had been repeatedly rejected during the Cultural Revolution. Few young cadres received the promotions that Wang Hung-wen had demanded, and few if any moderate officials were dismissed from office. If anything, the effect of the criticism of the distribution of power in the bureaucracy was to the leftists' detriment, for the leftists received few important positions on the new State Council or on the Standing Committee of the National People's Congress, both of which were organized at the end of the year.

Still, the campaign did have some marginal effect on the Chinese politi-

cal scene. It may have prevented, or at least delayed, any further rehabilitations of prominent central Party leaders dismissed during the Cultural
Revolution. The experiments with university admissions examinations
were halted, and no further modification of Cultural Revolution programs
was announced. Most important, the revolutionary great debate provided
a new form of open-door rectification, one that the leftists would use again
on the eve of Mao's death.

The Campaign to Study the Dictatorship of the Proletariat

In January 1975, after much delay, the Chinese finally convened their
Fourth National People's Congress, the first such meeting in ten years, to
adopt a new state constitution and to confirm the central state leadership.
Chou En-lai's report to the congress stressed economic modernization
rather than revolution.[60] He called for the comprehensive modernization
of agriculture, industry, national defense, and science and technology—
the so-called four modernizations—by the end of the century. He was also
uncompromising on organizational questions. At the end of his report, in
listing the tasks facing the Party and government, he mentioned the need
for discipline, unity, and Party leadership, and he criticized what he described as tendencies toward "splittism" and intrigue. He made no mention of mass supervision of the bureaucracy or of going against the tide.

The leftists nevertheless used the National People's Congress as the occasion to launch the second campaign in their counteroffensive against the
moderates, just as they had used the Tenth Party Congress to launch their
first. Chang Ch'un-ch'iao's report on the revision of the state constitution
was much less outspoken than Wang Hung-wen's report on the Party constitution in 1973, but it did contain one revealing passage. By claiming that
the superstructure still lagged behind the economic base, Chang seemed to
imply that even more egalitarian and populistic programs would be possible. And by claiming that the leadership in some enterprises was not in the
hands of Marxists, he laid the basis for yet another leftist rectification
campaign, directed this time against the basic levels.[61]

The theme of the leftists' second campaign was fully revealed on February 9, when a *Jen-min jih-pao* editorial introduced an "important instruction" by Chairman Mao on the question of theory. In essence, Mao's
directive stated that it was time to study the theory of the dictatorship of
the proletariat and to understand why it was necessary to exercise such a
dictatorship over the bourgeoisie. The editorial went on to say that it was
China's task, through that study, to work ceaselessly to "dig up the soil
that breeds revisionism."* Where might such soil be located?

---

*Jen-min jih-pao, 9.ii.75, in *Peking Review*, 14.ii.75, pp. 4–5. Mao's directive read, in
part, as follows: "Why did Lenin speak of exercising dictatorship over the bourgeoisie? Lack

Viewed as an answer to this question, the campaign that followed this editorial, which was highlighted by lengthy theoretical articles by Chang Ch'un-ch'iao and Yao Wen-yüan, was as interesting for what it did not say about organizational issues as for what it did.[62] The leftists did not trace the roots of revisionism to bureaucracy, as Lin Piao had done during the Cultural Revolution. Instead, they employed an economic analysis. The origins of revisionism, according to Chang and Yao, lay in "bourgeois rights," particularly the right to receive unequal pay for unequal work. It was the concept of bourgeois rights that led to a graduated wage system and thus created inequalities. Revisionism emerged when people began to develop an interest in maintaining those graduated wage systems and sought ever higher material benefits. To prevent revisionism, therefore, it would be necessary to impose restrictions on that part of the bourgeois rights that still existed. Otherwise, as Yao Wen-yüan explained, inequality would increase, economic polarization would occur, and those who benefited from the inequalities would eventually openly restore and develop the capitalist system.

This may have been a powerful argument for equality, but it was not a particularly strong attack on bureaucracy as a form of organization. Although the Chinese bureaucracy still employed a graduated pay scale, it was not singled out for criticism on that score, and Chang Ch'un-ch'iao even refrained from reintroducing his 1958 proposal that cadres once again be paid according to the supply system. Discussions of the quest for material advantage in a society governed by bourgeois rights did mention that some Party members and government officials had become corrupt, but the campaign did not stress the point.* Interestingly, the campaign placed more emphasis on the ways in which material incentives might lead to the degeneration of ordinary workers and peasants than on the corruption of Party and state cadres. In sharp contrast to their position during the Cul-

---

of clarity on this question will lead to revisionism." The Chairman later issued additional instructions along the same lines. One argued that the graduated wage system in China and the use of money to buy commodities both laid the foundation for a resurrection of capitalism. Another cited Lenin's warning that small-scale production "engenders capitalism and a bourgeoisie continuously—daily, hourly, spontaneously, and on a mass scale." It cautioned that this process of embourgeoisement was well under way in China, and that it was affecting industrial workers, government officials, and Party members alike.

*Chang did claim that there was a "bourgeois wind" blowing among certain leading cadres who "approve of the dictatorship of the proletariat at a certain stage and within a certain sphere and are pleased with certain victories of the proletariat, because these will bring them some gains; once they have secured their gains, they feel it is time to settle down and feather their cozy nests." This foreshadowed an argument the leftists would make more forcefully in 1976: some cadres who had supported the "new democratic revolution" by which the Chinese Communist Party had come to power did not fully support the goals of the socialist revolution and of socialist transformation.

tural Revolution, therefore, the leftists in 1975 traced the origins of revisionism to the economic base rather than to the political superstructure.[63]

Nor did the campaign to study the dictatorship of the proletariat even generate the same kind of revolutionary great debate that had characterized the criticism of Lin Piao and Confucius. One possible explanation is that the leftists did not receive permission to attempt to mobilize the same degree of mass participation as they had in 1974. Another is that the campaign was directed at the demands for higher wages that had been expressed during the criticism, and that the position taken by the leftists on this issue in 1975 was simply not one that attracted much worker support. For whatever reason, the campaign remained a low-keyed affair that had less lasting impact on the succession struggle than the revolutionary great debates of either 1974 or 1976.

THE MODERATES' SECOND PROGRAM, 1975

Chou En-lai's report to the National People's Congress moved the question of economic modernization to the top of the Chinese political agenda. To consider plans for achieving the "four modernizations" by the turn of the century, the State Council and the Central Committee convened a series of meetings throughout 1975, some of which dealt with problems in particular sectors of the economy, and others of which dealt with intersectoral planning and coordination. Of the documents and reports discussed at these meetings, three are most important. The only one of the three that was published at the time was a report by Hua Kuo-feng, then vice-premier in charge of agriculture, to a national conference on agricultural mechanization (the so-called Tachai conference) held in September and October.[64] The other two, drafted under the supervision of Teng Hsiao-p'ing, then ranking vice-premier in charge of all economic planning, were entitled "On the General Program for All Work of the Whole Party and the Whole Country" (the General Program)[65] and "Some Problems in Accelerating Industrial Development" (the Twenty Points).[66] The three documents dealt principally with economic issues, but they also embodied a revised version of the moderates' organizational program of 1971–73. In essence, the moderates were now explicitly rejecting the leftists' proposals for continuing revolutionary great debates and were advocating a closed-door rectification campaign throughout the country that would be directed against leftist sympathizers at all levels of the Party.

Before turning to the moderates' proposal for a rectification campaign, however, we should first note an additional element in the moderates' program that would also arouse the opposition of the leftists: the Twenty Points, besides discussing rectification in factories and industrial enterprises, also contained passages that called for increasing central direction and control over the Chinese economy.

The recentralization advocated by the moderates was by no means sweeping. In fact, the Twenty Points praised the transfer of enterprises from central to provincial control during the Cultural Revolution and proposed that, with a few exceptions, all enterprises in the country should either be placed under provincial control or else be "put under the dual leadership of both the central and local authorities, with the latter being held chiefly responsible." In defining the ideal scope for central planning—general policies, production targets, investment quotas, distribution of essential commodities, total wage bill, and prices—the Twenty Points did little more than reassert what had been established policy since the decentralization reforms of 1957–58.

But the Twenty Points did contain some other passages that would have strengthened the authority of the center over the provinces. First, they strongly criticized the tendency shown by provincial leaders and enterprise managers since the Cultural Revolution to ignore or evade central directives:

At present some localities and units have ignored the overall interests and the unified regulations of the central authorities by willfully formulating policies in violation of state plans, wantonly changing the direction of production of the decentralized enterprises, discontinuing the relationships of coordination and cooperation previously established, failing to complete the missions of transferring products to higher levels, arbitrarily adding basic construction projects and enlarging [their] size . . ., and wantonly securing and expending materials and funds.

The document also hinted that provincial authorities had increased the size of their labor force and altered commodity prices without central authorization. Thus, the Twenty Points insisted that it was mandatory to restrengthen unified state planning. Central plans and policies would have to be carried out in a disciplined manner, and any readjustment of plan would have to be reported for approval through stipulated channels.

Second, the Twenty Points concluded that one reason for the attenuation of central control over the economy was the abolition of the regional Party bureaus during the Cultural Revolution. It was proving impossible, the moderates argued, for the central authorities to monitor the economic activities of all the provinces. Accordingly, the Twenty Points proposed the reestablishment of some kind of regional economic planning and supervisory agency in each of six "coordinated regions."

These proposals for tighter central control over the economy, however, occupied a less important place in the moderates' organizational program than did their call for a Party rectification campaign and their opposition to the revolutionary great debates advocated by the leftists. The General Program and the Twenty Points rejected each of the key leftist themes of the time—"rebellion is justified," "going against the tide," and "blooming and contending through wall posters and great debates"—in an attempt to ensure discipline and stability. The Twenty Points, in particular, placed severe restrictions on the leftists' capacity to mobilize such criticism in the factories: "All political movements in the enterprises must be conducted under the condition that production is persistently carried on." The various propaganda teams, writing squads, and theoretical groups that formed the nucleus of the leftists' campaigns were to be disbanded without exception.

Instead of a revolutionary great debate, the moderates envisioned a sweeping rectification of the Party aimed at strengthening the leadership of Party committees at all levels. The target of this rectification was to be the leftists, on the grounds that they were engaging in factionalism and were disrupting unity. As the General Program described them, the leftists were "practicing revisionism while holding the antirevisionist banner," trying to strike down good cadres, promoting "the so-called struggle between new and old cadres" and "the so-called struggle between Confucianists and 'Legalists,'" and talking "only about revolution, and not production." These leftists, the General Program said, would have to be transferred to other positions, or even purged altogether. Otherwise, "these class enemies" would make it impossible to fulfill the task of consolidating the proletarian dictatorship at the grass-roots level.

The three moderate documents provided for different rectification techniques for different parts of the Party, but the common denominator was that the rectification campaign would be a closed-door affair. In the factories, the Twenty Points said, the rectification would be directed against three targets: the cadres, presumably of a basically correct orientation, who had become "soft, lazy, lax, fearful, or dispirited" under the continued attacks of the leftists; the cadres who, taking advantage of the chaotic conditions in some enterprises, had engaged in embezzlement or corruption; and the leftists themselves, who were described as "unreformed petty intellectuals." As the Twenty Points said in discussing this third category of cadres, "These persons, completely ignorant of politics and completely inexperienced in production, are carping and caviling, doing nothing but purging others, chanting bombastic words while doing nothing concrete, and constantly tagging others with the labels of 'restoration of the old,' 'retrogression,' [and] 'conservative force.'"

The rectification campaign was described as an inner-Party movement to be conducted under the leadership of Party committees at the higher level. Large numbers of provincial, special district, and county cadres were organized into work teams and sent to the countryside, where they would investigate the performance of the basic-level cadres. The goal was to educate errant cadres, not to punish or purge them. As Hua Kuo-feng explained, "It is necessary to help basic-level cadres remain relatively stable so as to familiarize themselves with the situation, and make long-term plans for their work."

At higher levels the emphasis was to be placed on the rectification of cadres at the county level through a combination of ideological and organizational consolidation. On the ideological side, each year for five years the county Party committees were to conduct a closed-door rectification in which they would study documents and solve practical problems arising in their work. On the organizational side, within one year the provincial, special district, and municipal Party committees were to undertake a readjustment of the county Party committees that would eliminate "bourgeois factionalists" and "evil elements" from membership. No mention was made of any form of mass participation in this rectification campaign.

THE LEFTISTS' SECOND COUNTEROFFENSIVE, 1976

In the economic planning conferences held throughout 1975, the moderates were able to win support for the adoption of policies—particularly in the areas of factory management, education, and science—that departed still farther from the "newborn things" of the Cultural Revolution. As in 1971–73, greater stress was placed on academic standards in higher education. Urban students were permitted in some cases to proceed directly from high school to college without spending time in the countryside. Mass participation in scientific activities was deemphasized, and renewed attention was given to pure research. Rules and regulations were reestablished in factories, and the authority of factory managers was reasserted.

It was virtually inevitable that these trends would produce some kind of response from the leftists. Unable to win the debate inside the planning meetings themselves, the leftists resorted to other devices. They denied publicity to moderate policies and programs through their influence over the press. And they used the mass media to mobilize popular resistance to the moderates' programs. This counteroffensive began in the summer of 1975 with a campaign to criticize the classic novel *The Water Margin*, which was described as a tale of capitulation to class enemies. It assumed a less allegorical form later in the year when a campaign was mounted against efforts to reverse the verdicts of the Cultural Revolution. By providing an occasion to defend the "newborn things" of the Cultural Revolution, this second campaign gave the leftists a convenient opportunity to condemn the new policy initiatives undertaken by the moderates in 1975, particularly in science and education.

Just as the campaign against the reversal of verdicts was gathering momentum, the death of Chou En-lai in January 1976 focused the struggle between leftists and moderates on the choice of a new prime minister. The struggle resulted first in compromise. Neither Teng Hsiao-p'ing, the principal moderate candidate, nor Chang Ch'un-ch'iao, the leading leftist contender, was named premier. Instead, the position of acting premier was given to Hua Kuo-feng who, despite his presentation of the moderates' rectification program at the Tachai conference the previous year, was still seen as a centrist candidate tolerable to both factions. But the April riots in Tienanmen Square in Peking, which followed the suppression of a popular tribute to Chou En-lai, led to a temporary defeat for the moderates. Teng Hsiao-p'ing, made a scapegoat for the rioting, was dismissed from all his Party and governmental positions. Although a hastily convened Politburo meeting named Hua, rather than one of the leftists, as permanent prime minister, the removal of Teng still provided the occasion for the most intense leftist campaign in China since the height of the Cultural Revolution.

The anti-Teng campaign continued many themes from the past leftist efforts. Lin Piao, Confucius, and *Water Margin* all came in for renewed criticism, as did the moderate policies in science, education, industrial management, and foreign trade adopted in 1975. But the anti-Teng campaign also contained a strong attack on the moderates' proposed rectification movement, a condemnation of the moderates' effort to strengthen central control over the economy, and a bitter criticism of veteran officials, one of the moderates' principal bases of support, as being the most important source of revisionism in China.

The leftists offered two characterizations of the Party rectification campaign proposed by Teng Hsiao-p'ing and Hua Kuo-feng in 1975. First, they described it as a thinly disguised effort to dismiss the younger cadres who had attained office as a result of the Cultural Revolution and to replace them with "unrepentant capitalist roaders" who would be more supportive of the moderates' "revisionist" policies. Throughout the first nine months of 1976, therefore, the leftists made a direct appeal to younger cadres, claiming that Teng Hsiao-p'ing had threatened their jobs and that they could remain in office only by supporting the leftist cause. Teng Hsiao-p'ing was quoted, probably accurately, as having described younger cadres who had been given rapid promotions as having "come up by helicopter." And he allegedly had said that since young cadres lacked practical experience, they should be sent to the basic levels for protracted on-the-job training, and then should only receive promotions step by step. If this kind of recruitment policy were followed, the leftists argued, the three-in-one combination of old, middle-aged, and young would be impossible to realize at higher levels of the Party, for by the time officials received their step-by-step promotions to positions at the provincial or central level, they would no longer be young. The leftists went on to argue that, although younger officials might not have had years of experience, they were the least conservative, the richest in "combat spirit," and the most practiced in the struggle against revisionism. And, the leftists charged, this was precisely why Teng Hsiao-p'ing wanted to remove them from important positions.[67]

Second, the leftists drew explicit analogies between the proposed rectification campaign and the conduct of the Socialist Education Movement under Liu Shao-ch'i's Revised Later Ten Points. Just as Liu Shao-ch'i had attacked corruption at the basic levels in order to protect revisionism at higher levels, Teng Hsiao-p'ing was now trying to use a Party-wide rectification campaign to prevent any resistance to the abandonment of the reforms of the Cultural Revolution. The emphasis on the rectification of Party committees at the county level and at the grass roots was described as "directing the spearhead of attack downward" and as "opposing the corrupt officials only and not the emperor." The use of work teams and closed-door rectification techniques was also described as a "bourgeois reactionary line" and, in a clear reference to the Revised Later Ten Points, as "the experience of T'ao-yüan."[68]

The leftists did all they could to block the rectification campaign, or at least to redefine its purposes. They were apparently able to prevent the Central Committee from issuing a directive on the rectification, as it was supposed to have done in April 1976. They encouraged provincial leaders to drag their feet in implementing the campaign. And in some areas the leftists were able to persuade work teams to leave the basic levels and return to their offices to rebel against the reversal of verdicts.[69] The purpose of any rectification, they said, should be the elimination of revisionism at the higher levels, not an assault on factionalism at lower levels: "In rural work, the first priority is criticism of Teng Hsiao-p'ing, the second priority is criticism of Teng Hsiao-p'ing, and the third priority is still criticism of Teng Hsiao-p'ing."[70]

In denouncing the discussion of central-provincial relations in the Twenty Points, the leftists caricatured Teng Hsiao-p'ing's position almost beyond recognition. He had actually praised the transfer of industrial enterprises back to provincial control during the Cultural Revolution and had said that only a few key enterprises and key construction projects should remain under the direct jurisdiction of the central ministries, but the leftists charged that what he really had in mind was to take "most of the big enterprises and the lesser ones working in coordination with them in all parts of the country" and turn them back to central ownership. The bulk of Chinese industry would therefore have been placed under the direct and exclusive control of the relevant central ministries, and the "controlling power of the Party Central Committee and the local Party committees over the economy" would have been "eliminated." This would have been tantamount to following the example of the trusts established in the mid-1960's by Liu Shao-ch'i.[71] In fact, the leftists were quite accurate in their analysis. By late 1979 Chinese leaders had gone far beyond the proposals for economic reform contained in the Twenty Points and had reestablished the very trusts of which the leftists had warned in 1976.

These characterizations of Teng's proposals were often supplemented by a more sophisticated argument. The leftists first appealed to provincial leaders, warning them that their discretionary powers in economic and financial affairs would be limited by Teng's proposals. They charged that the provincial governments would no longer be able to transfer commodities from one enterprise to another as freely as they had in the past to meet changed production conditions, to make changes in their budgets, or to make independent investments.

The leftists also appealed to nationalistic sentiment, saying that Teng's demand for tighter control over the economy was part and parcel of a broader plan to promote large-scale, capital-intensive industry by importing advanced technology from the West. Just as the decentralization measures of 1957–58 and the Cultural Revolution had been linked to the development of small-scale local industry, they argued, so was Teng proposing tighter central control over the economy in order to mobilize and allocate the greater sums of investment capital required for large-scale, modern Western industry. For this reason, Teng's views on provincial-central relations were often described as an important part of his "comprador-bourgeois" economic program, which would allegedly have turned China into a "raw materials supply base for imperialism and social-imperialism, a market for their commodities, and an outlet for their investment."[72]

The most important element of the leftists' final campaign—the criticism of veteran officials as being the most important source of revisionism in China—emerged somewhat later than the others, developing full force only in the summer of 1976. Interestingly, the leftists did not take advantage of the 105th anniversary of the Paris Commune in March to launch their assault on veteran officials, but waited for another anniversary two months later, the tenth anniversary of Mao's directive of May 16, 1966. The commemorative article introduced a new quotation from Mao Tse-tung on the theme that high officials often betray the revolution because they want to protect their own interests, and that there should be continuous revolution against this trend: "There are always sections of the people who feel themselves oppressed: junior officials, students, workers, peasants, and soldiers don't like big shots oppressing them."[73] This quotation provided the leftists with the two themes they would stress forcefully and repeatedly throughout the summer: bureaucracy was the source of revisionism, and mass mobilization was the only way to prevent the bureaucracy from setting China on a revisionist course.

The first theme, of course, was a return to the position Mao and Lin Piao had taken in 1966–67, and was somewhat of a departure from the views expressed by Yao Wen-yüan and Chang Ch'un-ch'iao the year before. Indeed, several leftist articles published in mid-1976 actually rejected Chang and Yao's earlier position that revisionism in China stemmed as much from the persistence of "bourgeois rights" and the "small-producer" mentality of the peasantry as from the bureaucracy. Instead, these articles argued that the main danger of revisionism resided inside the Party, not outside it: "We must not only see that the old bourgeoisie and its intellectuals still exist in society and that large numbers of the petty bourgeoisie are still in the course of remolding their ideology, but we must be *especially aware of the bourgeoisie hidden inside the Party*, that is, those Party persons in power [who are] taking the capitalist road."[74] To support this conclusion, the July 1 Party Day editorial contained an extended quotation from the statement Mao had written in 1965 that described the relationship between the bureaucracy and the workers and peasants as an antagonistic contradiction, and that claimed that the cadres taking the capitalist road were "sucking the blood of the workers."[75] This was soon followed by a more recent directive from Mao: "You are making the socialist revolution, and yet don't know where the bourgeoisie is. It is right in the Communist Party—those in power taking the capitalist road."

But though the leftists returned in 1976 to the position that bureaucracy was the major locus of revisionism in China, they did not give the same reasons for this as Mao and Lin had given in 1966–67. That is to say, they did not trace revisionism to the structural characteristics of bureaucracy: hierarchy, routinization, division of labor, and specialization.* Rather, they presented an historical argument. Most veteran officials had joined

*This is not to say that there were absolutely no structural critiques of bureaucracy during this period. A few leftists, drawing on the 1975 criticism of "bourgeois rights," suggested that the "system of grades and ranks under which people line up according to their grades and seniority" was one of the origins of revisionism in China. See Radio Peking, 24.ii.76, in Foreign Broadcast Information Service, *Daily Report: People's Republic of China*, 26.ii.76, pp. E1–7; and *Jen-min jih-pao*, 23.vii.76, in *Survey of the People's Republic of China Press*, no. 76–35 (1976), pp. 167–69.

the Party before the collectivization of agriculture and the nationalization of industry. They had joined the Party, the leftists said, not because they were attracted by the Party's socialist and communist goals, but because the Party was leading a "new democratic revolution" against imperialism, the landlords, and the Nationalist government. Despite years of education and rectification, their political philosophy had never really progressed beyond that point. Leftist articles expressed the point clearly: "Though they live in a socialist society, their thinking remains in the stage of the democratic revolution."[76] The leftists argued that it was therefore inevitable that a large number of these veteran officials would become revisionists. Some leftists apparently asserted privately that as many as 75 percent of the older officials would end up, sooner or later, on the capitalist road.[77]

This diagnosis of the origins of revisionism in China was followed by a second familiar theme, the need for mass mobilization to identify the revisionists and to strike them down. An important editorial in *Jen-min jih-pao* on May 29 entitled "The Masses Are the Real Heroes" asserted that it was ordinary people throughout the country who had first recognized Teng Hsiao-p'ing's revisionism and claimed that this demonstrated that the Cultural Revolution had "enhanced their immunity to revisionism and their fighting capacity to combat it."[78] The leftists put forward the argument that the masses should be encouraged to rebel against revisionist policies, criticize the capitalist-roaders in the Party, and assume responsibility for constantly supervising Party and state officials through such organizations as the trade unions and the militia. One article said that all basic-level units in China should become battlefields for criticizing revisionism and the bourgeoisie.[79] Another warned against the emergence of revisionism in the Central Committee and urged that leftists mobilize the masses against the revisionists.[80] Still another commended a situation in which "the masses not only can ignore but even criticize the erroneous orders issued by the 'officials.'"[81] The leftists acknowledged that constant struggle against revisionism might be tiresome, but insisted that it was necessary: "Are you getting tired of struggle? Do you feel that there have been 'about enough' struggles, and that it is time to engage in peaceful construction? If so, you have exactly tallied with the desire of the capitalist-roaders."

The revolutionary great debate promoted by the radicals in the summer of 1976 created economic disruption and political disorder throughout the country. Officially, this debate was still to be conducted according to the rules established during the criticism of Lin Piao and Confucius: no fighting groups, no repudiation of Party leadership, no decrease in production. Despite these provisions, leftists instigated slowdowns and strikes in many cities and along important railway lines, using the slogan "Refuse to produce for the wrong political line."* They organized demonstrations against provincial leaders and sit-ins in some Party and government offices. These activities, it was later charged, were coordinated by representatives dispatched from Shanghai and Peking, and planned and instigated by underground "liaison offices" established in selected cities and provinces.[82]

There is some evidence to suggest that even the "Gang of Four" were dismayed by the amount of disruption that their supporters created. The four may have realized that a renewal of the Cultural Revolution would have alienated a large number of Chinese who were tired of chaos, and that a wholesale assault against all officials would have deprived them of the support of some of the leading centrists in the Party. Thus, some of the most virulent leftist articles expressed support for the restrictions against fighting groups that distinguished revolutionary great debates from cultural revolutions.[83] And, in a speech attributed to him by the Taiwan government, Chang Ch'un-ch'iao reportedly warned of an "ultraleftist trend of thought" that was attacking too many cadres, disrupting the economy, and veering toward anarchism. Such a trend was impractical and dangerous. "A chaotic bombardment can make an attack fail, not succeed," Chang is reported to have said.[84]

Whether or not the strikes and demonstrations of the summer of 1976 were sanctioned by the "Gang of Four," they did not work out to the four's advantage. Nor did the leftists' insistence that the criticism of Teng Hsiao-p'ing continue despite devastating earthquakes that struck China in July.[85] Instead, these events caused a coalition of moderates, centrists, and military commanders to form against the leftists. Within a month of Mao's death on September 9, Wang Hung-wen, Chang Ch'un-ch'iao, Chiang Ch'ing, and Yao Wen-yüan had been dismissed from the Politburo, and a number of other central leftists had been placed under arrest. Though the revolutionary great debate may have generated some popular indignation about Teng Hsiao-p'ing's "revisionist" programs among some workers and students, it was unable to mobilize the secure base of support that was needed to prevent the purge of the "Gang of Four."

Throughout the period from 1969 to 1976, then, the leftists generally refused to take a radical approach to the bureaucratic dilemma: they were loathe to make a radical critique of bureaucracy, as they had during the Cultural Revolution, or to advocate the Paris Commune as a model to

---

*In the railway system, the leftists introduced the slogan, "Better to have socialist trains run late than [to have] revisionist punctuality." *Peking Review*, 26.xi.76, p. 16.

replace the bureaucracy. There were scattered exceptions, of course, such as Peking leftists' critique of bureaucracy during the criticism of Lin Piao and Confucius, but these did not receive the support of the "Gang of Four." Either leading leftists like Chang Ch'un-ch'iao and Yao Wen-yüan no longer believed that a radical attack on the bureaucracy would generate much support, or else, once drawn into leadership positions during the Cultural Revolution, they now no longer wanted to destroy it.

Indeed, the leftists presented an explanation of revisionism that placed its roots not inside the bureaucracy, but in the principle of distribution according to labor and in the salary differentials that it created. When the leftists did emphasize the bureaucratic origins of revisionism, as they did in 1976, they tended to diagnose the problem as lying in the historical experiences and personal backgrounds of leading officials—a problem that could be remedied through restaffing or through reeducation—rather than as being inherent in the structural characteristics of bureaucracy.

The organizational program proposed by the leftists during this period, as exemplified by the revolutionary great debates, would have emphasized constant mass criticism of bureaucratic officials and their policies, organized around changing ideological themes and guided through articles and editorials in the leftist-controlled press. The debates were therefore most similar to the Cultural Revolution committee, among the four models of mass participation developed during the Cultural Revolution. In contrast to the Paris Commune model, the debates did not entail the elimination of bureaucracy or the election of officials. In contrast to the revolutionary committees, the debates did not require that the masses have substantial direct representation in Party or revolutionary committees (it is interesting, in this connection, that the leftists' recruitment policy emphasized the promotion of younger officials rather than the appointment of mass representatives). And, in contrast to the Red Guards, the terms of the debates included specific prohibitions against the formation of organized fighting groups that could move from one basic-level unit to another. The revolutionary great debates, therefore, were closest in spirit to the Cultural Revolution committees. In each case, the basic idea was to generate regular mass criticism of revisionism from the grass roots.

The moderates' program, in contrast, centered around a series of closed-door rectification campaigns intended to purge the Party and government of leftists, to restore inner-Party discipline and unity, to facilitate the rehabilitation of cadres dismissed during the Cultural Revolution, and to justify the modification or abandonment of many of the "newborn things" of the Cultural Revolution. The leftists' version of rectification was a bottom-up affair emphasizing mass criticism of revisionist officials and revisionist cadres, but the moderates' program called for top-down rectification in which tendencies toward factionalism would be eliminated through the exercise of strict Party and administrative discipline.

On one level, then, the principal organizational issue of the mid-1970's was a familiar one: a debate between the proponents of open-door and closed-door rectification. But this debate over rectification did not stem principally from an abstract analysis of the most effective ways of improving the performance of the bureaucracy. Instead, the debate reflected the two groups' recognition that the choice of rectification techniques would have a significant, even decisive, effect on their struggle for political power. Both sides appeared to share the view that a high level of mass mobilization, as required by an open-door rectification campaign, would tend to weaken the moderates' influence over the bureaucracy because of the leftists' greater capacity to organize large numbers of supporters and create serious political turmoil and economic disruption. A closed-door movement, on the other hand, would tend to strengthen the moderates' ability to impose discipline and unity on the Party and state apparatus.

Even though the leftists were able to launch a series of debates between 1974 and 1976, they were not successful in maintaining their political power after Mao's death in September 1976. Their failure to do so illustrates one of the serious shortcomings of open-door rectification techniques in China. The leftists were able to mobilize a degree of mass support during the rectification campaigns of the mid-1970's, but they were unable to translate that support into effective political power. In essence, the leftists learned the same lesson that Mao had in the early months of the Cultural Revolution: mass criticism could identify programs and cadres that mass organizations or factions considered to be revisionist, but it could not force officials to change their policies, remold their political philosophies, or resign from office. In the Cultural Revolution, Mao had ultimately been required to sanction the overthrow of the entire Party and state apparatus and to order the army to enforce his decision. Neither Mao nor the army was willing to offer comparable support to the leftists in 1975–76. Instead, the instruments of power—as opposed to the instruments of protest—remained in the hands of the moderates.[86]

11
Conclusion

In the introductory chapter we identified three perspectives through which Chinese organizational policy might be analyzed. Bureaucracy, we said, might appear on the Chinese political agenda as an administrative problem, as a political issue, or as a social dilemma. In the conclusion we will summarize what we have learned about these three dimensions of analysis, and then offer a general evaluation of Chinese bureaucracy under Communist rule.

BUREAUCRACY AS A SOCIAL DILEMMA

In the revised edition of their textbook, *Comparative Politics*, Gabriel Almond and G. Bingham Powell summarize the quandary that bureaucracy has produced for industrialized societies. "The truth of the matter is that modern, complex, interdependent societies cannot get along without bureaucracies, and it also seems to be practically impossible to get along with them."[1] As we have seen, this dilemma has been particularly intense in contemporary China. On the one hand, the proposition that a modern society cannot get along without bureaucracy is fully congruent with most of China's political traditions and with the Leninist and Stalinist models of organization that Soviet advisers brought to China in the 1950's. On the other hand, the notion that bureaucracy is difficult to live with is reinforced by the Taoist traditions of ancient China, by the utopian antibureaucratic components of Marxist-Leninist ideology, and by the problems the Chinese Communist movement experienced with bureaucracy right from the formation of the first Soviet base area.

How, then, have the Chinese attempted to manage the social dilemma posed by bureaucratic organizations? Our first conclusion is that the Chinese, at one time or another, have adopted all four of the approaches to the bureaucratic dilemma that we outlined in Chapter 1. During the mid-1950's, the Chinese experimented with rationalization: rules and regulations were promulgated, a complex network of bureaucratic auditing and monitoring agencies was established, career lines were systematized, and specialized bureaucratic agencies were allowed to proliferate. Many later attempts to control the excesses of bureaucracy can also be understood as instances of rationalization: the reduction of staff implemented in 1955, the decentralization measures of 1957–58, and the partial recentralization of the early 1960's all being cases in point. Even elements of the organizational reforms of the Cultural Revolution, particularly the simplification of bureaucratic structure and the decentralization of economic management, are best read as examples of a rationalizing approach to the bureaucratic dilemma.

The Chinese have occasionally considered taking a radical tack in dealing with the social and political dilemmas posed by bureaucracy. During the Cultural Revolution some leaders proposed the complete destruction of the bureaucracy and its replacement by a much more participatory and less hierarchical form of political system. In keeping with the writings of Marx, Engels, and Lenin, these new nonbureaucratic organizations were to be modeled after the Paris Commune and were to involve the direct election and recall of all officials by the people, the elimination of all salary differences between cadres and ordinary citizens, and the limitation of officials' discretionary powers in performing their work.

The continuing use of rectification campaigns is an example of internal remedialism in China. These campaigns, as first developed systematically by the Chinese Communist Party in 1942–44, are based on the assumption that an organization's problems stem from the personal values and political orientations of its officials, and that solving them therefore depends on a thorough indoctrination of cadres through study, criticism, and self-criticism. Examples of this kind of rectification since 1949 include the Party rectification campaign of 1950, the basic-level rectification of 1951–53, the New San-fan campaign of 1953, the campaign against conservatism at the end of 1955, the campaign against waste and conservatism in 1957–58, the Socialist Education Movement as envisioned by the Revised Later Ten Points of 1964, the county reform campaign of 1965, the movement to study the works of Mao in 1965–66, and the proposals for rectification made by the moderates in 1975.

Finally, the mobilization of the masses to serve as organizational monitors has been the principal way in which the Chinese have adopted the external remedial approach to the bureaucratic dilemma. This kind of mass mobilization has been based on the assumption that popular participation in Party and state affairs provides a reliable method for discovering, criticizing, and rectifying organizational problems. Examples of mass mobilization as a remedial strategy include the solicitation of criticism from non-Party cadres and intellectuals during the Hundred Flowers period, the formation of poor and lower-middle peasant associations under the Early Ten Points, the Cultural Revolution committees as envisioned in 1966, and the proposals in 1956–57 that mass organizations be given greater autonomy from the Party and that people's congresses be given greater powers to oversee the state bureaucracy.

Indeed, the Chinese have been so inventive in their organizational strategies that this fourfold scheme will not encompass them all adequately. If we express this point diagrammatically, the four competing approaches to the bureaucratic dilemma actually constitute only the four poles of a diamond, as shown in figure 1, p. 332. The Chinese experience suggests that we should also consider five additional categories, each of which is a combination of elements from two of the polar strategies. Once this is done, the diamond shown in figure 1 is transformed into the more complex diagram shown in figure 2. These five additional categories can be defined as follows:

Regularized external remedialism involves limited mass supervision of the bureaucracy within a formal organizational framework. Examples include the establishment of a network of supervisory correspondents in the early 1950's as part of the Ministry of Supervision, and the active solicitation of letters from the people to the press and to bureaucratic agencies, a program that has continued throughout the history of the People's Republic.

Regularized internal remedialism refers to formal and routine procedures for cadre indoctrination. Like rectification, it seeks to promote ideological commitment, effective work styles, and selflessness among cadres, but it attempts to do so through less disruptive procedures. Examples include the systems of political education devised in the early 1950's and continued down to the Cultural Revolution, the routine hsia-fang campaigns of the mid-1950's and early 1960's, the system of regular cadre participation in physical labor inaugurated in 1958, and the political departments established in the bureaucracy in 1964–65. The May Seventh cadre schools, instituted toward the end of the Cultural Revolution, also represent regular ideological study and physical labor, but in a new organizational format.

Open-door rectification, like external remedialism, encourages mass involvement in organizational reform, but links it to an ongoing Party rectification campaign. Open-door rectification can also be more easily subjected to Party control than can pure external remedialism. The 1947–48 rectification campaign provided the prototype for open-door rectification, which was later applied to the San-fan campaign of 1951–52, to the Socialist Education Movement under the Later Ten Points, to the Fifty Days in 1966, and to the rebuilding of basic-level Party organizations after the Cultural Revolution.

Radical external remedialism refers to forms of mass monitoring that exercise greater autonomy and greater authority than those that appear under the pure form of external remedialism. The Red Guard movement is

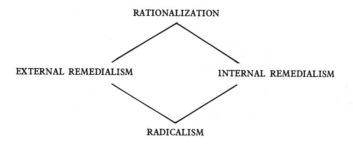

FIG. 1. *The "Polar" Approaches to the Bureaucratic Dilemma*

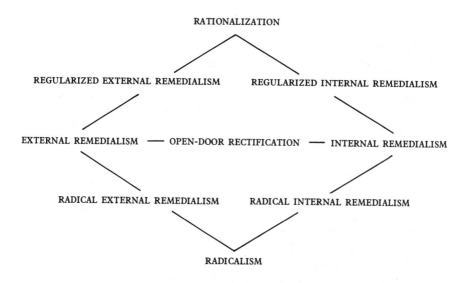

FIG. 2. *Nine Approaches to the Bureaucratic Dilemma*

the best example of radical external remedialism, but mass representation on revolutionary committees between 1967 and 1971 and the revolutionary great debates of 1973–76 also fall into this category.

Radical internal remedialism refers to organizational reforms that move staffing patterns, organizational structure, and operating procedures even further away from pure Weberian bureaucracy without actually approaching the "immediate democracy" of the Paris Commune model. Examples would be the proposals in 1958 and 1967–68 for the abolition of graduated salary systems, the experiments with "crash planning" in the High Tide and the Great Leap Forward, the denigration of specialists and technicians during the Great Leap and the Cultural Revolution, and the proposals made during the Cultural Revolution that organizational discipline could be ignored if the orders did not conform to the thought of Mao Tse-tung. Wholesale abolition of rules and regulations, such as occurred during the Great Leap and the Cultural Revolution, would also fall under this category.

The nine approaches to the bureaucratic dilemma—the four polar strategies and the five combined strategies—are summarized graphically in figure 3 (p. 334), together with the examples mentioned in the text.

Although the Chinese have experimented with all nine approaches to the bureaucratic dilemma at various times since 1949, our second principal conclusion is that internal remedialism has been the center of gravity of Chinese Communist organizational policy, just as it was the center of gravity of China's imperial tradition. Despite their antibureaucratic rhetoric, the Chinese have generally accepted the need for some kind of bureaucratic structure to guide their society's social and economic modernization. The experiments with radicalism during the Cultural Revolution were short-lived, the Chinese leadership quickly concluding that they represented extreme and unworkable positions. At the same time, the Chinese have believed that rationalization would be a necessary and desirable approach to the bureaucratic dilemma, but that it could offer only a partial solution. Rationalization might help increase the technical rationality and efficiency of the bureaucracy, but it could not by itself create the levels of performance the Chinese wanted. The Chinese have repeatedly tried to control the undesirable consequences of bureaucracy by introducing non-bureaucratic components into the structure and operations of the Party and state.* In the process, they have created what, following Ezra Vogel, we might call a "politicized bureaucracy."[2]

*For a valuable, and more detailed, comparison of Weberian bureaucracy and Chinese bureaucracy, see the two articles by Martin King Whyte, "Bureaucracy and Modernization in China: The Maoist Critique," *American Sociological Review*, 38 (1973), 149–63; and "Iron Law Versus Mass Democracy: Weber, Michels, and the Maoist Vision," in James C. Hsiung, ed., *The Logic of "Maoism": Critiques and Explication* (New York, 1974).

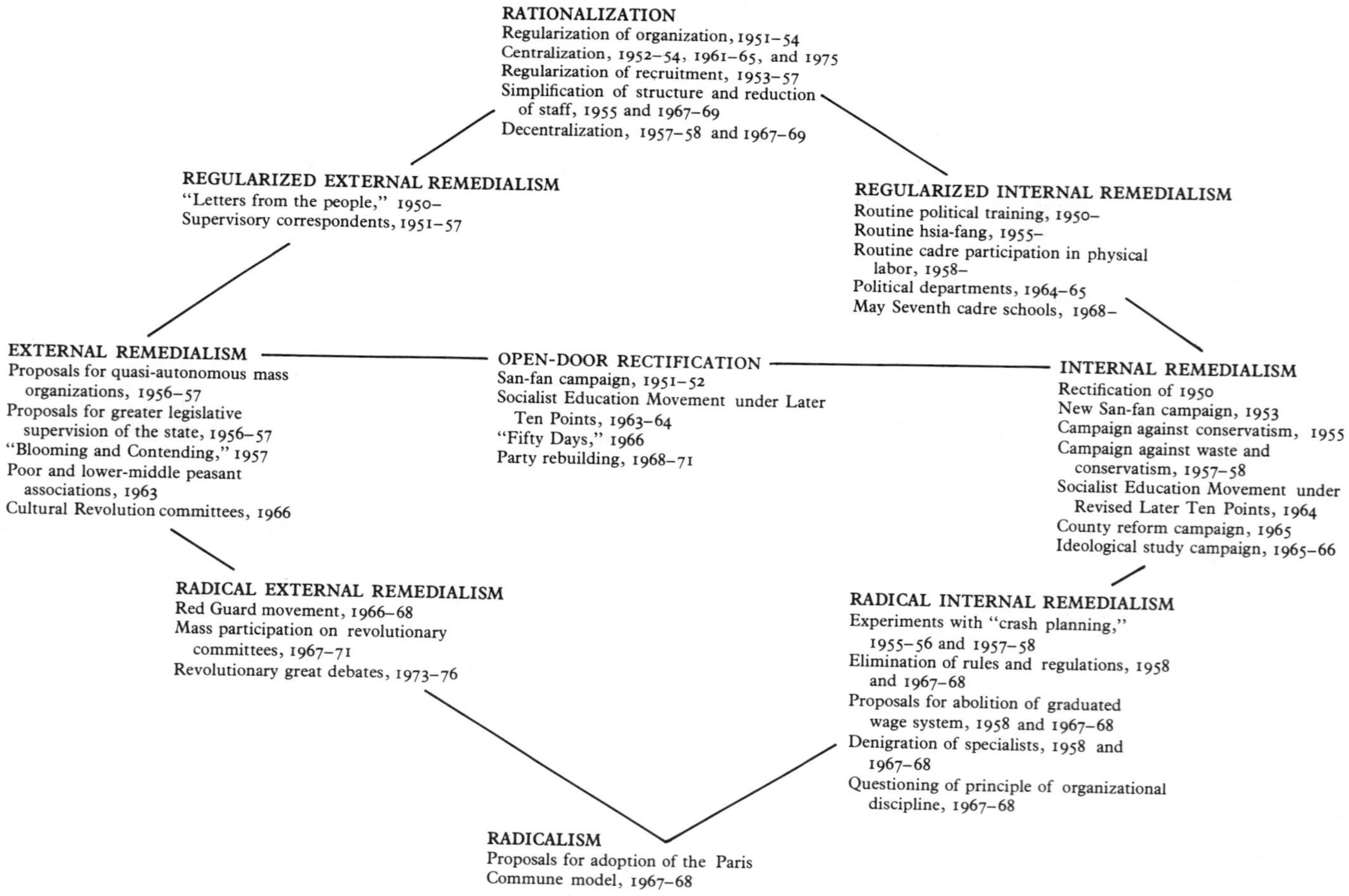

RATIONALIZATION
Regularization of organization, 1951–54
Centralization, 1952–54, 1961–65, and 1975
Regularization of recruitment, 1953–57
Simplification of structure and reduction of staff, 1955 and 1967–69
Decentralization, 1957–58 and 1967–69

REGULARIZED EXTERNAL REMEDIALISM
"Letters from the people," 1950–
Supervisory correspondents, 1951–57

EXTERNAL REMEDIALISM
Proposals for quasi-autonomous mass organizations, 1956–57
Proposals for greater legislative supervision of the state, 1956–57
"Blooming and Contending," 1957
Poor and lower-middle peasant associations, 1963
Cultural Revolution committees, 1966

REGULARIZED INTERNAL REMEDIALISM
Routine political training, 1950–
Routine hsia-fang, 1955–
Routine cadre participation in physical labor, 1958–
Political departments, 1964–65
May Seventh cadre schools, 1968–

INTERNAL REMEDIALISM
Rectification of 1950
New San-fan campaign, 1953
Campaign against conservatism, 1955
Campaign against waste and conservatism, 1957–58
Socialist Education Movement under Revised Later Ten Points, 1964
County reform campaign, 1965
Ideological study campaign, 1965–66

RADICAL INTERNAL REMEDIALISM
Experiments with "crash planning," 1955–56 and 1957–58 and 1967–68
Elimination of rules and regulations, 1958 and 1967–68
Proposals for abolition of graduated wage system, 1958 and 1967–68
Denigration of specialists, 1958 and 1967–68
Questioning of principle of organizational discipline, 1967–68

OPEN-DOOR RECTIFICATION
San-fan campaign, 1951–52
Socialist Education Movement under Later Ten Points, 1963–64
"Fifty Days," 1966
Party rebuilding, 1968–71

RADICAL EXTERNAL REMEDIALISM
Red Guard movement, 1966–68
Mass participation on revolutionary committees, 1967–71
Revolutionary great debates, 1973–76

RADICALISM
Proposals for adoption of the Paris Commune model, 1967–68

Fig. 3. *Chinese Approaches to the Bureaucratic Dilemma, 1949–76.*

Although the Chinese have used a variety of internal remedial measures, the most important have been recruitment of officials on the basis of their political standpoint, rectification and indoctrination of officials to maintain their ideological commitment, and the use of mass campaign techniques to carry out policy. Because of their shared values, officials are supposed to work in a more disciplined, zealous, and efficient way. And because those values emphasize selflessness and public service, problems of corruption and alienation are supposed to be minimized. Finally, through the application of the campaign style of policy implementation, the bureaucracy will, in theory at least, operate in a more flexible, efficient, and coordinated manner.

The Party's continued reliance on internal remedialism is not surprising, for it was an important feature of the Chinese Communist revolutionary movement.* The need for committed Communist cadres who were ready to make sacrifices for the sake of the revolution and able to work in a coordinated and efficient manner despite poor communications between scattered base areas led to the development of techniques of indoctrination and rectification. In the same way, the scarcity of material and financial resources in the base areas promoted the formulation of the campaign style as a way of converting policy into actuality. In addition, the emphasis on rectification and indoctrination can also be traced to the Confucian values of traditional China, which held that government should be conducted by a leadership recruited on the basis of a demonstrated commitment to a well-defined set of shared moral principles.

To what extent have the Chinese attempted to control bureaucracy by making it responsive and accountable to some kind of external authority? The answer to this question constitutes our third principal conclusion: Chinese leaders have been limited in their use of external remedialism by their distrust of any form of supervision that is not controlled by the Party. Consequently, the Chinese have not actively sought to develop independent legislatures, courts, interest groups, or news media. As we have seen, when the state control system, headed by the Ministry of Supervision, threatened to become independent of Party control, it was first stripped of its authority and then abolished. Similarly, the proposals in the mid-1950's that people's congresses and trade unions might serve as some form of watchdog over the bureaucracy were never adopted.

This is not to say that the Chinese have not used external remedialism as

---

*Compare Helen Constas's discussion of "charismatic bureaucracy," the organizational form she says is most likely to result from the institutionalization of a charismatic revolutionary movement, in "The U.S.S.R.—From Charismatic Sect to Bureaucratic Society," *Administrative Science Quarterly*, 6 (1961): 282–98.

an approach to the bureaucratic dilemma. In the early years of the People's Republic, the Party itself was to be an external monitor over the state bureaucracy. In theory, it was to remain a relatively nonbureaucratic organization, and its relation to the government was to be both detached and critical. Indeed, *Jen-min jih-pao* once likened the Party to a theater audience that would watch a play and then make criticisms and suggestions about the play and its performance.[3]

But the Party's effectiveness as an organizational monitor was steadily reduced in the 1950's—particularly during the Great Leap—as the Party assumed more and more of what had previously been the state's responsibilities. The earlier separation between Party and state, so essential to the Party's ability to supervise and control the governmental bureaucracy, almost entirely disappeared as the Party's committees and departments became so deeply implicated in decision making that they could no longer serve as a critical audience. As might have been predicted, the Party turned playwright, and it also selected and directed the players. Although it might thus control the state, its new role posed a new question: Who would control the Party bureaucracy itself?

The Chinese have used a second external mechanism, popular supervision, to control both the Party and state bureaucracy. This, in turn, has taken three forms: the mobilization via the press of popular criticism of the bureaucracy, as during the Hundred Flowers movement and the revolutionary great debates of the early 1970's; the establishment of mass organizations—such as the poor and lower-middle peasant associations, the Cultural Revolution committees, and the Red Guards—to monitor the state and Party apparatus; and the selection of mass representatives to serve on the revolutionary committees formed in 1967 and 1968.

But the effectiveness of these forms of popular supervision has ultimately depended on the sanction of the Party. The very establishment of popular supervisory organizations and the mobilization of mass criticism of the bureaucracy have required the approval of at least a portion of the Party elite.[4] And the impact of criticism has depended on the response of the officials being criticized—or on the response of their superiors, at least. If the criticism is rejected, then the masses have no recourse. If the criticism passes the limits established by the Party, as it did during the Hundred Flowers period, then it is likely to be suppressed. Maurice Meisner has pointed out in his discussion of popular participation in the Cultural Revolution that the "right to rebel" was "not a right inherent in the people but one given them by the authority of the deified Mao, and thus one that would be revoked by him."[5] What our analysis suggests is that, in the final analysis, the performance of the Chinese bureaucracy has been determined not by any effective external controls, but by the internal mechanisms of the bureaucracy itself.

BUREAUCRACY AS A POLITICAL ISSUE

Bureaucracy has continually occupied an important place on the Chinese political agenda since 1949, but the dimensions of debate over organizational policy have changed substantially over time, as have the relative importance and contestability of specific organizational issues. To clarify the evolution of the bureaucratic issue in Chinese politics, we can divide the years between 1949 and 1967 into four periods.* During the period of consolidation and institutionalization (1949–55), organizational issues were relatively noncontroversial. But during the period when the costs and problems associated with bureaucratization became more apparent (1955–59), Chinese leaders began to disagree openly and intensely about the best methods to prevent alienation between the governors and the governed. In the aftermath of the Great Leap Forward (1959–67), bureaucratic issues became intimately linked with the growing dispute over socioeconomic policy and over the possible emergence of revisionism in China. Then, during and after the Cultural Revolution (1967–76), organizational questions became closely intertwined with the struggle for succession to Mao Tse-tung. Let us consider each of these four periods in somewhat greater detail.

Consolidating and Institutionalizing a New Regime (1949-1955)

For the first six years of the People's Republic, there seems to have been general agreement among Chinese leaders that the principal organizational tasks facing the Chinese Communist Party were first to consolidate the existing Party organization, and then to build a larger, more regularized, and more bureaucratic Party and state apparatus. There also seems to have been little doubt about the proper mechanisms for undertaking these two principal tasks. The two Party rectification campaigns of the 1940's served, with modifications, as models for consolidation; and the Soviet Union's structure of government served, again with modifications, as the model for regularization and bureaucratization.

This is not to say that there was no debate over organizational issues during this period. During the Rectification of 1950, for instance, there was some disagreement as to whether the principal problem was commandism among basic-level cadres or bureaucratism among middle-level

---

*A more elaborate version of the argument presented in this section can be found in Harry Harding, "The Organizational Issue in Chinese Politics, 1949–1975," in *Proceedings of the Fifth Sino-American Conference on Mainland China* (Taipei, 1976).

cadres, and whether the principal offenders were newly recruited officials, former Nationalist bureaucrats, or veteran Communist cadres. During the San-fan movement, debate focused on how serious corruption was, whether it should be attributed to cadres or to the bourgeoisie, and whether its elimination required a full-scale rectification campaign.

Thus, there was controversy over the nature and severity of organizational problems and over the proper remedies to prescribe. In comparison to later periods, however, this debate was limited. The major shifts in organizational policy in the early 1950's (e.g., the turn from intense rectification in the San-fan to more moderate rectification in the New San-fan, and the shift from concern with local-level commandism to concern with higher-level bureaucratism) seem to have been caused more by a relatively unified leadership responding to a changing organizational environment, and to unintended consequences of their previous actions, than by controversy and debate among a fractured leadership.

Facing the Consequences of Bureaucratization (1955-1959)

As the process of regularization and institutionalization begun in the early 1950's reached its conclusion, the organizational issue underwent an important change. Where the organizational problems had once been those of a young, postrevolutionary regime, by 1955 they had become those of an older, institutionalized political system. As in the previous period, there was general consensus on the principal organizational task at hand: it was necessary to combat the undesirable side effects of bureaucracy, such as inefficiency and popular alienation, and thereby to improve the system's ability to provide effective leadership and maintain popular support. But despite this underlying consensus, there was increasingly sharp disagreement over the best ways to control or eliminate these consequences of bureaucratization. As we have seen, there were four competing viewpoints in the middle 1950's: the first called for greater rationalization of the bureaucracy through simplification of structure, decentralization, and revision of irrational regulations; the second favored intensified political and ideological education, tighter Party discipline, and even an inner-Party rectification campaign; the third argued for "democratizing" the existing channels by which the people could make their views known to the Party and the state; and the fourth stood specifically for providing non-Party officials, intellectuals, and members of the "democratic parties" with more opportunity to offer criticism and suggestions to the Party.

During this period, organizational issues were also controversial because of the effect of competing organizational reforms on the distribution of power within both the Party and state bureaucracy, and among the Party, the government, the mass organizations, the people's congresses, and the democratic parties. The competing approaches and proposals of different leaders seem to be based very largely, although not entirely, on their positions in the political system and the interests of the agencies and organizations they represented. Thus, of the major participants in the organizational discussions, Chou En-lai and Li Hsien-nien seems to have represented the interests of the state bureaucracy as a whole, Ch'en Yün and Hsüeh Mu-ch'iao the opinions of the central planners and economic ministries, Ch'ien Ying and Liu Lan-t'ao the views of the state and Party control agencies, Tung Pi-wu the interests of the people's congresses, Chang Po-ch'ün the views of the democratic parties, and Lai Jo-yü the interests of the labor unions. Mao Tse-tung, Liu Shao-ch'i, and Teng Hsiao-p'ing, in contrast, seem to have assumed the responsibility of trying to aggregate these specific proposals into broader policy packages. But beyond this, Mao's personal sponsorship—in the face of substantial opposition—of criticism of the Party by intellectuals and the democratic parties indicated that he was beginning to assume a more active role as an initiator of policy in the organizational arena, just as he had done on agricultural issues a few years before.

Although the principal issue between 1955 and 1959 was how to combat the undesirable consequences of bureaucratization, organizational questions were also linked increasingly to debates over socioeconomic policy. Chinese leaders tried to influence policy by manipulating the operating procedures of the bureaucracy and the content of organizational rectification campaigns. Mao tried in 1955 to encourage more rapid economic development and socialist transformation by promoting a campaign against conservative work styles within the Party. He believed that a "high tide" of development and transformation could be achieved if officials circulated information more widely, coordinated their activities better, improved their understanding of local conditions and model units, looked for ways of reducing bureaucratic waste and inefficiency, and conducted planning in a more democratic manner. The following year, Mao's opponents sought to slow down the rate of collectivization by launching a campaign against arrogance and rashness in the Party.

In 1958, when Mao wanted once again to accelerate the pace of economic development, he launched another rectification campaign in the bureaucracy. Its emphasis on eliminating waste, raising production targets, improving bureaucratic communications, and making planning more democratic, made this campaign against waste and conservatism quite similar to that of 1955. But it introduced new elements as well. Abstract principles and political work were to be emphasized in planning; planners were asked to consider whom they served; and bureaucrats were ordered to study the desirability of radical rather than gradual change. The introduction of these new principles into bureaucratic policymaking was an important organizational technique for promoting the Great Leap Forward.

Linking Organizational Issues with Socioeconomic Policy (1959-1967)

In the aftermath of the Great Leap Forward, the debate over organizational issues began to polarize as organizational questions became closely entwined with growing differences over socioeconomic issues. There at least had been a general consensus about the principal organizational task at stake during the previous two periods, but that consensus was now gone. There was a major division between 1959 and 1965 over whether the Party and state organizations were simply plagued by corruption and inefficiency or had become revisionist. And this division was directly connected with the debate over the new socioeconomic policies of the early 1960's.

Those who believed that revisionism was a serious danger in China sought to conduct rectification to prevent its emergence within the bureaucracy. To this end, Mao installed political departments in economic agencies in 1964, began a rectification campaign at the county level in 1965, and initiated a movement to study his own writings in 1965–66. In each case, his intention was to force a critical examination of the policies adopted since 1961, that is, to force cadres to "bring politics to the fore" and consider whether the policies they were following really conformed with Maoist doctrine.

Those who supported the policies of the early 1960's, on the other hand, sought to break the link Mao had forged between rectification and policymaking and to redirect Mao's rectification campaigns toward other purposes. They argued that the flagging commitment of cadres at the basic levels to socialism and collective agriculture was much less of a problem than cadre corruption. And they said that the principal problem at the upper levels was not revisionism, but rather the declining efficiency and productivity of the bureaucracy. Mao had hoped to promote a reassessment of economic and social policy, but his rivals instead used the very campaigns he had launched to stimulate more enthusiastic and efficient administration of existing programs.

At the beginning of the Cultural Revolution, the link between organizational policy and socioeconomic policy became even clearer, as various leaders and groups discussed the question of which form of administrative organization would be most resistant to the emergence of revisionism. Mao's original position, as we have seen, was that revisionism could best be prevented if mass organizations such as poor and lower-middle peasant associations and Cultural Revolution committees could be established to supervise and monitor the bureaucracy. The leftists on the central Cultural Revolution Group and in the Red Guard movement, in contrast, argued that revisionism could be prevented only if bureaucracy was destroyed and China reorganized along the lines of the Paris Commune. Ultimately, a more moderate position prevailed—that effective policymaking and policy implementation could be assured through a combination of rationalization and rectification coupled with a limited degree of mass representation on revolutionary committees.

There were, in addition, some connections between organizational issues and the distribution of power and status within the bureaucracy during this period. The establishment of political departments in civilian economic agencies created conflict between the military officers dispatched to staff them and the civilian bureaucrats and managers whose political standpoint those officers were supposed to oversee. In addition, middle and lower-level officials may have felt threatened by Mao's proposals that poor and lower-middle peasant associations be organized to uncover cases of corruption and revisionism in the countryside. But these connections did not become apparent until the Fifty Days of 1966, when important central and provincial leaders attempted to use work teams to prevent the rectification campaign in the universities and in the bureaucracy from threatening their own political survival. In the main, bureaucratic issues were prominent during this period because of their connections with socioeconomic policy issues, not their connections with political power.

Linking Organizational Issues with the Struggle for Succession (1967-76)

Between 1967 and 1976, more than at any other time in the history of the People's Republic, organizational issues were used instrumentally. Although some leaders doubtless were genuinely concerned about problems of corruption, weakness of central control over the provinces, factionalism at basic levels, and the work style of the military, the prevailing trend during this period was to use organizational issues as weapons with which to fight other battles. Chinese leaders contending for the succession to Mao Tse-tung used organizational issues and advanced organizational programs mainly to build secure power bases and to reduce the support available to their rivals. It was for this reason that staffing questions—the ratios by which seats of Party committees would be assigned to military officers, mass representatives, and cadres; the rate of rehabilitation of officials criticized during the Cultural Revolution; the policy toward the promotion of younger cadres—were particularly controversial during this period. Each group of contenders wanted to staff the Party and state with the kind of officials they believed would be most likely to support them. It was for the same reason that questions of control were so important. Lin Piao and the military officers around him wanted to maintain the autonomy of military representatives in the Party committees—to make the army, as Domes so shrewdly pointed out, a Leninist party within the Leninist Party—because they knew that a separate military chain of command would provide a more secure power base in the Party. The moderates tried to rehabilitate large numbers of veteran Party officials and place them in positions of authority throughout the bureaucracy. The leftists, in contrast, wanted to establish the right to "go against the tide" because their power depended on the ability of junior officials, workers, and students to disobey the policies and instructions of the moderate-dominated bureaucracy.

Organizational issues were also linked to socioeconomic policy by both the moderates and the leftists during this period. Both groups recognized that they would be more likely to prevail in debates over socioeconomic policy if they first won adoption of favorable organizational programs. Questions of staffing and discipline provided one such connection between organizational issues and socioeconomic policy. A bureaucracy staffed by younger officials recruited during the Cultural Revolution would be more likely to support the "newborn things" of that period than a bureaucracy staffed by rehabilitated older cadres. Conversely, the moderates' socioeconomic programs could be realized more effectively if they could restore strict organizational discipline in the Party than if lower-level cadres were permitted to "go against the tide" and "rebel" against policies with which they disagreed.

Rectification campaigns provided a second linkage between organizational policy and socioeconomic programs. The faction that determined the themes of inner-Party rectification could thereby determine the criteria used in policymaking throughout the bureaucracy. A campaign describing Lin Piao as a rightist, for example, would reinforce the programs of the Cultural Revolution, while a campaign that criticized him for ultraleftism would weaken them. A campaign against idealism and "apriorism," such as the moderates proposed in 1970–72, would have enabled their followers in the bureaucracy to criticize the "newborn things" of the late 1960's, while a campaign against pragmatism and empiricism would have suppressed such views. The radicals' campaigns against retrogression, capitulationism, and reversal of verdicts in the mid-1970's were clearly designed to protect the socioeconomic programs of the Cultural Revolution against attack by the moderates, just as later campaigns to "seek truth from facts" were intended to expunge the influence of the "Gang of Four." It was for this reason that the definition of Party rectification campaigns was so controversial an issue from the death of Lin Piao in 1971 to the purge of the "Gang of Four" in 1976.

A survey of these four periods suggests that there have been a number of recurring organizational issues in Chinese politics—the standards to be applied for promotion and recruitment in the bureaucracy, the proper relation between central and provincial authority, the question of whether to assign responsibility for poor organizational performance to basic-level cadres or to their superiors, and so on. From a broader perspective, however, the single most controversial and enduring issue between 1949 and 1976 was Mao's repeated proposal that the Party and state bureaucracies be reformed through external criticism by groups that he himself had admitted were politically unreliable. Three times Mao deliberately mobilized groups outside the Party that he believed to be uncertain in their commitment to Marxism-Leninism and asked them to serve as instruments of organizational reform—the intellectuals in 1957, the peasants during the Socialist Education Movement, and the students in 1966. He posited that calling on these groups to criticize the Party would help give them a good political education, demonstrate his confidence in them, and thereby strengthen their commitment to socialist ideology. To rely on the unreliable, he argued, was both an effective method of organizational reform and a means of indoctrinating a sector of society that was wavering politically and ideologically. Mao's willingness to approve, even if not personally to initiate, the revolutionary great debates of the early 1970's also demonstrates his continuing interest in mass supervision as a means of controlling and reforming bureaucracy in China.

In all three instances, Mao's proposals generated enormous opposition from his colleagues in the Party. Few other leaders were willing to accept his conclusion that the masses, particularly wavering elements among the masses, could serve as reliable instruments of organizational reform. Of the major central leaders, the one who seemed closest to Mao's position on this issue, paradoxically, was Teng Hsiao-p'ing. Teng's report to the Eighth Party Congress expressed his support for Mao's proposal that the Party solicit the criticism of the democratic parties and the intellectuals; and, to a substantial degree, Teng's Later Ten Points of 1963 embodied Mao's interest in using poor and lower-middle peasants as an instrument of organizational reform at the basic rural levels. After the Cultural Revolution, to be sure, when the leftists sought to use revolutionary great debates to weaken the position of the moderates, Teng shifted his position and promoted the use of closed-door rectification. But his apparent sponsorship of "democracy wall" in late 1978 and early 1979 was in keeping with his interest in permitting external criticism of the Party.

The views of two other central leaders deserve a brief summary here. The person who seems to have been most in favor of rationalization as an approach to the bureaucratic dilemma was not Liu Shao-ch'i, but Chou En-lai. Throughout the 1950's Chou consistently expressed a preference for rationalization or, less frequently, for continuing political education. Although he may have supported Mao on socioeconomic issues on the eve of the Cultural Revolution, there is no evidence whatsoever that he shared Mao's views on organizational matters. Indeed, Chou was involved in only the smallest way in any of the rectification campaigns of the 1950's or the early 1960's, including those that involved the state bureaucracy. It is significant, for example, that Po I-po, and not Chou, was placed in charge of the San-fan campaign; and that Hsi Chung-hsün, and not Chou, supervised the campaign against waste and conservatism in the State Council in 1958. Nor did he take an active part in the discussions of rectification in the early 1960's. He was actively involved in the Cultural Revolution, but that was out of sheer necessity, and his purpose was generally to restrict and control mass participation, rather than to expand it.[6] Once the Cultural Revolution was over, Chou was notable for his resistance to the leftists' demands for continued mass supervision of the bureaucracy. As indicated in the previous chapter, Chou's report to the Tenth Party Congress in 1973 did not contain a single reference to the need for the Party to accept criticism and supervision from the masses, even though Wang Hung-wen's report had given that very point special emphasis.

Like Chou, Liu Shao-ch'i was never particularly enthusiastic about mass supervision of the Party. He seems to have shared Lenin's distrust of the "spontaneity" of the masses, warning on several occasions of their low cultural level and of their tendency to become like "wild horses" if mobilized. His report to the Eighth Party Congress made clear that he was opposed to Mao's proposal for "blooming and contending," as did his symbolic absence from the photographs of the meeting at which Mao delivered his speech "On the Correct Handling of Contradictions among the People."[7] Similarly, his views on the role of the poor and lower-middle peasant associations in the Socialist Education Movement, and of the student movement during the Fifty Days, are hardly those of a man who favored popular criticism of Party cadres. But this is not to say that Liu was simply a proponent of rationalization, as Chou En-lai appears to have been. Instead, his preferred technique for controlling bureaucracy was rectification, even intense rectification, as long as it did not lead to "excessive struggle" and did not interfere with routine work. In this sense, he was the prototypical Party apparatchik in China, for his views coincided perfectly with the organizational center of gravity of the Chinese Party.

BUREAUCRACY AS AN ADMINISTRATIVE PROBLEM

In the introduction we identified eight types of organizational malady and suggested that bureaucracies can pose serious administrative problems when they develop these maladies. Which of the eight have the Chinese suffered from? When and why did they emerge? How serious were they? And what have the Chinese done to try to remedy them? The answers to these questions will lay the foundation for the evaluation of the performance of the Chinese bureaucracy that we will present in the final section.

Lack of Commitment

Chinese leaders have consistently tried to ensure that Party and state cadres be committed to the goals of the Party and the values of the revolution. But they have often been skeptical about the success of those efforts. At various times since 1949, members of the Party elite, especially Mao, have expressed serious doubts about the commitment of Party and state officials to socialist doctrine. The explanation of ideological deviance, however, has varied markedly over the past thirty years.

Consider first the question of basic-level rural cadres. In 1950–53, in 1957, and in 1962–66, basic-level cadres were said to be insufficiently committed to agricultural collectivization, overly concerned with increasing production, and willing to continue or restore individual family farming. But the explanation of this problem varied from one period to the next. In 1950–53 the lack of commitment was traced to the rudimentary ideological indoctrination of basic-level cadres and the relative unselectivity of the process that had put them in leadership positions. In 1957 it was traced to the influence of former landlords and rich peasants, who were said to be opposed to collectivization. And in 1962–66 it was blamed both on the corrupting influence of wealthier peasants and on "spontaneous capitalist tendencies" that existed among poorer peasants. In consequence of these diagnoses, since 1957 efforts to strengthen the commitment of basic-level cadres have rarely been aimed at officials alone. Instead, rectification in the countryside has always taken the form of a socialist education campaign of one kind or another in which both cadres and peasants have been encouraged to discuss the benefits of socialist and collectivist policies. This technique derives directly from the assumption that cadre deviations can be traced to the influence of the peasants, and from its corollary that cadre commitment can be guaranteed only if the ideology of the peasantry is simultaneously transformed.

The evaluation of the ideological commitment of higher-level officials has also passed through several stages since 1949. In the early 1950's the state bureaucracy was staffed by large numbers of retained Nationalist officials, most of whom clearly had little deep loyalty to the regime or commitment to its principles. Although some could be reeducated, the Party ultimately replaced most of them through the San-fan campaign of 1951–52 and the Su-fan campaign of 1955. At the same time, it was also recognized that many urban Party cadres had been recruited under rela-

tively lax procedures and, like rural officials, had had little systematic political training. Here the solution was to rely on regular political study
classes and the rectification campaigns of the early 1950's to educate cadres
in Party programs and principles.

Since 1955 there have also been recurring complaints about the commitment of higher-level officials—complaints that continued through the
Cultural Revolution. In the mid-1950's Mao concluded that working in a
bureaucracy created strong tendencies toward conservatism. Because
deskbound officials were divorced from reality, he argued, they were unable to understand the "new and advanced" experiences that could produce a faster rate of economic growth. Their desire for economic equilib-
rium led them to allow the passive or backward sectors of the economy to
hold the advanced sectors back. And because they worked in an environment structured by routine, they were disinclined to adopt new procedures, even those more efficient than the old.

By the mid-1960's Mao had come to the conclusion that bureaucratic
officials were not just conservative, but were actually revisionist. Lin
Piao's essay on the social foundations of revisionism traced this problem to
the hierarchically routine and specialized structure of the bureaucracy.
But Mao also appears to have been concerned with the special status that
cadres enjoyed in Chinese society. As a privileged elite, bureaucrats did
not only tolerate social and economic inequalities—they even sought to
preserve and extend them for the benefit of their children.

Once the Cultural Revolution had ended, however, this interpretation
of the origins of revisionist thinking among bureaucratic officials was substantially revised. The attacks on senior cadres in 1976 traced the development of revisionism in the Party and state not to the organizational
characteristics of bureaucracy, but rather to a historical phenomenon:
most veteran officials had joined the Party during the "new democratic
revolution," not the socialist revolution. The conclusion that time had
passed such leaders by, that their thinking was outmoded, implied that
younger leaders trained during the period of socialist construction and
tempered in the Cultural Revolution would not develop revisionist tendencies even if they were given important leadership positions.

The changing analyses of the commitment of Chinese cadres to
"socialist" principles, together with the shifting definitions of what those
principles actually are, suggest caution in assessing this aspect of China's
bureaucratic performance. Without extensive interviews of a broad sample
of Chinese officials, it is virtually impossible to know the political attitudes
of Party and state cadres with any certainty. But it is reasonable to conclude that many basic-level cadres have resisted the proposition that more
agricultural collectivization is better than less, and that they have been
sympathetic to peasant demands for greater material incentives and more

individual farming. It is also very likely that higher-level officials have been more conservative than Mao would have liked, and that many of them have sought to defend their economic and social privileges against egalitarian and populist programs. And there can be little question that officials at all levels have been deeply divided, just as the Party elite has been, over the applicability of leftist programs and Maoist principles to the modernization of China. Although the Party has been able to create and maintain a corps of relatively dedicated cadres throughout the period in which it has been in power, those cadres have reflected the uncertainty and disagreements that have plagued the Party's leadership at the highest levels.

Low Zeal and Poor Morale

Despite their efforts to promote "revolutionary enthusiasm," Chinese leaders have faced problems of lethargy and inactivity among Party and state cadres at several times since 1949. Poor morale has been particularly prevalent at the basic rural levels, where only limited material benefits accompany official posts, and where cadres have often been caught between the conflicting demands of their neighbors and their superiors. But similar problems have also occurred at upper levels, where the supercharged atmosphere of Chinese political life has often bred disillusionment and confusion.

Morale problems have emerged, first of all, when national economic policies have suffered serious setbacks, as in the aftermath of the High Tide and the Great Leap Forward. The demoralization caused by economic failure has often been compounded by the tendency of national leaders to deny responsibility for unworkable policies and to place the blame for economic difficulties on their subordinates. At such times, and particularly in the early 1960's, large numbers of basic-level cadres have demonstrated their dissatisfaction with Party policies by trying to resign their official positions altogether.

Intense open-door rectification campaigns have been a second cause of poor morale in the bureaucracy. During such periods as the Hundred Flowers, the Cultural Revolution, and the revolutionary great debates of the mid-1970's, cadres felt that they had been unfairly criticized by the people they were supposed to lead, and that their authority and prestige had been undermined. Fearful of further criticism, they performed their duties in a bland, inoffensive way in the hope of affronting as few people as possible. Thus, rectification, which was supposed to increase the dedication and commitment of bureaucratic officials, may have had results totally the opposite of those intended. We will return to this point later in the chapter.

Finally, the intense struggle for succession during the Cultural Revolution, the successive purges of high Party leaders, and the rapid changes in official line produced serious disillusionment during the late 1960's and early 1970's. Cadres were dismayed by charges that they had become a revisionist elite, and they were angered by the harsh treatment of officials in ideological study groups and May Seventh cadre schools. More than any other period, the ten years between 1966 and 1976 did serious damage to official morale, so it is not surprising that an important goal of organizational policy after the purge of the "Gang of Four" was to "unshackle" the enthusiasm of cadres who had been poorly treated during the Cultural Revolution.

Inadequate Skills

The problem of recruiting cadres and officials with adequate technical and administrative skills was a serious one for the Chinese Communist Party in the 1950's, one that they surmounted relatively slowly. For the sake of clarity, let us consider basic-level cadres and higher-level officials separately.

The shortage of qualified basic-level cadres was a chronic problem during the 1950's. Few peasants had elementary literacy and arithmetic skills, and those who did usually came from wealthier families and were considered politically unreliable. The few qualified peasants from acceptable backgrounds were often reluctant to assume the responsibilities of leadership positions. If they were willing, they would rapidly be promoted to jobs at higher levels. At the same time, the need for skilled rural leadership steadily increased. Collectivization and communization broadened the range of activities for which local cadres were responsible to include not only agricultural production, but also capital construction, social services, militia work, and local industry. The "green revolution" of the early 1960's meant that cadres in the Chinese countryside were also expected to master at least the rudiments of modern agricultural techniques.

The solution to this problem was undertaken in three stages, each one reinforcing the one that preceded it. The first was the hsia-fang of higher-level cadres, on a temporary or rotational basis, to strengthen the leadership at the basic levels. This program was first conducted on a large scale in the middle 1950's, and has continued with greater or lesser vigor since. The second was the hsia-hsiang of educated urban youths to serve as accountants and technicians in the rural areas. This program, too, can be traced to the middle 1950's, but it increased in importance in the 1960's and received particular emphasis after the Cultural Revolution. The third was the development of rural primary and secondary schools during the Great Leap and the Cultural Revolution. This program made it possible for the countryside to produce its own leaders without having to rely only on "importing" them from the cities or from higher levels of the bureaucracy.

Through these measures, the Chinese have been able to develop a fairly skilled corps of basic-level rural cadres, although the level of technical and scientific knowledge in the countryside could certainly be improved. The situation remains somewhat fragile, however. After the purge of the "Gang of Four," Chinese leaders cautioned against carrying out an excessively harsh purge of rural cadres, implying that the supply of skilled and qualified leaders was not such that a wholesale turnover of rural leadership could be undertaken successfully.

Shortages of administrative and technical skills were even more evident at higher levels. Throughout the 1950's and early 1960's, discussions of the contradiction between "talent" and "virtue," or between "red" and "expert," reflected the basic dilemma faced by the Party. Most of those who had the skills and knowledge the Party needed had come from bourgeois backgrounds, and many had been trained in Western universities or in Chinese institutions patterned after Western models. The handling of this contradiction followed a cyclical pattern. When mobilizational strategies of economic development encountered difficulties (as in 1956 and 1960–61), the advice of intellectuals was more actively sought, greater effort was made to recruit them into the Party, and their working conditions were improved. When the intellectuals were judged to have demonstrated their political unreliability (as in 1957 and 1967–76), or when they were believed to be taking a too conservative approach to economic problems (as in 1957–58), power would be transferred from specialists back to Party generalists.

Despite this cyclical pattern, the overriding secular trend has been toward a synthesis of "reds" and "experts." For one thing, Chinese leaders have come increasingly to recognize the need for continuous, ongoing expert advice on policy matters and for technical specialists to implement policy throughout the bureaucracy. For another, as the older intellectuals retired, as specialists trained in the Soviet Union or China began to take their place, as more intellectuals joined the Party, and as more Party cadres developed specialized skills of their own, the stark contrast between "red" generalists and "white" specialists that had marked the 1950's began to blur.

Nevertheless, the Chinese bureaucracy remains seriously short of the skilled officials it will need to lead China along the road of economic development. Only a small percentage are university graduates, and a relatively large proportion, especially in the more backward provinces, have only a primary-school education. Few have the specialized scientific or managerial knowledge they would require to perform their work most ef-

fectively. In addition, China's officialdom is aging: in 1980 most top provincial leaders were reportedly in their sixties, and few municipal or prefectural leaders were under forty-five. This does not mean only that many
cadres are simply too old to work with vigor and efficiency; it also implies
that few younger men and women have been given the experience to move
easily into high-level positions when their superiors die or retire.[8]

Moreover, though the Chinese appear to have resolved the question of
whether or not to use specialists in bureaucratic positions, the problem of
how and where to use them still remains. In the years to come, the Chinese
will have to decide whether specialists should be restricted to staff and
advisory positions, or whether they should be permitted to occupy such
important line positions as Party secretary and government minister. As
Doak Barnett predicted on the eve of the Cultural Revolution, the emerging issue is no longer the relationship between Party generalists and non-
Party specialists, as it was in the 1950's, but rather that between generalists and specialists within the Party itself. "Trends toward specialization within the Party itself are likely to challenge those Party generalists
who are preoccupied chiefly with general problems of ideology and organization and who have tended to monopolize the top leadership posts at
every level to date."[9] One can expect, therefore, that the Chinese will be
less concerned with the political reliability of specialists and more concerned with the problems of integrating them effectively into bureaucratic
organizations.

Loss of Control

The record of Chinese leaders in ensuring Party and state responsiveness to direction from higher levels has been remarkably good. This is
because they have developed an overlapping and reinforcing set of
mechanisms to maintain organizational discipline: systematic political indoctrination, selective recruitment policies, frequent rectification campaigns, and good systems of monitoring and reporting. Together, these
techniques have usually guaranteed that central policies will be administered with a high degree of speed and vigor. Indeed, on many occasions,
particularly in the 1950's, the problem of excessive control seemed far
greater than that of inadequate discipline. During periods of mobilization
such as the San-fan campaign, the High Tide, and the Great Leap Forward, cadres were likely to carry out Party policy too zealously, regardless
of objective limitations and popular reaction.

Despite this general pattern, however, there have been occasions when
maintaining organizational control has been a problem for Chinese leaders.
A review of the instances of noncompliance, sluggish compliance, or partial compliance with central directives suggests that such problems have
occurred under three sets of circumstances.

Problems have occurred, first of all, when policy directives were vague, particularly in periods of liberalization, consolidation, or retrenchment. In 1956–57 and the early 1960's, for example, central leaders called for a retreat from the unrealistic policies of the preceding campaign, but they gave few clear guidelines as to how far that retreat should proceed. Not surprisingly, the responses of lower-level officials sometimes went beyond what central leaders were prepared to tolerate. In such cases, the clear specification of central guidelines, coupled with disciplinary measures against those who had transgressed them, was usually enough to restore control.

Problems have occurred, as well, when there was serious division over policy among the central elite. The sluggish response of the bureaucracy to Mao's policy initiatives in the early 1960's and to the leftists' revolutionary great debates in the early 1970's stemmed from officials' realization that the central leadership was not unified behind these programs, and that it would be relatively safe to ignore unpopular directives or to implement them in an unenthusiastic manner.

And problems have occurred, finally, when the program in question ran counter to bureaucratic interests. Bureaucratic resistance to such programs as administrative retrenchment, hsia-fang, and open-door rectification could always be expected, since these programs could cost officials their staffs, their comfort, their status, or even their jobs. However, if the central elites were able to demonstrate that they were united behind such programs and expected results, this opposition could generally be overcome.

Inadequate Information

Just as they have usually been able to ensure bureaucratic discipline and compliance, so have Chinese leaders generally been able to acquire accurate and timely information about economic, social, and political conditions from their subordinates and staffs. The Chinese have developed redundant channels of communication to link Peking with the basic levels; the Party, the state bureaucracy, the mass organizations, the press, and, during certain periods, the army and the police have all been used to provide reports on local conditions. At the same time, information gathering occupies an important place in Chinese organizational theory. Officials are urged to make regular personal investigations of the areas and units under their jurisdiction, to hold effective and timely meetings, and to study sample or model units in depth.[10] Keeping horizontal and vertical channels of communication open, in other words, is part of the behavior that is expected of all Chinese cadres.[11]

On the other hand, distorted and inadequate information has also been a problem from time to time. During the early 1950's, for example, the shortage of trained cadres and the lack of effective statistical techniques and reporting procedures meant that the middle levels of the bureaucracy did not always have accurate information about conditions at the grass roots. Then, a few years later, the opposite problem emerged: because of the development and regularization of the statistical system and the centralization of the bureaucracy, officials in Peking were swamped with more information than they could process. And in the early 1960's officials at the middle levels were accused of being so preoccupied with routine office work that they were not engaging frequently enough in personal inspections of local conditions.

These structural problems were exacerbated by the effect of mobilizational techniques on information flow in the bureaucracy. During both the High Tide and the Great Leap, cadres were under great pressure not only to set unrealistically high targets but also to report the overattainment of these inflated goals. At the same time, the distrust of any kind of organizational routine and the belief that auditing and accounting procedures served only to hinder the enthusiasm of the masses meant that the statistical and reporting systems were seriously disrupted. As a result, the information that reached higher levels about local conditions during these two periods was very often inaccurate.

It would be fair to say, then, that the upward flow of information within the bureaucracy has often been less effective than the downward flow of orders and directives. Still, although these information problems have been serious, it is very important to recognize the speed with which the Chinese leadership became aware of them and acted to solve them. By undertaking personal inspections, by insisting on the accuracy of information, and by opening alternate communications channels, the Chinese leadership has usually been able to acquire more accurate and complete information in relatively short order.

Inefficiency

One of China's most persistent organizational problems has been bureaucratic waste and inefficiency. Ever since China's administrative structure was put in place in the early 1950's, there have been constant complaints about overstaffing, poor coordination, and excessive administrative costs in the Party and state bureaucracies. The problem of inefficiency was given prominence on the Chinese political agenda in 1951–52 during the San-fan campaign, in 1955–57 during the retrenchment drives, in 1957–58 during the campaign against waste and conservatism, and in 1967–69 during the latter part of the Cultural Revolution. It also received considerable attention during the Socialist Education Movement of the early 1960's.

Inefficiency is, to a large degree, endemic to all large complex organizations, and China certainly experienced virtually all of the phenomena mentioned in the discussion of inefficiency in Chapter 1: the belief that greater size and bigger budgets would enable a bureaucratic agency to do better work, the use of public employment to provide jobs to a swollen urban work force, the tendency for regular promotions to transfer too many officials to the middle levels of the bureaucracy and to leave too few at the basic levels, and the difficulty in coordinating departments that have overlapping or interdependent responsibilities despite their being formally distinct.

Other instances of inefficiency stemmed from the Soviet model of administration that the Chinese Communists adopted in the early 1950's. For one thing, the attempt to centralize economic planning and management under the First Five-Year Plan, as provided in the Soviet model, proved to be highly inefficient and created a swollen bureaucracy in Peking that could not adequately coordinate the plethora of economic activities for which it was nominally responsible. For another, the use of the Party to supervise the work of the government created another kind of waste and inefficiency. As the Party took on more and more policymaking and administrative functions, its own size and complexity inevitably grew, and yet there was little corresponding decrease in the size and complexity of the state apparatus. By the time of the Cultural Revolution, therefore, the Party and the government overlapped to such a degree that there was not only poor coordination between the two, but also substantial duplication of effort.

To cope with inefficiency, the Chinese have characteristically employed such devices as hiring freezes, budget cuts, transfer of staff to lower-level positions, amalgamation of government agencies, and organizational simplification. To meet the problem of overcentralization in the First Five-Year Plan, the Chinese instituted such programs as the decentralization in 1957–58 that continued with marginal changes through 1976. And to reduce the overlap between the Party and state bureaucracies, the Cultural Revolution attempted to amalgamate the two so that the governmental apparatus would become simply the administrative arm of the Party.

These reforms appear to have had significant short-term, but limited long-term, effects. After a program of administrative retrenchment was undertaken, substantial reductions in staff and budgets were always reported, but then shortly the size, complexity, and inefficiency of the bureaucracy all would begin to increase once again. In many cases, the targets established for administrative retrenchment were simply unrealistic—and thus unattainable. It is usually ongoing processes that produce inefficiency in large organizations. No single reform measure or campaign can be expected permanently to halt them, and in this the Chinese experience has been in no way special.

The one type of inefficiency that the Chinese appear not to have experienced stems from excessive dependence on routine. To be sure, Chinese leaders have periodically expressed their concern that organizational routines and regulations were preventing cadres from responding effectively to new political or economic conditions. These concerns have usually been expressed after a period of consolidation in which new organizational procedures were established and new operating guidelines were formulated. In such cases, the tendency has been to abandon most rules and guidelines during such mobilizational periods as the Great Leap, the High Tide, and the Cultural Revolution. Once the period of mobilization was over, the rules and guidelines would be reestablished. In this way, the use of campaign techniques in policymaking and policy implementation has kept the Chinese bureaucracy highly flexible. Indeed, the problem of excessive flexibility has usually been greater than that of excessive routine.

Alienation

The degree to which Chinese officials act as a privileged elite—arrogant, overbearing, and intolerant of criticism—is difficult to measure systematically and reliably. China has a lengthy tradition of bureaucratic elitism, but Chinese Communist doctrine has placed considerable emphasis on public service, face-to-face contact between officials and the public, and politeness and consideration in dealing with ordinary citizens. Still, the Chinese have identified alienation between officials and the public as a serious problem in three different periods.

In the early 1950's the shortage of trained cadres, the flush of victory, and the multitude of tasks facing the new regime contributed to arrogance and commandism on the part of many officials. Worry that the Chinese Communist Party might become "another Kuomintang" made alienation an important target of some of the rectification campaigns of the period, particularly the Rectification of 1950 and the New San-fan campaign of 1953. In addition, the recruitment of new cadres, the development of mass organizations, and the creation of a nationwide propaganda network were all designed to reduce the gap between leaders and led by improving the channels of communication.

By the middle 1950's, however, the problem of alienation not only remained unsolved, but appeared to many Party leaders to have reached near-crisis proportions. One lesson of Stalinism was the danger that the Party and state might rule by coercion rather than persuasion and thus become indifferent to the day-to-day needs of the people. After much debate, the Party decided to attack the problem by educating Party cadres in the proper methods of handling "contradictions among the people," but this aspect of the Hundred Flowers period soon became overshadowed by the shocking criticisms raised against the Party by students and intellectuals, and the issue of alienation virtually dropped from the Chinese political agenda for another decade.

The problem of alienation finally surfaced once again during the Cultural Revolution, in part because of Mao's belief that mass resentment against the bureaucracy could be traced to the arrogance and aloofness of officials dealing with the public as well as to their revisionist policies. Accordingly, one of the principal organizational reforms undertaken during the Cultural Revolution was the codification of a cadre work style that attempted to ensure that officials would not become an uncaring and arrogant elite. The provincial regulations adopted on the subject all provided for regular physical labor, face-to-face contact with the masses, solicitation of popular criticism and suggestions, and minimization of the material and psychological benefits of office.

What this summary suggests is that, like inefficiency, alienation is a problem endemic to any bureaucracy, one that cannot be eliminated with a single campaign or a single reform. The Chinese approach has been to raise it to prominence from time to time in an attempt to reduce bureaucratic arrogance and indifference to tolerable levels. How effective their approach has been remains a subject for future research.

Corruption

Like inefficiency, corruption has probably been one of the most persistent of the eight organizational pathologies we have considered in this study. There has been a chronic tendency for cadres to use their official positions to acquire special privileges for themselves, their families, and their friends. Nonetheless, graft, embezzlement, and bribery do not appear to have reached the same level in China as in many other Third World countries.

Corruption has been identified as a serious organizational problem on two occasions, during the San-fan campaign and during the Socialist Education Movement. The San-fan campaign was primarily directed against urban officials who accepted bribes and favors from merchants and industrialists in return for favorable government action to resolve labor problems, contract disputes, taxation difficulties, and supply shortages. The Socialist Education Movement was aimed largely at basic-level rural cadres who were using their official positions to gain extra goods and money for themselves and their families in the early 1960's. In both these cases, the opportunity and the motive for official corruption were present. In the early 1950's economic policies had not been clearly specified, and auditing and monitoring systems were still primitive. Businessmen, in turn, were coming under increasing government regulation, were not assured of securing favorable treatment if they worked solely through legal channels, and had the economic resources to engage in bribery. In the early 1960's the decay of the Party and of state auditing agencies that had resulted from the Great Leap Forward meant that rural cadres could engage in extortion or graft with the hope of going undetected. And the extremely bad economic conditions during the "three hard years" tempted cadres to try to extract extra material benefits from their leadership positions.

In both cases the response to the spread of corruption was swift and harsh. The Party used mass mobilization techniques to uncover cases of bribery, graft, and embezzlement, recognizing that they might not be discovered through regular investigatory procedures. Rectification, discipline, and dismissal were then applied to cadres who had engaged in corrupt activities. Corruption was also attacked indirectly by eliminating or alleviating the conditions that had brought it about in the first place. The nationalization of urban industry and commerce in 1955–56, for example, virtually eliminated the mercantile and industrial class that had engaged in bribery in the early 1950's. The gradual improvement of the agricultural economy in the 1960's and the rebuilding of basic-level Party committees similarly reduced the incentive and opportunity of rural cadres to engage in graft and extortion.

One should also mention the corruption that emerged in the aftermath of the Cultural Revolution. As with the other two cases we have been discussing here, the monitoring and disciplinary systems of the Party and state were then relatively weak, a condition that enabled cadres to engage in graft with little fear of being caught. Even more important, the ongoing struggle for power diverted attention from corruption to such a degree that the campaign launched against it in 1970–71 (the campaign to "strike at counterrevolutionaries and to oppose corruption and theft, speculation, and extravagance and waste") appears to have been used more to eliminate leftists from basic-level leadership positions than to deal with cases of corruption.[12] Perhaps as a result, complaints of corruption were prominently featured in the wall posters displayed during the criticism of Lin Piao and Confucius, and the elimination of corruption became a major concern of Chinese leaders after the purge of the "Gang of Four."[13]

Although the Chinese have done a creditable job in controlling outright graft, they have been much less successful in limiting the exercise of personal influence and the manipulation of personal "connections" (*kuan-hsi*). These include the attempt of one official to persuade another to provide special extralegal services, or the effort of an ordinary citizen to establish the kind of friendship with a cadre that might result in special benefits.

But the problem of connections has been a topic of serious discussion at only one time since 1949: during the criticism of Lin and Confucius there was an attack on the practice of "going through the back door" to gain college admissions or desirable work assignments. At most other times the Chinese have seemed to believe that the use of connections was a normal aspect of all political life.

TOWARD AN EVALUATION OF CHINESE BUREAUCRACY

How, then, can we evaluate the overall performance of the Chinese bureaucracy? How successfully have the Chinese leaders dealt with the bureaucratic dilemma in Chinese society?*

On the positive side, the Chinese Communist Party has been able to establish a complex network of political organizations that has effectively blanketed a large, diverse, and populous nation.† That organizational network has linked central and provincial leaders with the grass roots, has provided them (most of the time) with adequate information about local conditions, and has produced relatively swift compliance with their policy decisions. In turn, the organizational network established by the Chinese Communists has been able to promote a reasonably high rate of economic development and has created an even more impressive degree of social welfare and economic equality for a developing society.

In addition, Chinese leaders have been remarkably sensitive to the emergence of any form of bureaucratic pathology in their country, and they have generally taken swift and relatively effective countermeasures. In other words, the health and vigor of the Party and state have been important to the Chinese elite, and they have devoted considerable attention to solving organizational problems. They have codified a theory of

---

*There have been remarkably few attempts to evaluate the performance of the Chinese bureaucracy. The most comprehensive is A. Doak Barnett, *Cadres, Bureaucracy, and Political Power in Communist China* (New York, 1967), Pt. 4. An insightful, but much briefer, evaluation is Ezra F. Vogel, "Politicized Bureaucracy: Communist China," in Fred W. Riggs, ed., *Frontiers of Development Administration* (Durham, N.C., 1970). More narrowly focused studies of compliance and communications in the Chinese bureaucracy appear, respectively, in Victor C. Falkenheim, "County Administration in Fukien," *China Quarterly*, no. 59 (July–September 1974), pp. 518–43; and Michel Oksenberg, "Methods of Communication Within the Chinese Bureaucracy," *ibid.*, no. 57 (January–March 1974), pp. 1–39. For an evaluation of basic-level rural administration, see Benedict Stavis, *People's Communes and Rural Development in China*, Special Series on Rural Local Government, No. 2 (Ithaca, N.Y., 1974); and Norman T. Uphoff and Milton Esman, *Local Organization for Rural Development: Analysis of Asian Experience*, Special Series on Rural Local Government, No. 19 (Ithaca, N.Y., 1974).

†According to a study conducted at Cornell, China ranked first of sixteen Asian societies including present-day Japan, in terms of effective linkages among different levels of rural administration from the villages to the provinces. The study did conclude, however, that downward communication in China is more effective than upward communication. See Uphoff and Esman, *Local Organization for Rural Development*, pp. 28, 113.

organizational management, and they have taken great pains to communicate it to their own cadres. Indeed, Chinese leaders have usually been harsher critics of the performance of their own bureaucracies than have most outside observers.

Yet a balanced evaluation of Chinese bureaucratic performance would also have to include some serious problems. Since some of these, as noted earlier, have always been inherent in the management of large bureaucracies, we should not be surprised that the Chinese, although able to limit problems of inefficiency, corruption, and arrogance, have not been able to eliminate them. For, as Almond and Powell have pointed out, bureaucratic pathologies cannot be avoided completely.[14] They can only be mitigated. This means, however, that Chinese leaders will have to continue to be attentive to organizational problems—and inventive in their search for solutions—if the Chinese bureaucracy is to maintain the levels of performance it has enjoyed in the past.

Still other problems find their roots in China's historical traditions and in its level of economic development. A poor and backward society like China will inevitably suffer from shortages of trained and skilled officials as long as its educational system remains relatively small and primitive. (One should add that the Party's suspicion of "bourgeois intellectuals" has often prevented it from using available human resources in the most effective manner, and that Maoist educational policies have often hindered the training of qualified specialists.) Moreover, the traditions of the Chinese mandarinate have probably reinforced the tendencies of Communist officials toward elitism, abuse of power, and corruption.

A third set of shortcomings can be traced to the organizational theory and techniques employed by the Chinese Communist Party, particularly its reliance on indoctrination, rectification, and mass campaigns to ensure flexibility, commitment, and efficiency in the bureaucracy. All of these techniques have had serious unintended consequences. Indoctrination and rectification have often produced stifling conformity among officials, a reluctance to take risks or independent initiatives, and disillusionment and cynicism at frequent shifts in official line. The campaign style, in turn, has often led cadres to ignore routine work, provide their superiors with exaggerated and distorted information, apply directives blindly and unquestioningly, and employ coercion to force the people to accept rapid change. The techniques associated with "politicized bureaucracy" have thus, in Ezra Vogel's words, deprived Chinese leaders of the "stable balance wheel" that bureaucracies in many countries provide.[15]

One can also raise serious ethical questions about the Party's organizational techniques. Indoctrination and rectification may help guarantee a responsive and compliant bureaucracy, to be sure. But the personal costs associated with such mechanisms are also high. An organization that demands commitment to a single set of absolute political and social values as the basis for maintaining its coherence and effectiveness, and that is prepared to subject its officials to intense psychological and social pressures to achieve that commitment, can only trouble those who value intellectual freedom and individual human dignity.

Finally, an evaluation of the Chinese bureaucracy should not only examine its past performance, but should also look toward its future. Three questions are of particular significance here. First, if China is to become a fully modernized society by the year 2000, as its leaders now hope, will it be able to incorporate specialists and technicians into a bureaucracy hitherto dominated by administrative generalists? Will Chinese leaders be able to develop procedures for bringing technical and scientific information effectively to bear on policy questions? Or will specialists continue to be somewhat suspect because of their "elitist" education, their contacts with foreign countries, their lack of contact with China's huge peasant base, and (often) their privileged family backgrounds?

Second, will the campaigns, the rectifications, and the indoctrination that have characterized Chinese political life continue to be appropriate and effective as China becomes more modernized? Will campaigns that grew out of social and economic conditions in primitive rural bases in the 1930's and 1940's still be possible in an increasingly complex and advanced society? Will rectification and indoctrination be feasible in a bureaucracy that will have to rely on highly trained professionals for policymaking and administration?

Third, and perhaps most important, will China's bureaucracy exercise a selfish and oppressive rule over a quarter of humanity, or will it be responsive to something other than its own material and political interests? China today is a society without powerful legislative bodies, an independent press, autonomous mass organizations, or a visionary charismatic leader. Unless Mao's successors are willing to undertake fundamental institutional reforms, the prospects for subjecting the Party and state to effective external controls are bleak indeed. In the absense of such reforms, the performance of the Communist bureaucracy will depend largely on its own self-control, just as the behavior of China's imperial government depended largely on the self-discipline of its officials. In the past, bureaucratic self-control produced both periods of benevolence and periods of despotism. The question for the future is whether an ethos of public service will ensure humane government, or be too weak to prevent China from evolving into an unresponsive and inflexible authoritarianism.

Notes

Complete authors' names, titles, and publication data for works cited in the Notes are given in the Bibliography, pp. 397–406. The following abbreviations are used in the Notes.

AFP	Agence France Presse
CB	*Current Background* (U.S. Consulate-General, Hong Kong)
CC/D	*Documents of Chinese Communist Party Central Committee, September 1956– April 1969*
CCHH	*Cheng-chih hsüeh-hsi* (Peking)
CCJP	*Ch'ang-chiang jih-pao* (Wuhan)
CCP	Chinese Communist Party
CFCP	*Chieh-fang-chün pao* (Peking)
CFJP	*Chieh-fang jih-pao* (Shanghai)
CHCC	*Chi-hua ching-chi* (Peking)
CKCNP	*Chung-kuo ch'ing-nien pao* (Peking)
CLG	*Chinese Law and Government* (White Plains, N.Y.)
CPPCC	Chinese People's Political Consultative Conference
CPPCC/NC	National Committee of the Chinese People's Political Consultative Conference
CS	*Current Scene* (Hong Kong)
CW	Liu Shao-ch'i, *Collected Works of Liu Shao-ch'i*
ECMM	*Extracts from China Mainland Magazines* (U.S. Consulate-General, Hong Kong)
8NC/D	*Eighth National Congress of the Communist Party of China, Vol. 1: Documents*
8NC/S	*Eighth National Congress of the Communist Party of China, Vol. 2: Speeches*
FBIS	Foreign Broadcast Information Service. *Daily Report: Communist China* or *Daily Report: People's Republic of China* (Washington, D.C.)
FKHP	*Chung-hua jen-min kung-ho-kuo fa-kuei hui-pien*
GPCR/D	*CCP Documents of the Great Proletarian Cultural Revolution, 1966–1967*
HC	*Hung-ch'i* (Peking)
HH	*Hsüeh-hsi* (Peking)
HHPYK	*Hsin-hua pan-yüeh-k'an* (Peking)
HHYP	*Hsin-hua yüeh-pao* (Peking)
HHYPP	*Hsüeh-hsi yü p'i-p'an* (Shanghai)
HIWC	*Chung-hua-jen-min-kung-ho-kuo ti-i-chieh ch'üan-kuo jen-min tai-piao hui-i wen-chien*
HNJP	*Honan jih-pao* (Chengchow)
HWJP	*Hsin-wen jih-pao* (Shanghai)
IS	*Issues and Studies* (Taipei)
JMJP	*Jen-min jih-pao* (Peking)
JMST	*Jen-min shou-ts'e* (Shanghai, Tientsin, Peking)
JPRS	Joint Publications Research Service (Washington, D.C.)
KMJP	*Kuang-ming jih-pao* (Peking)
KSJP	*Kwangsi jih-pao* (Nanning)
LNJP	*Liaoning jih-pao* (Shenyang)
MMTTT	[Mao Tse-tung,] *Miscellany of Mao Tse-tung Thought*
MTTSH	[Mao Tse-tung,] *Mao Tse-tung ssu-hsiang wan-sui!*

NCNA	New China News Agency
NFJP	*Nan-fang jih-pao* (Canton)
NPC	National People's Congress
PR	*Peking Review* (Peking)
R.	Radio
SCMM	*Survey of China Mainland Magazines* (U.S. Consulate-General, Hong Kong)
SCMP	*Survey of the China Mainland Press* (U.S. Consulate-General, Hong Kong)
SCMP(S)	*Supplement to the Survey of the China Mainland Press* (U.S. Consulate-General, Hong Kong)
SPRCM	*Selections from People's Republic of China Magazines* (U.S. Consulate-General, Hong Kong)
SPRCP	*Survey of the People's Republic of China Press* (U.S. Consulate-General, Hong Kong)
SR	Mao Tse-tung, *Selected Readings from the Works of Mao Tse-tung*
SSST	*Shih-shih shou-ts'e* (Peking)
SW	Mao Tse-tung, *Selected Works of Mao Tse-tung*
SWB	*BBC Summary of World Broadcasts* (London)
10NC/D	*The Tenth National Congress of the Communist Party of China* (Documents)
TKP	*Ta-kung pao* (Tientsin, Peking, Hong Kong)
TPJP	*Tung-pei jih-pao* (Shenyang)
TTJP	*Tientsin jih-pao* (Tientsin)
URS	*Union Research Service* (Kowloon)
WHP	*Wen-hui pao* (Shanghai)
YCWP	*Yang-ch'eng wan-pao* (Canton)

CHAPTER I

1. Lewis, *Leadership in Communist China*, p. 1.
2. Mao, *SW* 3, pp. 153–61.
3. Ch'en, *Mao Papers*, p. 53.
4. For a discussion of the concept of "political agendas," see Cobb et al.
5. On the problems of introducing professionals into bureaucratic organizations, see Etzioni; Blau and Scott; and Hall.
6. Downs, p. 78.
7. For a discussion of information problems in large organizations, see Wilensky, chap. 3.
8. This section draws on Downs, especially chaps. 2, 13; Crozier, chap. 7; and Thompson.
9. Parkinson, p. 26.
10. Katz and Danet.
11. For a recent survey of political corruption, see Scott, *Comparative Political Corruption*.
12. The harmful and beneficial effects of corruption in a developing nation are discussed in Scott, "Essay on the Political Functions of Corruption"; Nye; Bayley; and Huntington, pp. 59–71.
13. For a concise summary of some of these "dilemmas of formal organization," see Blau and Scott, pp. 242–50.
14. Hilsman, p. 152.
15. Allison, chap. 3, especially p. 90.
16. Weber, *Theory of Social and Economic Organization*, p. 337.
17. *Ibid.*, p. 340.
18. *Ibid.*
19. Weber made these remarks at the convention of the Verein für Sozialpolitik in 1909. Quoted in Bendix, p. 464.

20. Weber, *Economy and Society*, vol. 1, app. 2, p. 1403.

21. John Stuart Mill, *Considerations on Representative Government* (1861), quoted in Dunsire, p. 72.

22. Walter Bagehot, *The English Constitution* (1867), quoted in Dunsire, p. 72.

23. Merton et al., pp. 361–71. The quotation is from p. 369.

24. On goal displacement, see Downs, pp. 103–7.

25. Illich, p. 9.

26. J. Toulmin Smith, *Local Self-Government and Centralization* (1851), quoted in Dunsire, pp. 69–70.

27. Merton et al., p. 396.

28. Dunsire, p. 31.

29. Summarizing Weber, *Theory of Social and Economic Organization*, pp. 412–15.

30. *Ibid.*

31. On the government structure and political philosophy of traditional China, I have found the following works especially useful: Balazs; Ch'u; Hsiao; Hucker; Metzger; Watt; Wu; and Yang.

32. On Marxist theory, see Avineri; and Tucker, *Marxian Revolutionary Idea*. For a general history of organizational policy under Lenin and Stalin, see Cocks, "Rationalization of Party Control"; and Schapiro. On the Soviet Union under Stalin, see Brzezinski; and Conquest.

33. The evolution of Chinese Communist organizational policy can be traced in Harrison; Lötveit; Kim; and Selden.

34. Metzger, pp. 255–69, 400–405.

35. Meyer, p. 327.

36. Schapiro, p. 623.

37. Price, chap. 6; Harrison, pp. 212–17.

38. On the Cheng-feng campaign, see Harrison, chap. 16; Selden, chap. 5; and Teiwes, "The Origins of Rectification." An official account can be found in Chao Han, pp. 18–23.

39. Many of the documents are compiled and translated in Compton.

40. The quotations are from Mao, *SR*, pp. 186, 191.

41. The official history of popular supervision of bureaucracy in the Soviet Union can be found in Turovtsev.

42. Schapiro, pp. 257–58.

43. Brandt, Schwartz, and Fairbank, pp. 226–39.

44. Compton, p. 163.

45. On the 1947–48 rectification campaign, see Teiwes, "Origins of Rectification"; Harrison, chap. 19; and Chao Han, pp. 23–26. The quotations are from Mao, *SW*4, pp. 230, 186.

46. Mao, *SW*4, p. 232.   47. Fung, pp. 102, 106.

48. Balazs, p. 8.   49. Feuer, p. 363.

50. Christman, p. 290.   51. Feuer, pp. 362–63.

52. *Ibid.*, pp. 360–61.   53. Christman, p. 292.

54. *Ibid.*, p. 362. For Marx's view, see pp. 362–63.

55. Tucker, *Lenin Anthology*, pp. 301–2.

56. Christman, pp. 295, 312–13.

57. Tucker, *Lenin Anthology*, p. 404.

58. *Ibid.*, p. 401.   59. Wiles, p. 335.

60. Lenin, 3: 69–143, 367–68.   61. Mao, *SW*1, p. 134.

62. Liu, *CW*1, pp. 81–87.

63. Christman, p. 302.
64. Lenin, 3: 771–72.
65. *Ibid.*, pp. 748, 776–88.
66. Cocks, "Rationalization of Party Control," p. 156.
67. See, for instance, Stalin, pp. 532–58, 750–61.
68. Mao, *SW* 4, p. 178.
69. Hucker, p. 51.

CHAPTER 2

1. See Eckstein, *Communist China's Economic Growth*, p. 26; and Barnett, *Communist China*, p. 236.
2. Mao, *SW* 5, pp. 26–32.
3. *Ibid.*, p. 39.
4. Cited in Chao Han, p. 27.
5. It was Chou En-lai who emphasized the importance of building mass organizations; *HHYP* 2.6 (x.50), pp. 1218–22. On the creation of China's mass propaganda network, see NCNA, 1.i.51, in *SCMP* 50 (17.i.51), pp. 7–10; and *JMJP*, 3.i.51, in *ibid.*, pp. 10–11.
6. For a discussion of the importance of these middle sectors to the CCP, see Thomas.
7. Mao, *SW* 5, pp. 35–36.
8. An Tzu-wen, in *HHYP* 10 (1952), pp. 23–26.
9. Kau, "Patterns of Recruitment," p. 99.
10. Vogel, "From Revolutionary to Semi-Bureaucrat," pp. 36–60.
11. *HHYP* 1.6 (iv.50), pp. 1346–50 (emphasis added). The channels of recruitment are also discussed by Chou En-lai, in *HHYP* 2.6 (x.50), pp. 1218–22; and An Tzu-wen in *HHYP* 10 (1952), pp. 23–26.
12. Schurmann, p. 170; An Tzu-wen, in *HHYP* 10 (1952), pp. 23–26.
13. Kuo Mo-jo, in *HHYP* 11 (1951), pp. 18–22. Kuo estimated that by 1956–57 China would need 150,000 high-level technical and administrative cadres, 500,000 middle- and basic-level technical cadres, 10,000 university and college professors, and some 1.6 million teachers.
14. According to An Tzu-wen, 59 percent of the college graduates in 1952 were assigned to "economic construction departments," but the bulk of these were placed in factories and mines, rather than in administrative offices; *HHYP* 10 (1952), pp. 23–26. For the view that all 66,000 university graduates became cadres, see Vogel, "From Revolutionary to Semi-Bureaucrat," p. 45; and Kau, "Patterns of Recruitment," p. 104.
15. The number of cadres who attended these schools is cited from An Tzu-wen, in *HHYP* 10 (1952), pp.23–26.
16. *JMJP*, 18.ix.49, cited in Kau, "Patterns of Recruitment," pp. 102–3.
17. Data are taken from Kau, "Patterns of Recruitment," p. 103; Falkenheim, "Provincial Leadership in Fukien," pp. 199–244; and Solinger, pp. 93–95.
18. On the emergence of activists during the Wu-fan campaign, see Gardner, pp. 477–539.
19. *Tang-ti tsu-chih kung-tso.*
20. An Tzu-wen, in *HHYP* 10 (1952), pp. 23–26; *JMJP*, 12.ii.53.
21. An Tzu-wen, in *HHYP* 10 (1952), pp. 23–26.
22. *Ibid.*
23. The Chinese version of An's report, first published in *JMJP*, 30.x.1952,

indicated that China had some 2.75 million cadres in September 1952. The official English version revised that figure to 3.31 million. I have chosen to use the latter figure. See *People's China*, no. 1 (1953), pp. 8–11.

24. *HH*, no. 1 (1951), in *SCMP* 161 (24–25.viii.51), pp. 25–27.

25. *HH*, no. 11 (1951), pp. 30–33.

26. On the reduction, see Vogel, "From Revolutionary to Semi-Bureaucrat," p. 39; on the increase, see An Tzu-wen, in *HHYP* 10 (1952), pp. 23–26; and *JMJP*, 14.ix.55, in *SCMP* 1134 (21.ix.55), pp. 13–17.

27. On the 1952 wage and supply increases, see NCNA, 1.vii.52, in *SCMP* 367 (3.vii.52), p. 24; and An Tzu-wen, in *HHYP* 10 (1952), pp. 23–26. On the institution of free medical care, see NCNA, 27.vi.52, in *SCMP* 365 (29–30.vi.52), pp. 27–28.

28. *JMJP*, 15.iii.52, in *SCMP* 302 (25.iii.52), pp. 9–13; *CCJP*, 24.vi.52, in *SCMP* 370 (9.vii.52), pp. 19–25; NCNA, 4.i.53, in *SCMP* 486 (7.i.53), pp. 12–14.

29. Vogel, "From Revolutionary to Semi-Bureaucrat," p. 55.

30. *Tang-ti tsu-chih kung-tso.*

31. Vogel, "From Revolutionary to Semi-Bureaucrat."

32. An Tzu-wen, in *HHYP* 10 (1952), pp. 23–26.

33. *HHYP* 4.4 (viii.51), pp. 778–80.

34. NCNA, 9.vi.51, in *SCMP* 113 (10–11.vi.51), pp. 11–12.

35. Mao, *SW* 5, pp. 45–49, 50–52.

36. Vogel, "From Revolutionary to Semi-Bureaucrat," p. 55.

37. Mao, *SW* 4, pp. 363–65.

38. Lin Piao's statement, published in *CFJP*, 20.vii.49, is cited in Robinson, *Lin Piao*, pp. 185–90.

39. For a discussion of these problems in Kwangtung, see Vogel, *Canton Under Communism*, pp. 78–79.

40. See, for instance, Liu Shao-ch'i's speech to the May Day rally in Peking in 1950; *HHYP* 2.1 (v.50), pp. 5–10.

41. None of these directives was ever published in full, but excerpts from the last, together with a summary of its contents, can be found in *HHYP* 2.3 (vii.50), pp. 505–6. The precise dates on which these directives were issued by the Central Committee are also unknown, but it is likely that they came out some time in April. See *JMJP*, 23.i.53, in *Chinese Communist Propaganda Review*, no. 39 (1.v.53), p. 10. At least two regional Party bureaus had launched rectification campaigns earlier in the year that also partially addressed these problems. One was in the northwest region and began in March; see *HHYP* 2.2 (vi. 1950), pp. 254–56. The other was in the central-south region; see Vogel, *Canton*, p. 59.

42. Mao, *SW* 5, pp. 26–32.

43. *JMJP*, 1.vii.50, in *HHYP* 2.3 (vii.50), pp. 504–5.

44. The directive in question was issued by the North China bureau and appears in *HHYP* 2.3 (vii.50), p. 506. For additional discussions of the campaign, see *JMJP*, 29.vii.50, in *HHYP* 2.4 (viii.50), pp. 778–81; and *HH*, no. 8 (1952), in *SCMP* 402 (26.viii.52), pp. 20–23.

45. *JMJP*, 29.vii.50, in *HHYP* 2.4 (viii.50), pp. 779–80.

46. Cadre meetings and study classes were the principal format of the campaign, but at least in the northwestern region, work teams were formed to investigate rent reduction and land reform. See NCNA, 9.iii.51, in *SCMP* 82 (11–12.iii.51), pp. 20–22.

47. Chao Han, p. 28.

48. Liu Shao-ch'i, in *HHYP* 2.1 (v. 50), pp. 5–10; *JMJP*, 1.vii.50, in *HHYP* 2.3 (vii.50), pp. 504–5.

49. *HHYP* 2.2 (vi.50), pp. 254–56.

50. *HHYP* 2.5 (ix.50), pp. 984–88.

51. *JMJP*, 24.ix.50, in *HHYP*, 2.6 (x.50), pp. 1246–48.

52. *HHYP* 2.2 (vi.50), pp. 254–56; *JMJP*, 29.vii.50, in *HHYP* 2.4 (viii.50), pp. 779–80.

53. *HHYP* 2.4 (viii.50), pp. 779–80. At this point, the percentage of elected delegates to the Peking representative conferences was slightly higher than the percentage of appointed delegates. Elections were either direct (by industrial workers, university students, and faculty) or indirect (by peasant associations, industrial associations, and youth and women's organizations). NCNA, 2.iii.51, in *SCMP* 76 (2–3.iii.51), pp. 16–18.

54. *JMJP*, 22.viii.50, in *HHYP* 2.5 (ix.50), p. 982.

55. Chao Han, p. 28.

56. NCNA, 9–10.iii.51, in *SCMP* 12 (11–12.iii.51), pp. 20–24.

57. Chao Han, p. 29.

58. For two analyses of the San-fan campaign, see Montell; and Chen and Chen.

59. Schapiro, p. 236.

60. *JMST* (1957), p. 146.

61. On the decision of the Third Plenum, see Mao, *JMJP*, 1.vii.50, in *HHYP* 2.3 (vii.50), pp. 504–5; and *HHYP* 2.5 (ix.50), pp. 986–87. Recruitment in rural areas was resumed in mid-1952, but halted again in mid-1953; see *JMJP*, 1.vii.52, in *CB* 191 (18.vii.52); *People's China*, no. 14 (1953), in *SCMP* 622 (31.vii.53), pp. 27–32.

62. Mao, *SW* 5, pp. 483–97.

63. On the conference on organizational work, see Thomas; and *JMJP*, 27.ii.53, p. 3. On the course of the campaign, see NCNA, 9.ii.53, in *SCMP* 514 (18.ii.53), pp. 10–15; *JMJP*, 1.vii.53, in *CB* 191 (18.vii.52); and Chao Han, pp. 29–34.

64. Mao, *SW* 4, p. 374.

65. On the conditions in the control system at that time, see *HHYP* 2.5 (ix.50), pp. 994–95; NCNA, 4.viii.51, in *SCMP* 150 (9.viii.51); and Schurmann, pp. 315–22.

66. *HHYP* 4.1 (v.51), pp. 31–33; *TPJP*, 1.xii.51, in *SCMP* 247 (3.i.52), pp. 9–16.

67. The first account in *JMJP* of Kao's speech of August 31 appeared on September 17, in *SCMP* 191 (10.x.51), pp. 12–13. The full text was carried in *TPJP* on December 1, and then in *JMJP* on December 14. On the September 18 party conference, see *JMJP*, 7.x.51, in *SCMP* 204 (28–29.x.51), pp. 15–16.

68. These economic data are drawn from *People's Republic of China: An Economic Assessment*, pp. 5, 124.

69. Mao, *SW* 5, p. 78.

70. *JMJP*, 20.xi.51, in *SCMP* 223 (27.xi.51), pp. 7–11.

71. Budget data are from Prybyla, p. 82. Administrative costs rose in absolute terms between 1950 and 1951, but fell as a percentage of the total budget.

72. *TPJP*, 1.xii.51, in *SCMP* 420 (20.xii.51), pp. 7–11.

73. *CCJP*, 13.xii.51, in *CB* 157 (8.ii.52), pp. 25–26.

74. *CB* 130 (25.x.51).

75. *CB* 134 (5.xi.51).

76. *TPJP*, 1.xii.51, in *SCMP* 240 (20.xii.51), pp. 7–11.

77. *JMJP*, 20.xi.51, in *SCMP* 223 (27.xi.51), pp. 7–11.

78. Mao, *SW*5, pp. 64–70.

79. On the meetings in the East China region, see NCNA, 11.xi.51, in *SCMP* 217 (16–17.xi.51), pp. 13–14; and NCNA, 17.xi.51, in *SCMP* 218 (18–19.xi.51), p. 15. On the meeting in the North China region, see NCNA, 16.xi.51, in *SCMP* 217 (16–17.xi.51), p. 12. On the meeting in the northwest region, see NCNA, 2.xii.51, in *SCMP* 228 (4.xii.51), pp. 10–12. On the meeting in the central-south region, see NCNA, 9.xii.51, in *SCMP* 232 (9–10.xii.51), p. 16.

80. On the meeting of the Government Administration Council, see *JMJP*, 15.xii.51, p. 1. On the directive of the CPPCC/NC, see NCNA, 30.xii.51, in *SCMP* 245 (30–31.xii.51), pp. 10–11. Mao's New Year's message can be found in *JMST* (1952), p. i.

81. NCNA, 9.i.52, in *SCMP* 255 (15.i.52), pp. 4–11.

82. *NFJP*, 23.i.52, in *SCMP* 267 (3–4.ii.52), pp. 8–14.

83. See, for instance, *JMJP*, 9.xii.51, in *SCMP* 247 (3.i.52), pp. 7–9.

84. *CFJP*, 30.xii.51, in *SCMP* 254 (13–14.i.52), pp. 14–19.

85. On Shih Liang, see *JMJP*, 8.i.52, in *SCMP* 260 (22.i.52), pp. 7–8; on Liu Ning-i, see *Kung-jen jih-pao*, 3.i.52, in *SCMP* 260 (22.i.52), pp. 9–10.

86. For a list of those dismissed during the campaign, see Montell, pp. 147–48.

87. According to An Tzu-wen, the San-fan was concluded at the central, regional, provincial, and district levels by June and July 1952, and at the county level by October 1952; NCNA, 9.ii.53, in *SCMP* 514 (18.ii.53), pp. 10–15.

88. *JMJP*, 24.i.52, in *SCMP* 270 (7.ii.52), pp. 7–15; NCNA, 10.viii.52, in *SCMP* 391 (10–11.viii.52), pp. 2–6.

89. Mao, *SW*5, p. 78.

90. NCNA, 9.ii.53, in *SCMP* 514 (18.ii.53), pp. 10–15.

91. *JMJP*, 2.iii.52, in *SCMP* 292 (11.iii.52), pp. 11–13; NCNA, 18.ii.52, in *SCMP* 359 (20.vi.52), pp. 14–18; and *JMJP*, 13.iii.53, in *SCMP* 532 (17.iii.53), pp. 12–15.

92. These unintended consequences of the San-fan campaign are described in detail in *JMJP*, 27.ii.53, p. 3.

93. The text of the directive was not published until 1977; Mao, *SW*5, pp. 84–86.

94. Contemporary references to the directive can be found in *CFJP*, 21.ii.53, in *SCMP* 521 (28.ii–2.iii.53), p. 25; *JMJP*, 27.ii.53, in *SCMP* 535 (20.iii.53), p. 17.

95. *JMJP*, 12.ii.53; NCNA, 9.ii.53, in *SCMP* 514 (18.ii.53), pp. 10–15.

96. For more on commandism in the effort to modernize agricultural techniques, see *JMJP*, 11.ii.53, in *SCMP* 512 (12.ii.53), pp. 2–4. On commandism in the formation of agricultural producers' cooperatives and in the formation of larger mutual aid teams, see NCNA, 22.iii.53, in *SCMP* 537 (24.iii.53), pp. 17–18. According to later accounts, commandism had been one of the factors that had produced a "blind and rash advance" in the formation of agricultural producers' cooperatives in late 1952 and early 1953; NCNA, 3.vi.53, in *SCMP* 584 (6–8.vi.53), pp. 17–19.

97. For a detailed discussion of these problems, see *JMJP*, 27.ii.53, p. 3.

98. *JMJP*, 12.ii.53.

99. NCNA, 9.ii.53, in *SCMP* 514 (18.ii.53), pp. 10–15.

100. For regulations adopted by the North China bureau to stop these kinds of economic activities by Party members and Party cadres, see *JMJP*, 26.ii.53, in *SCMP* 532 (17.iii.53), pp. 19–22.

101. *JMJP*, 12.ii.53.

102. The administrator in question was Huang I-feng, director of the communications department of the East China administrative committee, and president of the East China Institute of Communications. For details, see *CFJP*, 19.i.53, in *SCMP* 502 (29.i.53), pp. 1–5. For comment, see *JMJP*, 23.i.53, in *SCMP* 502 (29.i.53), pp. 8–12.

103. *JMJP*, 12.ii.53.

104. *Ibid.*

105. *JMJP*, 19.i.53, in *SCMP* 498 (23.i.53), pp. 11–13.

106. NCNA, 9.ii.53, in *SCMP* 514 (18.ii.53), pp. 10–15; *JMJP*, 12.ii.53.

107. NCNA, 9.ii.53, in *SCMP* 514 (18.ii.53), pp. 10–25; *JMJP*, 27.ii.53, p. 3.

108. *JMJP*, 13.iii.53, in *SCMP* 532 (17.iii.53), pp. 12–15.

109. *JMJP*, 26.vii.53, p. 1.

110. A summary of the methods used in the campaign can be found in NCNA, 9.ii.53, in *SCMP* 514 (18.ii.53).

111. *JMJP*, 13.ii.53, quoted in Walker, pp. 82–83; NCNA, 3.ii.53, in *SCMP* 508 (6.ii.53), pp. 5–6.

112. *JMJP*, 16.vii.53, p. 1. On work teams, see NCNA, 25.iii.53, in *SCMP* 539 (26.iii.53), pp. 7–8; and NCNA, 2.iv.53, in *SCMP* 545 (5–7.iv.53), pp. 4–5.

113. *JMJP*, 13.iii.53, in *SCMP* 532 (17.iii.53), pp. 12–15.

114. The role of the supervisory system in the New San-fan campaign was discussed at the Second National Conference on Supervisory Work, held in February 1953. See NCNA, 3.iii.53, in *SCMP* 523 (4.iii.53), pp. 3–6.

115. Like the January 5 directive, the March 19 directive was not published until after Mao's death. See *SW* 5, pp. 89–91.

116. *KSJP*, 23.iv.53, in *SCMP(S)* 598 (26.vi.53), pp. 22–24.

117. On the redefinition of the campaign, see *JMJP*, 27.vi.53, in *SCMP* 602 (3.vii.53), pp. 9–12; and *JMJP*, 26.vii.53, p. 1.

118. *JMJP*, 26.vi.53, in *SCMP* 607 (10.vii.53), pp. 14–17; *TTJP*, 29.vi.53, in *SCMP* 621 (30.vii.53), pp. 37–40.

CHAPTER 3

1. Mao, *SW* 5, p. 29.

2. NCNA, 10.viii.52, in *SCMP* 391 (10–11.viii.52), pp. 2–6.

3. See, for instance, *JMJP*, 1.vii.52, in *SCMP* 366 (1–2.vii.52), pp. 3–6; *JMJP*, 18.xi.52, in *SCMP* 456 (20.xi.52), pp. 9–11; and *JMJP*, 1.i.53, in *SCMP* 483 (1–3.i.53), pp. 1–4.

4. *JMJP*, 31.xi.68, in *SCMP* 4297 (13.xi.68), pp. 6–11. This statement of Liu Shao-ch'i, quoted during the Cultural Revolution, is undated, but it expresses the commitment to rationalization that was characteristic of the 1952–55 period.

5. The rejection of "organizational forms and work methods of rural state power" occurred at a conference on civil affairs work held by the Ministry of Interior in December 1953; see NCNA, 22.xii.53, in *SCMP* 717 (30.xii.53), pp. 4–6; and *JMJP*, 23.xii.53, in *SCMP* 717 (30.xii.53), pp. 6–10. The remark that direct action of military forces and the masses would have to be replaced by a more

systematic and methodical work style appears in an editorial on procuratorial work in *JMJP*, 21.v.54, in *SCMP* 821 (3.vi.54), pp. 20–22.

6. Borisov and Koloskov, pp. 74–79.

7. On the degree of autonomy of the regional governments, see Solinger, pp. 25–34.

8. *KMJP*, 25.xii.52, in *SCMP* 494 (17–19.i.53), pp. 36–38. See also Fingar, chap. 4; and Lardy, "Economic Planning in the People's Republic of China," especially pp. 95–97.

9. Mao, *SW* 5, pp. 108–10.

10. Official accounts of the Kao-Jao affair can be found summarized in NCNA, 18.ii.54, in *SCMP* 751 (19.xii.54), pp. 4–5; in *CB* 324 (5.iv.55), pp. 4–6; and in Mao, *SW* 5, pp. 154–71. For analysis, see Teiwes, "Evolution of Leadership Purges," pp. 122–35; Bridgham, "Factionalism in the Central Committee," pp. 203–35; and Schurmann, pp. 498–517.

11. NCNA, 16.xi.52, in *SCMP* 453 (15–17.xi.52), pp. 17–18. For contemporary commentary and analysis, see *TKP* (Hong Kong), 1.xii.52, in *SCMP* 462 (29–30.xi.52); and *KMJP*, 25.xii.52, in *SCMP* 494 (17–19.i.53), pp. 36–38.

12. Mao, *SW* 5, pp. 108–10.

13. The organizational principles adopted by the conference—the "eight phrases"—are listed and analyzed by Mao in a piece included in Ch'en, *Mao Papers*, pp. 68–69. Reference to the Conference on Organizational Work can also be found in Teng Hsiao-p'ing's report; see *8NC/D*, pp. 171–228.

14. NCNA, 19.vi.54, in *SCMP* 832 (19–21.vi.64), pp. 8–9.

15. *FKHP*, vol. 1, pp. 4–31.

16. For the two directives, see note 11 above.

17. NCNA, 22.vii.51, in *SCMP* 147 (1–2.viii.51), pp. 17–20.

18. NCNA, 8.vii.52, in *SCMP* 371 (10.vii.52), pp. 12–13.

19. *FKHP*, vols. 1, 2.

20. NCNA, 24.ix.54, in *SCMP* 899 (30.ix.54), pp. 6–10.

21. NCNA, 20.ix.56.

22. P'eng is quoted in a Red Guard newspaper, *Cheng-fa hung-ch'i*, 7.x.67; Tung is quoted in Chow, p. 92.

23. *HHYP* 10 (1952), pp. 23–26.

24. For a more detailed analysis of the reform of the salary system, see Vogel, "From Revolutionary to Semi-Bureaucrat," pp. 36–60.

25. This critique of the supply system is drawn from *SSST* 18 (1955), in *ECMM* 19 (19.xii.55), pp. 27–29.

26. *FKHP*, vol. 2, p. 223.

27. The 1952 figures are drawn from *HHYP* 10 (1952), pp. 23–26; the 1955 figures are from *SSST* 18 (1955), in *ECMM* 19 (19.xii.55), pp. 27–29.

28. The text of the regulation abolishing the supply system is in *FKHP*, vol. 2, pp. 684–85.

29. The wage grades are from *Chūgoku no keizai*, pp. 23–32, as cited in Vogel, "From Revolutionary to Semi-Bureaucrat," p. 50n.

30. *Ibid.*

31. *SSST* 18 (1955), in *ECMM* 19 (19.xii.55), pp. 27–29.

32. On the April increase in salaries, see NCNA, 14.iv.56, in *SCMP* 1270 (18.iv.56), pp. 18–20. On the December 1956 reduction in wages for high-level cadres, see Chou En-lai's report to the Fourth Session of the NPC on June 26,

1957, in *CB* 463 (2.vii.57); more details can be found in *Shang-ch'en-yüeh*, 10.i.68, in *SCMM* 616 (25.iii.68), pp. 16–20.

33. See Lin Feng's speech to the NPC in July 1955, in *CB* 351 (29.viii.55), pp. 1–7; and *JMJP*, 3.xii.56, in *SCMP* 1436 (21.xii.56), pp. 5–8.

34. *JMJP*, 1.vii.52, in *SCMP* 366 (1–2.vii.52), pp. 3–6.

35. NCNA, 30.v.52, in *SCMP* 346 (29–31.v.52), p. 28; NCNA, 11.iv.56, in *SCMP* 1277 (27.iv.56), p. 11.

36. *JMJP*, 12.ii.53, in *CB* 231 (1.iii.53).

37. Mao, *SW* 5, pp. 159–60.

38. The text of a Central Committee directive on cadre study programs for 1953–54, issued in April 1953, can be found in *SCMP* 559 (28.iv.53), pp. 19–22. See also *JMJP*, 31.i.53, in *SCMP* 518 (23–24.ii.53), pp. 25–27.

39. See Donnithorne, *China's Economic System*, pp. 176–77; and NCNA, 1.viii.52, in *SCMP* 392 (12.viii.52), pp. 9–10.

40. This discussion draws largely on *JMJP*, 22.xi.53, in *SCMP* 699 (2.xii.53), pp. 11–15; *CFJP*, 18.v.54, in *SCMP(S)* 847 (14.vii.54), pp. vi–ix; *JMJP*, 24.ii.54, in *SCMP* 758 (3.iii.54), pp. 15–18; *JMJP*, 11.vi.56, in *SCMP* 1320 (29.vi.56), pp. 8–9; and NCNA, 4.i.53, in *SCMP* 486 (7.i.53), pp. 12–14.

41. *JMJP*, 14.vi.52, in *SCMP* 371 (10.vii.52), pp. 9–11.

42. *JMJP*, 22.xi.53, in *SCMP* 699 (2.xii.53), pp. 11–15.

43. *Ibid*; *JMJP*, 25.vii.55, in *CB* 351 (29.viii.55), pp. 1–7.

44. *JMJP*, 18.iii.55, in *SCMP* 1015 (25.iii.55), pp. 11–15; Emerson, p. 213.

45. On the Procuracy, see the series of three articles by Ginsburgs and Stahnke.

46. On the confusion between the Procuracy and the Ministry of Supervision, see *JMJP*, 21.v.54, in *SCMP* 821 (3.vi.54), pp. 20–22.

47. The functions of the supervisory system are described in Schurmann, chap. 5; and Cohen, pp. 193–99. See also *FKHP*, vol. 2, pp. 77–80.

48. *JMJP*, 21.v.54, in *SCMP* 821 (3.vi.54), pp. 20–22.

49. On the extension of the supervisory system, see NCNA, 5.i.53, and *JMJP*, 6.i.53, both in *SCMP* 495 (20.i.53), pp. 19–24; and *FKHP*, vol. 2, pp. 479–83.

50. See Cocks, "Role of the Party Control Committee," pp. 49–96. The principal sources on the control commissions are "Resolution on the Establishment of Party Central and Local Control Committees," adopted by the National Conference of the Party on March 31, 1955, in *CB* 324 (5.iv.55), pp. 7–9; and the *Constitution of the Communist Party of China*.

51. A. Doak Barnett's otherwise comprehensive description of the Chinese state and Party apparatus in *Cadres, Bureaucracy, and Political Power* has only two passing references to the control commissions.

52. The directive is discussed in *CFJP*, 11.vii.52, in *SCMP* 377 (17–19.vii.52), pp. 16–18. For the date of the directive, see Chao Han, p. 31.

53. Mao, *SW* 5, pp. 108–9.

54. Mao, in Ch'en, *Mao Papers*, pp. 68–69.

55. *JMJP*, 18.iii.54, in *SCMP* 781 (3–5.iv.54), pp. 33–38.

56. Solinger, pp. 125–29.

57. *JMJP*, 19.i.53, in *SCMP* 498 (23.i.53), pp. 11–13.

58. On the supervisory correspondents, see NCNA, 25.viii.52, in *SCMP* 403 (27.viii.52), pp. 7–9; and Schurmann, chap. 5. On the procuratorial correspondents, see the three articles by Ginsburgs and Stahnke; on presenting complaints to Party control commissions, see Cohen, pp. 188–92.

59. See, in particular, *JMJP*, 18.xi.54, in *SCMP* 961 (5.i.55), pp. 29–35.

60. NCNA, 6.viii.55, in *SCMP* 1106 (10.viii.55), pp. 13–14.
61. Vogel, "From Revolutionary to Semi-Bureaucrat."
62. This resistance was apparently expressed at the National Conference on Financial and Economic Work, June-August 1953; Lieberthal, *Research Guide,* pp. 59–60.
63. Schurmann, chap. 5.
64. For Mao's endorsement of formalization, see *SW*5, p. 145. For his endorsement of centralization, see *SW*5, pp. 108–9. For his advocacy of greater technical skills in the Party and state, see *SW*5, pp. 159–60.
65. For P'eng's and Tung's views, see the citations in notes 20–22. For Lo Jui-ch'ing's position, see *CB* 345 (9.viii.55).
66. Mao, *SW*5, pp. 110–11, 166, 170.

CHAPTER 4

1. *JMJP*, 21.iv.55, in *SCMP* 1042 (6.v.55), pp. 21–23.
2. *CFJP*, 5.vii.55, quoted in Kau, "Recruitment and Mobility," p. 113.
3. *JMJP*, 17.iv.55, in *SCMP* 1042 (6.v.55), pp. 14–17.
4. *JMJP*, 21.iv.55, in *SCMP* 1042 (6.v.55), pp. 21–23.
5. *T'ung-chi kung-tso t'ung-hsün* (Statistical Work Bulletin), no. 23 (1956), in JPRS 17199 (8.i.63), pp. 11–24.
6. Mao, *SW*5, pp. 292–95.
7. *CHCC* 9 (1957), pp. 21–24.
8. See Fingar, chap. 7.
9. *HH*9 (1955), in *ECMM* 14 (14.xi.55), pp. 9–18.
10. Mao, *SW*5, p. 115.
11. Selden, pp. 212–16.
12. *JMJP*, 17.iv.55, in *SCMP* 1042 (6.v.55), pp. 14–17.
13. *JMST* (1956), pp. 235–36; *FKHP*, vol. 2, pp. 120–28.
14. Target figures are drawn from *FKHP*, vol. 2, pp. 117–19.
15. *Ibid.*
16. *JMJP*, 9.xii.56, in *SCMP* 1442 (3.i.57), pp. 10–12.
17. *FKHP*, vol. 2, pp. 113–17.
18. *Ibid.*
19. *Ibid.*
20. *HHPYK* 4 (1957), pp. 52–53; NCNA, 21.i.57, in *SCMP* 1464 (6.ii.57), p. 15.
21. *NFJP*, 24.ix.55, in *SCMP(S)* 1237 (29.ii.56).
22. *JMJP*, 9.xii.56, in *SCMP* 1442 (3.i.57), pp. 10–12.
23. *Ibid.*
24. *JMJP*, 18.xii.56, in *SCMP* 1442 (3.i.57), pp. 9–10.
25. Mao, *SW*5, pp. 184–207. Quotations are from pp. 187–88.
26. *Ibid.*, pp. 211–34.
27. *Ibid.*, pp. 201, 217.
28. Mao, in *IS* 10.8 (v.74), pp. 95–99; *SW*5, p. 334.
29. Mao, *SW*5, pp. 277–80.
30. See MacFarquhar, *Origins of the Cultural Revolution*, pp. 19–23.
31. Mao, *MMTTT*, pp. 27–29; Mao, *SW*5, pp. 238–41; Mao, in *IS* 10.8 (v.74), pp. 95–99.
32. Mao, *SW*5, pp. 238–41.   33. *Ibid.*
34. Mao, *MMTTT*, pp. 27–29.   35. Mao, *SW*5, p. 222.

36. *Ibid.*, pp. 277–80.   37. Mao, *MMTTT*, pp. 27–29.

38. Mao, *SW*5, pp. 277–80.

39. NCNA, 2.i.56, in *SCMP* 1210 (18.i.56), pp. 23–24.

40. *JMJP*, 6.xii.55, in *SCMP* 1188 (14.xii.55), pp. 5–10.

41. NCNA, 2.i.56, in *SCMP* 1210 (18.i.56), pp. 23–24.

42. *Ibid.*

43. *JMJP*, 15.i.56, in *SCMP* 1214 (24.i.56), pp. 13–16.

44. MacFarquhar, *Origins of the Cultural Revolution*, p. 30.

45. *JMJP*, 1.i.56, in *SCMP* 1201 (5.i.56), pp. 8–13.

46. MacFarquhar, *Origins of the Cultural Revolution*, p. 29.

47. *JMJP*, 20.vi.56, in *SCMP* 1321 (3.vii.56), pp. 11–14.

48. *Ibid.*

49. *JMJP*, 16.vi.56, in *CB* 392 (26.vi.56), pp. 1–18.

50. *TKP*, 24.iv.56, in *SCMP* 1289 (15.iv.56), pp. 7–9.

51. NCNA, in *SCMP* 1264 (10.iv.56), pp. 3–7.

52. Mao, *MMTTT*, p. 32.   53. Fingar, pp. 167–76.

54. Mao, *MMTTT*, p. 32.   55. Mao, *SW*5, pp. 292–95.

56. Bowie and Fairbank, pp. 128–44. See also Chou's political report to the CPPCC/NC on January 31, in *CB* 377 (15.ii.56), pp. 6–8; and Lu Ting-i's "Let One Hundred Flowers Bloom, Let One Hundred Schools of Thought Contend," in *JMJP*, 13.vi.56, in *CB* 406 (15.viii.56).

57. *JMJP*, 21.iii.56, in *SCMP* 1259 (3.iv.56), pp. 21–23.

58. NCNA, 12.iii.56, in *SCMP* 1259 (3.iv.56), pp. 17–19.

59. Mao, *SW*5, pp. 292–95.

60. The meetings are referred to in *8NC/D*, p. 310.

61. The draft was mentioned by Chou En-lai. See NCNA, 30.vi.56, in *CB* 398 (12.vii.56), p. 9.

62. *JMJP*, 18.xi.57, in *SCMP* 1665 (5.xii.57), pp. 1–10.

63. *8NC/D*, p. 310.

64. *CHCC* 9 (1957), pp. 21–24.

65. *HIWC*, p. 26.

66. Hsüeh himself claimed to be expanding upon Ch'en's views, which had been detailed in *8NC/S*, pp. 157–76. So, apparently, was Li; see *8NC/S*, pp. 288–303.

67. *8NC/D*, pp. 52, 56, 77–78.

68. *Ibid.*

69. *JMJP*, 18.xi.57, in *SCMP* 1665 (5.xii.57), pp. 1–10.

70. Lardy, "Centralization and Decentralization," pp. 25–60; and Lardy, "Economic Planning in the People's Republic," pp. 94–115.

71. *JMJP*, 18.xi.57, in *SCMP* 1665 (5.xii.57), pp. 10–14.

72. Merton et al., p. 396.

73. Mao, *SW*5, pp. 292, 297.

74. Mao, in *IS* 10.8 (v.74), pp. 95–99.

75. Mao, *SW*5, p. 226.

76. *Ibid.*, p. 246.

CHAPTER 5

1. The text of Khrushchev's speech can be found in *Anti-Stalin Campaign*, pp. 1–89.

2. *JMJP*, 5.iv.56, in Bowie and Fairbank, pp. 144–51.

3. Mao, *SW* 5, p. 341.
5. See note 2 above.
7. *Ibid.*, p. 116.
8. Mao, *SW* 5, p. 314; see also pp. 284–307, especially pp. 284–85, 306.
9. Mao, in *8NC/D*, pp. 7–11.
10. MacFarquhar, *Origins of the Cultural Revolution*, pp. 110–12.
11. *8NC/S*, pp. 288–303.
13. *JMST* (1957), pp. 132–33.
15. *8NC/S*, pp. 199–205.
17. *Ibid.*, pp. 153, 150.
18. *JMJP*, 29.ix.56, in *SCMP* 1435 (20.xii.56), pp. 11–17.
19. *8NC/S*, pp. 5–16.
20. *Ibid.*, pp. 79–97.
21. NCNA, 12.iii.57, in *CB* 444 (3.iv.57), pp. 1–8.
22. MacFarquhar, *Origins of the Cultural Revolution*, p. 115.
23. *8NC/D*, pp. 171–228.
24. *Ibid.*, p. 198.
25. *8NC/S*, pp. 236–47.
26. *Ibid.*, pp. 348–66. Li had made a similar argument at the NPC earlier in the year. See *HIWC*, pp. 288–98.
27. *8NC/S*, p. 363.
28. *CB*, 3.iv.57, pp. 23–27. Chang had foreshadowed these proposals in July 1956, when he had suggested that the CPPCC be given a formal supervisory role in state affairs. NCNA, 4.vii.56, in *SCMP* 1324 (9.vii.56), pp. 6–7.
29. *8NC/D*, pp. 263–328.
31. *Ibid.*
33. *Ibid.*, pp. 317–22.
35. *Ibid.*, p. 37.
37. *Ibid.*, p. 73.
39. *Ibid.*, pp. 102–3.
41. *Ibid.*, p. 174.
43. *Ibid.*, p. 181.
45. *Ibid.*, pp. 7–11.
47. *CC/D*, pp. 105–8.
48. *HIWC*, p. 21; NCNA, 29.vi.57, in *CB* 464 (5.vii.57), p. 3.
49. NCNA, 28.xi.56, in *SCMP* 1415 (21.xi.56), p. 5.
50. *HWJP*, 28.xii.56, in *SCMP* 1456 (23.i.57), pp. 16–18.
51. *JMJP*, 18.xii.56, in *SCMP* 1442 (3.i.57), p. 15.
52. *HHPYK* 3 (1957), pp. 16–18.
53. *HHPYK* 4 (1957), pp. 52–53.
54. NCNA, 26.i.57, in *SCMP* 1464 (6.ii.57), p. 15.
55. NCNA, 3.i.57, in *SCMP* 1451 (16.i.57), pp. 20–21.
56. NCNA, 27.i.57, in *SCMP* 1464 (6.ii.57), pp. 10–11.
57. NCNA, 26.xii.56, in *SCMP* 1448 (11.i.57), pp. 21–22; *HWJP*, 28.xii.56, in *SCMP* 1456 (23.i.57), pp. 16–18.
58. NCNA, 16.ii.57, in *SCMP* 1447 (26.ii.57), pp. 3–4.
59. NCNA, 2.xii.56, in *SCMP* 1442 (3.i.57), pp. 23–24.
60. NCNA, 17.i.57, in *SCMP* 1466 (8.ii.57), pp. 12–13; *NFJP*, 12.iii.57, in *SCMP* 1524 (7.v.57), pp. 16–17.
61. On Kansu, see NCNA, 22.iii.57, in *SCMP* 1504 (4.iv.57), pp. 15–16.

4. *Ibid.*, pp. 284–307, 384–421.
6. *8NC/D*, p. 37.
12. *Ibid.*, p. 294.
14. *Ibid.*
16. *Ibid.*, pp. 147–56.
30. *Ibid.*, p. 279.
32. *Ibid.*, pp. 310–12.
34. *Ibid.*, pp. 308–9.
36. *Ibid.*, pp. 75–78.
38. *Ibid.*, p. 101.
40. *Ibid.*, pp. 104–7.
42. *Ibid.*, pp. 186–87.
44. *Ibid.*, pp. 221–22.
46. *Ibid.*, pp. 126–29, 131–34.

62. See, for example, *JMJP*, 26.i.57, in *SCMP* 1467 (11.ii.57), pp. 6–8.
63. NCNA, 22.iii.57, in *SCMP* 1504 (4.iv.57), pp. 15–16.
64. On opposition to the campaign, see *JMJP*, 15.xii.56, in *SCMP* 1442 (3.i.57), p. 14; and *JMJP*, 26.i.57, in *SCMP* 1467 (11.ii.57), pp. 6–8.
65. *JMJP*, 7.xii.56, in *SCMP* 1442 (3.i.57), pp. 18–19.
66. NCNA, 6.xii.56, in *SCMP* 1442 (3.i.57), pp. 24–25.
67. *JMJP*, 22.i.57, in *HHPYK* 5 (1957), pp. 25–26.
68. NCNA, 17.i.57, in *SCMP* 1466 (8.i.57), pp. 12–13.
69. Teiwes, "Purge of Provincial Leaders," pp. 24–25.
70. NCNA, 3.iv.57, in *SCMP* 1519 (30.iv.57), pp. 3–4.
71. NCNA, 29.vi.57, in *CB* 464 (5.vii.57), p. 24.
72. NCNA, 11.ix.57, in *SCMP* 1611 (17.ix.57), p. 15; *JMJP*, 6.x.57, in *SCMP* 1631 (15.x.57), pp. 1–3.
73. *Jen-min chiao-yü* (People's Education), no. 84 (1957), in *ECMM* 89 (8.vii.57), pp. 26–31.
74. *Liang-shih* (Grain), no. 5 (1957), in *ECMM* 89 (8.vii.57), pp. 6–9.
75. *JMJP*, 1.i.57, in *SCMP* 1446 (9.i.57), pp. 6–9.
76. Mao, *SW*5, pp. 351–52.
77. NCNA, 23.ii.57, in *SCMP* 1483 (6.iii.57), pp. 16–22.
78. NCNA, 14.v.57, in *SCMP* 1536 (23.v.57), pp. 17–22.
79. Mao, *SW*5, pp. 352–53.
80. *Ibid.*, p. 345.
81. *Ibid.*, p. 353.
82. *Ibid.*, pp. 345, 353, 384–421, 422–35, 436–39; Mao, *MMTTT*, pp. 63–71.
83. Mao, *SW*5, pp. 396–99. See also p. 342.
84. *Ibid.*, p. 373.
85. *Ibid.*, pp. 404–6, 422–35.
86. Mao, *MMTTT*, pp. 64–65.
87. Mao, in *CLG*, 9.3 (Fall 1976), pp. 21–22.
88. *Ibid.*, p. 25.
89. Mao, *SW*5, p. 358. See also p. 374.
90. *Ibid.*, p. 345.
91. *Ibid.*, pp. 423, 429.
92. Mao, *MMTTT*, p. 64.
93. Mao, *SW*5, pp. 343–44.
94. Mao, *MMTTT*, p. 67.
95. *JMJP*, 23.iv.57, in *SCMP* 1518 (29.iv.57), pp. 1–5.
96. Mao, *MMTTT*, p. 67. The first major *JMJP* editorial summarizing Mao's speech on handling nonantagonistic contradictions was published on April 13. See *SCMP* 1512 (17.iv.57), pp. 1–5.
97. NCNA, 30.iv.57, in *SCMP* 1523 (6.v.57), pp. 40–42.
98. Ma T'ieh-ting, "Bureaucratism and the Radicalism of the Petty Bourgeoisie," in *Chung-kuo ch'ing-nien pao* (Chinese youth), 16.i.57, in *ECMM* 73 (11.iii.57), pp. 14–20.
99. NCNA, 19.iv.57, in *SCMP* 1518 (29.iv.57), pp. 39–40.
100. MacFarquhar, *Origins of the Cultural Revolution*, pp. 253–57.
101. Cf. Mao's statements in *SW*5, pp. 315, 348, 428; and in *8NC/D*, p. 9.
102. Mao, *SW*5, pp. 434–35. See also pp. 440–41.
103. *JMJP*, 5.iii.57, in *SCMP* 1511 (16.iv.57), pp. 24–36.
104. Solomon, *Mao's Revolution*, chap. 17.
105. *JMJP*, 5.iii.57, in *SCMP* 1511 (16.iv.57), pp. 24–36.
106. MacFarquhar, *Origins of the Cultural Revolution*, p. 178.

107. Liu, *CW*2, pp. 423–34.

108. *JMJP*, 7.i.57, in *CB* 452 (31.v.57), pp. 1–3.

109. *JMJP*, 6.iv.57, in *SCMP* 1519 (30.iv.57), pp. 1–3. See also Mao, *SW*5, p. 425.

110. *JMJP*, 23.iv.57, in *SCMP* 1518 (29.iv.57), pp. 1–5.

111. NCNA, 18.iii.57, in *SCMP* 1496 (25.iii.57), pp. 6–7.

112. *JMJP*, 21.iv.57, in *SCMP* 1521 (2.v.57), pp. 9–11; *JMJP*, 7.v.57, in *SCMP* 1531 (16.v.57), pp. 1–14.

113. See Harper.

114. NCNA, 17.iv.57, in *SCMP* 1517 (26.iv.57), pp. 1–4.

115. NCNA, 30.iv.57, in *SCMP* 1523 (6.v.57), pp. 40–42.

116. *JMJP*, 26.iv.57, in *SCMP* 1524 (7.v.57), pp. 1–4.

117. *Ibid.* For Li Wei-han's speech to the Eighth Party Congress, see *8NCIS*, pp. 348–66.

118. On the campaign in central government agencies, see *JMJP*, 1.v.57, in *SCMP* 1527 (10.v.57), p. 12; and NCNA, 9.v.57, in *SCMP* 1537 (24.v.57), pp. 5–8. On the campaign in the departments of the Central Committee, see NCNA, 30.iv.57, in *SCMP* 1525 (8.v.57); and *JMJP*, 2.v.57, in *SCMP* 1527 (10.v.57), p. 13.

119. NCNA reports from Shensi, Kiangsu, Hopei, Shantung, Tsinghai, Shansi, Peking, Liaoning, Heilungkiang, and Honan can all be found in *SCMP* 1527 (10.v.57).

120. On the first forum, see the collection of NCNA reports in *SCMP* 1543 (4.vi.57), pp. 2–37; on the second, see the reports in *SCMP* 1550 (14.vi.57), pp. 12–18. For the State Council meeting, see the reports in *SCMP* 1549 (13.vi.57), pp. 9–19.

121. Domes, *Internal Politics*, pp. 62–63.

122. See MacFarquhar, *Hundred Flowers Campaign*, pp. 145–53; and Doolin.

123. Mao, *SW*5, p. 447; and MacFarquhar, *Origins of the Cultural Revolution*, p. 220.

124. MacFarquhar, *Hundred Flowers Campaign*, pp. 210–11.

125. *Ibid.*, p. 49.

126. *Ibid.*, p. 212.

127. On the criticisms of cadre policy, see An Tzu-wen, in *CKCNP*, 20.ix.57, in *SCMP* 1623 (3.x.57). See also *CKCNP*, 18.xi.57, in *SCMP* 1676 (20.xii.57); and *SSST* 16 (1957), in *ECMM* 107 (12.xi.57), pp. 20–24.

128. See Teiwes, "Purge of Provincial Leaders," pp. 23–24.

129. MacFarquhar, *Hundred Flowers Campaign*, p. 68.

130. *Ibid.*, p. 44.

131. *Ibid.*, pp. 55, 65–66, 75, 87, 140, 211, 222.

132. *Ibid.*, p. 227.

133. One professor called the NPC and the CPPCC "paper flowers on the facade of democracy." *Ibid.*, p. 108.

134. *Ibid.*, pp. 46–47.

135. Teiwes, "Purge of Provincial Leaders," pp. 20–21.

136. See note 120. See also *HH* 15 (1957), in *ECMM* 104 (22.x.57), pp. 1–5; *SSST* 17 (1955), in *ECMM* 107 (12.xi.57); *HH* 17 (1957), in *ECMM* 107 (12.xi.57), pp. 4–13; and MacFarquhar, *Hundred Flowers Campaign*, pp. 42, 51, 227.

137. MacFarquhar, *Hundred Flowers Campaign*, pp. 47–48.

138. *Ibid.*, pp. 72, 142, 227.
139. *Ibid.*, pp. 56–57, 107.
140. *Ibid.*, chap. 7.
141. Teiwes, "Purge of Provincial Leaders."
142. Teiwes, "Rectification Campaigns and Purges."
143. Allison, p. 176.
144. Mao, *SW*5, p. 378.
145. *Ibid.*, pp. 438–39. In this passage Mao was speaking of the army, but there is little doubt that his analysis was applicable to the Party as well.
146. *Ibid.*, pp. 344–45.   147. *Ibid.*, p. 350.
148. *Ibid.*, p. 418.   149. *Ibid.*, pp. 436–37.

CHAPTER 6

1. Mao, *SW*5, pp. 448–50.   2. *Ibid.*, p. 467.
3. *Ibid.*, p. 457.   4. *Ibid.*, p. 466.
5. Mao, in Bowie and Fairbank, p. 392.
6. Mao, *SW*5, p. 498.   7. *Ibid.*, pp. 484–85.
8. *Ibid.*, p. 482.   9. *Ibid.*, p. 456.
10. *Ibid.*, pp. 458–59.
11. MacFarquhar, *Origins of the Cultural Revolution*, chap. 18.
12. Bowie and Fairbank, p. 323.
13. MacFarquhar, *Origins of the Cultural Revolution*, p. 302.
14. *Ibid.*, p. 291.
15. Bowie and Fairbank, pp. 341–63.
16. *Ibid.*, pp. 345, 360.
17. *Ibid.*, pp. 350, 354.
18. An Tzu-wen, in *JMJP*, 5.xii.57, in *SCMP* 1676 (20.xii.57), pp. 3–11.
19. NCNA, 26.xi.57, in *SCMP* 1668 (10.xii.57), p. 12.
20. *JMJP*, 25.i.58, in *CB* 491 (7.ii.58), pp. 1–34.
21. *JMJP*, 6.x.57, in *SCMP* 1631 (15.x.57), pp. 1–3.
22. *CKCNP*, 18.xi.57, in *SCMP* 1876 (20.xii.57), pp. 11–16.
23. Bowie and Fairbank, pp. 361–62.
24. *CCHH* 9 (1957), in *ECMM* 106 (4.xi.57), pp. 3–5.
25. *CCHH* 9 (1957), in *ECMM* 112 (23.xii.57), pp. 1–4.
26. *Ibid.*
27. Bowie and Fairbank, p. 350.
28. *Ibid.*, p. 353.
29. Mao, in Bowie and Fairbank, p. 392.
30. Bowie and Fairbank, p. 398.
31. *JMJP*, 25.i.58, in *CB* 491 (7.ii.58), pp. 1–34.
32. NCNA, 25.xi.57, in *SCMP* 1671 (13.xii.57), pp. 1–8.
33. Mao, *SW*5, p. 506.
34. NCNA, 23.vii.57, in *SCMP* 1589 (12.viii.57), pp. 13–14.
35. NCNA, 22.x.57, and 3.xi.57, in *SCMP* 1654 (19.xi.57), pp. 12–15.
36. NCNA, 25.xi.57, in *SCMP* 1671 (13.xii.57), pp. 1–8.
37. NCNA, 6.xii.57, in *SCMP* 1678 (24.xii.57), pp. 1–4.
38. NCNA, 6.xii.57, in *SCMP* 1678 (24.xii.57), pp. 4–7.
39. *JMJP*, 25.i.58, in *CB* 491 (7.ii.58), pp. 1–34.
40. NCNA, 28.x.57, in *SCMP* 1654 (19.xi.57), pp. 7–8.
41. NCNA, 1.xi.57, in *SCMP* 1654 (19.xi.57), pp. 9–10.

42. The May 14 directive was carried in NCNA, 14.v.57, in *SCMP* 1532 (17.v.57), pp. 2–4.

43. NCNA, 26.xi.57, in *SCMP* 1668 (10.xii.57), pp. 8–10; NCNA, 23.ii.59, in *SCMP* 1724 (5.iii.58), pp. 5–6.

44. *LNJP*, 11.xii.57, in *SCMP* 1723 (4.iii.58), pp. 10–12.

45. *JMJP*, 29.ix.58, in *SCMP* 1884 (29.x.58), p. 103.

46. For Kwangtung, see *JMJP*, 9.xii.57, in *SCMP* 1683 (3.i.58), pp. 28–29; for Anhwei, see *JMJP*, 9.x.57, in *SCMP* 1643 (1.xi.57), pp. 16–17.

47. NCNA, 29.x.58, in *SCMP* 1869 (7.x.58), pp. 1–2.

48. The term was used by Hsi Chung-hsün, who with his deputy Chi Yen-ming headed the State Council's hsia-fang task force. See NCNA, 25.xi.57, in *SCMP* 1671 (13.xii.57), pp. 1–8.

49. *Ibid.* See also *JMJP*, 9.x.57, in *SCMP* 1643 (1.xi.57), pp. 16–17; *HNJP*, 10.xii.57, in *SCMP* 1723 (4.iii.58), pp. 15–21; and NCNA, 23.ii.58, in *SCMP* 1724 (5.iii.58), pp. 5–6.

50. NCNA, 25.xi.57, in *SCMP* 1671 (13.xii.57), pp. 1–8.

51. *JMJP*, 25.i.58, in *CB* 491 (7.ii.58), pp. 1–34.

52. Mao, in *CLG* 9.3 (Fall 1976), p. 64.

53. Li Hsien-nien, in NCNA, 12.ii.58, in *CB* 493 (17.ii.58), p. 2.

54. Mao, in Schram, *Political Thought*, p. 408.

55. Liu Shao-ch'i, in Bowie and Fairbank, p. 429.

56. Mao, in Schram, *Chairman Mao*, p. 94.

57. Mao, in Ch'en, *Mao Papers*, p. 63.

58. See MacFarquhar, *Origins of the Cultural Revolution*, pp. 293–94; and *China: A Reassessment of the Economy*, p. 23.

59. Mao, *SW* 5, pp. 490–91.

60. Bowie and Fairbank, pp. 352–53.

61. NCNA, 7.xii.57, in *CB* 483 (16.xii.57), p. 9.

62. *Ibid.*, p. 6.

63. *JMJP*, 1.i.58, in *SCMP* 1685 (7.i.58), pp. 1–6.

64. Mao, in Schram, *Chairman Mao*, pp. 111, 113.

65. Mao, in Ch'en, *Mao Papers*, p. 63.

66. Mao, in Schram, *Chairman Mao*, p. 67.

67. NCNA, 8.iv.58, and *JMJP*, 2.iv.58, both in *SCMP* 1764 (5.v.58), pp. 4–9.

68. "Sixty Points," nos. 7, 10, 31–33, in Ch'en, *Mao Papers*, pp. 57–76; Mao, *SW* 5, p. 483; and Mao, in Schram, *Chairman Mao*, p. 106.

69. Mao, *SW* 5, p. 488.

70. "Sixty Points," no. 8, in Ch'en, *Mao Papers*, pp. 59–60.

71. "Sixty Points," no. 9, in Ch'en, *Mao Papers*, p. 60.

72. "Sixty Points," no. 4, in Ch'en, *Mao Papers*, p. 59.

73. NCNA, 28.x.57, in *SCMP*, 1654 (19.xi.57), pp. 7–8; NCNA, 1.xi.57, in *SCMP* 1654 (19.xi.57), pp. 9–10; NCNA, 19.i.58, in *SCMP* 1705 (4.i.58), pp. 2–8; Po I-po, in *CB* 494 (19.ii.58).

74. NCNA, 3.iii.58, in *SCMP* 1727 (10.iii.58), pp. 1–2.

75. See the introduction to the "Sixty Points," Ch'en, *Mao Papers*, pp. 57–58.

76. "Sixty Points," no. 23, in Ch'en, *Mao Papers*, pp. 66–67.

77. Mao, in Schram, *Chairman Mao*, pp. 98, 100.

78. Mao, *MMTTT*, pp. 129–32.

79. See, for instance, NCNA, 23.iii.58, in *SCMP* 1741 (28.iii.58), pp. 1–3;

NCNA, 30.iv.58, in *SCMP* 1773 (16.v.58), pp. 1–5; NCNA, 8.iv.58, in *SCMP* 1764 (5.v.58), pp. 4–7; and NCNA, 21.v.58, in *SCMP* 1787 (9.vi.58), pp. 1–4.

80. Mao, *MMTTT*, p. 89.

81. NCNA, 6.iii.58, in *SCMP* 1731 (14.iii.58), pp. 10–13; NCNA, 23.iii.58, in *SCMP* 1741 (28.iii.58), pp. 1–3; NCNA, 26.ii.58, in *SCMP* 1727 (10.iii.58), pp. 3–4.

82. Mao, *MMTTT*, pp. 80–81.

83. *Ibid.*, p. 79.

84. Bowie and Fairbank, p. 436.

85. *CKCNP*, 16.vi.58, in *SCMP* 1811 (15.vii.58), pp. 8–13.

86. Teng Hsiao-p'ing, in Bowie and Fairbank, p. 348.

87. Mao, in Schram, *Chairman Mao*, pp. 116, 119.

88. *KMJP*, 22.i.58, in *SCMP* 1727 (10.iii.58), pp. 27–29. See also NCNA, 16.ii.58, in *SCMP* 1716 (21.ii.58), pp. 2–3.

89. *FKHP*, vol. 7, pp. 331–32.

90. *FKHP*, vol. 8, pp. 96–99. For analysis, see Wang Kuei-wu, in *CHCC* 9 (1958), pp. 13–15.

91. Domes, *Internal Politics*, pp. 113–17; *China: A Reassessment of the Economy*, p. 23.

92. It should be pointed out that this passage is quoted from "Selected Edition of Liu Shao-ch'i's Counter-Revolutionary Revisionist Crimes," in *SCMM* 652 (28.iv.69), p. 29.

93. Mao, *MTTSH*, p. 275.

94. Mao, in Schram, *Chairman Mao*, pp. 144–45.

95. On balancing upward in the Great Leap, see *JMJP*, 28.ii.58, in *SCMP* 1731 (14.iii.58), pp. 1–4.

96. *JMJP*, 27.iv.58, in *SCMP* 1769 (12.v.58), pp. 2–5; Mao, in Schram, *Chairman Mao*, p. 106.

97. Mao, in Schram, *Chairman Mao*, p. 105.

98. Vogel, *Canton Under Communism*, p. 234.

99. Bowie and Fairbank, pp. 470–77.

100. NCNA, 31.viii.58, in *SCMP* 1846 (4.ix.58), pp. 1–2.

101. *JMJP*, 1.x.58, in *SCMP* 1870 (9.x.58), pp. 33–37.

102. Mao, *MMTTT*, p. 378.

103. *CHCC* 11 (1958), in *ECMM* 156 (26.i.59), pp. 24–28.

104. This information from refugee interviews is reported in Falkenheim, "Provincial Leadership in Fukien," p. 227.

105. Mao, in Schram, *Chairman Mao*, p. 142.

106. Mao, *MMTTT*, pp. 133–36, 140–48. On the breakdown of the statistical system, see *T'ung-chi kung-tso* (Statistical Work), no. 23 (1958), in *ECMM* 155 (23.i.58), pp. 52–53.

107. Joffe, *Between Two Plenums*.

108. Mao, *MMTTT*, pp. 133–36, 140–48.

109. *Ibid.*, pp. 170–72.

110. On the "five styles," see *URS* 28.12 (10.viii.62), pp. 199–200.

111. Mao, *MMTTT*, pp. 178–81. The revision was based on Mao's "Talk at the Seventh Plenum of the Eighth Central Committee," iv.59, in *MMTTT*, pp. 175–77.

112. For a chronology and analysis of these documents, see Ahn, "Adjustments in the Great Leap Forward," pp. 270–82.

113. *TKP*, 8.ix.61, in *SCMP* 2594 (9.x.61), pp. 1–3.
114. *JMJP*, 1.i.62, in *SCMP* 2653 (8.i.62), pp. 1–6.
115. Communiqué of the Ninth Plenum, in *CB* 644 (27.i.61), pp. 1–4.
116. *JMJP*, 29.iii.62, in *SCMP* 2716 (10.iv.62), pp. 10–13.
117. Ahn, "Adjustments in the Great Leap Forward."
118. Chao Kang, pp. 567–68.
119. See note 115 above.
120. Bastid, pp. 159–98; Ahn, *Chinese Politics and the Cultural Revolution*, pp. 140–45; Ahn, "Industrial Development in China."
121. Bowie and Fairbank, p. 574.
122. *JMJP*, 27.i.58, in *CB* 491 (7.ii.58), pp. 35–38.
123. Mao, *MMTTT*, pp. 77–84.
124. Bowie and Fairbank, p. 574.
125. See, for example, "Greet the Upsurge in Forming People's Communes," *HC* 7 (1958), in Bowie and Fairbank, pp. 457–59.
126. Articles drawing parallels between the people's communes and the Paris Commune include those by Wu Chih-p'u in *CKCNP*, 16.ix.58, in *CB* 524 (21.x.58), pp. 1–15; and by Ch'en Po-ta in *HC* 4 (1958), in *ECMM* 138 (11.viii.58), pp. 5–17.
127. Bowie and Fairbank, pp. 470–77.
128. An insider's account of this debate can be found in "The Confession of Wu Leng-hsi," *CLG* 2.4 (Winter 1969–70), pp. 74–75.
129. Mao, *MTTSH*, p. 248.
130. *JMJP*, 13.x.58, in *CB* 537 (5.xii.58), pp. 1–5.
131. *JMJP*, 18.x.58, in *CB* 537 (5.xii.58), pp. 15–17.
132. *JMJP*, 17.x.58, in *CB* 537 (5.xii.58), pp. 8–12.
133. *JMJP*, 13.xi.58, in *CB* 537 (5.xii.58), pp. 33–37.
134. *KMJP*, 2.xii.58, in *SCMP* 1923 (20.xii.58), pp. 2–5.
135. Bowie and Fairbank, p. 494.
136. *CLG* 2.4 (Winter 1969–70), pp. 74–75.
137. Bowie and Fairbank, pp. 597–99.

CHAPTER 7

1. Meisner, *Mao's China*, chap. 15.
2. For an account of organizational problems in the Chinese countryside in the early 1960's, see C. S. Chen; and Baum, *Prelude to Revolution*, pp. 1–21.
3. On the shortage of skilled and reliable cadres at basic levels, see Vogel, *Canton Under Communism*, pp. 282–82. On the campaign to strengthen rural leadership by sending down cadres from higher levels, see NCNA, 4.i.60, in *SCMP* 2172 (8.i.60), pp. 1–2; NCNA, 14.i.60, in *SCMP* 2184 (26.i.60), pp. 9–11; and Chao Han, in *HC* 2 (1960), in *ECMM* 200 (15.i.60), pp. 1–6.
4. *TKP*, 14.viii.65, in *SCMP* 3528 (31.viii.65), pp. 9–13.
5. See *TKP*, 7.vii.65, in *SCMP* 3509 (3.viii.65), pp. 8–12; and *TKP*, 12.viii.65, in *SCMP* 3533 (20.viii.65), p. 34.
6. See *YCWP*, 9.ii.66, in *SCMP* 3642 (21.ii.66), pp. 3–6; *JMJP*, 1.i.66, in *SCMP* 3616 (13.i.66), pp. 1–4; and *JMJP*, 15.xi.65, in *SCMP* 3589 (2.xii.65), pp. 1–4.
7. Baum and Teiwes, p. 89.
8. *JMJP*, 29.x.65.
9. *JMJP*, 18.x.65.

10. Chang, *Power and Policy*, pp. 145–46.
11. Ahn, *Chinese Politics and the Cultural Revolution*, chaps. 3–8.
12. Dittmer.
13. Teiwes, "Chinese Politics, 1949–1965."
14. Chang, *Power and Policy*.
15. Mao, in Schram, *Chairman Mao*, p. 193.
16. Dittmer, p. 678.
17. The resolution is printed in C. S. Chen, pp. 81–89.
18. Mao's views on the Socialist Education Movement, as held in the spring of 1963, can be found in *MMTTT*, pp. 314–24; and in Baum and Teiwes, pp. 55–71.
19. For more detailed discussions of these problems, see Baum, *Prelude to Revolution*, chap. 1.
20. *NFJP*, 25.v.63, quoted in Baum and Teiwes, p. 17.
21. Baum and Teiwes, pp. 72–94.
22. Baum, *Prelude to Revolution*, p. 63.
23. On the implementation of the Later Ten Points, see Baum, *Prelude to Revolution*, chap. 3; and Ahn, *Chinese Politics and the Cultural Revolution*, pp. 98–104.
24. The criteria are printed in Baum and Teiwes, pp. 95–101.
25. Baum, *Prelude to Revolution*, p. 63.
26. *SCMM* 652 (28.iv.69), p. 32.
27. The most detailed account of Wang Kuang-mei's visit to T'ao-yüan can be found in *JMJP*, 6.ix.67, in *SCMP* 4024 (20.ix.67), pp. 1–20. A less detailed but more entertaining account is to be found in *Cheng-fa kung-she* (Peking), no. 17 (1967), in *SCMP* 3958 (13.vi.67), pp. 10–23.
28. Excerpts from these speeches are in *8.13 Hung-wei-ping*, no. 68 (13.v.67), in *SCMM* 588 (14.viii.67), pp. 14–32. For more on Liu's views of the Socialist Education Movement, see his self-criticism in *CW*3, p. 362; and *CB* 834 (17.viii.67), pp. 23–24.
29. Baum and Teiwes, pp. 102–117.
30. Mao, *MMTTT*, pp. 337–38.
31. *Ibid.*, pp. 384–96.
32. Baum, *Prelude to Revolution*, chap. 5.
33. *8.13 Hung-wei-ping*, no. 68 (13.v.67), in *SCMM* 588 (14.viii.67), p. 28.
34. *CB* 824 (27.iv.67), pp. 10–12.
35. Baum, *Prelude to Revolution*, pp. 103–4, 111.
36. For Mao's comments, see *MMTTT*, pp. 408–32, 437–44. For the text of the Twenty-three Articles, see Baum and Teiwes, pp. 118–26.
37. Baum, *Prelude to Revolution*, pp. 138–40.
38. For representative articles, see *JMJP*, 15.xi.65, in *SCMP* 3589 (2.xii.65), pp. 1–4; *YCWP*, 2.xii.65, in *SCMP* 3600 (17.xii.65), pp. 1–11; *JMJP*, 1.i.66, in *SCMP* 3616 (13.i.66), pp. 1–4; *JMJP*, 1.i.66, in *SCMP* 3616 (13.i.66), pp. 4–6; and *JMJP*, 17.i.66, in *SCMP* 3628 (1.ii.66), pp. 5–8.
39. *JMJP*, 3.xii.65, in *SCMP* 3602 (21.xii.65), pp. 1–6. See also *JMJP*, 2.vii.65, in *SCMP* 3502 (22.vii.65), pp. 6–9.
40. One such meeting did, however, generate 3,100 separate "criticisms" of county cadres; see *JMJP*, 13.ii.66, in *SCMP* 3647 (1.iii.66), pp. 8–12. For an account of a similar meeting, see *JMJP*, 8.ii.66, in *SCMP* 3648 (2.iii.66), pp. 6–10.
41. Chiao's story can be found in *JMJP*, 7.ii.66, in *SCMP* 3639 (16.ii.66), pp. 1–2; and NCNA, 7.ii.66, in *SCMP* 3639 (16.ii.66), pp. 5–12.

42. *YCWP*, 25.iv.66, in *SCMP* 3691 (5.v.66), pp. 9–11.
43. *CC/D*, pp. 185–92.
44. *Mao Tse-tung chu-i chan-tou-pao* (Peking), no. 2 (23.ii.67), in *SCMP* 3903 (21.iii.67), pp. 7–10.
45. For representative articles on the campaign, see *JMJP*, 28.viii.64, in *SCMP* 3298 (15.ix.64), pp. 12–15; and *TKP*, 10.ii.65, in *SCMP* 3402 (23.ii.65), pp. 11–17.
46. *TKP*, 14.viii.65, in *SCMP* 3528 (31.viii.65), pp. 9–13.
47. For further discussion of the military reforms undertaken between 1960 and 1965, see Gittings, *Role of the Chinese Army*, chap. 12; Joffe, *Party and Army*, pp. 140–42; Joffe, "Chinese Army Under Lin Piao," pp. 343–74; and Ahn, *Chinese Politics and the Cultural Revolution*, chap. 6.
48. The spread of the political departments at the central level can be traced in *URS* 35.17 (29.v.64); *JMJP*, 7.vi.64, in *SCMP* 3249 (30.vi.64), pp. 1–3; and *CS* 4.15 (8.viii.66), p. 5.
49. *JMJP*, 17.x.65, in *SCMP* 3572 (4.xi.65), pp. 9–11.
50. Mao, in Ch'en, *Mao Papers*, p. 98; Mao, *MMTTT*, p. 329.
51. R. Peking, 16.xii.67, cited in Gittings, "Army-Party Relations," p. 395.
52. *TKP*, 16.vi.65, in *SCMP* 3495 (13.vii.65), pp. 5–7.
53. *TKP*, 12.i.66, in *SCMP* 3626 (28.i.66), pp. 1–11.
54. *SCMM* 639 (6.i.69), p. 15.
55. *TKP*, 12.i.66, in *SCMP* 3626 (28.i.66), pp. 1–11.
56. *TKP*, 27.xi.65, in *SCMP* 3595 (10.xii.65), pp. 4–6.
57. *JMJP*, 25.iii.66, in *SCMP* 3673 (6.iv.66), pp. 8–12.
58. For details, see Ahn, *Chinese Politics and the Cultural Revolution*, chap. 8; and Chang, *Power and Policy*, chap. 6.
59. E.g., the decision of the Central-South bureau, in *YCWP*, 1.ii.66, in *SCMP* 3635 (10.ii.66), pp. 1–5; the decision of the Peking municipal Party committee, in NCNA, 18.i.66, in *SCMP* 3625 (27.i.66), pp. 17–19; Shansi provincial conference on political work, in *JMJP*, 1.ii.66, in *SCMP* 3640 (17.ii.66), pp. 3–7; a meeting of the East China bureau, in *JMJP*, 7.iii.66, in *SCMP* 3660 (18.iii.66), pp. 1–5; and the decision of the North China bureau, in *JMJP*, 19.iii.66, in *SCMP* 3665 (25.iii.66), pp. 1–4.
60. *JMJP*, 14.xii.65, in *SCMP* 3609 (4.i.66), pp. 1–5; *YCWP*, 1.ii.66, in *SCMP* 3625 (10.ii.66), pp. 1–5; *YCWP*, 5.ii.66, in *SCMP* 3637 (14.ii.66), pp. 1–4.
61. *HC* 1 (1966), in *SCMM* 509 (31.i.66) pp. 1–3. See also *JMJP*, 14.xii.65 in *SCMP* 3609 (4.i.66), pp. 1–5.
62. *JMJP*,17.iii.66, in *SCMP* 3665 (25.iii.66), pp. 5–8; *JMJP*, 19.iii.66, in *SCMP* 3665 (25.iii.66), pp. 1–4; *KMJP*, 2.viii.65, in *SCMP* 3533 (8.ix.65), pp. 2–7.
63. *KMJP*, 2.viii.65, in *SCMP* 3533 (8.ix.65), pp. 2–7.
64. *JMJP*, 6.iv.66, in *SCMP* 3680 (19.iv.66), pp. 1–9.
65. *YCWP*, 5.ii.66, in *SCMP* 3637 (14.ii.66), pp. 1–4.
66. *Hsin Pei-ta* (Peking), 21.iii.67, cited in Lieberthal, *Research Guide*, p. 228.
67. *Hung-wei pao* (Canton), 27.ix.66, in *SCMP* 3796 (7.x.66), pp. 1–10.
68. *Tsao-fan yu-li* (Peking), 12.v.67, in *SCMP* 4006 (22.viii.67), pp. 7–12.
69. JPRS 43357 (16.xi.67), pp. 7–11.
70. *JMJP*, 21.iii.66, in *SCMP* 3671 (4.iv.66), pp. 6–10.
71. *KMJP*, 3.vi.66, in *SCMP* 3728 (29.vi.66), pp. 10–14.

72. For good accounts of this period, see Ahn, *Chinese Politics and the Cultural Revolution*, chap. 9; and Daubier, chap. 1.

73. On the Ministry of Culture, see *Wen-hua feng-lei* (Peking), no. 4 (5.iv.67), in *SCMP* 3953 (6.vi.67), pp. 1–5; on the Ministry of Finance and other bureaus in the finance and trade system, see *Pei-ching kung-she* (Peking), 12.iv.67, in *SCMP* 3954 (7.vi.67), pp. 39–40. For a discussion of the rectification campaign in the propaganda departments and the culture and education bureaus in the provinces, see Gray and Cavendish, pp. 118 ff.

74. Ahn, *Chinese Politics and the Cultural Revolution*, p. 216. On the role of the control commissions, see *Na-han chan-pao*, i.68, in *SCMP* 4141 (19.iii.68), p. 5.

75. *JMJP*, 24.vi.66, in *SCMP* 3728 (29.vi.66), pp. 1–4.

76. *JMJP*, 9.vii.66, in *SCMP* 3743 (21.vii.66), pp. 6–12.

77. R. Hofei, 16.vii.66.

78. On the restrictions placed on the movement in Tsinghua University, see Hinton, chaps. 4–5.

79. *JMJP*, 1.vii.66, in *SCMP* 3733 (7.vii.66), pp. 1–8.

80. See Daubier, p. 56.

81. This characterization of the leftists was provided by Yen Hsia, the leader of the work team dispatched to the Peking College of Construction Engineering. Yen is quoted in Liu, *CW*3, pp. 345–55.

82. *Huo-ch'i* (Shanghai), no. 2 (12.ii.67), quoted in Hunter, pp. 39–40.

83. Ch'en, *Mao Papers*, pp. 26–30.

84. *CB* 819 (10.iii.67), pp. 1–3. On the previous day Mao had compared the activities of the work teams to the suppression of the May Fourth Movement by the Peiyang warlords; Mao, in Schram, *Chairman Mao*, pp. 253–55.

85. Mao, in Ch'en, *Mao Papers*, p. 117.

86. For a fuller analysis of Mao's changing role in the Chinese political process, see Oksenberg, "Policy-making Under Mao," pp. 79–115.

87. Mao, in Ch'en, *Mao Papers*, pp. 86–92.

88. Mao, *MMTTT*, p. 323.

89. Schram, *Chairman Mao*, p. 193; Baum and Teiwes, pp. 72–94, 118–26; Mao, *MMTTT*, pp. 408–32, 437–44. See also Snow, pp. 191–223; Malraux, pp. 360–75; and "Khrushchov's Phoney Communism."

90. Mao, in Schram, *Chairman Mao*, pp. 193–95.

91. Mao, in Ch'en, *Mao Papers*, p. 102.

92. The communiqué is in *CC/D*, pp. 185–92.

93. Snow, pp. 221–22.

94. Mao, in Schram, *Chairman Mao*, p. 270.

CHAPTER 8

1. "Khrushchov's Phoney Communism," pp. 468–70.

2. See Mao, *MMTTT*, pp. 323, 351–60; and Mao, in Ch'en, *Mao Papers*, pp. 86–92.

3. Mao, in Ch'en, *Mao Papers*, pp. 24–26.

4. *JMJP*, 21.vii.66, in *SCMP* 3748 (28.vii.66), pp. 5–6; *JMJP*, 29.vii.66, in *SCMP* 3757 (10.vii.66), pp. 1–2.

5. *Decision of the Central Committee*, sec. 9.

6. *HC* 4 (1966), in JPRS 35137 (21.iv.66), pp. 5–22.

7. Mao, in Ch'en, *Mao Papers*, p. 24.

8. See, for instance, the confession of Yen Hsia in Liu, *CW*3, pp. 345–55.

9. For K'ang's speech, see *CB* 819 (10.iii.67), pp. 1–3. For Ch'en's speech, see *CB* 830 (26.vi.67), pp. 5–6.

10. The text of the directive can be found in *CB* 852 (6.v.68), p. 8.

11. *Decision of the Central Committee*, secs. 1, 9.

12. Mao, in Schram, *Chairman Mao*, pp. 256–61.

13. For evidence on this point, see Bennett and Montaperto, pp. 71–72.

14. Hunter, pp. 82–83; Hinton, p. 68.

15. Mao, in Schram, *Chairman Mao*, pp. 256–59.

16. See, for instance, *HC* 10 (1966), in *Great Socialist Cultural Revolution*, pp. 1–8; and *JMJP*, 20.viii.66, in *SCMP* 3767 (24.viii.66), pp. 6–7.

17. Bennett and Montaperto, chap. 5.

18. *JMJP*, 23.viii.66, in *SCMP* 3769 (26.viii.66), pp. 3–5.

19. Hunter, p. 156.

20. NCNA, 23.viii.66, in *SCMP* 3769 (26.viii.66), pp. 14–15.

21. *JMJP*, 23.viii.66, in *SCMP* 3769 (26.viii.66), pp. 3–5.

22. Bennett and Montaperto, pp. 85–87.

23. Hunter, pp. 90–92. 24. *GPCR/D*, pp. 77–80.

25. Hunter, pp. 96–97. 26. *Ibid.*, p. 134.

27. Lin's speech is in *CLG* 1.1 (Spring 1968), pp. 13–31. Mao's talks are in Ch'en, *Mao*, pp. 91–97; and Ch'en, *Mao Papers*, pp. 40–45.

28. Lin's speech is in *HC* 15 (1966), in JPRS 39532, pp. 4–7.

29. Bennett and Montaperto, p. 142.

30. *GPCR/D*, pp. 113–19, 131–35, 137–42.

31. For details on Shanghai, see Nee, pp. 326–31.

32. Mao, in Ch'en, *Mao Papers*, pp. 47–48.

33. *GPCR/D*, pp. 193–97.

34. *JMJP*, 22.i.67, in *PR*, 27.i.67, pp. 7–9.

35. *HC* 3 (1967), in JPRS 40086 (1.iii.67), pp. 12–21.

36. *Huo-ch'e-t'ou*, no. 7 (ii.67), in *SCMP* 3898 (14.iii.67), pp. 4–7.

37. NCNA, 13.ii.67, in *SWB* FE/2393/B/29–31.

38. R. Harbin, 8.ii.67, in *SWB* FE/2388/B/22–24.

39. R. Peking, 21.ii.67, in *SWB* FE/2399/B/26–30. See also the description of the Taiyüan Revolutionary Committee, NCNA, 4.ii.67, in *SWB* FE/2384/B/4–6.

40. R. Shanghai, 5.ii.67, in *SWB* FE/2385/B/14, 31–34; R. Tsingtao, 9.ii.67, in *SWB* FE/2389/B/41–42; R. Harbin, 16.ii.67, in *SWB* FE/2396/B/5–9.

41. NCNA, 16.ii.67, in *SWB* FE/2395/B/30–31.

42. For the texts of Mao's remarks, see *JMJP*, 10.ii.67, in *PR*, 17.ii.67, pp. 17–19; and Mao, *MMTTT*, pp. 451–55. Chang Ch'un-ch'iao's report of his meetings with the Chairman is in *Tzu-liao chuan-chi* (Canton), 10.ii.68, in *SCMP* 4147 (27.iii.68), pp. 1–10.

43. R. Shanghai, 5.ii.67, in *SWB* FE/2385/B/31–34.

44. Ch'i's remarks are contained in a pamphlet published by the "Liaison Headquarters" of the Central-South bureau, 5.xi.67, in *SCMM* 611 (22.i.68), pp. 12–18.

45. *Tzu-liao chuan-chi* (Canton), 10.ii.68, in *SCMP* 4147 (27.iii.68), pp. 1–10.

46. *GPCR/D*, pp. 325–26.

47. *Ibid.*

48. For a more detailed account of the formation of revolutionary committees in each of China's twenty-nine provinces, see Domes, "Role of the Military"; and Domes, *Internal Politics*, chaps. 12–14, especially pp. 200–205.

49. For accounts of such central "study classes," see, for instance, the pam-

phlet published by the "Liaison Headquarters" of the Central-South bureau, 5.xi.67, in *SCMM* 611 (22.i.68), pp. 12–18; and "Speeches by Leaders of the Central Committee," reprinted by the "October First Column of the Canton Red Guard Headquarters," x.67, in *SCMM* 611 (22.i.68), pp. 8–11.

50. For details of the purges in the army during the Cultural Revolution, see Chien; Nelsen, "Military Bureaucracy"; and Whitson, chaps. 7–8.

51. For a summary of the activities of main force units during the Cultural Revolution, see Nelsen, "Military Forces."

52. Statistical surveys of the composition of the revolutionary committees can be found in Domes, "Role of the Military"; and Baum, "China: Year of the Mangoes." The raw data are compiled in *CB* 863 (1.x.68), pp. 25–61.

53. *JMJP-HC-CFCP* joint editorial, 30.iii.68, in *SCMP* 4151 (2.iv.68), pp. 16–18.

54. *WHP*, 6.v.68, in *SCMP* 4190 (4.vi.68), pp. 19–21.

55. R. Peking, 21.ii.67, in *SWB* FE/2399/B/26–30.

56. "Whither China?" in Mehnert, *Peking and the New Left*, pp. 84–85.

57. *Ibid.*, pp. 88–89.

58. "Program," in Mehnert, *Peking and the New Left*, p. 76.

59. "Whither China?" in Mehnert, *Peking and the New Left*, p. 99.

60. *Wen-ko t'ung-hsün* (Canton), no. 12 (ii.68), in *SCMP* 4163 (24.iv.68), pp. 6–9.

61. Purges occurred in Honan, Peking, Shanghai, Kweichow, Tientsin, Kansu, Shantung, and Heilungkiang. See *Chung-hsüeh hung-wei-ping* (Canton), v.68, in *SCMP* 4194 (10.vi.68), pp. 1–3; *Hung nung-yu* (Canton), no. 3 (vi.68), in *SCMP* 4216 (12.vii.68), p. 7; and *Tung-fang-hung tien-hsün* (Canton), no. 3 (vii.68), in *SCMP* 4234 (8.viii.68), pp. 15–16.

62. *WHP*, 6.v.68, in *SCMP* 4190 (4.vi.68), pp. 19–21.

63. *WHP*, 22.iv.68, in *SCMP* 4178 (5.v.68), pp. 3–4.

64. *JMJP-HC-CFCP* joint editorial, 30.iii.68, in *SCMP* 4151 (2.iv.68), pp. 16–18.

65. Daubier, p. 248.

66. Domes, *China After the Cultural Revolution*, p. 14.

67. Mao, *MMTTT*, p. 470.

68. The decision was explained in an important article by Yao Wen-yüan in *HC* 2 (1968), in *PR*, 30.viii.68, pp. 3–6.

69. *JMJP*, 10.xii.69, in *SCMP* 4561 (19.xii.69), pp. 1–7.

70. R. Wuhan, 2.vii.70.   71. R. Changsha, 9.vii.69.

72. R. Changsha, 13.viii.69.   73. R. Chengchow, 12.xi.70.

74. Lin Piao, in Kau, *Lin Piao Affair*, pp. 462–64. Other articles published in the Chinese press during the Cultural Revolution elaborated Lin's argument by presenting more detailed criticism of the various structural characteristics of bureaucracy. On hierarchy, see *JMJP*, 6.iv.67, in SCMP 3920 (17.iv.67), p. 1; and *PR*, 19.iv.68, pp. 20–22; on the division of labor and specialization, see *JMJP*, 31.x.68, in *SCMP* 4297 (13.xi.68), pp. 6–11.

75. Mao, in JPRS 49826 (12.ii.70), pp. 40–43.

76. Meisner, "Leninism and Maoism."

CHAPTER 9

1. Robinson, "Chou En-lai and the Cultural Revolution," p. 204 n. 69, p. 213.

2. *HC* 4 (1967), in *PR*, 3.iii.67, pp. 5–9.

3. *JMJP*, 23.ii.67, in *PR*, 3.iii.67, pp. 19–21.

4. *GPCR/D*, pp. 335–38.

5. Kyodo, 14.ii.67, in *SWB* FE/2392/C/1; *Hung-t'ien-hsün* (Canton?), no. 3 (27.iii.68), in *SCMP* 4157 (11.iv.68), pp. 4–7.

6. Robinson, "Chou En-lai and the Cultural Revolution," p. 208; *GPCR/D*, pp. 335–38.

7. Rice, pp. 329–330.

8. Esmein, pp. 154–58.

9. Gurtov, p. 353.

10. *HC* 4 (1967), in *PR*, 3.iii.67, pp. 5–9.

11. *K'o-chi chan-pao* (Peking), 2.vi.67, in *SCMP* 4011 (29.viii.67), pp. 1–6.

12. *HC* 5 (1967), in *PR* 17.iii.67, pp. 14–16.

13. *K'o-chi chan-pao* (Peking), 2.vi.67, in *SCMP* 4011 (29.viii.67), pp. 1–6.

14. For accounts of these meetings, see *ibid.*; *Wen-ko feng-yün* (Canton), no. 2 (ii.68), in *SCMP* 4148 (28.iii.68), pp. 3–9; and *Tzu-liao chuan-chi* (Canton), no. 7 (28.ii.68), in *SCMP* 4154 (8.iv.68), pp. 1–11.

15. *Tzu-liao chuan-chi* (Canton), no. 7 (28.ii.68), in *SCMP* 4154 (8.iv.68), pp. 1–11.

16. Interview conducted by the author in December 1972. See also Robinson, "Chou En-lai and the Cultural Revolution," pp. 237–38.

17. *Tou-p'i t'ung-hsün* (Tungkuan hsien, Kwangtung), no. 19 (22.xi.67), in *SCMP* 4099 (15.i.68), pp. 14–15.

18. NCNA, 12.ii.68.

19. *Decision of the Central Committee*, p. 8.

20. Representative editorials and articles on this subject are to be found in *HC* 3 (1967), in *CB* 563 (13.iii.67), pp. 1–7; *HC* 4 (1967), in *PR*, 3.iii.67, pp. 5–9; *HC* 5 (1967), in *SCMM* 571 (10.iv.67), pp. 17–24; and *JMJP*, 21.x.67, in *SCMP* 4048 (26.x.67), pp. 1–4.

21. *JMJP*, 30.iii.69, in *SCMP* 4399 (22.iv.69), pp. 8–11; *JMJP*, 19.iv.69, in *SCMP* 4403 (28.iv.69), pp. 1–2.

22. R. Shanghai, 17.ii.67, in *SWB* FE/2397/B/16–19.

23. *WHP*, 19.ii.68, in *SCMP* 4135 (11.iii.68), pp. 3–4.

24. *Chi-yang wen-tzu* (Canton?), no. 1 (22.i.68), in *SCMP* 4125 (26.ii.68), pp. 1–4.

25. *Tsu-kuo*, no. 103 (1.x.72), p. 20.

26. Shantung in NCNA, 23.vi.67, in *SCMP* 3968 (27.vi.67), pp. 11–12; Shanghai in NCNA, 8.vi.67, in *SCMP* 3958 (13.vi.67), pp. 1–6; and in *JMJP*, 8.vi.67, in *SCMP* 3964 (21.vi.67), pp. 8–17; Kweichow in NCNA, 26.vi.67, in *SCMP* 3974 (6.vii.67), pp. 8–9; Heilungkiang in NCNA, 28.vi.67, in *SCMP* 3975 (7.vii.67), pp. 14–15; Peking in NCNA, 28.vi.67, in *SCMP* 3975 (7.vii.67), pp. 16–17; Inner Mongolia in NCNA, 3.vii.67, in *SCMP* 3980 (14.vii.67), pp. 1–3; Tientsin in NCNA, 13.xii.67, in *SCMP* 4081 (15.xii.67), pp. 14–15; Canton in *NFJP*, 7.iii.68, in *SCMP* 4140 (18.iii.68), pp. 1–3.

27. For representative articles on the study of model units, see *JMJP*, 13.iii.69, in *SCMP* 4382 (24.iii.69), pp. 6–11; *JMJP*, 31.iii.69, in *SCMP* 4401 (24.iv.69), pp. 9–11; *JMJP*, 30.i.70; and *JMJP*, 29.v.70, in *SCMP* 4681 (22.vi.70), pp. 1–11.

28. The three constantly read articles—"In Memory of Norman Bethune," 21.xii.39; "Serve the People," 8.ix.44; and "The Foolish Old Man Who Removed the Mountains," 11.vi.45—are to be found in Mao, *SR*, pp. 146–47, 252–53, and 260–63.

29. A collection of these directives can be found in Ch'en, *Mao Papers*.

30. *JMJP*, 12.x.67, in *SCMP* 4045 (23.x.67), pp. 1–3. For representative accounts of study classes during this period, see NCNA, 18.x.67, in *SCMP* 4049 (27.x.67), p. 11; and NCNA, 22.x.67, in *SCMP* 4047 (25.x.67), pp. 14–15.

31. NCNA, 1.iii.68, in *SCMP* 4131 (5.iii.68), pp. 18–19.

32. *Tsu-kuo*, no. 103 (1.x.72), p. 20.

33. *WHP*, 24.vi.67, in *SCMP* 3977 (11.vii.67), pp. 1–3.

34. *Wen-ko t'ung-hsün* (Canton), no. 12 (ii.68), in *SCMP* 4139 (15.iii.68), p. 3.

35. For a discussion of the doctrinal style of work fostered during the Cultural Revolution, see Harding, "Maoist Theories of Policy-Making and Organization"; and Harding, "Organizational Issue, 1959–72," chap. 9.

36. Specifically, cadres claimed that they lacked the time to engage in manual labor (R. Shanghai, 3.vi.72, in FBIS, 5.vi.72, pp. C1–2); in collective discussion of problems (*JMJP*, 8.v.69, in *SCMP* 4420 [21.v.69], pp. 6–8); in the mass line (*HC* 7–8 [1971], in *SCMM* 71–01 [viii.71], pp. 46–52); or in consultations with their subordinates (*HC* 7–8 [1971], in *SCMM* 71–01 [vii.71], pp. 12–18).

37. *WHP*, 13.v.68, in *SCMP* 4196 (12.vi.68), pp. 13–14.

38. For descriptions of the May Seventh cadre schools, see, for instance, Macciocchi, chap. 3; Mehnert, *China Returns*, chap. 7; Snow; and Wang.

39. For accounts of the Liuho school, see NCNA, 4.x.68, in *SCMP* 4276 (11.x.68), pp. 8–10; and NCNA, 16.x.68, in *SCMP* 4283 (22.x.68), pp. 13–16. For the directive, see Ch'en, *Mao Papers*, pp. 103–5.

40. *PR*, 11.x.68, p. 2.

41. NCNA, 14.xi.68, in *SCMP* 4295 (8.xi.68), pp. 22–23.

42. Wang, p. 527.

43. *JMJP*, 4.ix.69, in *SCMP* 4497 (17.ix.69), pp. 6–7.

44. NCNA, 16.x.68, in *SCMP* 4283 (22.x.68), pp. 13–16.

45. Interview conducted at the Eastern District May Seventh Cadre School, Peking, October 1976.

46. The term "revolutionary sabbatical" was coined in Committee of Concerned Asian Scholars, p. 100.

47. *8NC/D*, pp. 165–66.

48. Lin Piao, in *PR*, 28.iv.69, p. 20.

49. For representative warnings that the revolutionary committees should not try to make policy, see R. Changsha, 3.v.70, in *URS* 59.14 (19.v.70); and R. Peking, 19.v.70. For a broadcast with the complementary message—that the Party should not attempt to monopolize policy implementation, and that Party committees should not ignore the legitimate functions of the revolutionary committees—see R. Peking, 19.vi.70.

50. Mao, in Ch'en, *Mao Papers*, pp. 26–34.

51. *Ibid.*, pp. 152–53.

52. *Ibid.*, p. 155.

53. *HC* 12 (1969), in *SCMM* 669 (29.xii.69), pp. 12–16.

54. R. Kweiyang, 14.ii.67, in *SWB* FE/2395/B/18–22.

55. *WHP*, 2.iv.68, in *SCMP* 4168 (1.v.68), pp. 15–16.

56. *JMJP*, 31.x.68, in *SCMP* 4297 (13.xi.68), pp. 6–11.

57. The exception was the Office of National Defense Industry. See R. Hofei, 24.xii.72.

58. Barnett, *Cadres, Bureaucracy, and Political Power*, p. 9.

59. R. Harbin, 8.ii.67, in *SWB* FE/2388/B/22–24.

60. Snow, p. 14.

61. On Inner Mongolia, see *Wen-ko t'ung-hsün* (Canton), no. 12 (ii.68), in *SCMP* 4163 (24.iv.68), p. 5; on Heilungkiang, see R. Harbin, 8.ii.67, in *SWB* FE/2388/B/22–24; on Honan, see *Wall Street Journal*, 30.x.72, p. 18.

62. According to Chou En-lai, 80 percent of the 50,000 cadres reassigned from the central government were sent to May Seventh schools. See Snow, p. 14.

63. Mao, *MMTTT*, pp. 378–79.

64. *Ibid.*

65. *Ibid.*, pp. 373–74. For a fuller account of the debacle over agricultural mechanization in these years, see *CS* 6.17 (1.x.68); and Gray.

66. This discussion draws on Bastid; Donnithorne, "China's Cellular Economy"; Eckstein, *China's Economic Development*, pp. 355–62; and *CS* 6.22 (20.xii.68).

67. For differing interpretations of the degree of provincial autonomy in the early 1970's, see Chang, "Decentralization"; and Falkenheim, "Continuing Central Predominance."

68. For criticism of unsanctioned bartering among local enterprises and resistance to central planning, see *HC* 6 (1970), in NCNA, 8.vi.70.

69. R. Peking, 8.ii.67, in *SWB* FE/2390/B/18–20.

70. Niijima, pp. 44, 49.

71. For a summary of the criticism of the Weberian ideal-type during the Cultural Revolution, see Whyte, "Bureaucracy and Modernization in China"; and Starr, "Mao Tse-tung's Theory of Continuing Revolution," chap. 5.

CHAPTER 10

1. Mao, in Ch'en, *Mao Papers*, pp. 112–13.

2. *CC/D*, pp. 219–26.

3. For a well-balanced analysis of the advantages and disadvantages of the approach taken here, see Starr, "Tenth Party Congress."

4. Useful accounts of the 1969–76 period include Domes, "China After the Cultural Revolution"; Bridgham, "Fall of Lin Piao"; Goldman, "China's Anti-Confucian Campaign"; Wich; Lieberthal, "Internal Political Scene"; Starr, "Tenth Party Congress"; Chang, "Mao's Last Stand?"; and Harding, "China After Mao." See also the annual article on China in each January issue of *Asian Survey*.

5. See Gottlieb.

6. Domes, *China After the Cultural Revolution*, chap. 4.

7. *Ibid.*, p. 54.

8. The definition of the army's "fundamental task" is drawn from R. Changsha, 16.ii.71. The quotation from Mao comes from "Khrushchov's Phoney Communism."

9. The text of the draft constitution, released by the Taiwan government, was first published in *Background on China* (Taipei), no. B. 70–81 (4.xi.1970).

10. See, for instance, R. Tsinan, 21.i.72, in FBIS, 1.ii.72, pp. C15–18; R. Huhehot, 28.i.72, in FBIS, 8.ii.72, pp. F2–5; and R. Sian, 7.ii.72, in FBIS, 10.ii.72, pp. H5–6. These charges were also made while Lin was still in power; see, for instance, R. Canton, 31.vii.71, in FBIS, 4.viii.71, pp. B1–2.

11. *Chung-fa* no. 12 (1972), in Kau, *Lin Piao Affair*, p. 64.

12. See van Ginneken, p. 217.

13. *WHP* (Hong Kong), 8–25.xi.73, in Kau, *Lin Piao Affair*, p. 234.

14. Kau, *Lin Piao Affair*, p. 63.

15. Snow, p. 158.

16. Kau, *Lin Piao Affair*, pp. 63–64.

17. *Ibid.*, pp. 62–63; Lieberthal, *Research Guide*, pp. 275–76.

18. *HC* 1 (1971), in *SCMM*, 71–01 (i.71), pp. 45–50.

19. *HC* 2 (1971), *SCMM* 71–02 (ii.72), pp. 14–20.

20. *JMJP-HC-CFCP* joint editorial, 1.v.71, in *PR*, 7.v.71, pp. 10–12.

21. R. Canton, 31.vii.71, in FBIS, 4.viii.71, pp. B1–2.

22. R. Changsha, 8.viii.71, in FBIS, 10.viii.71, pp. D2–3.

23. R. Nanning, 10.vii.71, in FBIS, 12.viii.71, pp. D4–5.

24. The text of the document was published in *Chung-fa* no. 4 (1972), in Kau, *Lin Piao Affair*, pp. 78–95.

25. For this interpretation, see van Ginneken, pp. 272–74; and Domes, *China After the Cultural Revolution*, p. 132.

26. For a summary of that program, see Domes, "New Course in Chinese Domestic Politics."

27. See Lin Piao, in Kau, *Lin Piao Affair*, pp. 346–50, especially p. 347.

28. See *HC* 12 (1971), pp. 14–18.

29. R. Sian, 10.iii.72, in FBIS, 15.iii.72, pp. H1–5.

30. *China: A Look at the 11th Central Committee*, p. 4.

31. Domes, *China After the Cultural Revolution*, pp. 51–52, 73, and chap. 5.

32. R. Chengtu, 9.vii.72, in FBIS, 10.vii.72, pp. E1–2.

33. R. Shenyang, 30.i.72, in FBIS, 7.ii.72, p. G3; R. Foochow, 3.ii.72, in FBIS, 11.ii.72, p. C9; R. Hofei, 10.ii.72, in FBIS, 11.ii.72, pp. C5–9; R. Harbin, 5.ii.72, in FBIS, 16.ii.72, pp. G1–3.

34. See Teiwes, *Provincial Leadership in China*; and Scalapino, "CCP's Provincial Secretaries."

35. Chang, "Political Rehabilitation," pp. 331–40; R. Shenyang, 15.vii.72, in FBIS, 17.vii.72, pp. G1–2.

36. R. Shanghai, 3.vi.72, in FBIS, 5.vi.72, pp. C1–2.

37. See, for instance, R. Harbin, 8.vii.72, in FBIS, 10.vii.72, pp. G1–3; and R. Hofei, 12.xii.71.

38. R. Wuhan, 24.vi.73, in FBIS, 26.vi.73, pp. D1–3.

39. R. Sian, 27.i.73, in FBIS, 29.i.73, pp. H2–3; R. Tsinan, 4.v.73, in FBIS, 7.v.73, p. C5; R. Lanchow, 3.v.73, in FBIS, 7.v.73, p. H1.

40. R. Tsinan, 22.iv.73, in FBIS, 25.iv.73, pp. C1–2.

41. For representative articles and broadcasts, see R. Taiyuan, 31.i.72, in FBIS, 1.ii.72, pp. F2–3; NCNA, 30.i.72, in FBIS, 8.ii.72, pp. D4–5; and R. Haikow, 6.ii.72, in FBIS, 9.ii.72, pp. D2–3.

42. See Ni Chih-fu, in *PR*, 27.x.72, pp. 5–7.

43. R. Harbin, 9.viii.72, in FBIS, 10.viii.72, pp. G1–2. See also R. Hofei, 2.iii.72, in FBIS, 8.iii.72, pp. C1–2.

44. See Domes, *China After the Cultural Revolution*, p. 174.

45. R. Kweiyang, 24.i.73, in FBIS, 31.i.73, pp. E1–4.

46. R. Chengtu, 30.i.73, in FBIS, 31.i.73, pp. E3–5.

47. *JMJP*, 7.viii.73, in *PR*, 12.x.73, pp. 5–9.

48. *JMJP*, 18.viii.73, in FBIS, 20.viii.73, pp. B2–4, and 21.viii.73, pp. B1–2.

49. Wang Hung-wen, in *10NC/D*, pp. 40–57; and in *IS* 11.2 (ii.75), pp. 94–105.

50. Chou En-lai, in *10NC/D*, p. 6.

51. For useful summaries of this debate, see *China News Summary*, nos. 491 (1.xi.73), 492 (8.xi.73), 493 (15.xi.73), 494 (22.xi.73), 497 (13.xii.73), and 499 (3.i.74).

52. *JMJP-HC-CFCP* joint editorial, 1.i.74., in *PR*, 4.i.74, pp. 6–8.

53. *JMJP*, 2.ii.74, in *PR*, 8.ii.74, pp. 5–6.

54. See *China News Summary*, nos. 503 (7.ii.74) and 504 (14.ii.74).

55. AFP, 13.vi.74, in FBIS, 13.vi.74, pp. E1–2; AFP, 16.vi.74, and Reuters, 17.vi.74, both in FBIS, 17.vi.74, pp. E10–11; AFP, 17.vi.74, in FBIS, 18.vi.74, p. E3; Reuters, 28.vi.74, in FBIS, 28.vi.74, pp. E2–3.

56. AFP, 13.vi.74, in FBIS, 13.vi.74, pp. E1–2; AFP, 21.vi.74, in FBIS, 21.vi.74, pp. E2–3.

57. AFP, 4.vi.74, in FBIS, 5.vi.74, pp. E3–4; Reuters, 13.vii.74, in FBIS, 15.vii.74, pp. E3–4.

58. *JMJP*, 1.vii.74, in FBIS, 1.vii.74, pp. E1–2.

59. *Chung-fa* no. 21 (1974), in *IS* 11.1 (i.75), pp. 101–4.

60. *Documents of the First Session of the Fourth National People's Congress of the People's Republic of China*, pp. 45–65.

61. *Ibid.*, pp. 31–43.

62. The articles are in *HC* 4 (1975); and *HC* 3 (1975), respectively. Both were published as English-language pamphlets by the Foreign Languages Press in 1975.

63. Starr, "China in 1975," p. 48.

64. NCNA, 20.x.75, in FBIS, 23.x.75, pp. E1–11. There is a condensed version of Hua's report that excludes most of his references to rectification in *PR*, 31.x.75, pp. 7–10, 18.

65. The text appears in *Pan Ku* (Hong Kong), no. 103 (1.iv.77), in *SPRCM* 77–14 (1977), pp. 18–37.

66. The text appears in *IS* 13.7 (vii.77), pp. 90–113.

67. *JMJP*, 6.vi.76, in *SPRCP* 76–26 (1976), pp. 98–102; *JMJP*, 23.v.76, in *SPRCP* 76–26 (1976), pp. 54–57; *JMJP*, 7.i.76, in *SPRCP* 76–4 (1976), pp. 1–6; *JMJP*, 20.iii.76, in *China News Analysis*, no. 1044 (18.vi.76), p. 2; *HC* 4 (1976), in *SPRCM* 76–11 (1976), pp. 27–32; *JMJP*, 25.iv.76, in *SPRCP* 76–25 (1976), pp. 70–71.

68. *PR*, 7.i.77, pp. 11–12.

69. R. Canton, 24.xi.76, in FBIS, 29.xi.76, pp. H5–9.

70. R. Shenyang, 14.xii.76, in FBIS, 21.xii.76, pp. L7–10.

71. See, in particular, *HC* 7 (1976), in *PR*, 27.viii.76, pp. 6–9. See also *HHYPP* 8 (1976), in *SPRCM* 76–27 (1976), pp. 27–30; and *HHYPP* 9 (1976), in *SPRCM* 76–30 (1976), pp. 17–21.

72. *HC* 7 (1976), in *PR*, 27.viii.76, pp. 6–9.

73. *JMJP-HC-CFCP* joint editorial, 16.v.76, in *PR*, 21.v.76, pp. 6–10.

74. *HC* 6 (1976), in *PR*, 18.vi.76, pp. 7–10, 24 (emphasis added).

75. *JMJP*, 1.vii.76, in *PR*, 2.vii.76, pp. 7–8.

76. *HC* 3 (1976), in *SPRCM* 76–8 (1976), pp. 2–9; *HC* 2 (1976), in *SPRCM* 76–5 (1976), pp. 13–17; *HC* 7 (1976), in *SPRCM* 76–22 (1976), pp. 7–12.

77. R. Wuhan, 10.xi.76, in FBIS, 15.xi.76, pp. H4–5; NCNA, 29.xi.76, in FBIS, 30.xi.76, pp. E4–7.

78. *JMJP*, 29.v.76, in *PR*, 4.vi.76, pp. 11–12.

79. *JMJP*, 7.v.76, in *SPRCP* 76–20 (1976), pp. 118–23.

80. *JMJP*, 1.vii.76, in *SPRCP* 76–28 (1976), pp. 230–35.

81. *JMJP*, 23.vii.76, in *SPRCP* 76–35 (1976), pp. 167–69.

82. For accounts of leftist activities in various provinces, see R. Chengchow, 20.xi.76, in FBIS, 22.xi.76, pp. H1–3; NCNA, 11.xi.76, in FBIS, 18.xi.76, pp. G1–3; R. Nanchang, 29.xi.76, in FBIS, 1.xii.76, pp. G1–7; R. Wuhan, 8.xii.76, in FBIS, 9.xii.76, pp. H4–17; and NCNA, 28.xi.76, in FBIS, 29.xi.76, pp. E11–13.

83. *HC* 7 (1976), in *SPRCM* 76–22 (1976), pp. 7–12.

84. *CLG* 10.1 (Spring 1977), pp. 29–47.

85. *PR*, 26.xi.76, pp. 17–19.

86. For a fuller interpretation of the leftists' failure, see Harding, "China After Mao."

CHAPTER 11

1. Almond and Powell, pp. 276–77.

2. Vogel, "Politicized Bureaucracy," pp. 556–68. See also Hough, chap. 14; and the discussion of "L-structures" in Etzioni, chap. 9.

3. *JMJP*, 6.i.57, cited in Andors, p. 63.

4. Cf. Whyte, "Iron Law versus Mass Democracy."

5. Meisner, *Mao's China*, p. 324.

6. See Robinson, "Chou En-lai and the Cultural Revolution in China."

7. See MacFarquhar, *The Origins of the Cultural Revolution*, pp. 250–52.

8. *HC* 11 (1980), in FBIS, 17.vi.80, pp. L6–10.

9. Barnett, *Cadres, Bureaucracy, and Political Power*.

10. For a summary of communications processes within the Chinese bureaucracy, see Oksenberg, "Methods of Communication."

11. This point is the theme of Solomon's "Communication Patterns."

12. Domes, *China After the Cultural Revolution*, p. 78.

13. On the complaints against officials for bribery and corruption made during the campaign to criticize Lin Piao and Confucius, see AFP, 28.vi.74, in FBIS, 1.vii.74, pp. E3–4.

14. Almond and Powell, p. 279.

15. Vogel, "Politicized Bureaucracy," p. 567.

Glossary

blooming and contending. See HUNDRED FLOWERS MOVEMENT.

bureaucratism. As used by the Chinese, the tendency of officials to become inefficient, insensitive to public concerns, and ignorant of local conditions.

Cheng-feng campaign (1942–44). The first major Party rectification movement. It was designed to educate Party members from diverse backgrounds in a common ideology and outlook and to consolidate Party leadership after the inner-Party struggles of the 1930's. The campaign developed the basic techniques of CLOSED-DOOR RECTIFICATION that would be so important throughout the history of the Chinese Communist Party.

closed-door rectification. A type of campaign designed to improve organizational performance through study of selected documents, intense criticism and self-criticism, and small group discussions. In contrast to OPEN-DOOR RECTIFICATION, closed-door campaigns do not include participation by those outside the organization undergoing reform.

commandism. In Chinese usage, the tendency of bureaucratic officials to implement policy by force rather than persuasion.

Cultural Revolution (1966–69). A mass campaign launched by Mao Tse-tung to halt what he considered to be a tendency toward REVISIONISM in Chinese society. Ostensibly the Cultural Revolution involved the most radical criticism of bureaucracy in the history of the Chinese People's Republic, including demands that administrative organs be restructured along the lines of the Paris Commune. In actuality, the reforms undertaken during the Cultural Revolution were much more modest than the movement's rhetoric suggested. They included the formation of CULTURAL REVOLUTION COMMITTEES and REVOLUTIONARY COMMITTEES at virtually every level of administration, the reassessment of the political qualifications of all bureaucratic officials, regular cadre participation in ideological study and physical labor, retrenchment of bureaucratic staffs, and the decentralization of responsibility for economic planning from the central and regional authorities to the provinces.

Cultural Revolution committees. Originally intended as the forum for popular criticism of REVISIONISM during the CULTURAL REVOLUTION. Modeled after the Paris Commune, the committees were to be formed at the basic levels throughout the country to allow ordinary citizens to monitor and criticize the performance of local officials. They were not to replace the Party or government, but were to serve as a "bridge" between the Party and the people. The Cultural Revolution committees were soon replaced by the Red Guards and the REVOLUTIONARY COMMITTEES as the organizational instruments of the Cultural Revolution.

dogmatism. See SUBJECTIVISM.

empiricism. See SUBJECTIVISM.

external remedialism. As used in this study, the view that performance of bureaucracies can be improved by subjecting them to effective external control by non-bureaucratic organizations.

Fifty Days (1966). A brief but intense rectification campaign in June–July 1966 directed against "revisionist" officials in the central and provincial bureaus responsible for propaganda, culture, education, finance, trade, industry, and communications. The campaign was conducted in a supercharged political atmosphere amid growing demands by Mao and leftist officials that China be completely purged of REVISIONISM. To keep the movement under control, Liu Shao-ch'i banned or restricted popular participation and organized some 400 work teams composed of 10,000 officials to conduct the campaign inside the bureaucracy.

Five-anti movement (1962–64). A campaign launched at the Tenth Plenum as part of the SOCIALIST EDUCATION MOVEMENT and directed against corruption, speculation, waste, lack of coordination, and bureaucratic inefficiency in factories, enterprises, and Party and government agencies responsible for economic planning and management.

Great Leap Forward (1957–59). An attempt, like the HIGH TIDE, to promote rapid economic growth through mass mobilization. Despite the claims that the movement would quickly usher China into communism, the Leap's organizational policy contained few radical components. Instead, it involved a return to campaign styles of policymaking and administration, including a campaign against waste and conservatism (1958), a more flexible and rapid decision-making process, the extension of Party control over every policy issue, denigration of the roles of specialists in policymaking, and delegation to the provinces of power over the economy.

High Tide (1955–56). An attempt promoted by Mao Tse-tung in late 1955 to accelerate agricultural collectivization, industrial nationalization, and economic growth by reintroducing campaign techniques into the bureaucracy. These techniques included investigation of local conditions, faster circulation of information within the bureaucracy, comprehensive social and economic planning at every level of government, ambitious economic targets, and pressures to exceed even those goals. Cadres were accused of having "conservative work styles," and were urged to "speed up the tempo" and "achieve faster, greater, and better results" in all work projects.

hsia-fang. Literally, the "sending down" of officials to positions at lower levels of administration. Begun in Yenan in the mid-1940's, this method of organizational reform was reintroduced in several periods after 1949 especially in 1953–54, 1955, 1956–57, 1957–58 and during the CULTURAL REVOLUTION. The goals of hsia-fang, which have varied from one period to another, have included reducing administrative staffs and budgets at the upper and middle levels of the bureaucracy, strengthening leadership at the grass-roots levels, and providing officials with an opportunity for "reeducation" through physical labor.

Hundred Flowers Movement (1957). An OPEN-DOOR RECTIFICATION campaign sponsored by Mao Tse-tung to rid the Party of BUREAUCRATISM, SECTARIANISM, and SUBJECTIVISM. The campaign was particularly controversial because of Mao's insistence that the Party "open wide" to criticism, even from intellectuals and former capitalists who Mao admitted were wavering in their commitment to socialism, and his toleration of strikes and demonstrations as a means of expressing dissent. Despite the attempts of other Party leaders to keep the campaign under control, criticism expressed by students and intellectuals during the period of intense "blooming and contending" in May 1957 was more bitter than even Mao had expected. The movement was abruptly halted in June and replaced by a campaign against the "rightists" who had spoken out the month before.

internal remedialism. As used in this study, the view that organizational performance can be improved by deliberately introducing nonbureaucratic elements into the staffing and operations of a bureaucracy. These elements may include ideological indoctrination, the establishment of political criteria for public office, and the deliberate simplification of rules and regulations, and the implementation of policy through mobilization campaigns.

New San-fan campaign (1953). A campaign launched by the Central Committee in January 1953 against BUREAUCRATISM, COMMANDISM, and "violations of law and discipline" at all levels of administration. The campaign reflected the fact that the SAN-FAN CAMPAIGN had actually intensified, rather than resolved, problems of bureaucratic inefficiency and commandism. The methods employed during the campaign included work teams, ideological study, criticism and self-criticism, and limited mass participation. In general, it was a moderate movement restricted to CLOSED-DOOR RECTIFICATION.

open-door rectification. A type of campaign designed to improve organizational performance by inviting members of the public to criticize the behavior of bureaucratic officials. Compare CLOSED-DOOR RECTIFICATION.

poor and lower-middle peasant associations. Organizations formed during the SOCIALIST EDUCATION MOVEMENT of the early 1960's to provide a channel for popular control over basic-level Party and government organizations in the countryside. The reliability of these organizations became a major issue in the growing controversy between Mao Tse-tung and Liu Shao-ch'i that led to the CULTURAL REVOLUTION.

radicalism. As used in this study, the view that the social and political disadvantages of bureaucracy far outweigh the advantages, and that bureaucracies should therefore be replaced by organizations that are more participatory, less hierarchical, and less specialized.

rationalization. As used in this study, the view that an organization's performance can best be improved by bringing it closer to the bureaucratic ideal-type. This might be accomplished by creating a more efficient division of labor among the components of the organization, allocating power and responsibility more clearly, improving the skills of the organization's staff, adopting more effective rules and regulations, and establishing more stringent mechanisms for monitoring organizational performance.

Rectification of 1947–48. A campaign designed to rid basic-level leadership of cadres from landlord or rich peasant backgrounds and of officials who had engaged in corruption or abuses of power. The movement helped the Party to develop its techniques of OPEN-DOOR RECTIFICATION. Work teams dispatched from higher levels encouraged non-Party activists to criticize local cadres with bad class backgrounds or poor styles of work.

Rectification of 1950. A campaign initiated at the Third Plenum in June 1950 against the arrogance, BUREAUCRATISM, and COMMANDISM that had arisen in the Party after the seizure of nationwide power. The campaign was distinguished from its predecessors, the CHENG-FENG MOVEMENT and the RECTIFICATION OF 1947–48, in being more lenient and more tightly controlled.

revisionism. See SUBJECTIVISM.

revolutionary committees. Formed at the height of the CULTURAL REVOLUTION to replace Party committees and people's governments at virtually every level of administration. The revolutionary committees comprised a "three-in-one combination" of veteran civilian cadres, military officers, and popular representatives, but the distribution of power and position among these three groups varied considerably over time. The revolutionary committees were placed under the control of the Party apparatus when it was reestablished in the early 1970's and then abolished altogether shortly after the purge of the "Gang of Four."

revolutionary great debates. A device sponsored by leftist leaders during the mid-1970's to mobilize popular criticism of more moderate programs and policies, and thus to strengthen the leftists' political base. Although reminiscent of the period of "struggle and criticism" during the CULTURAL REVOLUTION, the revolutionary great debates were much milder in tone than the Red Guard movement, since the Party imposed restrictions on the formation of "fighting groups," and since participants in the debates were prohibited from attempting to "seize power" from the Party apparatus.

San-fan campaign (1951–52). The term is an abbreviation of "campaign against the Three Evils." An intense OPEN-DOOR RECTIFICATION, the San-fan campaign was directed against corruption, waste, and BUREAUCRATISM in both Party and government. It grew out of a continuing need to purify the ranks of the Communist movement after victory in the Revolution and to minimize the administrative expenditures of the bureaucracy during the Korean War. The campaign was treated as a "shock task" by most officials. It caused serious disruption of economic management and agricultural production in some areas and led to the punishment of 170,000 officials, but it did little to alleviate the problem of bureaucratism. The large number of cases of corruption discovered during the campaign led Party leaders to refocus attention on the "lawless" industrialists and merchants who had offered bribes to government and Party officials. The San-fan movement was thus transformed into the WU-FAN CAMPAIGN.

sectarianism. In Chinese usage, the tendency of some groups of officials to isolate themselves from, or look down on, other groups of officials. Usually sectarianism refers to cleavages between Party and non-Party officials within government bodies, but it can also refer to tensions between military and civilian cadres, strained relations between local cadres and officials sent in from outside, or even alienation of officials from the general public.

Socialist Education Movement (1962–66). A campaign designed to strengthen administrative organs throughout China, and to bolster commitment to socialist principles. In rural areas, the Socialist Education Movement was directed against cadre corruption and organizational decay. It also included several campaigns against inefficiency, excessive routinization, and REVISIONISM at upper levels of the bureaucracy, including the campaign to learn from the People's Liberation Army (1964–65), the campaign to study the thought of Mao Tse-tung (1965–66), and the FIFTY DAYS (1966). The Socialist Education Movement produced controversy at the highest levels of the Chinese leadership, particularly over the degree to which Party and state officials were following a revisionist course and the extent to which OPEN-DOOR RECTIFICATION in the form of POOR AND LOWER-MIDDLE PEASANT ASSOCIATIONS would be the appropriate solution for organizational problems in the countryside. The debates surrounding the movement were a major cause of the CULTURAL REVOLUTION.

Su-fan campaign (1955). A campaign directed against so-called hidden counterrevolutionaries in the Party and government. It provided the opportunity to dismiss from office most of the officials that the Communist regime had originally held over from the Nationalist government.

subjectivism. In Chinese usage, the tendency of officials or Party members to substitute their own partial or biased understanding of a situation for more objective analysis. Subjectivism may take any of several forms: dogmatism (the mechanical application of ideological prescriptions to a given problem), empiricism (the tendency to deal with a situation on its merits without referring to its broader ideological implications), or revisionism (the alteration of basic Marxist-Leninist principles in ways that threaten the restoration of capitalism).

"three-in-one combination." See REVOLUTIONARY COMMITTEES.

waste and conservatism. See GREAT LEAP FORWARD.

Wu-fan campaign (1952). The term is an abbreviation of "campaign against the Five Evils." An outgrowth of the SAN-FAN CAMPAIGN, the Wu-fan campaign was directed against bribery, theft of state property, theft of state secrets, cheating on contracts, and tax evasion on the part of private merchants and industrialists. The fines and other penalties levied during the campaign forced many private enterprises into state ownership.

Bibliography

Ahn, Byung-joon. "Adjustments in the Great Leap Forward and Their Ideological Legacy, 1959–62." In Chalmers Johnson, ed., *Ideology and Politics in Contemporary China*. Seattle, 1973.
———. *Chinese Politics and the Cultural Revolution: Dynamics of Policy Processes*. Seattle, 1976.
Allison, Graham T. *Essence of Decision: Explaining the Cuban Missile Crisis*. Boston, 1971.
Almond, Gabriel A., and G. Bingham Powell, Jr. *Comparative Politics: System, Process, and Policy*. 2d ed. Boston, 1978.
Andors, Stephen. *China's Industrial Revolution: Politics, Planning, and Management, 1949 to the Present*. New York, 1977.
The Anti-Stalin Campaign and International Communism: A Selection of Documents. Edited by the Russian Institute, Columbia University. New York, 1956.
Avineri, Shlomo. *The Social and Political Thought of Karl Marx*. Cambridge, 1968.
Balazs, Etienne. *Chinese Civilization and Bureaucracy: Variations on a Theme*. Translated by H. M. Wright. New Haven, 1964.
Barnett, A. Doak. *Cadres, Bureaucracy, and Political Power in Communist China*. New York, 1967.
———, ed. *Chinese Communist Politics in Action*. Seattle, 1969.
———. *Communist China: The Early Year, 1949–55. New York*, 1965.
Bastid, Marianne. "Levels of Economic Decision-Making." In Stuart R. Schram, ed., *Authority, Participation, and Cultural Change in China*. Cambridge, 1973.
Baum, Richard. "China: Year of the Mangoes." *Asian Survey*, 9 (1979): 1–17.
———. *Prelude to Revolution: Mao, the Party, and the Peasant Question, 1962–66*. New York, 1975.
———, and Frederick C. Teiwes. *Ssu-Ch'ing: The Socialist Education Movement of 1962–1966*. Center for Chinese Studies, Research Monograph No. 2. Berkeley, Calif., 1968.
Bayley, David. "The Effects of Corruption in a Developing Nation." *Western Political Quarterly*, 19 (1966): 719–32.
Bendix, Reinhard. *Max Weber: An Intellectual Portrait*. Garden City, N.Y., 1962.
Bennett, Gordon A., and Ronald N. Montaperto. *Red Guard: The Political Biography of Dai Hsiao-ai*. Garden City, N.Y., 1971.
Bennis, Warren G. *Changing Organizations: Essays on the Development and Evolution of Human Organization*. New York, 1966.
Berkley, George E. *The Administrative Revolution: Notes on the Passing of Organization Man*. Englewood Cliffs, N.J., 1971.
Bernstein, Thomas P. "Keeping the Revolution Going: Problems of Village Leadership After Land Reform." In John W. Lewis, ed., *Party Leadership and Revolutionary Power in China*. Cambridge, 1970.
———. *Up to the Mountains and Down to the Villages*. New Haven, 1977.
Blau, Peter M., and W. Richard Scott. *Formal Organizations: A Comparative Approach*. San Francisco, 1962.

Borisov, O. B., and B. T. Koloskov. *Soviet-Chinese Relations, 1945–1970*. Translated by Vladimir Petrov. Bloomington, Ind., 1975.

Bowie, Robert R., and John K. Fairbank, eds. *Communist China, 1955–1959: Policy Documents with Analysis*. Cambridge, Mass., 1962.

Brandt, Conrad, Benjamin Schwartz, and John K. Fairbank, eds. *A Documentary History of Chinese Communism*. New York, 1952.

Bridgham, Philip C. "Factionalism in the Central Committee." In John W. Lewis, ed., *Party Leadership and Revolutionary Power in China*. Cambridge, 1970.

———. "The Fall of Lin Piao." *China Quarterly*, no. 55 (July–September 1973), pp. 427–49.

Brzezinski, Zbigniew. *The Permanent Purge: Politics in Soviet Totalitarianism*. Cambridge, Mass., 1956.

Burchett, Wilfred. "Lin Piao's Plot—The Full Story." *Far Eastern Economic Review*, August 20, 1973, pp. 22–24.

CCP Documents of the Great Proletarian Cultural Revolution, 1966–1967. Hong Kong, 1968.

Chamberlain, Heath B. "Transition and Consolidation in Urban China: A Study of Leaders and Organizations in Three Cities, 1949–1953." In Robert A. Scalapino, ed., *Elites in the People's Republic of China*. Seattle, 1972.

Chang, Parris H. "Mao's Last Stand?" *Problems of Communism*, 25.4 (July–August 1976): 1–17.

———. "Peking and the Provinces: Decentralization of Power." *Problems of Communism*, 21.4 (July–August 1972): 67–74.

———. "Political Rehabilitation of Cadres in China: A Traveller's View." *China Quarterly*, no. 54 (April–June 1973), pp. 331–40.

———. *Power and Policy in China*. University Park, Pa., 1975.

———. "Provincial Party Leaders' Strategies for Survival During the Cultural Revolution." In Robert A. Scalapino, ed., *Elites in the People's Republic of China*. Seattle, 1972.

Chao, Han. *T'an-t'an Chung-kuo Kung-ch'an-tang-ti cheng-feng yün-tung* (A discussion of the rectification campaigns of the Chinese Communist Party). Peking, 1957.

Chao, Kang. "Policies and Performance in Industry." In Alexander Eckstein, Walter Galenson, and Ta-chung Liu, eds., *Economic Trends in Communist China*. Chicago, 1968.

Chen, C. S., ed. *Rural People's Communes in Lien-chiang: Documents Concerning Communes in Lien-chiang County, Fukien Province, 1962–1963*. Stanford, Calif., 1969.

Chen, Theodore Hsi-en, and Wen-hui Chen. "The 'Three-Anti' and 'Five-Anti' Movements in Communist China." *Pacific Affairs*, 26 (1953): 3–23.

Ch'en, Jerome, ed. *Mao*. Englewood Cliffs, N.J., 1969.

———, ed. *Mao Papers: Anthology and Bibliography*. London, 1970.

Chien, Yu-shen. *China's Fading Revolution: Army Dissent and Military Divisions, 1967–68*. Hong Kong, 1969.

China: A Look at the 11th Central Committee. Central Intelligence Agency, National Foreign Assessment Center, RP 77-10276. Washington, D.C., 1977.

China: A Reassessment of the Economy. Report of the U.S. Congress Joint Economic Committee. Washington, D.C., 1975.

Chow Ching-wen. *Ten Years of Storm: The True Story of the Communist Regime in China*. New York, 1960.

Christman, Henry M., ed. *Essential Works of Lenin*. New York, 1961.

Chugoku no keizai kanri taisei to kiko (The system and structure of economic management in China). Tokyo, 1964.

Chung-hua-jen-min-kung-ho-kuo fa-kuei hui-pien (Compendium of laws and regulations of the People's Republic of China). Peking, 1956–.

Chung-hua-jen-min-kung-ho-kuo ti-i-chieh ch'üan-kuo jen-min tai-piao ta-hui ti-san-tz'u hui-i wen-chien (Documents of the Third Session of the First National People's Congress of the People's Republic of China). Peking, 1956.

Ch'u T'ung-tsu. *Local Government in China Under the Ch'ing.* Stanford, Calif., 1969.

Cobb, Roger, et al. "Agenda Building as a Comparative Political Process." *American Political Science Review*, 70 (1976): 126–38.

Cocks, Paul. "The Rationalization of Party Control." In Chalmers Johnson, ed., *Change in Communist Systems.* Stanford, Calif., 1970.

———. "The Role of the Party Control Committee in Communist China." Harvard University, East Asian Research Center, *Papers on China*, vol. 22B. Cambridge, Mass., 1969.

Cohen, Jerome Alan. *The Criminal Process in the People's Republic of China, 1949–1963: An Introduction.* Cambridge, Mass., 1968.

Committee of Concerned Asian Scholars. *China! Inside the People's Republic.* New York, 1972.

Compton, Boyd. *Mao's China: Party Reform Documents, 1942–44.* Seattle, 1966.

"The Conflict Between Mao Tse-tung and Liu Shao-ch'i over Agricultural Mechanization in Communist China." *Current Scene*, 6.17 (October 1, 1968).

Conquest, Robert. *The Great Terror: Stalin's Purge of the Thirties.* New York, 1968.

Constas, Helen. "The U.S.S.R.—From Charismatic Sect to Bureaucratic Society." *Administrative Science Quarterly*, 6 (1961): 282–98.

Constitution of the Communist Party of China. Peking, 1956.

Crozier, Michel. *The Bureaucratic Phenomenon.* Chicago, 1964.

Daubier, Jean. *A History of the Chinese Cultural Revolution.* New York, 1975.

Decision of the Central Committee of the Chinese Communist Party Concerning the Great Proletarian Cultural Revolution. Peking, 1966.

Dittmer, Lowell. "'Line Struggle' in Theory and Practice: The Origins of the Cultural Revolution Reconsidered." *China Quarterly*, no. 72 (December 1977), pp. 675–712.

Documents of Chinese Communist Party Central Committee, September 1956–April 1969. Kowloon, 1971.

Documents of the First Session of the Fourth National People's Congress of the People's Republic of China. Peking, 1975.

Domes, Jürgen. *China After the Cultural Revolution: Politics Between Two Party Congresses.* Berkeley and Los Angeles, 1977.

———. *The Internal Politics of China, 1949–1972.* London, 1973.

———. "New Course in Chinese Domestic Politics: The Anatomy of Readjustment." *Asian Survey*, 13 (1973): 633–47.

———. "The Role of the Military in the Formation of Revolutionary Committees, 1967–68." *China Quarterly*, no. 44 (October–December 1970), pp. 112–45.

Donnithorne, Audrey. "China's Cellular Economy: Some Economic Trends Since the Cultural Revolution." *China Quarterly*, no. 52 (October–December 1972), pp. 605–19.

———. *China's Economic System.* New York, 1967.

Doolin, Dennis. *Communist China: The Politics of Student Opposition.* Hoover Institution Study No. 2. Stanford, Calif., 1964.

Downs, Anthony. *Inside Bureaucracy*. Boston, 1967.

Dunsire, A. *Administration: The Word and the Science*. London, 1973.

Eckstein, Alexander. *China's Economic Development: The Interplay of Scarcity and Ideology*. Ann Arbor, Mich., 1975.

——. *Communist China's Economic Growth and Foreign Trade: Implications for U.S. Policy*. New York, 1966.

Eighth National Congress of the Communist Party of China. Vol. 1: Documents; Vol. 2: Speeches. Peking, 1956.

Emerson, John Philip. "Manpower Training and Utilization of Specialized Cadres, 1949–68." In John W. Lewis, ed., *The City in Communist China*. Stanford, Calif., 1971.

Esmein, Jean. *The Chinese Cultural Revolution*. Translated by W.J.F. Jenner. Garden City, N.Y., 1973.

Etzioni, Amitai. *A Comparative Analysis of Complex Organizations: On Power, Involvement, and Their Correlates*. New York, 1961.

Falkenheim, Victor C. "County Administration in Fukien." *China Quarterly*, no. 59 (July–September 1974), pp. 518–43.

——. "Peking and the Provinces: Continuing Central Predominance." *Problems of Communism*, 21.4 (July–August 1972): 75–83.

——. "Provincial Leadership in Fukien: 1949–66." In Robert A. Scalapino, ed., *Elites in the People's Republic of China*. Seattle, 1972.

Feuer, Lewis S., ed. *Marx and Engels: Basic Writings on Politics and Philosophy*. New York, 1966.

Fingar, Thomas. "Politics and Policy-Making in the People's Republic of China, 1954–55." Ph.D. dissertation, Stanford University, 1977.

Fung Yu-lan. *A Short History of Chinese Philosophy*. Edited by Derk Bodde. New York, 1966.

Gardner, John. "The *Wu-Fan* Campaign in Shanghai: A Study in the Consolidation of Urban Control." In A. Doak Barnett, ed., *Chinese Communist Politics in Action*. Seattle, 1969.

Ginsburgs, George, and Arthur Stahnke. "The Genesis of the People's Procuratorate in Communist China, 1949–1951." *China Quarterly*, no. 20 (October–December 1964), pp. 1–37.

——. "The People's Procuratorate in Communist China: The Institution in the Ascendant, 1954–1957." *China Quarterly*, no. 34 (April–June 1968), pp. 82–132.

——. "The People's Procuratorate in Communist China: The Period of Maturation, 1951–1954." *China Quarterly*, no. 24 (October–December 1965), pp. 53–91.

Gittings, John. "Army-Party Relations in the Light of the Cultural Revolution." In John W. Lewis, ed., *Party Leadership and Revolutionary Power in China*. Cambridge, 1970.

——. *The Role of the Chinese Army*. London, 1967.

Goldman, Merle. "China's Anti-Confucian Campaign, 1973–74." *China Quarterly*, no. 63 (September 1975), pp. 435–62.

——. "Party Policies Toward the Intellectuals: The Unique Blooming and Contending of 1961–2." In John W. Lewis, ed., *Party Leadership and Revolutionary Power in China*. Cambridge, 1970.

Gottlieb, Thomas M. *Chinese Foreign Policy Factionalism and the Origins of the Strategic Triangle*. Rand Corp. Report R-1902-NA. Santa Monica, 1977.

Gray, Jack. "The Economics of Maoism." In *China After the Cultural Revolution.* Edited by *Bulletin of the Atomic Scientists.* New York, 1970.

———, and Patrick Cavendish. *Chinese Communism in Crisis: Maoism and the Cultural Revolution.* New York, 1968.

The Great Socialist Cultural Revolution in China. Vol. 7. Peking, 1967.

Gurtov, Melvin. "The Foreign Ministry and Foreign Affairs in the Chinese Cultural Revolution." In Thomas W. Robinson, ed., *The Cultural Revolution in China.* Berkeley and Los Angeles, 1971.

Hall, Richard H. "Professionalization and Bureaucratization." *American Sociological Review,* 33 (1968): 92–104.

Harding, Harry. "China After Mao." *Problems of Communism,* 26.2 (March–April 1977): 1–18.

———. "Maoist Theories of Policy-Making and Organization: Lessons from the Cultural Revolution." In Thomas W. Robinson, ed., *The Cultural Revolution in China.* Berkeley and Los Angeles, 1971.

———. "The Organizational Issue in Chinese Politics, 1959–1972." Ph.D. dissertation, Stanford University, 1973.

———. "The Organizational Issue in Chinese Politics, 1949–1975." In *Proceedings of the Fifth Sino-American Conference on Mainland China.* Taipei, 1976.

Harper, Paul. "Workers' Participation in Management in Communist China." Paper presented at the Annual Meeting of the American Political Science Association, 1970.

Harrison, James P. *The Long March to Power: A History of the Chinese Communist Party, 1971–1972.* New York, 1972.

Hilsman, Roger. *The Politics of Policy Making in Defense and Foreign Affairs.* New York, 1971.

Hinton, William. *Hundred Day War: The Cultural Revolution at Tsinghua University.* New York, 1972.

Hough, Jerry F. *The Soviet Prefects: The Local Party Organs in Industrial Decision-Making.* Cambridge, Mass., 1969.

Hsiao Kung-ch'üan. *Rural China: Imperial Control in the Nineteenth Century.* Seattle, 1960.

Hucker, Charles O. "Confucianism and the Chinese Censorial System." In David S. Nivison and Arthur F. Wright, eds., *Confucianism in Action.* Stanford, Calif., 1959.

Hunter, Neale. *Shanghai Journal: An Eyewitness Account of the Cultural Revolution.* New York, 1969.

Huntington, Samuel P. *Political Order in Changing Societies.* New Haven, 1968.

Illich, Ivan. "Why We Must Abolish Schooling." *New York Review of Books,* July 2, 1970, p. 9.

"Industrial Development in China." *Current Scene,* 6.22 (December 20, 1968).

Jen-min shou-ts'e (People's handbook). Shanghai, Tientsin, and Peking, 1950–.

Joffe, Ellis. *Between Two Plenums: China's Intraleadership Conflict, 1959–1962.* Michigan Papers on Chinese Studies No. 22. Ann Arbor, Mich., 1975.

———. "The Chinese Army Under Lin Piao: Prelude to Political Intervention." In John M. H. Lindbeck, ed. *China: Management of a Revolutionary Society.* Seattle, 1971.

———. *Party and Army: Professionalism and Political Control in the Chinese Officer Corps, 1949–1964.* Cambridge, Mass., 1965.

Johnson, Chalmers, ed. *Change in Communist Systems.* Stanford, Calif., 1970.

————, ed. *Ideology and Politics in Contemporary China*. Seattle, 1973.

Katz, Elihu, and Brenda Danet, eds. *Bureaucracy and the Public: A Reader in Official-Client Relations*. New York, 1973.

Kau, Michael Y. M., ed. *The Lin Piao Affair: Power Politics and Military Coup*. White Plains, N.Y., 1975.

————. "Patterns of Recruitment and Mobility of Urban Cadres." In John W. Lewis, ed., *The City in Communist China*. Stanford, Calif., 1971.

Kim, Ilpyong J. *The Politics of Chinese Communism: Kiangsi Under the Soviets*. Berkeley and London, 1973.

Klein, Donald W. "Sources for Elite Studies and Biographical Materials on China." In Robert A. Scalapino, ed., *Elites in the People's Republic of China*. Seattle, 1972.

————, and Lois B. Hager. "The Ninth Central Committee." *China Quarterly*, no. 45 (January–March 1971), pp. 37–56.

LaPalombara, Joseph G., ed. *Bureaucracy and Political Development*. Princeton, N.J., 1963.

Lardy, Nicholas R. "Centralization and Decentralization in China's Fiscal Management." *China Quarterly*, no. 61 (March 1975), pp. 25–60.

————. "Economic Planning in the People's Republic of China: Central-Provincial Fiscal Relations." In *China: A Reassessment of the Economy*. Report of the U.S. Congress Joint Economic Committee. Washington, D.C., 1975.

Lenin, V. I. *Selected Works in Three Volumes*. Moscow, 1971.

Lewis, John W., ed. *The City in Communist China*. Stanford, Calif., 1971.

————. *Leadership in Communist China*. Ithaca, N.Y., 1963.

————, ed. *Party Leadership and Revolutionary Power in China*. Cambridge, 1970.

Lieberthal, Kenneth G. "China in 1975: The Internal Political Scene." *Problems of Communism*, 24.3 (May–June 1975): 1–11.

————. *A Research Guide to Central Party and Government Meetings in China, 1949–1975*. White Plains, N.Y., 1976.

Lifton, Robert Jay. *Thought Reform and the Psychology of Totalism: A Study of "Brainwashing" in China*. New York, 1961.

Lindbeck, John M. H., ed. *China: Management of a Revolutionary Society*. Seattle, 1971.

Lippit, Victor D. "The Great Leap Forward Reconsidered." *Modern China*, 1 (1975): 92–115.

[Liu Shao-ch'i.] *Collected Works of Liu Shao-ch'i*. 3 vols. Kowloon, 1968.

Lötveit, Trygve. *Chinese Communism, 1931–1934: Experience in Civil Government*. Scandinavian Institute of Asian Studies Monograph No. 16. Stockholm, 1973.

Macciocchi, Maria. *Daily Life in Revolutionary China*. New York, 1972.

MacFarquhar, Roderick. "Communist China's Intra-Party Dispute." *Pacific Affairs*, 31 (1958): 323–35.

————, ed. *The Hundred Flowers Campaign and the Chinese Intellectuals*. New York, 1960.

————. *The Origins of the Cultural Revolution. Vol. 1: Contradictions Among the People, 1956–1957*. New York, 1974.

Malraux, Andre. *Anti-Memoirs*. Translated by Terence Kilmartin. New York, 1968.

[Mao Tse-tung.] *Mao Tse-tung ssu-hsiang wan sui!* (Long live Mao Tse-tung thought!) N.p., 1967.

[————.] *Miscellany of Mao Tse-tung Thought*. Joint Publications Research Service, Nos. 61269-1, -2 (February 20, 1974). Arlington, Va., 1974.

[————?] "On Khrushchov's Phoney Communism and Its Historical Lessons for the World: Comment on the Open Letter of the CPSU (IX)." In *The Polemic on the General Line of the International Communist Movement*. Peking, 1965.

————. *Selected Readings from the Works of Mao Tse-tung*. Peking, 1967.

————. *Selected Works of Mao Tse-tung*. 5 vols. Peking, 1967–77.

Mehnert, Klaus. *China Returns*. New York, 1972.

————. *Peking and the New Left: At Home and Abroad*. Center for Chinese Studies Monograph No. 4. Berkeley, Calif., 1969.

Meisner, Maurice. "Leninism and Maoism: Some Populist Perspectives on Marxism-Leninism in China." *China Quarterly*, no. 45 (January–March 1971), pp. 2–36.

————. *Mao's China: A History of the People's Republic*. New York, 1977.

Merton, Robert, et al., eds. *Reader in Bureaucracy*. New York, 1952.

Metzger, Thomas A. *The Internal Organization of Ch'ing Bureaucracy: Legal, Normative, and Communication Aspects*. Cambridge, Mass., 1973.

Meyer, Alfred G. *The Soviet Political System: An Interpretation*. New York, 1965.

Montell, Sherwin. "The *San-fan Wu-fan* Movement in Communist China." In Harvard University, Committee on International Regional Studies, *Papers on China*, vol. 8. Cambridge, Mass., 1954.

Montgomery, James D., and William J. Siffin, eds. *Approaches to Development: Politics, Administration, and Change*. New York, 1966.

Mouzelis, Nicos P. *Organisation and Bureaucracy: An Analysis of Modern Theories*. Chicago, 1968.

Nee, Victor. "Revolution and Bureaucracy: Shanghai in the Cultural Revolution." In Victor Nee and James Peck, eds., *China's Uninterrupted Revolution: From 1840 to the Present*. New York, 1975.

Nelsen, Harvey W. "Military Bureaucracy in the Cultural Revolution." *Asian Survey*, 14 (1974): 372–95.

————. "Military Forces in the Cultural Revolution." *China Quarterly*, no. 51 (July–September 1972), pp. 444–74.

Niijima, Atsuyoshi. "The Establishment of a New Commune State." *Chinese Law and Government*, 4 (1971): 38–60.

Nivison, David S., and Arthur F. Wright, eds. *Confuscianism in Action*. Stanford, Calif., 1959.

Nye, Joseph S. "Corruption and Political Development: A Cost-Benefit Analysis." *American Political Science Review*, 61 (1967): 417–27.

Oksenberg, Michel. "Methods of Communication Within the Chinese Bureaucracy." *China Quarterly*, no. 57 (January–March 1974), pp. 1–39.

————. "Policy-Making Under Mao, 1949–68: An Overview." In John M. H. Lindbeck, ed., *China: Management of a Revolutionary Society*. Seattle, 1971.

————, and Franco Pavoncello. "Recent Explorations in Elite Conflict in China." *Journal of Asian Studies*, 36 (1979): 333–38.

Parkinson, C. Northcote. *Parkinson's Law, and Other Studies in Administration*. New York, 1964.

People's Republic of China: An Economic Assessment. Report of the U.S. Congress Joint Economic Committee. Washington, D.C., 1972.

Powell, Ralph L. "Commissars in the Economy: The 'Learn from the PLA' Movement in China." *Asian Survey*, 5 (1965): 125–38.

Price, Jane L. *Cadres, Commanders, and Commissars: The Training of the Chinese Communist Leadership, 1920–1945*. Boulder, Colo., 1976.

Prybyla, Jan S. *The Political Economy of Communist China*. Scranton, Pa., 1970.

Reich, Charles A. *The Greening of America*. New York, 1970.

Rice, Edward E. *Mao's Way*. Berkeley and Los Angeles, 1972.

Riggs, Fred W. *Administration in the Developing Countries: The Theory of Prismatic Societies*. Boston, 1964.

———, ed. *Frontiers of Development Administration*. Durham, N.C., 1970.

Robinson, Thomas W. "Chou En-lai and the Cultural Revolution." In Thomas W. Robinson, ed., *The Cultural Revolution in China*. Berkeley and Los Angeles, 1971.

———, ed. *The Cultural Revolution in China*. Berkeley and Los Angeles, 1971.

———. *A Politico-Military Biography of Lin Piao: Part I, 1907–1949*. Rand Corporation Report R-526-PR. Santa Monica, Calif., 1971.

Scalapino, Robert A. "The CCP's Provincial Secretaries." *Problems of Communism*, 25.4 (July–August 1976): 18–35.

———, ed. *Elites in the People's Republic of China*. Seattle, 1972.

Schapiro, Leonard B. *The Communist Party of the Soviet Union*. 2d ed. New York, 1971.

Schram, Stuart R., ed. *Authority, Participation, and Cultural Change in China: Essays by a European Study Group*. Cambridge, 1973.

———, ed. *Chairman Mao Talks to the People: Talks and Letters, 1956–1971*. New York, 1974.

———, ed. *The Political Thought of Mao Tse-tung*. Rev. ed. New York, 1969.

Schurmann, Franz. *Ideology and Organization in Communist China*. Rev. ed. Berkeley and Los Angeles, 1968.

Scott, James C. *Comparative Political Corruption*. Englewood Cliffs, N.J., 1972.

———. "An Essay on the Political Functions of Corruption." *Asian Studies*, 5 (1967): 501–23.

Selden, Mark. *The Yenan Way in Revolutionary China*. Cambridge, Mass., 1971.

Snow, Edgar. *The Long Revolution*. New York, 1973.

Solinger, Dorothy. *Regional Government and Political Integration in Southwest China, 1949–1954: A Case Study*. Berkeley and Los Angeles, 1977.

Solomon, Richard H. "Communications Patterns and the Chinese Revolution." *China Quarterly*, no. 32 (October–December 1971), pp. 88–110.

———. *Mao's Revolution and the Chinese Political Culture*. Berkeley and Los Angeles, 1971.

Stalin, J. V. *Problems of Leninism*. Peking, 1976.

Starr, John Bryan. "China in 1975: 'The Wind in the Bell Tower.'" *Asian Survey*, 16 (1976): 42–60.

———. "From the Tenth Party Congress to the Premiership of Hua Kuo-feng: The Significance of the Colour of the Cat." *China Quarterly*, no. 67 (September 1976), pp. 457–88.

———. "Mao Tse-tung's Theory of Continuing the Revolution Under the Dictatorship of the Proletariat: Its Origins, Development, and Practical Consequences." Ph.D. dissertation, University of California, Berkeley, 1971.

———. "Revolution in Retrospect: The Paris Commune Through Chinese Eyes." *China Quarterly*, no. 49 (January–March 1972), pp. 106–25.

Stavis, Benedict. *People's Communes and Rural Development in China*. Special Series on Rural Local Government No. 2. Ithaca, N.Y., 1974.

Tang-ti tsu-chih kung-tso wen-ta (Questions and answers on Party organization work). Peking, 1959.

Teiwes, Frederick C. "Chinese Politics, 1949–1965: A Changing Mao." *Current Scene*, 12.1 (January 1974) and 12.2 (February 1974).

———. "The Evolution of Leadership Purges in Communist China." *China Quarterly*, no. 41 (January–March 1970), pp. 122–35.

———. "The Origins of Rectification: Inner-Party Purges and Education Before Liberation." *China Quarterly*, no. 65 (March 1976), pp. 15–53.

———. *Provincial Leadership in China: The Cultural Revolution and Its Aftermath*. East Asian Paper No. 4. Ithaca, N.Y., 1974.

———. "The Purge of Provincial Leaders, 1957–1958." *China Quarterly*, no. 27 (July–September 1966), pp. 14–32.

———. "Rectification Campaigns and Purges in Communist China, 1950–1961." Ph.D. dissertation, Columbia University, 1971.

Teng Hsiao-p'ing. *Report on the Revision of the Constitution of the Communist Party of China*. Peking, 1956.

The Tenth National Congress of the Communist Party of China (Documents). Peking, 1973.

Thomas, S. B. *Government and Administration in Communist China*. New York, 1953.

Thompson, James D. *Organizations in Action: Social Science Bases of Administrative Theory*. New York, 1967.

Thornton, Richard C. "The Structure of Communist Politics." *World Politics*, 24 (1972): 498–517.

Toffler, Alvin. *Future Shock*. New York, 1970.

Tucker, Robert C. *The Marxian Revolutionary Idea*. New York, 1970.

———, ed. *The Lenin Anthology*. New York, 1975.

Turovtsev, Victor. *People's Control in Socialist Society*. Moscow, 1973.

Uphoff, Norman T., and Milton Esman. *Local Organization for Rural Development: Analysis of Asian Experience*. Special Series on Rural Local Government No. 19. Ithaca, N.Y., 1974.

van Ginneken, Jaap. *The Rise and Fall of Lin Piao*. New York, 1977.

Vogel, Ezra F. *Canton Under Communism: Programs and Politics in a Provincial Capital, 1949–1968*. Cambridge, Mass., 1969.

———. "From Revolutionary to Semi-Bureaucrat: The 'Regularisation' of Cadres." *China Quarterly*, no. 29 (January–March 1967), pp. 36–60.

———. "Politicized Bureaucracy: Communist China." In Fred W. Riggs, ed., *Frontiers of Development Administration*. Durham, N.C., 1970.

Waldo, Dwight, ed. *Public Administration in a Time of Turbulence*. Scranton, Pa., 1971.

Walker, Richard L. *China Under Communism: The First Five Years*. London, 1956.

Wang, James C. F. "The May Seventh Cadre School for Eastern Peking." *China Quarterly*, no. 63 (September 1975), pp. 522–27.

Watt, John R. *The District Magistrate in Late Imperial China*. New York, 1972.

Weber, Max. *Economy and Society: An Outline of Interpretive Sociology*. Edited by Guenther Roth and Claus Wittich. Vol. 1. New York, 1968.

———. *The Theory of Social and Economic Organization*. Translated by A. M. Henderson and Talcott Parsons. New York, 1964.

Whitson, William W. *The Chinese High Command: A History of Communist Military Politics, 1927–71*. New York, 1973.

Whyte, Martin King. "Bureaucracy and Modernization in China: The Maoist Critique." *American Sociological Review*, 38 (1973): 149–63.

———. "Iron Law versus Mass Democracy: Weber, Michels, and the Maoist Vision." In James C. Hsiung, ed., *The Logic of "Maoism": Critiques and Explication*. New York, 1974.

Wich, Richard. "The Tenth Party Congress: The Power Structure and the Succession Question." *China Quarterly*, no. 58 (April–June 1974), pp. 231–48.

Wilensky, Harold L. *Organizational Intelligence: Knowledge and Power in Government and Industry*. New York, 1967.

Wiles, P.J.D. *The Political Economy of Communism*. Oxford, 1962.

Wu, Silas H. L. *Communication and Imperial Control in China: Evolution of the Palace Memorial System, 1693–1735*. Cambridge, Mass., 1970.

Yang, C. K. "Some Characteristics of Chinese Bureaucratic Behavior." In David S. Nivison and Arthur F. Wright, eds., *Confucianism in Action*. Stanford, Calif., 1959.

Index

Daubier, Jean, 260
Decentralism, problem of, 62
Decentralization, 9f, 149, 151; Mao on, 68; in mid-1950's, 107–14, 120f; Chou En-lai on, 109–12, 113; during Great Leap Forward, 175–77, 181–82, 329; in communes, 197; during Cultural Revolution, 289–92
Democratic centralism, 277–78
Democratic League, 125
Democratic parties: giving greater political voice to, 124–25; role in rectification of, 142–43; criticisms made by, 146–47
Democratization, proposals for, 122–24, 137, 141, 160
De-Stalinization, 87, 116, 117–29, 140, 149–50
Dictatorship of the proletariat: Stalin on, 20; Marx, Engels, Lenin on, 26–28; de-Stalinization and, 117; criticisms of, 148; Mao, and campaign to study, 315–17
Discipline, *see* Control mechanisms
Dittmer, Lowell, 201
Division of labor, problems in, 92–93
"Documentism," problem of, 93
Dogmatism, 139–40, 157; Mao on, 172. *See also* Subjectivism
Domes, Jürgen, 300
Downs, Anthony, 2n, 3, 5
Dunsire, A., 15

Early Ten Points, 202–3, 330
East China region, 45, 53, 68
Echelon: -by-echelon management, 110; distinction between level and, 268n
Economic conditions: during 1949–53 period, 32f, 40, 42f, 49–50, 65; Mao on, 32, 42, 54, 114–15, 176–77, 339; during 1952–55 period, 65–72 *passim*, 89–90; in Hundred Flowers period, 116, 119, 129f; in Great Leap Forward, 165–69, 178; in early 1960's, 196–97. *See also* Agriculture; Industry
Education, 65f, 134, 304, 320; Mao on, 24, 200; of cadres, *see* Cadres; Ideological study; May Seventh cadre schools
Education, Ministry of, 102f
Efficiency, *see* Inefficiency
Egalitarianism, campaign against, 183
Eighth Party Congress: First Session (1956), 71, 109, 112, 118–29, 137, 141, 150; Second Session (1958), 167, 174
Elections, *see* Popular participation
Eleventh Plenum (1966), 229, 236–39 *passim*, 268, 273

Elitism, bureaucratic privilege and, 146–47, 161, 162–63, 305n, 354–55. *See also* Alienation
Empiricism, 139. *See also* Subjectivism
Engels, Friedrich, 26f. *See also* Marxist-Leninist theory
Experts, Bureau of, 76
External remedialism, 194, 330, 335–37; as approach to bureaucratic dilemma, 16–17; in Chinese political tradition, 22–24; regularized, 331–34 *passim*; radical, 331–34 *passim*; defined, 402
Extortion, *see* Corruption

Factionalism: within revolutionary committees (Chou En-lai on), 271–72; among mass organizations, 274
Fifty Days, 225–59, 238, 268, 341, 402
Finance, Ministry of, 95, 132, 227, 270
Five-anti movement, 205–6, 217, 402
"Five communist styles," campaign against, 183, 197
"Five evils," the, 54
"Five excesses," the, 61–62
"Five-red" family backgrounds, 245
"571" document, 303–4, 309
Five-Year Plans: First, 65–72 *passim*, 76, 87, 89–90, 103f, 108, 353; Second, 104–9 *passim*, 167; Third, 224
Food Industry, Ministry of, 94n
Foreign Affairs, Ministry of, 219, 271
Foreign policy, moderates' program for (1971–73), 304–5
Foreign Trade, Ministry of, 301
Forestry, Ministry of, 94
"Four modernizations," 317
Fukien, 103

"Gang of Four," 326, 342. *See also* Chang Ch'un-ch'iao; Chiang Ch'ing; Wang Hung-wen; Yao Wen-yüan
Generalist-specialist relationships, 4, 350
Generational problems, cadre tensions resulting from, 38–40, 146, 156–57
Goal displacement, 13
"Going against the tide," 311f, 342
Goldman, Merle, 185n
Government: China's history of bureaucratic, 17–31, 193f, 235, 266; and Party relationships, 23–24, 48–53 *passim*, 65–86, 146f, 173–74, 187, 284–88, 293, 336, 353; regional, 34–35, 49f, 67–70; reorganizations of, 51–52, 70, 93n, 109; Mao on, 103, 173–74; proliferation of agencies of, 197; military representatives

Price, Jane, 21

Procuracy, 66, 78–80, 83, 189, 293

Professionalization, 8–9, 10, 105–7, 124–25. *See also* Specialists

Proletariat, *see* Dictatorship of the proletariat; Workers

Propaganda Department, 82, 155, 193, 223, 226

Provinces: relations between Party and government in, 98, 147, 199, 271; transfers of power/authority between center and, 111–12, 113, 175–77, 185–87, 290–92; administrative retrenchment in, 131, 133; planning process in, 167–68, 176, 182; revolutionary committees in, 271. *See also entries for individual provinces*

Public health, 101; Mao on, 200

Public Health, Ministry of, 102, 200

Public Security, Ministry of, 93, 270

Purges: in Soviet Union, 20; in Kiangsi period, 20–21; in 1950's, 44, 54, 148–49; in 1960's, 211, 214, 267–75. *See also* Rectification campaigns

Radicalism: as approach to bureaucratic dilemma, 15–16, 17, 30, 189–93, 330–34 *passim*; in Chinese political tradition, 24–28; during Cultural Revolution, 263–64, 333; defined, 403

Railways, Ministry of, 102, 219, 257, 287n

Rationalization: as approach to bureaucratic dilemma, 14–15, 16f, 30–31, 329–30, 332ff, 343–44; in Chinese political tradition, 28–30; organizational (1952–55), 65–86; Mao on, 85f, 114–15; proposals for (1955–57), 120–21, 137, 151–52, 338; Chou En-lai on, 151, 343–44; defined, 403

Recruitment policies, *see* Cadre policy

Rectification campaigns: before 1949, 21–22, 24; during period of consolidation, 43–62; Mao on, 43, 45, 52, 135–37, 153–55; in mid-1950's, 97–104, 114–15; during Hundred Flowers period, 116–52, 153–54, 263, 330; debates over Mao's proposals for, 138–44, 153–55, 201, 339–41; in late 1950's, 148–49, 155–63, 171–73; in early 1960's, 202–34; in early 1970's, 309–26, 342. *See also methods of*, *e.g.*, Closed-door rectification; Open-door rectification; *also targets of, e.g.*, Bureaucratism, Sectarianism, Subjectivism, *etc.; and also specific campaigns, e.g.*, Cultural Revolution, Hundred Flowers, *etc.*

Red Guard movement, 239–46, 256, 260–61, 268, 327, 331, 333; Mao's support of, 242, 265

Regions: government in, 34–35, 49f, 67–70; Party bureaus in, 34–35, 67–70, 185, 252n, 290–91; economic cooperation regions, 176. *See also entries for individual regions, e.g.*, Northwest, Southwest, *etc.*

Regularization, bureaucracy's, 66, 70–72, 83–84, 188–89, 191, 338; mass movements vs., 71–72. *See also* Rationalization

Reich, Charles A., 13n

Remedialism: as approach to bureaucratic dilemma, 16–17, 19–24, 31, 330–36. *See also* External remedialism, Internal remedialism

Retrenchment, *see* Administrative retrenchment

Revised Later Ten Points, 206–11, 229, 330

Revisionism, 39, 157; Mao's criticisms of, 199–201, 223–26, 230–32, 233ff, 267, 324, 340–41; purge of, in "Fifty Days," 226–29, 232; Cultural Revolution to halt, 235; origins of, 263–64, 316–17, 323–27 *passim*; combatting reemergence of, 311–12; leftists' explanation of, 327

Revolutionary committees, in Cultural Revolution, 252–60, 404; military's participation on, 253–54, 301–6 *passim*; mass organizations and, 254–57, 269–70; opposition to, 257–60; role of mass representatives on, 261–62, 285, 293f, 313, 333, 336, 341; Mao's endorsement of, 265; organizational restructuring and, 266, 286ff; inside the bureaucracy, 271–72; relationship of, to Party, 285

Revolutionary great debates: criticism of Lin Piao and Confucius conducted as, 313–15; economic and political disorder created by, 325–26; leftists' program exemplified by, 327; as example of radical external remedialism, 333; Mao's approval of, 343; defined, 404

Revolutionary rebel organizations, 268–69, 270. *See also* Red Guard movement

Rightist deviation: Mao on bureaucracy's, 98–100, 101n, 102; subjectivism as, 157; rectification of, 159–60. *See also* Antirightist campaigns; Conservatism; Revisionism

Robinson, Thomas W., 269n

Routinization, 6, 10, 198, 264

Rural Work Department, 82, 98

Rural work style, 22

Salaries, *see* Wage system

San-fan campaign (1951–52), 34, 42, 47–55, 63f, 81, 338, 344f, 355, 404